Creating German Communism, 1890–1990

Creating German Communism, 1890–1990

FROM POPULAR PROTESTS TO SOCIALIST STATE

ERIC D. WEITZ

PRINCETON UNIVERSITY PRESS

PRINCETON, NEW JERSEY

Published by Princeton University Press, 41 William Street,
Princeton, New Jersey 08540
In the United Kingdom: Princeton University Press, Chichester, West Sussex

Portions of the following work appeared first as "State Power, Class Fragmentation, and the Shaping of German Communist Politics, 1890–1933," *Journal of Modern History* 62:2 (1990): 253–97, © 1990 by University of Chicago, and "'Rosa Luxemburg Belongs to Us!': German Communism and the Luxemburg Legacy," *Central European History* 27:1 (1994): 27–64, © 1995 by Humanities Press International.

Library of Congress Cataloging-in-Publication Data

Weitz, Eric D.
Creating German communism, 1890–1990 : from popular protests to socialist state / Eric D. Weitz.
p. cm.
Includes bibliographical references and index.
ISBN 0-691-02594-0 (cloth : alk. paper). —
ISBN 0-691-02682-3 (pbk. : alk. paper)
1. Communism—Germany—History. 2. Communism—Germany (East)—History. 3. Germany—Politics and government—1871–. 4. Germany (East)—Politics and government. I. Title.
HX280.5.A6W385 1997
335.43'0943—dc20 96-20678 CIP

This book has been composed in Times Roman

Printed in the United States of America by Princeton Academic Press

1 2 3 4 5 6 7 8 9 10

1 2 3 4 5 6 7 8 9 10
(pbk.)

TO CAROL, LEV, AND BENJAMIN

"[S]ocial is just a nicer word for political."

Gabriele Cagliari, president of the Italian company ENI, quoted in the *New York Times*, 25 June 1992

CONTENTS

LIST OF ILLUSTRATIONS

Plates

FIGURES

LIST OF TABLES

ACKNOWLEDGMENTS

THE PRESENT WORK has its very distant origins in a dissertation completed at Boston University under Dietrich Orlow, who was a model advisor. My other graduate school teachers, Fritz Ringer, now Andrew Mellon Professor at the University of Pittsburgh, and Norman Naimark, now of Stanford University, have also been sources of great support, encouragement, and intellectual involvement over the years. When I first went to the Federal Republic of Germany to conduct research, Prof. Dr. Hans Mommsen of the Ruhr-Universität provided a stimulating environment and considerable practical help. In the German Democratic Republic, Prof. Dr. Erwin Könnemann of the Martin-Luther-Universität Halle-Wittenberg taught me a great deal, eased my way into archives, and got me access to restricted holdings. Even more importantly, he and his family provided a welcoming reception to an American family that had little idea of what to expect and arrived with a five-month-old baby and a "mountain of luggage," as he fondly relates time and again.

The research for this book has extended over many years, and I am grateful finally to have the opportunity to record my thanks to the numerous institutions and agencies that provided support. The German Academic Exchange Service (DAAD) made possible my dissertation research in the Federal Republic. Grants from the International Research and Exchanges Board (IREX) supported two research trips to the German Democratic Republic. A related project in comparative communism has found its way into the present work and was facilitated by a Bernadotte E. Schmitt Grant from the American Historical Association and a summer stipend from the National Endowment for the Humanities (NEH). In the final stages of research and writing, I was extremely fortunate to receive grants from the Joint Committee on Eastern Europe of the American Council of Learned Societies (ACLS) and the Social Science Research Council (SSRC) and from the National Council for Soviet and East European Research (NCSEER). St. Olaf College provided research leaves and sabbatical and other kinds of support. The grants extended by IREX, NEH, ACLS, SSRC, and NCSEER were made possible by funds appropriated by the United States government. Neither the U.S. government nor the granting agencies are responsible for the views expressed in this book.

Historians need libraries and archives and I have benefited from the knowledgeable staff at institutions in three (now two) countries. In both Germanys and at the local, regional, and national levels, the archivists were invariably helpful. I would especially like to thank Frau Dr. Inge Pardon, the former director of the former Institut für Geschichte der Arbeiterbewegung, who allowed me to work in the Zentrales Parteiarchiv of the Kommunistische Partei Deutschlands and Sozialistische Einheitspartei Deutschlands even though the archive was officially closed following a weeklong occupation by the Berlin police. The archivists at the Betriebsarchiv der Leuna-Werke were particularly helpful despite their immense surprise at the presence of an American researcher. The staff and the comfortable surroundings of the Bundesarchiv in Koblenz provided a pleasant respite after I had traipsed around local and firm archives in both Germanys, and work at the Hoover Institution Archives seemed positively luxurious. The librarians at the Interlibrary Loan Office of the University of Minnesota have filled more requests than they or I care to remember, but they always managed to procure even hard-to-find materials that I needed.

Writing is a solitary enterprise but intellectual engagement is not. Ron Aminzade and Mary Jo Maynes read the manuscript in its entirety, and when it was even longer than the present book, Donna Harsch, Dolores Peters, and Mark Weitz read selective chapters. I have benefited greatly from their incisive criticisms, along with those of two anonymous reviewers for Princeton University Press, and thank them for taking the time from their own busy schedules. Needless to say, any omissions and errors in the present work are my own. Unless otherwise indicated, translations are my own.

The discerning vision of Carol H. Weitz proved critical to the selection and processing of illustrations that complement the text, and I thank her as well. Quite some years ago now, Mary Nolan read my dissertation, and her criticisms helped me to rethink my account of the emergence of working-class radicalism in Germany. And for conversations that they probably do not remember but that helped me think about how to write the history of German communism, I would like to thank Ron Aminzade, Barbara Laslett, Helga Leitner, Mary Jo Maynes, Dolores Peters, and Eric Sheppard. Hal Benenson did not live to see this book in print. But it never would have been written without his support, encouragement, and engagement, and he would have understood that.

Aspects of this work have been presented at numerous conferences over the years. The commentators at these sessions provided very helpful criticisms, and I would like also to thank David Abraham, James Cronin, Gary Cross, Elisabeth Domansky, Geoff Eley, Laura Frader, Darryl Holter, Norman Naimark, Diethelm Prowe, Eve Rosenhaft, Laura Tabili, and Judith Wishnia. My colleagues in the History Department of St. Olaf College have also read numerous parts of this work in draft form, and they have provided both insightful comments and a collegial setting. I learned a great deal also from colleagues in the Program in History and Society at the University of Minnesota. Finally, I would like to thank two editors at Princeton University Press, Lauren Osborne and Brigitta van Rheinberg, whose confidence in the project kept me going and whose skills have made this a better book whatever its shortcomings.

Historians are trained to explore the meaning of the past. My family reminds me of the importance of the present and the future, and it is to Carol, Lev, and Benjamin that this book is dedicated.

LIST OF ABBREVIATIONS

AfS	*Archiv für Sozialgeschichte*
AHR	*American Historical Review*
AIZ	*Arbeiter-Illustrierte-Zeitung* (KPD illustrated weekly)
Alter Verband	Mineworkers Union
Antifas	Antifascist Committees
APZ	*Aus Politik und Zeitgeschichte*
AZ	*Arbeiter-Zeitung* (Essen SPD newspaper)
BAK	Bundesarchiv Koblenz
BAP	Bundesarchiv Potsdam
BASF	Badische Anilin- und Sodafabrik
BAV	Bauarbeiter Verband (Construction Workers Union)
BL	Bezirksleitung (district leadership of KPD or SED)
BLH	Bezirksleitung Halle
BLHM	Bezirksleitung Halle-Merseburg
BLPS	Bezirksleitung Provinz Sachsen
BLR	Bezirksleitung Ruhrgebiet
BLW	Betriebsarchiv der Leuna-Werke
BRD	Bundesrepublik Deutschland (Federal Republic of Germany)
BzG	*Beiträge zur Geschichte der Arbeiterbewegung*
CDU	Christlich Demokratische Union Deutschlands (Christian Democratic Union of Germany)
CEH	*Central European History*
Cominform	Communist Information Bureau
Comintern	Communist International
CPSU	Communist Party of the Soviet Union
DA	*Deutschland Archiv*
DAF	Deutsche Arbeitsfront (German Labor Front)
DDR	Deutsche Demokratische Republik (German Democratic Republic)
DMV	Deutscher Metallarbeiter-Verband (German Metalworkers Union)
DWK	Deutsche Wirtschaftskommission (German Economic Commission)
ECCI	Executive Committee of the Communist International
EKKI	Exekutivkomitee Kommunistische Internationale
FDJ	Freie Deutsche Jugend (Free German Youth)
GB	Rosa Luxemburg, *Gesammelte Briefe*
GG	*Geschichte und Gesellschaft*
GK VII. AK	Generalkommando VII. Armeekorps (General Command Seventh Army Corps)

GPS	*German Politics and Society*
GSR	*German Studies Review*
GStAKM	Geheimes Staatsarchiv preußischer Kulturbesitz Merseburg
GW	Rosa Luxemburg, *Gesammelte Werke*
HA Krupp, FAH	Historisches Archiv der Fried. Krupp GmbH, Familienarchiv Hügel
HA Krupp, WA	Historisches Archiv der Fried. Krupp GmbH, Werksarchiv
HIA, NSDAP	Hoover Institution Archives, NSDAP Hauptarchiv
HM	Halle-Merseburg
HStAD	Hauptstaatsarchiv Düsseldorf
HW	*History Workshop Journal*
IAH	Internationale Arbeiterhilfe (International Workers Aid)
IML	Institut für Marxismus-Leninismus
Inprekorr	*Internationale Presse Korrespondenz* (Comintern periodical)
IWK	*Internationale wissenschaftliche Korrespondenz zur Geschichte der deutschen Arbeiterbewegung*
JB	Prussia, MHG, *Jahresbericht der Preussischen Regierungs- und Gewerberäte und Bergbehörden, 1900–1928.*
JCH	*Journal of Contemporary History*
JMH	*Journal of Modern History*
KAPD	Kommunistische Arbeiterpartei Deutschlands (Communist Workers Party of Germany)
KJVD	Kommunistischer Jugendverband Deutschlands (Communist Youth Organization of Germany)
KL	Kreisleitung (county leadership of KPD or SED)
KLM	Kreisleitung Merseburg
KLS	Kreisleitung Saalkreis
KLW	Kreisleitung Weissenfels
KLZ	Kreisleitung Zeitz
KPD	Kommunistische Partei Deutschlands (Communist Party of Germany)
KPO	Kommunistische Partei-Opposition (Communist Party-Opposition)
LDP	Liberal-Demokratische Partei Deutschlands (Liberal Democratic Party of Germany)
LHSAM	Landeshauptarchiv Sachsen-Anhalt Magdeburg
LPAH	Landesverband Sachsen-Anhalt der Partei des Demokratischen Sozialismus, Landesparteiarchiv-Halle
LRLK	Landrat des Landkreises (County Magistrate)
LRLKE	Landrat des Landkreises Essen
LRLKM	Landrat des Landkreises Mansfeld
LRLKS	Landrat Saalkreis
LRLKW	Landrat des Landkreises Weissenfels
MdI	Ministerium des Innern (Prussian Ministry of the Interior)

MfS	Ministerium für Staatssicherheit (Ministry for State Security)
MHG	Ministerium für Handel und Gewerbe (Prussian Ministry of Trade and Commerce)
ND	*Neues Deutschland* (main SED newspaper)
NKFD	Nationalkomitee "Freies Deutschland" (National Committee for a Free Germany)
NKVD	People's Commissariat of Internal Affairs (Soviet Union)
NÖS	Neues Ökonomisches System (New Economic System)
NSDAP	Nationalsozialistische Deutsche Arbeiterpartei (Nazi Party)
OBE	Oberbürgermeister Essen (Mayor or Lord Mayor of Essen)
OBH	Oberbergamt Halle
OP	Oberpräsident (Provincial Governor)
OPM	Oberpräsident Magdeburg
OPPS	Oberpräsident Provinz Sachsen
PDS	Partei des Demokratischen Sozialismus (Party of Democratic Socialism)
PP	Polizeipräsident (Police Director)
PPE	Polizeipräsident Essen
PPen	Polizeipräsidenten (Police Directors)
PPH	Polizeipräsident Halle
PV	Polizeiverwaltung (Police Administration)
PVE	Polizeiverwaltung Essen
PVH	Polizeiverwaltung Halle
RAM	Reichsarbeitsministerium (Reich Labor Ministry)
RCP(b)	Russian Communist Party (bolshevik)
RdV	Rat der Volksbeauftragten (Council of People's Deputies)
RE	*Ruhr-Echo* (Ruhr KPD daily newspaper)
RF	*Rote Fahne* (main KPD daily newspaper)
RFB	Roter Frontkämpferbund (Red Front Fighters League)
RFMB	Roter Frauen- und Mädchen Bund (Red Women and Girls League)
RGO	Revolutionäre Gewerkschafts-Opposition (Revolutionary Trade Union Opposition)
RH	Rote Hilfe (Red Aid)
RK	Reichskommissar (Reich Commissar)
RKÜöO	Reichskommissar für Überwachung der öffentlichen Ordnung (Reich Commissar for the Supervision of Public Order)
RMdI	Reich Ministerium des Innern (Reich Ministry of the Interior
RP	Regierungspräsident (District Governor)
RPD	Regierungspräsident Düsseldorf
RPen	Regierungspräsidenten (District Governors)
RPM	Regierungspräsident Merseburg

SA	Sturmabteilung (Storm Troopers of Nazi Party)
SAPMO-BA	Stiftung Archiv der Parteien und Massenorganisationen der DDR im Bundesarchiv
SBZ	Sowjetische Besatzungszone (Soviet Occupation Zone)
SED	Sozialistische Einheitspartei Deutschlands (Socialist Unity Party of Germany)
SH	*Social History*
SKÜöO	Staatskommissar für Überwachung der öffentlichen Ordnung (State Commissar for the Supervision of Public Order)
SMAD	Sowjetische Militäradministration in Deutschland (Soviet Military Administration in Germany)
Sopade	Sozialdemokratische Partei Deutschlands/Exilvorstand (Exiled Executive of the Social Democratic Party of Germany)
SPD	Sozialdemokratische Partei Deutschlands (Social Democratic Party of Germany)
SSH	*Social Science History*
StAE	Stadtarchiv Essen
StAH	Stadtarchiv Halle
SVGK VII. AK	Stellvertretender Generalkommando VII. Armeekorps (Deputy General Command Seventh Army Corps)
UB	Unterbezirk (KPD or SED subdistrict)
UBL	Unterbezirksleitung (subdistrict leadership of KPD or SED)
Union	Union der Hand- und Kopfarbeiter (Union of Manual and Intellectual Workers)
USPD	Unabhängige Sozialdemokratische Partei Deutschlands (Independent Social Democratic Party of Germany)
VdgB	Vereinigung der gegenseitigen Bauernhilfe (Union of Peasant Cooperatives)
VfZ	*Vierteljahrshefte für Zeitgeschichte*
VKPD	Vereinigte Kommunistische Partei Deutschlands (United Communist Party of Germany)
VSWG	*Vierteljahrschrift für Sozial- und Wirtschaftsgeschichte*
ZfG	*Zeitschrift für Geschichtswissenschaft*
ZK	Zentralkomitee (Central Committee)
ZPA	Zentrales Parteiarchiv

Creating German Communism, 1890–1990

INTRODUCTION

> Ich habe für die DDR gelebt. . . . Arbeiter und Bauern werden erkennen, daß die BRD ein Staat der Unternehmer (spricht Kapitalisten) ist und daß die DDR sich nicht ohne Grund einen Arbeiter-und-Bauern Staat nannte.
>
> —*Erich Honecker*[1]

ERICH HONECKER was returned from political asylum in the former Soviet Union to the Federal Republic of Germany (Bundesrepublik Deutschland, or BRD) in July 1992. The former First Secretary of the Socialist Unity Party (Sozialistische Einheitspartei Deutschlands, or SED) and Chairman of the State Council of the German Democratic Republic (Deutsche Demokratische Republik, or DDR) was about to stand trial for manslaughter. He greeted reporters with the clenched fist salute, a gesture he repeated some months later in the courtroom.[2] In his statement to the court on 3 December and in interviews, he accused his accusers of creating a political show trial.[3] Erich Honecker was not on trial, he charged, but the cause of socialism. The "right-wing state," the Federal Republic, was determined, like its precursors, Imperial Germany, the Weimar Republic, and yes, the Third Reich as well, to destroy and discredit the very idea of socialism. Honecker placed himself in the long line of socialist victims of state persecution, including Karl Marx, August Bebel, and Karl Liebknecht. He reminded the public—and the court, of course—of the heroic struggles of socialists in the imperial period and communists in the Weimar Republic. He talked about the working class and its exploitation under capitalism, about the Communist Party of Germany (Kommunistische Partei Deutschlands, or KPD) as the single committed opponent of German fascism, about the achievements of the German Democratic Republic. He claimed to be "no historian," but the charges against him required that he summon the historical record.

The German public might have understood the clenched fist as a general symbol of communism. Few probably knew that it had been adopted in 1926 as the official salute of the KPD's paramilitary organization, the Red Front Fighters League (Roter Frontkämpferbund, or RFB), and from there had spread to communist parties around the world. When Honecker spoke of the "proletariat," "*Ar-*

[1] "I have lived for the DDR. . . . Workers and peasants will recognize that the BRD is a state of the employers (that is, capitalists) and that the DDR called itself, not without justification, a workers' and peasants' state." "Erich Honecker vor Gericht," 3 December 1992, in *DA* 26:1 (1993), 97–105, quote on 103–4.

[2] Photographs of Honecker in *Der Spiegel* 46:32 (3 August 1992): 19, and 46:50 (7 December 1992): 111.

[3] "Erich Honecker vor Gericht," and Reinhold Andert and Wolfgang Herzberg, *Der Sturz: Erich Honecker im Kreuzverhör* (Berlin: Aufbau-Verlag, 1990).

beiter und Bauern" (workers and peasants), and the ongoing "*Kampf*" (struggle) between socialism and capitalism, German citizens probably dismissed the terms as so much rhetoric of a bygone state, the former German Democratic Republic. Few probably paused to reflect on the historical origins of Honecker's language.

But Honecker knew and understood. He had joined the communist youth in 1926 and had become a full-fledged party member in 1929. With that one gesture, the clenched fist, and with his class-laden language, he staked out his identity as a communist of long standing, an individual whose struggles against capitalism stretched back to the Weimar Republic. In the political battles of the last decade of the twentieth century, Erich Honecker summoned the ideas and practices of the 1920s.

In the courtroom Honecker did more than appropriate history in his own defense. The former head of the Socialist Unity Party and the German Democratic Republic expressed the self-understanding that stood at the very core of German communism for much of its existence as party, movement, and state. The SED's forerunner, the KPD, founded at the very end of 1918, developed into the first mass-based communist party outside of the Soviet Union. In the Weimar Republic it acquired significant, though circumscribed, popular support, and became a formidable social and political force. It consistently attracted between 10 and 15 percent of the vote. In a few major cities and towns, its electoral support hovered between one-quarter and one-half of the electorate. Its wide-ranging affiliated organizations—the Red Front Fighters League, Workers Aid, the Red Women and Girls League, the Friends of Nature, choirs, theater groups, biking clubs, radio clubs, and many others—made its political and social presence even more palpable and placed the KPD firmly within the traditions of the German labor movement. Communists around the world ranked the KPD just behind the Russian Communist Party in significance, and in the 1920s and early 1930s counted on it to fight to successful conclusion the next battle of the worldwide proletarian revolution. The KPD's opponents, from social democrats and trade unionists to employers, state officials, and Nazis, defined their political identities, established their political agendas, and secured their political powers largely in opposition to German and international communism.

The Third Reich destroyed the mass-based, popular nature of German communism. The party was forced underground, its members killed or driven into concentration camps or exile. Many sustained a heroic but hopeless resistance against National Socialism. With the military destruction of the National Socialist regime in the spring of 1945, the party quickly reestablished its presence in both the Soviet and the western occupation zones. Communists resurfaced from the underground, emerged from Buchenwald and Sachsenhausen, and returned from the far-flung points of exile. In the workplaces and communities of industrial—and devastated—Germany, communists quickly assumed key roles. They helped to secure infrastructures, reestablish production and basic communal services, and organize local polities. The party began to redevelop its popular base, slowly in the western zones, rapidly and significantly in the east.

The most important group to return to Germany came back in the company of the Red Army. They had weathered the Third Reich and the Soviet purges. Already accustomed to following Soviet dictates, their experience in the Soviet terror had taught them that caution and loyalty enhanced the chances for survival and that political opponents could be dealt with by physical intimidation. But the ideological and political proclivities of German communists had been forged not just by their reading of Lenin, the internal dynamics of the international communist movement, and exile in Stalin's Soviet Union. The essence of their experiences as communists had transpired amid the political and social conflicts of the Weimar Republic and the massive repression of the Third Reich. They brought those experiences to the founding of the socialist state in 1949 and to the execution of the signature policies and precepts of the DDR for the forty years of its existence, namely, a class-oriented view of the world, a rigorous demarcation of state socialism from liberal capitalism, and strict central direction of the economy and polity. For a time the SED managed to create a stable and relatively prosperous socialist society. But ultimately, the policies derived from a strategy and a culture forged in the Weimar Republic, tempered in the Third Reich and the Soviet Union of the 1930s and 1940s, engendered the intense popular hostility that led to the regime's rapid and unexpected collapse in 1989/90.[4]

The book that follows is a history of a party and a society, and of the interconnections between the two. Precisely because German communism became a mass movement and a ruling party, its history refracts critical elements of Germany's social and political development in the modern era. I am particularly concerned in this study with the social forces that shaped the strategy and culture of German communism, and, in turn, the ways that the existence of a mass-based communist movement and a party-state shaped the contours of state and managerial authority in twentieth-century Germany. In many ways, this is a book about the contestation over order and discipline in German society. The discipline-crazed, submissive German is a much-cherished popular myth—the object of satire and admiration, the source of explanation for all events in German history from the Reformation to the Third Reich to the recent unification of east and west. Yet it is no exaggeration to argue that modern German history can very much be written as a history of ceaseless efforts to secure order against both deliberate, overtly political and "merely" informal, everyday challenges—challenges serious enough to worry the most brutal of dictatorships and the most stable of prosperous democracies.

In particular, this is a study about the efforts to discipline industrial labor and labor's challenges to order in the form of popular protests and communist politics. The KPD/SED became a mass movement and then a ruling party amid the intensely tumultuous political and social crises of the first half of the twentieth century. Germans lived through the recurrent breakdown and reconstitution of political authority, through military defeats and economic crises. German workers

[4] Note also Hermann Weber's comment: "German communism—its structures, mechanisms, and leadership corps—were already stamped in the first republic." "Aufstieg und Niedergang des deutschen Kommunismus," *APZ* B40/91 (27 September 1991): 25.

in the World War I era created the most sustained wave of popular activism in modern German history, a period in which the repertoires of protest expanded exponentially. Social democrats and trade unionists, employers and state officials searched frantically for ways to re-create discipline in the workplace and order in the larger society. The Third Reich provided its own solution to the problem of order, making socialists and communists the first victims of the brutal and murderous policies that defined the Nazi dictatorship.

Communists did not operate in conditions of their own choosing, and central to the following study is a spatial argument: the character of mass parties and movements is shaped not only by their ideologies and the social background of the members—important as these elements certainly are—but also by the political spaces within which they operate.[5] Factories and mines, neighborhood streets, city plazas and markets, households, battlefields, communal administrations, and national legislatures all constitute realms of political engagement and conflict. Parties and movements may choose to operate in any number of these spaces. But at least as often, they are driven into a particular configuration of spaces because of the larger political and social constellation and the unintended outcomes of political conflict. Unwittingly, the places of engagement shape the movement's political culture. Movements that arise within existing democratic structures have an array of spaces open to them, which may serve to absorb and moderate even the most militant-sounding group. Dictatorships, in contrast, severely constrict the range of political space, and even movements most committed to democracy will reproduce some of the authoritarian traits of their oppressors when they are forced to operate conspiratorially and clandestinely.

In its early years the KPD, drawing on the great wave of popular protest that followed World War I, operated in an array of spaces—the workplace, the streets, the battlefield, local and national legislatures. But labor and communist activism did not go unchallenged. Its adversaries created a "coalition of order," whose policies resulted in the spatial transformation of labor politics in the Weimar Republic, narrowing the KPD's field of operation. The coalition, by marshaling the state's weapons of coercion, after 1923 closed off the option of armed revolution, while the deployment of rationalization measures in the mines and factories created high unemployment that drove the KPD from the workplace.

As a result, the streets served increasingly as the decisive place of political engagement for the KPD. There the party gathered its supporters in demonstrations and combative confrontations with the police, fascist organizations, and even the Social Democratic Party (Sozialdemokratische Partei Deutschlands, or SPD) and employed workers. As the place of political contestation, the streets carried a

[5] I have been influenced here by the notion of "political opportunity structures" developed in American political science, as in Sidney Tarrow, *Power in Movement: Social Movements, Collective Action and Politics* (Cambridge: Cambridge University Press, 1994), and by human geographers' understanding of space, as in Eric Sheppard and Trevor J. Barnes, *The Capitalist Space Economy: Geographical Analysis after Ricardo, Marx and Sfarra* (London: Unwin Hyman, 1990); John A. Agnew, *Place and Politics: The Geographical Mediation of State and Society* (Boston: Allen and Unwin, 1987); and David Harvey, *Consciousness and the Urban Experience: Studies in the History and Theory of Capitalist Urbanization* (Baltimore: Johns Hopkins University Press, 1985).

distinctive logic. They helped forge a politics of display and spectacle, which encouraged ideological pronouncements and harsh physical engagements rather than the effective mediation of practical political issues. They contributed to the creation of a party culture that venerated male physical prowess as the ultimate revolutionary quality.

The Third Reich transformed yet again the spatial realm of communist politics. The sheer, brute repressive force exercised by the Nazis drove the KPD from the streets, its last cherished domain. Communist politics narrowed drastically to furtive and fleeting underground activities and to the Soviet Union, where the exiled leadership and thousands of other party members found refuge—and also imprisonment and execution during the Soviet terror. Physically and socially isolated and hunted by the Gestapo, many party members in the underground held desperately to the one fixed pole, communist politics as learned in Weimar. In the Soviet Union, the exiled cadres, even further removed from developments in Germany and contacts with activists in the resistance—however few in number—became ever more dependent on the Communist Party of the Soviet Union, ever more accustomed to an authoritarian mode of political engagement.

The political strategy and culture with which the KPD/SED became a popular movement and a ruling party had ideological as well as spatial and social-historical origins, and their geographical fount lay in Germany as well as in Russia and the Soviet Union. Rosa Luxemburg, the brilliant and fiery leader of the SPD's left wing before World War I, also provided much of the ideological orientation of the KPD. Profoundly committed to the creation of socialism in the here and now, Luxemburg refused to countenance compromise even with social democrats. She infused her politics with the language of unwavering hostility to the institutions of bourgeois society, of militant and irreconcilable conflict between the forces of revolution and reaction, of hard-fought class struggle and proletarian revolution as the sole and exclusive means of political progress. In the course of the Weimar Republic, the KPD joined—joined, did not replace—these positions, common to Luxemburg and Lenin, with Lenin's emphasis on a disciplined party organization and a powerful central state. By the late 1920s, the Luxemburgist-Leninist hybrid was increasingly subject to Stalin's particularly authoritarian interpretation of Leninism, but major elements of Luxemburg's orientation, shorn of the democratic sensibility with which she endowed them, retained their vitality in the KPD and SED.

Forged in the street battles of the Weimar Republic, the language—both German and Russian—of unceasing revolutionary engagement, and the bitter experiences of exile and repression, German communism took on a particularly intransigent cast. It developed a party culture characterized by a profoundly masculine, combative ethos; a "proletarianism" that idealized productive labor as the source of society's wealth and the working class as the wellsprings of a higher morality and the agent of social transformation; a voluntarism that demanded unceasing activism from the party and its supporters; an emphasis on central state power as the crucial instrument in the creation of socialism; and a rigorous demarcation of communism from all other political formations. This party culture cut through virtually all the factional divisions within the KPD of the 1920s and 1930s. Other European communist parties made the transition from sect to mass movement on the basis of the popular and national front strategies of the 1930s and 1940s. They forged alliances with nonproletarian groups and abandoned their revolutionary commitments for the politics of reform. However temporary and unstable these strategic departures, however contested their legacies, they remained the heroic moments of breakthrough that the parties commemorated and inscribed into their culture and politics in the succeeding decades.

But not the KPD. Its crucial and formative experience was the construction of the mass party in the Weimar years on the basis of an intransigent strategy of revolutionary militancy that became increasingly entwined with the authoritarian practices derived from the Soviet model. This legacy would be protected and glorified and carried over into the vastly altered circumstances of the Soviet occupation and the formation and development of the German Democratic Republic, and would drastically limit the KPD/SED's openness to other political strategies and ideas. Already in the 1930s, the KPD, of all the Comintern parties, proved the most hostile to the popular front strategy. Despite some trenchant reconsiderations during the Nazi and immediate postwar years, most of the German communists placed in power by the Red Army at the end of World War II drew almost instinctively toward the policies promoted by the Soviet Union, policies that accorded the central state the primary role in the construction of society and that demonized the bourgeois west. While some eastern European economies introduced elements of a market system as early as the 1960s and accepted private peasant agriculture, the DDR remained wedded to central planning and large-scale, socialized agriculture. A number of European communist parties, east and west, gradually abandoned many of the undemocratic practices enshrined in the communist movement in the interwar years. In contrast, the Socialist Unity Party retained its affection for such Leninist hallmarks as democratic centralism, the dictatorship of the proletariat, and the deep-seated hostility toward bourgeois political systems.

Instead of a politics shaped and limited by societal influences, politics in the DDR became largely the means of making, or trying to make, society. The politics of the SED-state drew very substantially on the party strategy and culture forged in the 1920s and 1930s and re-created in the late 1940s. Ultimately, a politics based on the ossified remains of an earlier period proved the undoing of the regime. Although the DDR's centrally planned economy was partly successful in the 1960s and 1970s in improving living standards, it proved unable to deal with the more complex economic realities of the 1980s. At the same time, the slight easing of political repression that began in the late 1970s failed to defuse the long-simmering resentment against the stultifying political practices of the regime. When the reforms initiated by Mikhail Gorbachev offered new political possibilities, the East German citizenry grasped the opportunity to overthrow its regime and with it, the legacy of German communism as formed in the Weimar Republic and cultivated in the German Democratic Republic.

This book has been written at a very particular moment, that of the political and historical demise of its subject. It also comes at a particular moment in the writing of German history, a moment when the paradigm that dominated the field from the

1960s into the 1980s, though never uncontested, has come under fire from an array of directions. The last generation has witnessed a veritable explosion of historical writing on Germany, and the subfields—women's history, labor history, social history in general—have multiplied dramatically. Few would deny the enormous vitality of both German and Anglo-American scholarship on Germany. Its origins and development have been recounted many times; the only need here is to lay out some salient points, and to identify three major areas of dispute: the *Sonderweg* discussion, the debate on German exceptionalism; *Alltagsgeschichte*, the history of everyday life; and poststructuralism.[6]

The generation of German historians that began writing in the 1960s bestowed lavish attention on the domestic, social underpinnings of political power. The dominant trends in German historical writing never had the apolitical bent fashionable for a while in American and British writing, nor the effort at total history that French *annaliste* writing had (at least in its origins). Looming over all the research and writing hung the intractable and unmovable image of the twelve years of the Third Reich.

Fruitful and illuminating as it has been, German historical writing has come under intense criticism in the last decade or so. First, as a form of social history, it displayed a peculiar neglect of the historical subjects themselves. With the intense concentration on the structures of political power, subordinate social groups were depicted as mere pawns in a manipulative game played out at the upper reaches of society. Second, the reality of National Socialist Germany loomed so large that, despite ritual protestations, almost all the history was written with 1933 in mind, depriving the imperial, revolutionary, and Weimar periods of their at least partly autonomous significance. To be sure, this "coming to terms" with the Nazi past was an immensely important task, politically and historically, in the face of the public and professional quiescence on the topic in the 1950s and the widely accepted view of the Third Reich as a mere aberration amid the centuries of the German past. At the same time, the concentration on 1933 made German history appear as a linear progression to the disasters of the Third Reich.

Third, the intense concentration on domestic politics and the domestic underpinnings of foreign policy resulted in an enormous neglect of the comparative sphere. German history, with its catastrophic termini of 1933 and 1945, has been accorded a unique, and deformed, path. This is, of course, the stuff of the "*Sonderweg*" (special path) discussion, labeled the historiographical topic of the 1980s but really part and parcel of German historical writing for decades. The outcome of the discussion remains unresolved, but there is an important methodological conclusion that has yet to be followed through in a systematic fashion. As Geoff Eley and David Blackbourn have argued most forcefully and, in my view, convincingly, the

[6] For recent discussions in English on the state of the historiography, see the special issue of *CEH* 22:3/4 (1989); Konrad H. Jarausch and Larry Eugene Jones, "German Liberalism Reconsidered: Inevitable Decline, Bourgeois Hegemony, or Partial Achievement?" in *In Search of a Liberal Germany: Studies in the History of German Liberalism from 1789 to the Present*, ed. idem (Providence: Berg, 1990), 1–23; and Larry Eugene Jones and James Retallack, "German Conservatism Reconsidered: Old Problems and New Directions," in *Reform, Reaction, and Resistance: Studies in the History of German Conservatism from 1789 to 1945*, ed. idem (Providence: Berg, 1993), 1–30.

Sonderweg argument hung on a superficial or idealized notion of the history of other western countries.[7] Serious comparative studies, informed by the historiographical advances of the last generation, have only just begun to appear in any significant dimension in German historical writing.[8]

Because German history has been so preoccupied with the structures and mechanisms of power, the area of popular culture and beliefs, of *mentalités*, has been relatively undeveloped. Only in the last decade, with the emergence of *Alltagsgeschichte*, much of which has occurred outside the formal historical discipline, have these areas received serious and insightful consideration. The best of this work has shown how politics penetrates into the most obscure realms of daily life. But despite the accolades that some have bestowed upon it, many works in the *Alltagsgeschichte* vein have been nonanalytical and merely antiquarian, and have failed to specify the nature of the power relations within which daily life unfolds.[9] At the same time, the severe criticism *Alltagsgeschichte* has drawn from the representatives of the formal historical discipline has clearly been overdone. The debate on *Alltagsgeschichte* points up not so much the need for a singular, "correct" approach to the study of the German past, but the immense and harmful chasm that exists between studies of the institutions of power and of the contours of everyday life.[10]

[7] David Blackbourn and Geoff Eley, *The Peculiarities of German History: Bourgeois Society and Politics in Nineteenth-Century Germany* (New York: Oxford University Press, 1984).

[8] Some important departures have been the project on the middle class directed by Jürgen Kocka and published in *Bürgertum im 19. Jahrhundert: Deutschland im europäischen Vergleich*, 3 vols., ed. idem with the collaboration of Ute Frevert (Munich: DTV, 1988); Fritz Ringer's work, including *Education and Society in Modern Europe* (Bloomington: Indiana University Press, 1979), *Fields of Knowledge: French Academic Culture in Comparative Perspective, 1890–1920* (Cambridge: Cambridge University Press, 1992), and *The Rise of the Modern Educational System: Structural Change and Social Reproduction, 1870–1920*, ed. Detlef K. Müller, Fritz Ringer, and Brian Simon (Cambridge: Cambridge University Press, 1987); Mary Jo Maynes's earlier work in education and her recent study of French and German working-class autobiographies, *Schooling for the People: Comparative Local Studies of Schooling History in France and Germany, 1750–1850* (New York: Holmes and Meier, 1985), and *Taking the Hard Road: Life Course in French and German Workers' Autobiographies in the Era of Industrialization* (Chapel Hill: University of North Carolina Press, 1995); and Gerhard A. Ritter, *Social Welfare in Germany and Britain: Origins and Development* (Leamington Spa: Berg, 1986). See also Tim Mason's plea, shortly before his death, for a return to the comparative study of fascism, "Whatever Happened to "Fascism'?" in *Nazism, Fascism and the Working Class: Essays by Tim Mason*, ed. Jane Caplan (Cambridge: Cambridge University Press, 1995), 323–31.

[9] For very positive reviews, Geoff Eley, "Labor History, Social History, *Alltagsgeschichte*: Experience, Culture, and the Politics of the Everyday—A New Direction for German Social History?" *JMH* 61:2 (1989): 297–343, and David F. Crew, "*Alltagsgeschichte*: A New Social History from Below?" *CEH* 22:3/4 (1989): 394–407. For a more critical stance, see my exchange with Eley, "Romantisierung des Eigen-Sinns? Eine e-mail-Kontroverse aus Übersee," *WerkstattGeschichte* 10 (1995): 57–64. For good collections, see *Alltagsgeschichte: Zur Rekonstruktion historischer Erfahrungen und Lebensweisen*, ed. Alf Lüdtke (Frankfurt am Main: Campus, 1989), and Alf Lüdtke, *Eigen-Sinn: Fabrikalltag, Arbeitererfahrungen und Politik vom Kaiserreich bis in den Faschismus* (Hamburg: Ergebnisse, 1993).

[10] A point made by Richard Evans already in 1978 in "Introduction: William II's Germany and the Historians," in *Society and Politics in Wilhelmine Germany*, ed. idem (London: Croom Helm, 1978),

Poststructuralist critiques have sometimes intersected with the positions taken by advocates of *Alltagsgeschichte*, but by denying any kind of substantive, knowable, material reality, poststructuralism really brings the entire historical enterprise into question. It founders especially in relation to the German case, a history marked so deeply by the bare materiality of genocide—as those historians of Germany receptive to poststructuralism have been quick to admit, leaving them in the rather strained position of advocating the methodology but not the epistemology of poststructuralism.[11] In other cases, proponents of poststructuralism have simply abandoned their own commitments when they venture into the terrain of German history.[12]

In this book I draw freely upon the immensely fruitful historical work of the last generation. But I also share many of the criticisms leveled at it in recent years. I will attempt here to hold continually in view the structures of power as they evolved in Germany, but also the partly autonomous life-worlds and practices of historical subjects. As mentioned above, I hope to make clear both the way that communism as a popular movement was shaped by the specific structures in which it emerged, and the way that men and women living and acting in the workplace, the streets, the household, the battlefield, and the formal political system also shaped those structures, not always to their own benefit. I attempt here to integrate more formal historical political economy with the social history of popular protest, gender analysis, and the symbolic representation of politics. And while this work is a study in German history, it is written with a comparative perspective in mind. Germany was indeed different from other western countries—different, but not unique. Its communist party became a mass party with a strategy that had markedly different nuances from those of other European communist parties that accomplished their own popular breakthroughs. But this is precisely what requires explanation, and I draw here on other studies of mine to specify along the way the KPD/SED's distinctive profile in relation to other communist parties and the comparative social histories in which mass-based communist parties emerged.

This work appears in the context not only of German history; it is also a study amid a huge literature on European communism. Here the historiography has been largely political in orientation. Deeply informative and ideologically charged, it has, however, often lacked the methodological and theoretical sophis-

11–39, and again by Geoff Eley and Keith Nield in "Why Does Social History Ignore Politics?" *SH* 5:2 (May 1980): 249–71.

11 See especially Jane Caplan, "Postmodernism, Poststructuralism, and Deconstruction: Notes for Historians," and Isabel V. Hull, "Feminist and Gender History through the Literary Looking Glass: German Historiography in Postmodern Times," in the special issue of *CEH* 22:3/4 (1989): 260–300.

12 See the strained essays of Hayden White, "Historical Emplotment and the Problem of Truth," and Dominick LaCapra, "Representing the Holocaust: Reflections on the Historians' Debate," in *Probing the Limits of Representations: Nazism and the "Final Solution,"* ed. Saul Friedländer (Cambridge, Mass.: Harvard University Press, 1992), 37–53 and 108–27.

tication that German historiography has come to display.[13] The opening of previously closed archives in the last few years seems to have resulted mostly in a great outpouring of rich empirical studies, but few new questions or approaches to the history of communism.[14]

In the now dated but still prevailing literature on European communism, two explanations are generally offered for the development of every communist party, including the German one. The first links every issue concerning the parties to the rise of Soviet or, more crassly, Stalin's personal domination over the international communist movement. The second, no less focused on the Soviet Union, nonetheless gives primacy to the major external events—the disruptions unleashed by World War I, the Great Depression and the rise of fascism, the onset of World War II, the establishment of Soviet power in eastern Europe—and their interpretation by the Soviet leadership. Historical analysis then becomes a simple matter of ascribing changes in party and Comintern strategies to the personal or collective whims of the Soviet leadership; to changes in Soviet domestic policies, which were immediately carried over to the International; or to Soviet strategic interests. This view originated in the political debates of the 1920s and then became especially pronounced in post–World War II scholarship.[15]

Obviously, the history of a movement that viewed the Soviet Union as the fount of all progress and that subjected individual parties to directives from Moscow cannot be divorced from Soviet developments and, especially, from the rise of Stalinism. The emergence of mass-based communist parties is hardly imaginable outside the crucible of the political and economic crises that virtually defined the first half of the twentieth century. Nonetheless, an interpretive schema focused exclusively on the Soviet Union, the political orientation of communist parties, and the major political events is overly simplistic and leaves many more questions unanswered than resolved. Most often, this schema entails a highly deterministic reading of communist history, a political narrative whose beginning and end points are already known. Especially in the older, Cold War–influenced version, political events, external to the histories of the parties themselves, serve as the driving factors that summon up predictable responses from the Comintern and the communist parties. The result is a picture of uniformity that masks the varieties of communism (which existed even at the height of Stalinism), ignores the important fact that

[13] This is, of course, a very broad generalization and is not meant to impugn individual works or the high quality of, for example, Anglo-American scholarship on Russian and Soviet history.

[14] See, for example, the *Jahrbuch für historische Kommunismusforschung*, as well as articles in such journals as *Deutschland Archiv*, *Aus Politik und Zeitgeschichte*, and *Beiträge zur Geschichte der Arbeiterbewegung*.

[15] Early examples, which established the interpretive framework for decades, are Franz Borkenau, *World Communism: A History of the Communist International* (New York: Norton, 1939) and Ruth Fischer, *Stalin and German Communism* (1948; New Brunswick: Transaction Books, 1982). See also the standard Comintern histories of Milorad M. Drachkovitch and Branko Lazitch, eds., *The Comintern: Historical Highlights* (New York: Praeger, 1966); Julius Braunthal, *History of the International*, vol. 2: *1914–1943* (New York: Praeger, 1967); Helmut Gruber, *Soviet Russia Masters the Comintern: International Communism in the Era of Stalin's Ascendancy* (New York: Anchor Books, 1974); and Fernando Claudin, *The Communist Movement: From Comintern to Cominform* (New York: Monthly Review Press, 1975).

individual parties had highly varied experiences with the different strategies and policies, and subsumes social into political history. The social context, to the extent that it is present at all, is treated as mere backdrop, its impact on party formation more assumed than explicated, or described in such general terms as to be of limited usefulness.

This kind of circumscribed political history, without question important in delineating certain aspects of communist history, cannot, however, address why, on the basis of particular strategies, some communist parties were able to make the transition from sect to popular movement. This void has been only partly addressed by the emergence, in the last generation, of social histories of labor that sometimes intersect with communist party history. These social histories, generally centered upon localities or regions, less frequently upon specific industries or even factories, have demonstrated the always imperfect fit between party and class. They have explicated the reasons why communist parties in different situations have been able to garner substantial popular support. But by and large, they have left unexamined the opposite flow: the way that a particular kind of popular base and social setting also shaped the character and strategy of individual communist parties.[16] By focusing so intently on localities and regions, they have redressed the Moscow-centeredness of older party and Comintern histories, but have often failed to link the local with the national and have sometimes ignored altogether the international dimension of European communism.

Few are the studies that have incorporated Perry Anderson's recommendation some fifteen years ago—that any history of communism has also to be a national and even transnational history of society—and German historiography has been no exception.[17] Positioned on the front line of the Cold War divide, the historiography of German and international communism in both Germanys always had immense political resonance. While in the DDR strict party controls eased a bit in some areas of historical investigation, the history of the KPD and SED lay too close to the state's claims to legitimacy to allow it free scholarly rein. To the very end of the regime in 1989/90, the history of the party remained one of untrammeled victories, of heroic struggles and stunning achievements. Critical engagement with the past reached only to the level of admitting a few mistaken emphases or overly hasty initiatives. Indeed, it is probably fair to say that as the regime's legitimacy came increasingly under question in the latter half of the 1980s, the recourse to a rigid and stultified history only intensified.[18]

[16] Reference to studies of German communism will be cited in due course. On the French and Italian cases, see Eric D. Weitz, *Popular Communism: Political Strategies and Social Histories in the Formation of the German, French, and Italian Communist Parties, 1919–1948*, Western Societies Program Occasional Paper no. 31 (Ithaca: Cornell University Institute for European Studies, 1992).

[17] Perry Anderson, "Communist Party History," in *People's History and Socialist Theory*, ed. Raphael Samuel (London: Routledge and Kegan Paul, 1981), 145–56.

[18] See the critical commentary of Hermann Weber: "Die SED und die Geschichte der Komintern: Gegensätzliche Einschätzung durch Historiker der DDR und der Sowjetunion," *DA* 22:8 (1989): 890–903, and "Geschichte als Instrument der Politik: Zu den Thesen des ZK der SED 'Zum 70. Jahrestag der Gründung der KPD,'" *DA* 21:7 (1988): 863–72, as well as the SED's own "70 Jahre Kampf für Sozialismus und Frieden, für das Wohl des Volkes: Thesen des Zentralkomitees der SED zum 70. Jahrestag der Gründung der Kommunistischen Partei Deutschlands," *ND*, 14 June 1988: 3–8.

West German historiography, while far more critical and varied in nature, has, like DDR historiography, been overwhelmingly political in orientation.[19] The dominant paradigm has long been the Stalinization thesis, articulated with great verve and empirical knowledge by Hermann Weber.[20] Ironically enough, his position has received a new lease on life by appraisals emanating from the former German Democratic Republic, which have been quick—too quick—to embrace a perspective castigated in the past as representative of "bourgeois, imperialist" historiography, and to explain every supposed deformation in the history of German communism as a manifestation of "Stalinism." In both its original articulation by Weber and the more recent, and even less compelling, reprise of the Stalinization perspective, the KPD, rooted originally in the social and political life of German labor, increasingly took on the character of its Soviet mentor. Practices developed out of backward, authoritarian Russian conditions were grafted onto German politics and society, and the initial democratic impulses of the party, articulated most forcefully by Rosa Luxemburg, were increasingly replaced by the dictatorial methods characteristic of Lenin and Stalin.[21] The authoritarian state socialism of the DDR marked the inevitable culmination of this process, the imposition on German soil of an alien form of politics.

While the impact of the Soviet Union on the KPD and SED can hardly be ignored—and will not be ignored in this work—the Stalinization perspective almost inevitably directs the causative gaze eastward, away from German conditions and to the forces—of lightness or of darkness, depending on the perspective—emanating from Moscow. But Soviet power explains only part of the history of German communism. The Soviets could never create a mass-based party. The ideologies and strategies emanating from Moscow had to be translated into practices and discourses that made sense to German workers. The significant question is how Bolshevik ideology and Soviet power interacted with the socio-

[19] But see Klaus-Michael Mallmann, "Milieu, Radikalismus und lokale Gesellschft: Zur Sozialgeschichte des Kommunismus in der Weimarer Republik," *GG* 21:1 (1995): 5–31, which has extensive references. Mallmann makes a strong case for the importance of the locality in shaping communism, but neglects to an excessive degree the national and transnational dimensions.

[20] Hermann Weber, *Die Wandlung des deutschen Kommunismus: Die Stalinisierung der KPD in der Weimarer Republik*, 2 vols. (Frankfurt am Main: Europäische Verlagsanstalt, 1969), as well as idem, *Kommunistische Bewegung und realsozialistischer Staat: Beiträge zum deutschen und internationalen Kommunismus. Hermann Weber zum 60. Geburtstag*, ed. Werner Müller (Cologne: Bund, 1988); idem, *Aufbau und Fall einer Diktatur: Kritischen Beiträge zur Geschichte der DDR* (Cologne: Bund, 1991).

[21] See Weber, *Wandlung* and *Kommunistische Bewegung*; Ossip K. Flechtheim, *Die KPD in der Weimarer Republik* (1948; Hamburg: Junius, 1986); Siegfried Bahne, *Die KPD und das Ende von Weimar: Das Scheitern einer Politik 1932–1935* (Frankfurt am Main: Campus, 1976); and Heinrich August Winkler's trilogy on Weimar labor, which generally follows Weber in relation to the KPD: *Von der Revolution zur Stabilisierung: Arbeiter und Arbeiterbewegung in der Weimarer Republik 1918 bis 1924* (Berlin: J. H. W. Dietz Nachf., 1984); *Der Schein der Normalität: Arbeiter und Arbeiterbewegung in der Weimarer Republik 1924 bis 1930* (Berlin: J. H. W. Dietz Nachf., 1988); and *Der Weg in die Katastrophe: Arbeiter und Arbeiterbewegung in der Weimarer Republik 1930 bis 1933* (Berlin: J. H. W. Dietz Nachf., 1990). For views from the former GDR and other ex-socialist countries, see many of the contributions to the 1990 symposium on Luxemburg in *BzG* 33:4 (1991).

political history of German labor and with the more general history of German society. German historiography on the KPD/SED, ensconced in the maneuverings of factions, in the personal and biographical element, in the unidimensional view of directives issued in Moscow and executed in Germany—that historiography, east and west, cannot begin to capture the complexity of the sociohistorical process that shaped German communism, and the process, no less significantly, whereby a mass-based communist party and then the party-state helped shape the larger contours of German society in both the Weimar and the Federal Republics, not to mention, of course, the area ruled by the party itself. Leaving aside ritual paeans to the need to ground German communism in its own historical context, West German historiography overwhelmingly interpreted the historical development of the KPD in the Weimar Republic and the SED in the German Democratic Republic as a process whose origins had to be located predominantly in Moscow. The historical development of the DDR was written out of German history in the twentieth century, only to find its way back—the prodigal son returning—in 1989/90. If German communists took to Stalinism with alacrity, if "[they] early on copied Soviet Stalinism with "*deutscher Gründlichkeit*' [German thoroughness]," then this process needs to be explained with recourse to German as well as Russian/ Soviet history.[22] "*Deutsche Gründlichkeit*," whatever its particular form, is not known to be a genetically inherited trait; it needs to be explained historically.

In the ten chapters of *Creating German Communism, 1890–1990* I draw particularly on my own archival research into the local and regional histories of the Ruhr and Prussian Saxony.[23] Both areas, and the major cities of Essen and Halle, were centers of Germany's industrial economy, and of KPD support in the Weimar Republic. But ultimately, the book is about German communism, not these two regions, and I give myself license to roam around other parts of the country.

Chapter 1 explores the patterns of state and managerial authority and the forms of working-class protest in Imperial Germany. Both employers and state officials pursued a combination of authoritarian and paternalistic policies designed to create stable and docile workforces. The mix of repression and social welfare created a dense web of relations that bound workers to the state and reinforced gendered understandings of the sexual and social division of labor. Workers resisted the all-encompassing claims of the state and employers through strikes, demonstrations, informal protests, and support for the SPD. As workers forged independent organizations and subcultures, they gave voice to democratic and egalitarian visions, but also reproduced the statist and gendered political conceptions that dominated German society at large. The KPD would build upon these practices to create the mass party in the 1920s, while employers and the state would develop their strategies of the prewar period to contain the threat of working-class radicalism and communism.

[22] Weber, "Aufstieg und Niedergang des deutschen Kommunismus," 39.

[23] The Prussian province of Saxony was distinct from the kingdom, later free state, of Saxony. With some territorial additions, the borders are similar to the present-day *Land* (state) of Saxony-Anhalt.

Chapter 2 explores the emergence of the great wave of popular protest triggered by the extreme conditions of total war. Working-class activism quickly escalated into direct challenges to the continuation of World War I and to the hierarchical order of the workplace and society. The rapid expansion of labor activism and Germany's defeat in World War I led to the German Revolution. As the old order collapsed, German labor experimented with new forms of political representation. Founded at the very end of 1918, the KPD emerged out of the confluence of the labor upsurge of the war and Revolution and the political development of the left wing of the SPD under Rosa Luxemburg.

The victories won by labor in the Revolution of 1918-20 did not go unchallenged. Chapter 3 examines the formation of the "coalition of order" that contested working-class power and influence in the Weimar Republic. The coalition came together especially in opposition to German communism. The strategies it pursued created the popular discontent that resulted in continual support for communism. At the same time, its strategy drove the KPD from the workplace, profoundly shaping the character of the KPD and, subsequently, the SED as well.

The workplace was, of course, of central importance to the party, and communist organizing efforts there are the subject of chapter 4. In the early years of the Weimar Republic, popular protest in the workplace provided a fruitful field of activity for the KPD, and the party garnered increasing support in the mines and factories of Germany. But its activities were hampered by the party's intense hostility to the existing trade unions and, after 1923 especially, by high unemployment, which enabled managers to purge their labor forces of communists. The result was the party's ultimate isolation from the workplace, a development of profound consequence for a party whose entire being rested on the idealization of the proletariat.

Driven out of the workplace, the party turned increasingly to the streets, the topic of chapter 5. Through an examination of a number of communist demonstrations, the chapter explores both the party's rootedness in the "traditional" practices of German labor and the political characteristics that derived from the concentration on combative conflicts in the streets. The logic embedded in the streets as the decisive space of political engagement led to a politics of display and spectacle, of militancy and masculinity. By emphasizing the streets and failing to pursue consistently practical work within the institutions of the Republic, the KPD foreclosed the possibility of attracting substantial support beyond the male proletariat.

More consistently than any other party in the Weimar Republic, the KPD called for women's emancipation. Some of its efforts, especially the campaign for the legalization of abortion, attracted support from feminists and other women outside the party's ranks. Yet the KPD also reproduced much of the standard gender ideology of the Weimar period and of the labor movement in general. Chapter 6 argues that the party's enthrallment with combative conflicts in the street gave German communism a profoundly masculine tenor, while the party's conflicting and contradictory constructions of femininity created an idealized and, given the realities of women's lives in the Weimar Republic, ultimately unattainable image. As a result, the KPD remained an overwhelmingly masculine political movement.

To be a communist in the Weimar Republic meant to live a life in the party—in its organizations, political campaigns, and cultural programs. Chapter 7 moves from the social context to the ideological and discursive terrains of party life. It explores what communism meant for the thousands who passed through the party. It examines in particular the creation of a communist culture in which the primary categories were class, struggle and solidarity, loyalty to the Soviet Union, hostility toward social democracy, and vitriolic factionalism. For many communists, support for the KPD meant a journey of sacrifice. But the party also offered people a place to forge identities, to have an impact on their world, to improve themselves.

Thousands of German communists were executed under the Third Reich and in Soviet exile, the period covered by chapter 8. Many more survived concentration camps. Despite the immense disasters, only hesitantly and very partially did the party undertake a critical dialogue with its past. Among workers, the combination of Nazi repression and social and economic policies managed to break the ties of previous political loyalties, rendering communist resistance activities extremely difficult and, ultimately, of marginal political significance. Many communists who survived the Soviet purges had become accustomed to the arbitrary, and often murderous, exercise of political power. In the twelve years of the Third Reich, the KPD layered onto the culture and strategy of the Weimar period an increasingly authoritarian orientation.

Yet the complete defeat of the Nazi regime, the presence of Allied occupying powers, and the immense destruction on German soil created an unprecedented situation, one that opened widely the political tableau. Chapter 9 explores the rebuilding of the party and the formation of the SED and then the DDR in the critical years 1945–49, a period marked by the uneasy coexistence of the politics of gradualism and the politics of intransigence. The language of democracy and a "German road to socialism"; the substantial, if limited, popular support won by the party in working-class areas; and its ensconcement in a wide variety of political spaces carried the potential of a moderating logic, one that might have led to the establishment of a "third way" system in the Soviet Occupation Zone. Ultimately, however, the logic of the Cold War led to the triumph of the politics of intransigence and the formation of an authoritarian, state socialist system in a truncated Germany. For German communists, this meant not only the subordination to Soviet designs, but also the reversion to their own past, to the political strategy and culture formed in the Weimar Republic.

Finally, chapter 10 examines key elements in the development of the DDR and the party-state's ongoing campaign to construct legitimacy. Central to this effort was the construction of a state with massive powers of direction. The SED also carefully cultivated KPD traditions and deployed strategies of discipline and order common to German regimes throughout the modern era. The continual recourse to the KPD of the Weimar Republic drastically limited the regime's inclinations and abilities to undertake new departures, leading ultimately to its collapse in 1989/90.

CHAPTER 1

Regimes of Repression, Repertoires of Resistance

[durch] diese Maßnahme [Arbeiterwohnsiedlungen] . . . wir uns . . . einen zuverlässigen und seßhaften Arbeiterstamm an die Werke fesseln und das Gefühl der Zugehörigkeit zu unseren Betrieben erwecken und befestigen.

—*Mine owner*[1]

[1. Mai 1890.] Wie war das nur möglich? An einem Arbeitstage wagten die Proletarierscharen nicht zu arbeiten, dem Unternehmer damit den Profit zu kürzen? Sie wagten zu feiern an einem Tage, der nicht von Staat oder Kirche als Feiertag festgelegt worden war?

—Ottilie Baader[2]

IN 1989, JUST BEFORE the collapse of the German Democratic Republic, the Socialist Unity Party's Institut für Marxismus-Leninismus began publication of a projected multivolume history of the party. The first volume, the only one to appear, did not start the narrative in 1946 with the establishment of the SED, not even in 1918/19, when its forerunner, the KPD, was founded. After a few introductory remarks that took the history back to the medieval period and the Reformation, volume one, "from the beginnings to 1917," began the narrative proper in the 1830s with the first glimmers of industrialization, a factory proletariat, and socialist ideology. The authors lavished their greatest attention, some three-quarters of the over eight hundred pages, on the development of the Social Democratic Party in Imperial Germany.[3]

The *History of the SED* was, of course, an exercise in self-legitimation, an

[1] "Through these measures [workers' housing colonies] . . . we bind a reliable and settled core of workers to the firm and develop and solidify the feeling of belonging to our enterprises." Quoted in Helmut Seidl, *Streikkämpfe der mittel- und ostdeutschen Braunkohlenarbeiter von 1890 bis 1914* (Leipzig: Deutscher Verlag für Grundstoffindustrie, 1964), 29.

[2] "[1 May 1890.] You could already see workers out first thing in the morning dressed in their Sunday best. How was this possible? On a workday the proletarian herd dared not to work and to deprive the employer of his profit? They dared to celebrate on a day that neither the state nor the church had declared a holiday?" Ottilie Baader, "Der erste Weltfeiertag," in *Proletarische Lebensläufe: Autobiographische Dokumente zur Entstehung der Zweiten Kultur in Deutschland*, vol. 1: *Anfänge bis 1914*, ed. Wolfgang Emmerich (Hamburg: Rowohlt, 1974), 351.

[3] *Geschichte der Sozialistischen Einheitspartei Deutschlands*, vol. 1: *Von den Anfängen bis 1917*, ed. Institut für Marxismus-Leninismus beim ZK der SED (Berlin: Dietz, 1989).

effort to demonstrate the deep roots of the SED and its state, their natural and seamless development out of the long course of German history. If it reaches beyond the bounds of the historical imagination to assert that the SED was "the heir of everything progressive in the history of the German people,"[4] the claims of the party historians had, nonetheless, a certain basis: the KPD and SED emerged out of the organizations, politics, and culture of the social democratic labor movement. Social democracy constituted for German communism a powerful source of ideas and practices, and an intractable and troublesome opponent. German communism was formed in continual exchange with social democracy and can only be understood by examining what it absorbed and rejected from its socialist origins.

But social democracy and German labor were not synonymous. The SPD to a certain extent imposed a structure on the "life-worlds" of the German proletariat, a more rigorously formulated worldview and an array of organizations and institutions that had both emancipatory and disciplinary components. And the SPD itself did not suddenly emerge in pristine fashion, a fully formed crystalline entity. As a popular movement rooted in the working class, the SPD was itself shaped by the economic, political, and familial patterns that formed the proletariat in the era of high industrialization. The workplace, the streets, and the household were the crucial spaces in which the working class as a social entity and the political direction of the labor movement were constituted. These were the sites in which elites sought to discipline and control workers, but these sites also provided workers and the organized labor movement with the resources—physical, social, and intellectual—to contest the all-encompassing claims of the employers and the state.

This chapter explores the formation of the working class and the emergence of the social democratic labor movement in Imperial Germany. The emphasis is on the methods deployed by employers and the state to create stable, loyal, and subordinate workforces, and the repertoires of resistance forged by workers.[5] In the more intensely conflictual circumstances of the Weimar Republic, elites would resurrect and deepen many of the strategies developed in the prewar period in order to contain the threats posed by radicalized workers and a mass-based communist movement. Communists, in turn, would draw on, revise, and extend the forms of protest developed before 1914.

Workplace Regimes

In the 1890s, Germany surmounted the travails of the long depression of the last quarter of the nineteenth century and entered the great period of economic expan-

[4] From the SED program and used as the epigraph in *Geschichte der Sozialistischen Einheitspartei Deutschlands*.

[5] The title of the chapter and the terminology I use here are adapted from Charles Tilly's concept of "repertoires of contention" and Michael Burawoy's discussion of "factory regimes." See Tilly's account of the development of the term in "Contentious Repertoires in Great Britain, 1758–1834," *SSH* 17:2 (1993): 253–80, and Burawoy, *The Politics of Production: Factory Regimes under Capitalism and Socialism* (London: Verso, 1985).

sion that lasted until the outbreak of World War I.[6] As its economy forged ahead, Germany moved to the very forefront of the industrial powers of the world. Its economic preeminence rested on the traditional industries of the industrial revolution—coal, iron and steel, metalworking, and textiles—as well as the key sectors of the "second" industrial revolution—chemicals, electrical power generation, and electrotechnical products. The very rapid process of industrial expansion and the sheer size and concentration of many of the new enterprises created grave problems for German employers, who had to create a disciplined labor force out of a heterogeneous population, and who faced unprecedented challenges from workers and the emergent trade unions and Social Democratic Party.[7]

As a constituent element of the intense drive for profit, employers sought to establish an internal patriarchal regime defined by hard work, severe discipline, loyalty to the firm and the kaiser, and subordination. In return, many firms promised to provide for the well-being of their workers. Coercion and paternalism, effected through a panoply of new technologies, blatant repression, and social welfare programs, functioned as the inextricably entwined, constituent elements of the patriarchal regime.[8] The workplace served as the central site of these efforts, but their reach, in the employers' view, would extend beyond to workers' families, the local community, and the society at large. By creating a disciplined labor force in the factories and mines, the workplace regime would also create disciplined and loyal subjects—certainly not citizens.

Germany's remarkable industrial growth rate rested upon the confluence of favorable market conditions with a conscious employer strategy of rationalization—the adoption of technological and managerial innovations designed to create new products, lower the costs of production, and assert managerial powers in the labor

[6] For summaries of Germany's economic development in this period, see Knut Borchardt, "Wirtschaftliches Wachstum und Wechsellagen 1800–1914," in *Handbuch der deutschen Wirtschafts- und Sozialgeschichte*, vol. 2, ed. Hermann Aubin and Wolfgang Zorn (Stuttgart: Ernst Klett, 1976), 198–275, and Alan S. Milward and S. B. Saul, *The Development of the Economies of Continental Europe, 1850–1914* (Cambridge, Mass.: Harvard University Press, 1977), 17–70. The classic, and disputed, work on the long depression is Hans Rosenberg, *Große Depression und Bismarckzeit* (Berlin: Walter de Gruyter, 1967).

[7] For the major recent accounts, see Gerhard A. Ritter and Klaus Tenfelde, *Arbeiter im Deutschen Kaiserreich 1871–1914* (Bonn: J. H. W. Dietz Nachf., 1992); Gerhard A. Ritter with Elisabeth Müller-Luckner, eds., *Der Aufstieg der deutschen Arbeiterbewegung: Sozialdemokratie und Freie Gewerkschaften im Parteiensystem und Sozialmilieu des Kaiserreiches* (Munich: Oldenbourg, 1990); and Mary Nolan, "Economic Crisis, State Policy, and Working-Class Formation in Germany, 1870–1900," in *Working-Class Formation: Nineteenth-Century Patterns in Western Europe and the United States*, ed. Ira Katznelson and Aristide R. Zolberg (Princeton: Princeton University Press, 1986), 352–93. For insightful though partly overdone criticisms of the approach taken by Ritter and Tenfelde, see Geoff Eley, "Class, Culture, and Politics in the Kaiserreich," *CEH* 27:3 (1994): 355–75, and Kathleen Canning, "Gender and the Politics of Class Formation: Rethinking German Labor History," *AHR* 97:3 (1992): 736–68.

[8] For a concise summary of employer strategies, see Alf Lüdtke, "Arbeiterpolitik versus Politik der Arbeiter: Zu Unternehmensstrategien und Arbeiterverhalten in deutschen Großbetrieben zwischen 1890 und 1914/20," in *Arbeiter und Bürger im 19. Jahrhundert: Varianten ihres Verhältnisses im europäischen Vergleich*, ed. Jürgen Kocka (Munich: Oldenbourg, 1986), 202–12. For an encyclopedic synthesis, see Ritter and Tenfelde, *Arbeiter*, 354–425.

process.[9] The major industries of Rhineland-Westphalia and Prussian Saxony, two of the nations's most concentrated industrial regions—and centers of social democratic and, later, communist support—all were in the forefront of this process. Beginning most consistently in the last decade of the nineteenth century, German firms established departments staffed by engineers and administrators that independently determined piecework rates and in general set more rigorous controls on the work process.[10] The basic steel, machine tool, and chemical industries were notable for establishing finely graded pay and skill differentials among workers that were only partly governed by technological necessities.[11] Ruhr mines began to experiment with longwall mining, whereby large numbers of miners worked together in a concentrated area.[12] In Prussian Saxony, the lignite seams were close to the surface, enabling owners to use advanced earth-moving equipment to extract the coal. Industrial piecework systems and longwall and strip-mining enabled management to intensify the pace of work and extend its general supervision of employees. But rationalization by no means signified the universal dequalification of skilled labor. Mechanization in many industries created demands for new skills and required highly trained machinists to maintain and repair equipment.

Employers did not only innovate—they also relied on long-standing repressive practices that were expressively conveyed in factory codes. Employers continually revised them—Krupp issued complete codes in 1856, 1885, and 1890, along

[9] For details, see Irmgard Steinisch, *Arbeitszeitverkürzung und sozialer Wandel: Der Kampf um die Achtstundenschicht in der deutschen und amerikanischen Eisen- und Stahlindustrie 1880–1929* (Berlin: Walter de Gruyter, 1986), 49–72; S. H. F. Hickey, *Workers in Imperial Germany: The Miners of the Ruhr* (Oxford: Clarendon, 1985), 109–68; Dieter Schiffmann, *Von der Revolution zum Neunstundentag: Arbeit und Konflikt bei BASF 1918–1924* (Frankfurt am Main: Campus, 1983), 54–128; Franz-Josef Brüggemeier, *Leben vor Ort: Ruhrbergleute und Ruhrbergbau 1889–1919* (Munich: Beck, 1983), 75–141; Uta Stolle, *Arbeiterpolitik im Betrieb: Frauen und Männer, Reformisten und Radikale, Fach- und Massenarbeiter bei Bayer, BASF, Bosch und in Solingen (1900–1933)* (Frankfurt am Main: Campus, 1980), 20–107; Wilhelm Treue, "Die Technik in Wirtschaft und Gesellschaft 1800–1970," in *Handbuch der deutschen Wirtschafts- und Sozialgeschichte* 2:81–82. See also the very informative commemorative volumes published by German firms and industrial associations, *A. Riebeck'sche Montanwerke: Die Geschichte einer mitteldeutschen Bergwerksgesellschaft. Zum 25 Jahre Carl Adolph Riebeck und 50 Jahre A. Riebeck'sche Montanwerke AG, 1858–1933* (Munich: F. Bruckmann, 1933), 89–105; *50 Jahre Mitteldeutscher Braunkohlen Bergbau: Festschrift zum 50jährigen Bestehen des Deutschen-Braunkohlen-Industrie-Vereins E.V. Halle (Salle) 1885–1935* (Halle: Wilhelm Knapp, n.d.), 6–7, 59–60, 80, 497–98; and the English version of the volume published for the Krupp centenary in 1912, *Krupp: A Century's History of the Krupp Works, 1812–1912* (n.p., n.d.).

[10] Gunnar Stollberg, *Die Rationalisierungsdebatte 1908–1933: Freie Gewerkschaften zwischen Mitwirkung und Gegenwehr* (Frankfurt am Main: Campus, 1981), 32–42, and Heidrun Homburg, "Anfänge des Taylorsystems in Deutschland vor dem Ersten Weltkrieg," *GG* 4:2 (1978): 170–94.

[11] Steinisch, *Arbeitszeitverkürzung*, 62–64, 211–14; Schiffmann, *Von der Revolution*, 104–5; Stolle, *Arbeiterpolitik*, 29–30, 110, 153–69; Elisabeth Domansky-Davidsohn, "Der Großbetrieb als Organisationsproblem des Deutschen Metallarbeiter-Verbandes vor dem Ersten Weltkrieg," in *Arbeiterbewegung und industrieller Wandel: Studien zu gewerkschaftlichen Organisationsproblemen im Reich und an der Ruhr*, ed. Hans Mommsen (Wuppertal: Peter Hammer, 1980), 95–116; and for one machine tool plant in Halle, Irmtraud Dalchow, "Die Hallesche Maschinenfabrik und Eisengiesserei AG von ihrer Gründung bis zum Jahre 1918," *Aus der Geschichte der halleschen Arbeiterbewegung*, vol. 7, ed. Stadtleitung Halle der SED (Halle: Druckhaus Freiheit, n.d.), 43–45.

[12] Brüggemeier, *Leben vor Ort*, 110–11; Hickey, *Workers*, 164.

with numerous amendments—a sign of the constant struggle to assert the preeminence of the patriarchal regime over workers' lives.[13] In its Arbeits-Ordnung of 1910, the Badische Anilin- und Sodafabrik (BASF), for example, claimed for itself immense powers over workers' time and movements.[14] Not only did the workday range from ten and one-half to twelve-hour shifts, but workers were forbidden from leaving the premises at specified times, such as during the night-shift break. The company preserved the right unilaterally to order overtime, Sunday, and holiday work, and the much-despised extended swing shift during the weekly change of the day and night crews. Fines, a particularly blatant form of coercion much hated by workers, were carefully delineated. Workers faced wage reductions ranging from twenty pfennig to one-half the average daily pay in cases of lateness, negligent use of machinery, and disobedience toward supervisors. The ability to level fines for vaguely worded charges placed immense discretionary power in the hands of foremen and managers.

The ultimate weapon of coercion, dismissal, firms deployed at will, constrained only by the labor market and the relatively rare instances of solidarity strikes. Firings for political agitation probably increased after the turn of the century as employers organized themselves more thoroughly. They formed new associations (as in the 1908 establishment of the Mine Owners Association) and strengthened existing ones through the coordination of antiunion and antisocialist measures, including joint strike insurance funds, blacklists of union and SPD members, and industry-wide lockouts.[15] After strikes employers were increasingly firm in refusing to rehire workers who had stayed out, in particular those known as agitators and organizers.[16] And they imposed fines with a relish. In one count by the factory inspectors in 1913, 60–70 percent of factories in the Halle-Merseburg government district levied fines for lateness, absenteeism, and other infractions of work rules.[17]

But blatant coercion was not the only weapon in the employers' arsenal. They also implemented social welfare measures that were as crucial in the formation of the working class as the measures of repression. Employers were often motivated by the traditional Christian values of paterfamilias and charity, in which they took responsibility for the well-being of their charges. Such high-minded motivations easily combined with the mundane self-interest of creating stable, loyal workforces, especially in the era of extremely high working-class mobility.[18] It is

[13] Lüdtke, "Arbeiterpolitik."

[14] "Arbeits-Ordnung," 17 December 1910, BLW 1301.

[15] See especially Klaus Saul, *Staat, Industrie, Arbeiterbewegung im Kaiserreich: Zur Innen- und Aussenpolitik des Wilhelminischen Deutschland 1903–1914* (Düsseldorf: Bertelsmann Universitätsverlag, 1974), and Hans-Peter Ullmann, "Unternehmerschaft, Arbeitgeberverbände und Streikbewegung 1890–1914," in *Streik: Zur Geschichte des Arbeitskampfes in Deutschland während der Industrialisierung*, ed. Klaus Tenfelde and Heinrich Volkmann (Munich: Beck, 1981), 194–208.

[16] As after the 1911 strike in the central German coalfields: Königlicher LR[LKM] to MdI, 15 August 1911, GStAKM 77/I/2522/1/2/151.

[17] For some reports on this situation see Prussia, Ministerium für Handel und Gewerbe, *Jahresbericht der Preussischen Regierungs- und Gewerberäte und Bergbehörden* (hereafter *JB*) *1900*, 432, 464, 470–71, 494, and *1913*, 247–48.

[18] On the motivations of employer welfare programs, see Eugene C. McCreary "Social Welfare

notable that employer-backed programs languished somewhat in the 1890s and then expanded concomitantly with the development of more authoritarian actions after the turn of the century. Miners' housing colonies, for example, expanded dramatically after 1900, and in the same period BASF first instituted a comprehensive social welfare program.[19]

Company housing glimmered as the crown jewel of employer welfare programs. In Essen at Krupp, Germany's major armaments manufacturer, the firm housed some 16 to 18 percent of its employees between the turn of the century and World War I.[20] In the Ruhr generally only 7 percent of miners lived in company housing in 1893, but 22 percent did in 1914, and some mining districts had even higher rates.[21] In the lignite mining region of Prussian Saxony, the housing situation was even more acute because of the almost constant demand for labor, especially after the turn of the century. Year after year, Prussian mining officials noted with satisfaction the progress made, so that by 1913 they could report that in the Halberstadt mining district the companies had completely satisfied the need for adequate housing.[22]

In every instance, disciplinary codes for the company colonies supplemented the factory codes workers were subject to on the job. Parents were charged with ensuring the proper behavior of their children. Quiet hours were decreed after 10:00 P.M. Residents were required to sweep and mop at regular intervals. The regulations of the Bochumer Verein's home for single workers stipulated that the residents had to "obey unconditionally the directions of the administrator and the supervisor" and to help put out fires. They were forbidden from lying in bed with dirty clothes, and could only have visitors with the administrator's permission. The firm, obsessively fearful of conspiratorial conversations, even forbade men from visiting in one another's rooms and expected them to eat lunch on the premises.[23] At all company housing, leases were subject to arbitrary termination, a weapon often used against workers who threatened to strike.[24] Working children could only remain in the parents' household when they worked at the mine—a

---

and Business: The Krupp Welfare Program, 1860–1914," *Business History Review* 42:1 (1968): 24–49; Elaine Glovka Spencer, *Management and Labor in Imperial Germany: Ruhr Industrialists as Employers, 1896–1914* (New Brunswick, N.J.: Rutgers University Press, 1984); and Lüdtke, "Arbeiterpolitik." Geoff Eley argues, correctly I think, that paternalism was not merely a feudal relic, but a highly rational practice of capitalist employers. See David Blackbourn and Geoff Eley, *The Peculiarities of German History: Bourgeois Society and Politics in Nineteenth-Century Germany* (New York: Oxford University Press, 1984), 107–11. For a synthesis and a somewhat more cautious view on the modernity of employer welfare programs, see Ritter and Tenfelde, *Arbeiter*, 409–25.

[19] See the figures in Hickey, *Workers*, 53–54, and Schiffmann, *Von der Revolution*, 54. However, Lüdtke, "Arbeiterpolitik," 209, argues that these programs expanded continually from 1873.

[20] Heinrich Lechtape, "Der Einfluß des Weltkrieges auf die Bevölkerung der Stadt Essen (Ruhr)" (Ph.D. diss., Universität zu Greifswald, 1923), 121–22; *Krupp: A Century's History*, 261.

[21] Heinz Gunther Steinberg, *Die Entwicklung des Ruhrgebietes: Eine wirtschafts- und sozialgeographische Studie* (Düsseldorf: Landbezirk Nordrhein-Westfalen Deutscher Gewerkschaftsbund, 1967), 25, 55; Max Jürgen Koch, *Die Bergarbeiterbewegung im Ruhrgebiet zur Zeit Wilhelms II* (Düsseldorf: Droste, 1954), 81; and Hickey, *Workers*, 53–54, whose figures are even higher.

[22] *JB 1913*, 667.

[23] Hickey, *Workers*, 68.

[24] Seidl, *Streikkämpfe*, 29.

means of ensuring a continued supply of labor.[25] And BASF, in the *ultima ratio* of the patriarchal regime, ordered that only members of the company union be granted company housing and the liberty to work gardens on the firm's land.[26]

In the textile towns of Rhineland-Westphalia, company housing for women came equipped with supervisory personnel designed to ensure a "proper" moral setting. In some instances, mill owners subsidized homes supervised by religious personnel. Time was strictly regimented: at one home for female workers in Cologne, the employees were awakened at 5:15 A.M., given a limited amount of time to wash, eat, and make their beds, and forbidden from entering their rooms during the day. Residents required the housemaster's permission to leave the premises, and the doors were locked at 9:30 P.M. Another home banned "indecent conversation or singing," and reported violations of "propriety" to the firm. One factory owner explicitly expressed the returns he expected for providing clean and decent housing: "The workers should requite this solicitude through competence and consistency at work and through moral and decent conduct in and outside of the dormitory."[27]

While single women factory workers were most often housed in dormitories, mine owners used the workers' family economy to solidify the workplace regime. Miners generally received small plots of land, at minimal or no rent, to work as a vegetable garden. Such measures, certainly materially advantageous, also bound workers to the company. As one mine inspector observed:

> The settlement of workers in colonies has at least this advantage—not to be underestimated—over the building of scattered housing: it facilitates the maintenance of order and adequate cleanliness. All mines that own a large number of workers' dwellings have appointed housing administrators who are solely concerned with the control of such dwellings. . . . Tight supervision of workers' dwellings is particularly necessary for that large proportion of immigrant miners who have previously without exception lived in much worse housing and who only gradually learn to value the advantages of order and cleanliness.[28]

Clearly, to state officials and employers, housing colonies offered an ideal setting: with impunity they could intervene in the daily lives of workers and their families and bring to bear the moral tutelage they believed lay at the very core of their responsibilities. The stability of the larger social order rested on their instructing workers to value "*Ordnung*" and "*Sauberkeit*"—order and cleanliness—the twin-headed goddess of bourgeois society.

Unable to foresee the immense social disruptions of World War I and the

[25] Ibid.

[26] Schiffmann, *Von der Revolution*, 67.

[27] Kathleen Canning, "Class, Gender, and Working-Class Politics: The Case of the German Textile Industry, 1890–1933" (Ph.D. diss., Johns Hopkins University, 1988), 253–65, quote on 258. See also idem, "Gender and the Culture of Work: Ideology and Identity in the World Beyond the Mill Gate, 1890–1914," in *Elections, Mass Politics, and Social Change in Modern Germany: New Perspectives*, ed. Larry Eugene Jones and James Retallack (Cambridge: Cambridge University Press, 1992), 175–99.

[28] Quoted in Hickey, *Workers*, 68.

postwar reconstruction, German employers also sought to guarantee a stable workforce for the future, to ensure, that is, the social and physical reproduction of labor. In the prewar era, many firms hired sons of employees as apprentices, which bound multiple generations to the firm. Such programs also accorded with the family strategies of workers. Mine inspectors, for example, reported in 1902 that miners actively sought to find employment for their sons at the same mines at which they were employed.[29] Often, employers held on to their young employees through recessions that made their actual production redundant. As the mine inspector for the Dortmund I mining region reported, "the hiring of young people in the interest of educating a capable corps of miners can only be signified as advantageous."[30] But the adjective "capable"—*tüchtig* in German—implied a host of other virtues, at least in the view of employers and officials: loyalty, discipline, moral rectitude. By offering gratuities and medals for long years of service—faithfully recorded by the inspectors—firms sought to ensure stability through the life course of a single generation. BASF paid premiums after every five years of service, but they were collectable only in the jubilee year, the twenty-fifth year of employment! In 1913, 1,083 workers received payments that averaged sixty-nine marks, approximately two weeks' wages.[31]

The biological family figured prominently in the labor force reproduction strategies of many large firms; the metaphor of the patriarchal family proved no less significant. The "*Herr-im-Hause*" (lord of the manor) claim of Ruhr industrialists is the most well known, but many other companies propagated similar views. Many firms in the years before World War I began to publish their own newspapers specifically to promote the sense of the "company family." These newspapers reported on cultural events, significant life-course developments among employees, productivity achievements, holiday celebrations, and the like.[32] Often they were distributed by company unions. Whatever the source of distribution, all deployed the metaphor of the patriarchal family for the firm and the larger society.

In the family strategies of employers lay embedded ideologies of gender. The various benefits, monetary and otherwise, of company welfare programs were almost always predicated on the presumption of the male wage earner and the domestic female homemaker. In the heavily masculine industries of mining and metalworking, the companies themselves promoted the ideal of a family wage for at least the core group of workers. Krupp, which had a minuscule proportion of female employees prior to World War I, established schools for the female members of Krupp employee families. Typically, the courses taught women household management on the assumption that better managed households increased the value of wages and—like discipline in the workplace—generated order in the family and the larger society. The male worker, weary from a hard day by the

[29] *JB 1902*, 464. Bayer established a school to accompany its apprenticeship program and admitted only sons of employees. Ibid., 324–25.

[30] *JB 1901*, 408, see also 415–16; *JB 1902*, 468.

[31] Schiffmann, *Von der Revolution*, 58.

[32] Lüdtke, "Arbeiterpolitik," 209–10.

blast furnace, the lathe, or the coal seam, would find rest and recuperation in the well-managed home, enabling him to go off to work the next day refreshed. Handicrafts were also taught, and were seen as providing the skills that girls and women could apply at home to provide for the family and to sell craft products in the marketplace to supplement, but certainly not replace, the male wage.[33]

Programs directed at the female family members of male workers were obviously insufficient in industries with high female employment. In these cases companies linked workplace and home in new arrangements, which were designed to contain the threatening social impact of female labor by reproducing prevailing understandings of gender. In the highly feminized textile sector, employers established household instruction similar to that offered at Krupp, but designated for female employees. These efforts were encouraged by the revised labor code of 1891 and the activities of factory inspectors, who, like employers, viewed the training of competent housewives as essential to social stability. In some instances, courses were given within the factory itself and were taught by religious personnel. The structuring of work life and home life were to run together in creating stable families and dependable subjects. As factory inspectors wrote, "the purpose of factory work is that the girls become accustomed to perseverance, that they learn to be attentive, orderly, and neat and recognize that even the lowliest job is valuable in connection with the whole, that it is necessary and must be carried out with dedication, if the whole is not to suffer."[34] Some employers, again with the encouragement of the inspectors, supported municipal or charitable educational institutions for young women in which women were taught sewing, cooking, and other household skills. A few municipalities and employers mandated the enrollment of their female employees.[35]

Many firms provided rest homes, hospitals, libraries, and food cooperatives for their members, and these measures also expanded after 1900. Krupp in Essen presided over a large consumer cooperative that had its own bakery and slaughterhouse and sold food, clothing, and household items at reduced prices to the employees. Alfred Krupp made clear his belief that by granting workers material benefits, the firm would be able to shape their attitudes and bind them to the company: "the advantages we grant to the workers will accrue to the firm in the same measure as the workers enjoy them."[36] Such sentiments were supported by state officials, as the mining officer who wrote that "the employer who institutes welfare programs serves not only the well-being of his workers but also—consciously or unconsciously—his own interest."[37]

In the effort to ameliorate the impact of inflation, many firms bought large quantities of foodstuffs—potatoes primarily, but also bacon, margarine, vegetables, and occasionally even fresh meat, fish, and fruit—at wholesale prices, which they then resold to their workforces at cost.[38] The mines dispensed coal and

[33] McCreary, "Social Welfare," 85.

[34] Canning, "Class, Gender, and Working-Class Politics," 258–64, quote on 260.

[35] *JB 1902*, 342.

[36] Quoted in McCreary, "Social Welfare," 83.

[37] Quoted in Hickey, *Workers*, 60–61.

[38] *JB 1901*, 142–43.

wood to their employees, but even this relatively minor disbursement came with conditions. In 1894, the Von der Heydt mine in Ammendorf (near Halle) raised the prerequisite for the coal disbursements from one to five years of employment.[39] Typically, paid vacations, in the rare instances that they were available at all, were extremely limited in scope and tied to years of service. The Ilse-Bergbau-AG in central Germany offered a yearly vacation of six days to workers who had been employed for ten years and had carried out their responsibilities in an "objectionless manner and with satisfactory productivity."[40] One of Halle's largest machine-building plants, the Hallesche Maschinen- und Eisengiesserei, had a profit-sharing plan for its workers, as did one mining company east of Halle, a program unique for its time but continually lauded as a model by state officials. But here too participation was tied to years of service.[41]

Sickness funds sometimes preceded the passage of national legislation under Bismarck. Krupp, which had one of the earliest and most extensive, even had its own hospital to care for sick employees, to which was added a maternity hospital in 1910. BASF, like many firms, placed the fines it collected into the sickness fund, and made additional contributions above and beyond the legal requirements. Ill employees received supplementary allowances but had to have been employed continually for at least two years at BASF, and could not be members of other sickness funds—an effort to undermine the funds in which the unions and the social democrats exercised influence. Ill workers received one-quarter of their weekly wages paid from the third day of the illness up to twenty-six weeks. To ensure that they would not tarry in returning to work, the allowance was only paid after the illness or after four weeks had elapsed.

Firms also took measures to improve the health and safety of the work situation, partly under the pressure of state officials. Even the chemical industry, notorious for its dangerous working conditions, increased the capacity of its shower rooms and the number of on-site doctors and other medical personnel. BASF built a maternity hospital for the wives of workers with at least two years' service. In the particularly dirty sections of the factory, the bathing time was included in the paid workday. Cafeterias were built so that workers would not have to eat their lunch at their workplaces amid dangerous chemicals, though company-provided meals were ended as an economy measure in 1914. And like many large firms, BASF, in addition to the sickness fund, contributed to accident insurance and pension fund plans for its workers that supplemented the state-mandated programs, but were limited to workers who had had, depending on the program, a minimum of two or five years service to the company.[42] Krupp's extensive disability and retirement programs reached back to the 1850s.[43] Giving voice, once again, to the concern for, even obsession with, the biological and social reproduction of labor, Alfred Krupp wrote that he wished to reward those

39 Seidl, *Streikkämpfe*, 29–30.

40 Quoted in ibid., 30.

41 *JB 1900*, 189 and *1905*, 205–6; Dalchow, "Hallesche Maschinenfabrik," 43–45; and Seidl, *Streikkämpfe*, 30.

42 Schiffmann, *Von der Revolution*, 55–57.

43 McCreary, "Social Welfare," 75–78.

workers who gave "faithful service" to the firm with pensions, and to provide for the disabled so that the surviving children "might become in their turn wherever possible faithful workers and foremen."[44]

In the last years before the war, company unions increasingly became the vehicles for welfare programs. Employers deliberately drove another wedge between workers by bestowing only upon members of these unions such benefits as special Christmas and Easter bonuses, low-interest loans, access to company rest and vacation homes, pension supplements, and even, in some cases, subsidized foodstuffs. The company unions presided over cultural and social activities, which included, in the case of BASF, a choir, theater group, orchestra, and youth programs. As BASF officials wrote, these efforts were designed to

> bring together all those workers who are unorganized, patriotic, and committed to economic peace in opposition to the inflammatory and employer-hostile tendencies of the trade union organized [workers] . . . in order to promote, in peaceful agreement with the factory directorate . . . the common interests of workers and employers and the . . . improvement of the social and economic circumstances of the members.[45]

In their workplace regimes, employers promoted ideologies of class collaboration and patriarchal families. They exercised blatant repression and instituted paternalistic social welfare programs designed to create disciplined and subordinate subjects. They exerted a powerful, but by no means unqualified, hold on workers, as did the very similar programs instituted by the state.

State Regimes

While the repressive and paternalistic practices of employers intensified after 1890, and especially after 1900, the web of relations that bound workers to the state grew more dense. The threefold growth in the membership of the social democratic–aligned Free Unions between 1900 and 1913 and the electoral advance of the SPD, which in 1912 won about one-third of the electorate, gravely worried Germany's ruling elites. National trends were reaffirmed by developments at the local and regional level. In cities and towns throughout Rhineland-Westphalia, Prussian Saxony, and other industrial regions the SPD vote far exceeded its national showing. Even workers long known for their passivity and loyalty to the kaiser, such as the Mansfeld miners of Prussian Saxony, joined the unions in significant numbers and launched strikes for better working conditions and union recognition—to the utter dismay of both employers and state officials.[46]

In response to these developments the state and the employers stepped up their antilabor activity.[47] Confrontations with the police formed a regular part of May

[44] Quoted in ibid., 76.

[45] Schiffmann, *Von der Revolution*, 64–69, quote on 64.

[46] The authorities found the 1909 Mansfeld strike particularly ominous. See various reports in BAP, RMdI 7005.

[47] See especially Saul, *Staat, Industrie, Arbeiterbewegung*.

Day activities and during the wave of demonstrations that took place between 1906 and 1910 against the inequitable Prussian three-class voting system. The deployment of troops during strikes, as in 1909 in the Mansfeld copper-mining region, in 1911 in the central German lignite and bituminous coalfields, and in 1912 in the Ruhr, aroused intense resentment on the part of workers.[48] Despite the fact that the antisocialist laws had lapsed in 1890, administrative and judicial harassment of the organized labor movement continued unabated, and even intensified after 1910.[49]

Yet the relationship between workers and the state was never exclusively hostile and adversary, nor merely manipulative. The state at times intervened on labor's side during industrial conflicts, and the government ran an array of social welfare programs. These measures drew upon a patriarchal tradition that stretched back in an unbroken manner to the cameralism and enlightened absolutism of the seventeenth and eighteenth centuries, and were designed to ensure the internal stability of the authoritarian system in an era of profound social and political change. Along with material benefits, the welfare system entailed limited forms of representation for workers. In their daily lives beneficiaries of government-run programs, German workers remained predisposed toward statist doctrines even when they struggled against the existing state.

As is well known, the German state pioneered the formation of the modern welfare state. In 1883 the Reichstag, at Bismarck's behest, passed a health insurance program, which was quickly followed by the establishment of workers compensation for industrial accidents and pensions for the disabled and the elderly. While benefits were minimal—in 1891 the average pension amounted to 18 percent of the average annual income of an employed person—they did cover a substantial portion of the population and at least ameliorated the harsh conditions of industrial life. By 1890 virtually all wage earners were covered by accident insurance and disablement and old-age pensions; by 1914 most had sickness insurance as well.[50]

Many workers also came to count upon the state to aid them in other ways. In the Ruhr miners strikes of 1889 and 1905, for example, the intervention of the

[48] See Klaus Tenfelde, "Probleme der Organisation von Arbeitern und Unternehmern im Ruhrbergbau 1890–1918," and Hans Mommsen, "Soziale und politische Konflikte an der Ruhr 1905 bis 1924," both in *Arbeiterbewegung und industrieller Wandel*, 38–86.

[49] For some examples from the Halle-Merseburg region, see *Durch Kampf zum Sieg! Jubiläumsschrift der Sozialdemokratischen Partei in Halle und dem Saalkreis* (Halle: Hallesche Genossenschafts-Buchdruckerei, 1914), 162; Werner Piechocki, "Der Volkspark als Kultur- und Bildungsstätte der halleschen Arbeiter (1907–1914)," *Aus der Geschichte der halleschen Arbeiterbewegung*, vol. 6 (Köthen: Aufbau-Druckerei, 1968), 19–21; and Roswitha Mende, "Geschichte der Sozialdemokratie im Regierungsbezirk Merseburg von der Jahrhundertwende bis 1917" (Ph.D. diss., Philisophischen Fakultät des Wissenschaftlichen Rates der Martin-Luther-Universität Halle-Wittenberg, 1985), 253. For Essen, see the unpublished memoir by Heinrich Rabbich, "60 Jahre Essener 'Freie-Arbeiter-Jugend'" (ms., 1965), in Archivsammlung Ernst Schmidt (Essen).

[50] For a good summary in English, see Gerhard A. Ritter, *Social Welfare in Germany and Britain: Origins and Development* (Leamington Spa: Berg, 1986), figures 85–86. See also Ritter and Tenfelde, *Arbeiter*, 691–716, and for a distinctive analysis, George Steinmetz, *Regulating the Social: The Welfare State and Local Politics in Imperial Germany* (Princeton: Princeton University Press, 1993).

state won workers concessions in the face of implacable employer hostility.[51] In response to the 1889 strike, the government sponsored amendments to the Reich Industrial Code of 1891 and the Prussian Mining Code of 1892, which provided for more comprehensive factory and mine inspection and established minimum working standards which the inspectors were empowered to enforce. Employers were required to inform workers in detail of the terms of employment.[52] In addition, the Industrial Courts Law of 1890 established institutions with worker and employer representation to which workers could appeal to settle labor grievances and disputes. Mediation boards were also established in 1890 and extended in 1901, and were charged with helping to conclude collective wage agreements and to mediate strikes and lockouts.[53] After the 1905 strike, national legislation mandated the establishment of workers committees in the mines, limited overtime, and prohibited company checkweighmen from rejecting entire wagonloads of coal, a long-standing complaint of miners.[54]

State officials at times even took a stand in defense of workers' physical safety. During the 1905 miners strike in the Ruhr, the Arnsberg district governor demanded that the mines' private security guards exercise restraint in dealing with strikers.[55] And state officials also opposed some of the harsher punitive measures imposed by employers after strikes, as in 1889:

> An agreement has been made between the mine managements of the Ruhr coal district that no miner who has been dismissed from a pit in this district or has resigned will be taken on at another mine. This rigorous measure can only be strongly regretted. . . . It represents a quite unjustified restriction on the right of free movement of labour and . . . sharpens the social differences between employers and employees.[56]

The activities of the factory and mine inspectors are also evidence of the wide-ranging social welfare policy of the German state. The Prussian inspectorate was established in 1853, but additional legislation in 1878 and 1891/92 substantially widened the scope of its activity. Employers opposed inspection, believing that it violated the position of the "*Herr-im-Hause*." But government officials argued that the state had to ensure the well-being of the population and the enforcement of the labor provisions of the civil code, if need be against the employers. Indeed, officials often complained that employers displayed concern only for profits. The state, therefore, had a responsibility to defend the "common good" and mediate

[51] Albin Gladin, "Die Streiks der Bergarbeiter im Ruhrgebiet in den Jahren 1889, 1905 und 1912," in *Arbeiterbewegung am Rhein und Ruhr: Beiträge zur Geschichte der Arbeiterbewegung in Rheinland-Westfalen*, ed. Jürgen Reulecke (Wuppertal: Peter Hammer, 1974), 111–48, and Koch, *Bergarbeiterbewegung*, 100–101.

[52] Klaus Saul, "Repression or Integration? The State, Trade Unions and Industrial Disputes in Imperial Germany," in *The Development of Trade Unionism in Great Britain and Germany, 1880–1914*, ed. Wolfgang J. Mommsen and Hans-Gerhard Husung (London: George Allen and Unwin, 1985), 344.

[53] Ibid., 346, and Adelheid von Saldern, "Wilhelminische Gesellschaft und Arbeiterklasse: Emanzipations- und Integrationsprozesse im kulturellen und sozialen Bereich," *IWK* 13:4 (1977): 497.

[54] Koch, *Bergarbeiterbewegung*, 100–101.

[55] Hickey, *Workers*, 216.

[56] Ibid., 220.

between workers and owners.[57] By the turn of the century, governmental action had forced industrialists to accept state inspection. As one inspector laconically reported in 1900, only rarely did the police have to be called in to ensure the inspectors access to the workplace.[58] More often, the inspectors cited their fine working relationship with the employers as a basis for the continual improvement in the well-being of workers.[59]

In both Rhineland-Westphalia and Prussian Saxony inspectors continually pressed for adequate facilities for workers—washrooms, showers, dressing and luncheon rooms—and they were generally satisfied with the measures taken by the firms. The inspectors in Düsseldorf, alarmed about the high incidence of illness and child mortality among cigar workers, launched an investigation into working conditions.[60] Concerned about public health, they tracked infectious diseases and, in 1909, undertook an involved investigation to find out if workers ate breakfast before going to work.[61] Year after year, both factory and mine inspectors conducted detailed investigations of accidents and actively encouraged safety efforts in the workplace. Officials enforced state regulations with regard to working hours and conditions and especially sought to guarantee that women and minors undertook only those tasks legally permitted. Indeed, the officials often expressed a paternalistic concern about female employment, yet recognized that it could not be wished away:

> It is unfortunate when women who have to care for a household must also take work outside the home. Yet they must be given the possibilities of finding a position. It should not be overlooked that widowed or separated women, as well as those whose husbands as a result of illness, invalidity, or drunkenness are limited in their ability to earn a living, must in circumstances of necessity provide for the maintenance of their families.[62]

Yet they reported enough instances of youth working at jobs for which they were barred and women working extensive hours to indicate widespread noncompliance with protective regulations.

Like the employers, the inspectors sought the construction of a loyal and disciplined labor force. They applauded youth employment, so long as it did not violate the legal code, because work taught the young to become accustomed to discipline, punctuality, and obedience (*Ordnung, Pünktlichkeit und Gehorsam*).[63] But like women, youth had to be supervised. The inspectors' deep concern about the moral rectitude of youth is almost palpable in their reports. The mining inspector of the South Bochum region was a notable exception when he

[57] Saul, "Repression or Integration?" 343, and Jean H. Quataert, "Workers' Reactions to Social Insurance: The Case of Homeweavers in the Saxon Oberlausitz in the Late Nineteenth Century," *IWK* 20:1 (1984): 17–35.

[58] *JB 1900*, 164.

[59] *JB 1901*, 127, *JB 1902*, 452.

[60] *JB 1902*, 337.

[61] *JB 1909*, 440–41.

[62] *JB 1900*, 425.

[63] *JB 1901*, 430.

reported, with no irony intended, that "in general, the young workers make the impression of lively young fellows."[64]

Instead, most inspectors strove to exercise, and encouraged employers to exercise, moral tutelage over the young. Distrustful of the influence of adult workers, they demanded the establishment of separate rooms where young male workers could take their legally mandated breaks. Yet they cautioned that supervision was required because the youth had a tendency to get too raucous.[65] Since religious belief was presumed an essential component of these values, the mine inspector in the West Halle district felt compelled to report that one mining company was granted permission to keep the mine going on three consecutive Sundays so long as the workers were "not hindered from attending church services and that in place of Sunday they receive a twenty-four-hour rest period on a weekday."[66]

In their efforts to create a disciplined labor force, inspectors reproduced prevailing gender ideologies. They sought, for example, to ensure a "proper" moral atmosphere in the factories and mines, to regulate both work and personal life to create order in society.[67] Finding female employees of a sugar-refining plant working with their blouses off because of the heat, the inspectors, more concerned with morals than the conditions of labor, ordered the factory owner to make sure they were fully clothed or else not employ them. In another instance, the inspectors wanted to prosecute a young male worker in a pottery plant because he had gotten a female employee drunk. Because the woman was an adult and had willingly participated in the incident, he could not be prosecuted, and the inspectors had to be content with warning the owner to more closely watch over the morals of his workforce.[68] In the East Essen mining district of the Ruhr, the inspector reported on the one woman employed by the mines, ensuring, lest there be any doubt, that she "does not use the clothing and washrooms at the mine. A special lavatory is available." The inspector might have been more concerned with her working conditions: she had a twelve-hour shift and she prepared coffee and cleaned the kitchen. But there is another moral tale here: her workday began at 6:00 A.M. The inspector thought she should be allowed to begin at 5:30 A.M. so that the coffee would be ready before the men entered the mine "in order to prevent the miners from partaking of spirits."[69]

Expressing their own gendered understanding of the interconnections between the workplace economy and the family economy, the Merseburg inspectorate reported that it had granted an exception to the mandated working day in the case of a book-printing plant. Instead of the one-hour lunch break for all employees, it had permitted women a one-half hour break with an overall shortening of the day by the same amount of time. The workers themselves had requested this and the inspectors had agreed since it allowed more time for the women to take care of their household tasks: "a great part of the afternoon could be devoted to the provisioning

[64] Ibid., 421.

[65] Ibid., 129, and *JB 1902*, 450.

[66] *JB 1902*, 444–45.

[67] See Canning, "Gender and the Culture of Work."

[68] *JB 1901*, 118.

[69] *JB 1902*, 492.

of the household and the caring for the family." The inspectors argued that for all workers, "an earlier conclusion to the workday enables workers to care for the house and courtyard and, in certain circumstances, also the garden and field, and thereby provide for the family."[70] Their active intervention against overtime for women undoubtedly reflected the same concerns for biological and social reproduction.[71]

As often as the inspectors acclaimed the efforts of employers, they also came into conflicts with them. The inspectors took seriously their responsibility for improving working and living conditions. Between 1900 and 1914 they continually expressed concern about inflation, which undermined wage gains, and pressured employers to reduce the length of the workshift.[72] The extraordinary amount of overtime worked in the steel industry on the eve of the war aroused the ire of the factory inspector in Düsseldorf. In a thorough and informative report, the inspector rejected the industry's claim that overtime simply compensated for the absenteeism that resulted from military service, illness, or sheer lack of discipline. Instead, he sharply condemned the labor policies of the industry: "[T]he overtime that a substantial portion of the labor force in the factories of the basic steel industry works has reached such an extent that the health of these workers is seriously endangered."[73] At least some inspectors intervened on the side of labor when workers charged that they had been unfairly dismissed from their employment, and fined employers who violated the provisions on child labor and the ban on Sunday labor or night work for women, or recklessly endangered the safety of workers.[74] Stricter control of overtime by the inspectors had reduced the number of cases that continued longer than four hours and often resulted in violations of the provision that workers had to have at least eight hours rest between shifts.[75]

The inspectors also promoted a "rationalized" workday, one that had clearly delimited beginning and end points, and clearly marked-off breaks. Following a 1902 law affecting the stone-quarrying industry, the inspectors pressured for a regular, ten-hour workday, but gave up in frustration since most of the workers were Italians who "are not used to maintaining a defined worktime." Their work was seasonal in nature and dependent on weather conditions. They were paid by the piece, so the employers also had little interest in fostering a system in which workers would be paid by the hour.[76]

And while the government generally took a strong stand against the unions, those closest to the situation, the mine and factory inspectors, did not always oppose the idea of union recognition. Indeed, in the years between the turn of the century and 1914, they mediated an increasing number of industrial disputes, supported the establishment of workers committees in the factories, promoted the

[70] *JB 1901*, 131–32.

[71] For example, *JB 1902*, 326.

[72] *JB 1906*, 469–71; *JB 1907*, 228, 437; *JB 1908*, 223–24, 410–13, 421; *JB 1909*, 218; and *JB 1911*, 253.

[73] *JB 1913*, 483–500, quote on 495.

[74] For some examples, see *JB 1901*, 425–26, 438; *JB 1902*, 182, 326; and *JB 1911*, 237, 239, 248.

[75] *JB 1911*, 524.

[76] *JB 1902*, 331.

establishment of joint labor-management mediation boards, and in general reported increased dealings with labor representatives—a trend that presages later developments during the war and the Weimar Republic.[77] In at least some regions, regular workers as well as trade union officials also became increasingly open to the intervention of factory inspectors—a sign of their increasing reliance on the authority of the state. Indeed, the inspectors themselves sounded almost hurt when, in 1901 in the Merseburg government district, their efforts had come to naught: "The workers have not stepped beyond their reticence in relation to the factory inspectors, even though nothing has been left undone [to encourage them]. . . . The factory inspector in Merseburg held regular meeting times in Zeitz and Weissenfels and will continue to do so although his efforts have been little rewarded. Only ten individuals have found their way to talk to him."[78] But the Düsseldorf inspector, perhaps somewhat more enterprising, spoke before trade union and factory meetings, explaining to workers the tasks of the inspectorate and some of the regulations governing working conditions. His efforts seem to have paid off in the greater willingness of workers and worker representatives to approach the inspectors with their grievances. One of the very few female inspectors reported that women workers in the Düsseldorf region were increasingly willing to approach her.[79]

Finally, the local state also served an important welfare function. The usual urban problems that accompanied industrialization—severe overcrowding, insufficient and poor housing, clogged transportation networks, poverty—quickly rendered outmoded the minimalist governance practiced by city notables. Following 1890, many cities had at their helm activist mayors who broadened the scope of the local state and the geographic boundaries of their communities. Where the SPD was able to win substantial representation in local city councils, municipalities took on an even broader role, in some cases establishing unemployment insurance and public works programs.[80]

For the activists, conservative, liberal, and, sometimes, social democratic, urban reform constituted an absolutely central element of social stability, one that complemented the efforts of employers and the central state. In their view, a "healthy" city would nurture the "sound and sober" elements of the population, and separate the "worthy" poor, who deserved social support systems, from the lazy and malingering "underclass."[81]

The activist mayors fought long battles with recalcitrant city councils in which property owners, loathe to see taxes increase or planners alter the cityscape,

[77] *JB 1901*, 115, 134, 268; *JB 1902*, 330–31; *JB 1905*, 185, 368; *JB 1906*, 471–74; and *JB 1909*, 407.

[78] *JB 1901*, 127. This instance involved a factory inspector, but it may be that miners were more inclined to appeal to officials because of the long tradition of state protectionism. For a very interesting collection of miners' appeals, see *Bis vor die Stufen des Throns: Bittschriften und Beschwerden von Bergarbeitern*, ed. Klaus Tenfelde and Helmuth Trischler (Munich: Beck, 1986).

[79] *JB 1901*, 258–59. See also *JB 1902*, 321–22.

[80] Steinmetz, *Regulating the Social.*

[81] Brian Ladd, *Urban Planning and Civic Order in Germany, 1860–1914* (Cambridge, Mass.: Harvard University Press, 1990).

constituted the dominant bloc.[82] The key, inextricably entwined elements of reform involved housing and public health policies, although both reached their full scope only in the Weimar Republic. To improve these conditions necessitated, as a prerequisite, administrative reforms and a widening of city boundaries. The incorporation of villages and suburbs created more rational administrative lines and gave cities land to promote the building of new housing and to stake out parks, nature preserves, and the famed *Schrebergärten*—small garden plots situated, most often, on the outskirts of cities and offered to residents for a minimal rental—that can still be seen in many German cities. Municipalities implemented zoning measures, more stringent building codes, housing inspections, and improved public sanitation. Halle, for example, instituted in 1910—over the strenuous objection of property owners—a building code and housing inspections "which through the supervision of conditions of the living room, bedrooms, and kitchen, and all attached rooms, were to ensure health and morality."[83] Even the composition of the housing commission reproduced prevailing gender ideas. Halle's mayor Richard Robert Rive noted that it was headed by a woman in order to placate the opposition since "the care of the family home is much more the charge of the housewife than [of] the husband . . . [and] the landlords would have nothing to fear from this woman, who exercised no powers of coercion and indeed could have an effect only on the renters."[84]

To Rive, it hardly seemed worth commenting on the fact that renters were now subject in their place of residence to the disciplinary powers of the municipality. Similarly, the establishment in 1907 of a public health service and a school health service presided over by physicians improved the health standards of the population and provided for greater intervention in the daily lives of workers. Healthy bodies and decent housing, sound individuals and a stable social order, were inextricably entwined in the view of urban reformers.

For the working-class population, municipal reform bore the promise of improved living conditions, but also constituted another realm of state intervention in their lives, another source of disciplinary regulation. By assuming new powers, municipalities also became a new agency to which workers and the organized labor movement appealed for redress.

Working Conditions

Welfare programs and social reforms never altered the very basic fact: industrial labor was arduous, oppressive, and dangerous.[85] The medicine prescribed by

[82] The section on the imperial period of the memoirs of Halle's mayor from 1906 to 1934, Richard Robert Rive, is a long heroic narrative of his triumphs over the incompetence, ignorance, and narrow vision of the city councillors. See *Lebenserinnerungen eines deutschen Oberbürgermeisters*, Schriftenreihe des Verfeins zur Pflege kommunalwissenschaftlicher Aufgaben e.v. Berlin, vol. 5 (Stuttgart: W. Kohlhammer Verlag, 1960). This would seem to be typical for the genre.

[83] For the Halle example, see ibid., 156–82, quote on 157–58. Generally, see Ladd, *Urban Planning*.

[84] Rive, *Lebenserinnerungen*, 157.

[85] For the grand synthetic description, see Ritter and Tenfelde, *Arbeiter*, 263–536.

employers and the state were mere palliatives and insufficient ones at that; the subclinical dosages sent the patient on the hunt for alternative remedies. Factory and mine inspectors, well aware of the dangers of the situation, conducted in 1911 three special investigations in addition to their regular activities. Their reports on overtime, night work, and conditions in cement factories detail the harsh realities of working-class life.

In the metalworking industry in Halle, the inspectors reported that the daily workday had decreased to nine and one-half hours, which the workers greatly valued. But the twelve-hour shift was still the rule in electrical and gas works, paper factories, flour and sugar mills, and steel and chemical plants.[86] Underground miners in central Germany generally worked nine-hour shifts portal to portal, but twelve-hour shifts were typical for above-ground workers, who were increasingly common as mechanized earth-moving equipment made strip-mining possible. In the Ruhr the workday exclusive of the time taken to reach and return from the seam was eight to eight and one-half hours.[87] As the mines expanded and shafts became deeper, it could take workers as long as one hour to reach the coal face from the mine entry.

Night labor was quite extensive, especially in those industries that produced with continuous processes, as chemicals, or kept ovens going constantly, as in steel, glass, and brick manufacturing. The Ruhr steel industry, among others, maintained the notorious twenty-four-hour swing shift every two weeks when the day and night crews switched. The situation was only slightly better in the Mansfeld copper-smelting plants of central Germany. On a three-shift system, every week two-thirds of the workforce worked sixteen hours straight, while one-third had a day and a half off.[88]

In boom years overtime was a common feature of the daily routine. In the Düsseldorf government district, inspectors reported that workers averaged nearly two-thirds of an hour overtime per day in 1911—and that came either on top of a twelve-hour shift or on Sundays and holidays. The overall figures masked some even greater abuses—115,970 cases of overtime amounting to more than four hours, 73 percent of which occurred on Sundays. The inspector identified fourteen cases in which workers on the swing shift labored longer than the twenty-four hours that was "normal" in these circumstances.[89] The inspector concluded that the legal minimum of an eight-hour rest period between workshifts was often violated, yet workers were themselves often indifferent to the provision so long as they were paid.[90]

Reforms of the labor code beginning in the 1890s resulted in prohibitions on night and overtime labor for women and youth and limits to their workday. But the inspectors reported numerous exceptions and violations. In one notorious incident,

[86] *JB 1911*, 233, 235–36, 515, 526–29. BASF in Ludwigshafen had reduced the workday, but this was not the case in the chemical plants of Prussian Saxony and the Ruhr.

[87] Ibid., 685; Hickey, *Workers*, 127–35.

[88] *JB 1911*, 234.

[89] Ibid., 515, 519, 522–24.

[90] Ibid., 522–24.

a garment factory dismissed its female workers at 8:00 P.M. in accordance with the law, and then secretly had them start up again at 9:00 P.M. and work all through the night during the rush season.[91] Numerous cases of the illegal employment of child labor were also reported.[92] While the inspector in Halle found little evidence of women textile workers taking work home after their factory shift—a practice banned by the commercial code—the Düsseldorf inspector reported on extensive violations. Since the law banned only home work for the same firm for which one worked a regular factory shift, some women worked at home for other companies. Some women took work home that other family members allegedly completed. Inspectors also observed women during their breaks completing handwork for other factories that lay nearby. Neighboring factories had even thought of swapping workers: those employed at one factory during the day would take home work for the other at night and vice versa.[93] Clearly, only the most desperate economic circumstances could have compelled women, after a full ten-hour day in the factory, to complete piecework clothing production at home.

Industrial employment remained a highly dangerous occupation.[94] Reported accidents on the job involved approximately 4 percent of the factory labor force in Halle-Merseburg, approximately 7 percent in the Düsseldorf government district. Twenty-seven individuals were killed on the job in 1911 in the Merseburg government district; 229 suffered severe injuries. Two hundred and nine work-related accidents were fatal in the Düsseldorf district.[95] In the mines, the situation was still more dangerous. In 1911, over 10.6 percent of the miners in the West Cottbus subdistrict suffered accidents that kept them out of work for more than three days; nineteen were killed on the job. In the Naumburg subdistrict, 12.7 percent of miners suffered accidents that kept them out of work for more than three days; seven were killed. In the Dortmund I subdistrict, the accident rate reached 15.8 percent, and included fifty-nine fatalities.[96] According to workers' representatives, the average age of invalided miners continually decreased, from fifty-one years old in 1861 to 41.2 in 1903, a sure sign of worsening health and safety conditions.[97]

Explosions of various origins were common killers, as were electrical lines—which often were not insulated—and poisonous vapors. In the mines, falling stones, coal, and beams and runaway train cars were the major killers. Chemically and electrically caused fires were also high on the list, but deaths and

[91] Ibid., 237–40, 530–40, example on 531. The inspector levied only a 30 mark fine on the manager, while the owner got off scot-free because he allegedly knew nothing about the night work.

[92] Ibid., 239.

[93] Ibid., 238, 534–36.

[94] The yearly factory and mine inspector reports contain sections on workplace accidents and health concerns. The examples that follow are taken from the 1911 reports for the Halle-Merseburg and Düsseldorf government districts, and the Dortmund and Halle mining regions (Oberbergamtsbezirk Halle and Oberbergamtsbezirk Dortmund). Ibid., 240–52, 540–52, 671–94, 711–68.

[95] Ibid., 240, 540.

[96] Ibid., 682, 684, 715.

[97] Petition of the Commission of Seven (made up of representatives of the four mining unions) to Reichskanzler Bülow, 8 February 1905, in Tenfelde and Trischler, *Bis vor die Stufen des Throns*, 417.

severe injuries also resulted from a wide variety of other machines and processes. In separate incidents two workers fell into a centrifuge used in a dye factory, one of whom was killed while the other suffered a severely broken and permanently damaged arm.[98] Presses employed in a wide range of factories often damaged limbs, and dusts and vapors injured respiratory systems. Investigating health conditions in cement factories, inspectors acclaimed a new, modern plant that had mechanized some of the most objectionable parts of the work process, such as the filling of cement sacks, and had installed newly designed ovens that cut down on both fuel consumption and the dust exuded into the atmosphere of the plant. But at an older factory, the inspectors depicted workers virtually swimming in the cement dust as they shoveled by hand the freshly baked cement into sacks. They loaded the sacks onto wheelbarrows, wheeled them over to train cars, and then loaded them by hand into the car. These workers endured extreme variations in temperature, from the intense heat of the ovens to the cold outdoors as they made their way to the train car. Although the inspectors reported that doctors had concluded that the health conditions of cement workers were no worse than "similarly positioned workers," they also reported a "not insignificant" incidence of rheumatic fever and of respiratory ailments.[99] Reports by mining inspectors in 1911 on the satisfactory state of workers' health can only be viewed with skepticism, or with the understanding that the inspectors adopted an extremely narrow definition of work-related illness.[100]

Despite some notable improvements in the years just before World War I, industrial labor in Germany was still marked by long hours and dangerous working conditions. In addition, inflation set in around the turn of the century and undermined wage gains, rationalization resulted in an intensified pace of work, and housing conditions were extremely difficult.[101] The overall conditions of labor remained bleak. And precisely because both the state and the employers had based a good part of their claims to legitimacy on their ability to provide for the well-being and security of the population, the validity of the existing economic and social order came increasingly into question. It would take the immense upheaval of war to undermine more fully their legitimacy. But well before 1914 working-class discontent was on the rise, and found expression in both organized and informal acts of resistance against the policies and claims of both the state and the employers. Communists would draw on this reservoir of antipathy and expand further the repertoires of resistance.

[98] *JB 1911*, 541, 684.

[99] Ibid., 245–52, quote on 248.

[100] The inspectors from virtually every mining subdistrict in the Dortmund and Halle mining regions reported satisfactory health conditions in 1911. See *JB 1911*.

[101] On housing, see especially Hickey, *Workers*, 36–67; Lutz Niethammer, ed., *Wohnen im Wandel: Beiträge zur Geschichte des Alltags in der bürgerlichen Gesellschaft* (Wuppertal: Peter Hammer, 1979); and Franz-Josef Brüggemeier and Lutz Niethammer, "Schlafgänger, Schnapskasinos und schwerindustrielle Kolonie: Aspekte der Arbeiterwohnungsfrage im Ruhrgebiet vor dem Ersten Weltkrieg," in *Fabrik, Familie, Feierabend: Beiträge zur Sozialgeschichte des Alltags im Industriezeitalter*, ed. Jürgen Reulecke and Wolfhard Weber (Wuppertal: Peter Hammer, 1978), 135–75.

Repertoires of Resistance

Despite the towering presence of the state and the firm in their lives, German workers also sought to define the conditions of their own life and labor. They went out on strike, marched in demonstrations, joined the Social Democratic Party and the trade unions, slowed the pace of work, and played around on the job out of sight of supervisors and employers. From the 1890s onward the repertoires of resistance became both more intense and more variegated. New forms of protest became layered upon, but did not override, earlier ones. As in so many social arenas, modernity signified growing complexity rather than the complete triumph over earlier forms of activism and identities.[102]

The boundaries within which working-class protests unfolded were highly constricted. In the Imperial period, even the most militant strikes, let alone individual actions like switching jobs, were hardly revolutionary in character. Many workers, probably the majority, continued to venerate the kaiser and church. But the spectrum between revolution and sheer passivity is broad indeed. Through the large repertoire of actions they practiced, workers shaped their own social and political environment—not always to their benefit—and forced the state and employers continually to renegotiate the terms of social order. And just as employers and officials brought larger understandings of labor, gender, and society to the workplace and state regimes they created, so the visible manifestations of working-class protest had embedded in them patterns of class, gender, and family life.

Strikes

Strikes were the classic form of proletarian protest. Women as well as men engaged in strikes, and some of their efforts, as in the Crimmatschau strike of 1908, were decisive in altering the terms of political conflict in Germany.[103] Strikes were also community protests, and nowhere more clearly than in the mining industry. Behind the facade of a universally male labor force and male proletarian protest lay family structures that sustained strikers in an era when strike support was minuscule at best.

[102] I am arguing here against a notion of strikes as *the* modern form of working-class protest. This approach overlooks (1) the immense array of informal protests in the workplace, (2) the intimate connection between workplace and community struggles, work and family, and (3) the increasingly strong evidence of strikes as far back as the late eighteenth century. It is far more fruitful to examine the multiplicity of working-class actions rather than concentrate on one or another. For two important statements on the modernity of strikes, see Edward Shorter and Charles Tilly, *Strikes in France, 1830–1968* (Cambridge: Cambridge University Press, 1974), and Klaus Tenfelde and Heinrich Volkmann, "Zur Geschichte des Streiks in Deutschland," in idem, *Streik*, 9–30.

[103] Heinz Niggemann, *Emanzipation zwischen Sozialismus und Feminismus: Die sozialdemokratische Frauenbewegung im Kaiserreich* (Wuppertal: Peter Hammer, 1981), 125–33, provides a good summary of women's involvement in strikes, contesting the notion that strikes were primarily the province of male proletarians. See also Canning, "Class, Gender, and Working-Class Politics," who emphasizes women's involvement in wildcat strikes.

In the autumn of 1909, a strike broke out against the Mansfeld mining company, the dominant force in Eisleben (Prussian Saxony) and the surrounding region. Copper miners went out on strike not over wages, but because fifty of their fellow workers had been fired for socialist agitation.[104] State officials correctly labeled the struggle an "issue of power." The workers and the SPD-aligned Alter Verband, the major mineworkers union, were attempting to force the company to rehire the fired workers. The company replied that under no conditions would it endure a social democratic organization among its workers. The district governor expressed support for the company's unwillingness even to negotiate with the union, and noted that Germany could do quite well with a temporary decline in copper supplies, especially as copper prices were quite low. With an air of great regret, he wrote the Minister of the Interior that the Mansfeld workers had in earlier years been quite loyal to the kaiser and the nation.[105] They had not voted in great numbers for the SPD, and had opposed the agitation and activity of the SPD and the Alter Verband. Yet the strike had taken on quite dramatic proportions. Pickets interfered with those who sought to stay on the job, and the military had to be called in to help the police after crowds spent two days jostling and hooting working miners as they came off their shifts. Even Kaiser Wilhelm II was kept informed about the events.[106]

The strike lasted five weeks, an impressive display of solidarity against the massed forces of employer and state. In an effort to preserve the little remaining of the strike fund, the union had tried to get younger workers to seek employment outside the region. About three hundred did without success. While about half of the miners and only a small percentage of the copper mill workers struck, the impact on production was much greater because at numerous mines the most skilled miners were the ones who went out on strike. Weary and hungry, the miners voted unanimously to return to work under the old conditions.[107]

Two years later, in 1911, Mansfeld coal miners went out on strike along with fellow workers throughout the central German coalfield, an action of greater significance than the more well-known 1912 Ruhr miners strike. Three of the four miners unions called the strike and demanded a collective contract, wage increases, an eight-hour day, paid vacations, elimination of fines, and the establishment of joint labor-management employment offices, among other items.[108] Prompted by immediate issues, the strike came also amid rising concern over sporadic unemployment, underemployment, declining real wages, and the increasing mechanization of the mines, which resulted in a reduced demand for labor.[109]

[104] OPM to MHG, 6 October 1909, with Abschrift from the Königlicher LRLKM, 5 October 1909, BAP RMdI/7005/27–29.

[105] OPM to MdI, 24 October 1909, BAP RMdI/7005/60–67.

[106] MHG to Staatssekretär des Innern with Abschrift for Kaiser und König, 28 October 1909, BAP RMdI/7005/3–5.

[107] MHG to Staatssekretär des Innern with Abschrift for Kaiserlichen und Königlichen Majestät, BAP RMdI/7005/10–11.

[108] Abschrift, MHG to MdI, 15 May 1911, GStAKM 77/II/2522/1/2/118–21; *JB 1911*, 680, 683, 685–87; Seidl, *Streikkämpfe*, 126–27.

[109] Seidel, *Streikkämpfe*, 122–23.

Once again, the owners adopted a stance of implacable opposition. They refused to negotiate and declared that "the struggle is to be carried through . . . with determination [and] without any concessions until the strikers resume work." The companies warned that strikers would be dismissed and excluded from the miners pension fund and other benefits, and those residing in company housing evicted.[110]

But the owners did not rely merely on their own resources. The Mansfeld strike marked a new level of coordination between owners and the state. At a meeting in Weissenfels among the district magistrate, officials of the Prussian Mining Office, and mine owners, held just before the outbreak of the strike, the owners pleaded for the early and massive deployment of troops. The strike, argued the owners, threatened to be bitter and extensive. Sabotage and intense pressure on those willing to work were to be expected. The owners had agreed not to give in to the demands, especially as they revolved around the unions' bid for power:

> The strongest possible intervention of gendarmes at the very beginning . . . would convince the strikers of the earnestness of the situation. Those willing to work would in great measure feel protected. . . . The experience of other strikes has shown that it is worthwhile to nip the movement in the bud, since each minor success of the strikers disproportionately lengthens and intensifies the conflict and strengthens the power of the unions.[111]

In a rather unsubtle manner, the owners offered to help defray the costs of the use of troops so long as they were deployed early and massively. State officials acceded to their wishes.[112]

Strike participation ranged from about one-quarter to one-half of the labor force at the various mines.[113] Mine inspectors maintained that the overwhelming majority of strikers were young, unmarried "fellows," while the "sensible, older people" went about their work unaffected by the strike call of the union leaderships.[114] In a number of areas, as in the Naumburg region, the mine officials reported over one hundred incidents of legal action against strikers, mostly for supposed trespassing and violations of the commercial code. In the neighboring Zeitz subdistrict, the inspector reported that the strikers had a great deal of success in preventing strikebreakers from entering the mines, despite the presence of gendarme detachments.[115] The strike lasted fourteen weeks, and the miners went back having failed to secure their goals—at least those who were taken back,

[110] Ibid., 126.

[111] Abschrift, Weissenfels, 4 May 1911, GStAKM 77/II/2522/1/2/127–28. On the long-term cooperation between employer-backed and state security forces, see Ralph Jessen, "Unternehmerherrschaft und staatliches Gewaltmonopol: Hüttenpolizisten und Zechenwehren im Ruhrgebiet (1870–1914)," in *"Sicherheit" und "Wohlfahrt": Polizei, Gesellschaft und Herrschaft im 19. und 20. Jahrhundert*, ed. Alf Lüdtke (Frankfurt am Main: Suhrkamp, 1992), 161–86.

[112] As in Weissenfels and Zeitz, where officials reported the quick deployment of gendarmes to protect those still willing to work. Abschrift, MHG to MdI, 15 May 1911, and RPM to MdI, 12 May 1911, GStAKM 77/II/2522/1/2/118–21, 124–26.

[113] RPM to MdI, 12 May 1911, GStAKM 77/II/2522/1/2/124–26.

[114] Ibid.

[115] *JB 1911*, 683, 685–87.

since many owners used the strike to pare down their labor force, especially of the "most malicious instigators and agitators."[116] The strike's failure no doubt resulted from the employers' unity and the tight coordination between the owners and the state.

In the post–World War I period, the Mansfeld region would become a major center of intense and bitter labor conflicts, and of KPD support. Its notorious stature, made heroic in Communist Party accounts, desperate and dangerous in government reports, had its origins in the two great strikes of the pre–World War I era. The 1909 copper mining strike was particularly poignant. In the background lay an accumulation of grievances—over wages, inflation, the arbitrary exercise of power by the company, the intensified pace of work. In the Mansfeld copper mines, the seams were so narrow that most of the work was done lying or sitting, which only accentuated the difficult conditions of labor.[117] However, the spark that set off the action involved not basic working conditions, but the issue of just handling of fellow workers. The strike demonstrated the fleeting but real sense of solidarity, a sense of common identities and destinies, created by the conditions of labor and community life, without which socialist and, later, communist organizing would have been meaningless. Both strikes signified an effort by workers to reclaim their community from the overshadowing presence of the Mansfeld company, which so dominated life in the area. The key role of women in picket lines and demonstration columns provides clear evidence of the community-wide nature of the strike.

Mansfeld, as state officials regretfully noted, had once been noted for its loyalty, its *König- und Kaisertreue* workers. A sea change was underway, and it involved skilled workers, the very core of the Mansfeld labor force, as well as the unskilled, more itinerant miners. The deteriorating conditions of labor coupled with continued socialist agitation had indeed had an impact. Miners had gone a long way toward building their own, independent organizations—the trade unions that called the 1911 strike—and were better prepared to engage in open conflict. The high demand for coal and copper in Germany's great industrial boom and the shortage of skilled labor, about which virtually all companies complained, gave workers a growing sense of confidence.

In both strikes, however, workers lost, and that too provided a valuable lesson. The intimate connection between private power and state power was vividly expressed in the deployment of troops, an action that miners bitterly resented. Mansfeld workers were also faced with particularly unsympathetic officials—the regional official of the state mining office did not even see fit to discuss miners' long-held grievances in his yearly report. The official seemed to find the firm's distribution of coffee and cake to its workers, which had as in previous years "a very active clientele," just as important.[118] Yet such supercilious comments

[116] Königlicher LRLKW to MdI, 15 August 1911, GStAKM 77/II/2522/1/2/151.

[117] See Walter Hoffmann, *Der Mansfelder Kupferschieferbergbau: Ein Beitrag zur mitteldeutschen Wirtschaftsgeschichte*, ed. Mitteldeutschen Kulturrat e.v. Bonn (Meisenheim am Glan: Anton Hain, 1957), 52–53.

[118] *JB 1909*, 575–76.

could not mask the great nervousness about labor unrest displayed by both employers and officials on the eve of World War I.

Demonstrations

Demonstrations were probably the most common form of collective protest in Imperial Germany, and their politically charged nature often made them the focal point of conflict between security forces and workers. In demonstrations workers laid claim to the streets of their communities and challenged the time rhythms prescribed for them by their employers. Demonstrations marked both their self-assertion as individuals and as a group in a social and political order that expected them to be quiescent and thankful and the integration, not just of individual workers, but of entire families into labor movement activism.

Demonstrations often accompanied strikes. Picket lines outside the mine or factory constituted a particularly active—and dangerous—form of demonstration, since they were designed not as symbolic statements, but physically to prevent nonstrikers from entering the workplace. Miners often marched on city hall or the local office of the mining officials in conjunction with their strikes. These marches most explicitly moved protests from the productive sphere into the political realm and marked workers' claim to the space of the workplace and the urban environment.

But many working-class demonstrations emerged independent of the workplace. Between 1906 and 1910, successive waves of demonstrations took place against the inequitable Prussian three-class voting system.[119] The struggle became a major point of contention within the SPD, with the increasingly isolated left wing of the party arguing that the party had to promote continually the mass actions of the "suffrage storm," as it was called. Like many urban areas, Halle, the major city of Prussian Saxony, was the site of repeated demonstrations in these years, including some that had led to bloody clashes with the police. In 1910, it became the site of one of the most notorious incidents of conflict between workers and the armed power of the state.[120] In conjunction with the Prussian Landtag election of 1910, social democratic meetings had been held throughout the Halle-Merseburg region. Resolutions called on the party leadership to unleash a campaign against the Prussian electoral system. On 27 January, the Halle party organization, one of the strongest in the region and nation, echoing the terms of the SPD left wing, called on the party to use the "political demonstration strike" in the electoral campaign. A demonstration soon thereafter,

[119] Carl E. Schorske, *German Social Democracy 1905–1917: The Development of the Great Schism* (Cambridge, Mass.: Harvard University Press, 1955), 171–87, still has the best description of the movement for electoral reform in Prussia.

[120] The following is drawn from Mende, "Geschichte der Sozialdemokratie," 132–34, 178–81, 225–35, and idem, *Karl Liebknecht und Rosa Luxemburg im Bezirk Halle*, ed. Kommission zur Erforschung der Geschichte der örtlichen Arbeiterbewegung bei der Bezirksleitung Halle der SED (Halle: Druckhaus Freiheit, 1981), 33–41.

attended by between 2,500 and 3,000 people, called on the party Executive "finally to take account of the situation and to use the mass strike."[121] Over the next few weeks, the number of demonstrations and meetings escalated. The local SPD newspaper printed Rosa Luxemburg's call for a political mass strike to create a democratic republic, an article banned from the central party press.

The intensity of the demonstrations had already led to heightened police mobilization and some skirmishes. On 13 February 1910, crowds gathered in the marketplace in Halle for yet another demonstration. They unfurled banners calling for free and fair elections. Like so many social democratic gatherings, this had something of a festive air about it. Entire families were present, and many no doubt had the intention to retire later to the Volkspark, the SPD meeting house, library, and beer garden. They were already at the point of dispersing to five different meeting places around the city. Instead, the police charged the crowd, and as the situation worsened, the police officials called on the army for reinforcements. Apparently prepared for a confrontation, army units were already quartered at the police station, and artillery had been brought up to a nearby hotel. The police and military repeatedly charged the crowd, five times just between 11:00 A.M. and 12:00 noon. Rather than dispersing, the crowd, provoked by the police, continually regathered and hurled stones and whatever other objects at hand at the police and army units.

While most of the police were occupied with the crowd in the market square, a group of 2,500 men marched toward the square, but could not breach the police lines. Instead, the group massed at the nearby municipal theater. The crowd listened to speeches and sang the "Workers' Marseillaise." Reinforcements that included army troops were called in. On horseback and with swords drawn, the police charged the crowd and chased people down side streets as they fled the tumult. Still the conflict continued, as the police themselves reported: "Scattered individuals attempted now, without plan, to head toward the market, but were stopped at the approaches by the police units. The order to disperse, issued three times, was answered with violence and [provocative] actions, so that at seven different spots . . . sabres . . . had to be used."[122] Until 4:30 P.M., the police continued to charge groups of citizens, increasingly in an indiscriminate fashion.

Amazingly, no one was killed, but forty were wounded and eighty arrested. The following Thursday, a great protest was held in the Volkspark. About ten thousand people demonstrated against police brutality and for a continuation of the struggle against the Prussian electoral system. Bloody Sunday, as it came to be called, stimulated sympathy demonstrations throughout the region and nation and brought prominent SPD politicians to Halle. Soon after the events Karl Liebknecht spoke in Halle, to which he returned quite often during the year, helping to secure the position of the left wing within the local organization. With another lawyer, he also

[121] Quoted in Mende, "Geschichte der Sozialdemokratie," 220.

[122] Quoted in Mende, *Karl Liebknecht und Rosa Luxemburg im Bezirk Halle*, 36. The "Workers' Marseillaise," written by Jakob Audorf, served as the unofficial anthem of the SPD. For text and commentary, see Vernon Lidtke, *The Alternative Culture: Socialist Labor in Imperial Germany* (New York: Oxford University Press, 1985), 112–14.

took up the defense of those arrested on Bloody Sunday, but forty-three nonetheless received prison sentences.

The events of Bloody Sunday revealed the intransigence of the state, whose police and soldiers attacked peaceful demonstrators with impunity. At the same time, the demonstration conveyed the determination of some workers to compel changes in the political structure of Imperial Germany, and the celebratory nature of their actions. It is not accidental that this major demonstration was called on a Sunday when most workers had their one full day off. Bloody Sunday began as a family outing with women and children well in attendance alongside men. When the conflict turned violent, both men and women responded in kind, though the judicial records indicate that only men were indicted. If strikes were the classic form of male labor protest, demonstrations cut through gender divisions to unite proletarian families against the forces of order. Far from being incidental to the world of labor politics, these demonstrations, by joining work and politics, proletarian labor and family life, integrated entire families into the labor movement. In part for this reason, Halle became a model "*Hochburg*" (fortress) of the SPD in Imperial Germany, a city in which the party became extremely well situated in the full array of institutions of proletarian life—trade unions, consumer cooperatives, cultural and sports associations, the family itself. In the Weimar Republic, the KPD inherited the SPD's prominent position and turned Halle—"Red Halle," as it became known—into its own "Hochburg." The long and direct experience of army and police brutality—in strikes and demonstrations in Halle, Eisleben, and many of the other communities—propelled social democrats in Prussian Saxony to the left wing of the SPD before World War I, into the Independent Social Democratic Party during the war, and into the KPD afterwards.[123]

Informal and Everyday Resistance

Organized protests were not the only means by which workers contested the regimes of repression presided over by employers and the state. Workers engaged also in informal actions, individual and collective, through which they carved out some autonomy, forged identities, and, occasionally, articulated a different kind of social order than the regulated world of the factory and the polity. These actions were eminently political in the sense that they revolved around power—the control of time, space, and bodies. But informal resistance occurred within a highly circumscribed framework: the state and workplace regimes that so powerfully structured workers' lives. One should be cautious and not ascribe too much significance to informal protests.[124]

123 Compare the contrasting experience of the labor movement in Göttingen, which appears almost placid in comparison with Halle. Adelheid von Saldern, *Auf dem Wege zum Arbeiter-Reformismus: Parteialltag in sozialdemokratischer Provinz Göttingen (1870–1920)* (Frankfurt am Main: Materialis, 1984).

124 These remarks are directed at *Alltagsgeschichte*, a great deal of which paints popular resistance in celebratory hues and loses sight of the profoundly limiting impact of the structures of state and

The most pronounced form of everyday resistance involved changing jobs. Company social welfare programs had increased the stability of the workforces, according to the mine and factory inspectors. Nonetheless, lateral mobility remained astoundingly high, and inspired unceasing complaints from employers and officials. The freedom of movement of labor, enshrined in the 1871 constitution, provided workers with a cherished means of exercising independence in search of better pay or a more reasonable foreman, especially in periods of high demand for labor.[125] In the numerous mining regions of central Germany and the Ruhr, inspectors reported that miners regularly ignored the fourteen-day notice they were required to give when leaving their employment—152 out of 167 at one mine.[126] In another example cited by the inspectors, a metalwares factory employed 348 workers in 1911, but in the course of the year had had to hire 565 individuals. In one cement factory in the Merseburg district in 1908, 191 workers were hired and 200 left in one year; the average employment level was 200.[127] These were typical, not exceptional, examples. One lathe operator, probably off the median scale, had the distinction of having had fifty different jobs in twenty years![128]

In piecework systems, workers had long found ways to subvert management's calculation of wage rates. Bosch, for example, had initially established a group piecework system in which the leader was paid the wage based on the entire output of the group. He then distributed the pay among the individual members. The firm soon abandoned this practice when it discovered that fast workers slowed down to the pace of their less adept colleagues.[129] Efforts by employers to control wages by revising piecework rates or by doctoring the time and wage calculations required eternal vigilance—and that vigilance was itself a kind of resistance.[130] For all the

---

society. Even Alf Lüdtke's innovative and insightful work is not free of these shortcomings. This is less true of his more recent publications, which, significantly, cover the Third Reich—an instance where it is impossible to overlook the blatant exercise of power. The English-language reviews of *Alltagsgeschichte* by David F. Crew and Geoff Eley are, in my view, a bit too laudatory. See Crew, "*Alltagsgeschichte*: A New Social History from Below?" *CEH* 22:3/4 (1989): 394–407, and Eley, "Labor History, Social History, *Alltagsgeschichte*: Experience, Culture, and the Politics of the Everyday—A New Direction for German Social History?" *JMH* 61:2 (1989): 297–343. See also my exchange with Eley, "Romantisierung des Eigen-Sinns? Eine e-mail Kontroverse aus Übersee," *WerkstattGeschichte* 10 (1995): 57–64. Many of Lüdtke's important essays have now been collected in *Eigen-Sinn: Fabrikalltag, Arbeitererfahrungen und Politik vom Kaiserreich bis in den Faschismus* (Hamburg: Ergebnisse, 1993).

[125] Inspectors were well aware of the reasons why workers changed jobs. See, for example, *JB 1907*, 223. For a detailed study, Dieter Langewiesche, "Wanderungsbewegungen in der Hochindustrialiserungsperiode: Regionale, interstädtische und innnerstädische Mobilität in Deutschland 1880–1914," *VSWG* 64:1 (1977): 1–40.

[126] *JB 1901*, 392 and 433 for examples from the Halberstadt and East Essen mining regions.

[127] *JB 1911*, 246.

[128] Eugen May, "Lohndreher im Akkord," in Emmerich, *Proletarische Lebensläufe*, 338.

[129] Stolle, *Arbeiterpolitik*, 159.

[130] See, for example, the autobiographical excerpts in Emmerich, *Proletarische Lebensläufe*, 338–43, and the more extensive excerpt of Eugen May in English translation, *The German Worker: Working-Class Autobiographies from the Age of Industrialization* (Berkeley and Los Angeles: University of California Press, 1987), ed. and trans. Alfred Kelly, 370–88. On the constant negotiations over piecework rates in the mines, see Hickey, *Workers*, 140–43.

exploitation intrinsic to the piecework system, some workers preferred it precisely because of the leeway it afforded them. Quarry workers, as mentioned previously, preferred the irregular rhythms and relative independence of the piecework system to the "rationalized" ten-hour workday mandated by legislation and promoted by officials.[131]

Young workers were a particular cause of concern to employers and state officials.[132] An array of practices associated with the act of labor was supposed to teach them discipline and obedience, yet often youth and their families found ways of subverting the efforts. Young workers were supposed to carry with them their wage books, a means of keeping tabs on them, yet they were often ignored altogether by minors. Inspectors also complained that youth were too distant from parental control and exercised little discipline and too much independence over their earnings. Calls by some employers and the inspectors that wages be paid to youth only when countersigned by a parent or guardian had proven unworkable since, to the chagrin of the inspectors, neither parents nor the youth demonstrated much interest.[133] Unpredictable actions continually frustrated employers and officials: a father complained to the inspectorate that an employer paid his daughters' wages directly to them without his permission. The inspector's efforts to rectify the situation led to the "unforeseeable result" that the two daughters left their father's house.[134]

Young, single workers, resistant to limits on their liberties, often refused to live in company-provided housing, despite its cleanliness and inexpense. The inspectors noted "Unfortunately the unmarried workers [of a chemical plant in Bitterfeld] only reluctantly make use of this well constructed, healthy, and certainly inexpensive dormitory. They feel their independence and freedom limited; they prefer shabby, often unhealthy, and expensive lodgings as boarders."[135] The innumerable conflicts with supervisors constituted another terrain of daily resistance, as working-class autobiographies and other sources make clear. Female textile workers talked back to supervisors and gossiped and engaged in horseplay in the bathroom, out of sight of the harsh factory regime.[136] During festival days, workers stayed away from the factory or mine and imbibed excessive amounts of alcohol.[137] Albert Rudolph, a mechanic employed at the Imperial Shipyard and a trade union functionary, found himself hauled before the authorities, who gruffly asked him how he had spent the previous Sunday. He refused to answer, telling

[131] *JB 1902*, 331.

[132] On the identification of a "crisis of youth" in Imperial Germany, see Derek Linton, *Who Has the Youth Has the Future* (Cambridge: Cambridge University Press, 1990); Detlev J. K. Peukert, *Grenzen der Sozialdisziplinierung: Aufstieg und Krise der deutschen Jugendfürsorge von 1878 bis 1932* (Cologne: Bund, 1986); and Jürgen Reulecke, "Bürgerliche Sozialreformer und Arbeiterjugend im Kaiserreich," *AfS* 22 (1982): 299–329.

[133] *JB 1901*, 129–30; *JB 1902*, 179; and *JB 1911*, 240.

[134] *JB 1911*, 538–39.

[135] *JB 1901*, 146. See also *JB 1902*, 189.

[136] Canning, "Gender and the Culture of Work," 188.

[137] Lynn Abrams, *Workers' Culture in Imperial Germany: Leisure and Recreation in the Rhineland and Westphalia* (London: Routledge, 1992), 37–43.

them that they had no business inquiring as to how he spent his free time away from work. The interrogation-like questioning continued, but Rudolph maintained his silence, although he knew that they knew he had spoken in favor of the eight-hour day at a public rally in Bremerhaven on that day. After weeks of waiting, he was fired—in particularly vindictive fashion, on the day before Christmas. He responded in kind—just to make life difficult for his superiors, he refused the offer of two weeks' pay and stayed on the job for the legally mandated fourteen days.[138]

Rough and tumble violence also defined an area of protest against the prevailing commitment to "law and order." Violence could be random and unfocused, but could also have a specific political purpose when directed at strikebreakers and foremen. The constant concern on the part of the employers and authorities to protect strikebreakers is one indication of the latent but ever present danger of political violence, even amid the orderly world of German social democracy and trade unionism. Violence might be individual in nature as well. Eugen May, in his some fifty jobs between 1900 and 1920, left behind a trail of brawls with foremen and masters—not the most politically astute form of resistance, but part of the repertoire nonetheless.[139] Rough violence might also be used against fellow workers, a kind of teasing or hazing through which workers carved out some time and place of their own amid the highly regulated world of the factory and asserted their collective identity as workers.[140]

Despite the harsh regulatory codes of most factories and mines and the close supervision of workers by employers and the police, the efforts to discipline labor were only partly successful. Not only in strikes and demonstrations, but also in everyday practices in the factories and mines, workers contested the all-encompassing claims of the state and the employers.

The Social Democratic World

The intense hostility of the state and employers toward the SPD, their unceasing efforts to make social democracy and social democrats pariahs in German society, meant that almost any action in support of the party—voting for its candidates, participating in the workers bicycle club, or joining the party itself—constituted one other act in the repertoire of resistance. Although labor support for the Catholic Center, liberal, and even conservative parties remained strong, the SPD's dynamic growth after 1890 and its self-identification as a workers party made it appear to be the exclusive vehicle for working-class grievances and hopes.

Socialism was never simply a political party formed to contest elections. In the

[138] Albert Rudolph, "Die Entlassung," in Emmerich, *Proletarische Lebensläufe*, 335–37.

[139] See the excerpt in Emmerich, *Proletarische Lebensläufe*, 338–43, and a more extensive one in the English translation by Kelly, *German Worker*, 370–88.

[140] See especially Alf Lüdtke, "Cash, Coffee-Breaks, Horseplay: *Eigensinn* and Politics among Factory Workers in Germany circa 1900," in *Class, Confrontation, and the Labor Process: Studies in Class Formation*, ed. Michael Hanagen and Charles Stephenson (Westport, Conn.: Greenwood, 1984), 65–95, and "Organizational Order or *Eigensinn*"? Workers' Privacy and Workers' Politics in Imperial Germany," in *Rites of Power: Symbolism, Ritual, and Politics since the Middle Ages*, ed. Sean Wilentz (Philadelphia: University of Pennsylvania Press, 1985), 303–33.

vanguard of the mass movements characteristic of the twentieth century, German socialism established an array of ancillary organizations and activities, from sports associations, lecture series, theater groups, and glee clubs to the political party and its associated trade unions.[141] In the interstices of strikes, demonstrations, and electoral campaigns lay the daily construction of a movement that sought to penetrate all areas of its members' lives.

But what did socialism mean to workers? To begin with, it provided a class-oriented way of understanding the world, the significance of which can hardly be underestimated. The specific social democratic articulation of class built upon the life experiences of workers, who in the workplace and the community encountered daily the inequalities and injustices of German society. The use of "*Arbeiter*" (worker) in everything from gymnastic associations and choirs to newspaper titles established linguistically the class identity of the movement. The terms "*Genosse*" and "*Genossin*" (the male and female forms of comrade), used in daily discourse in the party, established a collective class and party political identity among the members. Similarly, the founding of distinctive social and cultural associations generally involved the separation from preexisting, cross-class organizations, especially after the turn of the century. In Bremen, for example, social democrats walked out of the local Goethebund after a speech by Werner Sombart on historical materialism and founded their own Goethe society. Even in the cultural realm, socialists argued, there was no neutral ground.[142]

The language of class served also to elevate labor. Work was productive and creative: those who made society's material riches had the right to society's cultural and political riches as well. To what extent labor was indeed idealized by laborers is almost impossible to ascertain. Certainly, work was difficult, demanding, and dangerous for most Germans. But the cult of labor developed by the socialist movements, founded on long-hallowed religious traditions, clearly resonated with those who spent the greater part of their lives laboring—if for no other reason than it gave meaning to their daily existence. In festivals the various trade unions celebrated their craft by marching with samples of their wares and tools.[143] Johann Most's "Who Hammers Brass and Stone," a popular song of the socialist movement, idealized creative labor and its practitioners, and lamented the proletariat's sorry situation:

[141] This is the subject of so much historical research on social democracy, and it is impossible to provide adequate references. Two model studies in English are Mary Nolan, *Social Democracy and Society: Working-Class Radicalism in Düsseldorf, 1890–1920* (Cambridge: Cambridge University Press, 1981), and Lidtke, *Alternative Culture*. See also the special issues of *GG* 5 (1979) and *JCH* 13 (1978) devoted to workers' culture.

[142] See von Saldern, "Wilhelminische Gesellschaft und Arbeiterklasse." The separation of the SPD from the liberal movement occurred irrespective of the specific political tendency within the party. But for a more complex picture of the relations between liberals and labor, see Ralf Roth, "'Bürger' and Workers, Liberalism and the Labor Movement, 1848–1914," in *Between Reform and Revolution: Studies in German Socialism and Communism between 1840 and 1990*, ed. David E. Barclay and Eric D. Weitz (Providence: Berghahn, forthcoming).

[143] Lidtke, *Alternative Culture*, 90–91, and Klaus Tenfelde, "Mining Festivals in the Nineteenth Century," *JCH* 13:2 (1978): 377–412.

Who hammers brass and stone?
Who raiseth from the mine?
Who weaveth cloth and silk?
Who tilleth wheat and vine?
Who lives himself in sorest need?
It is the men who toil,
The Proletariat.[144]

Similarly, the iconography of the hand—often two hands linked together—and the powerful arm stood both for brotherhood and the power and productivity of labor.[145] The hammer, so often pictured as well, served as the extension of the hand, unifying human labor and the tools created by men. The clenched fist, an increasingly common symbol of the labor movement, extended proletarian strength into overt political struggle. The masculine character of the iconography, the representations of men as the creators of wealth and the bearers of progress, demonstrated far better than party pronouncements the intertwining of gender and class, the definition of class in terms of masculinity.

The social democratic understanding of class also entailed order and discipline, a focal point of much historiographical and political criticism of the SPD. As Vernon Lidtke reports, choir directors and gymnastic leaders had almost dictatorial control during practice sessions and rehearsals, which were highly regimented. Bylaws emphasized strict order and discipline.[146] The SPD's conception of the family—"*die ordentliche Familie*"—enshrined order and patriarchalism.[147] Many of the songs of the labor movement were based on older patriotic melodies. These often connected the socialist movement to the liberal patriotism of the pre-1871 era, but served also to blur the distinctions between a specifically socialist and the nationalistic-authoritarian ethos of Imperial Germany. And most of all, the class struggle required, in the party's view, a disciplined party and class, a kind of popular but orderly army, the *levée en masse* of socialism.

By entwining class with discipline, the SPD reproduced some of the least attractive features of Imperial Germany. But it is important also to recall that the dirt and disorder that pervaded so much of proletarian life might have made the self-constructed order of club life a welcome relief, and the liberal-humanistic understanding of patriotism countered the specifically authoritarian-nationalistic version of patriotism promoted by the ruling elites of Imperial Germany.[148]

From working-class autobiographies and the SPD press there exists little evi-

[144] Quoted in Lidtke, *Alternative Culture*, 116.

[145] See especially the very interesting essay by Gottfried Korff, "From Brotherly Handshake to Militant Clenched Fist: On Political Metaphors for the Worker's Hand," *International Labor and Working Class History* 42 (1992): 70–81.

[146] Lidtke, *Alternative Culture*, 51–52.

[147] Richard J. Evans, "Politics and the Family: Social Democracy and the Working-Class Family in Theory and Practice before 1914," in *The German Family: Essays on the Social History of the Family in Nineteenth- and Twentieth-Century Germany*, ed. Richard J. Evans and W. R. Lee (London: Croom Helm, 1981), 256–88.

[148] See also Lidtke's discussion in *Alternative Culture*, 124–28.

dence that workers understood socialism to mean workers' control of production. There is, however, a very clear and deeply felt sense of injustice—at bleak, unending toil in dark and dirty conditions, constant scampering to make ends meet, rapacious capitalists, and arrogant and oppressive officials.[149] For workers, socialism meant justice, and was often defined in the negative—an end to economic inequalities and, even more importantly, to the arbitrary exercise of power by employers and the state.[150]

Fritz Pauk, a young tobacco worker, reports on becoming a socialist when the owner of the factory fired an upstanding and capable worker on discovering that he was a socialist, though previously the owner and the socialist worker had gotten along famously:

> one day on the job it was like a murder scandal. The old one ran around like a crazy person and cursed: No, no, that I never would have even dreamed, that in this workplace there could be a social democrat. Listen up, what this Saxon has given me for good advice. I came to him and asked why our good Kaiser Wilhelm cigars . . . weren't moving any longer. He had the nerve to say to me, I should try it with his picture of Bebel. . . . He can't stay in this workplace, he's got to get out immediately!

Pauk then watched the Saxon leave the premises "with proud steps." More importantly, Pauk recognized that a "great injustice" had been done, and realized that a good worker arbitrarily fired because he was a socialist meant that socialists could not all be criminals and vagabonds.[151]

Alfons Petzold, working in a confectionery factory, depicted an owner who sometimes beat his workers. Among themselves, workers described their situation as "Russian conditions" in which "the statutes of the factory regulations were draconically strict, the director applied them in a cruel, arbitrary manner. . . . He was the almighty in the factory." He treated his workers "like dogs" and was not above ordering childbearing women to carry heavy loads up ladders. Advancement through the ranks and to higher wages was impossible. The sense of aggrieved justice is palpable, made worse when a colleague informs Petzold that the director dismissed even good workers after three or four years in order to prevent communication and solidarity from developing among them. The newly hired, the boss knew, needed their wages too desperately to risk a strike.[152] Autobiographers less articulate than Petzold expressed their understanding of socialism simply: it inspired workers "to struggle against injustice."[153]

[149] Working-class autobiographies express these sentiments quite clearly. See the collections edited by Emmerich, *Proletarische Lebensläufe*, and Kelly, *German Worker*, as well as the major study by Mary Jo Maynes, *Taking the Hard Road: Life Course in French and German Workers' Autobiographies in the Era of Industrialization* (Chapel Hill: University of North Carolina Press, 1995).

[150] The topic of Barrington Moore's much-cited work, *Injustice: The Social Bases of Disobedience and Revolt* (White Plains, N.Y.: M. E. Sharpe, 1978).

[151] Fritz Pauk, "Jugendjahre eines Tabakarbeiters," in Emmerich, *Proletarische Lebensläufe*, 324–25.

[152] Alfons Petzold, "Schutzmauern vor dem Klassenbewußtsein in Emmerich, *Proletarische Lebensläufe*, 326–28.

[153] Wilhelm Reimes, "Sozialismus und Christentum" in Emmerich, *Proletarische Lebensläufe*, 284.

In miners' grievances surfaced a sense of injustice felt especially keenly by those who experienced the transition from the well-protected, high stature of mining in the preindustrial age to the position of common proletarian labor.[154] Again, it was the *arbitrary* exercise of power that is so often the cause of grievances—beatings of workers, including minors, by supervisors; the imposition of overtime or an extension of the regular shift; the rejection of entire wagonloads of coal because of an overproportion of stone and other excess materials.[155]

In a long letter to the Prussian Ministry of Commerce in 1902, the socialist-led Alter Verband described a situation of "extraordinary excitement" at mines in Wattenscheid when the companies imposed the ten-hour shift "*against* the will of the workforce." The stable boys would not comply, and when they "refused . . . to lead the horses out of the stall, an *overseer* fell upon them with a stick and beat one of the boys so badly that he broke out in tears. The adult miners, including the boy's father and brothers, became greatly agitated. At the mass rally people cried out: 'Strike! Lay down the tools!'" The head of the Alter Verband succeeded in calming the workers, but only with the assurance that the state officials would be informed directly of the scandal, "and intervene to take measures for the protection of the workers." The letter went on to issue a not very veiled warning to the officials, reminding them that the great strike of 1889 had also begun in the Gelsenkirchen-Wattenscheid region, and also because of the mistreatment of stable boys.

Furthermore, the incident (at Zeche Holland) was only one of many, and came at a time of wage reductions and dismissals, as in 1889: "Each week we receive in our office poignant complaints about the *brutal behavior of supervisors*, who ever more often have engaged in *actions* that involve the *bodily mistreatment of workers* and the most objectionable *curses*. What effect these actions have, we saw in 1889." To add to the grievances, overseers rejected in an arbitrary fashion entire wagonloads of coal. When workers complained, the supervisors responded "with rudeness."[156] Resentment at the arbitrary and brutal actions—*willkürliche und brutale Behandlung*—of foremen and managers permeated miners' grievances time and again.[157]

The arbitrary alteration of the workshift also provoked the ire of miners. Invoking their own experience of the family economy, they described in a petition the disruptions in family life caused by a mere half-hour change in the daily start and end of the shift, which meant that those on the second shift might reach home around midnight: "Our wives or mothers must wake up and prepare the evening meal. Their sleep is disturbed and then, not rarely, they have to get up again between three and four to cook coffee for those on the morning shift. In families

[154] The theme of Klaus Tenfelde's major study, *Sozialgeschichte der Bergarbeiterschaft an der Ruhr im 19. Jahrhundert* (Bonn-Bad Godesberg: Neue Gesellschaft, 1977).

[155] Along with the important secondary studies on Ruhr mining, see especially the superb collection of documents edited by Tenfelde and Trischler, *Bis vor die Stufen des Throns*.

[156] From *Deutsche Bergarbeiter-Zeitung* 14:16 (1902) in ibid., 400–402.

[157] See a very similarly worded complaint just a little over a year later from the Alter Verband to the employers' association, the Bergbauverein, in ibid., 407–13.

in which one works the morning and another the afternoon shift—and such families are not rare—everyone's nighttime rest is disturbed."[158]

Similarly, the reduction of benefits aroused the sense of injustice that pervaded miners' grievances. In November 1910, the Pörtingsiepen mine (in the South Essen subdistrict) in place of the coal distributed free of charge to miners substituted briquettes of bituminous coal that must have been of inordinately poor quality, because they "are not useful for a fire in the house. Using them in the furnace and oven of a household results in a haze of smoke many times worse than the usual coal. . . . [T]he entire home and even the meal are covered in smoke. The housewife is unable to cook in the usual manner. The health of entire mining families suffers unendingly." Again protesting against the arbitrary actions of the owners, the miners' representatives wrote, "The mine administration has arbitrarily substituted low-quality coal briquettes in place of hard coal without consulting the workforce. As a result an immense bitterness prevails among the workers."[159]

If capitalism was defined by injustice, the socialist future would be marked by justice and equality. Even the titles of socialist newspapers reflected the faith in the future, as with *Die Neue Zeit* (*The New Era*) and *Gleichheit* (*Equality*). The symbolism of red, worn and carried in all sorts of activities—by cyclists, singers, and gymnasts; as scarves, sashes, and armbands; held aloft as banners; used to decorate meeting halls—symbolized not only revolution, but also the brightness of the morning sun, the future and illumination.[160]

The sense of optimism and faith in the future, the belief in justice and equality, connected socialism to the humanism and republicanism of the nineteenth century. Working-class autobiographers described their understanding of socialism in the familiar language of the Enlightenment, the French Revolution, and the German student movement of the early nineteenth century. Josef Peukert, for example, wrote, "[Socialism is] a humanitarian idea . . . defined by the poles of truth and justice. The most important endeavor of an individual is to become free, so far as possible, from all prejudices and spiritual barriers and to prepare for a truly free societal condition of universal human fraternity."[161] Another working-class autodidact, Franz Bergg used the well-worn metaphors of illumination to describe his encounter through literature and art with the world of classical Greece, and thence to the future socialist order:

> That bygone world imparted such a beam that it blinded my soul, that I forgot entirely the real world around me, and I built in the clouds, far from earth, islands and mountains of bliss. . . .

158 Appeal of the leadership of a mass meeting of the Alten Verbandes from the Mittelbexbach Mine to the Bayerische Oberbergamt, 1 March 1910, in ibid., 445–47.

159 Appeal of Workers Committee of Zeche Pörtingsiepen to Bergrevier Essen, [stamped 16 January 1911], in ibid., 452–53.

160 Both points made by Hartmut Zwahr in a very interesting essay, "Der rote Distelfink unter der Pickelhaube: Namen, Symbole, Identitäten Geächteter im 19. Jahrhundert" (ms., German Studies Association annual meeting, 1990).

161 Josef Peukert, "Aufklärung und Klassenkampf," in Emmerich, *Proletarische Lebensläufe*, 264–65.

> Socialism swelled my soul as the red morning of the future. Warmed by its luster, it filled me with genuine inspiration. I decided to do my part, to struggle to help liberate . . . humanity from its spiritual and bodily oppression . . . to give back to the poor proletariat its ideals.[162]

Illumination, brilliant glows, streams of light—these were the metaphors for the future.[163]

The invocation of German humanism moved the language and experience of socialism beyond the narrow boundaries of class to encompass a vision of human liberation. The artistic programs staged by local party organizations generally involved the cultural icons of German society—poetry by Goethe, Heine, Freiligrath, music by Beethoven, Mozart, Schubert, and others in the classical repertoire.[164] The "cult of the flag" noted by Vernon Lidtke in working-class associational life, as well as the use of patriotic names, sometimes regional, sometimes national, like "Germania," "Teutonia," or "Saxonia," identified workers with the liberal nationalism of the early nineteenth century. A goddess of freedom, present at all sorts of social democratic festivals, joined the labor movement to the republicanism of the French Revolution and the nineteenth century[165]—and would be conspicuously absent from communist marches in the Weimar Republic.

Even the religious vernacular in which socialism was so often presented by its orators bore an Enlightenment tenor:

> I heard Bebel, the elder Liebknecht, and other inspirational prophets of the worldwide workers' religion . . . and saw in the political and trade union movement the slow, difficult, but certain advance of the new spirit. . . .
>
> [The workers' movement] has . . . become a new spiritual home. . . . Freedom, equality, justice—they are . . . to me not only political, but above all humanitarian-ethical postulates.[166]

And as with the Enlightenment, religiously tinged language did not stand in contradiction to a scientific world view. Darwin was a favorite of social democrats, as he was of Marx and Engels, often in a more popularized version such as A. Dodel's *Moses oder Darwin?*[167]

The SPD's commitment to the icons of classical German and European culture

[162] Franz Bergg, "Antike Götterwelt und Karl Marx," in Emmerich, *Proletarische Lebensläufe*, 272–73.

[163] Heinrich Georg Dikreiter, "Die Idee des Zukunftsstaates," in Emmerich, *Proletarische Lebensläufe*, 286.

[164] Lidtke, *Alternative Culture*, 179; Nolan, *Social Democracy and Society*.

[165] Lidtke, *Alternative Culture*, 89–90.

[166] Ernst Preczang, "Tendenzdichtung und das Reinmenschliche," in Emmerich, *Proletarische Lebensläufe*, 288–89.

[167] Richard Richter, "Das Altarbild der neuen Weltanschauung," and Moritz Theodor William Bromme, "Lektüre eines sozialdemokratischen Arbeiters," in Emmerich, *Proletarische Lebensläufe*, 287 and 294.

has often been assailed.[168] Yet to condemn all this as simply the reproduction of bourgeois culture is enormously one-sided. By appropriating bourgeois culture, socialists and workers laid claim to it—and that was emancipatory, for individuals and the movement. At least some rank-and-file workers seized the opportunities made available to them and developed their intellectual faculties, their appreciation of the arts, and their abilities to articulate their views in the public realm. The SPD's cultural program also contested, by implication, the narrow class-exclusivist claim that *Bildung* had become in the late nineteenth century, a concept of *Bildung* that had long since lost its emancipatory content and had come to represent the epaulets of status and privilege for the educated middle class.[169] By appropriating bourgeois culture, the SPD moved socialism beyond its class-specific to universalist claims.

Socialism meant also a life of commitment to the party. For functionaries and intellectuals, this entailed the unending round of meetings, writing, rewriting, checking proofs, purchasing paper and ink, dealing with typesetters, arranging for the distribution of party publications, and keeping up a frenetic pace of speaking engagements. For Rosa Luxemburg, the personal and political flowed together. In her letters she moved effortlessly from expressing the deepest affection for and intense aggravation with Leo Jogiches, her amorous and political partner, to the details of party work.[170] But not only socialist intellectuals were immersed in the party. Regular workers, once they had made the commitment to the socialist movement, lived a life of meetings, leaflet distributions, Sunday retreats, hikes, lectures, speaking engagements, and, not rarely, prison. The Halle SPD established a workers educational and cultural association in the 1890s, which presided over a choir, theater, gymnastics association, and women's and youth groups. During the 1905 Russian Revolution, the association hosted evenings of poetry by Gorky and Russian music. In 1906, it ran theater evenings, photography exhibits, a Rembrandt festival, and lectures on Mozart, Heine, Russian history, the peasant wars of the Middle Ages, the Napoleonic Wars, Morocco, and workers and alcohol. The local party sponsored museum trips, outings, classes on books, writing, and health, and a library. In 1910/11, the cultural efforts became more systematic, and were opened to the public. Lectures were two and one-half

[168] For balanced assessments, see Dieter Langewiesche, "The Impact of the German Labor Movement on Workers' Culture," *JMH* 59:3 (1987): 506–23; idem, "Politik—Gesellschaft—Kultur: Zur Problematik von Arbeiterkultur und kulturellen Arbeiterorganisationen in Deutschland nach dem 1. Weltkrieg,' *AfS* 22 (1982): 359–402; Lidtke, *Alternative Culture*; and von Saldern, "Wilhelminische Gesellschaft und Arbeiterklasse." Hartmann Wunderer, *Arbeitervereine und Arbeiterparteien: Kultur- und Massenorganisationen in der Arbeiterbewegung (1890–1933)* (Frankfurt am Main: Campus, 1980), takes the more critical line. For a more comprehensive study that moves the topic beyond the organized labor movement, see Abrams, *Workers' Culture*.

[169] See Fritz Ringer, *Fields of Knowledge: French Academic Culture in Comparative Perspective, 1890–1920* (Cambridge: Cambridge University Press, 1992), 95–108.

[170] Rosa Luxemburg to Leo Jogiches, 21 March 1895 and 28 March 1895, in Rosa Luxemburg, *Gesammelte Briefe*, vol. 1, ed. Institut für Marxismus-Leninismus beim ZK der SED (Berlin: Dietz, 1989), 53–54, 60–67.

hours long and began at 8:30 in the evening. Attendance of five to seven hundred was considered low.[171]

The wave of construction of party and trade union halls after 1900 facilitated the SPD's incorporation into the daily lives of its members.[172] The Halle Volkspark, for example, opened in 1907. Like many others, the Volkspark was a highly impressive structure with a great meeting hall including gallery and concert stage; smaller meeting rooms; and, of course, given the important role of exercise in the liberal and socialist movements of the nineteenth century, a gymnastics room.[173] In good German fashion, there was also an immense restaurant and, outside, a beer garden with a music pavilion and space for 3,800 people to sit at tables. A smaller garden was also built for the many special programs run for children.

The large size of the structure and the architectural melange of neo-Gothic and nineteenth-century urban expressed the immense ambition and optimism of the Halle socialists. They made space for huge numbers of people to meet, agitate, and socialize. The beer garden in particular integrated the party into family life, since it provided the setting for a family outing on a Sunday or holiday. Situated in the northern part of the city, on the edge of more prosperous sections, the Volkspark also marked the SPD's political and social claim to the entire urban setting. Located close to the zoo—that classic public space of the bourgeois world—the Volkspark provided working-class families with the opportunity of a Sunday stroll through the zoo and then retreat for refreshments to the Volkspark. Parallel to the party's appropriation of classical culture, the compendium of zoo and Volkspark served as the space within which workers both asserted their claim to the larger urban setting and retreated to the class-specific identification that the Volkspark provided.

By structuring its partisans' lives, socialism also gave meaning to them. Activists forged their own identities in the context of their struggles as socialists. The commitment to a higher cause gave their life purpose, which, sometimes, could result in delirious joy. Working-class autobiographies express this, when, for example, the authors discuss their participation in May Day demonstrations. Especially in the 1890s, to participate in a May Day demonstration meant risking dismissals, the blacklist, and police beatings. To challenge such force required great courage, and resulted in exhilaration when one prevailed against the odds and over one's own fears. For each of the workers who described his or her participation in May Day activities, there is a virtually invariable script: as they contemplate whether or not to participate, each goes through a period of self-doubt and self-scrutiny, fearful of the consequences—loss of a job and the ability to support the family, often including ill and bedridden parents, perhaps even prison. Surmounting the fears, they take a stand—often in opposition to parents or spouses or fellow workers.

[171] Piechocki, "Volkspark," 21–23.

[172] See Elisabeth Domansky, "Der 'Zukunftsstaat am Besenbinderhof,'" in *Arbeiter in Hamburg: Unterschichten, Arbeiter und Arbeiterbewegung seit dem ausgehenden 18. Jahrhundert*, ed. Arno Herzig, Dieter Langewiesche, and Arnold Sywottek (Hamburg: Erziehung und Wissenschaft, 1983), 373–85.

[173] Piechocki, "Volkspark."

The sense of solidarity with workers around the world (or at least in Europe and North America), as well as with one's own fellow workers and neighbors, only accentuated the sense of joy. Adelheid Popp, in one of the best-known working-class autobiographies, describes such sentiments: "Among my colleagues [other women workers] were a few who were related to the master. . . . I had won them over for May Day. I had inspired them for the goals for which we were to stop work. . . . It was a little revolution! Wives, daughters, sisters of the supervisors—all for May Day."[174] Ottilie Baader, living with her father, established her own independence and identity through participation in socialist politics: "I had gradually freed myself from my father. That wasn't easy. . . . One day, with a burst of energy, I announced: 'I'm going tonight to the meeting of the bootmakers!' My father must have been completely surprised at my determination, but he kept quiet and let me go alone."[175] Wenzel Holek, called upon by fellow workers to speak at their May Day rally, hesitated even though it fell on a Sunday in 1892, fearful that a public speech would lead him, once again, to lose his job. He spoke nonetheless, and the weather was at first threatening. Then the sun broke through the clouds—a fine May Day symbol. But Holek was fired, and was effectively blacklisted because his date of dismissal was stamped in his labor book, a sure sign to prospective employers.[176]

Adelheid Popp's "little revolution," the acts of personal, courageous self-affirmation, melded individuals with their class.[177] The sense of purpose in a life dedicated to socialism was intertwined with the sociability of a life spent with comrades. Though the memories were perhaps embellished with time, Heinrich Rabbich's warm description of the socialist youth movement in Essen before the war rings true: "Here [in the youth room of the *Arbeiter-Zeitung* house] developed the exciting, cheerful life of youth. In connection with lectures or other events we had nonstop sociable encounters. Games of all kinds led to rich conversations."[178] Pranks were also part of the stock-in-trade of the youth movement—taunting the police, swiping the saber of a policeman and hanging it in the window of the socialist bookstore, pulling the emergency brake on a train full of strikebreakers on their way from Essen to Hamburg. For some, at least, the sense of danger that arose from confrontations with the police and leaflet distributions in hostile areas constituted part of the attraction of socialism.[179]

For the women like Adelheid Popp, Ottilie Baader, Clara Zetkin, and many others, the social democratic movement provided an added dimension of meaning. Through socialism they found the means of self-assertion against the gender as well as class and political inequalities under which they lived—in the party as

[174] Adelheid Popp, "Der Kampf um die Arbeitsruhe," in Emmerich, *Proletarische Lebensläufe*, 353–54.

[175] Baader, "Der erste Weltfeiertag," in Emmerich, *Proletarische Lebensläufe*, 350–51.

[176] Wenzel Holek, "Austritt am 2. Mai," in Emmerich, *Proletarische Lebensläufe*, 354–55.

[177] See in general all of the descriptions of May Day in the autobiographical excerpts in Emmerich, *Proletarische Lebensläufe*, 350–60.

[178] Rabbich, "60 Jahre Essener 'Freie-Arbeiter-Jugend,'" 2.

[179] Ibid., 3–4.

well as in the society at large. In party doctrine, the oppression of women was only a by-product of class oppression, and would inevitably wane with the triumph of socialism. Much of the party discourse on women and men remained confined within the gendered language of revolutionary republicanism. SPD leaders tended to have the most traditional of family lives—even August Bebel, the author of *Women and Socialism*, whose wife was eulogized by Karl Kautsky as a "conscientious and understanding housewife and mother."[180] The social democratic vision of sexuality and the family had deep affinities with the liberal idealism of the nineteenth century. In place of marriage founded on material necessity, socialism would free individuals to form unions based on love and morality. The romanticized vision of spiritual unions, almost asexual in character—or perhaps a sublimated sexuality—was worthy of the famous passage in Goethe's *Sorrows of Young Werther*, where the tragic hero and his beloved swoon enraptured as they say to one another, "Klopstock."

However limited, the SPD's concept of the family and female equality had also sharp emancipatory edges that marked off the SPD from the other major political movements in Imperial Germany. However infrequently realized, its rhetoric presented a vision of equality within the family and of women's self-assertion, which, for the activist women, constituted a vital part of the essence of socialism.[181] As the resolutions of the party's 1896 congress expressed it: "the woman as equal, equally producing and equally striving, marching forward with her husband as companions and [developing] her individuality as a human being, but at the same time able to fulfill to the highest measure her tasks as wife and mother." In place of the rights of the father over the family would emerge: "the equality of husband and wife, [in place of] monogamy as a command whose strict practice applies only to women, the freely determined moral fulfillment of both sexes."[182]

If monogamy was the ideal, premarital sex was rarely demonized.[183] And while Wilhelm Liebkencht viewed birth control as immoral, his views found no universal support within the party. The SPD was the only party that before World War I contested the official ban on artificial means of birth control, opposed the legal ban on abortions, and argued, if inconsistently, that sexuality and family planning should be left to individual couples and individual moralities. Clara Zetkin, like Lenin and Liebknecht, argued that socialists had an interest in greater numbers of workers and should, therefore, oppose neo-Malthusian efforts to limit the population. She also condemned as "egotistical" parents who limited the number of their children. Yet when she voiced these opinions at a public rally in Berlin in 1913, she found little support from the mostly female audience, which instead cheered an

[180] Niggemann, *Emanzipation*, 277–78.

[181] For a much more balanced interpretation of the SPD's position on gender equality than is generally current in the literature, see Mary Jo Maynes, "*Genossen und Genossinnen*: Gender Identity and Socialist Identity in Imperial Germany," in Barclay and Weitz, *Between Reform and Revolution*.

[182] From the SPD 1896 party congress, quoted in Niggemann, *Emanzipation*, 240–41.

[183] In general on the SPD vision of the family and sexuality, see Niggemann, *Emanzipation*, 237–81, and Maynes, "*Genossen* and *Genossinen*."

SPD doctor who advocated birth control as a means of improving the physical health of the proletariat.[184]

Yet all was not sweetness and light. There were enemies abroad in the land. The shining beams of illumination had to pierce the darkness of evil:

> It is a heavy fight that we are waging,
> Countless are the troops of the enemy,
> Even if flames and danger
> May break loose over us,
> We do not count the number of enemies,
> Do not worry about danger,
> We follow the path of courage
> On which Lassalle leads us.[185]

The employers and the state were the main targets of socialist anger and frustration, but so were fellow workers who remained resistant to the socialist message. Spies were, of course, deeply resented. When discovered, they were sent packing "with a sound thrashing."[186] The Center Party, so often in competition with the SPD for workers' loyalties, aroused the special ire of socialists, and it was often difficult to keep attacks on political Catholicism distinct from attacks on Catholics.[187]

The deeply felt anger at the injustices of the imperial system was as much a part of the impetus to socialism as the lofty vision of a bright and hallowed future. Indeed, injustice and oppression required struggle—*Kampf*, a term at least as prevalent as *Arbeiter* in socialist discourse. *Kampf* permeated all aspects of party life, even the names of cultural and sports associations like the cycling groups called "Rote Husaren des Klassenkampfes" or "Rote Kavallerie."[188] The language and experience of *Kampf*—in the workplace, the streets, the polity—lent to social democracy a special militancy feared by elites and lauded by its partisans.

Conclusion

Socialism provided men and women with rhetorical and practical strategies to contest the efforts by employers and the state to render them passive and obedient objects. Socialism gave them a language of rights and citizenship in a society that rarely spoke in those terms. The utopian vision at the center of Marxism, of a just world free from social conflicts, had meaning to those who experienced the arbi-

[184] Niggemann, *Emanzipation*, 267–69.

[185] Lidtke, *Alternative Culture*, 112–13.

[186] Rabbich, "60 Jahre Essener 'Freie-Arbeiter-Jugend,'" 5.

[187] See, for example, *Die Arbeiterbewegung im Ruhrgebeit: Eine Gabe an den Parteitag 1907 vom Sozialdemokratischen Verein Kreis Essen* (Dortmund: Buchdruckerei der Arbeiter-Zeitung, 1907).

[188] Lidtke, *Alternative Culture*, 61–62.

trary exercise of power on the shop floor and in the streets of industrial communities around the country. In the hard-fought struggles over wages, hours, and piecework rates, over May Day celebrations and equal suffrage, they forged repertoires of resistance that encompassed strikes, demonstrations, battles with foremen, and party activities. Many were the workers whose sense of justice and equality, and whose outrage at their absence, were nurtured by the manifold cultural activities of the party, in which they read and heard the prose and poetry of Lessing and Heine, Schiller and Freiligrath.[189] Many female socialists found support and further developed their ideas by reading August Bebel's *Women and Socialism*, though few came to socialism by reading it.

Elites forged their own repertoire, a collection of strategies that entailed blatant repression and social welfare programs and increasing coordination between employers and the state. Never were these strategies completely successful. Both working-class resistance and the parsimony of employers and the state, who could never provide quite enough welfare, limited the efficacy of the regimes of repression. But probably more through coercion than beneficence, they were able to contain the labor movement and defeat many of the vibrant challenges to the injustices and inequalities of the workplace and state regimes.

In other ways the strategies of employers and, especially, state officials had a major impact on workers and the labor movement. Workers remained tied to the state through the wide range of government-directed social welfare programs, and both popular activism, and the more specific activities of labor leaders, became increasingly oriented toward the state. Both the unions and the SPD had, by the 1890s, given up any essential opposition to the social welfare programs, and, in fact, called for their expansion and improvement. Furthermore, party and union officials participated in administering the programs, and used their positions to aid workers and, in the process, recruit members.[190] Increasingly, union representatives and, at times, ordinary workers turned to factory and mine inspectors and the industrial courts to redress workplace grievances, and sought the implementation of the eight-hour day through governmental legislation and regulation.[191] SPD representatives came to view the local state as a class-neutral arena open to social democratic participation.

For German workers the state—even the capitalist state—could improve living conditions, intervene positively in labor disputes, and, in general, serve as the engine of social transformation. The daily, working-class experience with a paternalistic and authoritarian state thus underpinned the statist conceptions that dominated the German labor movement from the Lasalleans of the 1860s, to the Kauts-

[189] Although many workers found penny novels far more appealing. See Dieter Langewiesche and Klaus Schönhoven, "Arbeiterbibliotheken und Arbeiterlektüre in Wilhelminischen Deutschland," *AfS* 16 (1976): 135–204, and Hans-Joseph Steinberg, "Workers' Libraries in Imperial Germany," *HW* 1 (1976): 166–80.

[190] Gaston V. Rimlinger, *Welfare Policy and Industrialization in Europe, America, and Russia* (New York: John Wiley and Sons, 1971), 126–30, and Ritter, *Social Welfare*, 72–82.

[191] *JB 1904*, 203–4; *JB 1906*, 227–28; *JB 1907*, 217–18; and Steinisch, *Arbeitszeitverkürzung*, 88–89, 96–103.

kian Marxism of the SPD, and, subsequently, to the Marxism-Leninism of the KPD. To this common statist tradition the KPD would add a voluntarism rooted in the social life of a working class battered by war, inflation, and rationalization.

But the KPD did not invent voluntarism in the 1920s. Probably no other aspect of the socialist legacy was as important for communism as the cult of militant struggle. As we shall see, in the 1920s it permeated every aspect of KPD life and became identified with a particularly masculinized ethos of physical battles in the streets. Indeed, in comparison with the fighting spirit and vituperative rhetoric of both the French Revolution, especially in its radical phase, and the communist movements of the twentieth century, the language and practice of pre–World War I socialism seem notably restrained. The language that makes pariahs out of whole classes of people, foreclosing any possibility of their inclusion in the larger community, never completely characterized social democracy.[192] The more radical tendencies were kept in check by the SPD's partial incorporation into the political institutions of Imperial Germany, but perhaps even more importantly, by the manifold links with the classical liberal humanist culture of the nineteenth century. Communism may have learned about struggle from social democracy, but only in the most formalistic sense did it follow the SPD's enthrallment with liberal humanism. Politics would indeed resound in a new key after World War I.

[192] See, for example, William H. Sewell Jr., *A Rhetoric of Bourgeois Revolution: The Abbé Sièyes and "What Is the Third Estate?"* (Durham: Duke University Press, 1994).

CHAPTER 2

War and Revolution and the Genesis of German Communism

Das patriarchalische System . . . ist tot.

—*Krupp official*[1]

IN THE EVENING of 4 August 1914, the Reichstag voted unanimously for war credits, thereby providing the financial means for the German army to begin its march through Belgium and into France and initiate the first of Germany's twentieth-century efforts at empire building. Of the six major parties in the Reichstag, uncertainty existed only about the SPD's decision. But meeting in caucus the day before the Reichstag vote, the SPD voted 78 to 14 to join the univocal chorus in favor of war.[2]

The German army's sweep westward and slower march eastward precipitated four years of unprecedented destruction and the accumulation of unheard of powers in the hands of the state. The proclamation of martial law in the first days of the war placed the nation under the direct control of the military, while the visible hand of the state channeled scarce economic resources—including labor—to the war economy and rationed food supplies and other essential consumer goods. The state's social welfare role expanded at the same time that its authoritarian capacities became more pronounced through the army's direct repression of strikes, demonstrations, and other manifestations of public discontent with the war effort. Companies that produced for the war effort grew dramatically and competed viciously with one another for labor and other resources. Their repressive side also became more pronounced as the demands of war production inspired them to extract ever more out of their workers. At the same time, companies found themselves forced to procure housing and food for their expanding and increasingly malnourished workforces.[3]

[1] "The patriarchal system . . . is dead." "Die Arbeiterschaft der Kruppschen Gußstahlfabrik: Zur Denkschrift 'Die Firma Krupp im Weltkriege'" (ms., n.d.), HA Krupp, WA VII/f1105/Kd75/115.

[2] For the most detailed and revisionist account, see Wolfgang Kruse, *Krieg und nationale Integration: Eine Neuinterpretation des sozialdemokratischen Burgfriedensschlusses 1914/15* (Essen: Klartext, 1993).

[3] On all these issues see Ludwig Preller, *Sozialpolitik in der Weimarer Republik* (Stuttgart: Franz Mittelbach Verlag, 1949), 34–85; Gerald D. Feldman, *Army, Industry, and Labor in Germany, 1914–1918* (Princeton: Princeton University Press, 1966); Jürgen Kocka, *Klassengesellschaft im Krieg: Deutsche Sozialgeschichte 1914–1918* (Göttingen: Vandenhoeck und Ruprecht, 1973); Gunther Mai, ed., *Arbeiterschaft in Deutschland 1914–1918: Studien zu Arbeitskampf und Arbeitsmarkt im Ersten*

In short, the combination of blunt repression and social welfare that defined the workplace and state regimes of Imperial Germany became still more pronounced during World War I. The drive to forge a disciplined working class, loyal to the firm and to the kaiser, received added ideological impetus from the call to sacrifice for the Fatherland threatened by external enemies.

But the impact of the war promoted, as well, the powerful upsurge of labor activism that contributed to the destruction of the imperial system and the severe, though temporary, diminution of managerial authority. By assuming such broad powers and asserting such all-encompassing claims over labor, both the imperial state and private employers became the targets of discontent when, soon after the onset of war, living and working standards deteriorated massively and, in the end, the German army came home in defeat. The Social Democratic Party and the trade unions, collaborators in the war effort, found their claims to representation challenged by their own constituents. Ultimately, the very nature of total war, fought to preserve the workplace and state regimes of Imperial Germany, underpinned labor's vibrant challenge to the restrictions under which it lived and worked.[4]

The Communist Party of Germany was born amid the conflagration of total war and mass working-class protest, as this chapter will show. For all of its later transmutations, German communism, like its European counterparts, remained a child of the war—and the demise of the East German state in 1990 can properly be seen as one marker of the closure of the era begun in 1914.[5] The disastrous wartime conditions radicalized a substantial number of workers, and the great upsurge of strikes, demonstrations, and armed revolutions—from Russia on across the continent—seemed to herald the new society. The vast destructiveness of the war also lent a tenor of brutality to communist politics, as it did to many other political groups. The vision of heroic soldiers fighting for the Fatherland found distorted reverberations in the idealization of the disciplined, combative male proletarian taking up the rifle of revolution. The ideologues of German communism, Rosa Luxemburg the most prominent among them, found in four years of total war the ultimate proof for the inhumanity of capitalism and the corruption of social democracy. They formulated a political language and strategy based in Marxist ideology, but sharply colored by the experiences of war, mass strikes, and armed revolution. To resolve the profound crises of German society, Luxemburg and her comrades offered still greater levels of proletarian

---

Weltkrieg (Düsseldorf: Droste, 1985); Ute Daniel, *Arbeiterfrauen in der Kriegsgesellschaft: Beruf, Familie und Politik im Ersten Weltkrieg* (Göttingen: Vandenhoeck und Ruprecht, 1989); and Richard Bessel, *Germany after the First World War* (Oxford: Clarendon, 1993).

[4] The argument of Kocka's influential *Klassengesellschaft im Krieg*. For a more general statement that more forcefully locates the wartime changes in the context of the general social developments attendant with the "second industrial revolution," see James E. Cronin, "Labor Insurgency and Class Formation: Comparative Perspectives on the Crisis of 1917–1920 in Europe," in *Work, Community, and Power: The Experience of Labor in Europe and America, 1900–1925*, ed. James E. Cronin and Carmen Sirianni (Philadelphia: Temple University Press, 1983), 20–48.

[5] See Klaus Tenfelde, "1914 bis 1990—Einheit der Epoche," *APZ* B40/91 (27 September 1991): 3–11.

activism designed to destroy capitalism and create, in the here and now, the socialist future—positions the KPD promoted throughout the Weimar Republic.

Labor and War

After soldiers and sailors, labor was the most vital resource in World War I. Labor found itself pursued, wooed, and dragooned by the state and employers in the unending effort to keep the army in the field supplied with bullets, shells, and uniforms. Firms producing for the war economy expanded substantially. But the workplace regimes so carefully constructed before 1914 were placed under siege, challenged by the extraordinarily high labor mobility of the war years, which, by sheer numbers alone, undermined the painstaking efforts to build loyal labor forces; by the inability of firms and the state, in the extraordinary economic conditions of wartime, to meet their lofty social welfare promises; and by the activism of labor itself, which burst through the limits imposed by employers and officials. And just as companies and the state drew upon their prewar policies in the increasingly frenetic effort to build labor discipline, so labor drew upon—but also dramatically expanded—the repertoires of resistance created before 1914.

Two cities and their surrounding areas are emblematic of the efforts by employers and the state to maintain their regimes, and of labor's challenge—Essen and Halle, the Ruhr and Halle-Merseburg. Both cities were centers of industrial production well before the war and were situated in two of Germany's major factory and coal-mining regions. Essen housed Germany's major armaments producer, the Krupp firm; Halle held a large number of critical, medium-sized metal-working plants. South of Halle, at Leuna, BASF, with major backing from the state, built a large plant to manufacture synthetic nitrogen for munitions production, one of the major examples of forced wartime industrialization. Both areas, not accidentally, also became major centers of KPD support in the Weimar Republic.

Krupp and Essen

At the end of July 1914, the Krupp firm, preparing for the expected war, announced its commitment to provide for the families of its employees who were drafted into the army. Workers would remain entitled to the benefits provided by the firm's pension and sickness funds, and existing, uncollected fines would be dropped. Once called up, workers would get half of their average wages for the next two wage periods and a one-time present of thirty marks for married workers and ten marks for single workers.[6] Krupp hereby demonstrated its paternalistic ethos and its integration into the national war effort. The reality would soon be otherwise for a company whose semiofficial stature as the "*Waffenschmiede des Reiches*" (Arms Forge of the Reich) only heightened its allure, a company that served as a model of patriarchal social practices and blatant repression.

[6] "Arbeiterschaft der Kruppschen Gußstahlfabrik," 11–12.

In August 1914 the Krupp plant in Essen employed 41,761 people, of whom 36,379 were workers.[7] During the war, the size of the workforce expanded nearly three times to approximately 107,000, and this figure does not even account for the tremendous turnover within these years. According to the firm's own history, from August 1914 to December 1918, approximately 248,000 individuals were hired and 249,000 left the firm's employment.[8] In the four years prior to the outbreak of the war, labor turnover had averaged 45 percent a year; during the war, the average rose to 104 percent.[9]

To fill its incessant demand for labor, Krupp searched far and wide for workers. Women constituted less than 3 percent of Krupp's labor force in August 1914. At the highpoint of the war effort in 1917, 28,664 women worked at the plant, slightly more than one-quarter of the total labor force.[10] To process more rapidly the high number of female employees, the firm shifted their registration from the company's Family Counseling office to the regular Labor Registration office—one further sign of the breakdown of patriarchalism and the modernization of female labor in the war.[11] Large numbers of youths were hired, as well as foreigners from neutral areas. The firm received prisoners of war from the army and impressed workers from the occupied countries.[12] However, the intensive recruitment campaigns launched in many German cities achieved only meager results.[13] In some instances, the firm was downright incensed, as when it recruited, transported, housed, fed, and gave work to a group of the unemployed from Hannover. A number of them, after being fed, then refused to work, an attitude, management charged, that "needs to be condemned all the more fervently" because the firm had had to hire foreigners to fill its labor needs. Krupp than requested that the city welfare office take action against these malingerers—whose names it provided to the officials—"with all available means."[14]

The unceasing demand for labor caused incessant conflicts between factory management and the army command.[15] The army had initially drafted every able-bodied man, but as the war bogged down the need for skilled labor became apparent. The strains did not ease even when the army began to return skilled workers from the front and assigned an officer to the factory on a permanent basis to oversee exemptions. Indeed, according to the firm's own history, the conflict between the military and industry became increasingly strident as the war contin-

[7] HA Krupp, WA 41/6-4, 6-5.

[8] "Arbeiterschaft der Kruppschen Gußstahlfabrik," 5, table 2.

[9] Johannes Marcour, "Arbeiterbeschaffung und Arbeiterauslese bei der Firma Krupp" (ms., 1921), HA Krupp, WA IV/1501/15.

[10] "Arbeiterschaft der Kruppschen Gußstahlfabrik," 5, table 2.

[11] Memo, Gußstahlfabrik, Direktorium to the Betriebe, 18 May 1915, HA Krupp, WA 41/2-140.

[12] On this issue generally, see Ulrich Herbert, *A History of Foreign Labor in Germany, 1880–1980: Seasonal Workers/Forced Laborers/Guest Workers* (Ann Arbor: University of Michigan Press, 1990). For evidence on Krupp's involvement in forced labor, see Nordwestliche Gruppe des Vereins Deutscher Eisen und Stahlindustrie to Geheimrat Hugenberg, 10 November 1916, HA Krupp, WA IV/1242.

[13] "Arbeiterschaft der Kruppschen Gußstahlfabrik," 15–16.

[14] Fried. Krupp AG to Städtische Armenverwaltung (Essen), 19 February 1915, StAE 102/I/1080.

[15] On this issue generally, see Feldman, *Army, Industry, and Labor.*

ued.[16] The company complained that troop commanders were often reluctant to release anyone, and sometimes sent the wrong people back; or when exchanges were arranged, would only release workers after new recruits arrived at the front; or would send back entire groups with the same skill or large numbers at the same time for whom the company was unprepared.[17] As late as October 1918, the army was still pressing for new recruits. Through that last year of the war, 30 percent of Krupp employees born between 1898 and 1900 were drafted.[18] And in that strange cluster of roles in which the military could sometimes serve as the protector of workers against the more onerous claims of employers, the army command warned Krupp and other employers that Belgian workers were to be paid at the same level as German workers, and encouraged them to treat the Belgians with respect and decency in order to ensure that more of their countrymen would voluntarily come to Germany to work.[19] The army even argued, against employers, that freely hired workers could not be forcibly detained in Germany.[20]

The huge influx of workers undermined the old, stable core of the Krupp workforce, the *Stammbelegschaft*, who were fairly well swamped by the new recruits—a trend deeply regretted by the company.[21] As one factory manager wrote, the earlier workforce had been "firmly rooted and settled," but the wartime workforce "under the compulsion of its immense growth . . . [was] predominantly fleeting and uprooted"—important terms in German culture, in which "rootedness" and "blood and soil" were often contrasted with the looseness and danger of the transient.[22] With very few exceptions—women in general, two large groups of workers from the rural areas of Lippe, and skilled workers from Bavaria—the firm was not greatly pleased with its newly recruited workers.[23] They were not used to and not very amenable to the discipline and workpace—the "*Kruppschen Drill*"—of the firm.[24] Age and health and "moral" criteria had been put aside, and many of the workers obtained under the civilian mobilization law were, from the firm's perspective, underage, overage, or handicapped, or had criminal records. Of the workers repatriated by the army, many, apparently, were malingerers who were only using Krupp as a way station home and often did not possess the skills that they claimed. From the industrial cities, only semiskilled workers, at best, could be recruited.

[16] Wilhelm Berdrow, "Die Firma Krupp im Weltkriege und in der Nachkriegszeit," vol. 1 (ms., 1936), HA Krupp, FAH IV/E10/21–24, 71–72.

[17] "Arbeiterschaft der Kruppschen Gußstahlfabrik," 21–26.

[18] Ibid., 25–26.

[19] SVGK VII. AK to government officials and industrial associations, 12 July 1917, StAE 102/I/1087.

[20] Ibid., 20 July 1917.

[21] This is almost a constant refrain in the official (but unpublished) firm history, Berdrow, "Firma Krupp," as well as another internally written manuscript that provided much of the raw material for Berdrow, "Arbeiterschaft der Kruppschen Gußstahlfabrik."

[22] Berdrow, "Firma Krupp," 73.

[23] "Arbeiterschaft der Kruppschen Gußstahlfabrik," 14, 16, 33–35; Berdrow, "Firma Krupp," 225–30.

[24] Berdrow, "Firma Krupp," 72–73, 230.

While the sheer volume of new recruits undermined the workplace regime, so did the firm's inability to provide adequate social welfare measures for its workers. As discussed in chapter 1, Krupp had had one of the most extensive social welfare programs of any German firm. Before 1914, a substantial proportion of the workforce found lodgings in company housing, and the firm's hospital, pension, cooperative, and other amenities certainly eased the material difficulties of working-class life and incorporated workers into the reigning ideology of the company. But none of this could be sustained at adequate levels in wartime, despite huge efforts by the firm. At the most basic level, the food situation in Essen quickly deteriorated.[25] By the winter of 1916–17, weekly rations amounted to only 1,500 grams of bread and 150 to 250 grams of meat, though supplies often failed to meet even these levels. Children five to seven years old were allotted only one-quarter of a liter of milk three times a week. By the summer of 1918, official rations covered only 25 percent of the protein, 19 percent of the fat, 59 percent of the carbohydrates, and 50 to 70 percent of the overall calories required by an adult.[26]

Clearly, no one could survive on official rations alone. Krupp, like many other firms, provided supplementary food allotments, especially to its miners and furnace workers. Thousands of workers were fed at least one meal in giant company cafeterias. But none of these measures could alter the basic fact that sufficient food stocks did not exist. Even Krupp, with its enormous resources and solid contacts in Berlin, was often unable to procure the foodstuffs needed for its allotments.[27]

Nor could the firm any longer adequately house its workers. In 1910, 18 percent of the firm's workforce lived in company housing, which was of good quality and charged rents significantly below the market rate.[28] Close to nine thousand workers were drafted in 1914 alone, close to forty thousand during the entire four years of war.[29] Their families could hardly be evicted, while the vast influx of workers put enormous strains on the city's and the company's housing stock. At first, Krupp rented schools, halls, and other buildings and converted them into dormitory-type sleeping quarters.[30] A few regular houses, additions to existing Krupp colonies, were built, but for the most part the company constructed large dormitories designed to accommodate vast numbers as quickly as possible.[31]

[25] See StAE 102/I/1088, passim; Hubert Schmitz, "Ausgewählte Kapitel aus der Lebensmittelversorgung der Stadt Essen in der Kriegs- und Nachkreigszeit," *Beiträge zur Geschichte von Stadt und Stift Essen* 58 (1939); and *Chronik der Stadt Essen*, 1914–19 (typescript, StAE) which contains substantial excerpts from the reports of the city's Food Supply Committee.

[26] *Chronik 1917*, 67; *Chronik 1919*, 99; Schmitz, "Ausgewählte Kapitel," 135–36, 165–67.

[27] Memos from the Directorate, 24 October 1916, 14 November 1916, 11 December 1916, and others, HA Krupp, WA 41/2-142. The Directorate admitted that the measures undertaken by the firm were insufficient. "Arbeiterschaft der Kruppschen Gußstahlfabrik," 99, and Berdrow, "Firma Krupp," 151.

[28] "Aufnahme auf den Kruppschen Werken beschäftigten Personen nach dem Stande in der Wochen von 23. bis 28. Mai 1910," HA Krupp, WA 41/6-8.

[29] "Arbeiterschaft der Kruppschen Gußstahlfabrik," 13.

[30] Ibid., 98–99; Berdrow, "Firma Krupp," 237–38.

[31] "Arbeiterschaft der Kruppschen Gußstahlfabrik," 98–99; *Führer durch die Essener Wohnsiedlungen der Firma Krupp* (Essen: Graphische Anstalt der Fried. Krupp AG, 1920), 8.

Large cafeterias were often built along with these structures, so that by October 1918 the firm had five cafeterias and thirty-six male and eight female dormitories. Together they housed around twenty-four thousand individuals and fed thirty-four thousand a day.[32] An almost incredibly sized building, designed to sleep twenty-two thousand and feed twenty-seven thousand, was only finished as the war ended, so it was never put into use.

While the strict regulations that governed the regular Krupp housing colonies also prevailed in the dormitories, the return for workers—adequate housing—became an ever more elusive dream. Clearly, the promise of decent living standards in return for hard work and loyalty to the firm and kaiser became mere mythmaking for the tens of thousands of workers crammed into army-like barracks. The regular colonies, with their curved streets, flower gardens, churches, recreation halls, and libraries, became the province of an ever declining proportion of the labor force. Reflecting on the war years and the Revolution, a Krupp official reached the obvious conclusion: "The patriarchal system . . . is dead."[33]

Its death, however, came at the hands not only of the anonymous forces of war and inflation, overcrowding and mobility. Workers themselves contributed to the murder, taking upon themselves actions that destroyed the cover of social peace that for a century the Krupp firm had sought to construct. While in comparison to other areas and factories Krupp remained relatively quiescent during the war, the mere occurrence of strikes at all—for the first time in the history of the company—marked an enormous breach in the workplace regime.

The first strike against Krupp broke out in the company-owned Emscher-Lippe mine in August 1916. The action was part of a larger strike wave that extended from Dortmund to Gelsenkirchen.[34] In the midst of martial law Krupp miners displayed an extraordinary level of solidarity.[35] Only 56 out of 740 men went down into the pits, and most of them were supervisory personnel. Typically, the strike was touched off by discontent with the food situation, in particular the lack or insufficient quantity of bacon and fat. The Workers Committee negotiated with management, but was roundly attacked at a mass meeting for not defending the interests of the workforce—one of the first public signs of the growing division between workers and their representatives. After two days, the miners voted unanimously to return to work. Whether they won concessions is not made clear in the documents.

Sporadic strikes broke out at a variety of Ruhr mines through the autumn of

[32] Berdrow, "Firma Krupp," 238; *Führer*, 9.

[33] "Arbeiterschaft der Kruppschen Gußstahlfabrik," 115.

[34] See Hans Spethmann, *Zwölf Jahre Ruhrgbergbau: Aus seiner Geschichte von Kriegsanfang bis zum Franzosenabmarsch 1914–1925*, vol. 1: *Aufstand und Ausstand bis zum zweiten Generalstreik April 1919* (Berlin: Reimar Hobbing, 1928), 20 ff. The very first wartime strike had broken out at the Essen mine Neu-Cöln on 7 July 1916. For a recent and thorough analysis of Ruhr miners, Karin Hartewig, *Das unberechenbare Jahrzehnt: Bergarbeiter und ihre Familien im Ruhrgebiet* (Munich: Beck, 1993).

[35] On the strike at Emscher-Lippe, see Gewerkschaft Emscher-Lippe to Zechenverband, 19 August 1916, HA Krupp, WA IV/1253.

1916. At Krupp, small-scale protests that contested managerial and military powers began to emerge.[36] Then, in 1917, the factory itself, for the first time in the history of the firm, experienced a strike. It began in the artillery works on 12 February 1917.[37] The workers claimed that they could not keep laboring without more food. From the end of December, potato rations had been cut from seven to five and then to three pounds, and then failed altogether in February. The bread rations had been cut as well. When management disclaimed responsibility for the food problem, the workers demanded higher wages and complained about the disparity in the pay scales of various trades and the low wages among helpers. Although one company report claimed that older "more reasonable" workers were opposed to the strike, other evidence indicates that the action attracted a broad range of support. It began among skilled mechanics and semiskilled bench workers, but also mobilized young and newer workers from outside Essen. Women were also involved in the strike, and, indeed, were targeted by company officials as among the major problems. All told, approximately 7,500 workers participated in the action. And they won from the company higher wages and promises of increased food rations.

In a manner typical of the great periods of popular protest, workers learned by example about the efficacy of strikes.[38] Miners struck when they failed to secure increases granted production workers; coking plant workers did the same when miners won raises. The February strike, for example, spread quickly from the artillery workshop to the Sälzer-Neuack mine, which was owned by Krupp and located within the factory grounds.[39] The prairie fire character of the strikes was also fueled by the perceived inequalities in wages, which upset the fairly fixed prewar wage spreads between skilled and unskilled, women and men. Krupp managers, writing in mid-1915, assessed the wage levels as satisfactory, but noted that the wages of older, skilled workers were being pressured by the relatively high wages used to attract new workers, many of whom lacked the requisite skills.[40]

The company was so worried by the strikes that Krupp von Bohlen und Halbach felt compelled to write Reich Chancellor Bethmann-Hollweg. The strike movement has taken on a very serious character, wrote Krupp, "and during the last week

[36] Heinrich Rabbich, "Protokoll: Gespräch mit Heinrich Rabbich 27.7.77: Novemberrevolution 1918 in Essen" (interview conducted by Ernst Schmidt), Archivsammlung Ernst Schmidt 1918-7, and Josef Orlopp, "Die Munitionsarbeiterstreik 1917 in Essen," in *Die Novemberrevolution und die deutschen Gewerkschaften*, 2. Halbband: *Erinnerungen aus Veteranen der deutschen Gewerkschaftsbewegung an die Novemberrevolution (1914–1920)* (Berlin: Tribüne, 1958), 132.

[37] See Krupp von Bohlen und Halbach to Reichskanzler Bethmann-Hollweg, 28 February 1917; "Zusammenfassung der Berichte der Ressortchefs und Betriebsführer über die Streikbewegung in der Artilleriewerkstätten in der Zeit von 12. bis 19. Februar 1917," 9 March 1917, both in HA Krupp, FAH/IV/C178; and "Arbeiterschaft der Kruppschen Gußstahlfabrik," 73–75.

[38] For an insightful theoretical discussion on cycles of protest, see Sidney Tarrow, *Power in Movement: Social Movements, Collective Action and Politics* (Cambridge: Cambridge University Press, 1994).

[39] Krupp to Bethmann-Hollweg, 26 February 1917; memo from Herrn Jüngst of Sälzer-Neuack management, undated, both in HA Krupp, FAH IV/C178.

[40] Büro für Arbeiterangelegenheiten to Herrn Dirketor Vielhaber, 17 June 1915, HA Krupp, WA 6-105.

or so both short and long work stoppages have broken out or been threatened in the most varied units of the plant." In order to get workers to return to their jobs, the firm had had to promise a regular disbursement of bread and flour and had granted pay and ration increases: "Given recent events, I have great reservations about whether these promises can be carried out by the appropriate governmental agencies. In such a case, the workers' respect for the company management and for government officials, as well as their trust in future promises, will leave much to be desired."[41] Krupp, unwittingly, was sounding the death knell of the workplace regime. No longer able to secure its paternalistic role, the firm strengthened its repressive hand. It drew up plans for the military protection of key points in the factory, should unrest break out, and proposed that workers involved in even the threat of unrest be drafted and forced to carry out their work under martial law.[42]

Nevertheless, strikes continued. In April 1917, strikes that began in the mechanical units spread to other branches, and the workers gained more concessions from the firm.[43] In July, two hundred women employed in munitions production were fired for refusing to work.[44] In August, strikes broke out again at Sälzer-Neuack.[45] Here, the deep level of solidarity was quite evident because miners went out not over wages and food, but in support of four of their fellow workers who had been fired. The miners found half-hearted support from the military, which opposed the firings in order to win a quick resumption of work.[46]

When the greatest strike wave of the war years broke out in January 1918, the Ruhr remained relatively quiescent, despite the expectations of an eruption.[47] In the mines, strikes were limited to the eastern part of the region centered around Dortmund and Bochum, and reached only a few Essen mines.[48] At Krupp, about seven to eight thousand workers in a variety of units walked off their jobs. But the company was deeply worried by the nature of the action.[49] The workplace regime had been challenged in 1916 and 1917 by workers demanding higher wages and adequate food supplies. Now the strikes had taken on a clear political dimension. The large number of leaflets and their wide, though obviously surreptitious, distribution in the Krupp factories and mines were seen as grave dangers, violating the company's control over the flow of ideas within its domain. One member of the Directorate asked the military to publish a pamphlet tying these leaflets to "English

[41] Krupp to Bethmann-Hollweg, 26 February 1917, HA Krupp, FAH IV/C178.

[42] Memo Gußstahlfabrik, "Vorbeugende Maßnahmen bei Arbeiterunruhen," 19 March 1917, HA Krupp, WA IV/1431.

[43] Orlopp, "Munitionsarbeiterstreik," 38–41.

[44] Oberkontrolle J.-No. 740 to Herrn Vielhaber, 6 July 1917; memo from Büro für Arbeiterangelegenheiten, 7 July 1917, HA Krupp, WA 41/6-168; "Arbeiterschaft der Kruppschen Gußstahlfabrik," 75.

[45] Jüngst to Krupp, 6 August 1917; Krupp to the Direktorium, 17 September 1917, HA Krupp, WA IV/1242. See also Spethmann, *Zwölf Jahre* 1:46–47.

[46] This prompted Krupp's chief executive officer, Alfred Hugenberg, to complain to the highest levels in Berlin that the military's actions weakened the authority of the firm. Hugenberg to Jüngst, 9 August 1917; General von Gayl to Krupp, 23 August 1917, both in HA Krupp, WA IV/1242.

[47] Oberstleutnant Figge to GK VII. AK, 28 January 1918, HA Krupp, WA 41/6-168. Figge was permanently stationed at the factory.

[48] Spethmann, *Zwölf Jahre*, 1:53, 64–65.

[49] Figge to GK VII. AK, 7 February 1918, HA Krupp, WA 41/6-168.

gold."[50] One of the leaflets, distributed under the imprimatur of the Independent Social Democratic Party (Unabhängige Sozialdemokratische Partei Deutschlands, or USPD) Reichstag fraction, argued that the Brest-Litovsk treaty between Russia and Germany revealed the true, imperialist war aims of Germany, and called for a peace without annexations and self-determination for all nations. An unsigned leaflet called for a mass strike and the overthrow of the government. Another charged that the German bourgeoisie, the German Junkers, and the German government constituted the true enemies. Still another called on workers to elect representatives on the Russian and Austrian models (i.e., establish workers councils), but to be sure not to elect any "government socialists."[51] These demands surfaced again in the summer of 1918 during miners strikes that included the Krupp-owned mines.[52]

The practice and threat of strikes induced management and government officials to grant workers material concessions, often at the behest of the army, which was determined to maintain production at all costs. The authorities thereby confirmed the value of strikes and bestowed upon workers a growing awareness of their own power. In a sense, working-class activism became the substitute for the exalted social welfare policies of the company and the government, which utterly failed to meet their stated claims. By strikes, demonstrations, and, later, food riots, petty thievery, and armed revolution, workers sought to force their employers and state officials to fulfill their paternalistic obligations. In so doing, they destroyed the essence of paternalism and burst the limits of the workplace regime; they became active subjects rather than dependent objects. Ultimately, though briefly, workers even abandoned their demands on the company and state and sought to refashion social relations altogether through workers' control. The learning experience for many workers during the war was that in times of trouble, they had to rely on their own collective activism to force improvements in their conditions—a lesson that drew on more sporadic actions before World War I and on the socialist idealization of proletarian labor. In the 1920s, communists would acquire a strong presence at Krupp and in Essen, to the utter dismay of company officials who pined away for the return of prewar conditions.

Leuna and Halle-Merseburg

In 1916 BASF began building a huge factory just outside the village of Leuna to manufacture synthetic nitrogen as a substitute for saltpeter, a key component of munitions. Germany's normal supplies of saltpeter had come from Chile, but these had been interrupted by the British blockade. Just before the war, the Haber-Bosch synthesization process had been invented, but existing output was too small. The German government provided substantial subsidies for the construction and operation of the new plant and a guaranteed market.[53]

[50] Member of the Direktorium to the Oberstleutnant, 29 January 1918, HA Krupp, WA 41/6-168.

[51] Spethmann, *Zwölf Jahre* 2:53, 56–57; copies of leaflets in HA Krupp WA, 41/6-168.

[52] Jüngst to Fried. Krupp AG, 19 August 1918, HA Krupp, WA IV/1253; Spethmann, *Zwölf Jahre* 1:67, 72–74.

[53] Beginning in 1925, BASF became the central component of the German chemical giant I. G.

Leuna itself was still a village when construction began, but it lay within one of the major industrial regions of Germany, Halle-Merseburg, the center of substantial coal-mining reserves (mostly lignite) and chemical, machine building, and metals-processing factories. The state and the company chose Leuna because, situated in central Germany, it was distant from enemy lines and had substantial water and coal supplies and excellent transport connections.

BASF, a firm in the vanguard of technological developments, presided over a workforce at its headquarters in Ludwigshafen that, like Krupp's, was the beneficiary of extensive social welfare provisions and the victim of a severe and disciplined workplace regime.[54] At Leuna, however, a new workforce had to be rapidly created. The entire region endured the usual wartime problems of overcrowding and insufficient food supplies; at Leuna, material conditions were even more desperate, and the forced pace of munitions production left little time or capital to direct at social provisions.[55] The company's patriarchal ideology rang increasingly hollow, leaving only the authoritarian practices in place. The emblematic workplace regime of BASF at Ludwigshafen was destroyed by the same processes as at Krupp—extraordinarily high workforce mobility; the company's inability, perhaps unwillingness, to meet its social welfare claims; and working-class resistance. Instead of a model enterprise, BASF built a factory that became a center of working-class radicalism and communist influence.

As at Krupp, BASF's first problem lay in finding workers. The core of the labor force consisted of a few hundred men brought from Ludwigshafen, a *Stammbelegschaft* valued for its skills and experience with company discipline. The agricultural areas around Leuna supplied some workers, but not in sufficient numbers. About one-half of the workers came from the surrounding industrial towns—Halle, Weissenfels, Naumburg, Zeitz—while others were recruited

---

Farben. The government-backed loans that BASF used to build the plant were later paid back during the inflation years, making the plant a virtual present from the state to the company. For the history of Leuna and BASF, see especially the studies conducted in the ex-DDR: *Geschichte der VEB Leuna-Werke "Walter Ulbricht" 1916 bis 1945*, ed. Kreisleitung der SED des VEB Leuna-Werke "Walter Ulbricht" (Leipzig: Deutscher Verlag für Grundstoffindustrie, 1989); *Geschichte der VEB Leuna-Werke "Walter Ulbricht" 1945 bis 1981*, ed. Kreisleitung der SED des VEB Leuna-Werke "Walter Ulbricht" (Leipzig: Deutscher Verlag für Grundstoffindustrie, 1989); Eberhard Stein, "Salpeter für Ludendorff und die IG: Zwei Beiträge zur deutschen Stickstoffchemie im Ersten Weltrieg," ed. IML an der Technischen Hochschule für Chemie Leuna-Merseburg (n.p., 1963); *Kämpfendes Leuna (1916–1945): Die Geschichte des Kampfes der Leuna-Arbeiter* Teil 1: 1. Halbband, ed. Kreisleitung der SED VEB Leuna-Werke "Walter Ulbricht" (Berlin: Tribüne, 1961); G. Meisel, "Der Kampf der Werktätigen des Leunawerkes in den Jahren 1919–1921" (Ph.D. diss., Institut für Gesellschaftswissenschaften beim ZK der SED, 1961); and Eberhard Stein, "Die Entstehung der Leuna-Werke und die Anfänge der Arbeiterbewegung in den Leuna-Werken während des Ersten Weltkrieges und der Novemberrevolution" (Ph.D. diss., Martin-Luther-Universität Halle-Wittenberg, 1960). See also Peter Hayes, *Industry and Ideology: IG Farben in the Nazi Era* (Cambridge: Cambridge University Press, 1987) and Helmuth Tammen, *Die I. G. Farbenindustrie Aktiengesellschaft (1925–1933): Ein Chemiekonzern in der Weimarer Republik* (Berlin: Verlag Helmuth Tammen, 1978).

[54] Dieter Schiffmann, *Von der Revolution zum Neunstundentag: Arbeit und Konflikt bei BASF 1918–1924* (Frankfurt am Main: Campus, 1983).

[55] On the dire material situation in Halle, see Richard Robert Rive, *Lebenserinnerungen eines deutschen Oberbürgermeisters*, ed. Schriftenreihe des Vereins zur Pflege Kommunalwissenschaftlicher Aufgaben e.v. Berlin, vol. 5 (Stuttgart: W. Kohlhammer, 1960), 280–92.

through the Auxiliary Service Law from more distant cities in Saxony and from Berlin. Close to half of the workers were repatriated soldiers; 1,368 were women; and almost nine hundred prisoners of war were employed. BASF constructed a labor force notable for its familiarity with industrial labor, if not with chemicals production, in areas with long traditions of labor movement organizing. Since the Leuna works were in an almost constant state of construction, building workers, often employed by subcontractors, labored in close proximity to production workers and added a particularly potent force of protest.

Production began in February 1917. By April 1917, almost one year from the start of construction, the firm employed over twelve thousand workers, though only about one-fifth of these were actually involved in production. Under the forced pace of wartime production, working conditions were exceedingly difficult. According to one source, eighty-four-hour weeks were common, as were the twenty-four-hour swing shift and compulsory overtime.[56] The combination of large numbers of workers inexperienced with chemicals production, excessive hours, and a rapid tempo contributed to excessively high accident rates. According to company statistics, in 1917 1,082 work-related accidents occurred, of which twenty-eight were fatal, and in 1918 1,243 accidents, of which twenty-one were fatal.[57] Many production workers labored in half-completed units that were exposed to the elements.

At Ludwigshafen BASF's extensive array of social welfare programs included a company hospital, company housing, and company-sponsored choir and sports teams. The firm granted premiums, bonuses, and vacations tied to years of service. Many of these benefits were channeled through the Werksverein, the company union. Yet the conditions at Leuna made it impossible to replicate these programs. The *Stammbelegschaft* brought from Ludwigshafen became an isolated island rather than the magnet for a new, loyal and disciplined workforce.

Good company housing at Leuna remained the preserve of white-collar workers, foremen, and a very few privileged workers. The vast majority, some seven thousand workers, lived cramped together in hastily constructed barracks, accentuating the sense of compulsory labor within a militarized system. As one history of working-class protest at Leuna described the barracks: "Around thirty men were housed in a narrow room without ventilation. The beds were stacked all over one another, and a single dreary lamp [hung] on the ceiling. Washing facilities were insufficient. In summer the air was overheated and suffocating; in winter, because of poor heating, ice cold."[58]

Women were housed in separate female barracks where conditions were scarcely better, company supervision even stricter. Female and male employees who lived in the surrounding areas often endured excessively long commutes, sometimes two hours in each direction, because of the government's inability to undertake repairs and regular maintenance of public transportation in wartime and the military's first claim on rolling stock. In the best of circumstances, this meant

[56] *Kämpfendes Leuna*, 56.

[57] Ibid., 56–57.

[58] Ibid., 61, and generally 59–63.

that workers could be away from home sixteen hours a day. In addition, the large number of workers housed in barracks were also dependent on the company for their meals. The poor quality and insufficient quantity aroused bitter protests, and became a key point around which class resentments, class identities, and class politics crystallized.

Unable to provide adequate social welfare provisions, BASF accentuated the repressive side of the workplace regime. Two-thirds of the labor force worked under military discipline, either as soldiers repatriated for a distinct period of time or as civilians recruited under the Auxiliary Service Law.[59] The soldiers even worked in uniform. Furthermore, the military command in Weissenfels helped the firm check on the experiences of workers and recruit workers from petit bourgeois and agricultural backgrounds. In the women's barracks, women and girls were crowded twenty into a room. Whoever wanted to leave had to register and receive a pass, and received heavy fines if she returned late.[60] The expression that became a virtual aphorism among workers in the 1920s—"Zuchthaus Leuna" (Leuna Penitentiary)—had its origins in the very real living conditions of Leuna workers in World War I.

The firm's regulations, the "Arbeitsordnung," issued on 6 June 1918, made clear the continued, authoritarian nature of labor relations in Germany and the firm's absolute determination to maintain its workplace regime amid the upheavals of the war and the challenges posed by workplace struggles.[61] These regulations supplemented those issued in 1910 (discussed in chapter 1), but were much lengthier, running to twenty-three pages and 126 clauses.

In minute detail, the specific items asserted the company's control over workers' time and bodies. Only the firm doctor, for example, could decide if a worker's illness necessitated a limitation in his or her work. The work schedule and requisite breaks were carefully detailed. The regular workday lasted from 7:30 A.M. to 6:00 P.M., with a one and one-half hour lunch break. Those on twelve-hour shifts labored from 6:00 A.M. or P.M.; the biweekly twenty-four-hour swing shift ran from 6:00 A.M. Sunday to 6:00 A.M. Monday. For women, Saturday work ended at 5:00 P.M., "as stipulated in the [state] commercial code." Wages were to be paid only for the actual work time. Even those who endured the twenty-four-hour shift were paid for twenty-two hours, unless they worked without a break. At least twice daily, supervisors were to ensure that workers were at their designated places; those who put in overtime were to be controlled three times a day. As a sign of the firm's generosity, the factory closed at 5:00 P.M. on the Saturday before Easter, Pentecost, Christmas Eve, and New Year's Eve, and workers were to be paid for the last hour along with a 25 percent bonus.

Subsidies were paid for transportation and for workers who lived away from home, an effort to create and maintain the workforce by providing at least some

[59] Ibid., 53.

[60] Ibid., 53, 57.

[61] The following discussion is drawn from "Arbeitsordnung," 15 June 1918, BASF Kommission für Arbeiterangelegenheiten, Ludwigshafen am Rhein, and "Arbeits-Ordnung," BASF, Ludwigshafen am Rhein, 17 December 1910, BLW 1301.

compensation for the difficult transport and housing situation. To assert its control over wage levels and dispel any illusions about workers' "rights" to these bonuses, the firm refused to pay transportation bonuses during temporary shutdowns. Workers were grouped into all sorts of categories that served to exclude many of them from the charmed circle of those who received bonuses. Only after five years of unbroken service did workers receive vacations—three days at half pay plus an allowance of 3.50 marks. In the ultimate display of generosity, the company announced that it would pay the members of the BASF choir if they missed work to sing at the burial of a fellow employee.

BASF's regulations described in excruciating detail the responsibilities of workers and the controls they labored under. The labor system was harsh, and the exigencies of total war reduced social provisioning to the benefits derived from gravesite performances. Severe food shortages and inequitable distribution only heightened the grievances. Workers at Leuna responded with nearly incessant protests, which shattered the remains of the workplace regime. Construction workers, skilled laborers with a strong fraternal corporate tradition, initiated many of the actions, which production workers then imitated. The presence of numerous companies at one worksite added layers of complexity to labor relations at Leuna, but also demonstrated the communicative possibilities among different kinds of workers in a situation of intense deprivation.

At the end of September 1916, only some four months after ground was broken for the construction of the factory, building workers went on strike and won wage improvements. Only a few days later, a mass meeting of construction workers called for additional wage increases, the elimination of piecework pay, equal overtime rates for Sundays and holidays for all subcontracting firms, and a limit of the daily workday to eleven hours. Again the companies—BASF as well as the subcontractors—were forced to relent and meet the demands.[62] Yet even this agreement did not still working-class agitation, for in January and February 1917 a mass movement designed to limit overtime spread from construction workers to metalworkers, and hundreds, if not thousands, simply refused to put in the overtime demanded of them. In April 1917, one-quarter of the approximately seven thousand workers employed directly by Leuna walked off their jobs after ten hours, refusing the overtime demanded by the company, after bread rations had been reduced.[63]

Like every other company with more than fifty employees, BASF had been forced by the Auxiliary Service Law to accept the formation of an elected workers committee. Its very existence in conjunction with constant worker protests resulted in an unending series of long, wearying negotiations among Leuna management, the managements of the subcontracting construction firms, the military, and worker representatives. Through 1917, company officials bitterly fought even the most minor concessions. Their exasperation with continually escalating worker demands—and with the fact that some workers were earning

[62] *Kämpfendes Leuna*, 68.

[63] Ibid., 80–81.

as much as the greater portion of white-collar workers—is palpable even through the opaque, bureaucratic language of managerial reports. Anytime one group of workers won benefits from the company, another group quickly followed suit. A fifteen pfennig bonus to the wage packet was enough to inspire cascading protests from all sorts of workers—factory production workers, construction workers hired by member firms of the Construction Employers Association, construction workers employed by other subcontractors.[64] By 1918, the unending wave of strikes broke even BASF's tenacity. Management seemed wearily resigned to the continuing wage spiral and sought only to limit its magnitude.[65]

Workers learned something different—that autonomous activism brought results. All the "normal" weapons at the firm's disposal in labor conflicts—lockouts, mass dismissals, deployment of security forces—had become useless given the absolute primacy placed on military production and the absolute centrality of labor. Behind the facade of strength, management's power was on the wane. When the military forced the firm to accept mediation, BASF found itself left in the lurch by the very state its products were supposed to defend. The firm could not stand alone against the pressure of a state determined to maintain military production at all costs and had to accept negotiations with worker representatives.

Wages were not the only issue of dispute. Food took on immense political meaning and figured prominently in the negotiations. In July 1917, worker representatives conveyed complaints that foremen and white-collar workers were receiving better food in their cafeterias than regular workers, and demanded a single dining room for everyone. Management denied any inequality in food provisioning, and worker representatives seemed to agree that the complaints were based on unfounded rumors. Clearly, though, the food situation was explosive enough that all kinds of stories circulated and were worrisome to management and labor leaders alike. The firm finally agreed to eliminate small variations in provisioning—not by giving more to workers, but by removing napkins and tablecloths from the dining room frequented by foremen and white-collar workers.[66]

But this issue also was not laid to rest by one negotiation, and it seems that the firm was a bit disingenuous in its claims that the same food was provided to all employees. Dr. Dehnel, the firm director who always led the negotiations, claimed—two days before the German Revolution—that in reality, a single meal had existed for a long time and that "only the manner of preparation was different in the managers' cafeteria." Worker representatives countered that "through actions of the kitchen personnel the meals for foremen and supervisors had been

[64] The long-running disputes about this are documented in "Niederschrift über die 7. Besprechung mit dem Arbeiterausschuß," 22 August 1917, BLW 1301/93–101; "Niederschrift über die ausserordentliche Sitzung des Arbeiterausschußes am 6. September 1917," BLW 1305/84–88; "Niederschrift über die zehnte Besprechung mit dem Arbeiterausschuß," 22 December 1917, BLW 1305/3–12; "Lohnbewegungen 1916–18," BLW 1301; and a somewhat different account in *Kämpfendes Leuna*, 87–91.

[65] This observation is based on reading the stenographic reports of the negotiations in BLW 1305 and 1307, as well as the very interesting document, "Lohnbewegungen 1916–18" (n.d., 6 pp. typescript), BLW 1301.

[66] "Niederschrift über die sechste Besprechung mit dem Arbeiterausschuß," 21 July 1917, BLW 1305/112–14.

better prepared than the meals for workers." After long discussions, the firm agreed that the same meal would be prepared for all and that workers would have the right to eat in the cafeteria frequented by foremen and white-collar workers—provided that they registered beforehand and brought their own utensils.[67] Complete equality the company was still not ready to grant. However, two days later, with Germany in revolution, the firm, alongside its acceptance of the eight-hour day and the abolition of overtime and Sunday work, finally agreed to provide the same meal for all employees. The stenographic report of the last negotiation of the war years laconically (and in typical bureaucratic style) relates: "On the plant directorate side, the demands of the workforce are agreed to."[68]

If the demand for better quality food was not exactly revolutionary, nor was it merely a "bread and butter" issue. Embedded in the demand for a single cafeteria lay a challenge to the class and status hierarchies that were constitutive of the workplace regime and of German society in general. Moreover, workers had learned that their demands could be efficacious, especially when backed with the reality or threat of a strike.[69] As the management of one mining company in the Halle-Merseburg region remembered this period, "uprisings of the workforce were the order of the day."[70]

The wartime strikes were not sudden explosions of an immiserated proletariat. Clearly, workers responded to the very real material deprivations that they suffered. However, strikes can be repressed and workers can be shot down or marched off to prison and the army. They sometimes were, but the centrality of labor to the war effort made it impossible for the forces of order to revert to a policy of repression alone. The army, the state, the companies—all needed workers more than ever. Slowly, the company became aware of the precarious situation. State and industry were forced continually to renegotiate the terms of social peace. Management foisted the blame, when possible, on union leaders, the army, and the state. Hesitantly, reluctantly, bitterly, BASF had to give in to the autonomous demands of workers and become party to the inflationary spiral in the effort to maintain production and social order.[71]

[67] "Niederschrift über die Besprechung mit den beiden Arbeiter-Ausschüssen und dem Ernährungsausschuß," 7 November 1918, BLW 1307/68 ff.

[68] "Niederschrift über die Sitzung mit den Delegierten der Arbeiterschaft der Leunawerke am 9. November 1918," BLW 1307.

[69] For a model study of how workers and their adversaries learn in the course of a strike, see Tim Mason, "Gli scioperi di Torino del marzo 1943," in *L'Italia nella seconda guerra mondiale e nella Resistenza*, ed. Ferratini Tosi et al. (Milan: Franco Angeli Libri, 1988): 399–422. Hence, it was not the process of working-class concentration per se during the war that was so significant, as Kocka argues in *Klassengesellschaft im Krieg*. Kocka maintains that the common experience of material deprivation coupled with the heightened communicative possiblilites of wartime established the preconditions for radicalism and revolution. But Kocka sees these as automatic processes and leaves little room for the mediating element of human consciousness and human agency, and for the learning experience of workers in wartime.

[70] *A. Riebeck'sche Montanswerke: Die Geschichte einer mitteldeutschen Bergwerksgesellschaft. Zum 25. Jahre Carl Adolph Riebeck und 50. Jahre A. Riebeck'sche Montanwerke AG 1858–1933* (Munich: F. Bruckmann, 1933), 113.

[71] See "Lohnbewegungen 1916–1918," BLW 1301.

In the end, it was the workers themselves—at Leuna, Krupp, and elsewhere in Germany—who destroyed the patriarchal workplace regime by moving increasingly boldly as they saw the efficacy of their own actions. Certainly, not all workers engaged in protest actions and many remained loyal to the firm. But the initiative lay with the rebellious ones, who forced the management of Krupp and Leuna to respond. The fact that wage hikes and increased food rations resulted not from the beneficence of the companies meant that workers had destroyed the very essence of the patriarchal system.

In the learning process of the war years, many workers also took inspiration from news, however fragmentary, of the Russian Revolution and strikes and mutinies in many other countries. But perhaps more importantly, they drew on their prewar experiences. The strikes of the war were mass strikes, but militants played key roles—shop steward metalworkers in Berlin and at Krupp, construction workers, with a long record of strikes, at Leuna. More than in most other areas, resistance in the workplace at Leuna was closely connected with the overt political radicalism in the surrounding region, which penetrated both party and union. Within the union cartel, the metalworkers and construction workers unions played the dominant roles, and both had strongly radical casts. Many individuals involved in both unions found work at Leuna, despite the effort of the company and military to screen out radicals, and the trade unions developed a strong presence in the plant as well. As a result, strikes developed a strong political articulation, and radicals moved into positions of leadership within the Workers Committee and the trade union locals, typified best perhaps by Bernard Koenen, one of the leaders at Leuna, who went on to a long career in the KPD and SED. Among this increasingly assertive working class, the KPD would find strong support—at Leuna and in Halle-Merseburg and at Krupp and in the Ruhr.

Rosa Luxemburg and the Beginnings of German Communist Politics

"In the first moments on 4 August, I was beside myself, almost broken," wrote Rosa Luxemburg to her elderly and revered colleague, Franz Mehring.[72] Her distress and lassitude did not last long. She soon roused herself to feverish activity designed to organize the socialist opposition to the war. She found support only among a small group of other left-wing social democrats, many of them deeply devoted to her, who would go on to form the core of the KPD.[73] In March 1915 they began to constitute themselves as the International Group, and the next month managed to produce a single issue of a tabloid, *Die Internationale*, edited

[72] Luxemburg to Franz Mehring, 31 August 1915, in Rosa Luxemburg, *Gesammelte Briefe*, vol. 5 (hereafter *GB*:5), ed. Institut für Marxismus-Leninismus beim ZK der SED (Berlin: Dietz, 1984), 70–72.

[73] On the left radicals during the war, see Peter Nettl, *Rosa Luxemburg*, abridged ed. (London: Oxford University Press, 1969), 365–436; Heinz Wohlgemuth, *Die Entstehung der Kommunistischen Partei Deutschlands 1914 bis 1918* (Berlin: Dietz, 1968); *Die Oktoberrevolution und Deutschland*, ed. Kommission der Historiker der DDR und der UdSSR (Berlin: Akademie, 1958), which has some interesting reminiscences as well as scholarly accounts; and Helmut Trotnow, *Karl Liebknecht (1871–1919): A Political Biography* (Hamden, Conn.: Archon Books, 1984), 134–77.

by Luxemburg and Mehring. In January 1916 the International Group began clandestine distribution of its political tracts, the "Spartacist Letters." From this title the International Group gradually acquired the name of the Spartacus Group.[74] In April 1917, when centrist and left social democrats split off from the SPD to form the Independent Social Democratic Party, the Spartacus Group joined the new group as an autonomous organization. Closely watched by the police, the radicals had an immensely difficult time even meeting and distributing their literature, and the major leaders—Luxemburg, Karl Liebknecht, Leo Jogiches—spent much of the war in the kaiser's prisons.

Luxemburg provided the major intellectual impetus to the Spartacists, and the positions she delineated would constitute central elements of the ideological and rhetorical orientation of the KPD and SED. She had developed her political ideas in the context of the pre–World War I Polish, Russian, and German socialist movements. She came to prominence first in the revisionist controversy around the turn of the century with her spirited defense of revolutionary politics and her equally spirited attacks on Eduard Bernstein and his effort to move social democracy down the path of reform. During the 1905 Revolution in Russia she found inspiration in the mass activism of Russian and Polish workers, which led her to develop further her incisive critique of bureaucratism in the German and international socialist movement. Luxemburg argued that not party directives, but the spontaneous actions of workers, culminating in the mass strike and revolution, would serve as the means of political transformation. Her rhetoric in her most famous pamphlet, "The Mass Strike," soared into celebrations of mass activism in the streets.[75] While never rejecting the importance of the party, Luxemburg's idealization of spontaneous activism shaded into anarchist and anarcho-syndicalist strands of politics. The very notion that the SPD, the beacon of ideological clarity and the *parti modèle* for other members of the Second International, could learn from the "less advanced" Russian and Polish workers marked a dramatic break from the standard line of socialist thought in Germany.

For Luxemburg, the SPD's capitulation to the war effort only confirmed the critique she had developed prior to 1914. Indeed, the line of causation was crystal clear: the triumph of bureaucracy and reformism in the party before World War I paved the way for its utter betrayal of the socialist cause in 1914, leaving the SPD with bloodstained hands. The war had at least forced reformism to display its true colors; the situation was now clear. The task ahead lay in forging a revivified socialist politics that would center around mass activism and would countenance no compromise on the road to revolution—a course that a socialist leadership worthy of its name would help incite and support.[76]

[74] For the political tracts, see the reprint *Spartakusbriefe*, ed. Institut für Marxismus-Leninismus beim ZK der SED (Berlin: Dietz, 1958). They were first published together in 1925.

[75] See especially Luxemburg, "Die Revolution in Rußland," (1905) in Rosa Luxemburg, *Gesammelte Werke* (hereafter *GW*) 1/2: *1893 bis 1905*, 6th printing (1970; Berlin: Dietz, 1988), 500–518; idem, "In revolutionärer Stunde: Was weiter?" in *GW*:1/2, 554–72; and, most famously, idem, "Massenstreik, Partei und Gewerkschaften," (1906) in *GW*:2: *1906 bis Juni 1911*, 5th printing (1972; Berlin: Dietz, 1990), 91–170.

[76] The most complete expression of Luxemburg's ideas during the war is her long pamphlet "The

But of what would this clarification consist? What did a revived socialist politics mean? Luxemburg was anything but clear about the particulars, and pointedly refused to delineate a political "recipe." Indeed, to do so would have violated her fundamental faith in popular action. As she wrote in her renowned antiwar tract, the "Junius" pamphlet:

> Revolutions are not "made," and great popular movements are not produced with technical recipes from the pocket of the party offices. . . . Whether great popular demonstrations and mass actions, whatever their form, really take place is decided by an entire collection of economic, political, and psychological factors . . . that are incalculable and which no party can artificially produce. . . . The historical hour posits each time the suitable forms of the popular movement and *itself creates new*, improvised, and previously unknown methods of struggle, and sorts and enriches the arsenal of the people unconcerned with all the pronouncements of the parties.[77]

On some level, a socialist politics worthy of the name simply meant struggle, hard, honest commitment to the socialist cause and the rejection of any compromise with the class enemy or the class traitors. It also meant that the fight against the war was inextricably entwined with the struggle for socialism.[78] The task of the international socialist movement consisted, therefore, of "bringing together the proletariat of all countries to an active revolutionary power."[79] The most she could propose in the way of particulars was a socialist leadership that provided clarity about the political situation.[80] In the "Junius" pamphlet she quoted her earlier, important tract, "The Mass Strike," in a way that almost presciently described the role she established for the Spartacus Group and the KPD in the German Revolution, and the KPD's self-conception throughout the Weimar Republic:

> the tactic of social democracy [should] never stand *below* the level of actual power relations, but . . . [should] hurry along the relation, that is the most important task of the "leadership' in the period of the mass strike. . . . A decisive, resolute, forward-striving tactic of social democracy summons up in the masses the sense of security, of self-trust, of desire for struggle.[81]

Crisis of Social Democracy," popularly known as the "Junius" pamphlet for the pseudonym she employed in its publication. But her letters are in many ways far more revealing about the development of her ideas, and I use them extensively in the following discussion. I use the German text of the "Junius-Brochure," "Die Krise der Sozialdemokratie," in *GW*:4, 5th printing: *August 1914 bis Januar 1919*, ed. Institut für Marxismus-Leninismus beim ZK der SED (1974; Berlin: Dietz, 1990), 49–164. See also the outline, "Entwurf zu den Junius-Thesen," in ibid., 43–47; her exchange with Karl Liebknecht and Julian Marchlewski in December 1915, in *GB*:5, 89–92; and letters to Carl Moor, 12 October 1914; Hans Diefenbach, 1 November 1914; and Franz Mehring, 31 August 1915, all in *GB*:5, 15–16, 19–20, 70–72.

[77] Luxemburg, "Die Krise der Sozialdemokratie," *GW*:4, 148–49.

[78] Luxemburg, "Entwurf zu den Junius-Thesen," *GW*:4, 45. The draft was adopted by the International Group on 1 January 1916.

[79] Ibid.

[80] Luxemburg, "Die Krise der Sozialdemokratie," *GW*:4, 149.

[81] Ibid., 149–50.

The ultimate historical battle that Luxemburg promoted, the struggle between capitalism and socialism, demanded the deepest dedication and commitment, and Luxemburg was unsparing in the demands she placed on herself, her closest friends, and "the masses." As she wrote to Franz Mehring: "Frau Eva [Mehring's wife] was correct: We were much too mild. But I swear, I will improve. I feel entirely like a porcupine and burn to let loose the quills."[82] Even when her closest colleagues proved disappointing, when "Karl [Liebknecht] can't be pinned down because he runs around like a cloud in the sky, Franz [Mehring] has little understanding for action that is not literary, mother [Clara Zetkin] reacts with panic and black pessimism," Luxemburg always found the inner resources to continue her political activism.[83]

But even Luxemburg's powerful intellect and deep sense of commitment did not work in isolation. She drew sustenance from the burgeoning labor protests in the Ruhr, Halle-Merseburg, and elsewhere in Germany and abroad, which buoyed her spirits and confirmed her faith in mass politics.[84] The great demonstration that took place on her release from her first prison term moved her deeply and provided solid evidence of the dissolution of the internal peace proclaimed by the kaiser at the outset of the war.[85] To her close colleagues, she communicated the briefest news of strikes and other manifestations of discontent—she did not even need to say how much they meant to her.[86] Always attuned to developments in the east, Luxemburg quickly recognized the significance of both Russian revolutions of 1917, which meant for her mass activism, the very antithesis of the "organizational cretinism" of the German labor movement and the dawning of the socialist future.[87] The Russian Revolution was a "bright choir of larks. . . . our own cause . . . which there wins and triumphs. It is world history in the flesh and blood, which fights its battles and dances, drunken with joy, the carmagnole."[88] The "wonderful things in Russia work on me like an elixir," she wrote to Marta Rosenbaum.[89] To her friends who failed to appreciate the significance of Russian developments for Germany, she was unstinting in her criticism.[90]

But for those who betrayed the cause, her socialist colleagues in the SPD and USPD, Luxemburg had only contempt—a sentiment sustained not only by the

[82] Luxemburg to Franz Mehring, 31 August 1915, *GB*:5, 70–72.

[83] Luxemburg to Kostja Zetkin, 6 February 1915, *GB*:5, 40.

[84] See Luxemburg to Helene Winkler, 11 February 1915; Marta Rosenbaum, 9 February 1917; Luise Kautsky, 15 April 1917; and Marta Rosenbaum, 29 April 1917, all in *GB*:5, 46, 167–68, 207–8, 226–27. See also the Spartacist Letters for a sense of how the upsurge of labor activism gave sustenance to the left radicals, as in "Politische Briefe," no. 22, 12 August 1916, in *Spartakusbriefe*, 192.

[85] Luxemburg to Clara Zetkin, 9 March 1916, *GB*:5, 105–6.

[86] As in a letter to Clara Zetkin, 3 July 1916, *GB*:5, 129.

[87] Or "parliamentary cretinism," both terms she used often in reference to social democracy. For one example, "Zur Russischen Revolution," *GW*:4, 341.

[88] Luxemburg to Luise Kautsky, 15 April 1917, *GB*:5, 207–8.

[89] Luxemburg to Marta Rosenbaum, 29 April 1917, *GB*:5, 226.

[90] For example, Luxemburg to Marta Rosenbaum, 29 April 1917, *GB*:5, 225–26.

deepest political disagreements, but also by the SPD's refusal even to defend radicals like Luxemburg and Liebknecht against the repressive actions of the state. Like Lenin, her special fury was often reserved for the centrists, the "swamp" as she continually labeled them, but she did not spare the dominant right-wing group. Her rhetoric soared as she depicted the horrors of the war and castigated social democracy for its utter collapse in the face of imperialism and chauvinism:

> In the present war . . . the Krupp firm in Essen . . . takes care of the "earthly" factors; the "spiritual" are charged . . . to the account of social democracy. The service it has given . . . to the German war leadership since 4 August is immeasurable. . . . Never has a war had such a Pindar, never has a military dictatorship found such Mameluks, never has a political party given up so ardently everything that it was and possessed on the altar of a cause that it swore . . . a thousand times it would struggle against until the last drop of blood. . . . Precisely the powerful organization, precisely the much-prized discipline of German social democracy, proved itself in the fact that the four-million strong body turned in twenty-four hours on the command of a handful of parliamentarians and harnessed a wagon against the storm that had been its life's goal.[91]

Even toward friends like Mathilde Wurm, who supported the USPD, Luxemburg could be scathing:

> Your letter made me absolutely wild because short as it was every line showed clearly the extent to which you are imprisoned by your milieu. Your weepy tone, your laments and sighs for the "disappointments" that you have experienced—allegedly because of others, instead of looking in the mirror to see the misery of humanity in its clearest image!
>
> You are "not radical enough," you suggest sadly. "Not enough" is hardly the word! You aren't not "radical" enough, just "spineless." It is not a matter of degree, but of kind. "You" are a completely different zoological species from me, and never have I hated your miserable, acidulated, cowardly, and half-hearted existence as much as I do now. . . . I swear to you, as soon as I can stick my nose out [of prison] I shall hunt and pursue your company of frogs with trumpets, whips, and bloodhounds—like Penthesilea, I wanted to say, but you by God are no Achilles.[92]

Luxemburg's absolute fury at those who renounced the cause alternated with a remarkable serenity, a belief in the masses and in history, a certainty that the war would lead ultimately to the revolutionary transformation that she clung to as an article of faith. As she wrote to Marta Rosenbaum in 1916:

> The success of these conscious efforts to influence the masses depends now, when everything seems so absolutely hopeless, on the deeply hidden compression springs of history. I know from historical experience, and also from personal experience in Russia, that precisely when on the outside everything seems smoothly in order . . . a complete reversal is in preparation. . . . Never forget: We are bound by laws of historical development that never fail, even when sometimes they don't exactly follow schema F,

[91] "Der Wiederaufbau der Internationale," in *GW*:4, 22–23.

[92] Luxemburg to Mathilde Wurm, 28 December 1916, *GB*:5, 150–51. I have partly used Peter Nettl's translation in *Rosa Luxemburg*, 408–9.

which we have correctly laid out. And for every moment: keep your head high and don't let your courage sink.[93]

Yet Luxemburg did not believe that the German radicals should form their own party—unlike Lenin, for whom an immediate party split was always the favored option. While Lenin articulated the "party of a new type," Luxemburg looked to the past, to the SPD of the "outlaw period," the 1880s, when it supposedly functioned as a revolutionary, class-conscious party. As she wrote to Alexander Winkler, who provided financial support for the publication of *Die Internationale*:

> here in Berlin and in many party locals . . . there reigns a real thirst for a social democratic word *in the old sense*. The mass of party comrades . . . have unlearned unconditional trust in their leaders, since these have failed so miserably. . . . Without stormy struggle [the clarification process] will of course not take place, but I hope that *the old tradition* will prove itself stronger than the "new course."[94]

To Helene Winkler she wrote that "we [the left radicals] defend *the old soil and the glorious traditions* of the party."[95]

Luxemburg's hesitations about forming a new party were the subject of strong criticisms by others, notably the Bremen and Hamburg left radicals, whose positions shaded further into syndicalism than Luxemburg's, and, subsequently, by the official communist movement.[96] Yet on the commitment to a revivified socialist politics, a deep-seated hostility toward social democracy, a firm belief that the catastrophe of war had placed socialism on the political agenda, a certainty that the Russian Revolution had opened up a new era in human history—on all of these issues Luxemburg's positions had deep affinities with Lenin's. Both also shared a revolutionary intransigence that brooked no compromise. And both claimed to find the tracks of their political ideas in the burgeoning march of working-class protest across the continent. In the German Revolution Luxemburg thought she found the setting that could turn ideas and hopes into reality. But the fulfillment of the task would require a new party, a position she reluctantly came to accept.

Broadening the Public Sphere: The German Revolution, 1918–20

At the end of October 1918, sailors in Kiel revolted against orders to set out to sea. Unwilling to engage in last-minute heroics, the sailors initiated the revolu-

[93] Luxemburg to Marta Rosenbaum, 9 February 1917, *GB*:5, 167–68. She wrote similarly to Mathilde Wurm, 16 February 1917, *GB*:5, 175–76.

[94] Luxemburg to Alexander Winkler, 11 February 1915, *GB*:5, 45. Emphases added.

[95] Luxemburg to Helene Winkler, 11 February 1915, *GB*:5, 46. Emphases added.

[96] On the views of the left radicals, especially the Bremen and Hamburg groups, see Hans Manfred Bock, *Syndikalismus und Linkskommunismus von 1918–1923* (Meisenheim am Glan: Anton Hain, 1969), and Rudolf Lindau, "Zu Fragen der Räte und der Linken in der deutschen Arbeiterbewegung," and Karl Drechsler, "Das Verhältnis zwischen Spartakusgruppe und Linksradikalen 1917/1918," in *Oktober Revolution und Deutschland*, 135–38 and 223–36.

tion that brought Imperial Germany to its inglorious end. For labor, the Revolution of 1918–20 signified the dramatic widening of the political tableau. The strike actions of the war years had gone a long way toward destroying the workplace regime. Now the state regime became the object of contestation. Repertoires of protest multiplied and came to include new weapons of coercion and popularly sanctioned transgressions of the criminal code. The political imagination soared as workers and their representatives groped their way toward new institutional and ideological arrangements.[97] At the same time, the old forces of order, now sometimes complemented by social democrats, sought ways to reconstitute their regimes of domination in the altered circumstances of republican politics, social reform, and armed revolution.

The KPD was founded within this matrix of intense popular activism and acute conflict over the regimes of German society. The vast broadening of the public sphere created by popular protest—the unending, hyperactive series of mass meetings, demonstrations, strikes, armed rebellions, electoral campaigns—offered communists fruitful fields of activity.[98] Under the initial intellectual guidance of Rosa Luxemburg, they defined a strategy that sought constantly to elevate all the varied manifestations of working-class activism into the ultimate battle with capitalist society. But the KPD's adversaries, from social democrats to army officers, proved able to limit decisively the party's interventions, and thereby helped shape the politics of German communism. The KPD, in short, did not emerge in pristine ideological form whether the primal fount is located in Moscow or Berlin. A child of war, the KPD's character was further shaped in the German Revolution and, subsequently, in the Revolutions's Thermidor. German communism was made by the commingling of party strategy defined largely by Luxemburg and Lenin and the multifocal struggle over the shaping of the regimes—the institutions and ideologies—of German society.

The Revolution begun by sailors at Kiel quickly spread to the port cities, and from there throughout Germany.[99] In Berlin, militant workers, organized in the Revolutionary Shop Stewards Movement, were already planning a revolution and were soon followed by the Spartacus Group, but events overtook all of them. Hundreds of

[97] William H. Sewell Jr.'s comments on the way the nature of collective action and state formation are mutually constitutive have influenced my approach here. See "Collective Violence and Collective Loyalties in France: Why the French Revolution Made a Difference," *Politics and Society* 18:4 (1990): 527–52.

[98] This in itself is not a contentious point, but few writers on German or European communism have made the social forces and political context explicit, critical, and formative of communism in their studies. Some of the recent work on the social history of the Russian Revolution and on the Soviet period are important pathbreakers here, as is the work of Eve Rosenhaft, *Beating the Fascists? The German Communists and Political Violence, 1929–1933* (Cambridge: Cambridge University Press, 1983), for the KPD.

[99] For the most recent synthetic accounts, Heinrich August Winkler, *Von der Revolution zur Stabilisierung: Arbeiter und Arbeiterbewegung in der Weimarer Republik 1918 bis 1924* (Berlin: J. H. W. Dietz Nachf., 1984), and Ulrich Kluge, *Die deutsche Revolution 1918/1919: Staat, Politik und Gesellschaft zwischen Weltkrieg und Kapp-Putsch* (Frankfurt am Main: Suhrkamp, 1985). For a brilliant and engaging literary rendition, see Alfred Döblin's *Ein Verratenes Volk*, in English as *A People Betrayed* (New York: Fromm, 1983).

thousands poured into the streets of Berlin and other cities demanding an end to the war and democratic reforms. In towns and cities and factories and mines throughout Germany, workers formed democratically elected councils to represent their interests, and soldiers did the same in the army. With the situation rapidly spiraling out of control, on 9 November Chancellor Prince Max von Baden named Friedrich Ebert, the chairman of the SPD, his successor. From the Reichstag building Philipp Scheidemann proclaimed the German Republic—to the great consternation of Ebert, who considered the move premature—while at the palace Karl Liebknecht proclaimed a socialist republic. Ebert formed a "popular government" composed of other social democrats and, after some maneuvering, USPD representatives. Two centers of political authority emerged—the SPD-USPD government, the Council of People's Deputies (Rat der Volksbeauftragten, or RdV), and the workers and soldiers councils capped, temporarily, by the local Berlin council.

Under Ebert's leadership, the RdV directed its attention at the immensely difficult task of readjustment and reconstruction. The war had to be brought to conclusion, the population kept supplied with food and coal, and the army and economy demobilized.[100] Stability, orderly transition, and the resumption of production were the SPD's priorities. Drastic social changes, it believed, would only intensify the chaos, threatening to bring to Germany the ever-feared "Russian conditions." Two days after assuming power, representatives of the new government signed the armistice with the allies. In a series of domestic agreements, the SPD recognized the traditional power centers of German society, hoping to win their cooperation. In the so-called Ebert-Groener pact, the SPD promised to guarantee the integrity of the army and the officer corps; in return, the army recognized the new government. By calling on the officials of the imperial system to remain at their posts, the SPD reaffirmed the position of the bureaucracy. And in the private but clearly state-supported Stinnes-Legien agreement, the major employers association granted the unions the recognition for which they had long struggled, the eight-hour day, and the establishment of joint labor-management boards to handle disputes; de facto the unions confirmed private property relations and managerial power.[101] At the same time, the SPD government issued a series of wide-ranging political and social reforms, including free, equal, and universal suffrage and the eight-hour day.

Politically, the SPD strove to curb the powers of the councils and sought, instead, the convening of a democratically elected constitutional convention that would provide the legal underpinnings for the new parliamentary regime. While the SPD sought to contain the revolutionary process, the array of the German left—militant workers, Spartacists, Independents, syndicalist left radicals—sought to push it forward. The conflicts over the direction of the Revolution were

[100] See Gerald D. Feldman, "Economic and Social Problems of the German Demobilization 1918–19," *JMH* 47:1 (March 1975): 1–23, and most thoroughly, Bessel, *Germany after the First World War*.

[101] On the Stinnes-Legien agreement, see Gerald D. Feldman, "German Business between War and Revolution: On the Origins of the Stinnes-Legien Agreement," in *Entstehung und Wandel der modernen Gesellschaft: Festschrift für Hans Rosenberg zum 65. Geburtstag*, ed. Gerhard A. Ritter (Berlin: Walter de Gruyter, 1970), 312–41.

fought out in countless mass meetings, strikes, and party deliberations, and then, in mid-December, at the National Congress of Workers and Soldiers Councils, which convened in Berlin. With the SPD dominant, the Congress essentially confirmed the approach of the RdV: elections to the constitutional convention were called for 19 January 1919 and a proposal to institutionalize the council system as the basis of the Republic was voted down. Furthermore, the Congress voted to recognize the government as the national political authority until the Constitutional Assembly convened. A proposal giving the Executive the power to affirm or veto laws was turned down. As a result, the USPD refused to participate in the election of the Executive, enabling the SPD to consolidate its control to an even greater extent. Soon afterwards, the USPD also withdrew from the government.[102]

Yet the radical elements were not completely quashed. The Executive of the Councils was granted the power to elect the government and supervise parliament. Also, the Congress adopted the so-called "Hamburg Seven Points," which amounted to the democratization of the army in direct contravention of the still-secret Ebert-Groener pact. Presciently, the Congress also called on the government to begin the socialization of "ripe" industries, especially mining.

Moreover, at the local and regional level workers often pushed the situation much further than the SPD desired. At the center of the revolutionary conflicts lay the workers and soldiers councils and popular efforts to socialize the mines and other industries. The character of the councils varied greatly, from the rare instances of revolutionary seizures of power and the consequent displacement of local officials to quite moderate efforts to manage the immense problems of postwar reconstruction through collaboration with the existing authorities. In Essen, for example, the local workers and soldiers council cooperated with the established authorities to secure order, which meant for both bodies removing female workers from the industrial labor force, encouraging demobilized soldiers not to use Essen as a way station home, and deporting every conceivable outsider from the city proper.[103] To accomplish these tasks, the Council never doubted that

[102] On all these events, see the still useful account of Eberhard Kolb, *Die Arbeiterräte in der deutschen Innenpolitik* (Düsseldorf: Droste, 1962), as well as Kluge, *Deutsche Revolution*; Winkler, *Von der Revolution*; and especially on the SPD, Susanne Miller, *Die Bürde der Macht: Die deutsche Sozialdemokratie 1918–1920* (Düsseldorf: Droste, 1978).

[103] The activities of the Essen Workers and Soldiers Council are documented in the following: communiqué, LRLKE, 11 November 1918, HStAD 15279; stenographic reports of meetings between the Workers and Soldiers Council and the regular city council, StAE 102/I/1093; leaflets and orders issued by the Workers and Soldiers Council in StAE 102/I/1093; report of a meeting of the city's Verkehrs-Deputation, 10 November 1918, StAE 102/I/1096; "Bericht über die Demobilmachung der Arbeiterkräfte bei der Firma Krupp, erstattet in der Sitzung des Arbeiter- und Soldatenrats mit der Stadtverwaltung am 19. November 1918," StAE 102/I/1093; memos, Gußstahlfabrik, 12 and 15 November, 9 and 27 December 1918, HA Krupp, WA 41/2-144; *Chronik der Stadt Essen 1918* and *1919*; Hans Luther, "Zusammenbruch und Jahre nach dem ersten Krieg: Erinnerungen des Oberbürgermeisters der Stadt Essen," *Beiträge zur Geschichte der Stadt und Stift Essen* 73 (1958): 24–25; *AZ*, 9 and 13 November 1918; and Fritz Baade, "Die November-Revolution von 1918," in *Die Heimatstadt Essen* 12 (1960/61): 49–60. The Essen events follow the general revolutionary pattern in the Rhineland as described by Helmut Metzmacher, "Der Novemberumsturz in der Rheinprovinz," *Annalen des historischen Vereins für den Niederrhein* 168/169 (1967): 135–265.

it had to rely on the technical skills of the established officials. Hence, it made no move to displace Mayor Hans Luther or the city bureaucrats. The results, on one level, were quite remarkable: within three weeks, fifty-two thousand workers were transported out of the city. By the end of January 1919, Krupp's workforce had declined from its wartime high of 107,000 to 38,000, only slightly higher than its prewar level, and only five hundred women remained on the company's payroll.[104]

In Halle the workers and soldiers council had from the outset a more radical complexion.[105] Independents dominated the council and were also well situated in the leadership of the trade unions. At the mass meeting that constituted the workers council, the crowd called for the "overthrow of capitalism. . . . [and] victory of the socialist proletariat" and for the establishment of a "free people's state."[106] The Council then issued the requisite appeal for calm and order, but, significantly, disarmed the police and vested its own security organs with the responsibility for ensuring order. However, it did little else to replace the existing bureaucracy. While the Essen Workers and Soldiers Council became co-opted into the process of administration, the Halle Council divorced bureaucratic management from political power. State officials, however, understood the realities of politics far better, and within two days reversed their recognition of the Council's full assumption of power. For months a battle raged between the Halle Council and the old authorities, a conflict ultimately resolved by force of arms.

As revolutionary politics go, the Essen Council's moves were certainly timid. They indicate the faith, widespread in the labor movement, in politics as rational, bureaucratic management. The Halle Council thought it sufficient simply to proclaim its own power over the activities of the regular municipal administration. Nonetheless, however limited the actions of the Essen and Halle councils, both exercised administrative and political power that had been attained through the autonomous, popular activism of workers and soldiers. By creating the councils, popular protest broadened the public sphere and recast politics beyond the narrow

[104] Berdrow, "Firma Krupp," 287, 291. For more detail see Eric D. Weitz, "Social Continuity and Political Radicalization: Essen in the World War I Era," *SSH* 9:1 (1985): 49–69.

[105] The revolutionary events in Halle are discussed in Karl-Heinz Leidigkeit and Jürgen Hermann, *Auf leninistischem Kurs—Geschichte der KPD-Bezirksorganisation Halle-Merseburg bis 1933*, ed. Bezirksleitung Halle der SED, Kommission zur Erforschung der Geschichte der örtlichen Arbeiterbewegung (Halle: Druckhaus "Freiheit," 1979), 31–42; Erwin Könnemann et al., *Halle: Geschichte der Stadt in Wort und Bild* (Berlin: Deutscher Verlag der Wissenschaften, 1983), 78–80; Eberhard Schultz, *Der Kampf um die revolutionäre Massenpartei der Arbeiterklasse in ehemaligen Regierungsbezirk Halle-Merseburg (1917–1920)*, Beiträge zur Geschichte der Arbeiterbewegung im Bezirk Halle (Halle: n.p., 1972), 15–31. See also *Dokumente und Materialien zur Geschichte der KPD-Bezirksorganisation Halle-Merseburg bis 1933*, ed. Bezirksleitung Halle der SED, Kommission zur Erforschung der Geschichte der örtlichen Arbeiterbewegung (Halle: n.p., 1982), 16–21. Interestingly, the memoirs of Halle's mayor, Rive, *Lebenserinnerungen*, are fairly silent on the revolutionary period. He could not contend, as could his Essen colleague (and friend) Hans Luther, that he had successfully incorporated the Council into the city administration, thereby blunting its revolutionary drive. In addition, Rive suffered the indignities of numerous attacks on his residency and demands from crowds that he come before them. See "Bericht über die während dieses Jahres vorgekommen Unruhen," OBH to RPM, 11 April 1919, StAH Centralbüro I/B/12/I-1918/51 ff.

[106] Quoted in Leidigkeit and Hermann, *Auf leninistischem Kurs*, 35.

conceptions of state officials and social democrats. Workers and their representatives groped toward new definitions of the political that involved greater competence for popular institutions and control over the economy and polity.[107] In creating the potential for a more radical reshaping of the political and social order, the councils provided much of the impetus for the formation of the KPD.

Like the councils, the great strike wave that began in December 1918 and, with ebbs and flows, lasted until April 1919 also radically reshaped the contours of politics.[108] The strikes began among miners and centered around demands for a shorter workday and higher wages. But the strikes quickly moved beyond material issues. By electing their own delegates at mass meetings, workers claimed representative powers and challenged managerial prerogatives. At the Essen mine Victoria Mathias, for example, workers explained that they had empowered their own committee to negotiate because "the entire workforce no longer trusts the unions to protect its interests."[109] With such statements, workers declared their rejection of all the forms of representation historically and politically current—a patriarchal system of state and company domination, as well as the standard social democratic and trade union practice of bureaucratic, albeit democratic, representation of workplace interests with its embedded practice of class collaboration. Instead, workers declared their self-representation and self-activity, and thereby blurred the lines between the economic and the political.

Moreover, the Victoria Mathias miners, as many others, raised all sorts of other demands that challenged managerial prerogatives. They demanded that their elected workers committee have the power to decide on disciplinary actions and fines leveled against workers, to inspect company books, and to name people to the food

[107] The historiography of the 1960s and 1970s, pathbreaking in its day, criticized the SPD for its timidity and lack of imagination in relation to the councils. While the critique is sound, it is insufficient to focus only on the psychology and ideology of the SPD leaders. Their actions need also to be embedded in larger cultural and social patterns, such as the faith in bureaucratic management typical of many segments of German society. For important examples of the older historiography, see Miller, *Bürde der Macht*; Eberhard Kolb, ed., *Vom Kaiserreich zur Weimarer Republik* (Cologne: Kiepenheuer und Witsch, 1972); Reinhard Rürup, "Problems of the German Revolution 1918–19," *JCH* 3:4 (1968): 109–35; and his later revisit of the issues in "Demokratischer Revolution und 'dritter Weg': Die deutsche Revolution von 1918/19 in den neueren wissenschaftlichen Diskussion," *GG* 9:2 (1983): 278–301. Winkler's *Von der Revolution* is the culmination of this historiography, though he tends to be less critical of the SPD than others.

[108] See Peter von Oertzen, "Die Großen Streiks der Ruhrbergarbeiterschaft im Frühjahr 1919," *VfZ* 6:3 (1958): 231–62; Erhard Lucas, "Ursachen und Verlauf der Bergarbeiterbewegung in Hamborn und im westlichen Ruhrgebiet 1918/19," *Duisburger Forschungen* 15 (1971): 1–119; Ulrich Kluge, "Essener Sozialisierungsbewegung und Volksbewegung im rheinisch-westfälischen Industriegebiet 1918/19," *IWK* 16 (1972): 56–65; Hans Mommsen, "Die Bergarbeiterbewegung an der Ruhr 1918–1933," in *Arbeiterbewegung an Rhein und Ruhr*, ed. Jürgen Reulecke (Wuppertal: Peter Hammer, 1974), 275–314; Jürgen Tampke, "The Rise and Fall of the Essen Model, January-February 1919," *IWK* 13:2 (1977): 160–72; Jochen Henze, *Sechsstundenschicht im Ruhrbergbau 1918–1920: Ursachen und Verlauf eines Arbeitszeitkonflikts* (Freiburg: Burg, 1988); and Winkler, *Von der Revolution*, 159–82.

[109] Spethmann, *Zwölf Jahre* 1:146–47.

distribution office. They also demanded that all female workers be dismissed—indicating the limits to the revolutionary practices of the era.[110]

The strikes initiated in December turned into efforts to socialize the mines after the New Year. The events do not need to be related in much detail here. Beginning in the Ruhr and then in central Germany as well, massive numbers of workers went out on strike in support of the socialization demand, which quickly came to include both the mines and other "ripe" industries and calls for the establishment of a "council system." Krupp underwent the first complete strike in its history; Halle and much of central Germany experienced the first near-general strike in German history.[111] In the Ruhr, the movement was workplace-based and had strong syndicalist tones.[112] In central Germany, the efforts were initiated by a radical political leadership and entailed a more overtly political effort to control the state and through it the workplace.[113] But these distinctions are perhaps less important than the fact that the vocabulary of socialization and workers and soldiers councils had widespread appeal. At the height of the movement, some 307,000 Ruhr miners, about 73 percent of the workforce, went on strike. In central Germany the strike wave peaked earlier and encompassed about 75 percent of the entire industrial workforce of the region.[114] Communists, few in number in 1919, participated in the struggles in both areas and were represented on the so-called Commission of the Nine, the body established in the Ruhr to draft and implement socialization. Only the unleashing of the full military powers of the state—exercised with a large complement of brutality—crushed the strike movements. The experience of armed repression at the hands of social democratic–sanctioned military forces left a legacy of bitterness that the SPD never surmounted.

Whether the socialization movement was "truly" radical or not—the issue that exercised historians twenty years ago—is not the major point.[115] There is cer-

[110] Ibid.

[111] On the strike at Krupp, see [unsigned, undated memo], HA Krupp, WA 41/6-168; "Bekanntmachung," Gußstahlflabrik, 5 April 1919, HA Krupp, WA 41/6-168; [handwritten table], "Streik auf der Gußstahlfabrik," HA Krupp, WA 41/6-168; PPE to GK VII. AK, 10 April 1919, HStAD 15974; and *AZ*, 8 April 1919.

[112] Klaus Tenfelde, "Linksradikale Strömungen in der Ruhrbergarbeiterschaft 1905 bis 1919," in *Glück auf, Kameraden! Die Bergarbeiter und ihre Organisationen in Deutschland*, ed. Hans Mommsen (Cologne: Bund, 1979), 199–224.

[113] The events in central Germany have been less well explored than those in the Ruhr. The official report of the Prussian Constitutional Assembly's investigative committee is very revealing: Verfassungsgebende Preussische Landesversammlung, "Bericht des Untersuchungsausschußes über die Unruhen in Mitteldeutschland vom November 1918 bis zum 19. März 1919," 14 September 1920, which I read in GStAKM 169/DIX/D3/1/3. See also "Bericht über die während dieses Jahres vorgekommen Unruhen," OBH to RPM, 11 April 1919, StAH Centralbüro I/B/12/I/51 ff. For secondary accounts, see David W. Morgan, *The Socialist Left and the German Revolution: A History of the German Independent Social Democratic Party, 1917–1922* (Ithaca: Cornell University Press, 1975), 229–36; Leidigkeit and Hermann, *Auf leninistischem Kurs*, 76–82; and Winkler, *Von der Revolution*, 175–78.

[114] Figures in Winkler, *Von der Revolution*, 173, 176.

[115] See the references in n. 108 above.

tainly evidence enough for both interpretations. In one contemporary account of an Essen demonstration on 11 January, the miners appealed to Mayor Luther to declare the socialization of the mines.[116] Later a Reich chancellor and Reichsbank president, Hans Luther in Leninist garb strikes a rather incongruous image, and offers little evidence of a class-conscious proletariat taking destiny into its own hands. At the same time, the Commission of the Nine called for a workplace-based system of workers' control, a vision of socialism with strong syndicalist tones.[117]

The hallmark of the socialization efforts was their broad-based character and the substantial broadening of the public sphere that they represented. The movement emerged on the wings of the destruction of the patriarchal regime during the war, and at a crucial juncture in the making of the Revolution. At this moment, miners broke through, if in inchoate form, the boundaries of politics and of representation. They sought to restructure their own workplace and industry through the establishment of workers' control. This signified an effort to create new institutional forms within which popular deliberation over politics and economics would occur—that is, a broadening of the public sphere in the fullest meaning of the term. The arena would be inclusive, involving workers, employees, and managers. But it would be an exclusive arena in terms of gender. Precisely because revolutionary efforts focused on reordering the productive sphere—understood by virtually all the participants in the socialization debate, from radical workers to owners, as a masculine sphere, even though the reality was far more complex—the efforts at socialization excluded from consideration the reproductive realm and the issues associated with it. The wave of consumer protests over goods shortages and inflated prices, which had begun during the war and most often involved working women, was reduced to a problem of social order even by the Revolution's advocates.[118] They could envision the contours of a new society out of strikes, but not out of crowds of women at the marketplace forcing merchants to reduce their prices. The socialization movement, the most broad-based radical effort of the

[116] *Chronik 1919*, 47.

[117] See the pamphlet put out by the Neunerkommission, "Die Sozialisierung des Bergbaues und der Generalstreik im rheinischen-westfälischen Industriegebiet," esp. 8–9, 29, StAE Ja 440. This position was echoed by Karski (Julian Marchlewski), who was appointed an advisor to the Neunerkommission. See his *Die Sozialisierung des Bergbaues*, Vortrag gehalten auf der Konferenz der Bergarbeiter-Delegierten des rheinisch-westfälischen Industrie-Gebietes am 5. März 1919 in Essen (Essen: Bezirksleitung der "Kommunistischen Partei" für Rheinland-Westfalen, 1919), 12, 24.

[118] On women's involvement in protests and the reshaping of the public sphere in the war, see Belinda Davis, "Reconsidering Habermas, Gender, and the Public Sphere: The Case of Wilhelmine Germany," in *Society, Culture, and the State in Germany, 1870–1930*, ed. Geoff Eley (Ann Arbor: University of Michigan Press, forthcoming); Hartewig, *Unberechenbares Jahrzehnt*, 218–44; idem, "'Eine sogenannte Neutralität der Beamten gibt es nicht': Sozaler Protest, bürgerliche Gesellschaft und Polizei im Ruhrgebeit (1918–1924)," in *"Sicherheit" und "Wohlfahrt": Polizei, Gesellschaft und Herrschaft im 19. und 20. Jahrhundert*, ed. Alf Lüdtke (Frankfurt am Main: Suhrkamp, 1992), 297–322; and Daniel, *Arbeiterfrauen*. But note Kruse, *Krieg und nationale Integration*, 177–78, who criticizes Daniel for arguing that women were particularly affected by the war and were the primary force behind the antiwar movement, while organized labor tended to be far more integrated into the war effort. For a profound though somewhat too monolithic interpretation of the gendered nature of the war and the meaning of modernity, see Elisabeth Domansky, "Militarization and Reproduction in World War I Germany," in Eley, *Society, Culture, and the State in Germany*.

revolutionary era, re-created, indeed, probably strengthened, the existing gender regime.

Hence, the political practices of workers in the winter of 1918/19 are as revealing of content as putative ideological assertions.[119] Rather than see revolution as a highly fluid situation within which working-class consciousness and politics are made, historians like Hans Mommsen, Heinrich August Winkler, and Ulrich Kluge apply a standard of radicalism so exacting, so idealized, that no real, living and breathing working class could ever pass the test.[120] In their understandings, workers had virtually to march under banners inscribed with Lenin's portrait to meet the definition of radicalism. But in broadening the definition of the political to encompass the workplace and, in essence, mingling the political and economic spheres through representation in both, workers in their actions demonstrated the radical potential embedded in the councils and the socialization movement.

The councils and socialization signified the radical possibilities of the German Revolution of 1918–20. The repression of the movements marked a critical way station in the SPD's integration into the state and in the political fragmentation of the German working class. The alliance among the state, now including the SPD, the army, employers, and trade unionists became more tightly drawn, sealed by a compact of bloody repression against working-class radicalism. SPD ministers unleashed the military and consulted with industrialists, seeking their support in a time of crisis and raising the specter of still greater revolutions to come if they did not fall in line behind the SPD government.

In one instance, representatives of the chemical industry association participated in a meeting with social democratic Reich Labor Minister Bauer on 10 March 1919, just after the suppression of the general strike in central Germany. Writing to BASF management at Leuna, the association reported: "The Minister [Bauer] left no doubt about the difficulties and the seriousness of the situation in which the government at the moment finds itself, and directed a pressing appeal to those present to support the government in its efforts to become master of the situation, and in that way to enable the government to carry out its policies."[121] For the moment at least, industry, sharing those fears of more radical revolution, was content to support the government's course.

Formulating Communist Politics: Rosa Luxemburg and the Foundation of the KPD

Rosa Luxemburg was released from prison on 9 November 1918 and reached Berlin on 10 November, one day after the formation of the socialist govern-

[119] At the same time, this also indicates that discussions of the public sphere that focus only on discourse are much too narrow in conception.

[120] Mommsen, "Bergarbeiterbewegung"; idem, "Soziale und politische Konflikte an der Ruhr 1905 bis 1924," in *Arbeiterbewegung und industrieller Wandel: Studien zu gewerkschaftlichen Organisationsproblemen im Reich und an der Ruhr*, ed. idem (Wuppertal: Peter Hammer, 1980), 62–86; Winkler, *Von der Revolution*; and Kluge, *Deutsche Revolution*.

[121] Quoted in *Kämpfendes Leuna*, 163.

ment.[122] She wasted little time. She went immediately to the printing plant that some Spartacists under Liebknecht had occupied, where she sought to persuade the workers to print *Die Rote Fahne* (*Red Flag*), their new tabloid.[123] Quickly she convened her closest collaborators: Karl Liebknecht, who had been released from prison in mid-October; Leo Jogiches, like Luxemburg released on 9 November; and the members of the group who would go on to play major roles in the KPD—Paul Levi, Ernst Meyer, Wilhelm Pieck, August Thalheimer, Hugo Eberlein, Hermann and Käthe Duncker, and Paul Fröhlich. Only Clara Zetkin and Franz Mehring, the elders among the Spartacists, were absent due to illness and the ravages of age. The group around Luxemburg was in many ways emblematic of the German labor movement—skilled workers, a few individuals from poor backgrounds who had managed to become school teachers or low-level white-collar workers, and intellectuals. They had behind them years of experience in the SPD; many had been Luxemburg's students before the war at the party school in Berlin and were her devoted followers. On 11 November, at a meeting in a Berlin hotel, they formally constituted the "Spartacus League."

Luxemburg laid out a political course for the Spartacists and the KPD that drew upon the ideas and sensibilities she had formulated well before 1914, developed further during the war, and that now, amid the Bolshevik Revolution, the end of World War I, and the German Revolution, took on even greater urgency: support for mass activism, active propagation of revolution, a determination to derail a socialist politics of reform and, instead, to build through revolution, a socialist society in the here and now.[124] She had little doubt about what was at stake: she understood the Bolshevik Revolution as a world-historical event, one that could be matched in Germany if the proletariat took up the cause. The failure to do so would mean, once again, the descent into barbarism, a barbarism perhaps even worse than the carnage of World War I.[125]

The task of the Spartacists therefore lay in pushing the revolution beyond the limited goals of parliamentary democracy and social reform elaborated by the "Scheidemänner" (one of her contemptuous terms for social democrats) to a true socialist revolution. Her language and ideas, articulated in the heat of revolution and in response to biting and even vicious criticism from the SPD and USPD, became, if anything, more fervent. Unwilling to countenance compromise even with other socialists, Luxemburg infused communist politics with the language of unwavering hostility to the institutions of bourgeois society, of militant and irreconcilable conflict between the forces of revolution and reaction, of hard-fought

[122] Nettl, *Rosa Luxemburg*, 442, says she was released on 9 November. Other sources give 8 November as the date, e.g., *Chronik: Geschichte der deutschen Arbeiterbewegung*, part 2: *Von 1917 bis 1945*, ed. Institut für Marxismus-Leninismus beim ZK der SED (Berlin: Dietz, 1966), 26.

[123] Nettl, *Rosa Luxemburg*, 449.

[124] For a more extended analysis see my article, "'Rosa Luxemburg Belongs to Us!' German Communism and the Luxemburg Legacy," *CEH* 27:1 (1994): 27–64.

[125] "Socialism or descent into barbarism!" a slogan she used often in the last months of her life, was by no means mere rhetoric. She and many others believed it deeply. For one usage, see "Was will der Spartakusbund?" *GW*:4, 444.

class struggle and proletarian revolution as the sole and exclusive means of political progress. Again she offered very little in the way of particulars and virtually no guidance to a party and movement that, for most of its existence, would have to navigate in the mundane, nonrevolutionary political world and in a multiclass society in which workers would never constitute more than around one-third of the population. Instead, she promoted an uncritical evocation of the power of mass activism and an unyielding commitment to a politics of totality. Luxemburg denigrated every kind of limited politics, any politics that substantively focused on everyday concerns and that, tactically, centered around political alliances.

All of these positions intersected with Lenin's views, at least those of the "classical" period of the Bolshevik Revolution of 1917–21. Progressively shorn of the democratic content with which they were endowed by Luxemburg, they were incorporated into the politics of German communism. For all of her democratic and humanistic sensibilities, Luxemburg, no less than Lenin, furnished ideological and linguistic support for an intransigent politics of confrontation fought out in the streets of Berlin, Halle, Essen, and other industrial centers during the Weimar Republic, and, in the German Democratic Republic, of the absolute demarcation of state socialism from liberal capitalism.[126]

So on 30 December 1918, in the midst of the German Revolution and under Rosa Luxemburg's intellectual guidance, the founding congress of the KPD convened in Berlin.[127] Initially, it had been called only as a national conference of the Spartacus League, but in the interim, the USPD had refused to call its own conference, other left radicals had constituted a new party—the International Communists of Germany—and the revolutionary situation had continued to intensify. Even those Spartacists opposed to the idea of the formation of a new party, Rosa Luxemburg prominent among them, had gradually, and somewhat reluctantly, shifted their views. Only Leo Jogiches and a few lesser-ranking leaders remained adamant in their opposition, ever fearful that a new party would only be another left-wing splinter organization devoid of all popular support.

The group that convened in Berlin was anything but uniform in its outlook. The largest segment of the 127 delegates were supporters of the Spartacus League, but well represented were also the Bremen and Hamburg left radicals, who inclined more toward syndicalist politics yet found in the revolutionary Jacobinism of the Spartacists and the Bolsheviks a temperament much suited to their own. The delegates were overwhelmingly skilled workers and intellectuals and relatively young. On 1 January 1919, they proclaimed retroactively (on Karl Liebknecht's initiative) the national conference to be the founding congress of the new party, which after much debate adopted the name Communist Party of Germany.

Many of the delegates present at the creation did not contribute for long to the development of the KPD. According to Hermann Weber's account, of the approx-

[126] For more detail, see Weitz, "'Rosa Luxemburg Belongs to Us!'"

[127] See Hermann Weber, ed., *Der Gründungsparteitag der KPD: Protokoll und Materialien* (Frankfurt am Main: Europäische Verlagsanstalt, 1969).

imately ninety-nine individuals known to have been present (out of 127) Luxemburg and Liebknecht were murdered two weeks later, Jogiches ten weeks after that; three other delegates were murdered in the course of 1919. Ten became inactive politically. Of the remaining eighty-three, only twenty-nine were still active in the KPD in 1933. Thirty joined various KPD splitoffs in the course of the Weimar Republic; seven left the KPD under other circumstances; six died between 1919 and 1933; no information was available concerning the remaining eleven. In 1946, twenty-one belonged to the SED.[128]

Nonetheless, and despite the many strategic and personnel shifts that the KPD would undergo between 1919 and 1945, the delegates at the founding congress gave voice to many—though certainly not all—of the political themes that would resonate throughout the history of the KPD. In so doing, the Congress naturally drew upon the positions that the International Group had articulated since 1914 and that Luxemburg had developed so intently in her writings between her release from prison and the convening of the Congress. Political differences among the delegates were pronounced, particularly on the issues of revolutionary terror and electoral participation. Over Luxemburg's vociferous objections, the Congress voted to boycott the upcoming elections to the Constitutional Assembly.[129] Many delegates demanded a more clear-cut statement in support of revolutionary terror. But in the end, the Congress confirmed Luxemburg's draft, "What Does the Spartacus League Want?" as the program of the KPD, and Luxemburg remained the dominant intellectual voice at the Congress. In her major address she gave expression to the utopian hopes and the immense self-confidence of the German left in the winter of 1918/19:

> Now, comrades, today we are experiencing the moment when we can say: We are again at Marx's side, under his banner. When we today declare in our program: the immediate task of the proletariat is nothing less than . . . to make socialism fact and reality, to eliminate capitalism root and branch, then we place ourselves on the same ground on which Marx and Engels stood in 1848 and from which they . . . never diverged.[130]

Two weeks later, Luxemburg and Liebknecht were dead, assassinated by right-wing military bands operating with the sanction of the SPD government. Radical workers in Berlin, drawing sustenance from mass demonstrations in opposition to the RdV's dismissal of the USPD police commissioner of Berlin, Emil Eichhorn, had decided to launch an uprising. The young KPD felt compelled to support the revolution despite severe reservations.[131] The right-wing bands that crushed the uprising used the occasion to murder Luxemburg and Liebknecht. In her last, powerful article, "Order Rules in Berlin," Luxemburg defended the so-

[128] Ibid., 36–37.

[129] For the debate, see ibid., 90–134.

[130] Ibid., 179.

[131] See Nettl's account in *Rosa Luxemburg*, 477–94. Liebknecht, mercurial as ever, apparently fell in with the revolutionary enthusiasm of the Berlin militants. Luxemburg reportedly considered the whole operation a mistake.

called Spartacist Uprising. Invoking her own, unquestioning faith in the ultimate victory, and writing, at the same time, her own epitaph, she concluded:

> The leadership has failed. But the leadership can and must be newly created by the masses and out of the masses. The masses are the decisive ones, they are the rock out of which the final victory of the Revolution will be constructed. The masses were on the heights, they have filed this "defeat" with the other historical defeats that are the pride and the power of international socialism. And from this "defeat" will bloom the future victory of socialism.
>
> "Order rules in Berlin!" You obtuse gendarmes! Your "order" is built on sand. Tomorrow the Revolution will "again climb the heights" and, to your horror, announce with trumpet blasts:
>
> *I was, I am, I shall be!* [132]

The Emergence of the Mass Party

The assassinations of Karl Liebknecht, Rosa Luxemburg, and, some weeks later, Leo Jogiches were a devastating blow to the young KPD. Liebknecht and Luxemburg, for all their temperamental and political differences, were well known and effective leaders. Jogiches was a master of organizational detail. All three were solidly rooted in the traditions of the prewar labor movement. Their loss certainly made the party more susceptible to external influences.

To add to the difficulties, the social democratic RdV used the Spartacist Uprising as a pretext to ban the KPD.[133] For the next ten months it existed underground, a shadow of a party, with pockets of support here and there—Stuttgart, Chemnitz, Berlin, a few other cities. Moreover, the differences of opinion evident at the founding congress did not dissipate over the succeeding months. Paul Levi, who succeeded Luxemburg as the leader of the party, engineered the exclusion of the left radicals who continued to oppose electoral participation. They formed the Communist Workers Party of Germany (Kommunistische Arbeiterpartei Deutschlands, or KAPD), which, over the next few years, provided the KPD with serious competition for the loyalties of radical workers.

Meanwhile, a few days after the Spartacist Uprising, Germans went to the polls to elect the Constitutional Assembly. The SPD became the strongest party in the country with 37.9 percent of the vote, and formed a government with the Catholic Center Party and the German Democratic Party, the so-called Weimar Coalition. The USPD polled only 7.6 percent of the electorate.

The formation of a democratic government seemed to augur well for the country. The Constitutional Assembly settled down to fulfill its charge while the government awaited the final peace treaty to the war. But the situation around the country remained exceedingly tense. The socialization strikes were only the most public forms of unrest. A veritable civil war raged in Germany through much of

[132] "Die Ordnung herrrscht in Berlin," *RF*, 14 November 1918, *GW*:4, 536.

[133] On the KPD in this period, see Ossip K. Flechtheim, *Die KPD in der Weimarer Republik* (1948; Hamburg: Junius Verlag, 1986), 107–26.

1919 as government security forces clamped down on strikes and suppressed efforts to establish radical council governments in various localities. Workers fled the unions in disgust, and the USPD attracted increased support. The government's obsession with order aroused deep misgivings among many social democrats. Strikes in all sorts of industries stood at a high level, despite the repressive actions of the state. The Ruhr and Halle-Merseburg remained under a state of emergency through 1919 and into 1920. Nonetheless, miners were back on strike in January 1920 demanding a six-hour day, supplementary payments, worker involvement in managerial decisions, and an end to the state of emergency.[134] The authorities reported that only the presence of the military prevented additional strikes at Krupp and a number of Essen mines, while small-scale, armed skirmishes between workers and security forces had become deeply worrisome.[135] Precarious food and coal supplies in the winter of 1919/20 only added to the difficulties, and the effects of inflation had begun to provoke serious concern.[136] And the Versailles Peace Treaty, signed in the summer of 1919, aroused universal anger in Germany that was often directed at the SPD.

With rising unrest and some indications that plans for another mass strike were in the works, the government again declared an intensified state of emergency for the Ruhr.[137] At the end of January 1920, Minister of the Interior Carl Severing and the army command issued a proclamation prohibiting picketing and workforce meetings. Strike committees were ordered dissolved, and any workers who engaged in passive resistance—working six hours and then quitting the shift—were to be fired. If rehired, they would lose all privileges of seniority. Once again, workers were warned that if they went out on strike, they would be compelled to work under martial law.[138]

It was not an auspicious policy for a socialist-led government, especially since the Republic's more serious problems came from the right, not the left, as Ebert, Severing, and their colleagues soon discovered. On 13 March 1920 right-wing military bands, the so-called Freikorps, marched into Berlin in an effort to overthrow the Republic and establish a right-wing dictatorship under Wolfgang Kapp.[139] The SPD-led government fled to Dresden and then Stuttgart, while the trade union federations—social democratic, Catholic, and liberal—issued a call for a general strike in support of the legitimate government. The SPD members of the government then echoed the call, and the massive movement that ensued completely paralyzed the country.

After only a few days in power, Kapp was forced to flee. But the forces un-

[134] PPE to RPD, 24 January and 9 February 1920, HStAD 15976.

[135] Ibid.

[136] As the reports of factory and mine inspectors indicate: *JB 1919*, *JB 1920*.

[137] The state of emergency had existed since the suppression of the socialization strikes in April 1919, and had been allowed to lapse only for three weeks in December. Flechtheim, *KPD*, 114.

[138] See the text in Spethmann, *Zwölf Jahre* 2:62–63.

[139] See Johannes Erger, *Der Kapp-Lüttwitz Putsch: Ein Beitrag zur deutschen Innenpolitik 1919/20* (Düsseldorf: Droste, 1967); Dietrich Orlow, "Preussen und der Kapp-Putsch," *VfZ* 26:2 (1978): 191–236; and Winkler, *Von der Revolution*, 295–342.

leashed by such an extensive action could not so easily be controlled. Disaffection with the national SPD's policies and bitterness with the army's tactics in repressing the working-class movement had been building for over a year. In the Ruhr, the strike movement quickly developed from a defensive action against the Kapp Putsch to an offensive centered around calls for the implementation of a host of unfulfilled demands that had arisen in the course of the Revolution.[140] Throughout the region, workers councils took power. A workers militia, known as the Red Army, emerged spontaneously and attracted somewhere between fifty and one hundred thousand troops. In a series of armed clashes, it successfully cleared the Ruhr of the Reichswehr and Freikorps and disarmed the security police. However disparate and inchoate the actions, the movement reflected broad-based working-class support for some form of council system, the abolition or at least control of the army and the establishment of a workers militia, some form of socialization, and a purge of reactionaries from the bureaucracy.

The general strike defeated Kapp, but not the SPD-led government, which returned to Berlin and then deployed the full complement of state power against the movement in the Ruhr. The details do not need to detain us, but the outcome was of great importance for the future of the KPD. The SPD's actions aroused such bitterness among workers that a substantial segment began to move to the left, to the USPD and, subsequently, the KPD, while deep dissension within its own ranks marred the effectiveness of the party. The SPD called new elections for June, which led to the USPD's emergence as a mass-based party and the SPD's withdrawal from the national government.

The KPD remained a tiny party on the margins of political life. In the autumn of 1919 it counted 106,656 members; one year later, its membership was down to 66,323.[141] The party's confused response to the Kapp Putsch and the uprising in the Ruhr—a constant wavering between condemnation and support—did little to pull it from its isolation.[142] But the implosion of the USPD, long suffering from severe internal divisions, saved the KPD from political obliteration.[143] Lenin's infamous "Twenty-One Conditions" for adhesion to the Third International served their precise purpose: they precipitated the USPD's final convulsions. The Twenty-One Conditions mandated that all member parties of the International model

[140] See Erhard Lucas, *Märzrevolution 1920*, 3 vols. (Frankfurt am Main: Roter Stern, 1970–78); Georg Eliasberg, *Der Ruhrkrieg von 1920* (Bonn-Bad Godesberg: Neue Gesellschaft, 1974); Morgan, *Socialist Left*, 320–47; and Erwin Könnemann and Hans-Joachim Krusch, *Aktionseinheit contra Kapp-Putsch* (Berlin: Dietz, 1972). For an important collection of documents, see Erwin Könnemann, ed., *Arbeiterklasse siegt über Kapp und Luttwitz* (Glashütten/Taunus: Auvermann, 1971).

[141] Hermann Weber, *Die Wandlung des deutschen Kommunismus: Die Stalinisierung der KPD in der Weimarer Republik* (Frankfurt am Main: Europäische Verlagsanstalt, 1969), vol. 1, 362.

[142] Lucas, *Märzrevolution* 3:24–25, 85–96, 99–100, 109–10, 132–34; Könnemann and Krusch, *Aktionseinheit*, 251–69, 431–75; and Flechtheim, *KPD*, 117–21.

[143] On the USPD, see Morgan, *Socialist Left*; Robert Wheeler, "The Independent Social Democratic Party and the Internationals: An Examination of Socialist Internationalism in Germany, 1915–1923" (Ph.D. diss., University of Pittsburgh, 1970); and Eugen Prager, *Geschichte der U.S.P.D.: Entstehung und Entwicklung der Unabhängigen Sozialdemokratischen Partei Deutschlands* (Berlin: Verlagsgenossenschaft "Freiheit," 1921).

themselves after the Russian Communist Party and conform to Bolshevik tactics. Both the KPD and the SPD began courting USPD members in the weeks prior to the party's October congress in Halle, where the delegates were scheduled to decide whether or not they should accept Lenin's postulates. The SPD launched a concerted campaign against the Bolsheviks. Essen's SPD paper wrote about "Pope" Lenin and warned "Moscow is militarism. Moscow is permanent war, the politics of power, the absence of freedom. Moscow is the muzzle, dictatorship, terror, Moscow is blood. Moscow is the justification for every crime of the reaction."[144]

The stakes were high when the delegates convened at Halle. Gregory Zinoviev represented the Russian party. Rudolf Hilferding and Lenin's old Menshevik opponent Julian Martov warned the Independents against allying with the Bolsheviks. By a vote of 237 to 156, the delegates voted to accept the Twenty-One Conditions, paving the way for merger with the KPD. In the weeks and months that followed, the two sides battled for control of the local organizations. The Halle-Merseburg USPD and the Halle city organization went solidly for adhesion to the Conditions, just as they had moved cohesively from the SPD to the USPD in 1917.[145] Greater variation prevailed in the Ruhr. In Essen, the USPD's functionaries had voted in favor of the Twenty-One Conditions before the congress, a decision, according to the police, supported by the vast majority of the rank and file, though some second thoughts did emerge.[146] In December, the two parties formally merged, and for about a year thereafter the new party was called the United Communist Party of Germany (Vereinigte Kommunistische Partei Deutschlands, or VKPD—for simplicity's sake, I will continue to use "KPD").

Conclusion

Through the collapse of the USPD, the Communist Party of Germany became a mass-based party, despite the loss of tens of thousands of Independents who did not follow their comrades into the KPD. It counted over 350,000 members, an array of newspapers, strong representation in the unions and parliaments, and solid bases in most of Germany's industrial areas, and especially in Halle-Merseburg, the Ruhr, Saxony, Hamburg, and Berlin.[147] The party still barely functioned as a cohesive organization, and sharp differences of opinion prevailed on any number of issues. But if the KPD's politics were not yet worked out in detail, the membership shared a general orientation shaped by the experiences of war and revolution and the language and ideology of Rosa Luxemburg and the Spartacus Group. An abiding contempt, even hatred, for social democracy; a

[144] *AZ*, 15 September 1920.

[145] Leidigkeit and Hermann, *Auf leninistischem Kurs*, 113–25.

[146] LRLKE to RPD, 26 October 1920 and PPE to RPD, 15 November 1920, HStAD 15818; *AZ*, 13 September 1920.

[147] In March 1921 the KPD counted some 359,000 members, but the figure declined to 224,689 over the next year and a half. Weber, *Wandlung* 1:362.

belief in the efficacy of armed revolution and possibilities of constructing socialism; a commitment to voluntaristic, activist politics; support for revolutionary Russia; a commitment to proletarianism as ideology and culture—these constituted the critical elements of the KPD's political strategy and culture. It would remain a party deeply colored by the hard political struggles of the war and Revolution; its development would be shaped further by the transformations in the Soviet Union and, closer to home, by the reconstruction of order undertaken by employers and the state.

CHAPTER 3

Reconstructing Order: State and Managerial Strategies in the Weimar Republic

> [D]ie Initiative [liegt] wieder in Händen der Behörden und in den führenden Persönlichkeiten.
>
> —*Police administration Eisleben*[1]

FOR EMPLOYERS and state officials, the signs of disorder were everywhere, and they did not cease with the end of the Revolution of 1918–20. Mass meetings called during working hours, widespread petty thievery, insolence toward factory guards, constant conflicts over wages and working conditions, strikes, armed revolution, active and emancipated women, and, ultimately, the appearance of a mass-based communist party—all invoked the specter of a world gone awry.

The vast broadening of the public sphere that these actions and developments exemplified did not go unchallenged. Driven together by common fears, real and imagined, of chaos and Bolshevism, the old forces of order—army officers and state officials, industrialists and agrarian capitalists—forged a tenuous, but no less real, coalition of order with social democrats and trade unionists. The strategy they devised was neither easily imposed nor completely successful. Order had to be continually renegotiated and required the absorption of at least some of the demands raised in popular struggles. The constituent elements of the coalition fought bitterly over the substance and extent of democracy and social welfare. But together they sought ways to reconstitute order and discipline in society. They built a more efficient state security apparatus, rationalized production, extended both private and public social welfare, and sharply delimited the vibrant, raucous public sphere created in the Revolution and replaced it with corporatist and parliamentary modes of representation.

The KPD served as the primary bonding agent of the coalition. Against its continual efforts to foment unrest and to create a Soviet Germany, the members of the coalition came together and developed their strategy of domestic containment. The very existence of the KPD as a mass-based party, the deep-seated, unrelentingly hostile opposition it engendered, decisively shaped the contours of the Weimar Republic's political and social economy. At the same time, the reconstruction of order profoundly shaped the nature of German communism. The discontent generated by military repression, economic rationalization, and insufficient social welfare produced continual popular support for the radical politics of the KPD. Perhaps most significantly, the reconstruction of order resulted in the

[1] "[T]he initiative again lies in the hands of the authorities and of the leading individuals." PV Eisleben to RPM, 14 April 1924, LHSAM C20/Ib/4648/4/89.

spatial transformation of labor and communist politics. The superior firepower of the state drove the KPD from the battlefield, while rationalization coupled with the impact of the Great Depression drove the party from the workplace. Consequently, the streets came to serve as the KPD's primary space of political mobilization, which encouraged a politics of display and spectacle, a politics of ideological pronouncements and physical confrontations. The specific character of the reconstitution of authority thereby contributed decisively to the creation of a communist party with a particularly intransigent cast, a party almost instinctively hostile to compromise and the champion of an ethos of male physical prowess as the decisive revolutionary quality.

This chapter will examine in some detail the reconstruction of order in the Weimar Republic. Much of the discussion is drawn from developments in the Prussian province of Saxony, an area of major industrial importance and a center of KPD support. It offers a particularly instructive example of the cooperation and conflicts between state officials, many of whom were social democrats, and employers in the effort to curb communist influence and reconstitute authority.

Creating the Security State: From the Kapp Putsch to the March Action

The Kapp Putsch created a great republican coalition against right-wing efforts to overthrow forcibly the Weimar Republic. But the workers uprising that quickly ensued also raised concerns about a radical left-wing revolution. Ever fearful of yet another walkout or demonstration that mushroomed into a general strike, an armed uprising, or a communist putsch, state authorities moved rapidly to strengthen the security forces—revolution had become a learning experience for the state and its allies, not just for radical workers. The national and state governments reorganized the police and created heavily militarized units, the Sicherheitspolizei (Sipo, or security police) and the Schutzpolizei (Schupo, or protective police). Both units were designed as highly mobile and well-armed forces trained to intervene in civil disturbances.[2] In social democratic–governed states like Prussia, these forces came under the direction of SPD officials, who were hoping to re-create in more modern guise the national guards of the revolutions of 1848, the citizen-defenders of the new republican state. Elsewhere, as in Bavaria, the state police forces were formed essentially out of right-wing military bands, and were far from the loyal defenders of the Republic that the Weimar Coalition had expected.

Alongside improved versions of the police, new kinds of security units were formed with the express purpose of contesting working-class protests. The Technical Emergency Squads (Technische Nothilfe, or TN), organized first by right-wing bands, quickly became incorporated into the official state structure.[3] They

[2] See Richard Bessel, "Militarisierung und Modernisierung: Polizeiliches Handeln in der Weimarer Republik," in *"Sicherheit" und "Wohlfahrt": Polizei, Gesellschaft und Herrschaft im 19. und 20. Jahrhundert*, ed. Alf Lüdtke (Frankfurt am Main: Suhrkamp, 1992), 323–43.

[3] Erwin Könnemann, *Einwohnerwehren und Zeitfreiwilligenverbände: Ihre Funktion beim Aufbau*

were designed to keep essential factories and mines working during strikes. Officials were given broad discretionary powers to designate a certain enterprise or area "*lebenswichtig*" (colloquially, critical to the public interest), which enabled them to ban strikes, prosecute strike agitators, and commit troops and the Technical Emergency Squads.[4]

The Reich and Prussian Commission for the Supervision of Public Order, founded in 1919 but increasingly active in 1920, served as another critical element in the creation of the security state. The law placed the commissions, with a commissar at their head, within the ministries of the interior. Their range of competence was most in evidence during states of emergency, when they were granted extraordinary powers, generally in conjunction with the military command, which they used to ban strikes, demonstrations, and communist newspapers. The commissars also issued weekly and at times daily reports that were circulated and discussed at the highest levels of government. The reports are a goldmine of information, but they were not written for the pleasure of the historians of the future. They were designed to coordinate and quicken the flow of information about radical politics and public unrest—an absolutely critical task in the security state that facilitated the more rapid deployment of the police and army. The reports demonstrate that the authorities were extremely well informed about the internal workings of radical groups and the manifestations of popular protest.[5]

The manifold levels of the *Länder* (state) and Reich bureaucracies—provincial governors, district governors, district magistrates, commerce officials—provided the bulk of information to the commissars of public order, who channeled the data to the ministries of the interior and, if need be, the rest of the government.[6] By the beginning of 1921, all sorts of other state agencies were keeping tabs on popular unrest and KPD activities. Even the Ministry of Trade and Commerce got into the act by ordering its mining officials to file daily reports when some sort of communist-inspired uprising was expected. Should unrest threaten, officials had to "intervene promptly with all the powers at our disposal against the pernicious influences."[7] Officials recognized that time was of the essence—that strike movements and armed uprisings had to be countered quickly before they got out of hand.

Local SPD members also provided domestic intelligence, especially when "their" people occupied higher state offices, indicating that integration into the state structure traveled deep down the party hierarchy.[8] Many municipalities like

eines neuen imperialistischen Militärsystems (November 1918 bis 1920) (Berlin: Deutscher Militärverlag, 1971), 173–86.

[4] SKÜöO to all Regierungskommissare, 28 January 1920, LHSAM C20/Ib/4603/2–3. For one example concerning a strike at a railroad repair shop, see RPM to MHG, 8 March 1920, GStAKM 120/BB/VII/1/3/30/120.

[5] The reports are available in various archives, e.g., BAP RAM, and are also now available on microfiche.

[6] See, for example, Meldestelle, OPM to RPen in Provinz, 22 April 1920, which contains a form for the Regierungspräsidenten to fill out in cases of unrest.

[7] MHG to OBH, etc., 11 January 1921, GStAKM 120/BB/VI/193/1/1–2.

[8] As in one report, RKÜöO to Reichskanzler, etc., 21 June 1920, BAP RAM 2817/14–20, in which the Reich Commissar cites information from Halle SPD leaders.

Essen introduced their own offices designed to process rapidly security information.[9] The Halle police, who could not quite get over the habits of the imperial period, kept track of every demonstration and mass meeting, and observed not just the KPD, but liberal and right-wing groups as well. Their reports to the district governor (Regierungspräsident), almost unbelievably thorough, run to seventeen volumes in the archives.[10]

The newly developed security measures were put to the test in early 1921. The setting, not accidentally, was Prussian Saxony and, specifically, the Halle-Merseburg region. Labor indiscipline had reached almost unimaginable levels and the boundary between political and criminal activities had become quite nebulous. Strikes great and small plagued all sorts of employers. Job shirking and rampant petty thievery added to their woes. Employers and government officials thought the situation wildly out of control. Moreover, the USPD had gone over almost en masse to the KPD, which found in Halle-Merseburg its first true *Hochburg* (fortress). The even more radical KAPD also had significant support in the region.

While communists had firm support in Halle-Merseburg, social democrats led the Prussian state government and occupied the security offices, including the all-important Ministry of the Interior and the Reich and Prussian Commission for the Supervision of Public Order, both, for much of the time, in the hands of Carl Severing.[11] A longtime official of the metalworkers union, Severing had demonstrated in 1919 and 1920 his willingness to use force to suppress radical workers. The provincial governor (Oberpräsident) of Prussian Saxony was Otto Hörsing, also a longtime SPD official known for his hostility to the radical left.

The event in question has been known as the KPD's March Action, but it really belongs to the Prussian state.[12] The enormity of the labor uprising during the Kapp Putsch had served as a warning signal. Now, the state was determined to crush working-class radicalism and impose order before the situation escalated into another revolutionary battle.

The KPD, through its own misguided actions, handed Prussia all the pretext it needed. Unity with the USPD had actually strengthened the wing of the party that believed the working class to be innately radical. Revolution lay on the agenda and

[9] See the documents in HStAD 15369.

[10] The reports are housed in LHSAM C20/Ib/4648.

[11] Though at the specific moment of the March Action, Dr. Robert Weissmann was Reich and Prussian Commissar for the Supervision of Public Order.

[12] The following account is drawn from RPM to MHG with Denkschrift, 11 May 1921, GStAKM 120/BB/VI/193/1/6–28; Preussischer Landtag, "Die wörtliche Berichte und die Sitzungen des Untersuchungsausschußes zur Feststellung der Ursachen, des Umfangen und der Wirkungen des kommunistischen Aufstandes in Mitteldeutschland in März 1921" (hereafter LT Proceedings) in GStAKM 169/DIX/D3/4/2; Preussischer Landtag, "Bericht des Untersuchungsausschußes über den Ursachen, den Umfang und die Wirkungen des kommunistischen Aufstandes in Mitteldeutschland in März 1921" (hereafter LT Report), GStAKM 169/DIX/D/4/2. For secondary studies, see Stefan Weber, *Ein kommunistischer Putsch? Märzaktion 1921 in Mitteldeutschland* (Berlin: Dietz, 1991), and Sigrid Koch-Baumgarten *Die Märzaktion der KPD 1921* (Cologne: Bund, 1987), which have supplanted the older account by Werner Angress, *Stillborn Revolution: The Communist Bid for Power in Germany, 1921–1923* (Princeton: Princeton University Press, 1963), 105–66.

required only decisive action by communists, who would be quickly followed by the masses of workers. The more temperate wing of the KPD, led by Paul Levi, who had assumed the mantle of leadership after Luxemburg's murder, found itself increasingly isolated. In January 1921 the party launched then quickly abandoned an effort to forge a united front with the SPD and the trade unions. In its place, the KPD, with the active encouragement of Comintern representatives in Berlin, the Hungarian Béla Kun notable among them, adopted the so-called theory of the offensive, which provided strategic gloss for the revolutionary optimists in the party.

While communists began preparing for an uprising, the state, in close contact with private employers, began to prepare a police action. In the middle of March directors of the Leuna works and other firms in the region approached state officials, not for the first time, claiming that they were no longer capable of eliminating the "rule of force" exercised by groups of workers in their enterprises. Every action taken by management was countered by a strike, and the level of theft had become extraordinarily high, they charged. The directors of Leuna threatened to shut down the factory altogether if the situation was not changed.[13] Directors of other firms voiced similar concerns and threats. As the State Commissar for the Supervision of Public Order, Dr. Weissmann, later testified, as a result of the meeting government officials decided to undertake a police action "finally to take charge of the criminals, who appropriate property that is not theirs and generally disregard the criminal code . . . and to reestablish calm and order."[14] In subsequent testimony, Weissmann explicitly linked communism and criminality by pointing to the widespread looting that plagued the area and the fact that "the communist workers essentially ruled the region and dominated the majority of workers who were willing to work."[15] Typically, Weissmann also linked the conditions to the presence of foreign agitators, Russians notably among them.

Certainly, managerial authority was under siege from the strikes, job shirking, and theft that had become endemic to the Halle-Merseburg region.[16] The Leuna director, Dr. Oster, later testified that workers actively resisted the firm's efforts to reduce thefts by strengthening controls at the plant gates. As one example, he mentioned that the firm had permitted workers to take scrap wood as a kind of social welfare measure since fuel was in short supply. But when it announced that workers caught taking anything more than scrap would be treated as thieves, workers went out on strike and shoved and beat up the guards at the gates.[17] Communists propagandized that materials at the factory constituted the workers' own property. The firm negotiated with the works council, which agreed to place its own men and other elected representatives at the gates. Still, looting only escalated in the succeeding weeks. "Whatever was not solidly nailed down was taken out," according to Oster.[18]

[13] Testimony of SKÜöO Dr. Weissmann, LT Proceedings, 9 May 1921, 3.

[14] Ibid., 4–5.

[15] Ibid., 14 September 1921, 392.

[16] LT Report, 3–4.

[17] According to Weissmann's testimony, LT Proceedings, 14 September 1921, 392–93.

[18] Ibid., 15 September 1921, 513.

Events of a very similar nature transpired at the Mansfeld firm, the site of major prewar strikes (discussed in chapter 1) and center of political unrest in the Weimar Republic.[19] In February 1921, just prior to the March Action, company directors and Prussian mining officials reported that thievery in the Eisleben mining region, completely dominated by the Mansfeld company, had increased dramatically. All sorts of materials and products were being spirited out of the worksites, including silver and copper. The firm had first attempted to set up an internal security force with its own employees, but they proved unwilling to act against fellow workers. Then Mansfeld called in a private security service, which deployed eight guards, a move that set off a revolt at the mine. The ensuing strike only ended when the firm agreed to remove the security guards after their contract ran out and to grant workers half pay for the days they were on strike—a concession that particularly galled management. Mining officials described the situation as very tense with grave dangers of further unrest. The goal was a "communist-Bolshevik" revolution, and "Russian Jews" were among the leading agitators in the Mansfeld region.

The authorities decided to deploy the police in the Mansfeld area. Oster requested the same for Leuna. In his testimony before the Prussian Landtag committee that subsequently investigated the March Action, he claimed he had said to provincial governor Hörsing:

> I guarantee you . . . if you intervene in Eisleben [the Mansfeld region], [the situation] will blow up in Leuna also. Couldn't you do both? When that was denied I said: then better you come to us first, since according to my information it is not as pressing in Eisleben as by us. And in the springtime in view of the agrarian economy it is especially important. [Leuna manufactured synthetic nitrogen for fertilizers.][20]

Oster also demanded the intervention of Reichswehr troops as well as police forces, a more serious level of engagement that state officials were reluctant to consider. They feared that the army, with its track record of brutality, would provoke workers to more extensive resistance.

Whatever the tactical differences—Eisleben or Leuna or both, army or police or both—state officials and employers had a common interest in suppressing crime and communism in Prussian Saxony. On 19 March 1920, heavily armed police forces moved in and occupied the industrial regions of Prussian Saxony.[21] Industry representatives again demanded the immediate deployment of Reichswehr troops with heavy artillery, contending that the Schupo alone could not handle the situation.[22] Hörsing and Severing resisted until they had no choice.

[19] The following account is drawn from Abschrift, Preussische Bergrevierbeamte, 5 February 1921, BAP RMdI 13397/334–41, and documents in LHSAM C20/Ib/4699/4: "Resolution," Hettstedt, 3 February 1921, 16–17; Mansfeldsche Kupferschieferbauende Gewerkschaft to OPPS, 9 February 1921, 19–21; [resumé of a meeting of Mansfelder company and the works council], 17 February 1921, 25–26; Meldestelle OPPS to SKÜöO, 18 February 1921, 27–30.

[20] LT Proceedings, 15 September 1921, 513.

[21] On the events see Weber, *Kommunistischer Putsch?* 82–191; Koch-Baumgarten, *Märzaktion*, 57–111; and Winkler, *Von der Revolution*, 514–20.

[22] As in Hallescher Bergwerksverein als Beauftragter des gesamten Mitteldeutschen Braunkohlenindustriebezirks to RMdI, 27 March 1921, and Landbund to RMdI, 1 April 1921, BAP RAM 13399/24, 57–58

Workers responded far more dramatically and violently than state officials had expected, even though the March Action never quite became the popular uprising of communist legend. The incursion of the Prussian police also forced the KPD into action ahead of schedule. The party issued calls for a general strike and a proletarian revolution. Workers in Mansfeld, Leuna, and elsewhere went out on strike and entered into battle with the police. Max Hölz, already a legendary figure among radical workers and a member of the KAPD, organized the military campaign in the Mansfeld mining region. Hugo Eberlein, the head of the KPD's military apparatus, traveled from Berlin to Halle to organize sabotage. Leuna workers fabricated their own tank and explosives.

But against combined police and army units the uprising had no prospects of success. On 29 March 1921 the security forces launched an artillery barrage against workers holed up in the Leuna factory. Calls for negotiations and efforts to turn over the plant peacefully had been rejected by the commanding officers at the scene, and also, apparently, by company directors.[23] The forces of order wanted a vivid demonstration of their powers, and they were prepared to risk substantial destruction of BASF's assets. In this venture, they had the support of leading social democrats, including Hörsing and Severing. The workers inside had no choice but to surrender, which marked the end of the campaign except for one final battle with Hölz's forces on 1 April. About 145 individuals were killed in the entire conflict and about 34,700 workers were placed in custody.[24] Many of them suffered terribly at the hands of the army and police, who exercised a virtual white terror.

Officials were clearly pleased with the success of the action. Prone to exaggerate the extent of communist influence beforehand, many were now too quick to assume its decline. The county magistrate (Landrat) of the Saalkreis, the area around Halle, wrote to the provincial governor at the beginning of May that there had been a "notable shift in the mood and outlook of communist workers." Many have ceased to display the red star on their jackets and shirts and have dispensed with the swagger typical especially of communist youth. Moreover, a "widespread psychological depression" is evident. The "circles infected by belief in the Soviets" now recognize that they face a state power that "cannot be chased away by sudden local attacks . . . and that possesses the will and the power to counter any rebellions. . . . Even they now see and accept that Soviet magic brings them no cure."[25]

Officials knew, of course, that the KPD commanded the support of only a minority of the working-class population. But the passivity of the majority in the

[23] LT Proceedings, 23 April 1921, 57–58, and Weber, *Kommunistischer Putsch?* 159–64.

[24] Figures from Winkler, *Von der Revolution*, 517.

[25] LRSK to OPM, 9 May 1921, LHSAM C20/Ib/4648/5I/100–102. See also the reports and communiqués in BAP RMdI 13400: OP and RK to MdI, 20 July 1921, 46–47; OP and RK to MdI, 18 August 1921, 51–55; OP and RK to MdI, 27 August 1921, 56–57; RMdI to OP, 30 August 1921, 44. See also, Meldestelle bei dem OPPS to RKÜöO, 17 August 1921, BAP RMdI 13398/80–84. The district governor in Merseburg also argued that the KPD had suffered a grave defeat, but sounded a cautionary note in opposition to the police director of Halle, who thought that the party was no longer capable of undertaking any great actions. RPM to Meldestelle, OPPS, 22 October 1921, LHSAM C20/Ib/4647/12–14.

face of communist "terror campaigns" gave them deep cause for concern and provided the ultimate rationale for the rapid display of force. As the district governor of Merseburg put it, communists were aided by the "astonishing inability of the peaceable workforce to resist. Not once did they attempt an earnest defense against the terror of the radical elements."[26]

Some officials and employers involved in the March Action knew that "communist terror" provided only part of the explanation for the deep-seated discontent in Halle-Merseburg. Social democrats, mine and factory inspectors, other state officials, and Leuna directors all spoke of industrialization at "an American pace," by which they meant the extremely rapid and concentrated rise of industry and, consequently, the lack of a settled and experienced, and therefore more "reasonable," workforce.[27] Leuna director Oster correctly identified construction workers as the initiators of many actions at the factory, but for the wrong reasons. Since they were not firmly tied to the factory—or any single firm, for that matter—construction workers were, in his view, rootless, the very antithesis of the settled, stable, and loyal workforces that companies like BASF had sought to construct in the imperial period and now wanted to re-create in the altered circumstances of the postwar world. To Oster and others like him, a transient labor force went virtually hand in hand with radicalism and indiscipline.[28]

But the reality was not quite what the participants believed. Oster and state officials, including social democrats, failed to recognize that beneath the veneer of transiency lay a working class with a shared experience of extremely arduous working conditions, grave material difficulties only worsened by the war and postwar crises, and, by 1921, strikes, demonstrations, and armed rebellions. Leuna certainly underwent explosive growth, but as discussed in the previous chapter, a very large proportion of the labor force was composed of workers who had long been employed in industry. Construction workers especially had built atop their common experiences well-organized trade unions, which provided them with the resources to engage management in conflicts and the self-possession to swipe materials from the job site. Prussian Landtag delegates seemed astonished when a works councillor of the Mansfeld firm testified that the postwar workforce was very little different from that of the pre-1914 period, that the same workers who had gone on strike at Mansfeld in 1907, 1910, and 1912 were still there fighting in 1919 and 1920.[29] Neither SPD officials nor employers could understand a workforce socially little different from others, but politically

[26] RPM to MHG, 11 May 1921, GStAKM 120/BB/VI/193/1/6–28. See also Oster's testimony, LT Proceedings, 15 September 1921, 520–21, 524.

[27] See, for example, the testimonies of Oberpräsidialrat Breyer on 9 September 1921 and Staatssekretär und Reichsentwaffnungskommissar Dr. Peters on 10 September 1921, LT Proceedings 226 and 251; the testimony of Minister of the Interior Severing in "Niederschrift über die von dem Untersuchungsausschuß zur Nachprüfung der Ursachen, des Umfangs und der Wirkungen des kommunistischen Aufstandes in Mitteldeutschland in März 1921 in mündlicher Verhandlung erhobenen Beweise," GStAKM 169/DIX/4/2/95; and LT Report, 7–8.

[28] LT Proceedings, 15 September 1921, 511. The USPD works council chairman Daniel basically reprised Oster's analysis, complete with all the charges of communist terror. See ibid., 532–49.

[29] Ibid., 26 September 1921, 706.

inclined toward radicalism. And if "peaceable" workers exercised so little resistance, it was not only because of communist compulsion, but also because they shared with their more activist colleagues at least a distaste for the system of moderate republicanism and revived managerial power that defined the Weimar Republic already in 1921.

After the March Action, the authorities evinced a new sense of confidence, though they continued to keep a close eye on the situation and reported on the "very depressed" mood of the population and "quite worrisome" situation in many parts of the province, especially where communists continued to lead the working population.[30] But at least for a while, order had returned to Prussian Saxony, an order built upon the cooperation of social democratic state officials, social democratic trade unionists, Catholic and liberal reformers, army officers, and employers.

Certainly, tactical differences existed among them, which reemerged in the months following the March Action. Employers and the more conservatively inclined government officials, many of whom were holdovers from the imperial state, wanted the KPD and its press banned outright.[31] Social democratic officials worried that such overtly repressive actions would simply make martyrs out of the communists and increase general working-class hostility toward the Republic. SPD officials tended to have more moderate and rational estimations of the possibilities of another communist insurgency, while employers and their conservative allies in the government were prone to sound the warnings of another left-wing putsch at every possible moment.[32] SPD officials had learned to be wary of

[30] RPM to OPPS, 25 March 1922; Beigeordneter der Landespolizeibehörden Provinz Sachsen to OPPS, Meldestelle, 23 June 1922, LHSAM C20/Ib/4647/28–29, 34–35.

[31] As in BASF to MdI, 23 April 1921, BAP RMdI 13399/153–54; RPM to MHG, 11 May 1921, GStAKM 120/BB/VI/193/1/6–28; BASF to MdI, 23 April 1921, Reichswirtschaftsminister to MdI, 29 April 1921, RMdI to RK in Magdeburg, 9 May 1921, BAP RMdI 13399/153–54, 184, 185; BASF to SKÜöO, 24 May 1921, Meldestelle OPM to SKÜöO, 3 June 1921, BASF to RKÜöO, 15 June 1921, RP Magdeburg to OPPS, 28 June 1921, LHSAM C20/Ib/4701/4–5, 6, 11–12, 14; PVH to RPM, LHSAM C20/Ib/4648/5I/114–15. The governor of the Saxony Province apparently felt compelled to meet at least some of the demands of the employers and agreed to ban the KPD press for three days during a strike in the Mansfeld region and to keep Schupo troops posted at the Leuna works.

[32] Hörsing in particular seems to have been caught in the middle of conflicting tactical lines. Through 1920 he advocated a police action, which he thought could be quite limited and contained. At the same time, he pleaded against President Ebert and Minister of the Interior Severing for maintaining the state of emergency in the region. He also came into constant conflict with the Reichswehr over the scope of his powers. The army resisted his efforts to remove certain particularly reactionary officers and opposed his arrest of some Freikorp activists. He resisted sweeping efforts to disarm workers unless similar actions were carried out against the right. See some of the documents in BAP RMdI 12256: Meldestelle beim OP to SKÜöO, 7 May 1920, 5–7; SKÜöO to MdI, 14 May 1920, 9; OP und RK Magdeburg to MdI, 11 May 1920, 30a–33. See also many of the documents in BAP RMdI 13397 and 12257, and OP und RK Magdeburg to MdI, 4 June 1920, BAP RMdI 12256, 300–301. In the latter volume, there are numerous efforts by the Reichswehr in the months following the Kapp Putsch to demonstrate that a Red Army in fact existed and intended a putsch, while civilian government officials argued that these were exaggerated and baseless rumors.

employers who brought before them yet another report of an impending KPD uprising, which were often founded on statements by unreliable informants.[33]

Whatever the tactical differences, the members of the coalition of order were bound together by a common hostility to communism and working-class radicalism. And the lessons of the March Action were clear to all involved: closer coordination between employers and the state; rapid information flows; when necessary, rapid deployment of troops; dismissal of workers involved in radical actions.[34] Various levels of the state continued to keep a close watch on the KPD and produced extremely detailed and informative reports, including information on finances, structure, and personnel of the KPD and its affiliated organizations.[35] When necessary, the authorities deployed open force, as in the KPD's October 1923 uprising and in many minor skirmishes. Repeatedly, the authorities expressed satisfaction that their energetic measures had weakened the KPD, and, with evident relief, that passivity had set in among workers.[36] But the authorities knew also that any easing of the situation depended on continual economic progress, and especially low unemployment and inflation.

Those hopes were dashed by the hyperinflation of 1923 and the high unemployment that resulted from rationalization and the Great Depression. But the coalition of order held its ground until nearly the very end of the Republic. The Kapp Putsch had divided social democrats and trade unionists from the old forces of order. The March Action brought them together in opposition to the KPD and working-class indiscipline, and thereby served as a critical moment in the reconstitution of the politics of order.

For the KPD, the creation of the security state brought it face to face with an opponent far more formidable than the czarist state overthrown by the Bolsheviks in 1917. The coalition of order foreclosed the possibility of a successful armed uprising against the state. But it was unable to drive from the landscape sullen, endemic social and political conflict. And the SPD's alliance with the police, the army, and the employers undermined its popular support, which redounded in part to the benefit of the KPD. German communists could claim to have defended workers against the police who came "not with the usual weapons . . . but with machine guns and hand grenades," against those who wanted to make workers labor under the watchful eye of "bloodthirsty [police] officers," and against the "brutal" Otto Hörsing, the "jailkeeper" for counterrevolutionary military bands.[37]

[33] For one example, PVH to RPM, 15 January 1923, LHSAM C20/Ib/4648/5II/1–3.

[34] See, for example, RPM to MHG, 11 May 1921, GStAKM 120/BB/VI/193/1/6–28, a detailed set of recommendations. The MHG replied that they were discussed in the Ministry of the Interior, and many of the measures had already been adopted. MHG, Vermerk, 29 May 1921, GStAKM 120/BB/VI/193/29. See also MdI to RPen and PPen, 24 May 1921, LHSAM C20/Ib/4603/21, and report of meeting to RAM, MdI, OPM, RPM, etc., 4 July 1921, GStAKM 120/BB/VI/193/41–43.

[35] For some examples, see PP Stuttgart, "Rote Hilfe" (103 pp.), HIA, NSDAP 41/812.

[36] The situation reports of the RKÜöO repeat this theme constantly from 1924 onwards.

[37] *Mansfelder Volks-Zeitung*, 21 March 1921; *Klassenkampf*, 22 and 24 March 1921, all in *Dokumente und Materialien zur Geschichte der Arbeiterbewegung im Bezirk Halle*, ed. Bezirksleitung Halle der SED (Halle: Mitteldeutsche Druckerei Freiheit, 1965), 110, 112, 113.

Order through Social Welfare

The members of the coalition of order knew that the battle against communism and general working-class unrest could never be waged by security means alone. *Sozialpolitik*—social welfare policy—constituted another essential element in the reconstruction of authority. In this realm, the divisions among the constituent elements of the coalition of order were far greater than in the common commitment to a security state. Social democrats and Catholics, employers, state officials, and Protestant reformers all sharply contested the ultimate aims of social welfare. They fought over the designation of the agents and the paymasters—whether the state, the firm, or private, religious associations should be the arbitrators and executors of welfare policy. But the objects of social welfare were the same for all groups: the working class, and, more specifically, working-class men, women, youth, and families, each of which was the target of specific policies and discourses.

Social democrats had, unsurprisingly, the most far-reaching conception of social welfare.[38] In their view, it constituted an absolutely essential means of raising working-class living standards and thereby ameliorating the harsh effects of industrial society. But they also endowed social welfare with grand historical meaning. Organized by the new democratic state, social welfare represented a step further along the historical evolution toward socialism. It served to create citizens, materially secure, active members of the state. Those outside the pale, those for whom the rigors of industrial life meant descent into abject poverty and dissolution, would be elevated back into the *Volk* by humane and rational-scientific programs. This meant not merely material supports, but state intervention into all aspects of family life, including health, sexuality, childrearing, and education, to create an "orderly family." The material and social crises of World War I and postwar reconstruction seemed to make such wide-ranging intervention even more necessary, as social democrats, along with virtually every other political and social group in Weimar Germany, invoked the continual specter of a crisis of the family, of youth, of women.[39] Social welfare would rationalize so-

[38] See especially David F. Crew, "'Eine Elternschaft zu Dritt'—staatliche Eltern? Jugendwohlfahrt und Kontrolle der Familie in der Weimarer Republik 1919–1933," in *"Sicherheit" und "Wohlfahrt": Polizei, Gesellschaft und Herrschaft im 19. und 20. Jahrhundert*, ed. Alf Lüdtke (Frankfurt am Main: Suhrkamp, 1992), 267–94; idem, "German Socialism, the State and Family Policy, 1918–33," *Continuity and Change* 1:2 (August 1986): 235–63; David E. Barclay, *Rudolf Wissell als Sozialpolitiker 1890–1933* (Berlin: Colloquium, 1984); and also Helmut Gruber's very interesting study, *Red Vienna: Experiment in Working-Class Culture, 1919–1934* (New York: Oxford University Press, 1991).

[39] On the major impact of the war and postwar crises and the focus on female bodies, see especially Elisabeth Domansky, "Militarization and Reproduction in World War I Germany," in *Society, Culture, and the State in Germany, 1870–1930*, ed. Geoff Eley (Ann Arbor: University of Michigan Press, forthcoming); Atina Grossmann, *Reforming Sex: The German Movement for Birth Control and Abortion Reform, 1920–1950* (New York: Oxford University Press, 1995); Kathleen Canning, "Feminist History after the Linguistic Turn: Historicizing Discourse and Experience," *Signs* 19:2 (1994): 384–97; Young-Sun Hong, "The Contradictions of Modernization in the German Welfare State: Gender and the Politics of Welfare Reform in First World War Germany," *SH* 17:2 (1992): 251–70; Ute Daniel, *Arbeiterfrauen in der Kriegsgesellschaft: Beruf, Familie und Politik im Ersten*

cial relations, from those within the family to those in the industrial sector where corporatist-type interest bargaining would ameliorate the most crass and brutal forms of class conflict.[40] By creating a positive loyalty to the republican state, a reasonable standard of living, corporatist representation, and orderly, humane, and stable family lives, social welfare would undermine the appeal of communism and prepare citizens for the transformation to socialism.

Religious and liberal reformers did not always share the SPD's grand historical vision, but they also viewed social welfare as an absolutely necessary means of compensating for the rigors of industrial life, now made worse by the crises of war and postwar reconstruction. Social welfare would bind the different classes of society together in a people's community (*Volksgemeinschaft*), a hierarchical, corporatist, but unified social order, and thereby ameliorate the harsh social conflicts of modern life. Religious activists feared and opposed a state monopoly of social welfare, especially a supposedly atheistic state identified with social democracy. For Protestants and Catholics, social welfare had a charismatic and spiritual, rather than a material, rational, and functional character.[41] The personal example of upstanding individuals would "save" those who were materially, morally, and spiritually lost. The state, in this vision, should subsidize social welfare, but leave its direction in the hands of religious associations. Liberal reformers, in contrast, approached the SPD's vision by calling for a functionalist-rationalist *system* of social welfare that would both preserve order and make for a more efficient use of human capital and a healthy *Volkskörper*.[42]

Employers also did not share the SPD's grand historical vision of social welfare, and they complained continually about the costs imposed upon them by Weimar social policy. For large employers especially, social welfare meant the firm's own *Sozialpolitik*, by which the company sought to win workers' loyalties by providing low-cost housing, company-run consumer cooperatives, leisure-time activities, and educational programs. Such measures were part of the managerial revolution of the 1920s, the emergence of scientific management and the effort to win workers' positive loyalty to the firm.[43] But as we saw in chapter 1, German companies also had bank accounts' work of experience with welfare programs, in some cases dating as far back as the mid–nineteenth century. During World War I, many firms, of necessity, had expanded their programs further

Weltkrieg (Göttingen: Vandenhoeck und Ruprecht, 1989); and Cornelie Usborne, "Pregnancy Is the Women's Active Service: Pronatalism in Germany during the First World War," in *The Upheaval of War: Family, Work, and Welfare in Europe, 1914–1918*, ed. Richard Wall and Jay Winter (Cambridge: Cambridge University Press, 1988), 389–416.

[40] See Charles S. Maier, *Recasting Bourgeois Europe: Stabilization in France, Germany, and Italy in the Decade after World War I* (Princeton: Princeton University Press, 1975).

[41] Crew, "'Eine Elternschaft zu Dritt,'" 271; Hong, "Contradictions of Modernization," 257–62.

[42] Hong, "Contradictions of Modernization;" Detlev J. K. Peukert, *Grenzen der Sozialdisziplinierung: Aufstieg und Krise der deutschen Jugendfürsorge von 1878 bis 1932* (Cologne: Bund, 1986).

[43] See Mary Nolan, *Visions of Modernity: American Business and the Modernization of Germany* (New York: Oxford University Press, 1994), 179–205, and Heidrun Homburg, *Rationalisierung und Industriearbeit: Arbeitsmarkt-Management-Arbeiterschaft im Siemens-Konzern Berlin 1900–1939* (Berlin: Haude und Spener, 1991).

and had gotten into the business of procuring food supplies and housing for their employees. After the war, economic instability and labor unrest sent many on a more intense hunt for ways to create more loyal and stable workforces. *Sozialpolitik* was one part of the answer, though its efficacy suffered from continual financial constraints.

To make individual workers loyal and efficient, companies maintained and expanded the various incentives that they had instituted before World War I. Invariably, the benefits were meted out according to years of service, like paid vacations after five years of work and bonus payments after twenty-five. But companies also recognized that individual workers did not exist unto themselves. To bind them to the firm necessitated intervention in family life as well, to create a still more conservative version of the "orderly family" presided over by the male worker. Company housing offered the best possible setting for controlling and "improving"—morally and materially—working-class lives. Construction waned in the inflation years, but revived in the middle and late 1920s and in conjunction with an overall employer offensive against the independence and autonomy of workers. Typically regulations forbade loud and boisterous behavior and unauthorized visitors. Normative conceptions of the family were reinforced by the expectation that wives of workers would be at home. Company security officers generally patrolled housing colonies and were known to evict at a moment's notice those found with communist literature. Consumer cooperatives and vacation homes for loyal workers were also designed to help secure a solid family life for the male wage earner, thereby ensuring the social and physical reproduction of labor.[44] By gaining the loyalty of the whole family, firms expected that the male wage earner would labor more efficiently and seek to remain with the firm. As in the prewar period, women, both employees and wives of male employees, were offered streams of advice on efficient household management.

Finally, officials drew upon a long tradition of state paternalism to support reinvigorated social welfare as a means of re-creating orderly subjects and social stability in an era of profound disturbance. While companies sought to bind workers to the firm within a larger framework of nationalism, officials naturally sought to bind workers first and foremost to the nation and state. They drew upon the policies and discourses of the Bismarckian era, but developed far more ambitious conceptions of social welfare. After 1890, and especially after World War I and the widespread hysteria about population decline and the wounding of the *Volkskörper*, officials recognized that *Sozialpolitik* had to be far more embracing and had to intervene in family life in a more systematic manner than previously. For state officials, the crises of the early years of the Weimar Republic only accentuated their tendency to use the tools of the bureaucracy and the central state to create an integrated, organic society. As they watched the populace reel from crisis to crisis, they laced their calls for order with a paternalist concern for the fate of the nation and its people.

[44] Alf Lüdtke, "'Ehre der Arbeit': Industriearbeiter und Macht der Symbole. Zur Reichweite symbolischer Orientierungen im Nationalsozialismus," in *Arbeiter im 20. Jahrhundert*, ed. Klaus Tenfelde (Stuttgart: Klett Cotta, 1991), 381–82, n. 99.

Writing just after the March Action, the district magistrate of the Saalkreis, for example, appealed for a wide-ranging social welfare program to aid workers and advocated his pet project, granting or leasing workers small plots of land. He touted his own achievements in the district: the establishment of a children's home, subsidies for housing construction, and, with evident pride, "a network of twenty-four local welfare offices . . . in which [people work] with diligence and joyful devotion." (That these offices might also become targets of demonstrations and riots he did not envision.) If the magistrate overestimated his personal influence, he nonetheless gave expression to the long-standing paternalism of the Prusso-German bureaucracy: "Positive efforts should be undertaken to achieve a reconciliation of the embittered and the desperate with the present. . . . From numerous individual observations I believe that I have been able to win the personal trust of even communist workers, so that I look with hope on the further development of political relations in the Saalkreis."[45]

The combination of the bureaucracy's long-standing paternalistic notions with the SPD's comprehensive conception of *Sozialpolitik* led to a vast expansion of the state's social welfare role. The Constitution guaranteed workers the right to organize and recognized collectively bargained contracts as legally binding. Factory inspectors and other government officials became involved in negotiating labor conflicts and often recommended decisions beneficial to workers, a policy continued after the stabilization crisis of 1923/24, when government arbitration of labor disputes generally awarded workers wage increases and began to impose a gradual decline in the workshift. By 1928, real wages had for the most part returned to their prewar levels, in large part because of governmental action.[46] An early decree issued by the revolutionary government in 1918 confirmed and expanded the eight-hour agreement signed by the unions and the employer associations. Legislation increased the scope of social insurance coverage, culminating in 1927 when the Reichstag passed a combined unemployment insurance and labor exchange program, one of the great milestones of welfare policy.[47]

[45] LRLKS to OPM, 9 May 1921, LHSAM C20/Ib/4648/5I/101–2.

[46] In disputes of major economic and political importance, as in the Ruhr coal mines, leading government officials consistently became involved. But the factory and mine inspectors mediated an immense number of less dramatic conflicts and were clearly overwhelmed by the task. See *JB 1919*, 317; *JB 1920*, 325. In both the coal and chemicals industry, real wages finally surpassed the prewar level, though the steel industry was an exception to the pattern. See Rudolf Tschirbs, *Tarifpolitik im Ruhrbergbau 1918–1933* (Berlin: Walter de Gruyter, 1986), 366–68; Dieter Schiffmann, *Von der Revolution zum Neunstundentag: Arbeit und Konflikt bei BASF 1918–1924* (Frankfurt am Main: Campus, 1983), 193–95; and Bernd Weisbrod, *Schwerindustrie in der Weimarer Republik* (Wuppertal: Peter Hammer, 1978), 136–41. For a detailed examination of state-directed arbitration, see Johannes Bähr, *Staatliche Schlichtung in der Weimarer Republik: Tarifpolitik, Korporatismus und industrieller Konflikt zwischen Inflation und Deflation 1919–1932* (Berlin: Colloquium, 1989).

[47] For a fine summary of the development of unemployment support in Germany, see Richard J. Evans, "Introduction: The Experience of Unemployment in the Weimar Republic," in *The German Unemployed: Experiences and Consequences of Mass Unemployment from the Weimar Republic to the Third Reich*, ed. Richard J. Evans and Dick Geary (New York: St. Martin's Press, 1987), 1–22. On the labor exchanges see Klaus J. Bade, "Arbeitsmarkt, Bevölkerung und Wanderung in der Weimarer Republik," in *Weimarer Republik: Belagerte Civitas*, ed. Michael Stürmer (Königstein/Ts.: Anton Hain, 1980), 160–87. Gerhard A. Ritter provides a good summary of the Republic's social policies

At the local level the state's interventionist role expanded dramatically.[48] The Reich Youth Welfare Law of 1922 provided for state support for the establishment of youth offices and subsidies for private welfare agencies that dealt with the young. Designed to protect and aid youth, the law also opened the way for the increased exercise of power on the part of social work professionals. By designating young people as "endangered" or "dissolute," they could investigate conditions in the family and, ultimately, remove children to foster homes or orphanages. If physicians active in the school health program identified a child whose health and well-being were neglected at home, local officials or designated social work professionals visited the home to investigate the problem and to ensure that medical recommendations were being followed. Often, the "clients" defiantly rejected such interventions.

Welfare legislation linked support to "individual need," which led directly to investigations of family circumstances that rarely remained limited to economics alone, but involved moral and social behavior as well. Local authorities investigated relatives of applicants to see whether they were able to support their aged kin, and women were assumed to be responsible for the task. When the Depression overloaded the unemployment insurance system, means tests were adopted for unemployment support as well. Public health and family planning clinics, many established with a combination of public and private support, promulgated an ideology and practice of sexuality that would be both mutually pleasurable and reproductively rational, thereby contributing to the stability of the family and, by extension, society.[49] Sexual counselors were given a mandate to intervene in the most intimate spheres of life.

Municipal housing estates, often the product of social democratic direction of municipalities or of joint trade union and municipal financing, were designed to "elevate" workers to higher standards of domestic culture, which sought to make them into passive consumers of rationally designed living spaces. To qualify for the materially improved surroundings, workers had to demonstrate an orderliness

---

in "Entstehung und Entwicklung des Sozialstaates in Vergleichender Perspektive," *HZ* 243 (1986): 61–67.

[48] The following is drawn especially from David F. Crew's various articles: "A Social Republic: Social Democrats, Communists, and the Weimar Welfare State, 1919–1933," in *Between Reform and Revolution: Studies in German Socialism and Communism from 1840 to 1990*, ed. David E. Barclay and Eric D. Weitz (Providence: Berghahn, forthcoming); "'Eine Elternschaft zu Dritte'"; "'Wohlfahrtsbrot ist bitteres Brot': The Elderly, the Disabled and the Local Welfare Authorities in the Weimar Republic 1924–1933," *AfS* 30 (1990): 217–45; "Bedürfnisse und Bedürftigkeit: Wohlfahrtsbürokratie und Wohlfahrtsempfänger in der Weimarer Republik, 1919–1933," *Sozialwissenschaftliche Information* 18:1 (1989): 12–19; "German Socialism, the State and Family Policy," as well as Elizabeth Harvey, *Youth and the Welfare State in Weimar Germany* (Oxford: Clarendon, 1993); Peukert, *Grenzen*; and idem, *Jugend zwischen Krieg und Krise: Lebenswelt von Arbeiterjungen in der Weimarer Republik* (Cologne: Bund, 1987).

[49] See Cornelie Usborne, *The Politics of the Body in Weimar Germany: Women's Reproductive Rights and Duties* (Ann Arbor: University of Michigan Press, 1992); Atina Grossmann, "The New Woman and the Rationalization of Sexuality in Weimar Germany," in *Powers of Desire: The Politics of Sexuality*, ed. Ann Snitow, Christine Stansell, and Sharon Thompson (New York: Monthly Review Press, 1983), 153–71; and idem, *Reforming Sex*.

and discipline in their personal lives, and as tenants had to submit to the supervision of their behavior.[50] Apartments designed for the two- or three-child nuclear family seemed to capture in brick and mortar the essence of rationalized sexuality.

In the imperial period workers had come to rely upon state support against the employers in labor disputes; the protective health and safety measures promoted by factory inspectors; and state-supported health, accident, and old-age insurance. In the Weimar period, workers expected all of that, and also the state-mandated eight-hour day, the government's beneficial arbitration of labor disputes, and comprehensive unemployment insurance. At the same time, social welfare policy became more interventionist, moving more directly into the "private" realms of reproduction.

Despite the vast differences that existed among the members of the coalition of order in relation to social welfare—and they were profound—there existed also a range of agreement, however tenuous, that made *Sozialpolitik* another arm in the common strategy designed to reconstruct order.[51] Whether the agent was the firm, the state, or a religious association, welfare policies were intended to be moral and educative—hence, disciplinary—and not merely supportive. The recipients were the objects of policy, even to a substantial degree in social democratic conceptions. Professionally trained staffs, whether in a municipality or a company's Bureau of Labor Affairs, executed policies to the recipients, who were rarely involved in planning and participation. Furthermore, social welfare targeted entire families, not just individuals, and policies and discourses were designed to reinforce a normative conception of the patriarchal family. All the advocates of social welfare argued, perhaps too glibly, that "sound" or "healthy" bodies meant healthy families and a healthy *Volkskörper*, a position that by the end of the 1920s slid too easily into eugenicist and racist ideologies.

Social welfare policies certainly benefited workers materially, a very basic conclusion too often overlooked or mentioned incidentally in the contemporary scholarly concentration on the disciplinary and repressive aspects of state intervention.[52] Under SPD influence or direction, the Weimar state vastly improved the protective measures available to workers. Social democrats were justifiably proud of the improvements in public health, construction of municipal housing, mater-

[50] See Adelheid von Saldern, "The Workers' Movement and Cultural Patterns on Urban Housing Estates and in Rural Settlements in Germany and Austria during the 1920s," *SH* 15:3 (1990): 333–54. Anthony McElligott critiques her position in "Workers' Culture and Workers' Politics on Weimar's New Housing Estates: A Response to Adelheid von Saldern," *SH* 17:1 (1992): 101–13, but I think he overstates the case.

[51] Hong, "Contradictions of Modernization," emphasizes the conflicts among the various participants in social welfare, especially Catholic and Protestant hostility toward state-run social welfare. But if one uses a broad concept of *Sozialpolitik*, including not only welfare (*Fürsorge*) per se, but also the myriad interventions relating to workers through the Reich Labor Ministry and the Prussian Ministry for Trade and Commerce, then the Christian position appears less one-sided. Many of the reforming actions of the Reich Labor Ministry were carried out by individuals associated with the Catholic Center Party, and the Catholic trade unions had no difficulty calling for state interventions.

[52] Gruber's *Red Vienna* as well as the works cited in n. 48 above are typical of this genre.

nity benefits, and unemployment insurance that they sponsored. At select firms, some workers for the first time had available to them paid vacations and company-subsidized food, clothing, and housing.

But in the end, welfare programs proved utterly insufficient, a final element that bound together the different groups in the coalition of order. Amid all the crises of the Weimar Republic, no matter who the agent—company, central state, municipality, Caritas, the Protestant Inner Mission—none could provide enough welfare to surmount the dire material straits of the working-class population and the related, wrenching social conflicts of the Weimar era.

At the same time, welfare policy bound nearly all workers to a conception of an activist, interventionist state. Following the defeat of the council option, neither communists nor social democrats could envision an alternative to a powerful state. Social democrats sought only a more effective version of the Weimar Republic. Communists, significantly, did not counter the SPD and the Weimar system with demands for a diminution of state power in syndicalist or council fashion. If the security state drove communists from the battlefield, the social welfare state created among all workers the sense that solutions came via the state. For the KPD and its supporters, the problem with Weimar was its insufficiencies as a welfare state, which the dictatorship of the proletariat would surmount.

Disciplined Labor through Economic Rationalization

The coalition of order, founded first on security concerns and social welfare, received new-found footing in economic rationalization. Some firms had improved their productive capacities earlier. But in general, the capital, labor, and material shortages of the war years, and the political uncertainties, financial speculations, and short-term economic advantages of the inflation period, had for the most part limited industry's desire and ability to apply new technologies. In 1923, however, the French occupation of the Ruhr and the accompanying crises of hyperinflation and then stabilization revealed the deep structural weaknesses of the German economy. Industry seized the opportunity to reassert its economic and political power.[53] Faced with excess capacity and relatively high production costs in an era of heightened international competition, employers, with state support, launched a thoroughgoing rationalization effort. They applied new technologies and methods of business organization, but also helped launched a discourse of functionalism and efficiency

[53] Fundamental on the inflation period and the economic and political character of the 1923/24 stabilization is Gerald D. Feldman, *The Great Disorder: Politics, Economics, and Society in the German Inflation, 1914–1924* (New York: Oxford University Press, 1993). See also Irmgard Steinisch, *Arbeitszeitverkürzung und sozialer Wandel: Der Kampf um die Achtstundenschicht in der deutschen und amerikanischen Eisen- und Stahlindustrie 1880–1929* (Berlin: Walter de Gruyter, 1986); Tschirbs, *Tarifpolitik*; Winkler, *Von der Revolution*, 605–734; Gerald D. Feldman and Irmgard Steinisch, "Die Weimarer Republik zwischen Sozial- und Wirtschaftsstaat: Die Entscheidung gegen den Achtstundentag," *AfS* 18 (1978): 353–439; and Gerald D. Feldman, *Iron and Steel in the German Inflation, 1916–1923* (Princeton: Princeton University Press, 1977).

that extended far beyond the factory and into the realms of family relations and sexuality.[54] In an era of "relative economic stagnation"[55] and intense social conflict, the import of rationalization was deeply contested, its impact highly ambiguous—except in the realm of labor, where industry's actions resulted in levels of unemployment so high that the social composition of the workforce fractured between the employed and the jobless. And it was the unemployed who came in large part to form the social basis of the KPD.

Technological innovations—longwall and strip-mining, larger-scale and continuous processes in manufacturing, serial production—constituted major, but not exclusive, elements of a general employer strategy designed to slash labor costs and assert managerial prerogatives over the labor process.[56] As in the prewar period, the combination of technological and managerial rationalization led to no universal dequalification of the workforce, for skilled workers still remained crucial to many labor processes.[57] More than sheer technological innovations, rationalization signified capital's increasing control over time and space.[58] As management expanded its supervisory functions, skilled workers lost a great deal of their earlier independence, and all workers became subject to an intensified pace of work.[59] In the mines management now assigned the hewers and the small workgroups that they led (the *Kameradschaft*) specific tasks, a sharp assault on their traditional independence underground. Piecework, on the advance

[54] On the elasticity of rationalization, see especially Nolan, *Visions*, and Grossmann, "New Woman." Other important recent studies are Homburg, *Rationalisierung und Industriearbeit*; Carola Sachse, *Siemens, der Nationalsozialismus und die moderne Familie* (Hamburg: Rasch und Röhring, 1990); and Gunnar Stollberg, *Die Rationalisierungsdebatte 1908–1933: Freie Gewerkschaften zwischen Mitwirkung und Gegenwehr* (Frankfurt am Main: Campus, 1981).

[55] Dietmar Petzina and Werner Abelshauser, "Zum Problem der relativen Stagnation der deutschen Wirtschaft in den zwanziger Jahren," *Industrielles System und politische Entwicklung in der Weimarer Republik*, ed. Hans Mommsen, Dietmar Petzina, and Bernd Weisbrod (Düsseldorf: Droste, 1974), 57–76, and Harold James, *The German Slump: Politics and Economics, 1924–1936* (Oxford: Clarendon, 1986).

[56] For details, Nolan, *Visions*, 137–53; Karin Hartewig, *Das unberechenbare Jahrzehnt: Bergarbeiter und ihre Familien im Ruhrgebiet 1914–1924* (Munich: Beck, 1993), 82–119; Tshirbs, *Tarifpolitik*, 244–59; Schiffmann, *Von der Revolution*, 319–91; Uta Stolle, *Arbeiterpolitik im Betrieb: Frauen und Männer, Reformisten und Radikale, Fach- und Massenarbeiter bei Bayer, BASF, Bosch und in Solingen (1900–1933)* (Frankfurt am Main: Campus, 1980), 190–204; Paul Wiel, *Wirtschaftsgeschichte des Ruhrgebietes: Tatsachen und Zahlen* (Essen: Siedlungsverband Ruhrkohlenbezirk, 1970), 119, 122, 215–16; Robert A. Brady, *The Rationalization Movement in German Industry: A Case Study in the Evolution of Economic Planning* (Berkeley: University of California Press, 1933).

[57] Alf Lüdtke emphasizes the complexity of the rationalization process in "Wo blieb die 'rote Glut'? Arbeitererfahrungen und deutscher Faschismus," in *Alltagsgeschichte: Zur Rekonstruktion historischer Erfahrungen und Lebensweisen*, ed. idem (Frankfurt am Main: Campus, 1989), 240–48.

[58] See David Harvey, *The Condition of Postmodernity: An Enquiry into the Origins of Cultural Change* (Oxford: Basil Blackwell, 1989), 228–30.

[59] See Nolan, *Visions*, 167–69; Tschirbs, *Tarifpolitik*, 256–58; Schiffmann, *Von der Revolution*, 107, 114–26, 123–24; Eric D. Weitz, "Conflict in the Ruhr: Workers and Socialist Politics in Essen" (Ph.D. diss., Boston University, 1983), 247–91; and Stolle, *Arbeiterpolitik*, 191–213.

since 1919, after 1923 became generalized throughout industry.[60] Wage differentials between the skilled and unskilled, which had narrowed significantly after the war, much to the distress of the employers (and some workers), diverged once again.[61] In one of their most bitter defeats, German workers lost the eight-hour day (seven hours in the mines) that they had won in 1918. The prewar workshifts were reinstituted—twelve hours in the factories, ten hours above ground in the mines, and eight to eight and one-half hours underground. A last-ditch effort by Ruhr miners in the spring of 1924 to maintain the seven-hour day ended in defeat, marking the end of the great labor upsurge that had begun in the summer of 1916.[62]

The impact of these changes on Germany's overall economic performance in the Weimar years remains much disputed. The "mania for rationalization" led to a great deal of misplaced investment. In a period of excess international capacity in coal, steel, machine tools, and chemicals—all the major industries of Rheinland-Westphalia and Prussian Saxony—the headlong rush to expand capacity further through high capital investment only worsened the contradictions under which the economy labored. But it is spurious then to conclude that rationalization was nothing more than a myth of the Weimar era.[63] It is quite clear that labor experienced the speed-up, longer workdays, and diminution of shop-floor control that were all a part of rationalization. And between 1926 and 1930 labor productivity per working hour rose 25 percent in metals processing, 18 percent in mining, 15 percent in basic steel, and 13 percent in chemicals.[64] Moreover, while business may never have reaped the profitability gains for which it hoped, many business leaders advocated rationalization as their last preserve of independence, a refuge from unceasing state intervention. A number of employers and quite a few engineers also viewed rationalization as the key element in a kind of productivist utopia in which technology and efficient labor would enable the nation to surmount the dire social conflicts of the past and present—and leave the hierarchical order intact.[65]

[60] For example, Steinisch, *Arbeitszeitverkürzung*, 436–37; Schiffmann, *Von der Revolution*, 105–9; and *50 Jahre Mitteldeutscher Braunkohlen Bergbau: Festschrift zum 50jährigen Bestehen des Deutschen-Braunkohlen-Industrie-Vereins E.V. Halle (Salle) 1885–1935* (Halle: Wilhelm Knapp, n.d.).

[61] The divergence reached about 40 percent: *JB 1923/24*, 264, 548.

[62] Hans Mommsen, "Die Bergarbeiterbewegung an der Ruhr 1918–33," in *Arbeiterbewegung am Rhein und Ruhr: Beiträge zur Geschichte der Arbeiterbewegung in Rheinland-Westfalen*, ed. Jürgen Reulecke (Wuppertal: Peter Hammer, 1974), 305.

[63] James, *German Slump*, writes, "Rather than a wave of technical advances and improvements, there was simply a sectoral maldistribution of investment that created overcapacity in some basic heavy industry and in textiles" (149). But see the much more considered judgments of Nolan, *Visions*, and Heinrich August Winkler, *Der Schein der Normalität: Arbeiter und Arbeiterbewegung in der Weimarer Republik 1924 bis 1930* (Berlin: J. H. W. Dietz Nachf., 1988), 32–34, 62–75.

[64] Wolfram Fischer, "Bergbau, Industrie und Handwerk 1914–1970," in *Handbuch der deutschen Wirtschafts- und Sozialgeschichte*, vol. 2, ed. Hermann Aubin and Wolfgang Zorn (Stuttgart: Ernst Klett, 1976), 805. See also the tables in Eva Cornelia Schöck, *Arbeitslosigkeit und Rationalisierung: Die Lage der Arbeiter und die kommunistische Gewerkschaftspolitik 1920–1928* (Frankfurt am Main: Campus, 1977), 258–62.

[65] See Charles S. Maier's classic article, "Between Taylorism and Technocracy: European Ideolo-

Reports from KPD enterprise cells, drawn up at the behest of the Central Committee, demonstrate the intensified exploitation that workers experienced in the mid-1920s. From the Mansfeld mines one of the party cells reported on the immense dismay of the miners at the return of the prewar workshift.[66] Although mechanization had eased the labor intensity of some tasks, workers were nevertheless more exploited, mining two to four tons of coal where they had previously mined one to two tons. Mechanization had also shifted the piecerate system to the advantage of the owners. At a brass foundry near Eisleben, the workday had jumped from eight to ten hours and the size of the workforce had been slashed to 60 percent of the 1923 level while output had increased 50 to 60 percent.[67] The work had also gotten more dangerous, leading to early invalidity.

From the Ruhr came similar reports. A worker at a Krupp-owned mine reported that management had adopted the longwall system. The work had become more exhausting, leading to a rise in illness rates. Miners were now expected to extract a preset amount per day, determined by management, forcing an even more intense pace of work and usually a longer day, since the miners had to fulfill their daily quota in order to qualify for their pay. Both underground and in the coking plants, more was being produced with fewer workers.[68] At Rheinstahl in Hilden, workers were producing two to three times the number of units in the same time as compared to 1913. As a sign of almost vindictive labor policies, Rheinstahl began one of its shifts at 3:00 A.M. and ran it until 5:00 P.M. Some of the workers lived in Düsseldorf, but no night trains ran. So they slept for a few hours in the evening at home, took the last train to Hilden, and then slept a few more hours in the dusty rooms of the molding unit in order to be present for the beginning of the shift.[69]

Perhaps most significantly, rationalization carried out in the context of relative economic stagnation resulted in a drastically reduced demand for labor. In the last quarter of 1923, 40 percent of the members of the German Metalworkers Union nationwide were unemployed, and although the figure declined to 4 percent in mid-1925, by early 1926 it was back up to 21 percent, while another 33 percent of the members were underemployed.[70] Krupp's workforce declined by over a quarter between 1923 and 1924, and in 1927 still counted only 28,800, lower than even the 1905 level.[71] Prussian factory inspectors wrote in 1925 of a "frightening" rise

gies and the Vision of Industrial Productivity in the 1920s," *JCH* 5:2 (1970): 27–61, and Homburg, *Rationalisierung und Industriearbeit.*

[66] [Untitled, undated, presumably 1925 or 1926], Betreibszelle Wolfsschacht, Mansfeld A.G., SAPMO-BA, ZPA I/3/11/21/172–75.

[67] [Untitled, undated, presumably 1925 or 1926], Messingwerk Gottsburt b/Eisleben [?], SAPMO-BA, ZPA I/3/11/21/176–77.

[68] "Bericht über die Konferenz der Betriebsräte des Kohlensyndikats am 10. Oktober 1926 in Essen," SAPMO-BA, ZPA I/3/18–19/12/186.

[69] "Bericht von der Konferenz der kommunistischen Betreibsräte der Werke des Stahl-Trusts am 10. Oktober 1926 in Essen," SAPMO-BA, ZPA I/3/18–19/12/195.

[70] Germany, Statistisches Reichsamt, *Vierteljahreshefte zur Statistik des Deutschen Reiches*, 32:4, 152–55; 33:1, 87–88; 34:2, 113–14; 34:3, 146–47; 35:1, 170–71; 35:2, 136–37.

[71] "Die Arbeiterschaft der Kruppschen Gußstahlfabrik: Zur Denkschrift 'Die Firma Krupp im Weltkriege,'" (ms., n.d.), HA Krupp, WA VII/f1105/kd75, table 3.

in unemployment and "extraordinarily numerous" cases of underemployment and many plant closings.[72] Overall, the Ruhr mining workforce declined by 33 percent from 1922 to 1928, the Prussian Saxony lignite workforce by the same percentage from 1922 to 1924.[73]

Industry's determination to slash labor costs created levels of unemployment so high that a stratum of the structurally unemployed was created in Germany some years before the onset of the world economic crisis. Rationalization fragmented the German working class not along the divide of skill, but between the steadily employed and the chronically and casually unemployed. The unemployed of the Weimar Republic did not compose a group economically and socially disenfranchised for generations; they were not members of a "culture of poverty." The unemployed constituted a substratum, newly created in the 1920s, of the industrial working class. Nor did the unemployed constitute a group homogeneous in its origins. Alongside the high levels of unskilled and youth unemployment, large numbers of skilled, experienced workers were rendered unemployed by the process of rationalization. A Krupp official, for example, bemoaned the fact that older, loyal, skilled workers had to be laid off as part of rationalization, but declared that the firm had no choice since with the "intensified demands of the new methods of work, they burdened the firm all too much with their deficient productivity."[74] Factory inspectors reported in 1925 that a large armature factory in the Merseburg district had to fire sixty-two older workers, most of whom had more than forty years service to the firm, because of their insufficient productivity.[75] The Bosch firm in Stuttgart laid off hundreds of its most skilled workers in 1926.[76] During the Depression Leuna management set up criteria for layoffs with the aim of eliminating "the over-age and less productive . . . [those who are] useless" in order to hold on to the "younger, more vigorous people."[77] And the sheer magnitude of the retrenchment in the Ruhr mines well before the Depression cost tens of thousands of skilled miners their jobs.[78]

Through their positions in the state and as trade union officials often engaged in corporatist-type relations with employers, the SPD joined with Weimar governments of all stripes in promoting rationalization. The state supported rationalization through subsidies for major industries and support for various research and educational institutes directly linked to the rationalization drive.[79] Typically, social democrats had a grandiose conception that joined rationalization and social

[72] *JB 1925*, 267, 563–66, 693–94.

[73] Wiel, *Wirtschaftsgeschichte*, 131; *JB 1923/24*, 649.

[74] Wilhelm Berdrow, "Die Firma Krupp im Weltkrieg und in der Nachkriegszeit" (1936), vol. 2, 76, in HA Krupp, FAH IV/E10.

[75] *JB 1925*, 276.

[76] Stolle, *Arbeiterpolitik*, 200.

[77] Auszug aus dem Soko [Sozial Kommission], Protokoll No. 65, 11 September 1929, BLW 1340.

[78] Tschirbs, *Tarifpolitik*, 252–53.

[79] On the state-supported Reichskuratorium für Wirtschaftlichkeit in Industrie und Handwerk, see Nolan, *Visions*, 131–37, and Peter Hinrichs and Peter Lothar, *Industrieller Friede? Arbeitswissenschaft, Rationalisierung und Arbeiterbewegung in der Weimarer Republik* (Cologne: Pahl-Rugenstein, 1976), 53–59.

welfare as the twin elements of a single policy. They envisaged a kind of productivist utopia marked by technological efficiency *and* material security, even prosperity, all of it guided along by an interventionist state. Social welfare policies—from unemployment insurance and state-mandated wage increases to sex counseling—would compensate for whatever deleterious impact rationalization had on workers' physical and moral well-being.

The reality was rather more prosaic. Through its support of rationalization and its social welfare policies, the state contributed to the fragmentation of the Weimar working class. The government's arbitration of labor disputes after the stabilization crisis of 1923/24 clearly benefited employed workers by granting them wage increases, but also contributed to high unemployment, because industry responded to the high wage costs imposed upon it by substituting machine for human power.[80] In addition, the strictures of the 1927 unemployment insurance law deliberately marginalized the long-term unemployed by removing their cases to the welfare rolls. By the time of the Depression, the authorities had virtually renounced any effort geared toward reintegrating the unemployed into the mainstream labor force, and concentrated instead on measures of control and discipline.[81] This division was further enhanced by divergent housing patterns. Many of the better-off workers moved into the municipal housing that was widely built in the Weimar era, and there developed something of a "respectable" working-class culture distinct from the "rougher" street culture.[82]

In Heinrich August Winkler's words, the milieu of the German working class no longer constituted a unified world.[83] As a result of rationalization and social welfare policies, a large group of the unemployed emerged who were isolated not only from the world of work, but also from the organizational and cultural traditions of the social democratic labor movement. And the fractures of this world became reproduced in the political divisions of the German labor movement.

For the KPD, the disastrous impact of rationalization helped provide new recruits and gave the party no end of propaganda material to deploy against employers and the Weimar state. Certainly, the KPD shared the technological optimism of the SPD, and from the distance of Moscow communists often touted German and American rationalization as the wave of the future that communist societies needed to adapt to their purposes.[84] But the immediate political advantages were far more important to

[80] Ernst Brandi, the head of the Bergbau-Verein, reflected business's position when he argued that industry had to exploit fully the cost-saving potential of technology, the only sphere in which it was not subject to government control. Quoted in Tschirbs, *Tarifpolitik*, 345–46.

[81] See Heidrun Homburg, "From Unemployment Insurance to Compulsory Labor: The Transformation of the Benefit System in Germany, 1927–33," and Elizabeth Harvey, "Youth Unemployment and the State: Public Policies towards Unemployed Youth in Hamburg during the World Economic Crisis," in *German Unemployed*, 73–107 and 142–71.

[82] See Dick Geary, "Unemployment and Working-Class Solidarity: The German Experience 1929–1933," in *German Unemployed*, 261–80; James Wickham, "Working-Class Movement and Working-Class Life: Frankfurt am Main during the Weimar Republic," *SH* 8:3 (October 1983): 315–43; and von Saldern, "Workers' Movement and Cultural Patterns."

[83] Winkler, *Schein der Normalität*, 697, and generally 694–97.

[84] See Nicholas N. Kozlov and Eric D. Weitz, "Reflections on the Origins of the 'Third Period':

the KPD than a lengthy exposition on the dialectical possibilities of rationalization, which, at any rate, could only be truly realized in communist societies. As the party's illustrated weekly put it in a feature article, "Capitalist rationalization, that means: the labor power of humans is replaced by machines. The unemployed can starve."[85] By linking rationalization and the United States, the KPD played upon nationalist sentiments. In one two-page pamphlet, the party charged "*Rationalization! Americanization of the Economy!*" The results for the population were immiseration: "*American factory and exploitation methods, American profits, but no American wages, only German hunger wages.*"[86]

The Leuna Example

"Zuchthaus Leuna" communists called it—Leuna penitentiary. A centerpiece of the BASF, then, from 1925, I. G. Farben, chemical empire, the Leuna factory provided workers with arduous working conditions and low wages. In the heart of Halle-Merseburg, the firm's harsh regime created a volatile working class among whom the KPD found a solid base of support. But the company and the state were determined to rein in Leuna workers. Leuna management used all the strategies discussed above: it exercised outright repression within the factory, implemented rationalization, and developed company social welfare programs. And it did it all in cooperation with the state. Ultimately, the firm succeeded in driving active labor radicalism from the factory, but not in creating a stable, loyal workforce.

Most basically, Leuna management sought to limit drastically the public sphere within its domain, to impede the flow of ideas, curtail the powers of workers' representatives, and eliminate the heady, unpredictable mass meetings at which working-class demands so often crystallized. The March Action had brought the firm closer to its goal, but even artillery barrages and a white terror failed to bring complete victory. Less than three months after the its conclusion, management complained once again to regional officials. The construction workers union had called a mass meeting during working hours, "which can only be seen as a deliberate provocation." Such actions, management charged, made it extremely difficult to work with the unions, as the government had requested.[87] Officials responded with a letter to the chairman of the union, requesting that he use his influence to prevent the continual occurrence of mass meetings during working hours.[88] Through his aides, the provincial governor then informed Dr.

Bukharin, the Comintern, and the Political Economy of Weimar Germany," *JCH* 24:3 (1989): 387–410.

[85] *AIZ* 10:1, 4–5.

[86] "Aufruf der Leuna-Arbeiter," [undated, presumably 1925 or 1926], SAPMO-BA, ZPA I/3/11/21/137–38.

[87] BASF to Oberregierungsrat Freysing, 6 June 1921, LHSAM C20/Ib/4701/25–27.

[88] Meldestelle OPPS to Vorsitzender des Bauarbeiter-Verbandes Herrn Koch, 9 June 1921, LHSAM C20/Ib/4701/28.

Oster, the director of the Leuna-Werke, that he was in full agreement with the complaint and had contacted the chairman of the union, who "will do what is necessary." Officials went on, in quite deferential fashion, to proclaim their willingness to be of help whenever necessary—but with the proviso that contacts between the firm and the provincial governor's office be kept secret:

> Highly honored Herr Doctor, in case you have any additional desires, I request you to direct them to me. In the next few days you will receive in secret and personally an important resolution of the VKPD, which concerns . . . tactics in the workplace and the political realm. After you have taken notice of them and consulted with your colleagues, I request that you destroy all the communications sent to you personally.[89]

Despite the state's professed willingness to help the firm, Leuna management remained dissatisfied with the level of action and adopted an increasingly hard line against all forms of worker representation. The firm complained that the unions still violated regulations by holding mass meetings during worktime. Along with other chemical companies, Leuna refused to allow the works council even to post notices.[90] In 1924, the firm reminded its managers that works council members who wanted to visit a particular plant unit had to register with the plant director beforehand. Directors were never to negotiate personally with the council members, but were to direct all matters to the Department for Labor Affairs.[91] The chemical industry association even called upon its members to provide no information on the activities of the works councils to the International Association for Labor Protection in Geneva.[92] And in one instance, the company complained bitterly about the fact that the works council chairman had published a call in *Klassenkampf*, the Halle KPD newspaper, for the collection of food to support strikers at the BASF plant in Ludwigshafen. This action, claimed management, constituted a gross violation of the works council law, which mandated that activities of the councils remain limited to the specific workplace. In a communiqué to the workforce, it said it would overlook this incident, but warned that future actions of this sort would lead the company to fire immediately the perpetrator, dissolve the works council, and hold new elections.[93]

BASF clearly desired a return to the prewar situation, the halcyon days when management reigned supreme (so they thought) and did not have to deal with the unions, works councils, and mass meetings—all the myriad forms of workers representation—and the workforce was so cowed that the company could dictate the daily routine in the plant without interference. Yet BASF and Leuna management could not venture to refuse any dealings with the legally recognized forms

[89] Meldestelle OPPS to Herrn Dr. Oster, 9 June 1921, LHSAM C20/Ib/4701/29–30.

[90] Arbeitgeberverband der chemischen Industrie Deutschlands Sektion Vb, Rundschreiben Nr. 1441, 14 June 1923, BLW 1323.

[91] Abteilung für Arbeiterangelegenheiten, Rundschreiben Nr. 255 to all Herrn Betriebsführer, 25 April 1924, BLW 1326.

[92] Arbeitgeberverband der chemischen Industrie Deutschlands Sektion Vb, Innere Abteilung, Rundschreiben Nr. 1123 to all members, 11 July 1922, BLW 1321.

[93] Aktenvermerk, Leuna-Werke, 9 May 1924, BLW 1327.

of representation, the councils and the unions. To do so would risk destroying completely its relations with the state and the SPD.

Certainly, the firm needed the state in its internal war against working-class unrest and communist influence. Only five months after the March Action the firm called in the police to search workers' barracks, where they found weapons, munitions, hand grenades, and fuses, as well as leaflets and articles with "provocative contents." Needless to say, the police seized all this material.[94] Nearly three years later, at a meeting of Reich ministers in March 1924, reports conveyed from the Leuna director of incidences of sabotage at the plant led the Prussian Minister of the Interior to dispatch immediately a unit of the Schupo, ban the distribution of leaflets (based on the Prussian press law of 1851), strengthen the police supervision of train stations and trains, deploy criminal police in the plant, and place the Technical Emergency Squads on alert. The last two actions were rescinded when management argued that the squads would be unable to run the plant and the presence of criminal police might incite the workers.[95] The cooperation forged in the March Action stood the firm in good stead in subsequent years.

The firm directed many of its repressive actions squarely at the KPD. When the party cell at Leuna managed in 1924 to publish its newspaper, *Der Leuna-Prolet*, management responded by quickly informing local authorities. In case he had forgotten, Leuna management reminded the Halle prosecutor that communists were seeking to recapture the position lost in March 1921, when Leuna was the center from which a reign of terror spread throughout central Germany. The publication of the paper was therefore more than just the firm's concern, but related to the general societal need for calm and order. Even the security of Germany's food supply rested on the undisturbed functioning of the Leuna plant, management argued. *Der Leuna-Prolet* called for sabotage of production and for "workers to launch the attack." Acts of sabotage had indeed resulted, the firm claimed. Well informed as usual, company directors provided the prosecutor with names of people involved in the production and distribution of *Der Leuna-Prolet* and of *Klassenkampf*.[96] By August 1924, the firm triumphantly announced that it had fully interdicted the distribution of *Der Leuna-Prolet*. Significantly, this was accomplished "in the closest cooperation and collaboration with the police officials of the surrounding cities."[97]

Following the March Action the workforce had endured seven purges designed to exclude communists and other radicals from the company's employment, yet the KPD had still managed to retain a presence in the factory.[98] In the more

[94] MdI to Preussichen Ministerpräsidenten und Staatsminister, 19 August 1921, GStAKM 1120/BB/VI/193/75.

[95] "Bericht über die Sitzung in Reichsministerium für Ernährung und Landwirtschaft," 24 March 1924, BAP RMdI 13398/230–31.

[96] [Leuna-Werke] to Herrn Ersten Amtsanwalt, Amtsgericht Halle, 24 December 1924, BLW 1327.

[97] "Jahresbericht der Werksaufsicht für das Jahr 1924," BLW 1326.

[98] Leuna-Zelle, "Über das Leune-Werk und seine Kommunistische Betriebszelle," [undated, presumably 1925 or 1926], SAPMO-BA, ZPA I/3/11/13/345.

conservative conjuncture of stabilization, however, the firm made a determined effort to complete the task. Lest anyone had doubts, management reminded all unit directors that the labor code of the firm made clear that "the distribution of printed materials during worktime and inside the factory, as well as any political or other activity which is not related to the work, is forbidden."[99] The police searched houses and apartments and seized copies of the communist papers. Even the appearance of a byline in *Klassenkampf* or possession of *Der Leuna-Prolet* could be cause for dismissal or arbitrary reassignment to a less desirable job.[100] By 1925, the KPD could only get the paper distributed at the train stations of surrounding towns during the shift changes and with the help of "constantly changing individuals, for the most part unemployed," who were relatively immune from the long arm of the firm's security force.[101]

Not only communists were subject to the harsh disciplinary regime of the Leuna works. The measures of control extended far beyond the circles of explicit radicals to encompass the entire workforce. Management issued order after order detailing the passes workers were required to carry, the system for assigning identification numbers to workers, and other methods of tracking, and thereby controlling, the workforce.[102] Fines, widely hated by workers in the imperial period, were levied for all sorts of infractions: fifty pfenning for twice arriving at work late, one mark for improper use of the centrifuge, fifty pfenning for false identity cards, fifty pfenning for washing hands before the end of the shift.[103]

Most importantly, the KPD's defeat in the March Action enabled the firm to expand its internal security forces, which, as we have seen, operated closely with the municipal and state police. With petty thievery still rampant, especially in the crisis year 1923, the firm tightened up controls at the factory gates, where guards were empowered to conduct arbitrary searches. In 1923, an average of 5,298 workers and 236 white-collar employees *per month* were investigated for thefts, and many were caught with "appropriated"—as communists termed it—goods.[104] All sorts of items were stolen—ammonium, soda, oil, metals, handtools, clothes, glass, paper, coal, among others. Items were hidden in socks, underwear, between the legs, around the neck, in specially sewn pockets, under the

[99] Direktion to Betriebsführer, Rundschreiben No. 22/1925, 12 May 1925, BLW 1330.

[100] For examples, see Aktenvermerk Leuna-Werke, 7 November 1924, BLW 1327; Ammoniakwerk Merseburg to the Arbeitgeberverband der chemischen Industrie Sektion Vb, Innere Abteilung, 14 July 1924, BLW 1327; "Jahresbericht der Werksaufsicht für das Jahr 1924," BLW 1326; "Jahresbericht der Werksaufsicht für das Jahr 1925," BLW 1330/14–15; "Jahresbericht der Werksaufsicht für das Jahr 1927," BLW 1335/17–18; "Jahresbericht der Werksaufsicht für das Jahr 1928," BLW 1337/21–22. KPD documents also make clear that the repressive policies of Leuna management were quite successful. For some examples, see "Aus dem Jahresbericht der Kommunistischen Partei Bezirk Halle-Merseburg vom 1. April 24 bis 31. März 1925," SAPMO-BA, ZPA I/3/11/13/269–70, and "Über das Leune-Werk und seine Kommunistische Betriebszelle," [undated, presumably 1925 or 1926], SAPMO-BA, ZPA I/3/11/13/343–49.

[101] "Jahresbericht der Werksaufsicht für das Jahr 1925," BLW 1330/14–15.

[102] See some of the Rundschreiben from the Direktion to all Betriebsführer, BLW 1326.

[103] Lohnbüro [Jahresbericht 1926], BLW 1332.

[104] Ammoniakwerk Merseburg 1923 [Jahresbericht der Firma], BLW 1323/60.

hat, in bicycle packs, in postal and soda packages, and in corned beef cans—all of which indicates that body searches were quite thorough. "On the basis of previous experience, wood sacks, coaches, and locomotives must be controlled especially thoroughly," management wrote and reported that the cooperation with the judiciary was quite good. In 1923, 141 persons were charged with theft, of whom the vast majority were condemned to fines or prison sentences or both.[105]

By 1924, the firm's security force triumphantly reported that strengthened security measures, notably at the firm gates, had cut the number of thefts in half; by 1926 they were only one-quarter of the 1923 level. Indeed, in 1924 a total of 108,400 cases of individual searches were carried out at the plant gates.[106] Strengthened control meant also increased training for the security personnel, who went through 264 hours of instruction and seven control discussions, and some were instructed in "suitable police grips (Juijitsu)."[107] Sometime in the intervening year, the security forces were also outfitted with guard dogs, who were used especially on patrol in housing colonies.[108] Along with the regular, uniformed guards, Leuna paid informers who attended meetings of the unions and labor parties and kept the company well informed about the activities of its adversaries. In 1927, management received reports on eighty such meetings and conversations.[109]

In 1925, the firm reported 4,359 violations of factory rules. In typical bureaucratic form, the firm carefully recorded the type and incidence of the violations. These included, along with theft, drunkenness, lateness, entering the factory with a rucksack, entering the factory too early, reading or sleeping on the job (eighty-six cases), leaving the window open or lights burning over night (1,512 cases), riding with a bicycle lamp lit (two cases), riding on handtrucks, pretending to work, carrying weapons, and carrying false identification papers. Clearly, the firm watched its workers carefully.[110]

Direct repression was only one weapon in the company's arsenal. The chemical industry, on the cutting edge of technological developments, played a key role in the rationalization drive. Following the formation of I. G. Farben in 1925, the Leuna works and other facilities in central Germany became increasingly important to the chemical trust.[111] Leuna began to manufacture synthetic gasoline as well as nitrogen. Mostly an unprofitable exercise, the firm required ever increasing subsidies from the state, which considered the process essential to Germany's national security since it would lessen the nation's dependence on imported oil and gasoline.

The continual expansion of the factory spared Leuna employees the mass un-

[105] Ibid., 60–61.

[106] "Jahresbericht der Werksaufsicht für das Jahr 1924," BLW 1326/9–10; "Jahresbericht der Werksaufsicht für das Jahr 1926," BLW 1332/11.

[107] "Jahresbericht der Werksaufsicht für das Jahr 1924," BLW 1326/12.

[108] "Jahresbericht der Werksaufsicht für das Jahr 1925," BLW 1330/4.

[109] "Jahresbericht der Werksaufsicht für das Jahr 1927," BLW 1335/16.

[110] "Jahresbericht der Werksaufsicht für das Jahr 1925," BLW 1330/8–9.

[111] See especially Helmuth Tammen, *Die I. G. Farbenindustrie Aktiengesellschaft (1925–1933): Ein Chemiekonzern un der Weimarer Republik* (Berlin: Verlag Helmuth Tammen, 1978).

employment that workers in many other industries experienced, at least until the Depression. But the high capitalization costs and low profit margins of the synthetic fuels program made the firm ever more intent to slash labor costs through rationalized production processes. The firm continually adopted the most advanced mechanization processes to reduce or limit the number of workers it had to hire. The system of passes and identification numbers and new methods of keeping wage records were all part of a stricter supervision of labor designed to raise worker productivity.[112] Premium and piecework pay systems became increasingly important after 1923. Even the laundry facilities were affected. The firm installed larger and more mechanized equipment, including a steam iron with high-pressure steam, and placed the entire workforce on a piecework system. By 1927, a completely rebuilt laundry with modern machinery and "a rational division of labor" resulted in much higher productivity.[113] In the midst of the Depression, the workforce was slashed to one-third its 1928 level, wages were cut, and premiums and piecework rates reduced.[114] At the same time, the firm extracted more labor out of each worker, a result not only of the Depression but of more intensive labor processes. According to company figures, between 1928 and 1933, production per worker increased by more than one-third; according to KPD sources, the figure approached two-thirds. In the generator section of the plant, eight men had to accomplish what twenty-four had done previously.[115]

Finally, Leuna management also used social welfare in the effort to control a workforce renowned for its indiscipline and inclination toward radicalism. Like many other companies, Leuna built housing for its workers. In the crush of construction begun in 1916, typical company housing at Leuna consisted of long barracks that housed single male workers, hardly the model of positive social welfare. These became notorious as hothouses of radicalism, and following the March Action most of them were razed.[116] Beginning in the mid-1920s, the company began to build more substantive housing. Typically, the housing colonies had schools, gymnasiums, stores, hospitals, bakeries, laundry facilities, and garden plots, and at least one had a swimming pool. Leuna also bought up and renovated existing housing stock in surrounding towns and cities. In the Thuringian woods it arranged for rest and vacation visits for its employees.

Leuna also granted paid vacations to workers, which increased with years of service. From the age of twenty, one and two years of service earned workers four vacation days a year, three years of service five days, and upward to ten years of service twelve days. If a worker left the firm of his own volition, he had

[112] See the collection of memos and directives in BLW 1330.

[113] "Angestellte- und Arbeiter-Angelegenheiten" [Jahresbericht 1924], BLW 1326/5; "Jahresbericht der Wirtschaftsbetriebe für das Jahr 1926," BLW 1332/17; "Jahresbericht der Wirtschaftsbetriebe [1927]," BLW 1335/20.

[114] *Kämpfendes Leuna (1916–1945): Die Geschichte des Kampfes der Leuna-Arbeiter*, Teil 1: 1. Halbband, ed. Kreisleitung der SED VEB Leuna-Werke "Walter Ulbricht" (Berlin: Tribüne, 1961), 485–97.

[115] Ibid., 480, 490.

[116] See Meldestelle OPPS to Pressedienst des Preussischen Staatsministeriums, 6 July 1921, LHSAM C20/Ib/4701/7.

no claims upon his vacation days.[117] Similarly, premiums were paid to workers at the end of each year according to length of service.

Periodically, the firm bought up large quantities of food stocks that it distributed free or at cost to its workers—a practice initiated by many firms in World War I and continued out of necessity during the intermittently desperate crises of the postwar decade.[118] The firm also had a soda water factory and put great store by its distribution of free coffee. In a paean to pedanticism, the company's yearly reports delineate the number of liters of coffee made each year, and the recipe.[119] Even the number of cups of coffee distributed was subject to control—presumably to prevent double-dippers—indicating that social welfare and social discipline were always intertwined. In the gleeful tones of the yearly report, managers reported in 1928 a savings over the pervious year of 1,449,104 liters of coffee worth RM 15,650.32.[120]

Whether free coffee meant all that much to workers is hard to determine. In any case, the documentary record of Leuna's social welfare program demonstrates rather haphazard, frenetic, and, ultimately, grossly insufficient efforts. Its housing stock was quite limited given the size of the workforce and populated disproportionately by scientists, technicians, other white-collar workers, and foremen. Among workers, the *Stammbelegschaft* brought from Ludwigshafen seems to have had privileged access to the better housing owned by the company.[121] Even the vacation and recuperation home in the Thuringian woods seemed geared for foremen and white-collar workers. In 1924, only eleven individuals were able to use it for vacations.[122] And in the Depression, the firm continually slashed its social welfare programs in an effort to maintain profitability.[123]

The 1920s may have been the great debut of modern, scientific management in which firms sought to win the positive loyalty of their employees. But at Leuna, old-fashioned repression proved far more significant than social welfare in containing working-class radicalism and communist influence.

Conclusion

The profound social and political conflicts of the Weimar Republic tested the coalition of order at many junctures. But the coalition remained intact until the summer of 1932 when Reich Chancellor Franz von Papen destroyed the SPD-led

[117] Rundschreiben Nr. 1/25, 2 January 1925, BLW 1330.

[118] Bekanntmachung des Betriebsrates, 25 October 1923, BLW 1324; Rundschreiben No. 214 and 224, Abteilung für Arbeiterangelegenheiten, 6 and 19 December 1923, BLW 1323.

[119] As in "Angestellten- und Arbeiter-Angelegenheiten [Jahresbericht 1924]," BLW 1326.

[120] "Jahresbericht der Wirtschaftsbetriebe," 14 March 1928, BLW 1335/6.

[121] These observations are based on the reports of the Abteilung für Arbeiterangelegenheiten and of the Wirtschaftsbetriebe contained in the firm's yearly reports for 1922, BLW 1321; 1923, BLW 1323; 1924, BLW 1326; 1925, BLW 1330; 1926, BLW 1332; and 1927, BLW 1335. The expansion of the firm in the latter part of the 1920s maintained the pressure on the existing housing stock.

[122] Wirtschaftsbetriebe, Angestellten- und Arbeiter-Angelegenheiten, [Jahresbericht 1924], BLW 1326/8–9.

[123] *Kämpfendes Leuna*, 491–92.

Prussian state government. As Heinrich August Winkler writes, "With a grain of salt one can speak of a basic 'deflation consensus' [between the SPD and the bourgeois parties in the Depression]—comparable to the 'inflation consensus' of the years 1919 to 1921 and to the 'rationalization consensus' of the mid-twenties."[124]

A number of salient points need to be made about the nature of this consensus, or the coalition of order, as I have termed it here. Each element in the strategy of containment entailed the expansion of central state power and, consequently, of distanced and bureaucratized forms of representation. Security measures in particular rested on close coordination between private employers and the state. In the most blatant instances, the state simply marshaled its weapons of coercion and closed down the possibilities of representation and working-class protest. Indeed, the industrial areas of the country experienced one state of emergency after another in the first years of the Republic. The state eliminated the workers and soldiers councils of the revolutionary period and sharply delimited the scope of powers of the legally constituted works councils. As at Leuna, the state joined with employers in challenging the right of workers to call mass meetings during the workday, thereby confirming management's power to regulate and control time over workers' efforts to reclaim part of the workday for their own concerns. And the state supported industry's drive for rationalization. An ideology and a program of economic and social reform, rationalization enabled management to exercise greater control over the labor force. For workers, it led to the fear and reality of unemployment and an intensified pace of work.

In place of the active—and chaotic—forms of representation workers invented in the Revolution and the early years of the Weimar Republic, the state sought to "rationalize" existing social relations through corporatist-style interest group representation and social welfare programs. The state sought to create legally established and socially acceptable channels within which class conflict could be contained and model, "orderly" families that would serve as the substratum of social order. The more radical and utopian vision embedded in the councils and in some feminist efforts fell by the wayside.

The strategy of reconstituting authority bore, therefore, strong continuities with managerial and state strategies in the imperial period, though the policies became far more systematic and widespread in Weimar. In both regimes, elites displayed an almost instinctual reliance on the tools of central state power to contain civil society, a process central to the entire experience of German history in the modern era.

The corporatist-welfare strategy reaffirmed, indeed, strengthened, both the class and gender divisions of German society because it made industrial workers and patriarchal families the objects of state policy—despite the incorporation of social democratic workers into the Weimar state, the extension of suffrage to women, and the active female involvement in the local state in the Weimar Republic. Moreover, the strategy of containment made the sphere of production the

[124] Winkler, *Schein der Normalität*, 818. The observation is approvingly quoted by Gerald D. Feldman, "The Weimar Republic: A Problem of Modernization?" *AfS* 26 (1986): 14.

crucial locus of interest group representation, while that of reproduction the object of state intervention—a program actively promoted by social democrats and trade unionists. No mechanisms were established for the representation of consumers or homemakers within the welfare state, and it was the rare industry, such as textiles, in which because of their sheer numbers women achieved a kind of independent representation.[125] As applied to the household, rationalization was seen as a way of making women's labors less burdensome. To the extent that it defined anew the household as women's sphere, this kind of rationalization was also a part of the effort to reconstitute order through the reaffirmation of existing gender relations. Moreover, the manifestations of women's protests—in strikes, but also in food riots and community-based activism—indicated the existence of a different public sphere, one less amenable to welfare state intervention than the workplace arena of strikes and works councils.

The strategies forged by the coalition of order never fulfilled the expectations of the members. State-mandated welfare inspired such hostility among employers that they ultimately renounced any kind of support for the Weimar Republic. Christian welfare advocates fought the SPD's drive to establish a state monopoly on *Sozialpolitik*. Social democrats and liberal reformers saw their hopes for a progressive social order dashed by the Depression and the rise of the Nazis. Social welfare never managed to create the fully rationalized beings that reformers anticipated.

Nonetheless, the coalition proved immensely successful in containing working-class radicalism. Its strategies, and especially those of repression, eliminated any prospects for a successful second revolution following the liberal republican one of 1918–20, or even for a radical reshaping of the Republic in line with the demands of the socialization strikes of 1919. Instead of revolution, the Weimar Republic found itself burdened with endemic social and political conflict that drained both supporters and opponents.

The mere existence of the KPD and of widespread popular protest and indiscipline served, then, to generate the expansion of state power in the Weimar Republic and the political coalition of order that underpinned it. At the same time, the efforts of the state and employers to reconstruct order decisively shaped the nature of German communism. Social welfare, whether practiced by the state or employers, fragmented the Weimar working class. Some workers benefited greatly from housing and public health measures and the intervention of state authorities in wage disputes. Social welfare, in short, proved capable of binding some workers to the firm or the state. But on every level social welfare proved grossly incapable of mastering the material and political crises of the Weimar era. Because of their insufficiencies, social welfare generated widespread popular discontent that redounded, in part, to the benefit of the KPD.[126] In many cities and towns, social democrats constituted a large proportion of the welfare officials with whom people

[125] See Kathleen Canning, "Gender and the Politics of Class Formation: Rethinking German Labor History," *AHR* 97:3 (June 1992): 736–68, and "Class, Gender, and Working-Class Politics: The Case of the German Textile Industry, 1890–1933" (Ph.D. diss., Johns Hopkins University, 1988).

[126] See Crew, "Social Republic."

came into immediate contact, which only provided greater sustenance for the deep-seated hostility between the SPD and KPD.[127] The appearance of heavily armed police and soldiers firing on strikers or demonstrators, often under the orders of social democratic officials, made unbridgeable the chasm between social democracy and communism.

Perhaps even more significantly, the strategy of order resulted in the spatial transformation of labor and communist politics. After 1923 the KPD never again attempted an armed uprising. By the late 1920s, the KPD had also been driven from the workplace. The drastic decline in demand for labor that accompanied rationalization enabled employers, with the support of the unions and the state, to fire communists and other radicals, a process only accentuated by the employment crisis of the Great Depression. By foreclosing the possibility of armed revolution and making workplace organizing nearly impossible, the policies executed by the coalition of order drove the KPD into the streets and into increasing reliance on the radical propensities of the unemployed. In a situation most ironic for a party whose entire meaning rested on the idealization of the proletariat and whose organizational structure supposedly rested on workplace cells, the KPD essentially lost its base in the factories and mines after 1923.

Instead, the streets came to serve as the KPD's primary space of political mobilization, as we shall see in greater detail in the next two chapters. There it cultivated a combative, voluntaristic politics that the party joined to a political vision based on the dictatorship of the proletariat. Ironically, the KPD re-created the German tradition of a powerful central state and long-standing working-class political practices centered around the ameliorative possibilities of state action. While Moscow set overall party direction, communist strategy was molded as it was played out on German soil.

[127] Crew, "Bedürfnisse und Bedürftigkeit," 13, notes that two-thirds of the volunteer staff in the Hamburg welfare office were members of the SPD's welfare commission.

CHAPTER 4

Contesting Order: Communists in the Workplace

> Mit ihrer wuchtigsten Waffe, die Arbeitsverweigerung, muß die Arbeiterschaft die Pläne der Reaktion durchkreuzen und die . . . Unterdrückung des Volkes verhindern.
>
> —*KPD leaflet*[1]

"THIS LAZINESS has finally got to stop!" shouted the director of a factory in Eilenburg (Prussian Saxony) when he walked on to the shop floor one July morning in 1921 and saw scores of workers milling about. The craftworkers at whom he yelled were incensed, deeply insulted that the director had called them "lazy," and demanded that he retract his words. The director refused; the workers then demanded their papers, which were more than willingly handed out. As they saw their colleagues about to leave the workplace in search of other positions, the remaining workers demanded their rehiring and, again, that the director retract his words. Once more, the director refused, so the entire workforce went out on strike. The director then promptly fired all of the strikers. Negotiations ensued with the unions and the works council. The workers who had demanded their papers remained fired, as well as two works councillors, who "failed to exercise their responsibility." The other workers were rehired. The documents do not reveal whether the director ever retracted his words.[2]

At a luxury auto firm in Diemitz (also in Prussian Saxony), two workers were fired for refusing to perform certain tasks. To force their rehiring, the rest of the workforce engaged in passive resistance. The union, the works council, management—all sought to convince the workers to return to their jobs. The workers refused, even challenged the right of the works council to represent them. Escalating the conflict, management demanded that workers accept the introduction of piecework within six weeks time. The workers completely refused. Management then locked out the entire workforce, about seven hundred people. The works council and state mediators sought to resolve the issue but without success. Management demanded that the workers accept the revised

[1] "With its most powerful weapon, the refusal to work, the working class must thwart the plans of the reactionaries and prevent the . . . suppression of the people." "Aufruf!" Streikleitung Halle, 15 March 1920, in *Dokumente und Materialien zur Geschichte der Arbeiterbewegung im Bezirk Halle*, vol. 1: *1917–1923*, ed. Eberhard Schultz, Bezirkskommission zur Erforschung der Geschichte der Arbeiterbewegung im Bezirk Halle (Salle) bei der Bezirksleitung Halle der SED (Halle: Druckerei Freiheit, 1965), 84–85.

[2] Report on ending of a strike in Kreis Delitzsch, probably to Meldestelle OPPS, 7 July 1921, LHSAM C20/Ib/4699/2.

wage structure before it would reopen the plant. The strike and lockout lasted nearly three weeks and ended in defeat for the workers, who had to accept the introduction of piecework. A mediation board was given the task of deciding whether workers would be paid for the days of the lockout and strike.[3]

In these two incidents and countless others played out in the routines of daily life in the Weimar Republic, workers directly contested management's attempts to establish exclusive control over the conditions of labor and state and managerial efforts to reestablish order in society. These were inherently political actions because they revolved centrally around power in the workplace.[4] The contestation for power occurred in innumerable small-scale activities, like job-shirking and blue Mondays; in countless strikes, many of short duration; and in the large-scale, mass protests like the socialization strikes of 1919 and the Ruhr metalworkers' struggle of 1928, all of which demonstrated that the strategies pursued by the coalition of order were never completely successful. Workers drew on practices that reached back to the nineteenth century, but in the supercharged setting of the Weimar Republic, workplace-based protests became more frequent and intense and the demands far more embracing. They also involved all kinds of workers, from the "classic" proletarians of the heavily masculine coal and steel industries to theater staffs and artisans.

Strikes and other shop-floor battles constituted a vital part of the raw material out of which the KPD manufactured its rhetorical and organizational program. These activities provided the substratum of popular protest that the KPD sought continually to elevate and transform into a more clearly defined ideological and political struggle against the capitalist economy and republican polity of Weimar Germany. At the same time, the KPD sought to bring popular protest within the confines of the party's own ideology, strategy, and organization, an enterprise that proved far less successful, particularly in the second half of the Weimar Republic. Many workers were unwilling to allow their actions to be politicized along communist lines, which lent a certain tenor of frustration and anger to the political culture of the KPD. Moreover, the panoply of weapons deployed by the coalition of order turned the workplace into a nearly impenetrable space for the party. And the KPD's own often misguided strategies further accentuated the political and social fragmentation of the working class and the party's ultimate isolation from the factories and mines of Weimar Germany. From a movement inextricably rooted in the workplace-based protests of labor, the KPD became a party of the unemployed working class, as we shall see in this chapter.

[3] PVH to RPM, 23 December 1920 and 7 January 1921, LHSAM C20/Ib/4648/5I/21, 26.

[4] The thrust of a good deal of labor and social history of the last generation has been to expand the concept of politics, and I am writing in that context. See Geoff Eley, "Is All the World a Text? From Social History to the History of Society Two Decades Later," in *The Historical Turn in the Human Sciences*, ed. Terrence McDonald (Ann Arbor: University of Michigan Press, forthcoming); idem, "Wie denken wir über die Politik? Alltagsgeschichte und die Kategorie des Politischen," in *Alltagskultur, Subjektivität und Geschichte: Zur Theorie und Praxis von Alltagsgeschichte*, ed. Berliner Geschichtswerkstatt (Münster: Westfälisches Dampfboot, 1994), 17–36; and Alf Lüdtke, *Eigen-Sinn: Fabrikalltag, Arbeitererfahrungen und Politik vom Kaiserreich bis in den Faschismus* (Hamburg: Ergebnisse, 1993).

Popular Protest in the Workplace

Strikes were the most pronounced form of working-class protest. The number of strikes reached a high point in 1919, remained at a very high level through 1925, declined in association with stabilization, revived somewhat in 1928, and then declined again in the wake of the mass unemployment of the Great Depression.[5] In strikes, workers deployed the resources available to them—their own labor power and the physical space of the factory or mine. They withheld their knowledge, skills, and physical exertions, and claimed control over the workplace through picket lines and proto-sit-ins. Even more than in the prewar period, strikes easily shaded into other forms of popular protest like demonstrations. When workers moved out of the factory or mine to march on city hall, the district governor's office, or the owner's residence, they laid claim to the entire space of the urban environment, not just the workplace.

Strikes acted like contagions, jumping from one area and one group of workers to another—a phenomenon that gave the authorities no end of worry and communists no end of hope and joy. The authorities watched with special closeness the regions of concentrated working-class populations, like the Ruhr and Halle-Merseburg, well aware that an uprising in one could immediately spread to the other. Communist leaders acted likewise, and their movements back and forth between the regions were carefully tracked.[6] In the middle of the hyperinflation of 1923, a series of wildcat strikes plagued the Leuna plant. Reprising the pattern of the wartime labor battles, construction workers at the factory demonstrated in front of the administration building for an advance, just as factory workers had gotten the day before, and for the full payment of their wages—their construction firm had run out of money, so BASF had to cover the shortfall. Two hours later, one thousand factory workers, mostly "radical young people," took up a demonstration at the same site, and demanded that the advance become a regular supplement to their wages; that mass meetings be held during worktime after each wage negotiation; and that the Cuno government be replaced by a "workers' and peasants' government." A few days later, workers in the main production unit demanded supplementary pay—ten million marks per person—and the demand then spread to workers at the power and gas units of the firm. The firm agreed, but had trouble disbursing the sums because it lacked the paper currency and had to print script instead, and because the employees in the wage office were themselves participating in a demonstration and unavailable to distribute the funds.[7]

[5] See the statistics in Dietmar Petzina, Werner Abelshauser, and Anselm Faust, *Sozialgeschichtliches Arbeitsbuch*, vol. 3: *Materialien zur Statistik des Deutschen Reiches 1914–1945* (Munich: Beck, 1978), 114.

[6] Lagebericht RKÜöO, 15 June 1921, BAP RAM 2817/297–335.

[7] See the various documents in BLW 1324: Aktenvermerk [undated and untitled]; Aktenvermerk, 11 August 1923; Betriebsrat und Belegschaft des Ammoniakwerkes, 13 August 1923; Aktenvermerk, 13 August 1923; Schiedsspruch des Schlichtungsausschußes Halle, 17 August 1923; Ammoniakwerk Merseburg to Kriegsarbeitsamt Merseburg, 22 August 1923; and "Ammoniakwerk Merseburg 1923," [Jahresbericht der Firma], BLW 1323/8–9.

And Leuna was not the only plant affected. Police reports from Prussian Saxony depict units dashing from town to town, neighborhood to neighborhood, in a somewhat frenetic effort to quell disturbances.[8] As was so often the case, miners in Prussian Saxony began a strike wave in August 1923, which then spread to almost all of Halle's labor force with the exception of postal and rail workers.[9] At times, it must have seemed that everyone who worked for a living had been bitten by the strike bug. Among those on strike at various times in the early 1920s were the choir at the local theater in Magdeburg, 160 cabinet makers in 16 shops (an average of 10 workers per shop), 10 stonemasons at one firm in Halle, 350 workers in 20 woodworking shops, and 21 paperhangers and painters at 4 firms.[10] Clearly, in the Weimar period not only the "classic" proletarians, miners and metalworkers, went out on strike.

For the KPD, every kind of strike meant an opportunity to elevate the level of conflict. Workers' vibrant protests, especially in the first phase of the Republic, seemed to confirm a party strategy built around the constant escalation of the struggle. No matter how few the number of workers, how isolated the particular industry, a strike served as a harbinger of more vital conflicts to come. However limited the goals, a strike provided a vital opening for party propaganda and organization.

The coercive element of strikes—often overlooked in labor histories—became more pronounced in the Weimar Republic, reflecting the general brutalization of public life as a result of World War I and the more intense nature of political conflict.[11] The authorities were prone to exaggerate the extent of pressure on nonstrikers and spoke continually of the "terror" practiced against those willing to work. But such instances were not infrequent and were embedded in the very nature of strikes. Especially in the winter of 1918/19, the spectacles of a foremen thrown down a mine shaft or placed in a wheelbarrow and rolled out of a factory onto a garbage dump constituted essential elements of strike actions. Younger workers brandished revolvers or clubs and forced recalcitrant individuals to join in a strike, or at least to stay home. Especially in mining communities, women took to the picket line and harassed police officers and strikebreakers. Reporting afterwards on the socialization strikes, the Essen police president described incidents at mines in which workers sabotaged the boiler rooms and threatened supervisors with revolvers and forcefully threw them into their homes. Some strikers went on to search the home of the director of the Mathias Stinnes mine, whom they hoped to capture. At the Krupp mine Helene und Amalie, armed

[8] Police reports, 13 and 14 August 1923, LHSAM C20/Ib/4647/49–53.

[9] BLHM, "Situationsbericht des Bezirks 11 Halle-Merseburg," 11 August 1923, SAPMO-BA, ZPA I/3/11/18/175–78, and OBH to RAM, 23 August 1923, BAP RAM 83/152–56.

[10] RP Magdeburg to MHG, 19 December 1919, GStAKM 120/BB/VII/1/3/30/21; PVH to RPM, LHSAM C20/Ib/4648/5I/125; strike reports, PPH to OPM, LHSAM C20/Ib/4699/5/191, 253, 254.

[11] Notable is Hans Mommsen's observation that force and terror were rare in the Revolution and that terror and the masculine cult of violence were promulgated by the counterrevolution. He probably underestimates the elements of coercion in the Revolution and the rapid development of a cult of violence on the left. See *Die verspielte Freiheit: Der Weg der Republik von Weimar in den Untergang 1918 bis 1933* (Frankfurt am Main: Propyläen, 1990), 62.

strikers forced other workers out of the mine shafts, which then led to armed conflict between strikers and the municipal guard.[12]

The violent nature of some strikes intersected with the KPD's own emphasis on revolution as armed confrontation and its masculinist ethos. Working-class activists, communists in particular, paraded their "roughness" as a badge of pride, a quality that marked them off from other social classes and political groups. The line between forcing workers out of the shop or mine, sabotaging plant equipment, roughing up hated supervisors, fighting the police or company guards, between all of that and armed revolution, inevitably became indistinct. Bernard Koenen, KPD leader at Leuna and in the Halle-Merseburg district, made clear the communist position on compulsion in his appearance before the Prussian Landtag committee that investigated the March Action:

> There has been a hue and cry about the treatment of people who were not particularly liked by the workforce because they did not want to go in the same economic or political direction with [the workers]. I must say that the behavior of workers in this matter has not been any different than what we organized workers engaged in before the war. In those factories in which the majority of workers are organized, we have claimed the right to exercise a certain compulsion over the others in order to bring them into our organization.[13]

With little subtlety, Koenen indicated that indeed a great deal of pressure had been exerted upon nonconformist workers. Leuna officials agreed—they complained that workers with other political views, and especially some who had been members of the various local security units such as the Sicherheitswehr or Einwohnerwehr, were pressured and terrorized.[14]

Sabotage, virtually unheard of before 1914, also occurred in the postwar period. Its extent is difficult to gauge, and employers were certainly prone to exaggerate its incidence and to label virtually any agitation for a strike as sabotage.[15] Nonetheless, there were instances in which workers during strikes refused to perform the maintenance work needed to ensure the continued operation of the workplace, leading in some instances to the flooding of mines and the destruction of high-temperature ovens in various branches of the metals industry. These actions expressed the rage felt by some workers, though the organized labor movement, communist and socialist, generally opposed such desperate tactics.

Yet select communists also underwent military training with explosives and

[12] These examples are from PPE to RPD, 17 October 1919, HStAD 15976.

[13] Preussischer Landtag, "Die wörtliche Berichte und die Sitzungen des Untersuchungsausschußes zur Feststellung der Ursachen, des Umfangen und der Wirkungen des kommunistischen Aufstandes in Mitteldeutschland in März 1921" (hereafter LT Proceedings), in GStAKM 169/DIX/D3/4/2/650, 16 September 1921.

[14] BASF to SKÜöO, 24 May 1921, LHSAM C20/Ib/4701/4–5.

[15] For example, "Bericht über die Sitzung in Reichsministerium für Ernährung und Landwirt," 24 March 1924, BAP RMdI 13398/230–31, in which Leuna officials complained, once again, that sabotage was on the rise in the plant and strikes threatened to break out. Quick to respond, the Prussian Minister of the Interior deployed the Schupo and the Technical Emergency Squads and banned the distribution of leaflets.

were not adverse to the extreme measures that some workers practiced.[16] At a strike at Leuna in the summer of 1920, seven ovens were apparently damaged because workers did not perform the maintenance tasks, and four to five months of repair work were required.[17] Koenen maintained that workers at Leuna performed essential maintenance work during the March Action strikes, but he also admitted that strike leaders at first had difficulty finding workers who would agree to undertake the tasks.[18] During the August 1923 strikes in central Germany, workers at a metalworking factory completely abandoned the plant, ruining the entire aluminum unit. Three months of repair work was required until the plant could become operational.[19] During the 1924 Ruhr miners strike, miners and their wives actively attempted to interfere with maintenance work. At two mines, Carolus Magnus and Mathias Stinnes, the miners actually voted to prevent, with force if necessary, emergency maintenance work. At Mathias Stinnes, the workers never really made an effort to implement their decision, but at Carolus Magnus and a few other mines the police had to intervene to protect maintenance workers from pickets.[20]

Workers in the 1920s struck over a wide variety of issues relating to power in the workplace, including the personnel of the labor force and of management, the scope of labor representation, the work schedule, and plant security. At one mine in the Halle district, workers walked out because the company hired the son of a pastor, whom the miners believed to be a police spy.[21] Often, workers demanded the removal of particularly hated foremen. At mines outside of Zeitz, workers went out on strike to demand the dismissal of a supervisor whom the miners considered negligent in his duties and partly responsible for an accident that killed twenty-four workers. In an impressive display of solidarity, 3,930 workers at seven mines walked out, and were at least partially successful—the supervisor was furloughed until a final determination on the cause of the accident could be made.[22] These actions signified workers' determination to participate in the selection of co-workers and supervisors, a direct attack on managerial prerogatives that communists always supported. Leuna officials complained that wildcat

[16] See, for example, the memoirs of Erich Wollenberg (typescript, HIA), who was active in the KPD's underground military apparatus and received training in the Soviet Union, and Beatrix Herlemann, "Der deutschsprachige Bereich an den Kaderschulen der Kommunistischen Internationale," *IWK* 18:2 (1982): 205–29.

[17] Lagebericht, RKÜöO, 3 August 1920, BAP RAM 2817/60–64.

[18] LT Proceedings, 16 September 1921, 559–60.

[19] BLHM, "Gesamtbericht über den Generalstreik in Mittel-Deutschland," 21 August 1923, SAPMO-BA, ZPA I/3/11/18/204–17.

[20] PVE to OBE, 12 May 1924 (two reports) and 14 May 1924 (two reports), StAE 102/I/1077; PVE to OBE, 13 May 1924, HStAD 16868/12; reports by city officials, 15 and 16 May 1924, StAE 102/I/1077.

[21] [Unititled, undated] LHSAM C20/Ib/4705/14.

[22] [Police reports] Kreis Zeitz to OPPS, 19 and 20 September 1921, LHSAM C20/Ib/4705/28, 29. In this instance, at least, the police were a bit more level-headed than usual, and cautioned the provincial governor against sending in police since negotiations were underway and emergency work was being carried out.

strikes, bad enough on their own, were often accompanied by "unfulfillable demands," such as calls for the removal of various foremen and directors.

Solidarity strikes were widespread, as in the two examples presented at the beginning of this chapter, as were strikes fought to defend workers councils and other forms of self-representation.[23] Especially in the first period of the Republic workers were able to win far-ranging powers for the councils. At Leuna, management was forced to free representatives from work (even prior to the passage of the works council law), and had to negotiate with the works councillors over a wide range of issues. The councillors patrolled the plant and, apparently, supervised the hiring of workers, examined the food served in the cafeterias, investigated accidents, and established a trusted corps of workers attached to the KPD and to the plant. Mass meetings during the workday were a regular event, which aroused the special ire of management, as we saw in the previous chapter.[24]

Finally, workers fought, incessantly, over wages and hours. Even when the crises of stabilization and depression sapped their energies and resources, some workers still managed to muster the ability to strike and thereby stake out claims to participate in decisions about the most basic elements of their working life. In so doing, they provided the KPD with unparalleled opportunities to present itself as the defender of the working class's most immediate interests.

Strikes were not the only forms through which workers contested managerial power. Workers also appropriated time by commemorating certain events despite management's efforts to maintain the regular work schedule. Many workers in the Ruhr commemorated the murders of Liebknecht and Luxemburg by leaving work early or not reporting for work. During the 1921 commemoration, nine hundred of 1,250 miners at Mathias Stinnes II left the midday shift three hours early to participate in the event; 250 out of one thousand in the night shift did not work at all.[25] At Leuna, where according to the contract three-quarters of the workforce had to vote for May Day as a holiday in order for the firm to close down, only 68 percent voted for a holiday in 1923. Nonetheless, more than one-third of the workforce refused to show up for work anyway, and in some units, including the main production unit, "almost the entire workforce failed to report for work."[26]

Workers also contested management's control of the daily schedule. Strikes for shorter workdays—as few as six and one-half hours in the mines during the winter of 1918/19—were the most obvious form of these claims.[27] In one rare instance, a strike at BASF's AGFA plant in Bitterfeld broke out because workers

[23] For one example of a three-month strike by woodworkers, Abschrift, RPM, 24 December 1919 and Abschrift, Gewerbeinspektor für den Stadtkreis Halle und den Saalkreis, 14 January 1920, GStAKM 120/BB/VII/1/3/30/79–80.

[24] On all these practices, KPD Leuna-Zelle, "Über das Leune-Werk und seine Kommunistische Betriebszelle," [undated, presumably 1925 or 1926], SAPMO-BA, ZPA I/3/11/13/343–44.

[25] PPE to RPD, 13 January 1921, HStAD 15412.

[26] Ammoniakwerk Merseburg to BASF, 14 May 1923, BLW 1324.

[27] See Jochen Henze, *Sechsstundenschicht im Ruhrbergbau 1918–1920: Ursachen und Verlauf eines Arbeitszeitkonflikts* (Freiburg: Burg, 1988).

wanted to work on a religious holiday during which the plant was scheduled to be closed.[28] Economic necessity no doubt played a role here, because "Bußtag" was not a paid holiday. But this strike, however singular its origins, also revolved around the contestation for power—who would decide the work schedule and holiday pay. Moreover, this strike, as so many others, quickly escalated into a major conflict over the nature of workplace representation. When workers showed up at the plant gates, disruptions developed, and the jittery employers quickly called for troops. Government officials declared a state of emergency and had troops occupy the factory and other parts of Bitterfeld. The workers, incensed at the incursion of the military, voted to strike until the government removed the military, lifted the state of emergency, and paid workers for the strike days, an action actively supported by the KPD. BASF then responded with mass firings, and the government, backing BASF, said that work had to be resumed and a few days of calm had to pass before it would withdraw the troops. The district governor had to be called in to get negotiations going, which led to an agreement that those workers fired because of their involvement in acts of violence would remain fired, though those whom the courts did not convict would be rehired. BASF lifted its mass firing order, but refused to pay for the strike days. The works council and the unions agreed that certain "unruly elements" had caused the uproar, which they regretted. But they also strongly condemned the decision to send in the troops, and charged that BASF used the incident to try to depose the works council. Like many others, this strike was largely unsuccessful, but it demonstrated how quickly workers were ready to challenge state and managerial powers and to assert their claims to democratically elected representation and to participation in determining the work schedule.

Workers also asserted their claims to time and property by calling mass meetings during working hours, making blue Mondays a regular practice, and stealing. To be sure, workers had stolen company goods in the Imperial period. Certain groups of workers, like longshoremen and construction workers, were especially renowned for pilfering. But in the early years of the Weimar Republic, petty thievery became endemic, and, as shown in the previous chapter, was viewed by employers and state officials as an immense problem. The Prussian Landtag committee investigating the March Action calculated losses in the millions as a result of thefts from fields, factories, and mines.[29]

[28] The following account is drawn from documents in BAP RAM 2060: Bezirksarbeiterrat Halle to RAM, 29 November 1919, 152; Bezirksrat der chemischen Industrie, der Metallindustrie, des Baugewerbes, des Eisenbahnwesen, Bezirksarbeiterrat Halle und Merseburg, etc., to RAM, 29 November 1919, 153; RPM [to RAM], 9 December 1919, 170; "Vermerk über die Besprechung mit den Vertretern der Bitterfelder Arbeiterschaft," RAM, 27 November 1919, 191–92; RPM [to RAM], 28 November 1919, 157; "Vermerk," RAM [n.d.], 198–99. See also Karl-Heinz Leidigkeit and Jürgen Hermann, *Auf leninistischem Kurs—Geschichte der KPD-Bezirksorganisation Halle-Merseburg bis 1933*, ed. Bezirksleitung Halle der SED, Kommission zur Erforschung der Geschichte der örtlichen Arbeiterbewegung (Halle: Druckhaus "Freiheit," 1979), 95–96.

[29] Preussischer Landtag, "Bericht des Untersuchungsausschußes über den Ursachen, den Umfang und die Wirkungen des kommunistischen Aufstandes in Mitteldeutschland in März 1921" (hereafter LT Report), GStAKM 169/DIX/D/4/2/3–4.

The political significance of petty criminality should not be overestimated, as is often the case in social histories of popular protest. Nonetheless, the line between criminality and political protest is often obscure. In the workplaces, thievery symbolized, if not workers' claim to ownership, at the very least their disregard for the property claims of the owners and managers. Some working-class groups attributed direct political meaning to thievery by seeing it as a form of struggle against capitalism, a position articulated by the KPD splitoff, the KAPD, and some syndicalist groups. The KPD's position on the matter was more ambiguous. Before the Prussian Landtag, Bernard Koenen condemned thievery and the rough treatment of porters that had occurred before the March Action. But Koenen also turned the tables on management by arguing that workers stole because management stole:

> Every worker knew that extensive under-the-table work is done for foremen, white-collar employees, factory managers, and higher officials, that workers were occupied with things that were not at all necessary for production. . . . For these very expensive matters [workers were given] passes [to leave the factory grounds] and this kind of work was seen as a privilege for a part of the workforce. All that created the atmosphere for thievery on a small scale.[30]

Piecework calculations also remained a constant terrain of conflict. Management charged that workers claimed excessive rates or slowed the pace of work. The solution, as with theivery, was more stringent supervision and fines for willful violations.[31] Leuna officials, as we have seen, also complained bitterly in the months before the March Action that workers arbitrarily violated the workshift and called meeting after meeting during worktime.[32] And through horseplay, arbitrary breaks, collusion to slow down the pace of work—through manifold, creative practices—workers sought to carve out some autonomy, however restricted, in the workplace.[33]

Popular protest in the workplace after 1920 continued the process begun in the Revolution of redrawing significantly the boundaries of politics and of representation. Only infrequently did workers articulate clear political positions. Most often their actions were motivated by economic concerns. Moreover, the impact of widespread unemployment already in the mid-1920s and the reassertion of managerial powers succeeded in repressing the most public forms of workplace-based protest. Fears of dismissal and general weariness with political upheavals contributed to the rapid decline in the number and frequency of strikes, a trend that the Depression only accentuated.

Nonetheless, strikes, blue Mondays, mass meetings on the factory floor, and job-shirking challenged directly the hierarchies of domination presided over by

[30] LT Proceedings, 16 September 1921, 640–41.

[31] For example, Abteilung für Arbeiterangelegenheiten Leuna-Werke, Rundschreiben Nr. 29, 4 April 1922, BLW 1321.

[32] BASF to SKÜöO, 24 May 1921, LHSAM C20/Ib/4701/4–5.

[33] On all these practices, see especially Lüdtke, *Eigen-Sinn*.

industrial managers and state bureaucrats, which limited decision making to restricted and powerful elites. These forms of protest and representation signified the expansion of the very definition of politics beyond the "normal" terrain of electoral contests and bureaucratic administration. Through popular protest, workers pushed at the outer limits of political practice and political thinking in Germany. They created a civil society far more activist and participatory, and, consequently, far more turbulent and chaotic, than anything seen in Imperial Germany; they articulated, however unclearly, a politics of working-class participation in the economy and polity. This does not mean that workers were "essentially" radical and that but for the deceitfulness of the SPD they would have all been communists, as in the old DDR interpretations of Weimar. The majority of workers remained committed to the SPD, the Catholic Center, or one of the liberal or conservative parties. But by posing the issue of power, working-class activism provided the popular basis upon which the KPD emerged as a mass-based party.

Communists in the Workplace

Throughout the early 1920s, both police and internal party reports indicate growing support for the KPD in the workplace and the successful construction of communist cells within the unions. In the major industrial regions of the Ruhr and Halle-Merseburg, for example, communists dominated a number of locals of the important mining and metalworkers unions (the so-called Alter Verband and the Deutsche Metallarbeiter-Verband [German Metalworkers Union], or DMV). KPD representation was also quite strong in the legally constituted works councils of both industries. The party had a strong presence also at the worksite and within the unions of construction, transport, carpentry, and even, in some localities, municipal workers. In Halle-Merseburg, one of the KPD's strongest regions, the party controlled most of the DMV locals, and held every seat on the executive board of the carpenters union district organization and nine out of eleven seats on the woodworkers executive board. In DMV elections in July 1923, communist candidates topped the lists in Düsseldorf, Bochum, and Oberhausen, all key Ruhr cities, and Berlin as well.[34] In some working-class districts, the KPD had been scoring impressive electoral victories since 1921.

The KPD found substantial support in other areas too. At Bayer in Ludwigshafen, following a series of defeats in which the firm reimposed piecework and a more stringent factory code (with the acceptance of the unions), the KPD

[34] These examples are drawn from various sources, including "Lagebericht," 4–10 December 1920, LHSAM C20/Ib/4648/51/3; BL KPD Rheinland-Westfalen Nord, "Gewerkschaftlicher Bericht für den Monat Januar," 21 February 1923, SAPMO-BA, ZPA I/3/18–19/55/11; BLHM, "Tätigkeitsbericht des Genossen Schoenlank von Dezember 1921," SAPMO-BA, ZPA I/3/11/13/28–29; BLR, "Gewerkschaftlicher Monatsbericht für die Monate Februar und März," 27 April 1923, SAPMO-BA, ZPA I/3/18–19/55/17–21; *RE*, 23–25 July 1923.

won control of the works council in early 1921. Over the course of 1921, it came to dominate the shop stewards at BASF and in March 1922 decisively won a factory council election on the Free Union list, which was usually dominated by social democrats.[35] In Stuttgart, Solingen, Chemnitz, and a number of smaller cities the KPD dominated the local organizations of the DMV and a few of the miners union in the Saar and Upper Silesia.[36]

Throughout the crisis year of 1923 the reports of the party's regional trade union sections evinced a growing sense of confidence and satisfaction.[37] Even amid the stabilization and rationalization crises of 1924 and 1925 there were, from the party's perspective, glimmers of brightness—solid communist fractions in a number of localities; the movement almost in toto of more radical, separatist mining groups into the regular miners union; good fractions in the DMV in Essen and Oberhausen, slow but steady improvement in Bochum and Duisburg; other solid fractions scattered among the municipal, wood, and construction workers unions, including occasional party control of the local, as in the Dortmund construction workers union.[38] In late 1925 internal KPD documents counted 190 KPD fractions in the 240 locals of the Construction Workers Union (Bauarbeiter Verband, or BAV) in the Ruhr. In about one-third of the 240 the KPD had the majority of members, and in about forty party comrades occupied the leadership positions—though many of these had not been confirmed by the BAV central leadership, which unleashed a storm of protest.[39] Party leaders in the Ruhr in 1926 reported that the KPD's influence in the unions was on the rise, and listed an array of locals of metalworkers, municipal workers, carpenters, and others that the party either controlled or within which exercised a great deal of influence.[40]

In Halle-Merseburg, one of the KPD's most solid areas, the party kept a firm hold on an array of local and regional union organizations despite the high unemployment of its members and political repression. Especially in the construction, metalworking, and chemical industries, intermittently in mining and the shoe industry, the KPD was well anchored in the workplace. In 1925, the KPD district leadership reported to the Central Committee that the party held in hand ninety-eight union locals. The party led all the works councils in the chemical industry, two-thirds in metalworking, and the majority in the Mansfeld iron ore mining district. The works councils in the shoe factories of Weissenfels were also in great majority communist, and the railroad works councils in Halle

[35] Craig Patton, "Patterns of Protest in the German Inflation: Labor Militance and Political Radicalism in Four Chemical Communities, 1914–1924" (ms., 1993), chap. 5, 37–39.

[36] Werner Müller, *Lohnkampf, Massenstreik, Sowjetmacht: Ziele und Grenzen der "Revolutionären Gewerkschafts-Opposition" (RGO) in Deutschland 1928 bis 1933* (Cologne: Bund, 1988), 48–49.

[37] For example, Abschrift, BL Gewerkschaft Ruhrgebiet to the Zentrale, Abt. Gewerkschaften, 4 September 1924, SAPMO-BA, ZPA I/3/18–19/55/36–38.

[38] BLR Gewerkschaft, "Bericht über den Stand der Fraktionen und ihre Arbeit im Bezirk Ruhrgebiet," 21 October 1925, SAPMO-BA, ZPA I/3/18–19/55, 70–72.

[39] BLR, "Bericht über die Bezirksleitungssitzung des Bezirks Ruhrgebiet am 30. December 1925," 20 January 1926, SAPMO-BA, ZPA I/3/18–19/12/119.

[40] BLR, "Bericht der Bezirksleitung," 9 December 1926, SAPMO-BA, ZPA I/3/18–19/11/210–13.

and Delitzsch had communist majorities.[41] Leuna's works council was long dominated by the KPD.

Despite the KPD's high, if circumscribed, level of popular support, the party had an immensely difficult time mobilizing its support and maintaining a consistent presence in the workplace. State and employer repression, high unemployment, and the insufficiencies and contradictions of the party's own strategy undermined its presence.

For the KPD, workplace organizing always had an instrumental character. Communist politics were anything but "workerist." Struggles in the workplace were designed to raise workers' consciousness and their propensity for activism, their "*Kampfstimmung*." Strikes and demonstrations were all preparatory for the ultimate revolutionary combat, the giant, voluntaristic battle that would bring on the new order. Hence, the party sought always to elevate strikes into general struggles against the Weimar system.

As a result, communist strategy had little to offer workers in moments of passivity and weariness. Even in the earlier, more activist period of the Republic, the authorities reported on widespread political passivity and popular exhaustion with political and economic struggles. While the KPD talked about resuming the struggle broken off in March 1921, "among the great majority of workers there is no inclination whatsoever to follow these cries of the communists."[42] Mining officials reported at the end of 1922 that in the West Halle mining region, workers evinced a certain "works councils and organizational weariness," and only the pressures of other organized workers kept many of them in the labor movement. Much of the discontent arose from the high dues they had to turn over to the unions.[43] Even in the first part of 1923, with the material situation rapidly deteriorating, the KPD, "with all of its manipulations," was having little success.[44] The situation had altered little five months later in the midst of the Ruhr crisis, with the police reporting from even strong communist districts that interest in communist agitation and gatherings had fallen off sharply, in large part because of the increasing power of employers, rising unemployment, and the KPD's lack of money and personnel.[45] By the autumn of 1924, the trade union section of the Ruhr reported to the party Executive (Zentrale), "one cannot really talk of fractions that truly function."[46] One year later, some recovery was evident, and the Ruhr trade union section reported that the party had 236 fractions within the unions of the region. But of these, "40 percent conduct fraction work poorly, 40 percent with insufficiencies, and 20 percent well."[47]

During the 1924 Ruhr miners strike, an instructor sent out from the Central

[41] All of these figures are from BLHM, "Aus dem Jahresbericht der Kommunistischen Partei Bezirk Halle-Merseburg vom 1. April 24 bis 31. März 1925," SAPMO-BA, ZPA I/3/11/13/272–73.

[42] Lagebericht RKÜöO, 5 July 1921, BAP RAM 2819/121.

[43] OBH to RAM, 8 November 1922, BAP RAM 83/232–36.

[44] Bericht, PV Eisleben to Meldestelle OPPS, 18 January 1923, LHSAM C20/Ib/4648/4/29–31.

[45] Ibid., 15 May 1923, LHSAM C20/Ib/4648/4/41.

[46] Abschrift, BL Gewerkschaft Ruhrgebiet to the Zentrale, Abt. Gewerkschaften, 4 September 1924, SAPMO-BA, ZPA I/3/18–19/55/36.

[47] BLR Gewerkschaft, "Bericht über den Stand der Fraktionen und ihre Arbeit im Bezirk Ruhrgebiet," 21 October 1925, SAPMO-BA, ZPA I/3/18–19/55/70.

Committee reported that the regional party had "completely forsaken" its responsibility to move the miners to a still more activist stance against the mine owners.[48] Around the same time the district leadership in Halle-Merseburg evinced a great deal of confidence, but soon conceded that the "workers' lack of courage is great." Numerous local union organizations simply disappeared under the pressure exerted by employers and the state. And by the summer of 1924, internal reports claimed that the Halle-Merseburg district "has totally gone under." Of a Red Central Germany, only the expression remains. Indeed, in a number of factories the right-wing Stahlhelm had become the dominant force.[49]

Even more seriously than "organizational weariness," unemployment simply ravaged the communist presence in the workplace. As discussed in the previous chapter, rationalization and stabilization led to a drastic decline in labor force needs. Even before the onset of the Depression the political economy of the Weimar Republic generated a stratum of the structurally unemployed. Management, generally in cooperation with the trade unions, the SPD, and the state, used the opportunity afforded by the employment crisis to rid their workforces of communists and other radicals. One KPD estimate from early 1924 indicated that 85 percent of the membership in the Ruhr was unemployed.[50] Among communist youth in the Ruhr, the unemployment rate at the end of 1925 stood at 40 percent, and the remaining 60 percent were employed in smaller firms, rather than the large-sized firms of the Ruhr that the party considered crucial to its efforts.[51] At the outset of 1926, the Ruhr leadership reported:

> Over 68 percent of the party members are unemployed. In some localities the entire party organization is unemployed. This means that we are more or less an unemployed party, or, better stated, we are the party of the unemployed and the Christians and the SPD are the party of the labor movement. . . . The unemployed comrades are inclined to all sorts of political nonsense which is easily explained by the fact that they are quite worn down by long unemployment and therefore are receptive to all sorts of voices.[52]

As a result, in its union work the party had behind it unemployed union members, but not the core of employed workers. And even where the party attracted widespread sympathy among workers, as was often the case, it proved much more difficult to catapult this sentiment into organizational successes. Of five hundred

[48] "Bericht aus dem Ruhrgebiet," 12 May 1924, SAPMO-BA, ZPA I/3/18–19/12/21.

[49] BLHM to the Zentrale-Orgbüro Abteilung, 4 August 1924, SAPMO-BA, ZPA I/3/11/20/59–60.

[50] BLR, "Politischer Bericht Bezirk Ruhrgebiet," 4 March [1924], SAPMO-BA, ZPA I/3/18–19/11/33. The figure certainly receded in the course of the year. According to another party report, the demand for skilled labor forced firms to rehire communist workers, but some of these had found alternative sources of income, such as small shopkeepers and the like, and refused to resume their jobs—much to the chagrin of the party with its emphasis on organizing in the factories and mines. At least some party leaders called for disciplinary measures against members who refused to resume their proletarian jobs. See "Bericht über Besprechung mit Genossen aus wichtigen Grossbetrieben des Ruhrgebietes," [undated, presumably 1924], SAPMO-BA, ZPA I/3/18–19/12/32.

[51] "Bericht über den Bezirk Ruhrgebiet," [undated, presumably late 1925 or early 1926], SAPMO-BA, ZPA I/3/18–19/12/95.

[52] BLR to ZK, 5 January 1926, SAPMO-BA, ZPA I/3/18–19/11/131.

new members recruited in the Ruhr in January 1926, 70 percent were unemployed.[53] In December 1928, well before the onset of the Depression, 20 percent of the membership in Halle-Merseburg was unemployed.[54] In January 1930, reports from the Ruhr indicate that only 41.9 percent of the members were employed in the workplace, and by November the figure was down to 22.6 percent.[55] This signified, as the party itself noted, an immense decline in the proportion of members still working in the factories and mines despite a strong, overall increase in the number of members. Moreover, the same party report warned that the figures probably underestimated the extent of unemployment among party members, since the figures failed to account for the underemployed and those behind on their dues and whose records had not been updated.[56] By January 1931, of 12,752 party members in Halle-Merseburg, 6,457 were unemployed (50.6 percent), and another 2,791 (21.9 percent) were underemployed.[57] As early as 1926, efforts to foment strikes or, at the very least, demonstrations, often became, in reality, demonstrations of the unemployed that had little impact on employed workers.[58]

High unemployment had an immense impact also on those who managed to hold on to their jobs, because it made them intensely fearful of engaging in open political work. As one KPD instructor wrote, "even the average politically active worker . . . prefers a one-percent risk of falling in battle . . . to a ninety-nine percent certainty of being dismissed by his employer for striking illegally and then being placed on the blacklist."[59] A number of firms actively promoted the right-wing Stahlhelm, sometimes forcing workers to join it in order to keep their jobs, as at Schalker Verein in Gelsenkirchen and Rheinstahl in Duisburg.[60] And in 1926, delegates to a party works council conference reported that the last three communists had just been fired from the Thyssen-Werk in Mülheim, a sign of true determination and efficiency on the firm's part.[61]

In the autumn of 1926 the KPD called conferences of communist works councillors in mining and steel, two industries absolutely central to party calculations. Of forty councillors invited to the mining conference, only seven showed up. In

[53] BLR, Abt. Pol.-Büro, "Politischer Bericht aus der Arbeit im Monat Januar," 12 February 1926, SAPMO-BA, ZPA I/3/18–19/11/142.

[54] BLHM, "Politischer und organisatorischer Bericht der KPD Bezirk Halle-Merseburg für die Monate November 1928 bis März 1929," SAPMO-BA, ZPA I/3/11/40/66–67.

[55] "Entwicklung der Mitgliederbewegung im Ruhrgebiet," [undated, received at the Comintern 8 January 1931], SAPMO-BA, ZPA I/3/18–19/14/94.

[56] Ibid.

[57] [BLHM], "Bericht über die Kontrolle im Bezirk Halle-Merseburg," 16 March 1931, SAPMO-BA, ZPA I/3/11/16/169b–70.

[58] BLR Pol-Leitung, "Bericht aus der Arbeit des Bezirks Ruhrgebiet im Monat Mai 1926," SAPMO-BA, ZPA I/3/18–19/11/155.

[59] Quoted in Eve Rosenhaft, *Beating the Fascists? The German Communists and Political Violence, 1929–1933* (Cambridge: Cambridge University Press, 1983), 47.

[60] "Bericht von der Konferenz der kommunistischen Betreibsräte der Werke des Stahl-Trusts am 10. Oktober 1926 in Essen," SAPMO-BA, ZPA I/3/18–19/12/195–96, 198. See also Conan Fischer, *The German Communists and the Rise of Nazism* (New York: St. Martin's Press, 1991) on the rise of right-wing influence within the workplace.

[61] "Bericht von der Konferenz der kommunistischen Betreibsräte der Werke des Stahl-Trusts am 10. Oktober 1926 in Essen," SAPMO-BA, ZPA I/3/18–19/12/194–95.

steel, the situation was no better: nine of thirty-two invitees appeared, and none of them from the major firms of Vereinigte Stahlwerke. (And the Central Committee representative considered only three of the nine really capable.) At least one of the reasons for the poor showing was that the delegates feared being saddled with more tasks by the party leadership.[62] At the end of 1927, an instructor sent out by the Central Committee attended a meeting of the party cell at Krupp and was anything but impressed. Although the cell had two hundred members, only fifty-two appeared at the meeting. "The comrades' inclination to struggle is incredibly slight," and there was no sign of any political or organizational preparation for the upcoming wage conflict in the industry. Even communists in leadership positions as works councillors were reluctant to take stands against the unions and the SPD, fearful that they would be thrown out of the union and fired.[63]

Little had changed a few months later when Arthur Vogt, a leading party functionary, attended a meeting of the Krupp cell. Hardly anyone spoke during the meeting, apparently a normal state of affairs. Virtually nothing had been done to support the party's candidates in works council elections, and many comrades even failed to vote. And to Vogt's chagrin, the KPD's local newspaper, the *Ruhr-Echo*, even published the results of the elections one day after the bourgeois press because comrades at Krupp had not bothered to inform themselves about the results and to communicate the information to the editors.[64] Even the lockout of Ruhr metalworkers in 1928, seemingly a fruitful opportunity for the party, failed to alter significantly the poor state of party work despite some successes in winning new party members and, in a few factories, mobilizing the workers.[65] In some factories, the number of party members among the workforce was so small as to be almost nonexistent. At the Vestag plant of Rheinische Stahlwerke, party leaders counted only ten comrades among a workforce of 11,000.[66] In mining the situation was still more desultory. At a party-called "Demonstration Day," part of an effort to activate miners for the approaching wage conflict, only 108 out of two thousand miners appeared, in Alten-Essen only five.[67]

The Leuna chemical works provides an instructive example of the successes and difficulties of communist activism in the workplace. Throughout the early 1920s,

[62] "Bericht über die Konferenz der Betriebsräte des Kohlensyndicats am 10. Oktober 1926 in Essen" and "Bericht von der Konferenz der kommunistischen Betriebsräte der Werke des Stahl-Trusts am 10. Oktober 1926 in Essen," SAPMO-BA, ZPA I/3/18–19/12/191, 192, 193.

[63] "Bericht über unsere Tätigkeit in der Lohn- und Arbeitszeitbewegung Nordwest Dezember 1927," SAPMO-BA, ZPA I/3/18–19/13/45–46.

[64] "Bericht über die Sitzung der Kruppzelle am 28. März 1928," 2 April 1928, SAPMO-BA, ZPA I/3/18–19/13/77–78.

[65] "Bericht über die Arbeitern der Partei und über sonstige Vorgänge im Aussperrungsgebiet (Ruhrgebiet)—Unterbezirk Gelsenkirchen für die Zeit vom 29. November bis 5. Dezember 1928," 11 December 1928, SAPMO-BA, ZPA I/3/18–19/13/182–85. On the mixed results of party efforts, see some of the additional instructor reports, e.g., SAPMO-BA, ZPA I/3/18–19/13/150–52, 186–95, 205–10.

[66] "Erfahrungen und praktische Beispiele aus dem Ruhrkampf," 12 December 1928, SAPMO-BA, ZPA I/3/18–19/13/186.

[67] "Bericht über das Ruhrgebiet: Unterbezirkssekretär-Konferenz am Montag 19. März [1928]," SAPMO-BA, ZPA I/3/18–19/13/65–67.

the KPD had a powerful presence in the plant, which was renowned among workers for its horrendous conditions. In January 1924, internal KPD reports spoke still of a strong and determined oppositional mood in the factory. But some months later, the local party leadership complained bitterly about the state of the Leuna organization and of the party in general.[68] Not only was the enterprise cell work of the party stagnating, but it was slipping backwards and the responsible leader was not up to the task.

> In our district the peculiar fact prevails that in almost all of the large firms relatively few communists are employed. Although our influence on the works councils is strong—we even have a majority of the works councils in our hands—the enterprises are dead, hardly any workplace cells exist. . . . For months now [we have] not had the slightest connection between the workplaces and the district leadership . . . maybe with the exception of Leuna.

In a fit of frustration, the report continued:

> Given the revolutionary tradition of the population of this district it must be possible, through the foundation of workplace cells and through their politicization, to bring the largest part of the workforce once again behind the party.
>
> The story of the Leuna cell in the last months is a real drama. The *Leuna-Prolet* . . . was a pathbreaking journal in Germany. Through repressive measures, but even more because of the lack of interest on the part of responsible comrades in the district leadership . . . for four months the newspaper did not appear.[69]

Only with pressure from the Executive and the district leadership was it finally possible to resume publication.

When Leuna's management in May 1924 extended the workday to nine hours for about four thousand of the plant's workforce, all the efforts by the party leadership to foment resistance fell on deaf ears. Because of the intense repression, protest demonstrations could not be held so they were called for the various surrounding communities where Leuna workers lived. Many had to be called off because of lack of interest; even in Halle only three hundred workers appeared. The mood among the workers, complained party leaders, was "extraordinarily passive."[70] Meetings the following days only underscored how successful Leuna management had been in suppressing its workers. Party comrades said that since the March Action, the KPD had lost strength in the plant because of the "strong terror" exercised by management. The control and spying system had been developed into an art form, and one party report estimated three hundred spies in the plant. Workers could not even leave their stations without being reported, hence a great fear and caution ruled the workforce. Now when works council members wanted to speak to the workers, they had to receive permission from manage-

[68] "Bezirk Halle-Merseburg," [undated, presumably December 1924], SAPMO-BA, ZPA I/3/11/13/144–45.

[69] "Bericht Situation in der 'Chemischen Industrie,'" 10 March 1924, SAPMO-BA, ZPA I/3/11/13/168.

[70] "Bericht über den Stand der Bewegung im Leunawerk," 2 June 1924, SAPMO-BA, ZPA I/3/11/13/222.

ment, which then observed all conversations[71]—a far cry from the situation in 1919 or 1920, when works councillors patrolled the plant at will. Moreover, some of the most experienced party members, found with copies of the *Leuna-Prolet*, had fallen victim to the strict controls exercised by management and had lost their jobs.[72] Of a workforce of around twelve thousand, the KPD cell counted only about sixty men.[73]

By the end of 1924, an instructor sent out by the Central Committee reported that one could not really speak of a party cell at Leuna.[74] All of the most capable party members had been fired. Furthermore, the geographic dispersal of the workforce made it extremely difficult to mobilize party supporters at Leuna. Local organizations sought to enlist Leuna workers in their campaigns, and sometimes even avoided informing party officers of the Leuna workers in their districts. An all-out conflict had developed between the enterprise cells, the supposed organizational basis of the KPD (and other communist parties) since 1924, and the neighborhood cells and districts over the bodies and energies of communists employed at Leuna.[75] But the tight control in the plant gave the lie to the efforts to make enterprise cells the organizational basis of the party. The KPD literally had no choice but to organize Leuna workers in their neighborhoods, where there existed more freedom of movement and expression than behind the factory gates.

In 1929, party leaders reiterated all the old problems of communist work at Leuna—poor coordination, strict repression, fear of unemployment, geographic dispersal, failure to carry through on campaigns, numerous members in arrears of dues. One participant at a cell meeting finally broke out in frustration:

> Seventy-five percent of the things that have been spoken about are nothing new. When a representative of the Central Committee is here, the comrades talk in accord with the speaker. When no one is there [from the Central Committee], they have another idea. Then black is painted black. When a representative is present, they have all sorts of proposals, see many practical possibilities for [party] work, but then at the next meeting they say again the opposite.[76]

Party officials estimated that six to seven hundred communists were employed at Leuna in the winter of 1928–29, yet only about one hundred had actually been identified.[77] No doubt the others feared for their jobs and preferred to lie low. As a further sign of the difficulties of communist work in the plant, the

[71] "Bericht, Betriebszellenversammlung Leuna," 6 June 1924, SAPMO-BA, ZPA I/3/11/13/225–27, and "Berichte über Grossbetriebe im Bezirk Halle-Merseburg in der Zeit vom 8.-11. November 1924," SAPMO-BA, ZPA I/3/11/13/241.

[72] "Bericht Situation in der 'Chemischen Industrie,'" 10 March 1924, SAPMO-BA, ZPA I/3/11/13/168.

[73] "Bericht, Betriebszellenversammlung Leuna," 6 June 1924, SAPMO-BA, ZPA I/3/11/13/225.

[74] "Die Leuna Zelle," 11 December 1924, SAPMO-BA, ZPA I/3/11/19/8–10.

[75] "Bericht über die Versammlung der Leunazelle am 6. November 1929," SAPMO-BA, ZPA I/3/11/19/185–86.

[76] Ibid., quote on 188.

[77] "Bericht über den Stand der Arbeit der Zelle in den Chemiebetrieben des Bezirks Halle-Merseburg (17. und 18.1.1929)," SAPMO-BA, ZPA I/3/11/19/143.

press run of the cell newspaper, *Der Leuna-Prolet*, had declined from five to three thousand.[78] The party's strong position within the works council suffered a precipitous decline after 1924, and in 1930 it lost its majority, as table 4.1 demonstrates. The decline in votes for the communist list almost matched the layoff of five thousand workers, indicating that employers continued to use economic crises to rid the workplace of radicals.[79] In 1931, the KPD cell at Leuna lost eighty members in nine months, most of them through layoffs. The onetime stronghold of the KPD was reduced to a cell of forty members, of whom only twenty were active.[80]

But it was not only the actions of employers, the state, and trade unionists that weakened the communist position in the workplace. The KPD's own ideological proclivities served also to undermine the party's presence. The Luxemburgist-Leninist hostility to the established trade unions, disparaged as bureaucratic, reformist institutions, made it difficult to convince the membership of the importance of party work within the unions, even in the period when official Comintern and KPD policy called upon members to join the existing unions (predominantly, the SPD-aligned "Free Unions" and the Catholic Center Party–aligned Christian unions). No matter what the official line at any moment, the party had always to contend with deep-seated rank-and-file discontent with the unions, especially in the more radical KPD districts like the Ruhr.

Pointedly, a large proportion of the communist rank and file was not organized into trade unions—40 percent in the Ruhr, according to one estimate.[81] In March 1925, the Ruhr leadership reported, with evident relief, that active resistance to union membership had all but ceased. Nonetheless, some 20 percent of party members had still not found their way back to the Free Unions. Moreover, some comrades simply lied to party controllers about their supposed union membership, while others, "mostly older comrades . . . .refuse, and to be sure out of deeply seated sentiments, to return to the free unions."[82] An instructor sent out to the Ruhr by the Central Committee in the autumn of 1924 reported that no one had any idea about the level of union organization of party members. When asked, they would always claim to be union members, but could not produce their membership book. "It is sheer deception," he concluded.[83]

Even when the party dominated local union organizations, the KPD had to deal with the more radical strivings of the rank and file. In 1924, the DMV in Essen, dominated by the KPD, wanted to secede from the parent body and organize a

[78] Ibid.

[79] Rosenhaft, *Beating the Fascists?* 46.

[80] "Bericht über die Kontrolle im Bezirk Halle-Merseburg," 16 March 1931, SAPMO-BA, ZPA I/3/11/16/170.

[81] Abschrift, BL Gewerkschaft Ruhrgebiet to the Zentrale, Abt. Gewerkschaften, 4 September 1924, SAPMO-BA, ZPA I/3/18–19/55/37.

[82] BLR an die Zentrale der KPD Polbüro, "Politischer Bericht," 3 March 1925, SAPMO-BA, ZPA I/3/18–19/11/89–90.

[83] "Bericht vom Bezirk Ruhrgebiet," 4 Oktober 1924, SAPMO-BA, ZPA I/3/18–19/12/49.

TABLE 4.1
Works Council Elections Leuna-Werke, 1924–33

	1924		*1925*		*1929*		*1930*		*1931*		*1933*	
	No.	*Pct.*	*No.*	*Pct.*	*No.*	*Pct.*	*No.*	*Pct.*	*No.*	*Pct.*	*No.*	*Pct.*
Electoral participation		92.3		92.1		92.7		93.2		93.4		95.3
Free Union	2,379	27.6	2,244	25.9	5,917	33.8	5,115	39.9	3,909	38.8	2,986	40.9
Communist	6,249	72.4	5,062	58.5	9,259	52.9	4,767	37.1	3,511	34.9	884	12.1
Company Union			1,347	15.6	1,736	9.9	2,220	17.3	604	6.0		
Christian Union					594	3.4	730	5.7	525	5.2	285	3.9
Stahlhelm									462	4.6	1,043	14.3
Nazi									1,062	10.5	2,094	28.7

Source: "Zahlenergebnisse der Arbeiter-, Angestellten- und Betriebsratswahlen 1924–1933," BLW 1327.

new, revolutionary trade union.[84] In Naumburg, the KPD completely controlled the construction workers cartel (Baugewerksbund), yet KPD members still wanted to separate from it because they believed that if they joined with the Union of Excluded [from the regular union] Construction Workers, they would be able to pursue better revolutionary activity—"a very particular point of view [*eigenartige Auffassung*]," according to the regional leadership, which exerted great efforts, ultimately with success, to dissuade the Naumburg workers from this course.[85]

Moreover, since the KPD sought always to escalate the level of conflict, it never knew how to end strikes. Its own rhetoric was so overwrought that its supporters could hardly expect anything less than complete victory, while its refusal to countenance limited goals alienated more moderate workers. In August 1923, for example, the KPD sought to develop the great strike wave into the prelude for the German reenactment of the October Revolution. But then, recognizing that the timing was not yet right, the party sought to channel the strikes into an economic course.[86] A wave of anger swept over party supporters, who shouted down KPD functionaries at mass meetings in the Ruhr and in Halle.[87]

Furthermore, the hostility to the established unions led the KPD (in alignment with Comintern directives) in the first (1919–23) and last (1929–33) phases of the Republic to establish independent, revolutionary unions, which it hoped would replace the social democratic, Christian, and liberal unions as the major institutions of workplace representation. Instead, with this policy the party sowed confusion and discontent among workers inside and outside the party and enabled employers and the unions to move more easily against communists.

In the first years of the Weimar Republic, over half of the party members in the Ruhr who were organized into trade unions were members of the separate Union der Hand- und Kopfarbeiter (Union of Manual and Intellectual Workers), so that "in the entire Ruhr region at the most eight to ten thousand party members come into question for trade union work."[88] The Union was a rather undisciplined organization that had all sorts of radicals within its ranks and gave the KPD no

[84] Bezirk Ruhrgebeit, Abteilung Gewerkschaft to the Zentrale and Politbüro, 20 March 1924, SAPMO-BA, ZPA I/3/18–19/55/28–29.

[85] "Bericht über die am 29.3.24 in Naumburg stattgefundene Sitzung der Industriegruppe Bau," SAPMO-BA, ZPA I/3/11/13/182.

[86] BLHM, "Situationsbericht des Bezirks 11 Halle-Merseburg," 15 August 1923, SAPMO-BA, ZPA I/3/11/18/185–86.

[87] On the strikes in Halle-Merseburg, see the various reports of the BL: "Situationsbericht des Bezirks 11 Halle-Merseburg," 15 August 1923; "Gesamtbericht über den Generalstreik in Mittel-Deutschland," 21 August 1923; "Bericht von der Bauarbeiterkonferenz des Bezirkes Halle am 26. August 1923," SAPMO-BA, ZPA I/3/11/18/184–86, 212–13, 218–20; "Oppositionelle Gewerkschaftskonferenz des Bezirks Halle-Merseburg," 23 March 1924, SAPMO-BA, ZPA I/3/11/52/23–32. At the 26 August 1923 meeting of construction workers, the discussion revolved around how to destroy the unions—to the chagrin of the KPD speaker. On the Ruhr strikes in May and August, see *RE*, 30 May and 22 August 1923; RPD to MdI, etc., 6 July 1923, HStAD 16934/18–20; PPE to RPD, 23, 26, 29 August, 4, 6 September 1923, HStAD 16573.

[88] BL Rheinland-Westfalen Nord, "Gewerkschaflicher Bericht für den Monat Januar," 21 February 1923, SAPMO-BA, ZPA I/3/18–19/55/6.

end of problems. The Union was, according to one party report, "a very clumsy body . . . which continually has to be pushed and directed by the party. Among these people hardly any are capable of undertaking any kind of independent steps or actions."[89] As a result, one Central Committee instructor recommended moving some experienced comrades from the DMV to the metalworkers section of the Union. Construction workers complained that the their organization was weakened by competition with the comparable body of the Union. In the mining sector, most communists were in the Union, and as a result, relatively few communists were organized in the much larger Alter Verband. In addition, competent personnel were always stretched thinly in the party, and the local leaders of the mining section of the Union were so incompetent that a large number of members "and not the worst" were intending to return to the Alter Verband, a cause of great concern to the party in this period.[90]

Moreover, no one seemed certain whether the Union was to be an out-and-out communist organization or a more radically inclined trade union that encompassed nonparty workers as well. The KPD leadership tried to promote the establishment of communist fractions in the Union as well, but members were resistant to the idea, seeing it as superfluous.[91] KPD members in the Union wore their membership as a badge of revolutionary virtue, and condemned their comrades who remained in the regular unions.[92] This distinction carried over to the response to Comintern directives: the same trade union report indicated that the communist opposition in the established unions responded favorably to the decisions of the Fifth Comintern Congress in 1924, which called on communists to enter the regular trade unions, while those in the more radical Union of Manual and Intellectual Workers opposed it. Even the employers association circulated a report which confirmed that the party was having grave difficulties convincing its own members as well as those of the Union that the Fifth Congress decision—encapsulated in the slogan "Join the free unions!"—constituted the correct line. The free unions themselves were carefully monitoring the situation and doing all that was possible to bar KPD members from entering their ranks.[93]

By 1924, the situation within the Union had reached a crisis stage and relations between the Union and the KPD leaderships had become extremely tense.[94] Both the Comintern and the KPD had realized that efforts to establish independent radical unions only isolated the party. The Union refused to accept the Comintern call to conquer the established trade unions and instead raised its own slogan, "Out of the unions!" Relations between communist cells and Union groups in the

89 Ibid., 7.

90 BLR, "Gewerkschaftlicher Monatsbericht für die Monate Februar und März," SAPMO-BA, ZPA I/3/18–19/55/19.

91 Abschrift, BL Gewerkschaft Ruhrgebiet to the Zentrale, Abt. Gewerkschaften, 4 September 1924, SAPMO-BA, ZPA I/3/18–19/55/36–38.

92 Ibid.

93 Arbeitgeberverband der chemischen- und Sprengstoff-Industrie, Rundschreiben G.Nr. 8, 2 October 1924, HIA, NSDAP 41/807.

94 For the following, see "Bericht über das Verhältnis der Partei und Union im Ruhrgebiet," 6 March 1924, SAPMO-BA, ZPA I/3/18–19/12/13–18.

workplace fractured completely. At one meeting, the Ruhr KPD leadership told comrades in the Union "short and sweet . . . that they either had to act as communists, or there would be no place for them in the Communist Party."[95] Finally, the KPD decided to break completely with the Union, which soon faded from significance.

But in 1928, the Comintern and the KPD revived the idea of an independent revolutionary union with the foundation of the Revolutionary Trade Union Opposition (Revolutionäre Gewerkschafts-Opposition, or RGO).[96] This decision derived from the shift in Comintern tactics to the "third period," the strategy based on the view that a renewed escalation of class conflict and a burgeoning revolutionary wave were on the horizon.[97] As a result, communist parties were called upon to escalate the class struggle and to break decisively with all reformist elements in the labor movement. While the decision came from Moscow, the sentiment in favor of independent unions was already widespread within the KPD. The RGO absorbed the energies of many communists, but also made their activism far more insular. As the party itself reported, the RGO leadership in the Ruhr was comprised, in fact, of the KPD district leadership secretary for trade union affairs, while at the local level the subdistrict secretaries handled RGO matters.[98] The RGO was no more successful than the Union of Manual and Intellectual Workers in replacing the existing trade unions. Only in a few areas and industries was it able to establish anything approaching a solid basis.[99] More often, participation in RGO activities enabled the regular trade unions to exclude radicals from their ranks. The RGO became increasingly an organization of the unemployed, which isolated the KPD still further from the workplace and from the larger group of workers outside the party's own ranks.[100]

An RGO-called strike in the Northwest Group of the metals industry in 1930 exemplifies the problematic character of separate communist trade union activity.[101] Participation was, to begin with, spotty. The police adopted a very aggressive stance and arrested strike leaders and pickets, while the SPD and Catholic-aligned unions refused to go along with the strike call. Strikers were then fired, communist works councillors and trade union officials removed from their positions. The coalition of order functioned effectively here, even in the midst of the Depression. At Krupp, Schupo officers stood at the plant gate and identified workers who had manned the picket lines, which meant certain dismissal. Krupp

[95] Ibid., 16.

[96] For a detailed history of the RGO, see Müller, *Lohnkampf.*

[97] See Nicholas N. Kozlov and Eric D. Weitz, "Reflections on the Origins of the 'Third Period': Bukharin, the Comintern and the Political Economy of Weimar Germany," *JCH* 24 (July 1989): 387–410.

[98] "Bericht über den Nordweststreik," 7 July 1930, SAPMO-BA, ZPA I/3/18–19/14/77.

[99] See Müller, *Lohnkampf,* 336–73.

[100] The RGO estimated in 1931 that the free unions had excluded 30,500 individuals. See Müller, *Lohnkampf,* 292–93, 338.

[101] The following is drawn from "Bericht über den Nordweststreik," 7 July 1930, SAPMO-BA, ZPA I/3/18–19/14/69–79. See also Müller, *Lohnkampf,* 140–50, who discusses the Nordwest and three other strikes.

and other firms also took advantage of the defeat to reduce further piecework rates. In the midst of the action, the claim that "the strike goes on, led by us with undiminished force" marked only brave words on the part of the Central Committee's instructor.[102] More telling was the same instructor's comment that nowhere was the party able to take the leadership from the hands of the SPD or DMV. In addition, many communist works councillors refused to follow party directives, clearly fearful of being fired and of supporting an action that they knew would isolate the party. Party leaders were quick to recognize some of the problems and attribute blame to the KPD's insufficient organizational capacities, but failed utterly to recognize the disasters inevitable with a strategy of building separate unions and engaging in separate workplace actions.

Despite all the immense weaknesses of the attempted strike, including the subsequent firing of some 2,500 activists,[103] the KPD still considered the effort a success. The KPD claimed that about fifty thousand struck, which was

> a great success for the party and the RGO, which at the same time shows how satisfactory the basis is for our systematic political and organizational work in the smelting and rolling mills of the Ruhr, so long as we succeed in creating the cadre of functionaries that is currently lacking. The workers are ready to follow us. They undoubtedly recognize the correctness of the RGO's and the party's slogans. Only because of the weak organizational basis of the RGO, they do not yet have the trust and the belief that it will be possible for the RGO to lead workers to victory against all their enemies.[104]

Since the KPD considered all strikes only a starting point for more general mobilizations, it sought to engage other party sections in the strike. Mostly, it tried to extend the strike to the mining industry and to organize support among the unemployed. The party leadership demanded that "all the units [of the KPD's unemployed committees] be set in force as shock brigades [*Stossbrigade*] of the RGO in the strike,"[105] and that mass demonstrations be held in conjunction with strikers at the gates to the mines and factories and in mine housing colonies.

By 1930, workers and the workplace had become difficult to organize. But the unemployed could be set in action, and the streets of a democratic polity offered far greater opportunities for mobilization than the dictatorially administered factory and mine. This was, though, a highly dangerous strategy, because it set the unemployed against the employed since the strike was by no means universal, and made it seem to the metalworkers and miners that "outsiders" were intervening in their own affairs. The KPD, however, determined to promote any form of mass activism, threw caution to the winds. Rather than serve as a basis of unify-

[102] "Bericht über den Nordweststreik," 7 July 1930, SAPMO-BA, ZPA I/3/18–19/14/72.

[103] Rosenhaft, *Beating the Fascists?* 46–47.

[104] "Bericht über den Nordweststreik," 7 July 1930, SAPMO-BA, ZPA I/3/18–19/14/78. The DMV estimated fifteen thousand, which, as Werner Müller says, is probably closer to the truth. See Müller, *Lohnkampf*, 143. The KPD also claimed great successes the next year from an RGO-inspired miners strike. See "Vorläufiger Bericht des Genossen Funk über den Bergarbeiterstreik im Ruhrgebiet und Oberschlesien," [undated, received 28 January 1931], SAPMO-BA, ZPA I/3/18–19/14/96–100.

[105] Bezirksausschuss der Erwerbslosen Ruhrgebiet, "Januar-Arbeitsplan," 5 January 1931, SAPMO-BA, ZPA I/3/18–19/59/8.

ing the unemployed and the employed in a common struggle, the call by the RGO on its own for a strike and the mobilization of the party's reserves of unemployed served only to accentuate the fragmentation of the working class in the Weimar Republic.

Since the Fifth Comintern Congress in 1924, enterprise cells were supposed to be the basic organizational units of all communist parties. This proved extraordinarily problematic. Even in the best of circumstances, the high levels of unemployment made it almost impossible to establish well-tuned enterprise cells. Moreover, neighborhood organizations and enterprise cells competed for the energies of committed activists. Factories and mines that operated on a shift system created other problems, since it proved impossible to get all members of a cell together at the same time. Party leaders considered 45 percent attendance at cell meetings quite good.[106] The high fluctuation of workers, as in the Ruhr mines, which on a regular basis might lose and replace one-quarter of their workers in a given year, made party and union organization still more difficult.[107]

Other examples only underscore the point.[108] The Duisburg docks employed about thirty thousand men, a very small proportion of whom were permanent employees. As on most docks, the majority of the workforce consisted of temporary help that would be hired when work was available. The KPD had some support among this unsteady labor force. The Duisburg port had about ten docks, and the party proposed that each dock have its own cell composed of permanent and temporary workers. This was clearly a convoluted and impractical solution, since intrinsic to the work was a very loose connection to a particular place of employment. In Essen, the party established seven cells at Krupp, each in a different unit of the sprawling factory, and gave each of the cells responsibility for an adjacent neighborhood. Unsurprisingly, "unclarity" existed about this organizational structure, which the Executive's instructor had to attempt to fix. For construction workers, among whom the KPD also had strong support, the party provided a still more convoluted organizational solution. These workers were particularly mobile. They moved around to different sites and worked for different contractors. At any job site, a wide variety of trades might be present. The party proposed that communist construction workers join cells according to their employer, not the work site. Given the frequency with which workers changed employers—a frequency comparable to miners—it is hard to see the sense behind this organizational structure.

Finally, the emphasis on workplace cells almost necessarily meant a neglect of women's issues. Despite the great public debate about women's labor in Weimar Germany, the majority of women were not employed in the paid labor force and

[106] "Bericht über den Bezirk Ruhrgebiet," [undated, presumably late 1925 or early 1926], SAPMO-BA, ZPA I/3/18–19/12/85.

[107] BLR, "Bericht der BL Ruhrgebiet," 9 December 1926, SAPMO-BA, ZPA I/3/18–19/11/193–94.

[108] The following is drawn from "Bericht über den Bezirk Ruhrgebiet," [undated, presumably late 1925 or early 1926], SAPMO-BA, ZPA I/3/18–19/12/86–88.

still fewer in the heavy industrial sectors of coal and iron that the party constantly idealized as the essence of proletarian labor. As will be discussed more thoroughly in chapter 6, the party condemned the individual household as the wellspring of petit bourgeois sentiments. Unable to function effectively in the workplace yet determined to the bitter end to make it the centerpiece of party life, the KPD only narrowed its own base of support.

With a deep level of frustration aggravated by the Depression, which, given the crisis-oriented strategy of the KPD, should have improved party prospects, party leaders in the early 1930s could only reiterate a long list of problems related to workplace organizing. A significant segment of the working class remained mired in passivity. Party functionaries inside the unions and the works councils lacked initiative. Party cells and party representatives in the workplace and district and subdistrict leaderships failed to coordinate their work. For fear of losing their jobs or of isolation from their fellow workers, KPD members in the workplaces refused to support party positions in the unions, in the works councils, and at mass meetings. Factory cells were nonexistent or did not function in coordination with the party fraction in the union. The unemployed movement and other KPD organizations and representatives worked in isolation from one another.[109]

But now, in the last years of the Republic, these complaints were accompanied by attacks on "right-wing" and "conciliator" elements within the KPD, a function of the Comintern switch to the intransigent strategy of the third period in 1928/29. The KPD was fighting on all fronts within the factories and mines—against SPD members now labeled "social fascists"; against the party "conciliators" who were especially strong in the unions in Halle-Merseburg; against the fascists who were making advances among workers; and, sometimes, even against the employers. Indeed, the party seems to have expended its greatest energies not just against the SPD—the oft-repeated condemnation of KPD politics in the last phase of the Weimar Republic—but also against factions within the party. It was not a cleverly designed strategy, and the expectation that the Depression would almost automatically radicalize workers for the communist revolution proved to be another KPD chimera, for the unemployed—as much research has shown—were as prone to passivity as activism, while many of those in the workplace, as we have seen, feared for their jobs.[110]

[109] "Bericht der Gewerkschaftsabteilung Halle-Merseburg vom 15.5. bis 31.7.1929," and "Bericht der Bezirks-Gewerkschaftsabteilung [Halle-Merseburg]," [undated, presumably 1930 or 1931], SAPMO-BA, ZPA I/3/11/52/124–41, 144–48. For similar complaints, see "Bericht über Grossbetriebe im Bezirk Halle-Merseburg in der Zeit vom 8.–11. November 1924," SAPMO-BA, ZPA I/3/11/13/241–47; "Bericht über Reise nach Halle am 12. Januar 1926;" BLR, "Bericht der Bezirksleitung," 9 December 1926; "Bericht von der Kontrolle des Bezirks Halle-Merseburg am 4. Januar 1930;" "Bericht über den Bezirk Halle-Merseburg," 11. Mai 1928, SAPMO-BA, ZPA I/3/11/19/30–33, 108–11, 192–94, 211; "Bericht der Gewerkschaftsabteilung Halle-Merseburg vom 15.5. bis 31.7.1929," SAPMO-BA, ZPA, I/3/11/52/124–48; "Bericht über die Kontrolle im Bezirk Ruhrgebiet am 21/22. November 1929," 6 December 1929, SAPMO-BA, ZPA I/3/18–19/14/39–42.

[110] See Heinrich August Winkler, *Der Weg in die Katastrophe: Arbeiter und Arbeiterbewegung in*

The situation was all the more vexing for party officials in Halle-Merseburg because there the KPD had managed to maintain a strong position within the unions and the works councils. Internal party reports ran through a long list of industries in which the communists in Halle-Merseburg were strongly represented—construction, mining, wood, graphics, leather, saddle making and upholstery, chemicals, metalworking, shoemaking, stoneworking—and found only a catalog of insufficient activism and missed opportunities. In mid-1929, with the impact of the Depression quite apparent, the party proved unable to extend its influence further in the spring union elections. Many KPD functionaries in the unions sought to keep the party at arm's distance, thinking that "the party should 'where possible avoid involvement' in union affairs." Partly, a generational conflict was at hand, since younger, "ambitious elements" were "kept at a distance" by older comrades who had long held union positions, and a "crass opposition" emerged over virtually every issue. Overall, "trade union legalism strongly marks almost all fractions," noted party officials. As a result, the communist fractions were often disunited in relation to the social democrats. Some party comrades in the unions misunderstood the united front tactic and even sought to establish electoral coalitions with the SPD in union and works council elections, to the horror of the KPD leadership. The local DMV, for example, remained ravaged by conflicts among different KPD factions and between the SPD and the KPD, and the SPD regional leadership seemed particularly determined to purge communists from official positions.[111]

But worst of all to the party leaders firmly committed to the intransigent policies of the third period was the fact that union work had become the preserve of the conciliators:

> Trade union work, instead of being a focal point for the entire party, has instead become the preserve of so-called trade unionists. It is no accident that the trade union specialists, who have gradually taken control out of the hands of the membership, have become a center for conciliator and calcified elements in the district. For the most part . . . they are trade union legalists and run from the terror of the union bureaucrats and from the difficulties of mass work.[112]

The "depth and extent of this right opportunism in trade union work" is "catastrophic," concluded one report.[113]

As a result, the party leadership initiated a systematic campaign to remove the

---

der Weimarer Republik 1930 bis 1933 (Berlin: J. H. W. Dietz Nachf., 1987), 19–22; Richard J. Evans and Dick Geary, eds., *The German Unemployed: Experiences and Consequences of Mass Unemployment from the Weimar Republic to the Third Reich* (New York: St. Martin's Press, 1987); and Peter D. Stachura, ed., *Unemployment and the Great Depression in Weimar Germany* (London: Macmillan, 1986).

[111] "Bericht der Gewerkschaftsabteilung Halle-Merseburg vom 15.5. bis 31.7.1929," SAPMO-BA, ZPA I/3/11/52/124, 125, 130–33, 138–39.

[112] "Bericht der Bezirks-Gewerkschaftsabteilung [Halle-Merseburg]," [undated, presumably 1930 or 1931], SAPMO-BA, ZPA I/3/11/52/144.

[113] Ibid.

older union functionaries, associated with the right and center, and replace them with a new, younger corps of party trade unionists. Many local groups simply fell apart, since it proved no easy matter to create this new leadership corps. The impact of this can hardly be underestimated. The KPD's position in the workplace had already been ravaged by unemployment and the coordinated actions of employers and trade unionists. As one party report noted, "with the mass firings the influence of the opposition [i.e., the KPD] has declined," while at the same time both the "social fascists" and the fascists had had strong successes in works council elections.[114]

Now the party further weakened its position through the factional conflicts, which led to the purging of those members most experienced in the workplace and the workplace-based institutions of the labor movement. In union after union in Halle-Merseburg, the KPD eliminated its "trade unionists."[115] In the mineworkers union, where, at the time of one report, the older party unionists still had their positions, the report, expressively conveying the intransigent policies of the third period, called for an unrelenting campaign against them: "In the mining industry union many important union and workplace positions are still held by comrades who . . . strictly refuse to implement party decisions and assignments. A radical purge of these elements from the party and the construction of union fractions must put an end to this situation."[116] Many of these people were often well-experienced and well-respected trade unionists—which, of course, was precisely the problem for the central party leadership. To destroy those cadres in the midst of mass unemployment was foolhardy at best. Shortly thereafter, the Nazis would finish the task.

Conclusion

For the KPD, almost every protest in the workplace bore the potential of a more generalized assault on the Republic. To every strike the KPD responded, in near-Pavlovian fashion, "General strike! Everyone out of the workplace!" Its claims found widespread, though circumscribed, support among workers already renowned for a high level of collective action. The practice and experience of hard political struggle—on the shop floor and on the picket line—accorded with the KPD's unceasing efforts to initiate and intensify mass protests. The KPD's continual attacks on the Republic, and on the SPD in particular, articulated the discontent of many workers who identified both with armed repression, hyperinflation, and unemployment.

Yet the KPD had an immensely difficult time mobilizing and sustaining its

[114] Ibid., 144, 145.

[115] A similar process occurred in other areas. In Stuttgart, the purge resulted in the KPD's loss of the DMV local it had long controlled. Until 1930 the national headquarters of the DMV was also located in Stuttgart, which gave the local there special importance. The KPD also lost the locals in Solingen, Remscheid, and Chemnitz. See Müller, *Lohnkampf*, 74–75.

[116] "Bericht der Bezirks-Gewerkschaftsabteilung [Halle-Merseburg]," [undated, presumably 1930 or 1931], SAPMO-BA, ZPA I/3/11/52/146.

support. Workers, prepared to fight with management over wages, hours, representation, work schedules, and many other issues, were not convinced en masse that communism or the Communist Party provided the means of solution. The successes scored by the coalition of order drastically reduced the ability of workers to engage in mass protest and radically diminished the KPD's presence in the workplace—a trend only aggravated by the onset of the world economic crisis and by the KPD's own factional conflicts. In the concise words of both Hermann Weber and Heinrich August Winkler, the KPD became "*the* party of the unemployed of the Weimar Republic."[117]

The transformation of the KPD from a party of the working class to a party of the unemployed gave German communism a very particular profile. Both the French and Italian communist parties achieved their popular stature by penetrating the workplace, along with the local polities, the national legislatures, and, in World War II, the resistance armies. They occupied multiple political spaces and, as a result, achieved significant support beyond the core male working-class base and functioned within the institutions of the nation.[118] The KPD, in contrast, became dependent on the sporadic activism of the unemployed, whose discontents the party was more than ready to channel into a kind of pseudorevolutionary strategy composed of street fights and demonstrations. The intransigent radicalism they displayed then intersected with the ideological radicalism that the KPD imbibed from Luxemburg and Lenin.

The KPD's strategic move from the workplace to the streets was an eminently sociopolitical process, not simply the result of the "structural logic" of capitalism, anonymous events like the Great Depression, the ideological proclivities of the KPD, or Soviet domination of the international communist movement. Economic rationalization, state and employer repression, and the incorporation of social democracy into the state—developments initiated by employers and managers, bureaucrats and politicians, trade unionists and social democrats—created the conditions that deprived the KPD of access to the workplace. These processes made the streets a congenial terrain for political engagement, but at great political cost to German communism.

[117] Winkler, *Schein der Normalität*, 447; Hermann Weber, *Die Wandlung des deutschen Kommunismus: Die Stalinisierung der KPD in der Weimarer Republik* (Frankfurt am Main: Europäische Verlagsanstalt, 1969), 1:351.

[118] See Eric D. Weitz, *Popular Communism: Political Strategies and Social Histories in the Formation of the German, French, and Italian Communist Parties, 1919–1948*, Western Societies Program Occasional Paper no. 31 (Ithaca: Cornell University Institute for European Studies, 1992).

CHAPTER 5

Contesting Order: Communists in the Streets

[Jede Straßen-Demonstration soll] . . . die Arbeiterschaft an Kämpfe mit den staatlichen Machtorganen gewöhnen.

—*State officials quoting KPD pamphlet*[1]

IN AUGUST 1923, miners in Essen, out on strike, began to march on the classic target of demonstrations, the city hall. En route, they were joined by thousands of unemployed workers. The demonstrators demanded higher pay and greater unemployment benefits, and a meeting with the mayor, Hans Luther. He refused. The police managed to disperse the crowd of thousands, which proceeded to the Labor Office, the agency responsible for disbursing unemployment benefits. The crowd stormed the building as the police pursued them. Municipal workers inside fled out of windows while the police forcibly occupied the building and ejected the demonstrators. The crowd reassembled outside and threw stones at the police, who drew their weapons. Shots were fired from both sides, but amazingly, no one was hit, though a number of people were wounded by nightsticks and stones. The police concluded, "Only through a very energetic intervention was it possible to disperse the tenacious demonstrators and protect the threatened officials of the Labor Office."[2]

In September and October 1932, communists in the Berlin neighborhood of Neukölln organized a rent strike because the Nazi Storm Troopers (Sturmabteilung, or SA) had moved into a tavern in the building. The tavern had once served as a left-wing locale, but the owner had seen his business plummet with the impoverishment of the neighborhood residents. The Nazis promised a turnover of at least one barrel of beer a day if the SA were given use of the premises. The owner agreed, and subsequently joined the Nazi Party. Neukölln had been a communist stronghold for years, but the Nazis also had a substantial presence. Communists viewed the SA move into the tavern as an incursion into "their" space. SA attacks on communists and general rowdiness only increased the level of anger. The rent strike was not a sufficiently powerful tactic, despite a high level of participation. Many residents, already on welfare, had their rent paid directly by the welfare office to the landlord, so they had nothing to withhold.

[1] "[Every street demonstration should] . . . accustom the workers to struggles against the agencies of state power." State officials quoting KPD documents in "Wie denkt sich die K.P.D. die Eroberung der Macht im Staat," HIA, NSDAP 41/807/5.

[2] PPE to RPD, 6 September 1923, HStAD 16573/96–97.

Others were quickly brought to heel by the threat of eviction. Local KPD leaders decided to escalate the conflict. On 15 October 1932 communist activists, many of them members of the paramilitary Red Front Fighters League (Roter Frontkämpferbund, or RFB) and the Fighting League (Kampfbund), gathered for a demonstration about one kilometer away from the tavern. One comrade secretly chained shut the back gate of the police station. Groups of men gathered at other places, and about thirty to fifty started marching toward the tavern shouting "Down with fascism" and singing the "Internationale." When they reached the tavern, some of the men took out revolvers and fired. Four people inside were wounded, including the tavern owner, who died a few days later.[3]

By the 1920s, demonstrations, like strikes, had become a time-honored form of working-class protest. As in these two incidents, demonstrations provided the occasion for raising specific demands, forging class and political identities, and displaying symbolically and physically working-class power.[4] Demonstrations developed spontaneously during heated political moments or as organized events planned by the labor parties or unions. They ranged from peaceful marches to armed provocations.

While demonstrations had a long lineage, in Weimar they also became invested with new forms and meanings, as these two incidents also show. Demonstrations became more frequent, more intense, and more confrontational. Moreover, in the course of the Republic the nature of demonstrations changed. In the first phase, they tended to be mass popular events with fluid party lines. But as a result of both heightened party political conflict and social fragmentation within the milieu of labor, demonstrations subsequently became far more the affairs of a specific party or a segment of the working class like the unemployed. The loci of demonstrations also changed. As both unemployment and urban political violence developed, the sites of political contestation increasingly shifted from the factory and mine gates to the local welfare office and the streets of confined working-class districts.[5]

For the KPD, demonstrations in the streets, like conflicts in the workplace, provided the substratum of popular protest upon which it became a mass party.

[3] I draw this description from Eve Rosenhaft, *Beating the Fascists? The German Communists and Political Violence, 1929–1933* (Cambridge: Cambridge University Press, 1983), 119–27.

[4] Amid a very large literature on rituals and, in particular, demonstrations, I have found especially useful Temma Kaplan, *Red City, Blue Period: Social Movements in Picasso's Barcelona* (Berkeley and Los Angeles: University of California Press, 1992); Mary Ryan, "Gender and Public Access: Women's Politics in Nineteenth-Century America," in *Habermas and the Public Sphere*, ed. Craig Calhoun (Cambridge, Mass.: MIT Press, 1992), 259–88; Mary Ryan, "The American Parade: Representations of the Nineteenth-Century Social Order," in *The New Cultural History*, ed. Lynn Hunt (Berkeley and Los Angeles: University of California Press, 1989), 131–53; and David I. Kertzer, *Ritual, Politics, and Power* (New Haven: Yale University Press, 1988).

[5] See David F. Crew's discussion of the politics of protest in the welfare offices, which included a high level of violence against welfare officials: "Bedürfnisse und Bedürftigkeit: Wohlfahrtsbürokratie und Wohlfahrtsempfänger in der Weimarer Republik, 1919–1933," *Sozialwissenschaftliche Information* 18:1 (1989): 12–19, and "Gewalt 'auf dem Amt': Beispiele aus der Wohlfahrtsverwaltung der Weimarer Republik," *WerkstattGeschichte* 4 (1993): 33–42.

The voluntaristic and confrontational elements of many demonstrations accorded with the party's own strategy of active conflict with the forces of order. The streets constituted the political space where the party intersected with dissatisfied workers and marshaled its own supporters in displays of power and combative confrontations with the police, fascist organizations, and even the SPD and employed workers. As with popular protest in the workplace, the KPD also sought to organize and direct popular protest in the streets, an enterprise fraught with difficulties. The party drew sustenance from demonstrations, but its efforts to organize those involved on a sustained basis and to endow every confrontation with revolutionary significance ran against the intrinsically haphazard and erratic nature of many street actions.

This chapter will examine three forms of activism in the streets: the demonstrations and street battles of the unemployed and the efforts to establish price control committees; two confrontations between communists and right-wing groups in Halle-Merseburg in 1923 and 1924; and the so-called Lenin-Liebknecht-Luxemburg commemorations. These three examples will show the intersections between popular and specifically communist protest, and the KPD's reshaping of demonstrations into party vehicles. The examples here fall mostly (though not exclusively) prior to 1928/29 and the onset of both the Comintern's "third period" and the world economic crisis, and deliberately so. They demonstrate a certain level of continuity in communist strategy despite the factional conflicts of the 1920s. And the examples show the way that the political space of the streets and the more general social historical nature of the Republic had substantially shaped the political culture of German communism even prior to the crisis of the Depression and the Stalinization of the KPD.

Unemployed Demonstrations and Popular Control Committees

Demonstrations of the unemployed were a permanent feature of the political and social landscape of Weimar society. But as with so much else, 1923/24 marked a major divide. In the early period, before the emergence of mass, systematic unemployment, demonstrations of the unemployed constituted just one other form of popular protest within the general labor upsurge.[6] The employed and unemployed managed on more than one occasion to join together in common actions and to link up with community-based struggles over prices and food supplies. After the stabilization crisis, however, the unemployed were more likely to act on their own, a process underpinned by the political and social fragmentation of the Weimar working class. For the KPD, the sporadic militancy of the unemployed constituted models of proletarian activism that the party sought continually to sustain, channel, and deepen.

[6] See the classic article by Gerald D. Feldman, Eberhard Kolb, and Reinhard Rürup, "Die Massenbewegung der Arbeiterschaft in Deutschland nach dem Ersten Weltkrieg," *Politische Vierteljahresschrift* 13:3 (August 1972): 84–105, which, however, makes too rigid a division between early and later protest and marks the closure of the first phase already in 1919, which is too soon.

Demonstrations by the unemployed had emerged first in 1919, and sporadically in 1920 and 1921. But the surprisingly low level of unemployment in the first postwar years made these only incidental occurrences.[7] Working-class and communist organizing remained within the more traditional spaces of the factory and mine. In 1923, however, the year marked by hyperinflation, unemployment emerged with a vengeance, and within a context of still intense labor activism. In Essen, the heart of the Ruhr, demonstrations by the unemployed had become an almost daily occurrence by midsummer 1923.[8] The gatherings often attracted as many as eight thousand people. Clashes with the police were common, and on more than one occasion events turned violent. These demonstrations shaded easily into other forms of direct action, such as plundering, food requisitions, and the enforcement of popularly sanctioned prices. They involved the unemployed and employed, women and men, and moved from the workplace to state offices to the marketplace.

In mid-August 1923, for example, rumors circulated in West Essen that a number of shops had large stocks of fats and meats. Workers from the Hagenbeck mine and their works council representatives descended upon the shops and demanded that the goods be brought to the mines and sold to the miners at moderate prices. The merchants agreed—the police account is notably reticent about the kind of compulsion used to extract this concession. When the authorities arrived on the scene, the deal had already been struck.[9] In another incident, miners employed at Zeche Ernestine in Stoppenberg took from a warehouse eight fifty-kilogram sacks of sugar, which they distributed among their fellow workers. The police managed to prevent further efforts to seize tobacco and cigarettes.[10] In a few mines, formal requisition commissions were established, and they went around to wholesalers and simply loaded up trucks; they then drove them back to the mine and sold the wares at reduced prices, often with prices geared to the number of family members.[11]

Not every case of plundering or every control action originated at the workplace, but they clearly involved workers or their family members. Toward the end of August, the police prepared for a demonstration of the unemployed, organized with the collaboration of communists, in which shops in the city center were to be plundered. In this instance, the effective deployment of the police prevented unrest, although the security forces faced a column three hundred meters long of men armed with clubs. Some merchants in Essen refused to take their wares to the market because crowds were either robbing them or forcing them to slash

[7] On the very successful demobilization and initially very low unemployment, which surprised many contemporary observers, see Richard Bessel, "'Eine nicht allzu große Beunruhigung des Arbeitsmarktes': Frauenarbeit und Demobilmachung in Deutschland nach dem Ersten Weltkrieg," *GG* 9:2 (1983): 211–29.

[8] See PPE to RPD, 20, 25 August, 6, 21, 25, 27 September 1923, HStAD 16573/48–49, 52–53, 55–56, 72–73, 96–97.

[9] PPE to RPD, 20 August 1923, HStAD 16573.

[10] PPE to RPD, 16 August 1923, HStAD 16573.

[11] BLR to Zentrale, 16 August 1923, SAPMO-BA, ZPA I/3/18–19/11/20.

their prices. In one case, a crowd of over one hundred men, women, and children began to break into a merchant's cellar and take his potatoes, but stopped when he promised to distribute the goods the following day. In the Essen suburbs, large crowds, often numbering in the hundreds, plundered potato fields. At one mine, enterprising residents of the area dug their own secret entrance and took out coal for their own use and to sell.[12] The Ruhr KPD reported that control committees had in some instances succeeded in having prices reduced by 50 percent.[13]

By October, the situation around the country, and especially in the Ruhr, had deteriorated drastically—much to the pleasure of the KPD, which, along with the Comintern, viewed the unrest as a harbinger of revolution. Within the space of a few days during the last week of October, crowds robbed railroad cars loaded with food, potato fields in the suburbs, a streetcar laden with food as it passed through the Krupp works, and stores in the city, and a pitched battle between police and Krupp workers erupted inside the factory gates, leading to another strike at this one-time bastion of loyalty to the kaiser and the firm.[14] Essen's police chief reported toward the end of the month that "public security in Essen and the surrounding area is highly endangered," and he expected the situation to worsen with more layoffs and price increases.[15] Whenever the police went into action, they were attacked with stones, sticks, and small arms. The police were extremely nervous, and a number of reports described them as severely overstrained and "at the end of their strength."[16] They expressed their greatest fears, which were symmetrical with the communists' greatest desires: "tomorrow [the grave possibility exists that] the partly communist-inspired workers [at Krupp], in conjunction with the many unemployed, who are also for the most part communists, will engage in serious unrest."[17]

One month later, the fears of the police were realized in a long day of confrontation at all the sites of working-class protest: municipal offices, the streets, the workplace, and the marketplace. Thefts of foodstuffs were rampant throughout the city, and often involved women and children. After preventing some thefts at the train station, the police discovered that an entire trainload of ten cars, all packed with food supplies, had been completely robbed. At the same time, demonstrations were taking place in neighborhoods and towns throughout the area, and a number had turned violent. In Essen, the police reported,

> already early in the morning . . . where the municipal Unemployment Support Office is located, large numbers of people gathered. The security officials were actually attacked by the demonstrators and had to use their arms. No one was wounded. In the afternoon the communists, in conjunction with the unemployed, held a rally at the Burgplatz. A

[12] All of these incidents are reported in PPE to RPD, 15 and 20 August and 21 September 1923, HStAD 16573/46–47, 72–73.

[13] BLR to Zentrale, 16 August 1923, SAPMO-BA, ZPA I/3/18–19/11/20.

[14] For these and other incidents see the collection of police reports in HStAD 16573 and 17072, and PPE to RPD, 26 October 1923 (two reports), HStAD 17076/157–59.

[15] PPE to RPD, 26 October 1923, HStAD 17076/157–58.

[16] Ibid. (two reports), HStAD 17076/157–59.

[17] Ibid., HStAD 17076/157.

huge crowd of people, many of whom streamed into the city from all around the area, filled the adjacent streets. The police had to disperse the large crowd. A substantial part then attempted to move to Graben-, Segeroth-, and Altendorferstrasse as well as the north train station, in order to plunder the shops there. In Altendorferstrasse the police were in fact attacked immediately with rifle and revolver shots, along with hand grenades and pieces of stone and ice. In Osterfeldstrasse the crowd constructed a barricade out of pavement stones, from which they shot and threw stones at the security officials. The order to fire was given. . . . At this moment a unit of French troops arrived to support the hard-pressed police. Three officers were wounded, two demonstrators were killed and twenty-five wounded.[18]

The activist nature and combative tenor of requisitions, unemployed demonstrations, plundering, and control actions seemed to communists the very essence of proto-revolutionary engagement that, once sufficiently channeled and organized by the party, could become part of the ultimate revolutionary struggle.[19] Workers took matters into their own hands. They attacked the state—in the form of the unemployment office and the police—and "bourgeois" merchants. They were combative and militant, and acted in a myriad of political spaces. The participants were women and men, adults and youth, the employed and unemployed—proletarian unity at its best, in communist eyes.[20] While the violence might have occasionally gotten a bit out of hand for the KPD, the actions too spontaneous and anarchic, the militancy displayed by demonstrators accorded with a party strategy centered on continually raising the level of conflict. In a directive to party organizations, the Executive at the end of 1923 cited two model actions, a clear sign of its support for the militant engagement of the unemployed:

> [In Heidelberg], when no [unemployment] support was paid out, the unemployed organized shock troops [*Stosstrupps*] of thirty to forty men. At a set hour they met at the same time in all parts of the city and carried out requisitions of food supplies. The police were completely helpless. In other towns, the unemployed formed troops of 50 to 100 men and went from one businessman and one peasant to another and demanded foodstuffs, which, under pressure, they gave to the masses. . . . The withholding of unemployment support should be met everywhere with self-help actions.[21]

The party's military communiqués and journals issued instructions for how to pursue combat in the streets.[22]

[18] PPE to RPD, 18 November 1923, HStAD 17076/160–61.

[19] Though there were also reservations, especially when such actions first emerged in 1919, 1920, and 1921. For some examples of party condemnation of plundering, see Silvia Kontos, *"Die Partei kämpft wie ein Mann!" : Frauenpolitik der KPD in der Weimarer Republik* (Frankfurt am Main: Roter Stern, 1979), 209–12.

[20] On the role of women in these actions, see Kontos, *"Die Partei kämpft wie ein Mann!"* 209–31, and Hans-Jürgen Arendt, "Zur Rolle der Frauen in der Kontrollausschußbewegung 1922/23," *Wissenschaftliche Studien der Pädagogischen Institute Leipzig* 1 (1971): 22–27.

[21] PPH to RPM, 14 February 1924, LHSAM C20/Ib/4648/5II/96.

[22] See, for example, the excerpts "Militärische Lehren der Oktoberkämpfe in Hamburg," [end of

The KPD also sought to institutionalize such actions through the organization of control committees and councils or committees of the unemployed. Typically, communist delegations in municipal councils would enter motions for the formal recognition of these groups, which would bestow upon the unemployed councils the right to negotiate with municipal administrations on such matters as unemployment benefits and public works programs and give the control committees the power to regulate prices. Very rarely, such efforts succeeded, though only for brief moments. KPD delegations also demanded that city councils approve higher benefits and subsidies for rent payments and utility bills.[23] The party also called continually for regional and national congresses of each of these groups—in 1924, a Reich Congress of Control Committees and a Reich Congress of the Unemployed and Underemployed Councils. None of these efforts had much success; in many cases, the control committees were subordinated to the works council movement, a clear reflection of the KPD's ideological emphasis on the productive sphere and its difficulties in conceiving how to organize women in particular.[24] Nonetheless, all of these actions served as powerful mobilizing tools and demonstrate how the party sought to build upon, and thereby channel and direct, forms of popular protest.

While the militancy of the unemployed and the KPD converged at moments, these kinds of actions also demonstrated the inherent limits of party strategy. The very nature of plundering, requisitions, and control actions brought the party into direct conflict with middle-class merchants, who were the easiest and most direct targets but by no means the root cause of food shortages and inflation. Requisitions hardly endeared communism to the agrarian population or the middle class, and communism came to be identified with a kind of semianarchistic criminality widespread in the 1920s. The KPD's support for the movement of the unemployed constructed the proletarian identity of the party, which intrinsically involved its sharp demarcation from and absolute unconcern for other social classes. These actions made it virtually impossible for the party to establish cross-class alliances—had it even wanted to.

The actions of the unemployed separated the KPD from other social classes; after 1923/24, they also increasingly separated the KPD from the employed working class. The rise of mass unemployment, intermittently between 1924 and 1929, then on a sustained and almost unimaginable level from 1929 to 1933, made the unemployed an ever more critical element in KPD calculations.[25] The KPD came

---

1923], and "Zur Taktik des Strassenkampfes im bewaffneten Aufstand," April 1931, in Hermann Weber, ed., *Der deutsche Kommunismus: Dokumente* (Cologne: Kiepenheuer und Witsch, 1963), 81–82, 105–6.

[23] See Beatrix Herlemann, *Kommunalpolitik der KPD im Ruhrgebiet 1924–1933* (Wuppertal: Peter Hammer, 1977), 90–107.

[24] See "Resolution der II. Frauenreichskonferenz der KPD zur Teuerung," 28 September 1922, in Arendt, "Zur Rolle der Frauen," 25, which first calls on all housewives, female workers, and female employees to support the works council movement and to join the struggle for the control of production and distribution.

[25] Siegfried Bahne, "Die Erwerbslosenpolitik der KPD in der Weimarer Republik," in *Vom Elend der Handarbeit: Probleme historischer Unterschichtenforschung*, ed. Hans Mommsen and Wilfried Schulze (Stuttgart: Klett-Cotta, 1981), 477–96, dates the emergence of the KPD's increasing aware-

increasingly to see the unemployed—with their intermittent but notably radical militancy—as the "true" revolutionary agents, despite frequent rhetorical reminders of the importance of organizing in the workplace. At the same time, the unemployed became increasingly a distinctive substratum of the working class—a process, as described in chapter 3, initiated by stabilization and rationalization and sustained by various elements of state policy.

As unemployment deepened, the practices of 1923/24 were revived, often with added force and anger. Demonstrations, the occupation of welfare offices, plundering or "proletarian shopping trips" as Berlin communists labeled them, the protection of tenants from eviction—all became a part of the texture of public life in working-class areas of Germany.[26] The party press reported such actions sympathetically, usually accompanied by warnings against "individual" acts of thievery or terror, but the general sympathy was unmistakable.[27]

There was another element to the actions of the unemployed, particularly when the unemployed and the communists were nearly coterminous, as in certain Berlin neighborhoods. Along with the usual run of unemployed actions, the protection of the neighborhood constituted a central aspect of communist activism.[28] The opponents were the police and, increasingly, the SA, which had its own strategy of street violence and was determined to challenge communist strongholds on their own turf.[29] Taverns and streets became the choice sites of political brawls as communists sought to protect "their" neighborhoods. Such actions again created problems for the central party leadership, but the militancy and engagement of the rank and file, even if misplaced, seemed to confirm a party strategy that always sought to intensify the level of conflict and to bring workers out into the streets. *Rote Fahne* eminently conveyed this approach when it trumpeted, "Hit the fascists wherever you meet them!"—a line picked up by local communists in countless actions.[30]

---

ness of the unemployed from 1925. (491) But I think he is wrong to focus exclusively on the ultraleft policies of the "third period" as the background for the party's emphasis on the unemployed (486). Both the social historical context—rationalization, depression, unemployment—and party strategy need to be kept in view. See also Rosenhaft, *Beating the Fascists?* and Anthony McElligott, "Mobilising the Unemployed: The KPD and the Unemployed Workers' Movement in Hamburg-Altona during the Weimar Republic," in *The German Unemployed: Experiences and Consequences of Mass Unemployment from the Weimar Republic to the Third Reich*, ed. Richard J. Evans and Dick Geary (New York: St. Martin's Press, 1987), 228–60.

[26] For examples see Herlemann, *Kommunalpolitik*, 173–87; Georg Fülberth, *Die Beziehungen zwischen SPD und KPD in der Kommunalpolitik der Weimarer Periode 1918/19 bis 1933* (Cologne: Pahl-Rugenstein, 1985), 360–75; and Rosenhaft, *Beating the Fascists?* 53–54.

[27] For example, Walter Ulbricht quoted in Rosenhaft, *Beating the Fascists?* 54.

[28] See Rosenhaft, *Beating the Fascists?* and for some examples from the Halle-Merseburg region, Karl-Heinz Leidigkeit and Jürgen Hermann, *Auf leninistischem Kurs—Geschichte der KPD-Bezirksorganisation Halle-Merseburg bis 1933*, ed. Bezirksleitung Halle der SED, Kommission zur Erforschung der Geschichte der örtlichen Arbeiterbewegung (Halle: Druckhaus "Freiheit," 1979), 419–22.

[29] As just one example, see the report of a Nazi meeting held in 1927 in Wedding, one of the centers of KPD support in Berlin, in *Nazism 1919–1945*, vol. 1: *The Rise to Power, 1919–1934*, ed. Jeremy Noakes and Geoffrey Pridham (Exeter: Exeter University Publications, 1983), 53–54.

[30] Rosenhaft, *Beating the Fascists?* 64–67, 142–43. The slogan was variously condemned and resurrected by the leadership, but found widespread support among the rank and file.

And the Central Committee, at least for a time, clearly sanctioned organized acts of terror, such as the murder of police officers and shoot-ups of SA-frequented taverns.[31]

Indeed, the KPD and Comintern came to view the unemployed and generally unorganized as more active and militant, as those elements "that appear now on the stage of the class struggle as the very earnest and decisive factors of the movement," rather than the "social democratic–infected" union members.[32] At the outset of 1931, party chairman Ernst Thälmann defended communist street violence by calling on workers to respond to Nazi terror with "the most offensive, physical mass struggle." In Thälmann's view, such actions would not only undermine the fascists, but would cause "social democratic workers [to] gain confidence in us, because they see that we are there and fight back." In the process, the party would "strengthen, forge, and steel our cadres for higher tasks in the revolution."[33]

By the autumn of 1931, however, the party leadership had begun to have some doubts, less about the efficacy of street violence than about the neglect of the workplace and the problems of "individual" actions. In a Central Committee resolution of 10 November 1931, the KPD felt compelled to warn its members against acts of individual terror, which it considered completely "un-Leninist," a reversion to the tactics of the petit bourgeoisie and anarchists and a diversion from the task of building mass struggles.[34] In 1932, the party leadership moved decisively against Heinz Neumann and other outspoken advocates of physical violence. Yet none of this signified that the party had given up on street battles, and within the rank and file there existed strong sentiments in favor of street tactics, especially among those directly threatened by Nazi violence.[35] As Thälmann argued, "the resolution of the Central Committee should not serve to weaken in the slightest the mass struggle of the proletariat and workers in defense against the murderous terror of the fascists."[36]

Yet a strategy focused on the unemployed and that seemed to support any act of combativeness—from seizing food and protesting evictions to armed attacks on fascists—only accentuated the fragmentation of the Weimar working class and narrowed the party's base of support. The KPD realized that the unemployed could not be organized in the traditional places of labor politics, the factories and mines.

[31] For one well-documented event, see Rosenhaft, *Beating the Fascists?* 118–27. The murder of two police officers at Bülowplatz was the most notorious incident. Retrospective justice was applied when Erich Mielke, the former head of the DDR's Ministry of State Security, was convicted in 1993 for the killings committed sixty-two years previously.

[32] I. Jusefowitsch and G. B. Smoljanski, quoted in Bahne, "Erwerbslosenpolitik," 487.

[33] Quoted in Rosenhaft, *Beating the Fascists?* 73.

[34] See Ernst Thälmann, "Einige Fehler in unserer theoretischen und praktischen Arbeit und der Weg zu ihrer Ueberwindung," *Die Internationale* 14:11/12 (1931): 481–509.

[35] See Rosenhaft, *Beating the Fascists?*

[36] Thälmann, "Einige Fehler," 505–6. See also Rosenhaft, *Beating the Fascists?*; Hermann Weber's introduction to the collection he also edited, *Die Generallinie: Rundschreiben des Zentralkomitees der KPD an die Bezirke 1929–1933* (Düsseldorf: Droste, 1981); and Horst Duhnke, *Die KPD von 1933 bis 1945* (Cologne: Kiepenheuer und Witsch, 1972), 18–47, all of whom provide close readings of the twists and turns in official party policy.

Instead, the party sought them out where they gathered—at the welfare agencies and offices where they went to register, to be examined, and to receive their payments. As one KPD directive (presumably in 1932) put it: "Committees of the unemployed . . . are to be elected in the registration, examination, welfare, or disbursement offices; in unemployed residencies; in people's and welfare kitchens; and in the neighborhoods. The decisive organizational basis of the unemployed movement must be the examination and registration offices."[37] As a result, the political space of communist organizing largely shifted out of the workplace and into neighborhood streets and local welfare offices, a kind of inversion of communist politics that ran completely against the supposed centrality of enterprise cells to the organizational structure of communist parties.

The unemployed committees were to have elaborate structures—a sign of the seriousness with which the KPD considered the organization of the unemployed and of the political phantasms that drove the party.[38] Each unemployed committee was to have a women's commission, which was to organize the female unemployed at the registration and examination offices, and engage them in the "*Kampffront*." Women were also to be organized in the neighborhoods, and local leaders—*Vertrauensleute*—were to be selected. In addition, each unemployed committee was to have subcommittees devoted to organization, agitation and propaganda, press, finance, youth, white-collar workers, workplace and trade union work, legal protection, and economic issues. That the unemployed rarely, if ever, could muster the organizational will and resources to create such an edifice seemed beyond the purview of party leaders. As in 1923/24, the unemployed committees had, in reality, transient memberships and loose, if any, structures, all of which correlated with the sporadic and militant forms of activism favored by the unemployed—a reality that the party leadership recognized and continually complained about.

Both the chronically unemployed and the casually employed lost more than the ability to earn a living: they were deprived also of organizational links with the trade unions and the legally constituted works councils, the institutions of the labor movement based in the workplace and dominated by the SPD. The unemployed lost their grounding in the combination of workplace, marketplace, and state-directed actions that had typified German labor activism in the past. They could no longer place demands upon the employers, nor could their grievances be articulated through the trade unions. The target of their activism shifted almost exclusively to the state. They came into conflict with the police, and demanded from state agencies improved unemployment and welfare benefits. To the extent that the KPD became a party of the unemployed, its terrain of activism also shifted out of the workplace.[39]

From the social welfare policies of the Republic the unemployed derived only the bare minimum needed to eke out a marginal existence, hardly enough to win

[37] "Der Aufbau der E.-Ausschüsse," HIA, NSDAP 41/810.

[38] Ibid.

[39] This is the argument of Rosenhaft, *Beating the Fascists?* but, as should be clear, I think that this process was not at all restricted to the Depression.

their loyalty to the Weimar system. The employed, in contrast, derived much more tangible benefits from state arbitration of labor disputes and unemployment insurance, which, despite the low level of benefits, served them well through bouts of episodic (though not long-term) joblessness. Those fairly steadily employed had, therefore, a fully legitimate basis to remain loyal to the Weimar system and the efforts of the SPD to create a more effectively social democratic state out of the Republic. Unlike the imperial period, when virtually all male industrial workers shared in common the material benefits conferred by the paternalistic state, the fragmented working class of the Weimar period participated in the welfare state in a grossly inequitable manner.

Still more serious, and decisive for the bitterness of the political divisions within the German labor movement: The unemployed and the communists came into conflict with a state identified with and oftentimes staffed by social democrats. The SPD's stature as the *Staatspartei* of the Weimar system was not merely symbolic. As discussed in chapter 3, in Prussia (and some other states) the SPD directed the police forces throughout the Weimar period, and the party's members often worked in the national, state, and local social welfare agencies. The socialist-led unions were, in the eyes of the unemployed, similarly suspect, for they had collaborated with firms in using the employment crisis to rid the workplace of radical workers and resisted efforts to integrate the demands of the unemployed into wage disputes.

Hence, the social fragmentation of the working class resulted in distinct paths of political activism and very different relations to the Weimar state. But at the same time, the paths of action taken by the unemployed of the Weimar Republic display some lines of continuity with the repertoire of working-class actions as far back as the nineteenth century. When they demanded public works projects, higher unemployment and welfare benefits, the confiscation and distribution of food supplies, a state-mandated reduction in the workday coupled with additional hirings, free transportation, forgiveness on water and electricity bills—these were all demands predicated on the expectation that the state had an obligation and the capacity to intervene on behalf of workers.[40]

Significantly, the unemployed in the 1920s and 1930s never came to articulate an antistatist ideology, even though they so often came into conflict with the Weimar state. The syndicalist notions embedded in the council system, with their emphasis on the workplace as the nucleus of the future social order, came to have little relevance for those removed from the productive sphere by structural unem-

[40] Gerald D. Feldman, "Saxony, the Reich, and the Problem of Unemployment in the German Inflation," *AfS* 27 (1987): 124, cites one telling example from Saxony in the summer of 1920, when the Labor Minister was forced to receive a delegation of the unemployed. One worker said, "the government should simply bring the workers into the factories, and then the unemployment would be relieved." For another early example, see PVH to RPM, 25 June 1921, LHSAM C20/Ib/4648/5I/132, and from the Ruhr in 1923/24, PPE to RPD, 29 August 1923, HStAD 16573/50; PPE to RPD, 6 September 1923, HStAD 16573/96–98; PPE to RPD, 21 and 25 September 1923, HStAD 16573/52, 72–73; PPE to RPD, 7 November 1923, HStAD 16765. For other examples of the demands and actions of the unemployed, see "Der Aufbau der E.-Ausschüsse," HIA, NSDAP 41/810, and "Material für die Erwerbslosenbewegung" and "Wie mobilisieren wir die Massen der Erwerbslosen zum Kampf um ihre Forderungen," HIA, NSDAP 41/811.

ployment. Instead, the ideological terrain of the German labor movement remained dominated by the explicitly statist notions of both the KPD and the SPD. The reformist strategy of the SPD, predicated on incremental gains derived from collective bargaining, state arbitration, and the legislative expansion of the welfare state, provided the unemployed with little hope of a solution to their problems. But the KPD's vision of an even more activist state—the dictatorship of the proletariat in its specifically Marxist-Leninist version—offered the unemployed a mechanism of surmounting the dire situation in which they existed and accorded with the long tradition of working-class political practice centered around an interventionist state.

The combative tenor of the actions of the unemployed only accentuated the masculine character of the movement—in contrast to the more fluid and diverse character of the unemployed demonstrations in the first period of the Republic. The gendered nature of the labor market had, in the first place, made the workplace and union organization inhospitable to women, so relatively few were eligible for unemployment benefits. Second, women were also discriminated against in the granting of unemployment benefits, so were less likely to appear at the places of mobilization. Third, in the deep economic crisis of the Depression years, the household burdens on women only increased, giving them less time for political activities. All of these factors ensured that, by the time of the Depression, the unemployed movement remained overwhelmingly male, which no doubt facilitated its incorporation into the KPD's masculinized political strategy of street battles and political violence.

"For Eilenburg—Eisleben," May 1923, and "Workers' Day" in Halle, 11 May 1924

Two demonstrations in the Halle-Merseburg region, separated by a year, show how much *Kampfstimmung* (fighting sentiment) was an essential aspect of the party's makeup, and how early, long before the emergence of the NSDAP and the endemic violence of the last years of the Weimar Republic, the politics of street battles had become a focal point of the KPD's political strategy.

In the first case, the events turned on a radical right-wing demonstration in Eilenburg, located in the Mansfeld region of Prussian Saxony.[41] A veterans brigade (the so-called Kriegsverein ehemaliger 27ziger) along with the Stahlhelm, Wehrwolf, and other right-wing bands had called the demonstration for 10 May. Eilenburg was a communist stronghold, so the demonstration was seen from the outset as a provocation. The local union cartel, dominated by the KPD, approved a communist-initiated proposal for a counterdemonstration. At first, the workers' demonstration was poorly attended—many people had wanted to watch the fascists parade, as they did in suitable military formation and outfitted with side

[41] The description of the following events is drawn from BLHM [to ZK], "Sonderbericht über die Vorgänge am Donnerstag, den 10. Mai 1923 in Eilenburg," and BLHM [to ZK] "Sonderbericht über die Vorgänge in Eisleben," 9 July 1923, SAPMO-BA, ZPA I/3/11/18/106–9, 155–57.

arms, clubs, rubber truncheons, metal splinters from grenades, and other weapons. According to the district KPD, the right-wingers planned beforehand to engage communists in battle.

They did not have to wait long. The first incident occurred just inside the city limits, when a communist bystander laughed at one of the marchers. He was then hit on the shoulder with a rubber truncheon, and another comrade, standing nearby, demanded that the police, also nearby, arrest the assailant. Two police officers as well as some KPD people ran behind the marchers in an effort to identify the one who had delivered the blow. According to the KPD account, the Stahlhelm leader then ordered, "Prepare to attack! The one in the blue cap, beat him dead! Fall out!" The communist who had appealed to the police was then beaten senseless. A number of bystanders who spoke out against the attack were also beaten, initiating a whole series of fights along the march route and elsewhere in the town. According to the communist account, the right-wingers began to attack bystanders almost at random, as well as more selective targets. Their discipline and overwhelming superiority of numbers gave them a "cheap victory."

But interesting for our purposes is the KPD analysis of the event. To the immense satisfaction of the leadership, the right-wing demonstration had served to arouse the workers of Eilenburg and the surrounding region out of their passivity. The next day, close to five thousand workers gathered for a mass protest meeting, more than attended similar events during the Revolution in Eilenburg. SPD spokesmen were shouted down, though local social democratic leaders were at least for a while ready to contemplate forming proletarian defense brigades with the KPD. A few days later, however, they reversed themselves, probably under pressure from the national leadership. In at least one factory, workers charged that one of their colleagues, a Wehrwolf member, had participated in the attacks. They demanded that he be fired, and management acceded. In this plant, the Eilenburg Motorwerken, workers also established a defense brigade under KPD leadership. With some satisfaction, KPD leaders concluded their report that "the events in Eilenburg have brought new life to our local group." Some twenty SPD members, along with other individuals, had gone over to the KPD.

The Eilenburg events were soon followed by a KPD countermove throughout the region. The party was well aware that fascists were gaining ground in the crisis year 1923, including among workers, through a "clever campaign of agitation in the workplace." According to party reports, the fascist upswing was noticeable especially in those areas that in March 1921 had been centers of revolutionary action. Right-wing groups were carrying out terror acts against workers. Hence, workers and the party had to respond to counter the fascist rise and to shift the tide in the region in the communist direction. To accomplish this, the party proposed to the union cartel in Eisleben, which was controlled by the KPD, that the date of a planned trade union festival be shifted from 17 to 24 June, the very day that the Stahlhelm was planning a march in Eisleben. The KPD proposed the slogan for the festival: "For Eilenburg—Eisleben." Nothing could more expressively convey the blow-for-blow political strategy of the KPD and the emphasis placed on confrontation and political violence.

Over three thousand Stahlhelmer in four columns marched on Eisleben. The KPD gathered seven thousand workers—only one thousand from Eisleben itself—"a glittering deployment of the KPD of our district." This time, the KPD successfully organized its countermoves. Communist demonstrators managed to cross the routes of the Stahlhelm columns, preventing them from joining together. For the entire day the Stahlhelm remained divided while workers marched in military fashion and held their trade union festival.

But the day was not over. A small group of workers were set upon by Stahlhelmer and badly beaten. The KPD paramilitary units—the Proletarian Hundreds—from Halle and other towns, as well as Eisleben, were alerted and quickly mobilized, "at first to secure the entire festival and to prevent panic." This apparently succeeded. In addition, three groups of five communists (the so-called Fünfergruppen) "beat Stahlhelm people in two very well-led attacks, so that they had to make their way to their meeting place with badly battered heads." Schupo officers then intervened, more against the Stahlhelm than the KPD. Of the party wounded, a few were the result of people "who lack discipline and believe that the Stahlhelm can be countered through individual force." All told, the communists suffered twelve wounded, the Stahlhelm twenty-six. In the evening, the comrades from Halle and other towns marched to the train station in "tight groups of one hundred" and did the same when they arrived in Halle. Here again they were attacked by Stahlhelmer with firearms, but the intervention of the Fünfergruppen set the Stahlhelmer to flight.

For the district leadership, the events in Eisleben were a great success. They had demonstrated the KPD's presence in the district and its offensive tactics. As a result of the events, Proletarian Hundreds had been established in the Mansfeld region—for the KPD, the surest indication of success. In addition, the action had caused discussion and further dissension in the ranks of the right. Yet the right-wingers were not only enemies—there were potential recruits to be had. The district leadership applauded the "Schlageter speech" by the Bolshevik and Comintern leader Karl Radek, in which he claimed the nationalist cause for the KPD.[42]

All of the characteristics of communist demonstrations were even more amply displayed in a major demonstration in Halle on 11 May 1924, the so-called "Workers' Day" ("Arbeitertag").[43] The KPD called for Arbeitertag in direct response to the announcement of a "German Day" ("Deutschertag") in Halle by a number of right-wing paramilitary bands, the Stahlhelm prominent among them, for 10 May 1924. The KPD mobilized all its forces, including communists from as far away as Berlin and Thuringia. The KPD demonstration was intended to be a major display of working-class strength and to challenge directly the ability of the radical right to make Halle "its" city, if only for a few hours. The KPD was to make its stand in one of the most left-wing of German cities. The preparations were to be

[42] For the text of the speech, see Weber, *Deutscher Kommunismus*, 142–47.

[43] The discussion that follows is drawn from a long internal party report, [BLHM to ZK], "Bericht über den Arbeitertag," SAPMO-BA, ZPA I/3/11/13/186–200, and from Leidigkeit and Hermann, *Auf leninistischem Kurs*, 201–4.

meticulous, the authorities and the right were to be foiled. The reality turned out otherwise, but the district leadership found the events exhilarating nonetheless.

With the demonstrations separated by only one day, members of both the communist and the right-wing contingents would undoubtedly cross paths in the city and the surrounding area. Indeed, conflicts between the two groups was an intrinsic element of the KPD's strategy, a way to demonstrate its superior power. The regional party leadership therefore organized the demonstration with a strong military cast. All preparations were conducted in close consultation with the KPD's military apparatus, whose district leader assumed organizational responsibility. In militaristic fashion, the demonstrators from outside the city proper were to gather at five distinct points and the columns would then march on the city, converging in the city center (the Marktplatz)—"to enliven the city and the street scene with their march and to disturb the fascists." Reliable comrades were to be armed to protect the demonstration columns.

The organizers were well aware that this plan would lead to serious confrontations with the fascists. To prevent the police from hindering the marchers, communists inside the city were to gather early in the morning at the Marktplatz and set off in their own march columns, thereby engaging the police and preventing them from dispatching squads to the city limits. Then the entire force would gather around noon at the Sportplatz and the Volkspark, followed by another march past the burial place of revolutionary militants and back to the center of the city. In the evening, the crowd would disperse—again with a march, though this time in loose groups toward the train station, from where the comrades from outside the city would depart. As the organizers wrote to the Central Committee, "The plan was adapted to the fascist march plan. Should it be accomplished successfully, then it would lead most probably to sharp conflicts with the fascists." To further the militaristic hues of the entire event, the party had set up a command center in an apartment in the city, complete with a communications division. From the command center, reliable comrades were to be dispatched to each of the five marching columns to ensure contact between base control and the demonstrators. In order to carry the plan out successfully, the Halle party organization also had to organize food and sleeping quarters for the many comrades expected from outside the city.

Yet from the very moment of its inception, the demonstration proved to be a fiasco. The military leader was incompetent; he often failed to show up at planning meetings and never carried through on his responsibilities. At the last moment, the leaders of the political and organizational divisions of the local party had to take over the organizational preparations.

The vaunted effort to maintain tight lines of communication failed also in other arenas. The central command was able only in part to maintain links with the five columns, and middle-echelon leaders lacked the instructions they were supposed to convey. The military preparations to protect the columns failed almost completely, a result of the "extraordinarily poor level of the military work in the district." These plans included sending "select, qualified groups to Halle. . . to stand in the front lines, along with the special groups of the district, in the struggle against the fascists." Presumably, this entailed comrades with military training who carried special (but unspecified) weaponry.

Efforts to interrupt the fascist demonstration also failed. The organizers had hoped to hinder the movement of trains with right-wing demonstrators aboard, but this effort utterly failed because of the KPD's almost complete lack of influence among locomotive engineers. Instead, the fascists marched unhindered into Halle on Saturday midday as the greatly strengthened police detachment simply watched. Despite a police order forbidding marches, the fascists marched in long columns, heavily armed and with black-white-red banners and swastikas flying. By evening they had fully occupied the major streets.

Communists from outside the city began arriving the same day, and confrontations with security forces quickly arose. The police barred demonstration marshals from the train station and simply arrested arriving communists. Although fascists controlled the major streets, delegations of communists nonetheless managed to march through the neighboring streets to the Volkspark singing communist songs, giving the "street scene a decisive proletarian character." All through the night and the following morning communists continued to arrive in the city. But when they gathered at the Volkspark, it was evident that the local communists had by and large stayed home. To the despair of the leaders, many of the newly arriving headed straight for their beds and provisions and for a good time away from home. Only with difficulty, and often not at all, could they be rounded up for the marches and demonstrations. Delegations failed to register with the leaders of the event, hence making it impossible to bring together at the same time all of the forces for a disciplined show of strength. Some delegations were quartered far outside of the city, so the police had an easy job preventing them from getting any closer.

Moreover, the entire plan hinged on the punctual massing of all available forces in order to disrupt the city. This part of the plan, however, became "a complete fiasco." Only two to three hundred workers showed up at 8:00 A.M. on Sunday in the Marktplatz, most of whom were party functionaries. Clearly, many workers had no intention of arising that early for a demonstration, party orders or not. At other gathering points, sometimes as few as ten or fifteen comrades appeared. The police then had an easy time closing off the Marktplatz and dispersing the demonstrators, while the marching columns, many of which lacked directions anyway, were prevented by the police from arriving in the Marktplatz. A number of bloody confrontations between the police and demonstrators occurred, both in Halle and the surrounding towns. Even had the police not interfered, many of these groups had only the vaguest ideas of where they were supposed to be—as party leaders themselves stated: "Here the absolutely unsatisfactory military preparations avenged themselves." In the city, meanwhile, the small columns of demonstrators had returned to the Volkspark after some relatively mild confrontations with the police and the fascists. Much to the disappointment of party leaders, they were unable to convince the comrades, some of whom were tired, to march again out of the Volkspark and, no doubt, to engage the police and fascists.

That turned out to be a major error, for the communists now ensconced in the

Volkspark were an inviting target for the vastly strengthened police forces. The police began to gather in the area. The party military leadership gave the order for people to leave the Volkspark, but that did not happen because of "the lack of discipline of the masses and the flagging energy of the marshals," so those inside were now surrounded. There the mood reached near-panic levels, helped along by talk of the pogrom-like attitude of the police and rumors of bloody conflicts between workers on the outside and the security forces. Certain hotheads among those in the Volkspark, in disregard for the overwhelmingly superior force of the police—which included Schupo units, armed with hand grenades and machine guns—sought to promote a confrontationist mood among the crowd and attacks on the police. The military leader had to be removed from his position, while other leaders snuck in and out of the Volkspark trying to calm the situation. Also, the weapons that many comrades carried had to be secured for fear of personal and house searches.

Negotiations began, but the communists inside at first refused to leave the Volkspark under the escort of the police. But nothing could be done in the Volkspark, only in the streets and in the city. The communists inside thereby extended their confinement by at least six hours and hindered the "effective struggle against the fascists." The party leadership was in full agreement that given the strength of the police forces and their heavy arms, an attempt to break out of the Volkspark would have resulted in immense casualties and probable failure. Finally, after long negotiations, the police let the workers leave the grounds of the Volkspark in columns of one hundred. As they reached the city—after midnight—the workers' columns and the fascists engaged in renewed combat, leaving wounded on both sides. All told, in Halle, Erfurt, and Leipzig, three workers were killed and nine wounded and hospitalized during these demonstrations. Many more suffered less serious wounds. Four hundred and fifty workers were taken prisoner, four Schupo officers were killed in Magdeburg and Halle, six were wounded and hospitalized. A large number of fascists were wounded and two were listed as missing.

The next day, Monday, there were demonstrations in Halle and throughout Germany in protest against the killing of workers. Six thousand workers in Halle gathered at the Volkspark. For the KPD, the Arbeitertag, with all of its chaos and disorganization, had at least served part of its purpose—the workers were now angry and aroused. The police observers were forced to leave the hall, so intense was the mood inside: "At the rally the workers gave no evidence of disappointment. In contrast, [they showed] a considerable excitement. The demonstrations were a success for the party." While communists gathered once again at the Volkspark, the fascists took advantage of the situation to attack the party's Produktivgenossenschaft (where its press and other resources were housed) and small groups of workers on the streets. Groups of workers and the Schupo fought with fascist bands made up of fifty to sixty individuals. From nearby windows the attackers opened up with firearms, and were answered by communists inside the Produktivgenossenschaft, who managed to fight off the fascists.

The party then called a protest strike for 15 May at 12:00 noon to coincide with the burial of the workers who had been killed in the weekend demonstrations. In Halle, over twenty thousand people followed the caskets—two thousand more than had voted for the KPD in the last election. According to the KPD report, many social democrats participated, and most large firms were forced to shut down. Even the police now prevented any attacks on the demonstrators and "a great number of them saluted the dead."

The confrontational intentions of Arbeitertag are clear. KPD leaders planned that their supporters would encounter rightist demonstrators and expected sharp conflict between their own forces and those of the police and the radical right. As state officials well understood, such demonstrations served a twofold purpose: they were designed as displays of party and proletarian power and to accustom the party's supporters to conflict, physical conflict in particular, with their opponents. Through physical combat workers would learn that still greater, more disciplined struggles were required.

Clearly, this strategy was highly gendered. The sources make no mention of the composition of the demonstrators, but it is clear from internal evidence that males comprised the overwhelming proportion of participants. The military-like planning, the provisions for sleeping quarters, the absence of any particular efforts to attract women's support, the intention to foment confrontations with the police and the fascists—all that shows the highly masculinized nature of the demonstration and of communist politics in general. As mentioned earlier, the confrontationist strategy was by no means the province of a particular wing of the party, although "Workers' Day" expressively conveyed the approach of the KPD left that dominated Halle-Merseburg from 1923 to 1925. Nonetheless, the events in Halle drew upon earlier episodes of confrontation between communists and rightists in the city and region and would be reprised in the later years of the Republic, both periods when the district organization was in the hands of the center and right.[44] The politics of street battles and the elevation of male physical prowess had become a fundamental feature of communism in the Weimar Republic almost irrespective of party factions.

Strikingly, despite all the failures and the anarchic situation, the party leadership considered the demonstration a great success. Those who failed in their responsibilities are depressed, claimed the district leadership. The workers in general have been aroused by the active steps of the party against fifty thousand fascists and ten thousand Schupo and Reichswehr officers. Many more copies of the party's newspaper have been sold, and the demonstrations in the succeeding days show how much support the party has won.

[44] In 1921, for example, well before the last phase of the Weimar Republic and its endless round of street violence between the KPD and NSDAP, communists in Halle disrupted meetings of the Stalhelm, which, like the KPD, had a strong presence in the city. PVH to RPM, 2 September 1921, LHSAM C20/Ib/4648/5I/184–85. In 1923, the Halle police reported numerous violent altercations between members of the Stahlhelm and Wehrwolf, on the one side, and communists on the other. "For Eilenburg—Eisleben" was only the most dramatic of the confrontations. See PPH to RPM, 14 May, 14 June, 14 July 1923, LHSAM C20/Ib/4648/5II/16, 24–25, 53.

> Workers' Day has led to an immense sharpening of the relations between fascism and the revolutionary workforce. Reports of intense conflicts between fascists and workers are coming in from numerous localities in the district, which for the most part have ended with serious woundings on the fascist side. . . . Workers' Day has above all else led to the recognition on the part of workers that the bourgeoisie and the fascist bands must be opposed with weapons in hand. In sum, Fascist Day in the district and the surrounding area has had a revolutionary impact. . . . Workers' Day has clearly shown that the Communist Party is ready with all means to lead the struggle against reaction and for the emancipation of the working class. It has brought confusion in the camp of the enemy and has decisively raised the influence of the party.[45]

This was an old story, the same one repeated after the defeat of every party-led insurrection. It exhibits the party's continual fixation on confrontation and violence, its belief that through the demonstration of revolutionary credentials the party would attract increasing support. But the holiday-like disorganization and indiscipline, with workers going off to find food and comradeship—at least until the situation turned violent—was evidence enough of how difficult it would be to generate solid organization and real advances out of this strategy.

The politics of confrontation served to accentuate the militaristic tenor of party life. Significantly, the events in Halle constituted a major impetus to the formation of the KPD's paramilitary unit, the RFB, a further sign of the militarization—and masculinization—of communist culture in the Weimar Republic.[46] At the same time, the party rank and file often lapsed into a languid passivity, an irony not lost on the leadership. Here in "Red Halle," a bastion of, successively, the SPD, USPD, and then KPD, where the party was better rooted than almost anywhere else in the daily lives and institutions of labor—in the unions, the cooperatives, the informal networks of sociability—where the KPD became almost without a struggle the heir to a rich tradition of working-class culture and oppositional politics, here the very strength of the party had engendered a certain kind of passivity. Clearly, the old social democratic strategy of erecting bastions of party strength in preparation for the assumption of power, while holding off the active engagement with the forces of order, still had resonance, largely because it was easy and placed fewer demands on people. Like the old SPD, the rank and file of the KPD oscillated between out-and-out combat with the agencies of order—though with the use of greater force on both sides than had been the case before 1914—and a kind of passivity that awaited great developments. But unlike the SPD, the KPD as a party sought to promote continually the activist, confrontationist side of working-class politics.

The Lenin-Liebknecht-Luxemburg Festivals

Not every demonstration was designed for physical confrontations, at least not initially. Demonstrations served also as moments for the reassertion of party

[45] [BLHM to ZK], "Bericht über den Arbeitertag," SAPMO-BA, ZPA I/3/11/13/198.

[46] See Leidigkeit and Hermann, *Auf leninistischem Kurs*, 203.

ideology and the construction and reaffirmation of class and political identities. Communists drew here on a rich tradition of working-class and more generally popular collective action that reached back at least to 1848, but endowed these actions with their own particular meanings.

The annual commemoration of Rosa Luxemburg's and Karl Liebknecht's assassination played an especially important role in this regard. These festivals provided the primary occasion for memorializing the party's founders, the moment when leaders offered testaments to their great revolutionary role, the press published excerpts from their writings, and the party's supporters were drawn into a sacred public ritual that consecrated the militant activism and conscientious socialist labor of the party's founding leaders and the succeeding generations. In this way, Liebknecht's and Luxemburg's legacy could then be used to lend legitimacy to party strategies (and later in the DDR, to state policies and the national identity of the socialist state and its citizenry).

These yearly festivals began immediately after the assassination of Luxemburg and Liebknecht on 15 January 1919. Ten days later, on 25 January 1919, tens of thousands of Berlin workers, the largest gathering Berlin had ever seen, marched to Friedrichsfelde to bury Liebknecht and an empty coffin for Luxemburg, whose body had not yet been found. Late that spring, on 13 June 1919, after her body had turned up in a canal, working-class Berlin reenacted the march and gave Luxemburg a proper burial.[47] The ritual marches to the gravesite in 1919 reproduced a long-standing tradition of funereal demonstrations in which the popular classes memorialized their leaders or the victims of repression and states and political parties sought to solidify their power or influence.[48]

The young KPD soon formalized these commemorations, making of them specifically party, rather than more generally popular, affairs. With Lenin's death, also in January, they became the so-called "LLL" (Lenin-Liebknecht-Luxemburg) festivals.[49] In Berlin, the "LLL" commemorations always included a march from the Frankfurter Allee to the gravesite at Friedrichsfelde, where along with Liebknecht and Luxemburg other socialist militants were buried. The march became a fixed feature of Berlin politics in the Weimar period, while outside of the capital local party districts organized their own commemora-

[47] See the account "'Unser Schiff zieht seinen geraden Kurs fest und stolz dahin bis zum Ziel': Impressionen am Wege unserer traditionellen Demonstration zur Gedenkstätte der Sozialisten in Berlin-Friedrichsfelde," *ND*, 10/11 January 1987, 9.

[48] See, for example, Mona Ozouf, *Festivals and the French Revolution* (Cambridge, Mass.: Harvard University Press, 1988), 61–82, which has some scattered discussions of funerals; the oft-repeated story of Victor Hugo's grand funeral in 1885, which purportedly helped solidify the Third Republic, in Hubert Juin, *Victor Hugo*, vol. 3: *1870–1885* (Paris: Flammarion, 1986), 307–26; and August Bebel's great funeral in Zurich as reported in *Vorwärts*, 17 August 1913 ("Der stille Bebel") and 18 August 1913 ("Bebels Leichenbegängnis").

[49] The order of the names was not merely alphabetical, but reflected the evaluation of the importance of each of the leaders, as propaganda directives to the party districts in late 1932 advised: "There cannot be a shred of doubt that Lenin stands ahead of Luxemburg and Liebknecht." Agitprop Abteilung des ZK der KPD, "Lenin, Liebknecht, Luxemburg: Rede-Dispositionen for LLL-Feiern und -Kundgebungen 1933," BAK R45/IV/39/201.

tions. In Halle-Merseburg, for example, the district leadership reported to the Central Committee that forty-four LLL-festivals in 1927, forty-five in 1928, had taken place, and that they had attracted wide participation.[50]

In the LLL-festivals, the KPD reaffirmed the intransigent aspects of party ideology by invoking Luxemburg's and Liebknecht's untrammeled commitment to an activist, revolutionary politics. *Rote Fahne*' s commemoration of them in conjunction with the 1933 anniversary of the assassination resonated with Luxemburg's inflamed rhetoric and revolutionary ideas:

> six million communists hold the flag high, which at that time fell from the hands of Luxemburg and Liebknecht. Six million communists stand armed in the spirit of Liebknecht and Luxemburg and with the weapons of victorious Leninism to struggle for a socialist Germany. . . .
>
> In the middle of a world ignited by the fire of war, in the middle of the cacophony of arms of the reactionary powers, in the center of capitalist rule in fascist Germany—today resounds the clear call of the proletariat, the call of the Germany of workers and peasants:
>
> With Luxemburg and Liebknecht—We are on the attack![51]

By staking out the offensive, by going "on the attack," the KPD of the Weimar Republic reprised Luxemburg's efforts to raise continually the revolutionary temper. It proved a simple task to cull quotes from her speeches and writings that echoed *Rote Fahne*' s own inflamed tones and that made commitment to revolutionary politics the essential criterion of socialist militancy.

Moreover, the street battles of the Weimar Republic seemed like the confirmation in practice of Luxemburg's overwrought rhetoric and celebration of the streets as the essential space of political engagement. *Rote Fahne* concluded one report of the LLL demonstration with a depiction of a street fight between communist demonstrators and "cocky and provocative" SA men, whom the crowd beat into retreat.[52] In the march to the gravesite, the prominent role of the Red Front Fighters League gave visual representation to the militancy of the socialist struggle. Disseminated through the party press, the depictions of idealized revolutionaries as physically powerful men marching in disciplined formation echoed Luxemburg's own gendered language, which identified clear revolutionary politics with masculinity.[53]

Luxemburg's bipolar concept of politics as a struggle between revolutionaries and counterrevolutionaries, with social democrats prominent among the latter, seemed perfectly incarnated in the social and political conflicts of the Weimar

[50] BLHM, "Politischer Bericht des Bezirks Halle-Merseburg für die Monate Dezember 1926–Januar 1927," SAPMO-BA, ZPA I/3/11/16/62, and BLHM, "Politischer Bericht des Bezirks Halle-Merseburg für die Monate November und Dezember 1927 und Januar 1928," SAPMO-BA, ZPA I/3/11/16/115–16.

[51] "In ihrem Geiste vorwärts! Auf nach Friedrichsfelde!" *RF*, 15 January 1933.

[52] "So ehrte das rote Berlin seine Toten!" *RF*, 17 January 1933.

[53] See Luxemburg, "Parteitag der Unabhängigen SP," 29 November 1918, in *GW*:4, 423, in which she accused the Independents of lacking "manly resolve."

Republic. With little difficulty, the editors of *Rote Fahne* in 1933 assembled quotations from Luxemburg and Liebknecht under the headline, "Forever indicted! Liebknecht and Rosa Luxemburg lash out at the social democratic leaders."[54] The memorials to Luxemburg and Liebknecht, and the use of Luxemburg's own language, served as constant reminders of the calumny of social democracy.

Typically, the KPD memorialized the martyrdom of Liebknecht and Luxemburg to inspire party supporters to still greater exertions on behalf of the party and the socialist cause. As one report trumpeted: "Rosa Luxemburg and Karl Liebknecht fell in the struggle for the proletarian dictatorship. The German working class will fulfill the living legacy of their dead leaders in the struggle for the proletarian dictatorship!"[55] In the days just before the tenth anniversary of the assassination of Luxemburg and Liebknecht, *Rote Fahne* published a series of tributes under the dramatic headline, "They are still not avenged!"[56] The lead article, with pictures of Luxemburg and Liebknecht, admonished party members, "Forward in the spirit of our pioneers [*Vorkämpfer*]."[57] As late as 1933, almost one and one-half years after Stalin had issued a blanket condemnation of Luxemburg and just before the Nazi rise to power, *Rote Fahne* again lionized her contributions to the revolutionary cause with an article commemorating the assassinations, complete with a drawing on the front page of Lenin, Liebknecht, and Luxemburg peacefully laid out in their coffins and the headline "Forward in their spirit!" (plate 5.1)[58] Such representations, often coupled with excerpts from her writings under such headlines as "Writings of Rosa Luxemburg that every worker should know,"[59] connected Luxemburg's politics of totality with the party's claim to embody "true" socialist politics—however much in other respects the party diverged dramatically from her conception of socialism.

Withstanding the January cold and rain to march in honor of Liebknecht and Luxemburg underscored the determination and commitment of the party's followers, just as Luxemburg and Liebknecht had been unwavering in their commitment to socialism. As the party daily reported just two weeks before the Nazi *Machtergreifung* radically altered the fortunes of German communism:

> Red Berlin marched to the graves of Karl and Rosa. . . .
>
> Many times we saw one person give another his gloves, a youth drape his coat over an old comrade marching next to him, or vice versa. The Workers Music Group provided the march beat, and most of them played with bare hands. The fingers of the

[54] *RF*, 15 Janaury 1933.

[55] "Vom Spartakus zum Bolschewismus," *RF*, 15 January 1930.

[56] *RF*, 13 January 1929.

[57] Ibid..

[58] Ibid., 15 January 1933. Stalin accused Luxemburg and the entire prewar SPD left of "Menshevik errors." Josef V. Stalin, "Zu einigen Fragen der Geschichte des Bolschewismus," *RF*, 22 November 1931. His intervention was soon followed by still more vicious attacks by various KPD and Comintern spokesmen.

[59] *RF*, 15 January 1930.

18. Jahrg. / Nr. 13 — 15 Pfennig — Berlin, Sonntag, 15. Januar 1933

Die Rote Fahne

Zentralorgan der Kommunistischen Partei Deutschlands (Sektion der Kommunistischen Internationale)

In ihrem Geiste vorwärts!

Auf nach Friedrichsfelde!

Plate 5.1 The KPD's "Lenin-Liebknecht-Luxemburg Festival." The three heroic leaders lie peacefully in their coffins as the powerful force of the Soviet Union ignites communism around the world. Germany, with six million communist voters, is already partly inflamed. The headline reads "Forward in their spirit!" *Source: RF*, 15 January 1933.

pipers became stiff, but they played anyway. With uncountable banners the columns marched on, from the north, the east, the south, the west, underway for miles and hours. The unemployed without breakfast, without coats, freezing inside and out, streamed together to the three meeting places.[60]

Proletarian solidarity and commitment to the cause—the essence of class and political identities for communists—were established through the act of demonstrating. The famous line from Luxemburg's last article, "Ich war—ich bin—ich werde sein" [I was—I am—I shall be], displayed on banners carried by demonstrators and at the monument to socialists militants at Friedrichsfelde, linked Luxemburg's unwavering commitment to the socialist cause with the current generation of party members and asserted the timeless character of one's political identity as a communist.

The militancy of the party was inextricably entwined with its internationalist commitments, and here also Luxemburg's politics and persona lent themselves to mobilization (plate 5.2). *Rote Fahne* described the 1933 commemoration in terms that reaffirmed commitment to the Soviet Union and to the larger universe of proletarian struggle:

Proletarians, when you march today, know that all of working-class Germany, the entire proletarian world, marches with you in spirit to the graves in Friedrichsfelde! Know that the names of Liebknecht and Luxemburg inflame millions of Russian workers in the construction of socialism! Know that the names Liebknecht and Luxemburg are holy to the last coolie of Shanghai and are honored in the immense provinces of China where the impoverished peasants have overthrown the yoke of the landlords and have established soviet power!

There, where Karl and Rosa lay side by side with many brave Berlin workers, the victims of white officers, the victims of the murderous SA, the victims of Zörgiebel and Grzesinski [respectively, the social democratic police president of Berlin and Prussian minister of the interior]—there march today men and women and youth of Berlin, communists and social democratic and unaffiliated workers, who swear to be worthy of the fallen proletarian heroes![61]

Finally, the memorialization of Luxemburg served also to establish the historical legitimacy of the party and its leaders (and, later, of the party-state in the post–World War II world). Even party chairman Ernst Thälmann, faithful Stalinist that he was, invoked the powerful meaning of Liebknecht and Luxemburg for the KPD some months after Stalin had disabused communists of such views:

We have no intention of diminishing the importance of Rosa Luxemburg, Karl Liebknecht, Franz Mehring, and the other comrades who formed the left radical wing of prewar social democracy. We have no intention of denying the true revolutionary character of these fighters and leaders or of denying their solid revolutionary traditions. And we certainly do not want to leave them to the social fascists, SAPers, or Brandlerers [the latter two smaller left-wing organizations composed mainly of ex-communists and ex–

[60] "So ehrte das rote Berlin seine Toten!" *RF*, 17 January 1933.

[61] "In ihrem Geiste vorwärts! Auf nach Friedrichsfelde!" *RF*, 15 January 1933.

„Die Märtyrer hat die Arbeiterklasse in ihr großes Herz geschlossen. Ihre Henker hat die Geschichte schon jetzt an jenen Schandpfahl genagelt, von dem sie zu erlösen alle Gebete ihrer Pfaffen ohnmächtig sind" (Karl Marx)

Vérünket és életünket a forradalomért mint Rosa és Károly

„Wie Karl und Rosa unser Blut und Leben für die Revolution!"

Karl Liebknecht ed il proletariato italiano

„Karl Liebknecht und das italienische Proletariat"

Plate 5.2 Luxemburg and Liebknecht hold a wreath over the proletariat streaming into a demonstration from the neighborhood and the factory. The quote from Marx reads: "The working class holds its martyrs close to its heart. History has already nailed their executioners to the pillory, before which all the prayers of redemption of their priests are powerless." Below the caricature are testaments in a variety of languages to the heroic founders of German communism. *Source: RF*, 15 January 1929.

> social democrats], who defame the dead. Rosa Luxemburg and the others belong to us, belong to the Communist International and the KPD, on whose founding they contributed.[62]

In the ultimate consecration of leaders and led, *Rote Fahne* reported the response to Wilhelm Pieck at the 1933 commemoration: "In front of the speakers' stand beamed the white head of our comrade Wilhelm Pieck. The Red Front cry roared out. Everyone greeted the comrade of Karl and Rosa. Everyone raised their fists and joined in the commitment to fulfill the work of our great departed ones."[63]

In the march to the gravesite, communists honored the founders of Bolshevism and of German communism. Lenin was admired, but Luxemburg and Liebknecht held special significance because of their involvement in the German labor movement and, of course, because of their martyrdom. The LLL commemorations inscribed Luxemburg and Liebknecht into party culture as the preeminent symbols of revolutionary politics, the martyred leaders who, whatever their theoretical weaknesses, died in the cause of the socialist future. The march expressed militancy, determination, commitment, the leitmotifs of the idealized communist life. But that was not all. The binary oppositions that infused Luxemburg's writings and speeches in particular and that became an intrinsic element of communist language and ideology—between revolution and reform, socialism and capitalism, revolutionaries and traitors—were articulated time and again in the January demonstrations. Through the cultural practices of the party and an array of media, these meanings were conveyed to party members and served as the setting for the formation of the class and political identities of communists in the Weimar Republic.

Conclusion

The KPD could not always generate the support it desired. Demonstrations could be depressing affairs—poorly attended, the glaring expression of weakness rather than the powerful display of proletarian solidarity. The police, professionally inclined to see major disturbances behind every voice of protest, nonetheless often reported poorly attended rallies, marches that had to be called off because not enough people showed up, dispirited speeches. This was especially the case after major protest efforts had failed, but even in 1921 following the assassination of the Center Party leader Mathias Erzberger, the Halle police noted that a jointly called demonstration attracted only five thousand people, less than the hoped-for success.[64] In late February 1924, the height of the stabilization crisis, the police reported, for the first time in years, that no significant political party activity had

[62] Thälmann at a meeting of the Central Committee in February 1932, quoted in "In ihrem Namen . . . ," *RF*, 15 January 1933, 2. Thälmann did go on, however, to reiterate the standard criticisms of Luxemburg.

[63] "So ehrte das rote Berlin seine Toten!" *RF*, 17 January 1933.

[64] See some of the reports from the PVH to RPM in LHSAM C20/Ib/4648/5I, including 13 August 1921, 178–79, and 2 September 1921, 185.

occurred in Halle. The great unemployed demonstrations sought by the party had failed to materialize. Local events were dismal—few showed up to rallies, speakers failed to appear, and participants began wandering away long before the end of the proceedings.[65] And plans in 1924 for great demonstrations in connection with "International Youth Day" apparently misfired altogether, which the party leadership blamed on the incompetence of the district leaders and the youth secretary.[66]

Yet workers took to the streets often enough, and they provided the party with a rich repertoire of activism. The party was never a free agent; its politics were not derived in unmediated fashion from the classic Leninist texts or from the experience of the Bolshevik Revolution. In imperfect but unmistakable fashion the KPD responded to the nature of events generally outside of its control by building upon forms of popular protest whose origins lay more in the conditions of proletarian life and the traditions of working-class protest and less in consciously designed political strategies. The creation of mass unemployment as a result of rationalization and depression, coupled with the repressive practices of employers, unions, and the state, drove communists from the workplace, as we saw in chapter 3. The streets, in contrast, offered a more freewheeling terrain of activism. Ironically enough, the prevailing democratic conditions of the Weimar Republic made the streets accessible to the KPD. In sharp contrast, authoritarian systems like fascist Italy drove communists into the workplace, which at least provided some measure of security for clandestine activities. For the KPD, the restructuring of the working class through rationalization and depression meant a far higher proportion of unskilled, semiskilled, and unemployed workers, who, in the party's view, had far greater revolutionary inclinations than the stratum of skilled workers that had once been the backbone of the labor movement.[67]

Communists also endowed these street protests with new meanings. As state officials well recognized, demonstrations were intended to be assertive affairs: to stake out communist claims to the streets no matter what the authorities or the fascists decided, to make of the streets a venue to display communist politics and communist determination, and to accustom workers to active struggle against the "enemy"—the state, fascists, the bourgeoisie, social democrats. In that way, demonstrations were to be used as "preludes to the great transformation."[68]

Yet here too the KPD was not a free agent. As a defined political space, the streets carried their own logic, one that did not operate independently of, rather intersected with, the larger social and political context. The political space of the

[65] PPH to RPM, 14 February 1924, LHSAM C20/Ib/4648/5II/114–15.

[66] Arbeitgeberverband der chemischen und Sprengstoff-Industrie, Rundschreiben G.Nr. 8, 2 October 1924, HIA, NSDAP 41/807.

[67] See, for example, "Resolution des XII. Parteitages der KPD," 9–11 June 1929, in *Zur Geschichte der Kommunistischen Partei Deutschlands: Eine Auswahl von Materialien und Dokumenten aus den Jahren 1914–1946*, ed. Marx-Engels-Lenin-Stalin Institut beim Zentralkomitee der SED, 2d ed. (Berlin: Dietz, 1955), especially section VI:22, 268–69.

[68] See, among others, the very interesting report drawn up by state officials sometime in the late 1920s from internal KPD documents, "Wie denkt sich die K.P.D. die Eroberung der Macht im Staat," HIA, NSDAP 41/807, and Lagebericht RKÜöO, 22 March 1921, BAP RAM 2818, 43–76.

streets encouraged, most generally, a politics of display and spectacle on the part of the KPD. Demonstrations were designed to be exhibitions of party power, a sense conveyed by the unemployed marching on and then occupying the welfare office; by the sight of thousands parading with larger-than-life posters of Luxemburg and Liebknecht; by a chorus of voices singing in unison proletarian songs; by banners held aloft; and by physical confrontations with the Stahlhelm, SA, and police. Such actions encouraged separate communist actions and ideological pronouncements, not the building of coalitions and the mediation of political disputes. The displays of massed proletarian power made it still more difficult for the party to attract other social groups, whose desire for identification with the working class was slight in the first place. The SPD's leading role in the Weimar system, and in Prussia in particular, meant that the police forces with which communists came into conflict were often under the command of social democrats, making coalitions even with other labor parties almost unthinkable. The intense communist hostility toward social democracy had its origins, therefore, not only in ideology, but also in the hard experience of physical conflict in the politicized spaces of urban streets and marketplaces. And the politics of the streets accentuated those militant, masculine elements of the KPD present at its founding, with the result that male physical prowess came increasingly to define the KPD's model of revolutionary militancy.

All of these tendencies predated the onset of the Depression and the Comintern's "third period," but received added sustenance from them. The KPD leadership, hesitant to advocate the open use of violence after a bloody confrontation in Berlin on May Day 1929, soon switched course. The radicalism of the third period strategy, the open violence exercised by the police and increasingly by the fascists, the enticing prospects of accelerating militancy in the streets, and the determination of the party rank and file to protect themselves and their neighborhoods against the incursions of the SA and the police all served to move the party toward growing acceptance and, occasionally, outright advocacy, of street violence.[69] The party's understanding and utilization of the streets as an arena of politics thereby contributed mightily to the creation of a communist party with a particularly intransigent cast, with an orientation deeply hostile to any forms of political alliances and highly amenable to Leninism and to Stalin's particularly authoritarian interpretation of Leninism.

[69] Rosenhaft, *Beating the Fascists?* 34–41 and passim. In 1931, the party even reissued a Comintern handbook for revolutionaries that discussed knives, brass knuckles, oil-soaked rags, axes, bricks, and boiling water, to say nothing of hand grenades and revolvers, as important weapons in the struggle (40).

CHAPTER 6

The Gendering of German Communism

Die ganze deutsche Arbeiterklasse muß sich geschlossen wie ein Mann hinter die [streikende] Hafenarbeiter stellen.

—*KPD Central Committee*[1]

MORE CONSISTENTLY than any other party in the Weimar Republic, the KPD advocated women's emancipation. In its public pronouncements and legislative proposals, the KPD asserted the full equality of men and women and demanded equal pay for equal work, the right to an abortion, wide-ranging social protection measures, and, in general, the complete and active participation of women in all realms of life.[2] Ideologically, the KPD seemed the legitimate heir of the bourgeois and socialist feminist movements of the late-nineteenth and early-twentieth centuries, and at an historical moment when the enormous impact of World War I had profoundly destabilized—and politicized—gender roles. The enormous loss of male lives coupled with the accelerated employment of women during the war and the rapid emergence of the "new woman" of the 1920s—active, slender, athletic, sexual, and amaternal—provoked widespread unease that, in some quarters, took on near-hysterical, apocalyptic hues bound up with fears of national decline.[3]

[1] "The entire German working class must stand united as one man behind the [striking] dock workers." "Solidarität mit den streikenden Hafenarbeitern!" ZK der KPD, 3 Oktober 1926, in *Zur Geschichte der Kommunistischen Partei Deutschlands: Eine Auswahl von Materialien und Dokumenten aus den Jahren 1914–1946*, ed. Marx-Engels-Lenin-Stalin-Institut beim Zentralkomitee der SED, 2d ed. (Berlin: Dietz, 1955), 215.

[2] Its most developed statements drew on the "Guidelines of the Comintern for the Communist Women's Movement," drafted by Clara Zetkin and passed at the Third Comintern Congress in 1921 and published in *Die Kommunistische Internationale* 15 (1920/21): 530–55. See also the KPD's 1931 "Protective Program for the Working Woman," in Hans-Jürgen Arendt, "Das Schutzprogramm der KPD für die arbeitende Frau vom 15. Oktober 1931," *BzG* 11 (1969): 291–311. In general on the Comintern and women, see Aurelia Camparini, *Questione femminile e Terza internazionale* (Bari: De Donato, 1978).

[3] See especially Elisabeth Domansky, "Militarization and Reproduction in World War I Germany," in *Society, Culture, and the State in Germany, 1870–1930*, ed. Geoff Eley (Ann Arbor: University of Michigan Press, forthcoming); Atina Grossmann, *Reforming Sex: The German Movement for Birth Control and Abortion Reform, 1920–1950* (New York: Oxford University Press, 1995); and Karen Hagemann, *Frauenalltag and Männerpolitik: Alltagsleben und gesellschaftliches Handeln von Arbeiterfrauen in der Weimarer Republik* (Bonn: J. H. W. Dietz Nachf., 1990). For interesting treatments of this topic elsewhere in Europe, see Mary Louise Roberts, *Civilization without Sexes: Reconstructing Gender in Postwar France, 1917–1927* (Chicago: University of Chicago

The KPD's stance in support of women's emancipation marked a direct challenge to those fearful of what seemed like gender confusion. Yet the KPD found little support among women and remained a predominantly male proletarian party. According to party statistics, in 1929, the high point, women comprised only 17 percent of the membership; in the last years of the Weimar Republic, the figure hovered around 15 percent.[4] The KPD had the most masculine electoral profile of any party in the Weimar Republic, while one of its archenemies, the Catholic Center Party, proved most successful in garnering female votes.[5]

It would be an easy matter to attribute the KPD's poor showing to "traditional" or "religious" sentiments among German women. Easy, but misleading, because this perspective presumes some unchanging entity that can be labeled "tradition," while traditions are constantly being invented and transformed, and assumes that men underwent a learning and politicization process in the upheavals of the World War I era to which women remained immune.

Instead, this chapter will focus on the KPD's construction of a gendered party culture that elevated male productive labor and male physical prowess to the revolutionary ideal, a process that accentuated the intransigence forged in other areas of party activism. In contrast, the understandings of women's roles were notably diffuse, even contradictory. Most often, the KPD rendered women as the oppressed but largely passive objects of capitalist exploitation. But women were also variously portrayed as active fighters, proletarian versions of the "new woman," or eternally maternal females. The diverse imagery reflected a deep-seated uncertainty about how to approach and organize women that extended in some instances to an utter neglect of women's issues—despite all the rhetoric in support of women's emancipation. At the same time, the KPD provided some women with a vibrant setting in which they could develop their own identities and capabilities.

Constructing Masculinity

In the course of the nineteenth century, the labor movement came to define work as a primarily masculine enterprise located at the point of production—a result of both the general separation of home and work, family and production in capitalist

Press, 1994); Susan Kingsley Kent, *Making Peace: The Reconstruction of Gender in Interwar Britain* (Princeton: Princeton University Press, 1993); and the rather different Soviet case, Wendy Z. Goldman, *Women, the State, and Revolution: Soviet Family Policy and Social Life, 1917–1936* (Cambridge: Cambridge University Press, 1993).

[4] Hans-Jürgen Arendt, "Weibliche Mitglieder der KPD in der Weimarer Republik: Zahlenmäßige Stärke und soziale Stellung," *BzG* 19 (1977): 654. Arendt provides the most thorough account, though many of the figures are estimates, as he points out. Despite the low percentage, the KPD in this period had the highest proportion of female membership of any of the communist parties in the developed countries.

[5] Gabriele Bremme, *Die politische Rolle der Frau in Deutschland: Eine Untersuchung über den Einfluß der Frauen bei Wahlen und ihre Teilnahme in Partei und Parlament* (Göttingen: Vandenhoeck und Ruprecht, 1956), 73–74.

Plate 6.1 A lathe operator: idealized male labor. *Source: AIZ*, 31 January 1928.

society and the Marxian (and more generally materialist) understanding of the productive sphere as the bedrock of social organization and the locus of politics. In consequence, the trade unions and the socialist parties articulated an intrinsically gendered self-understanding of the labor movement as an enterprise composed primarily of male industrial workers.[6]

The KPD reproduced and accentuated this tendency. Despite rhetorical paeans to the significance of female labor, the KPD press idealized male productive labor as the source of the material riches of society and the basis of the future socialist order. While women were depicted as oppressed and harried, the party's illustrated weekly, the *Arbeiter-Illustrierte-Zeitung* (AIZ), published innumerable depictions glorifying male labor—lathe operators, riggers, riveters, underground construction workers (plate 6.1).[7] Representations of the "construction of socialism" in the Soviet Union almost invariably showed men at the sites of heavy industry—steel factories, coal mines, electric power plants (plate 6.2). In the KPD's proletarian novels of the 1920s and early 1930s, men are either at the workbench or in the pits, or else they are at the front in revolutionary civil war. The men are invariably strong, determined, and skillful. They gaze upward, heroically, into the socialist future or concentrate deeply on their labor (plate 6.3). With these representations, the KPD built upon but also extended an ethos of proletarian masculinity centered on toughness—of body and will—and of political commitment.

In the nineteenth century, the labor movement had used tough masculinity to demarcate, and idealize, workers from the "foppish" or "aesthete" middle and upper classes. In Weimar these images also broadened the chasm between communists and social democrats. In communist caricatures, social democrats are soft, frightened, fat, and old, commingling with the bourgeoisie and the Junkers in genteel circumstances, while communists, women and men, are broad-shouldered and muscular (plate 6.4). Rosa Luxemburg's own gendered language—her depiction of the Independent Social Democrats as lacking "manly resolve"—was absorbed into communist party practice and rhetoric with little difficulty.[8]

The politics of armed revolution and street battles, with their elevation of physical

[6] Good examples from what is now a very large literature are Mary Jo Maynes, *Taking the Hard Road: Life Course in French and German Workers' Autobiographies in the Era of Industrialization* (Chapel Hill: University of North Carolina Press, 1995); Kathleen Canning, "Gender and the Culture of Work: Ideology and Identity in the World beyond the Mill Gate, 1890–1914," in *Elections, Mass Politics, and Social Change in Modern Germany: New Perspectives*, ed. Larry Eugene Jones and James Retallack (Cambridge: Cambridge University Press, 1992), 175–99; Sonya O. Rose, *Limited Livelihoods: Gender and Class in Nineteenth-Century England* (Berkeley and Los Angeles: University of California Press, 1991); Harold Benenson, "The 'Family Wage' and Working Women's Consciousness in Britain, 1880–1914," *Politics and Society* 19:1 (1991): 71–108; idem, "Victorian Sexual Ideology and Marx's Theory of the Working Class," *International Labor and Working Class History* 25 (1984): 1–23; Eric Hobsbawm, "Man and Woman: Images on the Left," in idem, *Workers: Worlds of Labor* (New York: Pantheon, 1984), 83–102; and Heinz Niggemann, *Emanzipation zwischen Sozialismus und Feminismus: Die sozialdemokratische Frauenbewegung im Kaiserreich* (Wuppertal: Peter Hammer, 1981).

[7] *AIZ*, 1926–32. Some particularly striking examples are in the following issues: 12 (1926), 15 (1926), 31 January 1928, 18 April 1928, 16 (1930).

[8] Rosa Luxemburg, "Parteitag der Unabhängigen SP," 29 November 1918, in *GW*:4, 423.

Plate 6.2 Soviet workers, the "shock brigades of socialism," gaze heroically into the future in front of the smokestacks of socialist development. *Source: AIZ* 16 (1930).

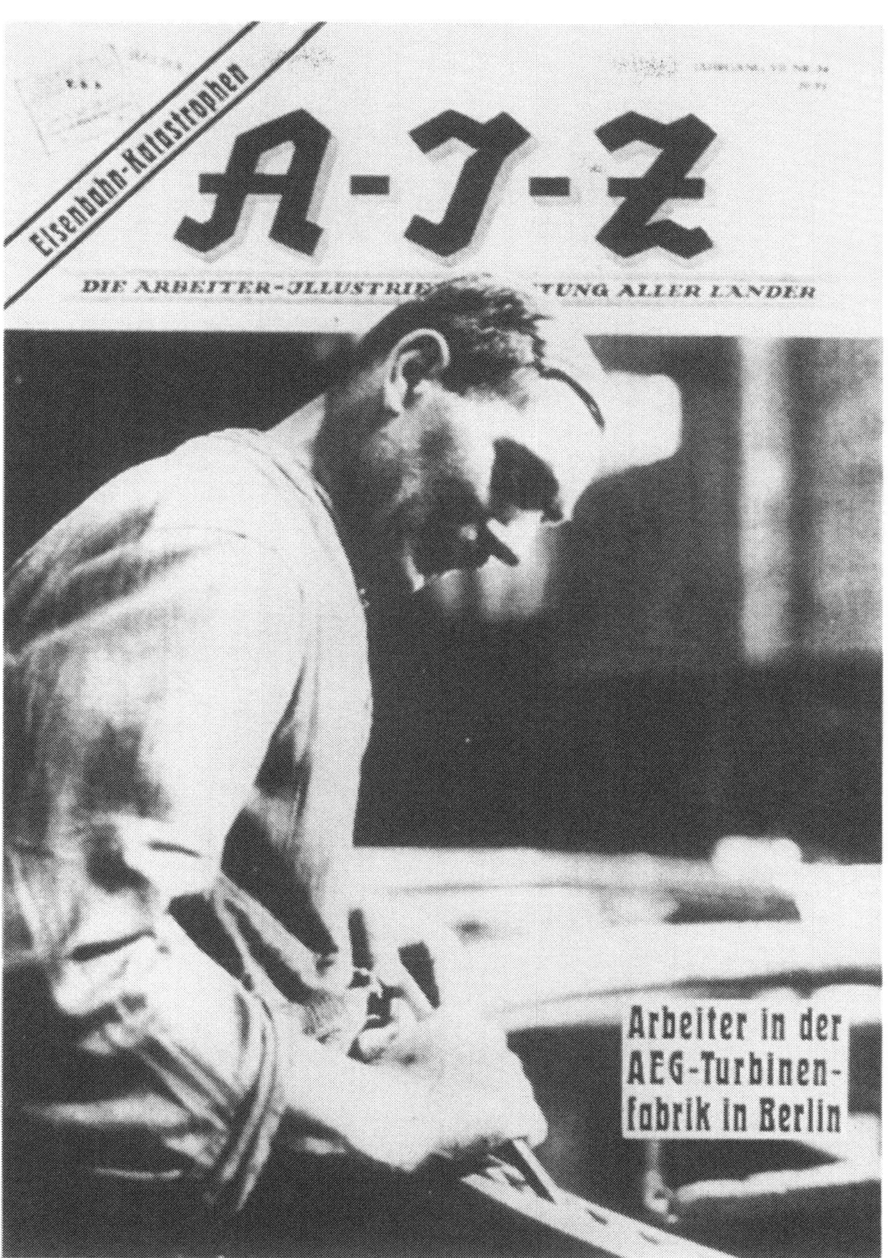

Plate 6.3 The male worker concentrates intensely on his labor and produces society's wealth. *Source: AIZ* 34 (1928).

Struggle for a free socialist Germany!

Proletarian, decide! [Note the police uniform of the SPD man.]

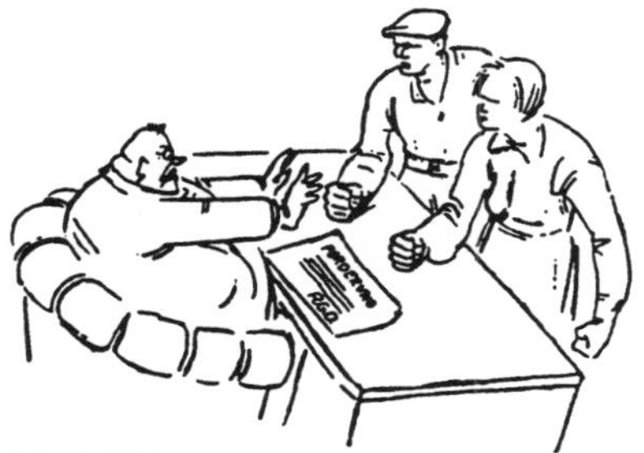

Only the RGO represents decisively the interests of the work force. Elect only red works councils! [Note that even the woman's arms and hands are exaggerated.]

Join the Fighting League Against Fascism! Only the Fighting League offers the security that these murderous fascist bandits will be held accountable for their bloody work.

Defend the Soviet Union!

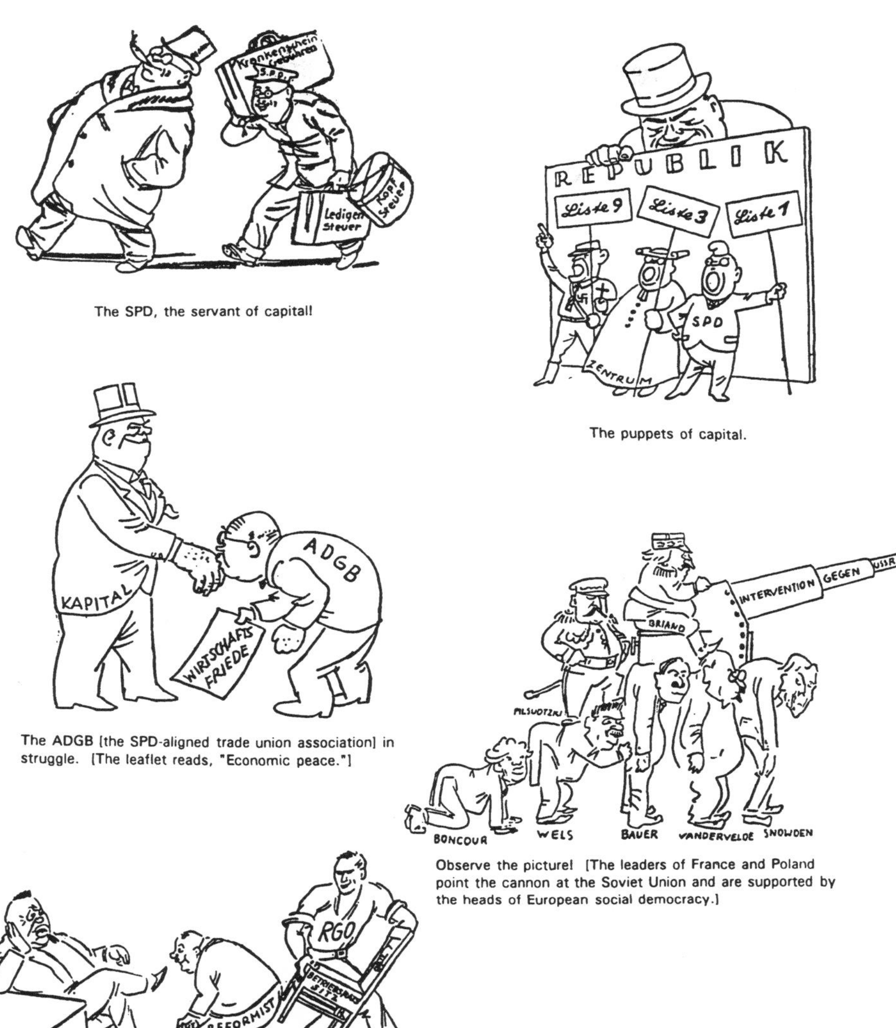

The SPD, the servant of capital!

The puppets of capital.

The ADGB [the SPD-aligned trade union association] in struggle. [The leaflet reads, "Economic peace."]

Observe the picture! [The leaders of France and Poland point the cannon at the Soviet Union and are supported by the heads of European social democracy.]

Throw the reformists out of the works councils! Elect only red works councils!

Plate 6.4 A set of caricatures from the Central Committee's Agitprop section shows communists as powerful and determined. Social democrats, in contrast, are weak, potbellied, smiling servants and supplicants. *Source:* "Illustrations-Vorlagen für Betriebs- und Häuserblock-Zeitungen," vols. 10, 11, 12, ed. ZK der KPD, Agitprop (Frankfurt am Main: Rhein-Main-Druck, [early 1930s]). BAK R45/IV/39.

prowess to the essential revolutionary quality, gave additional force to the masculine tenor of German communism. The Revolution of 1918–20, however spontaneous its outbreak and incomplete its effects, established the precedent of armed political struggle in Germany. In four of the first five years of the Republic, the KPD sought to found a socialist system through military means: the (misnamed) Spartacist Uprising of 1919, the Ruhr conflict that followed the Kapp-Putsch in 1920, the so-called March Action of 1921, and the uprising of October 1923.

None of these attempts succeeded. But they provided the KPD with its own militaristic legacy, one sustained by the sometime violence of the KPD's political rhetoric and by the individual and political martyrdoms ascribed to its military efforts in subsequent propaganda. In the midst of the March Action, the *Ruhr-Echo*, the local party paper in Essen, ran a banner headline, taken from the penultimate phrase of the party program and written by Luxemburg, "Thumb in the enemy's eye, knee on his chest!"[9] Following the event, *Rote Fahne*, the central KPD paper, proudly trumpeted the Comintern's pronouncement, "You have acted correctly!"[10] Party supporters acted in kind. At a rally in Halle a few months later, the crowd greeted the name of Otto Hörsing—the SPD provincial governor of Prussian Saxony and key strategist of the March Action—with the shouts, "Stand him up against a wall and shoot him!"[11] The workers killed at Leuna and elsewhere in central Germany in the March Action became the martyred heroes of German communism, as were the Hamburg workers killed in the ill-starred 1923 revolt—all of whom were honored in yearly commemorations on the anniversaries of the uprisings (plate 6.5).[12]

After the suppression of the 1923 revolt, the KPD never again attempted an armed uprising. Yet its militaristic ethos only intensified in the succeeding years. The KPD reiterated the ECCI's appellation as the "general staff" of the Comintern, the individual parties the avant guard of the battle.[13] The title of a short-lived KPD newspaper, *Rote Peitsche (Red Whip)*, established as a four-page publication for the 1928 electoral campaign (which quickly became a supplement to the *Ruhr-Echo*) expressively conveyed the rhetoric of militant violence that pervaded the KPD.[14] And the party bestowed lavish attention on its paramilitary organizations, primarily the RFB.[15] The *Arbeiter-Illustrierte-Zeitung*, for example, published photo after photo of uniformed men, banners flying, marching in disciplined military formation or at rallies amid countless red flags (plate 6.6).[16]

[9] *RE*, 29 March 1921.

[10] *RF*, 14 April 1921.

[11] Abschrift PVH to RPM, LHSAM C20/Ib/4648/5I/117.

[12] See Ernst Thälmann's commemoration, "Die Lehren des Hamburger Aufstandes," 23 October 1924, in *Zur Geschichte der Kommunistischen Partei Deutschlands*, 151–57.

[13] For example, *RF*, 18 October 1932.

[14] "Bericht über den Wahlkampf im Bezirk Ruhrgebiet," SAPMO-BA, ZPA I/3/18–19/13/124.

[15] See Kurt G. P. Schuster, *Der Rote Frontkämpferbund 1924–1929: Beiträge zur Geschichte und Organisationsstruktur eines politischen Kampfbundes* (Düsseldorf: Droste, 1975).

[16] These impressions are based on reading the *AIZ* from 1926 to 1932. Some especially revealing photos can be found in the following issues (the paper variously used volume and issue numbers,

Plate 6.5 The monument commemorates the Leuna workers killed in the March Action. Note the clenched fist, the RFB salute, and the inscription inside the star, "Through Struggle to Victory." *Source: Geschichte der VEB Leuna-Werke*, 90.

Only the character of the uniforms and banners enables a viewer to distinguish the RFB from the Nazi SA (plate 6.7). One sees the same determined men—women are completely absent in both the KPD and Nazi representations—the same emphasis on a muscular masculinity, and even photos of party leader Ernst Thälmann complete with jackboots and brown cap or standing above a sea of Red

dates, or a combination of the two): 10 (1926), 5 June 1927, 19 June 1927, 25 April 1928, 9 May 1928, 4 (1930), 31 (1930), 49 (1931), 24 (1932).

Plate 6.6 The militaristic style: proletarian men marching under the banner of the red flag.
Source: AIZ 24 (1932).

Plate 6.7 The dense, militaristic regalia make it difficult to distinguish the RFB from the SA. The men are in uniforms, complete with jackboots, and they stand at attention and give the clenched-fist salute. *Source: AIZ* 4 (1930).

Front fighters and red flags (plate 6.8). By invoking a rhetoric of violence and glorifying its own military efforts despite the string of failures, the KPD sought to join its traditions with the Soviet invocation of the October Revolution and the victorious Civil War as *the* heroic moments of Bolshevism and world socialism.[17]

No doubt, the KPD's militaristic ethos intensified through the party's interaction with National Socialism. The KPD sought to wean away some of the Nazi Party's constituency by elevating male combativeness to new heights of glory during the Depression. In so doing, the KPD invoked its own legacy, but also demonstrated its partial absorption of aspects of Nazi rhetoric and practice.[18] At its most extreme, the KPD press sometimes labeled Thälmann "*unser Führer*" (our leader), a clear mimicking of the authoritarian and militaristic elements of the NSDAP.[19] Both parties also glorified street combat, even as they fought one another for control of neighborhoods.[20] But even before the rise of the NSDAP the KPD had adopted the militaristic style of its right-wing competitors. As the Halle police noted in 1923, KPD demonstrations looked much like those of the Stahlhelm. Among both groups demonstrations were led by men who, in military fashion, laid walking sticks over their shoulders.[21]

Street battles, as described in the previous chapter, became one of the preeminent forms of communist activism. Here especially the party developed an ethos of tough proletarian masculinity. For communists in many areas of Germany, street fights against the Nazis and the police signified defense of their own neighborhoods and meeting places and training for the ultimate revolutionary battle. Street battles and RFB activities were often indistinguishable, and they constituted a substitute form of organization and activism for many of those who could no longer find a place within the unions or the works councils.[22]

The culture of political violence, so fundamental to the construction of masculinity, resulted not only from conscious party effort, but also from the general brutalization of daily life in World War I and in the manifold conflicts of the Republic. The actual experience of armed combat seemed to produce not a revulsion against political violence, but a desire to make the next round far more successful—a characteristic shared by the fascist right and the communist left. Large numbers of workers came home from the front accustomed to violence and with their weapons in hand, or secured arms in subsequent conflicts with the forces of order in the early years of the Republic. In some instances, workers made their own weapons, as at the Leuna plant during the March Action, when workers manufac-

[17] See Diane P. Koenker, William G. Rosenberg, and Ronald Grigor Suny, eds., *Party, State, and Society in the Russian Civil War: Explorations in Social History* (Bloomington: Indiana University Press, 1989).

[18] See Thomas Childers, "The Social Language of Politics in Germany: The Sociology of Political Discourse in the Weimar Republic," *AHR* 95:2 (1990): 350–51, and Conan Fischer, *The German Communists and the Rise of Nazism* (New York: St. Martin's Press, 1991).

[19] *RF*, 12 September 1930.

[20] See Eve Rosenhaft, *Beating the Fascists? The German Communists and Political Violence, 1929–1933* (Cambridge: Cambridge University Press, 1983).

[21] PPH to RPM, 14 June 1923, LHSAM C20/Ib/4648/5II/27.

[22] As the Ruhr KPD leadership noted: BLR, "Bericht der Bezirksleitung Ruhrgebiet," 9 December 1926, SAPMO-BA, ZPA I/3/18–19/11/197.

Plate 6.8 Ernst Thälmann in his RFB uniform above a sea of red flags. *Source: Zur Geschichte der Kommunistischen Partei Deutschlands.*

Plate 6.9 Proletarian struggle is armed struggle, as with these men who defend the Leuna-Werke against the police. *Source: Kämpfendes Leuna.*

tured a tank for use against the police, an event later mythologized in party propaganda and in the DDR. Later, weapons were seen as an essential element of self-defence as street battles with the SA spiraled out of control.[23]

But guns, like tanks, also had a mystique, and possession was one of the cherished symbols of commitment—and of masculinity—especially among RFB cadres. The proletarian-in-arms was a fixed feature of the communist press and literature (plate 6.9). Typically, the membership card for the RFB defined class in military terms by joining the traditional image of powerful proletarians wielding hammers with their uniformed counterparts standing guard, rifles at the ready (plate 6.10). The knowledge that, if discovered, possession of guns meant an almost immediate jail sentence only heightened the fascination that some men had with weaponry. It made them part of a conspiratorial society, an elite of men

[23] See also Rosenhaft, *Beating the Fascists?* 179–80.

Plate 6.10 Honorary membership card in the RFB. The KPD joins the nineteenth-century iconography of male labor with the combative imagery of the proletarian under arms. *Source:* HIA, NSDAP Hauptarchiv.

devoted to the revolutionary cause and bonded together by their ideas and the dangers they ran together.

Even women could be drawn into the fascination with guns—though by educating their young boys into their importance. One KPD pamphlet, supposedly quoting Lenin, advised mothers on how to speak to their children:

> You will soon be big. You will be given a rifle in [your] hand. Take it and train yourself diligently in the craft of weaponry. Your knowledge is necessary for the proletariat—not to shoot your brothers, the workers of other countries, as was the case in this war and as the traitors to socialism advise you to do. But [use your knowledge] to struggle against the bourgeoisie of your own country, to put an end to exploitation, poverty, and war—not through wishful thinking, but by disarming and defeating the bourgeoisie.[24]

In other ways workers also had experience with violence and militarism. The KPD's array of military and paramilitary organizations—the RFB, the proletarian hundreds, Kampfbrigaden, and others—offered many workers their first experience with the discipline of communist organization. In these organizations workers learned techniques of terror and sabotage, and sometimes carried them out. These were not actions peripheral to the main line of party work. In the course of the March Action, for example, leaders of the Halle-Merseburg KPD discussed seriously, sometimes with the participation of Executive member Hugo Eberlein, sabotaging munitions supply trains and cooperatives, for which it hoped to pin the blame on its adversaries.[25] Memoirs of party functionaries like Erich Wollenberg, active in various branches of the KPD's military units, depict a life of conspiratorial meetings, shoot-outs with the police, and constant movement to prevent capture.[26]

State officials, experienced with communist uprisings, were all too aware of the party's militaristic ethos and the attention devoted to its paramilitary units. The officials kept close tabs on these groups and were almost always well informed about their activities. When the RFB was banned in 1929, the KPD sought to maintain the organization by subterfuge, as officials well knew. In a long report from the early 1930s, officials described in intimate detail the organization of other paramilitary units and the use of supposedly "peaceful" organizations to further the military training of party cadres—Initiative Groups, Partisan Troops and Fighting Associations in the workplace, Unemployed Detachments, Fighting Organization against Fascism, Workers' Sports Association, and others in the communities.[27] Organized in military style and often providing weapons instructions for the members, all of these groups added to the militaristic ethos of the KPD, which became more and more pronounced through the decade. Re-

[24] BL[R], Frauenabteilung und Agitpropabteilung, "Krieg dem imperialistischen Kriege: Material für die Frauenschule des Bezirks Ruhrgebiet vom 23.–28. Juli 1928 in Essen," SAPMO-BA, ZPA I/3/18–19/38/19.

[25] "Aus dem Bericht des Genossen Lemck-Halle," 8 April 1921; "Aus dem Bericht des Genossen Bowitzky," 12 April 1921; "Material aus dem Hallenser Bezirk," [n.d., presumably April 1921], SAPMO-BA, ZPA I/3/11/13/4–5, 13, 16–17.

[26] Erich Wollenberg, memoirs (typescript, HIA).

[27] "Wie denkt sich die K.P.D. die Eroberung der Macht im Staat," HIA, NSDAP 41/807. See also Rosenhaft, *Beating the Fascists?* 88–110, on the array of substitute military organizations.

marking on the exercises of the communist sports clubs, which the KPD had split off from the SPD-dominated association in 1928, state officials noted that the training was geared toward street battles. The participants learned how to patrol, read maps, fire small weapons, and sling stones. Officials quoted internal KPD directives on the need to turn mass demonstrations into military exercises complete with security patrols and intelligence detachments.[28]

Some party members were aware that street fights and armed revolution were not quite the same thing, and that the sense of civil disorder they created might ultimately benefit the Nazis. But for a party schooled on the Luxemburgist-Leninist celebration of mass activism and whose cadres had undergone the experiences of war, armed revolution, and street battles, the specter of thousands of workers marching in military fashion and small groups beating up policemen and fascists was simply too enticing. In elevating such actions to the essence of revolutionary commitment, the KPD constructed a culture of masculinity defined by male productive labor and male physical prowess.

Constructing Femininity

No single image of femininity dominates KPD representations in the way the heroic and combative male proletarian provides a uniform and consistent construction of masculinity. Instead, a cacophony of images emerges from the party press, film, and literature of the Weimar period—harassed and oppressed mother, comrade marching shoulder to shoulder with the RFB, new woman of the 1920s, factory worker. The images do not work together, collage-like, to reveal a party that understood the complexities of women's lives and developed a comprehensive approach to reaching them in all of their social roles. Instead, they show a party groping unsteadily, lurching from one image to another in the search for some way to appeal to women. Moreover, the representations of women, however varied, appear far less frequently than those of men. They surface now and again in the pages of the *Arbeiter-Illustrierte-Zeitung*, as shadowy figures in proletarian novels and memoirs, as the afterthought at party conferences—despite all the resolutions in favor of women's equality and the organization of proletarian women.

Most often, representations of the German woman entailed Käthe Kollwitz–like depictions of oppression and depression—the proletarian housewife, old before her time, overwhelmed by poverty and motherhood and unending household labor, as in plate 6.11. John Heartfield's powerful statements against paragraph 218, the law that criminalized abortions, offer other examples of the melodramatic genre that predominated in the *AIZ* and other communist media (plate 6.12).[29] The women in these depictions are objects of sympathy and pathos, but rarely is the viewer offered representations of activist women. Presumably, women's emancipation from their dire straits would arise from the actions of their male relations and comrades.

[28] "Wie denkt sich die K.P.D. die Eroberung der Macht im Staat," HIA, NSDAP 41/807/4.

[29] See Patrice Petro, *Joyless Streets: Women and Melodramatic Representation in Weimar Germany* (Princeton: Princeton University Press, 1989), esp. 94–103 and 127–39.

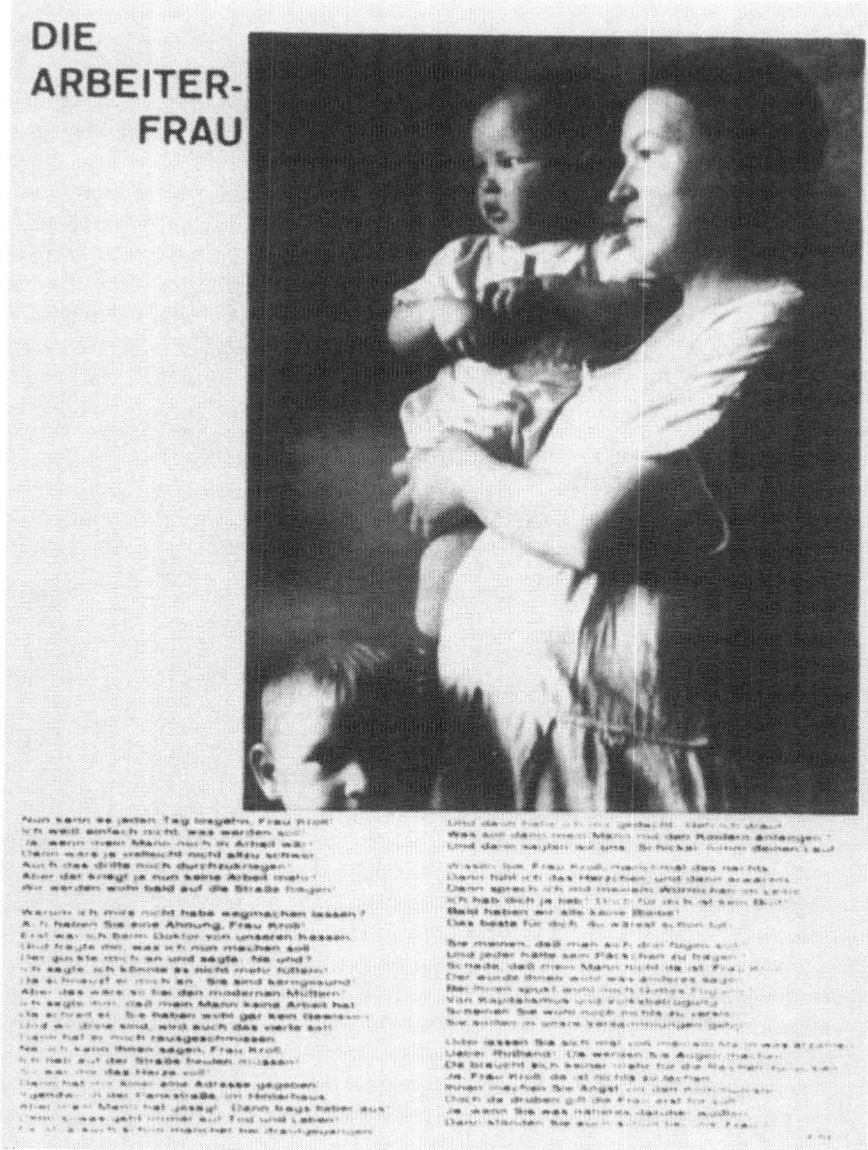
DIE ARBEITER-FRAU

Plate 6.11 The burdens of female proletarian existence in a state that criminalizes abortion. *Source: AIZ* 37 (1930).

Moreover, female labor is only rarely depicted in the heroic cast with which male labor is endowed. Women workers were depicted as oppressed by long hours and low wages, by the authoritarian relations of the office and department store, by the dirt and grime of factory labor, by barely concealed sexual exploitation. Rarely, if ever, does one see women as the skilled creators of wealth. They

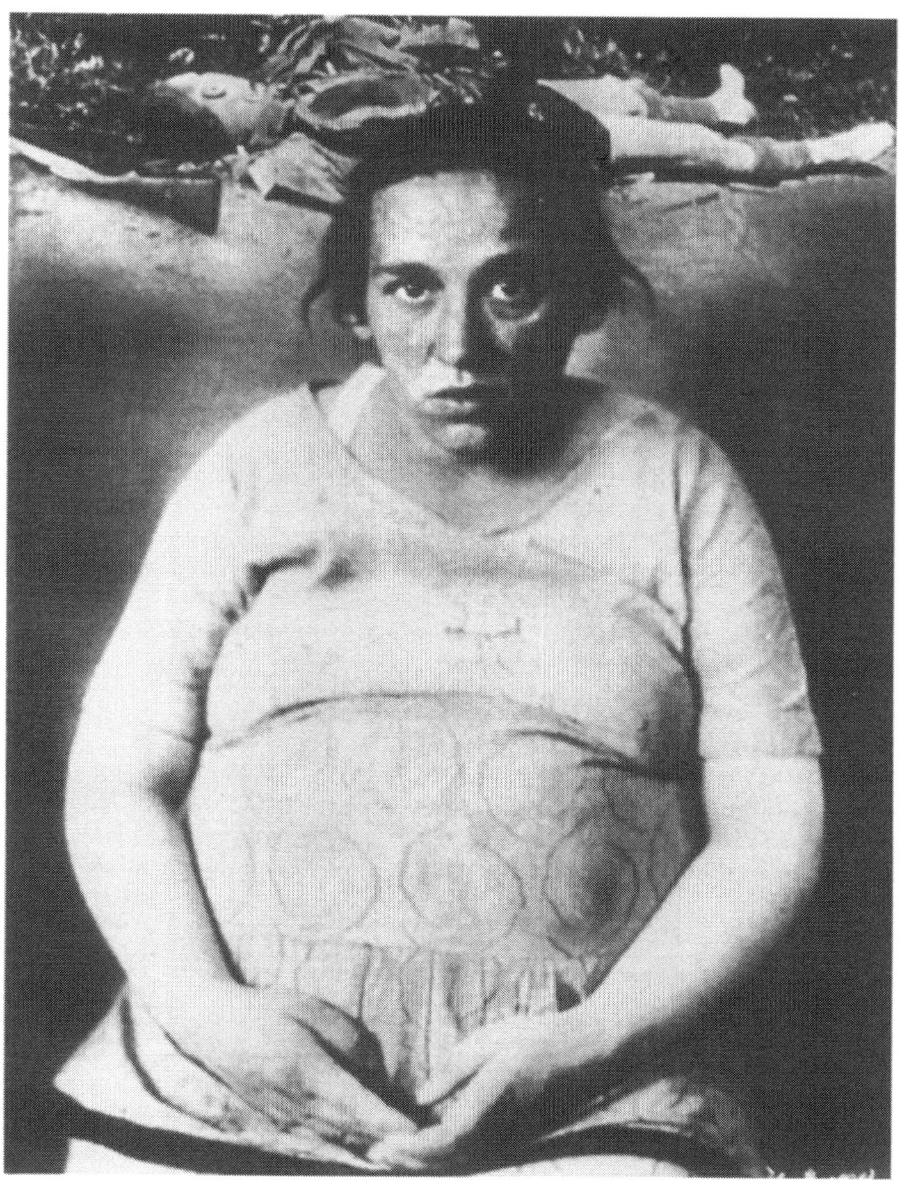

Plate 6.12. The miseries of female proletarian life. Behind the pregnant woman is a dead soldier. The caption reads "Forced to carry human material. Have courage! The state needs the unemployed and soldiers." *Source: AIZ* 9 (1930), by John Heartfield. © 1996 Artists Rights Society, New York/VG Bild Kunst, Bonn/The Heartfield Community of Heirs.

work in the interstices of the capitalist economy—as ticket collectors, office workers, saleswomen, home workers, and, occasionally, factory laborers (plates 6.13–6.14). This may have been a more or less accurate depiction of the female labor market of the 1920s.[30] But for a party that built its imagery on "heavy metal" as the wellsprings of proletarian solidarity and society's wealth, women's labor could only be seen as of secondary importance. They might work outside the home and in increasing numbers, but it was not upon their labor that the new society, with unlimited riches, would be created.

While representing proletarian motherhood as oppressive and women's paid labor as ancillary to "true" productive labor, the KPD denigrated the household as a backward province of precapitalist social forms and petit bourgeois values.[31] Individually rather than socially organized, the household was by definition a retrograde social organism, hence a site of the most backward political and social ideas—political passivity that oscillated with spontaneous, semianarchistic eruptions; loyalty to an unthinking socialist reformism or Catholicism; petit bourgeois individualism; pacifism.[32] Women as a group and the household as a retrograde political space constituted the ever-present others that threatened to undermine the (male) proletarian resolve forged in the workplace and the streets.

Full emancipation could only emerge from women's participation in the industrial economy. Concomitantly, household labor would be socialized in communal kitchens, nurseries, and laundries. As the KPD's women's newspaper, *Die Kommunistin*, put it in 1921:

> Women's work [in the paid labor force] is for us no necessary evil, but a necessary stage in the development of the petit bourgeois working-class housewife to a class-conscious proletarian. A woman who only sees her four walls, who thinks of nothing other than her stove and wash day, will, in ninety-nine out of one hundred cases, remain, despite all deprivation, backward and petit bourgeois in her thinking. She will understand nothing of the great transformation that is occurring in our time.[33]

This approach shaded all too easily into a kind of neglect of and contempt toward women in the household, although it remained the preeminent social sphere for women in the 1920s.[34] Even Clara Zetkin, generally quite sensitive to the need to organize women wherever they were to be found, voiced this kind of attitude:

> the housewives and mothers are in general less capable of resistance against the rising suffering, less armed than their brothers. They feel life's deprivations deeply, but they

[30] On the uneasy mix of tradition and modernity in women's lives in the Weimar Republic, see Grossmann, *Reforming Sex*; Hagemann, *Frauenalltag und Männerpolitik*; and Renate Bridenthal and Claudia Koonz, "Beyond *Kinder, Küche, Kirche*: Weimar Women in Politics and Work," in *When Biology Became Destiny: Women in Weimar and Nazi Germany*, ed. Renate Bridenthal, Atina Grossmann, and Marion Kaplan (New York: Monthly Review Press, 1984), 44–53.

[31] On this issue generally see Silvia Kontos, *"Die Partei kämpft wie ein Mann!": Frauenpolitik der KPD in der Weimarer Republik* (Frankfurt am Main: Roter Stern, 1979), esp. 131–41.

[32] Kontos provides suitable quotes in *"Die Partei kämpft wie ein Mann!"* 173–78.

[33] Quoted in ibid., 134.

[34] On the primacy of the household sphere, see Hagemann, *Frauenalltag und Männerpolitik*.

Plate 6.13 A woman rushes off to the office. Women are harassed and exploited by the job market, but there is nothing heroic about their labor. *Source: AIZ* 42 (1929).

Plate 6.14 The caption reads "Women as merchandise! Boss: 'Well, my dear child, your testimonials and recommendations are all very well. I have no job for you. But if you want to become my private secretary I can offer you a job with double the salary!'" *Source: Die Kommunistin*, 1 September 1922, in Usborne, *Politics of the Body.*

> are weak in their defense against them. They are sufferers instead of fighters. The evil legacy of many hundreds of years of subordination under men, of being penned in the narrowness of four walls, has narrowed her vision, made her will powerless. Just as she is so meek under the command of her husband, bows to the family, so little does she venture to rise against the remorseless abuses of the capitalists or the oppressions of the bourgeois state.[35]

Nonetheless, the KPD made some efforts to reach proletarian women in the home. The *AIZ* published a women's column entitled, for a few weeks in 1926–27, "Mother and Child," though that quickly changed to "The Working Woman"

[35] Quoted in Kontos, *"Die Partei kämpft wie ein Mann!"* 173.

(Die werktätige Frau). Whatever its title, the column offered women typical household advice—how to sew jackets or knit sweaters for the family, re-use old clothing, keep food without ice. The fashions depicted were plain and utilitarian. Women were also shown how to bathe, carry, and breast-feed their infants. Such advice mixed easily with overt party ideology: one column promoted raising children in a progressive manner "so that they become strong, self-confident individuals . . . who will be enemies of capitalism and builders of socialism."[36] In accord with other political tendencies in the Weimar Republic, the KPD advocated a "rationalized" household in which efficient work and modern technology would combine to ease the burden on women.[37] Women in the home were advised to work while seated and to adjust table and chairs to the proper height, to put dishes where they would not gather dust, to arrange the workspace of the kitchen efficiently, to make use of the newest appliances. The party almost always accompanied such advice with the caveat that most modern appliances were too expensive for the proletarian family, and the true rationalization of household labor could occur only in socially organized communal kitchens, laundries, and nurseries.[38]

While offering "traditional" household advice, the *AIZ* at times also promoted a proletarian version of the "new woman" of the 1920s.[39] Like her bourgeois counterpart, the proletarian new woman was youthful, healthy, slender, athletic, erotic. In the household she not only cooked and laundered, but also carried out electrical repairs, plastered, and painted windows.[40] Idealized Soviet women, especially Soviet athletes, often served as the model, but the German new woman also graced the party press (plate 6.15). Occasionally, the party even managed to provide some humor, as in plate 6.16, which shows the new woman better off suffering a crab bite than pregnancy. Often, she was shown juxtaposed with her precise opposite—the old, heavy-set, haggard-looking woman, who worked inefficiently and was worn down by years of backbreaking labor bent over the washtub, or the old, witchlike midwife ready to perform an abortion on a desperate woman.[41] By juxtaposing the

[36] "Dein Kind—Dein Kamerad!" *AIZ* 10, no. 51: 1030. In 1928–29, the women's column disappeared from the pages of the magazine altogether, and few photos appeared of women. For some other examples, see *AIZ*, 19 January 1927: 10; 16 Janaury 1927: 10; 2 February 1927: 12; 9 February 1927: 10; 20 February 1927: 10; "Unsere ganz Kleinen: Fragen der werktätigen Frau," 9, no. 45: 886; 6 March 1927: 10; "Lebensmittelschutz ohne Eis," 10, no. 22: 434; "Kleine Küchentricks," 10, no. 52: 1050.

[37] See, for example, *AIZ*, 4 April 1928: 7. The campaign for "rationalized" households cut through the political divisions of the Weimar period. See Hagemann, *Frauenalltag und Männerpolitik*, and Mary Nolan, "'Housework made Easy': The Taylorized Housewife in Weimar Germany's Rationalized Economy," *Feminist Studies* 16:3 (1990): 549–73.

[38] "Die werktätige Frau," *AIZ*, 5 June 1927: 10; 29 June 1927: 10; 20 July 1927: 12; "Alter und neuer Haushalt," *AIZ*, 4 April 1928: 7; "Um die Gesundheit der proletarischen Hausfrau," *AIZ*, 9, no. 39: 766.

[39] See Atina Grossmann, "The New Woman and the Rationalization of Sexuality in Weimar Germany," in *Powers of Desire: The Politics of Sexuality*, ed. Ann Snitow, Christine Stansell, and Sharon Thompson (New York: Monthly Review Press, 1983), 153–71; Petro, *Joyless Streets*, 104–39; Cornelie Usborne, *The Politics of the Body in Weimar Germany: Women's Reproductive Rights and Duties* (Ann Arbor: University of Michigan Press, 1992), 85–101; Ute Frevert, *Women in German History: From Bourgeois Emancipation to Sexual Liberation* (New York: Berg, 1989), 168–204.

[40] "Die Frau als Elektriker," *AIZ* 9, no. 20: 386; "Die Frau als Handwerker," *AIZ* 9, no. 26: 506.

[41] For example, "Die werktätige Frau," *AIZ*, 5 June 1927: 10; "Mordparagraph 218," *AIZ*, 13 July 1927: 7; "Alter und neuer Haushalt," *AIZ*, 4 April 1928: 7.

Plate 6.15 "Oh those girls!" Communist depictions of the new woman of the 1920s—slender, athletic, and physical. *Source: AIZ* 51 (1929).

old and the new, the KPD clearly presented itself as the party of change, of the new woman, of the future. The celebrations of youth served the same function, and bear an uncomfortable closeness to fascist representations (plate 6.17).

Body politics and class politics often ran together. The *AIZ* claimed that the old German Turnvereine (gymnastics associations) prescribed tight and rigid forms

Plate 6.16 Young, slender, lively, and not pregnant—the communist ideal of the 1920s. The caption reads: "better than being bitten by the stork!" *Source: AIZ* 24 (1931).

Plate 6.17 Youth looking to the future, a socialist future created by the party. The similarities with Nazi representations are overwhelming. *Source: AIZ* 25 (1930).

of movement in keeping with their rigid and outmoded political ideology. By implication, the revolutionary sports movement promoted new bodies and the new class, emancipation and socialism.[42] The *AIZ*, for its part, assured the proletarian housewife that she could exercise even without gymnastic equipment. All it takes is "one-quarter hour every morning, good will, and a sturdy towel. " The exercises were best done naked, "because then one has at the same time an air bath, [good] for the body, which, unfortunately, given our European morals, must languish most of its life in the constraints of clothing and coverings."[43] The weekly also advocated group gymnastics, and the depictions show women whose body movements were at one and the same time loose and free and collectively disciplined and organized.

Fashion constituted another site of the class struggle.[44] While "bourgeois decadence" finds its expression in luxurious and impractical clothing, which involves "wasteful excesses of material, . . . extravagant lines, . . . complicated style of preparation" and makes the woman an object of masculine desire, the working-class woman, "is neither the luxury creature of a man, nor does she follow the dictates of fashion, which maintain [bourgeois] class interests in refined form. But she has a natural need to dress in a pretty fashion, to wear beautiful colors and good material that highlight her figure."[45] The drawing that accompanied the article shows two decadent bourgeois women opposite two working women, whose clothes are plain but fashionable. They are the epitome of the proletarian new woman: slender, short hair, loose clothes that show the body form (plate 6.18). They even wear sports clothing, which should not be the exclusive preserve of the bourgeoisie.

The "masculinization of women" (*Vermännlichung der Frauen*), another aspect of the "new woman" and so much criticized in Weimar society, found a very particular expression in communist culture—women as combatants, marching shoulder to shoulder, or at least column to column, with men in the cause of socialism. For about a year after its founding, women were permitted to join the RFB. However, the high level of physical engagement made the RFB "unsuitable" for women, while its general appeal to women proved quite limited. Instead, the KPD organized the Red Women and Girls League (Roter Frauen- und Mädchen Bund, or RFMB) as a kind of female version of the RFB. Like the RFB, the RFMB was conceived to enlist workers beyond the party ranks in the proletarian cause, including the "struggle against the bourgeois women's movement."[46]

[42] "Frauengymnastik," *AIZ* 8, no. 42: 18.

[43] "Die Werktätige Frau," *AIZ*, 17 April 1927: 10. The editors, however, could not quite bring themselves to depict a naked woman. The sketches that show how to do the exercises are of a desexed child.

[44] The *AIZ* even ran one article supportive of cosmetic plastic surgery as a right of workers rather than a privilege of the wealthy. "Soziale Kosmetik," *AIZ* 8, no. 5: 7.

[45] "Die Mode-Reaktion," *AIZ* 8, no. 45: 14.

[46] Hans-Jürgen Arendt and Werner Freigang, "Der Rote Frauen- und Mädchenbund—die revolutionäre deutsche Frauenorganisation in der Weimarer Republik," *BzG* 21 (1979): 250, 254. The RFMB's highest membership level was 25,000, which it reached in 1927. Approximately four-fifths were not party members, and only half were female workers. Ibid., 254. See also Kontos, *"Die Partei kämpft wie ein Mann!"* 59–62, 139–43.

Die Mode-REAKTION

Sichere Existenz

REKORD

Nur 10 Pfennig täglich

Wundervoll lockiges Haar

Zerrüttung

Stottern

Bettfedern

Reizende Locken!

Plate 6.18 Class struggle on the fashion front. Overly attired bourgeois women on the left, the socialist new woman on the right. *Source: AIZ* 45 (1929).

In many ways the party's women's organizations adopted the militaristic style of the RFB. The members of the RFMB wore similar uniforms—with the addition of red kerchiefs—and marched together in disciplined formation.[47] At its Third

[47] Arendt and Freigang, "Roter Frauen- und Mädchenbund," 253. At times, however, the militaristic style was criticized, as at the KPD's Eleventh Congress (1927) and by Clara Zetkin. See ibid., 255–56.

Congress, the RFMB resolved to intensify the military training of its members and to support the establishment of the proletarian antifascist Young Guards. In 1930, when the KPD organized the Fighting Association against Fascism (Kampfbund gegen den Faschismus), RFMB groups joined it and formed women's detachments.[48]

Rhetorically also the KPD promoted the militarization of women. In one leaflet distributed by the women's section of the Ruhr district, the party advised women not to be passive bystanders in the inevitable civil war that will accompany the transition to socialism: "Women and children thirteen years old struggled at the side of men during the time of the Paris Commune. It cannot be otherwise in the future struggle for the suppression of the bourgeoisie. *Proletarian women will not look on passively as the well-armed bourgeoisie shoots down the poorly armed or unarmed workers.* As in 1871, they will take up arms."[49] Even Clara Zetkin made use of the military metaphors that became commonplace in the international communist movement: "[Women workers are] the elite of the female troops. They support the economic and political mass actions of the proletariat under the leadership of the communist party [and] help fight the great historical battle of the revolution."[50]

If women were to fight, then men had also to assume household responsibilities. At times in the 1920s and early 1930s the KPD articulated a vision of transformed family relations in which men participated equally with women in household labor. These "companionate marriages" were contrasted with social democratic "petit bourgeois" conceptions of the family in which the proletarian housewife was to remain confined to the kitchen.[51]

> The union activist or party worker who proves in practice that he has grown out of those petit bourgeois prejudices that consider the man's participation in household labor superfluous and "dishonorable" demonstrates that he holds high the command of proletarian solidarity also within his four walls. Every worker who through support of his wife contributes to her participation as an active cofighter for the cause of the proletariat has exercised a service to the labor movement—and not the slightest service![52]

But especially in the realm of sexuality the KPD emerged as the advocate of the new woman and staked out an emancipatory position with wide-ranging political and social possibilities. Its defense of a woman's right to an abortion placed it squarely in opposition to prevailing legal and moral codes and made it possible to imagine a society in which women would have greater control over reproduction. The party press published laudatory articles about Magnus Hirschfeld and other sexual reformers, and occasionally turned over the pages of the *AIZ* to sexologists like the physician Max Hodann.[53] In his article Hodann bluntly critiqued the hypocrisy and inhumanity of "bourgeois" morals and the

[48] Ibid., 254, 257.

[49] "Krieg dem imperialistischen Kriege: Material für die Frauenschule des Bez. Ruhrgebiet," BLR Frauenabteilung/Agitpropabteilung, 23–28 July 1928, SAPMO-BA, ZPA I/3/18–19/38/18–19.

[50] Quoted by Kontos, *"Die Partei kämpft wie ein Mann!"* 203–4.

[51] See ibid., 127–28.

[52] "Mehr Freizeit für die werktätige Frau!" *AIZ*, 12 October 1927: 7.

[53] "Magnus Hirschfelds Lebenswerk: Zum 60. Geburtstag des Forschers," *AIZ*, 23 May 1928: 13; Max Hodann, "Sexualforschung/Gebärzwang und Massenelend," *AIZ* 7, no. 30: 3.

notion that sexual relations should occur only within marriage. Like other sex reformers, Hodann advocated birth control and, when necessary, legal abortions to remove the fear of unwanted pregnancies, and companionate marriages in which men and women shared in the household responsibilities. The photos accompanying the article critiqued both the illusory bourgeois marital world depicted in films and the male proletarian "*Wohnstubenmonarchist*" (household tyrant) who can only say, "Blast it, isn't dinner ready yet?"[54]

Even more radically, *AIZ* published an excerpt from Otto Rühle's *Illustrierte Kultur- und Sittengeschichte des Proletariats* (*Illustrated Cultural and Moral History of the Proletariat*) that equated marriage and prostitution. There is, Rühle argued, no essential difference between the two, only a gradation of difference. "In marriage the man is served by female sexuality over the entire course of life. The husband is granted exclusive use in return for continual material support. . . . In prostitution the man is served by female sexuality intermittently. He shares with others the use in return for partial material support."[55] Like Hodann, Rühle criticized the hypocrisy of the bourgeoise who attacked sexual relations outside of marriage, leaving many people trapped in sexually unsatisfying marriages or condemned to no sexual life at all. Similarly, the party implicitly defended single women's right to a sexual life when *AIZ* ran an article that conveyed sympathy for the plight of a young woman who had to rent a room completely lacking in beauty and whose private life became subject to the rules and surveillance of the tyrannical landlord, who forbade visits, the gramophone, and any laughter whatsoever.[56]

The KPD also launched a public campaign against the 1930 papal encyclical on marriage, which explicitly defended the powers of men in the family and the subordinate role of women and reasserted the Church's opposition to abortion. Rallies and demonstrations were held around the country. The *AIZ* quoted the encyclical along with statements by working-class women that asserted their right to limit pregnancies and to have abortions and rejected implicitly the papacy's very explicit statement in support of patriarchal relations within the family.[57]

What then was the ideal of femininity constructed by the KPD? What was the female counterpart to the productive, powerful, and combative male proletarian? Certainly, the idealized woman was a proletarian committed to the cause of socialism and revolution and a full participant in all realms of social life. She worked in a factory, since participation in the productive realm constituted the necessary path to emancipation. At the same time, she was a housewife attuned to rationalized methods of work in the home and to constructing a supportive environment for the proletarian family—for the man when he came home from a hard day of labor and political struggle, for the children as they matured conscious of and confident in

[54] Max Hodann, "Kameradschaftsehe?" *AIZ* 8, no. 12: 4–5.

[55] "Ehe und Prostitution," *AIZ* 9, no. 20: 394.

[56] "Die Qualen der jungen Mieterin," *AIZ* 8, no. 9: 6.

[57] "So spricht der Papst: Arbeiterfrauen antworten," *AIZ* 10, no. 5: 84–85. See also Hans-Jürgen Arendt, "Eine demokratische Massenbewegung unter Führung der KPD im Frühjahr 1931: Die Volksaktion gegen den Paragraphen 218 und gegen die päpstliche Enzyklika 'Casti connubii,'" *ZfG* 19 (1971): 212–23.

their class and political identities. She was young and energetic and an object of beauty, but in a proletarian manner—not luxurious and ostentatious, but a beauty that derived from athleticism and health. She was sexually emancipated in that she had a right to the pleasures of a sexual life and could choose, by her own volition, to limit family size.

While many men could attain the party's construction of masculinity—they could be and often were combative workers—the feminine ideal was very much more elusive. The double burden of paid work and housework left little time and even less energy for daily exercise, political involvement, establishment of a nurturing home environment, attention to beauty, and a full sexual life.[58] Certainly, the KPD often critiqued the travails of proletarian women's lives. But one is left wondering whether the construction of an image so far from attainability accounts in part for the KPD's weak support among women.

Moreover, other aspects of party propaganda and party life often vitiated the KPD's emancipatory message. In the realm of reproductive rights the KPD demonstrated an instrumental approach consonant with its political tactics in other areas. In the party's view, paragraph 218 had to be overturned because it signified bourgeois society's oppression of the proletariat, and proletarian women in particular, not because any state's claims on women's bodies violated fundamental human liberties. As *Die Kommunistin* put the matter in 1921, "we recognize in full measure the right of the state in relation to the child."[59] This meant that the state had the responsibility to provide protection and welfare for the woman and child to ensure the well-being of coming proletarian generations, not, as Silvia Kontos emphasizes, to protect and secure the life and health of the woman. As Kontos goes on:

> This implied a reduction of women to their biological potential, which trailed only slightly the reactionary ideology of motherhood. It fell back upon a "female compulsion to motherhood," which a communist society had to help emerge. . . . Granting the state the right and responsibility in relation to the coming generations meant maintaining a principled societal claim upon women.[60]

At times, the KPD reverted to earlier condemnations of family limitation, as in 1931 when the Central Committee decried neo-Malthusianism as "cowardly, philistine, and reactionary theories whose object is to blame proletarian sexual dissipation instead of capitalist rule for the existing mass suffering and to lead the exploited masses astray from the path of revolutionary class struggle into the pitfalls of individual self-help."[61]

Furthermore, despite the advocacy of companionate marriages, the primary household role of women went largely unquestioned. Only two articles in a six-year span of the *AIZ* criticized men's regal bearing around the household and the

[58] See the wealth of detail in Hagemann, *Frauenalltag und Männerpolitik.*

[59] Quoted in Kontos, *"Die Partei kämpft wie ein Mann!"* 135.

[60] Ibid., 135–36.

[61] "Richtlinie der KPD zur Frage der Geburtenregelung," [1931], quoted in Usborne, *Politics of the Body*, 118.

suppression of women within it.[62] Typically, even these rare articles called on men to exercise "solidarity also within the household" so that women will be able to participate in the labor movement. One issue of *Rote Fahne* in 1920 advised men to send their women to party meetings and told them not to worry that the housework would not be completed. The women's improved morale would help them do their household chores more efficiently.[63]

Even as the party criticized men for their neglect of household and familial responsibilities, it offered the most traditional advice to women about making the home a supportive and pleasant environment. The *AIZ* described a typical working-class family in which the man and woman rush off to work, the children hurriedly have to get dressed to go to school or to a neighbor's to be watched.

> Aside from work outside the house, the employed woman very often has to take care of the household completely on her own. No one is to be blamed if she rarely . . . considers what she might do to help her exhausted husband relax and recuperate. This has nothing to do with the petit bourgeois preoccupation with comfort and coziness (*Gemütlichkeitssache*), but is a necessity for the working person—to allow him to unwind after work and the expenditure of so much energy. . . .
>
> The heavily burdened wife can arrange the meal with little accessories so that it tastes better to the family members and also to her. Men have no great fondness for the one-pot dish, but it will go down better if it's not simply thrown into a bowl and shoved on a table that is not particularly clean, which gives the husband the sense that he should feed rapidly like an animal. A bright table cloth, but one that doesn't get dirty as quickly as one that is completely bright, a pair of flowers on the table, and the mealtime is arranged quite nicely and is pleasing to the eye. The feeling of satiation lasts much longer than when the meal is hurriedly swallowed.[64]

Such efforts are necessary, the party's illustrated weekly went on, not to enable workers to serve capitalism better, but "to use every means to maintain our powers . . . in order to be armed for the struggle for our freedom."[65]

Dilemmas of Party Work among Women

Women's activism and the politicization of gender reached new levels of intensity during the Weimar Republic. Women were widely involved in plundering actions during the years of most intense crisis; in picket lines and other forms of strike support, especially in mining communities; in their own strikes as industrial workers; and in the great public campaign for the repeal of paragraph 218.[66] The KPD established an array of women's organizations; called conferences of women workers; launched a movement for elected female representatives in the workplace and the neighborhood; mobilized campaigns in support of reproduc-

[62] *AIZ*, 10 August 1927: 12, and 8:12 (1929): 4–5.

[63] Bridenthal and Koonz, "Beyond *Kinder, Küche, Kirche*," 58, n. 29.

[64] "Die werktätige Frau," *AIZ*, 10 August 1927: 12.

[65] Ibid.

[66] For examples, see Kontos, *"Die Partei kämpft wie ein Mann!"* 76–84.

tive rights, equal pay for equal work, and social welfare measures. Yet for all the efforts, the KPD proved singularly incapable of benefiting from the heightened public role of women and the fervent public discussion about women's roles and about sexuality. The obstacles to KPD organizing among women were great, and many were of the party's own making.

For the majority of proletarian women, the household remained the essential space of social life in the Weimar Republic. Impervious to this fact, the KPD and the Comintern, as discussed previously, argued that women's emancipation would develop only in tandem with their participation in the productive sphere. Despite items like the women's column of the *AIZ*, the party almost invariably appealed to women in the paid industrial labor force, although these remained a minority of proletarian women. The Halle-Merseburg KPD's workplan for International Women's Day in 1929 targeted women workers almost exclusively at the same time that party leaders complained that few female factory workers were to be found in the district. The district organization called for International Women's Day to be celebrated by strikes and new works council elections that would strengthen women's representation within the workplace. "Storm the *women's enterprises*!" ran one of the major slogans—not exactly the most effective appeal to the majority of women who did not labor in factories.[67] The Comintern's directive to make enterprise cells the basic organizational unit of the party, and then the movement of political space from the workplace to combative conflicts in the streets, necessarily meant the denigration of organizing work among women, since the party focused its efforts on spheres in which women were often not present.

Perhaps more significantly, the masculinized culture of the KPD created a climate unwelcoming to women and often resulted in a lack of sympathy among men for women's issues. In Essen in 1927, party leaders ordered male comrades to attend a meeting about the party's work among women. The men were incensed and expressed complaint after complaint. They wanted to know why they had to be at a meeting devoted to "women's matters." At the same time, some of the women clearly wanted the women's section to remain their province. As the Central Committee's instructor reported:

> The mistaken position of a number of male and female comrades concerning [party] work among women as a task solely for female comrades was expressed numerous times in this meeting. The leader of the women's section of the district leadership explained that she did not understand why the male comrades had been invited to a "women's meeting." At the beginning of the discussion there was a nasty mood among the women toward the men and vice versa, which led to numerous interruptions and sharp reproaches on both sides.

The Central Committee's instructor managed, not very convincingly, to pull some positive observations out of the meeting: "At the beginning of the talk the male comrades showed no interest in the questions about party work among

[67] "Arbeitsplan bis zum Internationalen Frauentag für den Bezirk Halle-Merseburg," [1929], SAPMO-BA, ZPA I/3/11/42/12–15.

women, but in due course they became interested and became convinced of its importance."[68] Yet in the discussion it became apparent that various party sections had had no involvement whatsoever with women's issues. At a meeting the next day in Cologne, the same kind of tone permeated the discussion. The men were "astonished and just about unwilling" to attend a meeting devoted to party work among women.[69]

The general indifference to women's issues and the ideological emphasis on the factory proletariat rendered women largely invisible to party organizers. In both the Ruhr and Halle-Merseburg, two of the most concentrated industrial regions of the country, party leaders complained that the low proportion of female factory workers hindered their efforts to organize women.[70] Yet in fact a substantial number of women did work in industry in both regions. Many more pursued the typical combination of part-time or temporary paid labor, home work, and household labor. The Ruhr leadership, however, remarked with an air of frustration that it had no choice but to work among housewives.[71] In Halle-Merseburg, work among factory women was of "secondary significance" because of the low proportion of female factory workers, the district leadership claimed. More with an air of resignation than frustration, it reported to the Central Committee that it concentrated on housewives and household servants and had had some successes attracting women to meetings and film evenings. Nonetheless, electoral results showed that the KPD did very poorly among women, and the RFMB remained very weak.[72]

Certainly, party leaders recognized some of the problems, and every level, from the Central Committee to the subdistricts, issued time and again a plaintive cry for better work among women.[73] Nonetheless, other party campaigns generally took precedence over women's issues. In 1927, even the planned celebrations for International Women's Week floundered because of a certain lack of interest and the fact that party members had had their fill of campaigns.[74] The situation was no better one year later. In 1928, a party instructor reported that International Women's Week in Essen was a complete fiasco, and not much better in other cities

[68] "Bericht über Parteiarbeiterkonferenzen zur Arbeit unter den Frauen," [April 1927], SAPMO-BA, ZPA I/3/18–19/35/1.

[69] Ibid., 2.

[70] "Aus dem Jahresbericht der Kommunistischen Partei Bezirk Halle-Merseburg vom 1. April 24 bis 31. März 1925," SAPMO-BA, ZPA I/3/11/13/271; "Bericht der Frauen-Abteilung Halle-Merseburg," [received at Central Committee 19 April 1929], SAPMO-BA, ZPA I/3/11/42/7–8; and BLR, "Bericht der Bezirksleitung," SAPMO-BA, ZPA I/3/18–19/11/208.

[71] BLR, "Bericht der Bezirksleitung," SAPMO-BA, ZPA I/3/18–19/11/208–9.

[72] "Politischer Bericht des Bezirks Halle-Merseburg für die Monate April/Mai einschließlich des Berichtes über die Wahlarbeit," 15 June 1928, SAPMO-BA, ZPA I/3/11/40/18–19, 25, and "Politischer und organisatorischer Bericht der KPD Bezirk Halle-Merseburg für die Monate November 1928 bis März 1928," SAPMO-BA, ZPA I/3/11/40/75.

[73] For a few examples, see "Monatsbericht des Bezirks 11—Halle-Merseburg für Monat März 1923," 14 April 1923, SAPMO-BA, ZPA I/3/11/18/89; "Aus dem Jahresbericht der Kommunistischen Partei Bezirk Halle-Merseburg vom 1. April 24 bis 31. März 1925," SAPMO-BA, ZPA I/3/11/13/271; and "Bericht der Gewerkschaftsabteilung Halle-Merseburg vom 15.5. bis 31.7.1929," SAPMO-BA, ZPA I/3/11/52/132.

[74] BLR, "Bericht der Bezirksleitung," SAPMO-BA, ZPA I/3/18–19/11/209, and "Politischer Bericht des Bezirks Halle-Merseburg für März/April," 14 May 1927, SAPMO-BA, ZPA I/3/11/16/72.

of the Ruhr. Yet he provided no explanation for the disaster, perhaps a sign of neglect on the part of the party.[75]

Even at firms with a large female workforce, such as I. G. Farben's Wolfen Filmenfabrik, party organization gave virtually no attention to women's specific interests and made no effort to bring women into the preparations for a strike.[76] In party districts throughout Germany female cadres were often designated for "appropriate" feminine tasks—as in recommendations that work in local welfare institutions "offers the class-conscious proletarian woman an important and rewarding field of activity."[77] Efforts to recruit new female members often degenerated into attempts to win over the wives of male comrades—not always with the support of the men.[78] In sectors where relatively few women were employed, as in mining or basic steel, the KPD simply was out of its depths, unsure how to approach housewives when the party's entire orientation revolved around the male proletariat, combative political violence, and, in the case of women, the firm commitment to their proletarianization. The gendered language of the party did not help, as in *Rote Fahne's* headline after the 1924 party congress: "Forward, comrades [*Genossen*, or male comrades], enough with the discussion, forward to work, all together as one man [*Mann*, not *Mensch*]."[79]

Aware of the difficulties, the KPD in the mid- and late 1920s sought new and various ways to expand its influence among women. The women's column of the *AIZ* constituted one such effort, as did the founding of the RFMB in the autumn of 1925 as the party's major vehicle for organizing women. But as even DDR historians admitted, the RFMB never became a mass organization and had only partial successes in a few cities. The RFMB's deliberate attempt to mimic the militaristic style of the RFB might have found support among some female activists, but not the broad mass of women.[80]

The limited success of the RFMB prompted the KPD to adopt a rhetoric and style specifically directed at women. Never did these techniques supplant the dominant masculinized ethos of the party. Yet in somewhat uneasy tension, a specific rhetoric of women's politics emerged alongside the masculinized politics of street battles.

[75] "Bericht über meine Anwesenheit im Ruhrgebiet vom 5. März bis 14. März und vom 18. März bis 3. April 1928," 4 April 1928, SAPMO-BA, ZPA I/3/18–19/13/87, and "Bericht über Parteiarbeiterkonferenzen zur Arbeit unter den Frauen," [April 1927], SAPMO-BA, ZPA I/3/18–19/35/1–2a.

[76] "Bericht der Zelle Film-Wolfen (18.1.32)," SAPMO-BA, ZPA I/3/11/19/223. About two-thirds of the workforce was female.

[77] BLR Frauenabteilung/Agitpropabteilung, "Praktische Winke für die Sozialpolitische Arbeit: Material für die Frauenschule des Bez. Ruhrgebiet," 23–28 July 1928, SAPMO-BA, ZPA I/3/18–19/38/11.

[78] "Auszug aus dem Jahresbericht der KPD Bezirk Halle-Merseburg 1924/25," SAPMO-BA, ZPA I/3/11/42/4–5.

[79] Quoted in Kontos, *"Die Partei Kämpft wie ein Mann!"* 55.

[80] See Arendt and Freigang, "Zur proletarischen Frauenbewegung," 1024. In the entire Ruhr, the RFMB had three thousand members, six hundred of whom were also party members. But only in five out of eighty-eight locals were communists not in the leading positions. BLR, "Bericht der Bezirksleitung," 9 December 1926, SAPMO-BA, ZPA I/3/18–19/11/198.

The party women's organization, for example, called for mobilizing women for May Day around the slogan "equal pay for equal work."[81] During the 1928 Ruhr metalworkers lockout, the KPD made a concerted effort to connect the conflict to women's own concerns, calling the metalworkers struggle "your struggle" and for a "common struggle of metal workers and working women to guarantee the victory."[82] It also tried, with some success, to organize women's support actions. The leadership seconded Marie Wiedmaier from Berlin to the Ruhr, and she launched a whirlwind organizational campaign. With her help, women held demonstrations and "flying" rallies, raised money for the International Workers Aid (Internationale Arbeiterhilfe, or IAH), cooked in the kitchens established by the IAH, and even, on a few occasions, won admission to union and workplace meetings.[83]

Local and regional party organizations also began to develop a more systematic approach toward organizing women. The Halle-Merseburg party in 1929 adopted new forms of agitation and propaganda, including women's evenings that entailed film showings, musical performances, lectures, and readings, often in combination. While these evening programs drew on long-standing practices of the labor movement, their direction at women in particular marked something of a departure, especially for a party long resistant to the separate organization of women. The evenings were a great success and spread from Halle to other towns in the district. Women functionaries were also active participants in the various educational programs designed for cadres. Perhaps for these reasons International Women's Week proved far more successful in 1929 than in previous years. All of the various political and cultural events were well attended, the party report claimed, and provided the KPD with an opportunity to present its ideas and program. Yet while many women apparently enjoyed film showings and lectures, few of them joined the party. The "organizational successes" were quite limited.[84]

Meetings often entailed talks by party leaders with little participation from the audience. The leaders complained about the passivity of the female audience—"the female comrades appeared without any inner preparatory work for the meeting and waited for the oracles from the course leader," as one report put it—but the problem lay at least as much in a party culture that allowed leaders to drone on endlessly.[85] Nor was it likely that a membership drive would have much success when the prize for the comrades who recruited the most new members consisted of a book about the Soviet Union.[86] Deceptions like letters to the editor of a party women's publication supposedly written by workers, but from the tone

[81] RFMB Gau Ruhrgebiet, "Unsere Aufgaben im Monat Mai!" 30 April 1930, SAPMO-BA, ZPA I/3/18–19/37/2.

[82] "Bericht über die Arbeit unter den Frauen während des Ruhrkampfes," 18 December 1928, SAPMO-BA, ZPA I/3/18–19/35/3.

[83] Ibid., 8.

[84] "Bericht der Frauen-Abteilung Halle-Merseburg," [received at Central Committee 19 April 1929], SAPMO-BA, ZPA I/3/11/42/7–8.

[85] "Bericht über den Kursus im Bezirks Halle-Merseburg am 4. Juni 23," SAPMO-BA, ZPA I/3/11/18/134.

[86] "Arbeitsplan bis zum Internationalen Frauentag für den Bezirk Halle-Merseburg," [1929], SAPMO-BA, ZPA I/3/11/42/14–15.

most probably by party functionaries, must have been transparent to most people, and would hardly have endeared the KPD to them.[87]

Inevitably, women in the party often felt that their efforts and concerns were shunted to the side by male comrades, who were generally less than supportive. Yet in spite of their complaints and all the insufficiencies of the KPD's work among women, at times the KPD did provide, almost inadvertently, a forum for some women to articulate their concerns and to develop their own identities. The KPD women's organization offered women an avenue to develop their talents and leadership abilities and a place for a broader circle of women to give expression to their burdens and desires. In 1929, the women's organization in the Ruhr held a public antiwar meeting.[88] The KPD's speaker gave the usual address that warned of the dangers of another war, which could only be forestalled by proletarian solidarity. But somehow, the meeting turned from a mundane political rally to a riveting and emotional experience as women gave voice to the miseries of proletarian life only worsened by the agony of war. They described intense poverty and the constant presence of death—of parents who died at too young an age, of siblings, of their own children. They lamented their fate as mothers forced to go off to work leaving a nine-year-old girl in charge of the household, and their own experiences as children whose parents were gone at work the entire day. Those who exercised power only created greater difficulties for them. Pastors and bureaucrats were remote, callous, and unhelpful. Company doctors ordered people back to work when sick, or claimed that on-the-job accidents were the result of illnesses. Rape was forestalled only by the brandishing of a butcher knife. Welfare payments, when available, barely held body and soul together. Pregnant women had to work until they were ready to deliver, and then had to undertake a desperate search for child care. Living on the street was preferable to shelters. And the war—the ostensible topic of discussion—had taken husbands and sons, and left others "fully broken," mentally and physically.

The party also provided women a forum to voice the difficulties of welding together family and party life. In the winter of 1927/28, the women's column of the *Ruhr-Echo*, the major party newspaper in the Ruhr, became the forum for a vibrant discussion. One woman wrote in complaining about the fact that her husband was always off at party gatherings, leaving her alone with a two-and-one-half-year-old child. She did not object to the fact that he was politically active, but did not think that he should entirely forget his family. The responses poured in, and not all of them were charitable. The letter writer (a "comrade D.") was told that she did not understand "the entire meaning of our struggle," and was advised that if she did not like going for a walk alone on Sundays, then she should join the party's demonstrations.[89] Another reader told her to be happy that her husband participated in party events, and to go off and read *Cement* (by

[87] *Die Delegierte: Merkblatt für Frauendelegierte in Stadt und Land* 1:7–8, [n.d., probably 1929], SAPMO-BA, ZPA I/3/11/41/14–20.

[88] The following is drawn from the fragment of a transcript of a meeting. [Untitled], 18 June 1929, SAPMO-BA, ZPA I/3/18–19/35/9–23.

[89] This and the following quotes are from "Für die proletarische Frau," *RE*, 6 January 1928: 4.

Gladkov), which would show her how Russian women had struggled to become free. One male metalworker wrote in to say that Sunday rallies are part of the class struggle, and if men do not concern themselves with politics, the situation will be worse for women. "Help your husband with his political work," was his solution to her dilemma. One woman, who had given up the effort to establish a "comfortable and cozy [*gemütliches*] home" for the political struggle, advised her: "Don't make life difficult for you and your husband. Struggle together, then it will be easier."

The woman who had written the original letter was not enthralled by the responses. She wrote back to say that she was in poor health and was happy to get a little fresh air when she was done with her housework. Now and again she had gone with her husband to meetings, but could hardly stand the air thick with smoke: "I ask the comrades to have consideration for women, and to stop smoking in meetings so one doesn't go home with a headache. . . . Now, to you dear women, as I can now confirm, walks are healthy and the doctor has ordered them for me. First take care of health, then politics. What good is it if with politics I end up in the cemetery?"

Some women, however, did respond with sympathy. One reader wrote in to complain about the "cold responses, which to be sure are well intended, and are also correct from the party standpoint, but are not at all sufficient for a woman who is compelled by the neglect of her husband to give up her own self."[90] The paper's editors, according to this reader, responded with slightly more feeling, but with the same essential position:

> I have noticed in reading the lines, how little women are understood. . . .
>
> I know how much pain and suffering lies behind comrade D.'s lines. I sympathize with her, when her husband stays away from his home far beyond the scope of his political work. It can't contribute to her recuperation that she can't be rid of her spiritual and domestic loneliness. And when material distress comes, which is mostly the case in proletarian families, then should a woman, ill and worn down by the economic situation, struggle and labor? A woman gives warmth and feeling, but to maintain these qualities she needs replenishment, a little nourishment, otherwise she . . . goes to pieces or herself becomes cold.
>
> And you write, dear comrade, how the family life of a militant [*Klassenkämpfer*] should be: comradeship, mutual help, etc. and give the advice: "Don't neglect your wife and the family, it is un-communist." . . . Hundreds of times the sentence has been written in meetings, books, and newspapers. Has it had any response from the men? Has it contributed only a little to improvement? And why not? I believe it would be better if we turned the sentence around. It shouldn't any longer be: "Husband, how do you treat your wife?" That is obsolete. It must be:
>
> *"Woman, how do you defend yourself?"*[91]

Another woman, responding with as much intensity, wanted to know what the editors thought a woman should do when her husband refused to participate in

[90] This and the following quotes from ibid., 20 January 1928: 4.
[91] Ibid.

the "enlightenment" of his wife, "when the man has lost the sense for home and family, as is the case with many men, including good communists. All the warnings and good advice don't help at all. . . . From the women's pages [of the newspaper] we women have the right to demand enlightenment and advice about how we should defend ourselves against everything that oppresses us." She then went on to describe her husband as a man who "always forces his dominating will upon me"—leaving readers certain about the sexual connotations of her lament.[92]

The editors of the *Ruhr-Echo* did respond with a certain degree of sympathy. Comrade D. "doesn't demand too much," they wrote. "It is not communistic when a man neglects his family." But quickly they tempered the note of sympathy with one of condescension.

> In the end, the class is composed of families and
> *the family is, not least, the most important cell of the class.*
> . . . [But] it is also correct that the wife has to learn to understand political life. Only then will she understand her politically active husband. Here is the most important demand that must be addressed to married party comrades: Help your wife to understand politics. Don't act in a dominating way toward your wife, but enlighten her with simple words. The oft-experienced attitude, that the man explains to his wife that she should not concern herself with politics, is counterrevolutionary and unworthy of a communist. By neglect of the family . . . we understand that a man fails in his first responsibility, a class responsibility: to influence his wife and his children in line with his worldview.

The editors called for much improved "methods of enlightenment," for greater conviction and patience in the effort.

> *Family life for a militant means: Comradeship between husband and wife, mutual help, and no one-sided domination of the one or the other, common party work, even at different posts, and at the same time that portion of free time for the completion of necessary family affairs, which can in no way be of unconcern to a revolutionary.*[93]

Party leaders in the Ruhr probably did not expect such an outpouring, nor such vociferous comments, when they published comrade D.'s letter. But she touched a nerve that reverberated through many aspects of party life—the general neglect of women's issues, even in the women's column of the party newspaper; the brave words about egalitarian relations that were rarely honored; the condescension of party leaders who assumed that men were innately revolutionary while women required "enlightenment."

Yet at the same time, the KPD, because of its commitment to equality, even if only rhetorical, opened up a forum for women that enabled them to voice publicly their concerns. And this was true not only in the letters columns of party newspapers, but also in relation to the party leadership. In Eisleben, women complained bitterly that the Central Committee had failed to carry through on its

[92] Ibid.
[93] Ibid., 13 January 1928: 4.

commitments to provide speakers for women's events—a complaint often aired at the local level in relation to all sorts of issues. To the local women, the Central Committee's actions constituted not only an organizational mistake, but a breach of faith that seemed to speak to the general neglect of women and women's issues in the party.[94] In Bitterfeld, women criticized the works councils for failing to support the political work of women.[95] Female functionaries in Essen, the seat of the *Ruhr-Echo*, seem to have challenged the party's emphasis on the RFMB as the major focus of organizing for women. They claimed that it took too much of their energies, and apparently conducted a campaign to undermine it. The male party leadership in Essen and the Ruhr complained bitterly that the women were uncooperative, stubborn, and wrongheaded and were undermining party work. While party work among women in the area was going well, in Essen female comrades carried out directives in a high-handed manner, alienating other women. They drew a sharp line between themselves and the RFMB and sabotaged it through passive resistance. If they join the RFMB,

> they nag and criticize the indifferent women, without working better themselves. Then soon they quit the RFMB.
>
> It is extraordinarily difficult to develop among female party comrades a basic understanding of fraction work in an organization that extends beyond the party. They engage in the greatest stupidities, then brag that everything had already been resolved, etc. Briefly stated, only a very few of the fractions work really well.[96]

To be sure, female party activists were not above a tone of condescension toward other women. They complained about the passivity of women in general, and the fact that too many female comrades failed to understand that political education and development had to take place in the context of the entire party, not just in the women's movement.[97] But although the sources do not allow for substantiation, it is certainly possible that party women also had other ideas about how the KPD's organizing work should be conducted. They might just have objected to the kinds of subterfuges that prevailed in all sorts of party fronts, the RFMB included, and to the clear intent not to allow the RFMB to develop into an organization that articulated women's interests.

Nothing depicts better the party's dilemmas in relation to women than the great campaign against the prohibition of abortion, paragraph 218 of the criminal code. In the campaign, which flowered in earnest in the midst of the Depression, the KPD demonstrated the breadth and limits of its commitment to both women's emancipation and to political organizing around women's issues.[98]

94 "Bericht der Frauen-Abteilung Halle-Merseburg," [received at Central Committee 19 April 1929], SAPMO-BA, ZPA I/3/11/42/7–8.

95 "Bericht über den Kursus im Bezirks Halle-Merseburg am 4. Juni 23," SAPMO-BA, ZPA I/3/11/18/135.

96 BLR, "Bericht der Bezirksleitung," 9 December 1926, SAPMO-BA, ZPA I/3/18–19/11/198.

97 "Auszug aus dem Jahresbericht der KPD Bezirk Halle-Merseburg 1924/25," SAPMO-BA, ZPA I/3/11/42/3–5.

98 The following is drawn from Atina Grossmann, *Reforming Sex*; idem, "Abortion and Economic

Of the major political parties, the KPD was certainly the most forceful and consistent advocate of women's right to an abortion and to the availability of birth control methods.[99] Its position marked a radical departure from the predominant political views in Germany, and even ran against some of Lenin's less enlightened statements on neo-Malthusianism. Numerous organizations of feminists, socialists, liberal reformers, physicians, and sex reformers were allied with the KPD on these matters. But only with the arrest in 1931 of two Stuttgart physicians, Friedrich Wolf and Elsa Keinle, did a mass movement in favor of abortion rights really emerge. The KPD, for one of the few times in its history, led a multiclass and multipolitical alliance in defence of the two physicians and in opposition to paragraph 218. The campaign was led by the party front organizations, the International Workers Aid and the Working Group of Social Welfare Organizations, which initiated the formation of a committee that counted about sixty other groups, including socialist, liberal, professional, and feminist organizations. About eight hundred local action committees were formed.[100] Demonstrations, rallies, discussions in the letters columns of newspapers, serialized novels, dramatic performances—an entire realm of the public sphere opened up in discussion of paragraph 218. The concluding line of Friedrich Wolf's widely performed play, *Cyankali*, "a law that turns eight hundred thousand mothers into criminals every year is no longer a law," became one of the rallying cries of the movement.

The KPD indicted paragraph 218 in the context of its condemnation of capitalist society, which forced women to have abortions because they were unable to support their children.[101] Capitalism therefore distorted and destroyed the "natural" sentiments of motherhood. The cases in which women were condemned to prison sentences offered the KPD plenty of examples to depict the vengeful and inhumane character of the Weimar judiciary, including instances in which women who already had given birth to even eighteen and nineteen children were sent to prison for having abortions. As the party noted, criminalization did not put an end to abortions, and the increasing desperation of the Depression years only added to the incidences. As one emergency order after another led to declining wages and the elimination of family and child supports, "nothing is left to working families other than naked want. . . . Hunger compels [women]. . .to suppress their maternal feelings and to kill the coming life." Only in the Soviet Union are women free to give birth as they desire, and there the birth rate is on the rise, unlike the capitalist lands, for in the Soviet Union all have enough to eat. Hence, the struggle against paragraph 218 is only a part of the struggle against the capitalist system: "Only when the working class has power will this paragraph disap-

---

Crisis: The 1931 Campaign against Paragraph 218," in Bridenthal, Grossmann, and Kaplan, *When Biology Became Destiny*, 66–86; Usborne, *Politics of the Body*, 156–213; Kontos, "*Die Partei kämpft wie ein Mann!*" 84–120; and Arendt, "Eine demokratische Massenbewegung."

[99] However, Usborne, in opposition to most commentators, makes a strong defense of the SPD's commitment to abortion reform. See *Politics of the Body*, 156–81.

[100] The figures are from Arendt, "Demokratische Massenbewegung," 217.

[101] I draw here on the text of a leaflet, "Frauen heraus zum Massensturm gegen den Mordparagrafen 218," [undated, presumably 1931], SAPMO-BA, ZPA I/3/18–19/37/12.

pear. Then women will freely control their bodies [*frei über ihren Körper verfügen*], and a new, healthy human species will grow up."[102]

But certainly not every opponent of paragraph 218 shared the KPD's confidence in a Soviet future, or believed that the ban on abortion had to be understood within the context of capitalist society. The party found itself with uncomfortable allies, women who articulated an autonomous feminism that challenged the primacy the KPD placed on class.[103] Within the ranks of the party women increasingly gave voice to an independent position that placed greater weight on gender than the party leadership was prepared to countenance. Nor was the KPD free from the eugenics-based population politics that many other groups, right and left, advocated. At the same time, by raising the slogan "Your body belongs to you," the KPD "implicitly and rather nervously defended the individual woman's right to choose. . . . The Communist left at least partially broke through the motherhood and eugenic consensus that extended into the ranks of left, feminist, and Sex Reform movements."[104]

Yet, as Atina Grossmann also writes, the KPD found itself with an insoluble dilemma. It had set in motion a broad-based coalition around women's issues, yet resisted the development of an autonomous women's politics, indeed, feared any action outside the realm of party-controlled cadre politics.[105] Numerous articles in *Rote Fahne* and local communist newspapers lauded the formation of action committees from below while reviling the social democratic leadership and equating (and confusing) the Brüning government, fascism, and social democracy.[106] Only the KPD, the party argued in one leaflet, "truly opposes the infamous and murderous paragraph [218]. The front of reaction reaches from the Nazis to the Social Democrats. And this front of fascism wants to use working-class children as cannon fodder for a new robber imperialist war, for the insatiable profits of the industrial and financial capitalists."[107]

Ultimately, the KPD, fearful of mass activism that lay beyond its control, pulled back from the movement and scuttled the broad-based coalition it had founded. Instead, it formed its own Unity Committee for Proletarian Sexual Reform, which soon waned into insignificance.

102 Ibid.

103 Grossmann, "Abortion and Economic Crisis," 74–80. Note also Petro's comments, *Joyless Streets*, 139, on the ambiguity of the messages in *AIZ*, which potentially enabled a reader to develop an identification with women and women's issues despite the overt emphasis on class.

104 Grossmann, "Abortion and Economic Crisis," 77.

105 Ibid., 78–80. This was not the first time that the KPD scuttled a broad-based coalition it had initiated. Much the same thing happened in 1927 during the quite successful campaign to expropriate without compensation the princely houses of Germany. A KPD-led coalition collected enough petitions to have the matter considered in a referendum—a remarkable achievement even though the referendum itself failed. But the party quickly drew back from the campaign, fearful that it would not be able to direct it. Jakob Walcher, in a very insightful letter to Nikolai Bukharin, at the time head of the Comintern (among many other tasks he exercised), critiqued the party on just this basis. See Walcher to Bukharin, 26 May 1927, SAPMO-BA, ZPA I/6/3/161/5–11.

106 For one example, see Kontos, *"Die Partei kämpft wie ein Mann!"* 89.

107 "Frauen heraus zum Massensturm gegen den Mordparagrafen 218," SAPMO-BA, ZPA I/3/18–19/37/12.

Conclusion

In the course of the Weimar Republic the KPD intensified the gendered understanding of politics and society that the socialist movements of the nineteenth century had developed. Despite its strong rhetorical support for women's emancipation, the party glorified male productive labor as the source of society's material wealth and male political combativeness as the means of surmounting the limits and exploitations of capitalist society and creating the socialist future. Women played ancillary roles in both arenas. They labored primarily in the home or in the interstices of the capitalist economy, neither the basis for proletarian solidarity, and acted as auxiliaries to the much-feted fighting organizations of the KPD, the Red Front Fighters League and its various clones.

Certainly, the general Marxist-Leninist enthrallment with the productive sphere, and the "heavy metal" sector in particular, contributed to the party's strongly masculine tenor. In the KPD's view, the subordination of women was only an epiphenomenon of the subordination of the proletariat in capitalist society. Since class was primary, the major representatives of the class—combative and assertive men—took precedence. Even the party's recipe for women's emancipation reflected the ideological denigration of the reproductive sphere—in order to become free, women had to become more like men, namely, they had to work in the sphere of production.

But the gendering of German communism derived not only from the party's ideological framework, nor solely from the discursive terrain as some kind of abstracted, independently powered social arena. The KPD's construction of gender was shaped also, and very decisively, by the spatial transformation of labor and communist politics discussed in previous chapters. Driven by the coalition of order from the workplace, the streets became the KPD's primary space of political engagement. When combined with the party's incessant invocation of revolution as the path to the future society and its denigration of the legislative arena, the turn to the streets made male physical prowess the essence of political action and commitment. While the party constantly sought to raise women's political activism, its subliminal message was that politics involved men primarily, and only the powerful need apply. Precious little space was left for the invocation of women's social roles as the basis of a political movement or of the future social order, and for sustained attention to the specifics of women's subordination in society.

As a result, the KPD's constituency remained limited to proletarian men, and primarily the unemployed among them. The gendered character of the KPD contributed greatly to its deep-seated political intransigence. A strategy based on creating civil disorder through male combativeness in the streets precluded political alliances, especially when the security forces were directed by social democrats. In the major instance when the KPD had the opportunity to win broad-based support from women—the campaign against paragraph 218—the party abandoned the movement for fear of diluting its primarily masculine, proletarian character.

Furthermore, by disparaging "practical work" in the legislatures, the party isolated itself from one of the realms in which it could have had a direct impact on women. Instead, it used the legislatures primarily for agitational purposes, to foster the intransigence it considered the very essence of politics. But these maximalist positions had even less resonance among women. In contrast, the French Communist Party beginning in the 1930s and the Italian Communist Party after World War II won much greater female support by utilizing effectively the local political arena to institute wide-ranging programs beneficial to women and families.[108]

Still, the KPD did articulate an emancipatory message. Its call for abortion rights, equal pay for equal work, and the full participation of women in society challenged most directly the prevailing gender codes of German society. It vastly broadened the "political imaginary," enabling people to envisage a world of egalitarian relations between the sexes. The party offered some women an avenue of activism and a vigorous forum that enabled them to articulate their oppressions and desires.

Yet these opportunities proved, in the end, of secondary importance. Instead, the gendering of German communism constituted one vital element of a party culture centered around class; hard, combative struggle; and loyalty to the Soviet Union, topics explored further in the next chapter.

[108] For a further development of this argument on a comparative scale, see Eric D. Weitz, *Popular Communism: Political Strategies and Social Histories in the Formation of the German, French, and Italian Communist Parties, 1919–1948*, Western Societies Program Occasional Paper no. 31 (Ithaca: Cornell University Institute for European Studies, 1992).

CHAPTER 7

Forging a Party Culture

Der Leninismus lehrt, daß man den Kampf aufnehmen muß.

—*Ernst Thälmann*[1]

To be a communist in the Weimar Republic meant to live a life in the party. In political battles and commemorative demonstrations; in meeting upon meeting of party enterprise cells, block associations, city-wide organizations, and sports groups; in organized cultural events—in all these arenas KPD supporters came into conflict with their opponents and encountered, on a daily basis, the language and ideology of German and international communism. Here the KPD forged a party culture and individuals fashioned their political and social identities. In conjunction with engagement in the physical and social spaces of workplace and street, people learned to be communists through their encounter with the party's formal pronouncements, discussions and arguments, and visual representations. The primary categories they learned were loyalty to the Soviet Union, commitment to the communist cause, and the centrality of class, struggle, and solidarity. But the party did not exist in pristine isolation, and these categories assumed much of their meaning from the dangerous opponents that lurked in every corner and continually threatened the KPD and the Soviet Union. Essential to the culture of communism was also a long catalog of enemies in which social democracy took pride of place. Some enemies had even infiltrated the party, and KPD members also learned unceasing and vitriolic factionalism as a way of life in the party.

Many of these categories were not new. The KPD inherited a class-oriented view of the world and a belief in struggle and solidarity from the nineteenth-century socialist movements. Depictions of callous and exploitative employers and government leaders had been the common fare of socialist propaganda since the 1830s. But in the 1920s and in the hands of communists, these categories acquired a new tenor and became invested with new meanings. The tones became harsher, more uncompromising. They reflected a new, more brutal kind of political conflict that emerged in World War I and the Bolshevik Revolution. The culture of communism grew more distant from the liberal-humanistic bourgeois culture of the nineteenth century, the world that had first spawned Marxism and the socialist labor movements.

[1] "Leninism teaches that one has to take up the struggle." Ernst Thälmann, "Die Lehren des Hamburger Aufstandes," 23 October 1925, in *Zur Geschichte der Kommunistischen Partei Deutschlands: Eine Auswahl von Materialien und Dokumenten aus den Jahren 1914–1946*, ed. Marx-Engels-Lenin-Stalin-Institut beim Zentralkomitee der SED, 2d ed. (Berlin: Dietz, 1955), 155.

This chapter, like the preceding one on gender, moves from the social context "on the ground," the political space of workplace and street, to the ideological, discursive, and organizational terrains of party life. The aim is to explore what communism meant for the thousands who passed through the KPD and how the party "fixed" a language and an ideology that would have decisive consequences for the development of German communism as party, movement, and state through the long span of the twentieth century.

The Light from the East

In the course of the Weimar Republic, the Soviet Union came to exert increasing authority over the KPD.[2] Moscow set overall strategy and broke and made KPD leaderships. Paul Levi, Ernst Reuter, Ernst Meyer, Heinrich Brandler, and Ruth Fischer—party leaders between 1919 and 1925—all foundered when, for various reasons, they lost the backing of the Russian Communist Party (RCP[b]; from 1923, the Communist Party of the Soviet Union, or CPSU).[3] KPD factions rose and fell depending on the Comintern's assessment of the tactics appropriate for a particular period and, more often and more fatefully, on personal and political alignments between German communists and their Russian mentors.

The Communist International (Comintern) hierarchy served as the major avenue of Soviet control, a development implicit in its very founding in 1919 and especially in Lenin's promulgation of the "Twenty-One Conditions" in 1920, which mandated that all members model themselves on the Russian party. KPD leaders journeyed increasingly often to Moscow to consult on major matters with the Executive Committee of the Communist International (ECCI), dominated, of course, by the Russian party leaders. The ECCI delegated agents to the KPD Politburo who often enjoyed special powers. Hundreds, perhaps thousands, of German communists journeyed to the Soviet Union in the course of the 1920s and 1930s to receive technical and political training. Some came home disillusioned; many more acquired enhanced stature within the KPD by virtue of their Soviet experience. By the end of the 1920s, training at one or another of the various academies and institutes attached to the Comintern, the CPSU, or the Red

[2] The theme of most historical writing on the KPD, and especially Hermann Weber, *Die Wandlung des deutschen Kommunismus: Die Stalinisierung der KPD in der Weimarer Republik*, 2 vols. (Frankfurt am Main: Europäische Verlagsanstalt, 1969), and Ossip K. Flechtheim, *Die KPD in der Weimarer Republik* (1948; Hamburg: Junius, 1986).

[3] For biographical backgrounds see the entries in Weber, *Wandlung* 2: 84–86 (Heinrich Brandler), 117–20 (Ruth Fischer), and 221–22 (Ernst Meyer); Rosa Meyer-Leviné, *Inside German Communism: Memoirs of Party Life in the Weimar Republic* (London: Pluto, 1977), also on Ernst Meyer; Charlotte Beradt, *Paul Levi: Ein demokratischer Sozialist in der Weimarer Republik* (Frankfurt am Main: Europäische Verlagsanstalt, 1969); Peter Nettl, *Rosa Luxemburg*, abridged ed. (Oxford: Oxford University Press, 1969); Willy Brandt, *Ernst Reuter: Ein Leben für die Freiheit* (Munich: Kindler, 1957). David E. Barclay is preparing the definitive biography of Reuter-Friesland, the early KPD leader and post–World War II SPD mayor of Berlin.

Army had become virtually a prerequisite for advance within the KPD hierarchy.[4]

Ernst Thälmann, the last and longest-lasting leader of the Weimar KPD, epitomized the enhanced Soviet domination of the German party.[5] A dockworker and trade union functionary from Hamburg, Thälmann was installed as party chairman in 1925. His working-class background, including a rough but empathetic personality and a minimum of formal education, won him genuine affection from many rank-and-file communists. In fact, his selection as chairman demonstrated the increasing proletarianization of the KPD, since four of the six preceding leaders were intellectuals and a number of them Jewish as well. Thälmann also conveyed that complete commitment to the socialist cause that the party sought always to develop in its members.

Inclined toward rebellion from an early age, Thälmann found the intransigent radicalism of the KPD quite congenial. He aligned himself with the KPD's left-wing factions, which in the early years of the Weimar Republic thought revolution turned merely on the decisive will of the party and the proletariat. But when the Comintern abandoned the left-wing faction under Ruth Fischer, which had steered the KPD into near isolation by the end of 1924, Thälmann followed the Soviet path and was chosen to head up the new leadership. Early on, he threw in his lot with Stalin in the Russian factional conflicts and drove the KPD to increasing reliance on the Soviets. As Stalin consolidated his control, the deadweight of Soviet authoritarian practices came increasingly to characterize the KPD as well. Mimicking Russian methods, power in the KPD came to center in the ever more restricted Politburo dominated by Thälmann and in the Comintern agents responsible for the German party. Increasingly, support for the Soviet Union became the litmus test for communist loyalty. Anyone who challenged political decisions taken at the center—the KPD Politburo, the Comintern, Stalin himself—could be castigated as "disloyal" to the party and international communism. The democratic facets of Luxemburg's ideology waned in favor of the more dogmatic, deterministic, and sterile aspects of Marxism-Leninism. The intransigence of the KPD, forged out of the Luxemburgist-Leninist ideological matrix and the experience of hard political struggle in the Weimar Republic, now became entwined with the authoritarianism that marked the Stalinist revolution from above in the Soviet Union.

But for party members, the Soviet Union was not the nefarious force of so many historical accounts, the agent of backward, authoritarian ideas and practices that it imposed upon radical but democratically inclined communist parties around the world. Even before the so-called Stalinization of the KPD, radical workers in Germany looked to Russia and the Soviet Union as the heralds of revolution, the model that Germany would have to follow. As the coalition of order in Germany secured its powers, the Bolshevik model won increasing reso-

[4] See Beatrix Herlemann, "Der deutschsprachige Bereich an den Kaderschulen der Kommunistischen Internationale," *IWK* 18:2 (1982): 205–29.

[5] See the biographical entry in Weber, *Wandlung* 2: 318–20.

nance among German communists, a form of political and psychological compensation for their own failed efforts to overthrow capitalism. The Soviet Union, in contrast, had engaged the construction of socialism and was the site of peace and prosperity and the abolition of exploitation. It commanded solidarity.

How did communists learn loyalty to the Soviet Union? By the early 1930s, the functionaries had learned that opposition led quickly to exclusion from the KPD, a kind of internal personal and political exile that only the most self-assured felt they could endure. On a broader and more "positive" level, the party media lavished attention on "revolutionary Russia." When communists went back to their founders, Karl Liebknecht and Rosa Luxemburg, they discovered paeans of support to the nascent Soviet Union. Luxemburg's attitude toward Bolshevism was by no means uniformly negative, as those who have only a cursory knowledge of her unfinished pamphlet, "The Russian Revolution," believe. The Revolution inspired and enthralled her. In "The Russian Revolution" she lauded the Bolsheviks for their revolutionary audacity, their refusal to follow the chimera of majority rule, and their "iron resolution."[6]

In subsequent KPD press accounts, the Soviet Union was a bastion of peace and progress in which men and women gave of themselves heroically to build socialism. The Soviet Union was the "socialist fatherland of workers of all countries."[7] Soviet workers and peasants have "chased their exploiters to the devil. . . . Russian workers have food to eat, while in Germany workers go hungry. In Russia peasants have land, while in Germany hundreds of thousands of settlers and small peasants wait for an acre to feed themselves."[8] In a kind of hero worship that had deep psychological appeal to many workers and functionaries, Lenin and Stalin were lauded for their devotion to the proletarian cause, their "genial" direction of the international workers movement.

Not only were material riches available to all in the Soviet Union. Women were free and did not have to endure back-alley abortions and the fear of criminal prosecution. They could give birth as they desired, and socialism had resulted in prosperity and a rising birth rate, the exact opposite of trends in the capitalist countries.[9] Report after report in the party press depicted excellent child care and educational facilities in the Soviet Union, socialized housework, and outstanding public health. Children were happy, women were the very epitomy of the "new woman," and families were wholesome (plates 7.1–7.3). The men, meanwhile, were busy building socialism, models of committed proletarians who joined together across racial and national lines to fight for their class. They gaze heroically together into the future in front of the smokestacks of industrialization (plate 7.4) and march in the Red Army in defense of peace and socialism.

[6] Luxemburg, "Zur russischen Revolution," *GW*:4, 338, 341.

[7] "Über die Verschärfung der Widersprüche des Kapitalismus, die Kriegsgefahr und die Aufgaben der Kommunistischen Partei Deutschlands: Aus der Resolution des ZK-Plenums," February 1932, in *Zur Geschichte der Kommunistischen Partei Deutschlands*, 317.

[8] "Aufruf der Kommunistischen Partei zur Wahl," 2 April 1924, in Hermann Weber, ed., *Der deutsche Kommunismus: Dokumente* (Cologne: Kiepenheuer und Witsch, 1963), 317.

[9] Ibid.

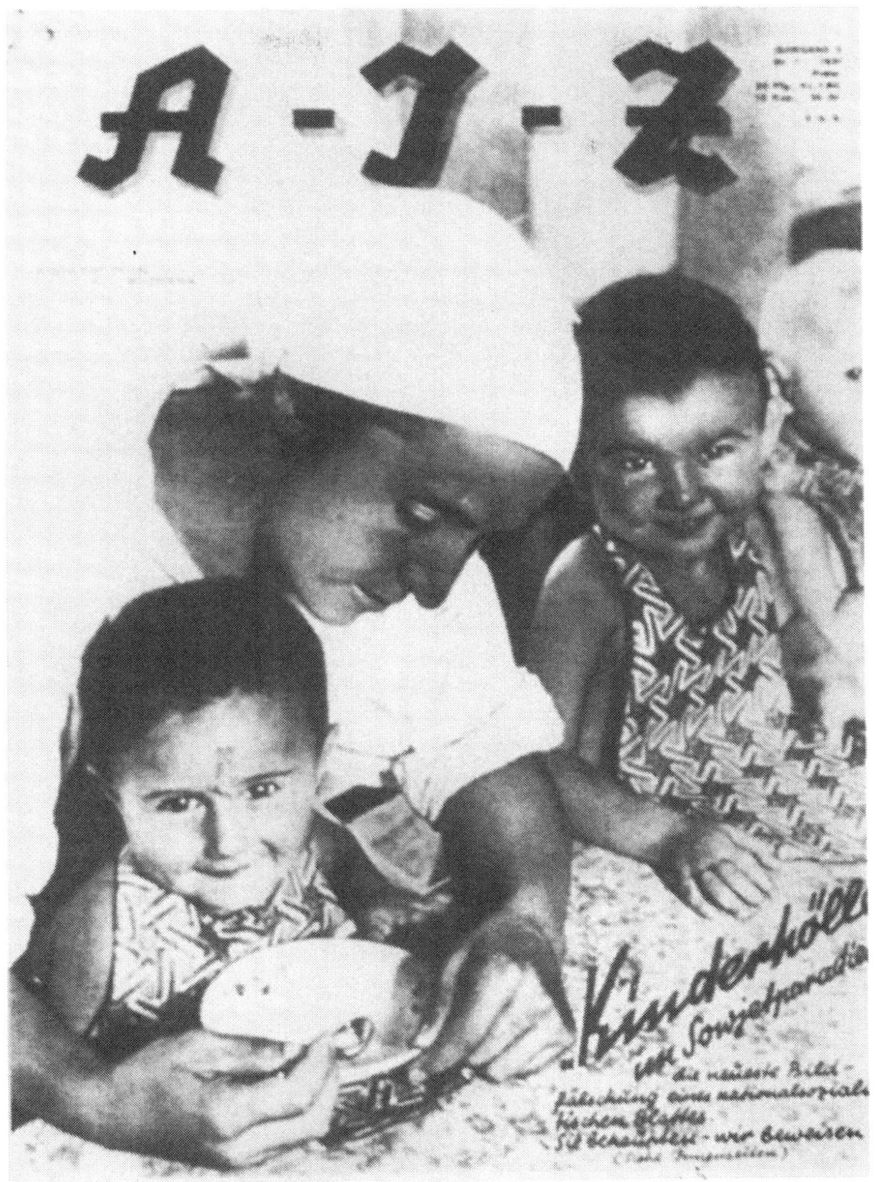

Plate 7.1 Children in the Soviet Union are happy and well fed in state-run nurseries and kindergartens. *Source: AIZ* 7 (1931).

Plate 7.2 The female Russian athlete symbolizes the bright, youthful socialist future. *Source: AIZ* 48 (1928).

Plate 7.3 Family life in the Soviet Union is wholesome and happy, as among these peasants. *Source: AIZ* 30 (1929).

SCHÜTZT DEN SOZIAL

Einen Schutzwall um die Sowjet-Union zu ziehen, das ist die Aufgabe, die uns allen gestellt ist. In der Stunde, wo der Imperialismus mitten ins Herz der Sowjet-Union zielt, ist sie berechtigt, vpm Proletariat andere Dinge als

nur Gelübde und Sympathiekundgebu
muß den ruhmreichen Spuren des sov
es verstanden hat, im Zeichen von M

Plate 7.4 Proletarian men of all ethnic and racial backgrounds gaze upward heroically as they build socialism. *Source: AIZ* 30 (1931).

German communists did not only read about the Soviet Union. Solidarity with the Soviet Union became inscribed in the cultural and political practices of the party. In one of the first popular front campaigns, the KPD raised money and food for revolutionary Russia gripped by famine in 1920. Communists every year celebrated the anniversary of the Bolshevik Revolution and commemorated Lenin's death along with Luxemburg's and Liebknecht's in the LLL festivals. Communist children leafletted their school colleagues to invite them to events honoring the Soviet Union. Party competitions offered prizes—a trip to the Soviet Union, or, less captivatingly, a book on the subject. Already in the 1920s workers' and children's delegations visited the Soviet Union, and raising the necessary funds served as one other form of public mobilization.[10] Visits to revolutionary Russia were not always an inspiring experience, but they proved inspirational to many KPD members who wrote suitable reports for the party press upon their return. In numerous campaigns the party mobilized support for the "socialist fatherland," often trumpeting the slogan, "Hands off the Soviet Union!"[11] Party cells in German and Russian factories established relations in which they corresponded and sent aid to one another. And many communists, as mentioned, went to the Soviet Union for training in Soviet military academies, the Comintern, and International Workers Aid, and also in various other party and technical capacities. German remained a lingua franca in the Comintern into the 1930s, easing the way for German communists.

Solidarity with the Soviet Union was made more urgent by the constant threats it endured, from English imperialists and American finance capital to the German bourgeoisie and every other reactionary force around the world. "[Soviet Russia] is flesh of the flesh and blood of the blood of working people . . . [where] the working class is proving that it . . . has the power to govern and . . . can secure to all workers a free, humane, and happy existence."[12] Solidarity with the Soviet Union therefore required "the greatest vigilance, energy, and resolution!"[13]

In practical terms, this meant armed solidarity along with the usual run of resolutions and demonstrations. The KPD's military apparatus actually made plans for coming to the military aid of the Soviet Union in the event of war.[14] Less practical, but no less important, Erich Weinert's and Hans Eisler's *Kampflied* (fighting song), "Der heimliche Aufmarsch" (The Secretive March), composed in 1929, called on workers and peasants to take up arms in defense of the Soviet Union.

[10] BLR, "Bericht der Bezirksleitung," 9 December 1926, SAPMO-BA, ZPA I/3/18–19/11/226–27.

[11] For one of the first times as a call by the Executive, see "Hände weg von Sowjetrußland: An das Proletariat Berlins," 8 May 1920, in *Zur Geschichte der Kommunistischen Partei Deutschlands*, 93–94.

[12] "Es lebe die Sowjetunion und der Kampf um den Frieden! Nieder mit allen kapitalistischen Kriegshetzern!" 25 February 1927, in *Zur Geschichte der Kommunistischen Partei Deutschlands*, 222–23.

[13] "Aufruf der KPD zur Unterstützung der Roten Armee," 6 August 1920, in Weber, *Deutscher Kommunismus*, 122.

[14] See the three documents excerpted by Weber in *Deutscher Kommunismus*, 130–34.

Around the world races a whisper.
Worker, don't you hear it?
Those are the voices of the war ministers.
Worker, don't you hear it?
The coal and steel producers are whispering.
The chemical war producers are whispering.
On all the continents there is whispering.
Mobilization against the Soviet Union!

[refrain:]
Workers, peasants, take the rifle,
Take the rifle in hand!
Destroy the fascist bandit army,
Set all hearts ablaze.
Plant your red banner of labor
In every field, in every factory!
Then arises out of the ruins of the old society
The socialist world republic!

Worker, listen up, they're cultivating the field
And crying, "For nation and race!"
That is the war of the rulers of the world
Against the working class;
For the attack against the Soviet Union
Is the stab in the heart of the revolution,
And the war, which now races through the countries,
Is the war against you, prolet!

[Refrain.][15]

Like other *Kampflieder*, "Der heimliche Aufmarsch" is fast-clipped and martial-sounding. It joins the KPD's fervent devotion to the Soviet Union with the party's own militaristic ethos and makes war the essence of proletarian activism.

The Soviet model inspired in many communists an uncritical support, a belief that the first socialist state had to be defended physically and ideologically no matter what the circumstances. That kind of devotion, when coupled with the entire ideological matrix of Marxism-Leninism-Stalinism, accentuated the authoritarian tendencies of the KPD. The space for a democratic political culture within the party, though never completely extinguished, narrowed drastically as Soviet control intensified. But the Soviet model proved inspirational because to German communists, Russian workers and peasants had seized the moment, had, through their own activism, overthrown an oppressive regime and engaged the task of constructing a better future. For KPD members, Soviet workers and peasants had blazed the path; it remained for their German counterparts to follow.

[15] "Der heimliche Aufmarsch," lyrics by Erich Weinert, music by Hans Eisler, composed 1929. See Erich Weinert, *Gesammelte Gedichte*, vol. 3 (Berlin: Aufbau-Verlag, 1971), 480–81, by permission. Note also: "Eisler: Lieder mit Ernst Busch," Nova recording 8 85 004.

CLASS

The KPD was, first and foremost, a proletarian party. By self-identification, membership, language and ideology, cultural activities—everything about the party resonated with class. Class was the essential determinant of politics and the primary source of identification. "Proletarians!" "Working Men and Women!" "Long live the proletarian Soviet Union!" "For the Dictatorship of the Proletariat!"—the language of class cascaded through all aspects of party life. The imagery of class—the proletarian turning a lathe or wielding a jackhammer, workers marching together on strike or battling the police—saturated the party press. The associations of party-proletarian life enveloped the membership. "Hinein in die Gewerkschaften!—Join the trade unions!" "Join the Workers Sports Association!" "Long live the Red Front Fighters League!" Class gave meaning to history and politics, to the present and the future. The proletariat was the creation of historical progress, the object of capitalist exploitation, and the force that would determine the future. To be a communist meant to be devoted to the cause of the working class, and to set one's own life on a course of progress leading to a better future for the collectivity.

For most party members, class was not only an ideology but, even more fundamentally, an experience, one encountered on the shop floor and in the neighborhood, in households among families, and bodily. As working-class and communist autobiographies and memoirs make clear, class meant primarily an experience of deprivation and exploitation: of dire want at home; the hunt of young proletarian men for a bed to rent; the eternal search for work; beatings in school and by the police; minimal schooling and dashed hopes for a Gymnasium education; tyrannical foremen and anonymous, avaricious bosses. For many women, the experience of class meant the unending double burden of housework and paid labor, of cooking and cleaning and sewing along with long hours bent over factory machinery.[16] Class was experienced bodily: through the pangs of hunger and hard, sweated labor in the factories and mines of industrial Germany.[17] Rationalization only intensified the demands on the body as work had to be executed at faster tempos. The bodily losses were greater also, with fingers and other limbs lost to machines, and for women, the damage to their own and their children's bodies by laboring in factories until nearly the moment of childbirth and almost immediately afterwards. And class was experienced in the common struggles on the picket line, in demonstration columns, and in bread riots.

[16] See the autobiographical excerpts in Wolfgang Emmerich, ed., *Proletarische Lebensläufe: Autobiographische Dokumente zur Entstehung der Zweiten Kultur in Deutschland*, vol. 2 (Hamburg: Rowohlt, 1975), and *Mein Arbeitstag—mein Wochenende: Arbeiterinnen berichten von ihrem Alltag 1928*, ed. Alf Lüdtke (1930; Hamburg: Ergebnisse, 1991). For an important analytical statement about how to use these kinds of sources, see Mary Jo Maynes, "Autobiography and Class Formation in Nineteenth-Century Europe: Methodological Considerations," *SSH* 16:3 (1992): 516–37, along with other essays in the special two-issue collection of articles on narrativity in *SSH* 16:3 and 16:4 (1992).

[17] On the bodily dimensions of class, see Kathleen Canning, "Feminist History after the Linguistic Turn: Historicizing Discourse and Experience," *Signs* 19:2 (1994): 368–404.

TABLE 7.1
Social Structure of KPD Membership, 1927

	No.	*Pct.*
Skilled industrial workers	57,154	39.9
Unskilled industrial workers	40,346	28.2
Agricultural workers	3,164	2.2
Peasants	143	0.1
Middle class*	3,164	2.2
Lower-level officials	1,088	0.8
Clerks	2,477	1.7
Artisans and tradesmen	13,702	9.6
Labor movement employees	3,737	2.6
Party employees	2,348	1.6
Other	15,935	11.1

*Middle class includes middle-ranked officials, free professionals, and small-business people.

Source: Kaasch, "Soziale Struktur," 1052.

The bare realities of exploitation and deprivation gave rise to a sense of injustice that drove some workers to communism.

If class was evident in language, ideology, and experience, it was also manifest in the very composition of the KPD as a primarily male proletarian party. Despite a very substantial fluctuation in membership, the party's social profile remained quite constant. Close to 70 percent of party members identified themselves as industrial workers—even if they were unemployed—as table 7.1 demonstrates. Undoubtedly a significant proportion of those listed as artisans and tradesmen, employees of labor movement organizations, and "other" were also at least of working-class origin, bringing the party's proletarian membership closer to 80 percent. The members were also relatively young, certainly in relation to other political parties with the notable exception of the Nazis. In 1927, 64.5 percent of the KPD members were under forty years of age.[18] A good part of the party's dynamism no doubt came from its melding of youth with a substantial segment of workers with long experience in the labor movement. The gendered character of German communism, the definition of class through masculinity, is made patently clear in table 7.2, which shows the proportion of female members ranging between 10 and 15 percent for most of the years of the Weimar Republic.

Electorally, the KPD's support came also primarily from proletarian districts.

[18] Wienand Kaasch, "Die soziale Struktur der KPD," *Die Kommunistische Internationale* 9:19 (1928): 1051.

TABLE 7.2
Female Proportion of KPD Membership, 1919–33

	No. Total	*No. Female*	*Pct. Female*
1919	106,656	5,000	4.7
1920	78,715	6,000	7.6
1921*	200,000	20,000	10.0
1923	294,230	32,856	11.2
1924*	150,000	18,700	12.5
1925	114,204	14,800	13.0
1927	124,729	16,200	13.0
1928*	120,000	14,700	12.3
1929	124,511	21,100	16.9
1930*	176,000	26,400	15.0
1931	246,554	37,000	15.0
1932	287,180	43,100	15.0
1933*	300,000	45,000	15.0

*Total membership figures approximate.
Source: Arendt, "Weibliche Mitglieder," 654.

At the most general level, the most industrialized areas of Germany provided the greatest tallies for the KPD.[19] Locally, the party drew its greatest support from working-class electoral precincts, and especially from those with a higher concentration of unskilled workers, as figures 7.1 through 7.3 demonstrate for the industrial city of Halle.[20] The SPD, in contrast, had made some inroads among other social classes. The proportion of skilled workers tended to have a neutral

[19] See Jürgen Falter, *Hitlers Wähler* (Munich: Beck, 1991), and Alfred Milatz, *Wähler und Wahlen in der Weimarer Republik* (Bonn: Bundeszentrale für politische Bildung, 1965).

[20] The graphs were constructed out of electoral and sociological data for each of Halle's seventy-three electoral precints. I used the officially sanctioned Halle address book to count and classify the occupations of the residents of each precinct. The regression lines were calculated and plotted by the graphing program.

There are obvious limitations to this approach. The address book only lists heads of households, so the occupations of other family members and boarders are not known. Nonetheless, the method does provide a fairly accurate picture of the sociology of the electorate. Sources: for the electoral data, *Hallische Nachrichten: General Anzeiger für Halle und die Provinz Sachsen*, 8 December 1924; for the geographic composition of the precincts, ibid., 2 December 1924; for the sociological data, *Adressbuch für Halle a.d.S. und Umgebung 1925* (Halle: August Scherl Deutsche Adressbuch-Gesellschaft, 1925). Many thanks to Prof. Dr. Erwin Könnemann, Halle, for procuring a copy of the *Adressbuch* and arranging for its export to me.

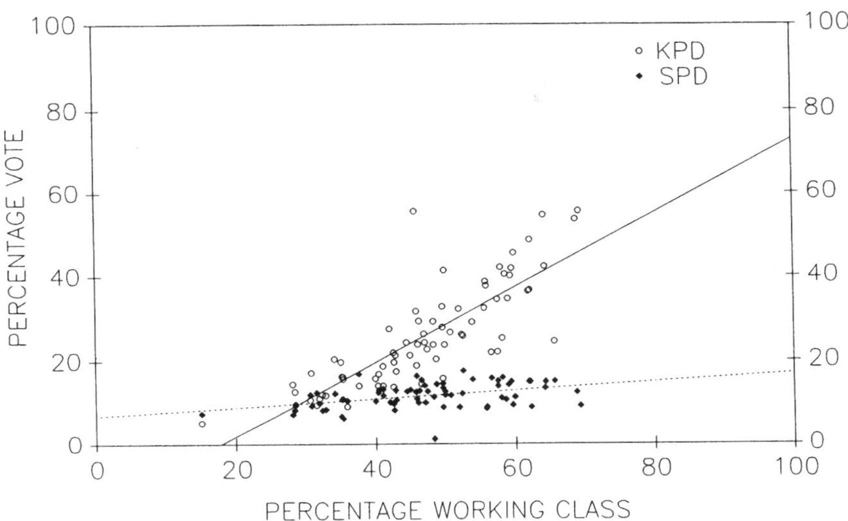

Figure 7.1 Halle Reichstag Election December 1924: KPD/SPD Vote by Percentage Working Class

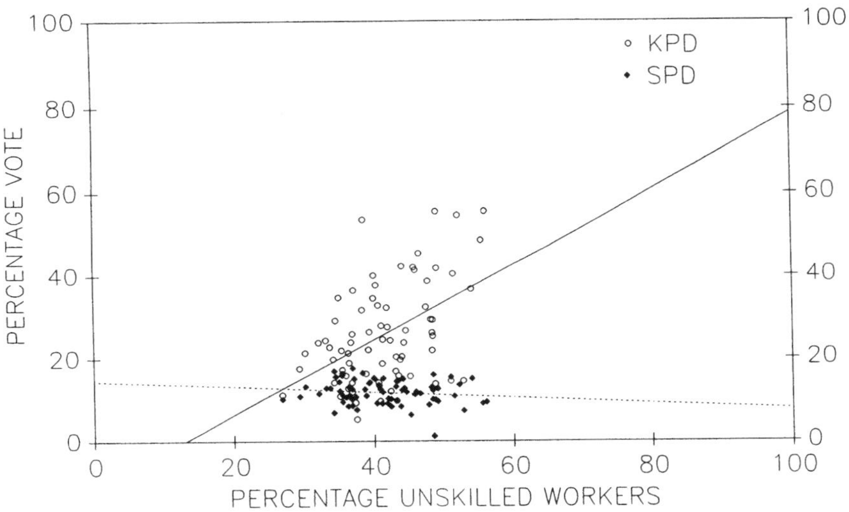

Figure 7.2 Halle Reichstag Election December 1924: KPD/SPD Vote by Percentage Unskilled Workers

impact on SPD support, while its votes declined slightly as the concentration of the unskilled increased.

The intensely proletarian character of the KPD made it quite difficult, indeed, nearly impossible, for the party to win support from other social groups. The language of class had very little to offer small shopkeepers, white-collar workers,

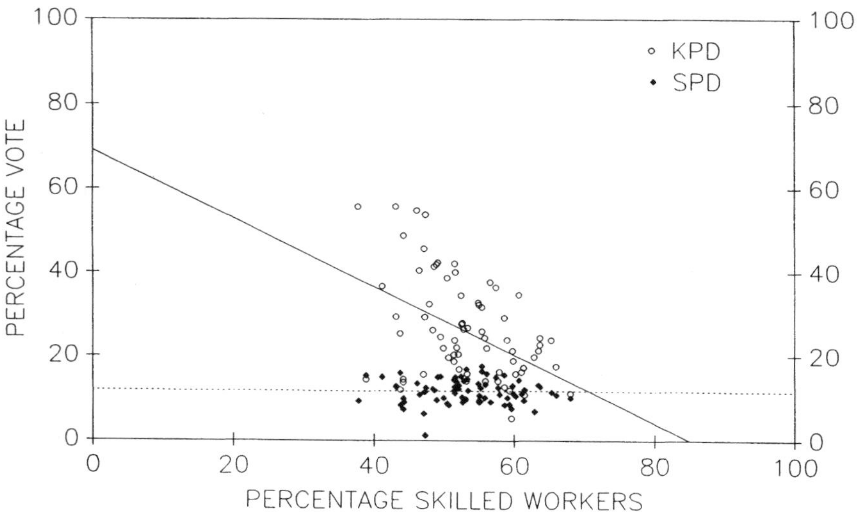

Figure 7.3 Halle Reichstag Election December 1924: KPD/SPD Vote by Percentage Skilled Workers

or landholders. The visible evidence of communists marching in the streets or engaging in fights induced the specter of even greater civil disorder that would threaten their livelihoods and way of life.

Nor was the KPD much concerned about building cross-class alliances. Instead, the party held to a classically Marxian notion that assumed the polarization of society into two essential classes, the proletariat and the capitalist. KPD chairman Ernst Thälmann claimed that only a politics focused on the working class, a politics that signified revolution and the construction of the dictatorship of the proletariat, could win the support of the middle strata.[21] The patent absurdity of such views went largely unexamined, but their impact was decisive. They injected a tenor of proletarian superiority into the party that undermined even the occasional efforts to construct political alliances and reach out to other social groups.

If class was so central to German communism, what of nationalism? German communists certainly understood themselves as defenders of the nation. But to communists, the "national interest" was identical with working-class, or, occasionally, more generally popular interests. Concretely, the national cum class interest mandated programs and policies beneficial to workers, good diplomatic relations with the Soviet Union, and, ultimately, a Soviet Germany. In contrast, capitalists were often portrayed as the traitors of the nation. All the major diplomatic events of the Weimar period—the Versailles Treaty, the Ruhr occupation, the Dawes Plan, the Locarno Treaties, the Young Plan—were used to demonstrate the treasonous actions of the upper classes, who sacrificed the national

[21] Ernst Thälmann, "Einige Fehler in unserer theoretischen und praktischen Arbeit und der Weg zu ihrer Ueberwindung," *Die Internationale* 14:11/12 (1931): 491, 496.

territory and the economic well-being of the population to their own avaricious instincts.

At particular moments, however, especially in 1923 and the early 1930s, the party propagated more conventional nationalist sentiments in an effort to capture right-wing support. "To Everyone!" began one KPD appeal during the Ruhr crisis, one of the very few times it did not use "*Arbeiter*" or "*Werktätige*" ("workers" or the somewhat more general "working people").[22] "Down with the government of national humiliation and treason!" began one KPD leaflet that same year.[23] Karl Radek's infamous "Schlageter-Speech," in which he commemorated the death of a right-wing activist and sought to claim the national cause for the KPD, was widely distributed in the party press and found substantial, though by no means unqualified, support.[24]

In its most developed nationalistic statement, the "Programmatic Statement for the National and Social Liberation of the German People" in 1930, the KPD clearly adopted the rhetoric of the nation in an effort to win wider support and contest the growing power of the NSDAP. The phrases "national liberation," "subjugation of Germany," "high treason" committed by social democracy, "sale of the national interests of the working masses of Germany," "dictated peace of Versailles," "tearing apart and plundering of German territory"—all echoed the language of the right.[25]

While the KPD lent to nationalism its own definitions and episodically and opportunistically adopted the terminology of the right, the language and practices of nationalism never surpassed or surmounted class in importance.[26] The KPD remained, preeminently, a class-oriented, proletarian party intimately tied to the Soviet Union. Indeed, its fixation on class made the KPD incapable of ever convincingly laying claim to the national interest, especially in a society in which the industrial working class constituted, at most, slightly over one-third of the population. Other communist parties, in the drastically altered circumstances of World War II and the Resistance, proved able to take up the national mantle and build multiclass movements and alliances. The KPD, enraptured with the proletariat, remained profoundly limited by class.

Kampf und Solidarität — Struggle and Solidarity

Class was inextricably entwined with struggle. In line with the classical Marxian texts, the KPD argued that in struggle the proletariat would become a class for

[22] "An Alle! An die deutsche Oeffentlichkeit!" 23 May 1923, in *Zur Geschichte der Kommunistischen Partei Deutschlands*, 133.

[23] "Nieder mit der Regierung der nationalen Schmach und des Volksverrats!" May 1923, in Weber, *Deutscher Kommunismus*, 140–42.

[24] The text, published in *RF*, 26 June 1923, can be found in Weber, *Deutscher Kommunismus*, 142–47.

[25] "Programmerklärung zur nationalen und sozialen Befreiung des deutschen Volkes," 24 August 1930, in Weber, *Deutscher Kommunismus*, 58–65, quotes on 58, 59, 60.

[26] Here I think Conan Fischer, *The German Communists and the Rise of Nazism* (New York: St. Martin's Press, 1991), while providing a host of interesting detail, greatly overstates the case.

itself and fulfill its world historical role. Hence, the language of *Kampf*—struggle or fight—runs through all communist propaganda and literature: *Klassenkampf*, the title of the party newspaper in Halle; "Roter Kampfblock der Werktätigen" (Red Fighting Bloc of all Workers), the party slogan for the 1928 election; "Geschlossene Kampfront" (United Fighting Front), the title of a typical appeal; "Kampf" or its derivatives in almost every paragraph of a manifesto issued during the Ruhr occupation; "Heraus zum Kampf!" "Auf zum Kampf!" "Durch Kampf zum Sieg!"[27]

In struggle solidarity is forged. Solidarity rang out as the clarion call of the KPD, the basic instinct of the proletariat that it was the party's responsibility to nurture and develop. As in so many other realms, the KPD built upon the practices that emerged, if intermittently, out of the conditions of proletarian life, in this case the need for mutual help engendered by poverty and harsh working conditions. The party leadership issued one appeal after another for workers to exercise solidarity. "For the demands of the striking railroad workers! . . . Solidarity with those who struggle!" "Solidarity with striking aniline workers!" "Solidarity with striking dock workers!" Often, solidarity bore a specifically masculine meaning in keeping with the gendered character of German communism. Chemical workers "stand as one man against the employer class." Other workers were called upon to "help your brothers in struggle."[28]

"Comrade" in the male and female forms ("*Genosse*" or "*Genossin*") served as one of the essential rhetorical elements of solidarity. It was used among party members along with the informal "you" (*du*) as a sign of closeness and familiarity based on similar life experiences and a common commitment to the struggle, and as a mark of demarcation from everyone else, especially social democrats. On occasion, though, the term could be applied more broadly—"class comrades" or even "social democratic worker comrades"—particularly when the KPD sought to rally support from the SPD rank and file.[29]

Struggle had to be active and resolute, a voluntaristic approach that greatly distanced the KPD from the determinism of the SPD. The use of the active voice and vigorous-sounding verbs was not accidental. The working class had to "conquer" its freedom under the flag of the communist party.[30] Bourgeois democracy

[27] These quotes are from [BLR], "Bericht über den Wahlkampf im Bezirk Ruhrgebiet," [1928], SAPMO-BA, ZPA I/3/18–19/13/115; "Geschlossene Kampfront!" 10 January 1923, in *Zur Geschichte der Kommunistischen Partei Deutschlands*, 116–18; "Aufruf der Internationalen Konferenz zu Frankfurt am Main," 18 March 1923, in ibid., 130–32; "Heraus zur Massendemonstration gegen die Hindenburgdiktatur!" in ibid., 178–79; and Ludwig Turek, "Ein Prolet erzählt," in Emmerich, *Proletarische Lebensläufe*, 265.

[28] Quotes are from "Für die Forderungen der streikenden Eisenbahner!" 5 February 1922, and "Solidarität mit den streikenden Anilinarbeitern," 2 December 1922, in *Zur Geschichte der Kommunistischen Partei Deutschlands*, 103–4, 109–10; and "Solidarität mit den streikenden Hafenarbeitern!" *RF*, 3 October 1926.

[29] For example, "Heraus in Massen gegen den Fürstenraubzug! An die sozialdemokratischen Arbeiter!" 9 October 1926, in *Zur Geschichte der Kommunistischen Partei Deutschlands*, 212.

[30] "Manifest des XI. Parteitages der Kommunistischen Partei Deutschlands," 7 March 1927, in *Zur Geschichte der Kommunistischen Partei Deutschlands*, 227.

was to be "unmasked" as a "dictatorship of trust capital." The working class had to "take up" the revolutionary class struggle to destroy the existing state, establish the proletarian dictatorship, and construct the socialist economy and society.[31] German workers had a choice: coalition and alliance with the ruling class in a new imperialist war, or "through revolutionary struggle to the conquest of political power by the working class."[32] The military metaphors are evident; they resound also in the pithy phrase of the "third period," "class against class."[33]

Workers were to be aroused to struggle through pathos and outrage, through a melodrama of suffering at the hands of exploitative owners and their nefarious allies.[34] The rhetorical devices prevalent in the socialist movement since the early nineteenth century found renewed vibrancy in the propaganda of the KPD. When chemical workers went out on strike soon after a disastrous explosion at the BASF plant in Oppau, which killed more than four hundred people, the KPD invoked the tragedy and the specter of widowed wives and fatherless children as a call to solidarity: "The workers of the chemical industry work constantly in life-threatening conditions. The Oppau catastrophe, which cost the lives of hundreds of wage slaves of the aniline kings, shoved hundreds of families into the greatest misfortune, snatched away husbands from their wives and fathers from their children, is still engraved in memory."

But immediately afterwards, the rhetoric switches from pathos to outrage. Owners were accused of deriving profits from financial swindles, a charge made only more poignant by the contrast drawn between suffering workers and easy-living employers, between families as the expression of working-class life and anonymous exploiters: "The worker families affected by the catastrophe descend into poverty. The billions in profits, which the shareholders sack away . . . are minted out of the sweat and blood of aniline workers."[35] At its best, the KPD's rhetoric proved a worthy successor to Rosa Luxemburg's captivating, melodramatic prose.

Kampf and *Solidarität* also resonate through the visual representations of the party. The striking covers of the *Arbeiter-Illustrierte-Zeitung*, many created by John Heartfield, convey the militant sense of struggle—powerful proletarian arms and fists, rifles drawn, bayonets slashing upward (plates 7.5–7.6). *Kampf* be-

[31] See [BLR], "Bericht über den Wahlkampf im Bezirk Ruhrgebiet," [1928], SAPMO-BA, ZPA I/3/18–19/13/115–36.

[32] "Vor einem neuen imperialistischen Krieg," 27 July 1927, in *Zur Geschichte der Kommunistischen Partei Deutschlands*, 234.

[33] The phrase itself originated with Jules Humbert-Droz, the official in charge of the Comintern's Latin Secretariat. See *De Lénine à Staline: Dix Ans au Service de l'Internationale communiste 1921–1931. Memoires de Jules Humbert-Droz*, vol. 2 (Neuchâtel: Editions de la Baconnière, 1971), 227–82, and Eric D. Weitz, "Bukharin and 'Bukharinism' in the Comintern, 1919–29," in *Nikolai Ivanovich Bukharin: A Centenary Appraisal*, ed. Nicholas N. Kozlov and Eric D. Weitz (New York: Praeger, 1989), 59–91.

[34] See Patrice Petro, *Joyless Streets: Women and Melodramatic Representation in Weimar Germany* (Princeton: Princeton University Press, 1989), on melodrama as politics.

[35] "Solidarität mit den streikenden Anilinarbeitern!" 2 December 1922, in *Zur Geschichte der Kommunistischen Partei Deutschlands*, 109.

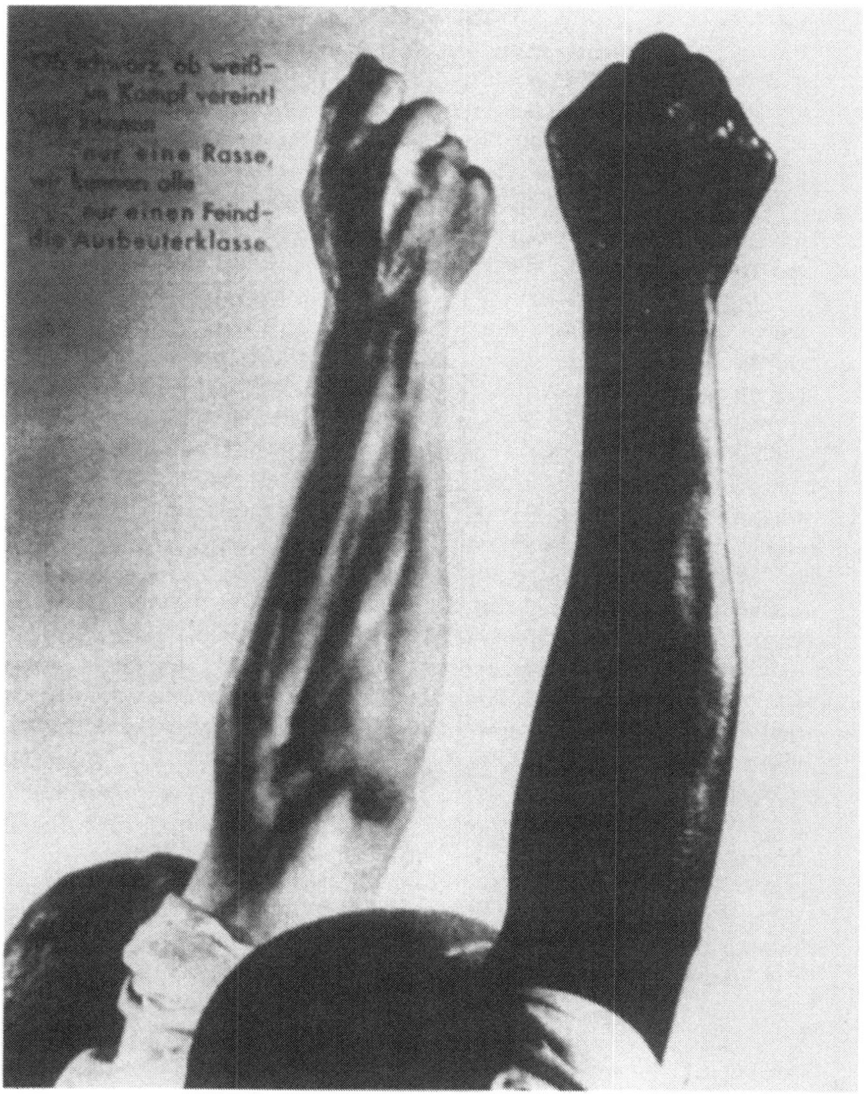

Plate 7.5 Class is defined by the struggles and solidarity of powerful men across racial and national lines. *Source: AIZ* 26 (1931), by John Heartfield. (c) 1996 Artists Rights Society, New York/VG Bild Kunst, Bonn/The Heartfield Community of Heirs.

comes, quite literally, physical struggle, and the rhetoric, with its constant invocation of battles, campaigns, and weaponry, served to reinforce the militarism of the party. Heartfield's representations depict the virulence of struggle and struggle as a social act, almost invariably of men.

Solidarity was not only rhetorical and visual. It meant also "practical

Plate 7.6 The essence of proletarianism. Rifles drawn, bayonets at the ready, the working class defends the Soviet Union. *Source: AIZ* 31 (1930).

solidarity"—strikes in support of other workers, which occurred only infrequently, but also marches and demonstrations, leaflet distributions, and, importantly, collections of money and material goods, which later on in the decade occurred most often under the auspices of the front organizations Red Aid and International Workers Aid. Exercising solidarity meant also getting resolutions passed in support of striking workers elsewhere—in works council meetings, in the municipal councils, on the shop floor.

Communists also acquired their individual identities through struggle and solidarity—a leitmotif of working-class autobiographies of the nineteenth and twentieth centuries and of the KPD's proletarian novels of the late 1920s and early 1930s. Struggle against poverty, oppressive households, exploitative foremen and bosses, tyrannical fathers, policemen, and judges—the forces of oppression run together in communist literature. In struggle, the individual is united with the party, class, and history, and thereby achieves his (and it is most often *his*) identity through the collective.

Werner Eggerath, as a nineteen-year-old returning from the front, went looking for work. "There on the gate of the factory I stood as one of the many millions who streamed home after the end of the war and appeared so superfluous and helpless."[36] Then he was hired as a boiler worker, shoveling coal to keep the turbines of an electrical power plant running. To the common experience of war came now the common experience of hard, oppressive labor in heat and humidity. He encountered a man who was already a Spartacist, and in communism he found a new and deeper meaning to solidarity:

> The word Spartacist, at that time [the Revolution] a frightening word, acquired for me an entirely new tone. Spartacus, that was the name of the leader of the slave revolt in ancient Rome. "Spartacus, that is fire and spirit," Karl Liebknecht had said. Spartacus, that is determination and power, Spartacus, that is the concept of struggle against suppression and exploitation, for freedom and human rights. With all the excitement and enthusiasm of youth I grabbed at these ideas as one who had been starving. Everything that until now had developed in me unconsciously, this hatred against injustice, the desire for . . . free development, now acquired form and content. I saw the path to the realization of my dreams.[37]

For Ludwig Turek, the heavy and hot labor making stone and cement pipes at Hoesch in Dortmund constituted the basis for a solidarity of resentment at the oppressive conditions.

> Everyone here felt the same! Ask any Hoesch proletarians who are involved with production whether they have any desire to work, whether they don't have a wish that they secretly carry that will be their salvation, their salvation from this unending, debilitating drudgery!—"Goddamned shit!" . . . "Cursed hell!" . . . They all feel the unbearability of the conditions of proletarian life. But it is useless so long as they don't exercise a

[36] Werner Eggerath, "Nur ein Mensch," in Emmerich, *Proletarische Lebensläufe*, 196.
[37] Ibid., 198.

more effective kind of criticism beyond curses and swears, [don't develop] a revolutionary worldview with the firm commitment to act![38]

Those who violate solidarity pay the price. In Turek's description, it was a miner who had managed through all sorts of side occupations to stash away enough money to buy a small plot of land. He died a year later—consumption as a result of overwork, leaving his wife and children indebted and impoverished.[39] Here an early death was the ultimate revenge for the violation of solidarity.

In the hands of the police one also found solidarity with fellow inmates. In Otto Gotsche's proletarian novel about the March Action, the main character sees his comrades beaten senseless, arms and noses broken, faces smashed, as the police exercise their revenge. Fritz comforts his fellow inmate who can get no rest because of the pain from the broken arm the police had given him. "Lie quietly comrade. . . . The ones they drag out in the night you never see again." Fritz himself lay in the dark, fearful of the certain execution that awaits him. But then he sees the light, the solidarity in struggle that gives him meaning and hope.

> Oh gently, gently. We haven't fled, we haven't been defeated! And even if they throw us in jail—we are here and remain here! And the day of freedom approaches! The Golgatha path of the German working class is not finished. . . .
>
> Fragments of the powerful words of Karl Liebknecht crashed like thunder and aroused the will to live. An inner voice stirred the real being inside him. Fritz! You're not even seventeen, aren't you ashamed to think of death? . . . The road to victory is broad, it is difficult, but it is there to be taken. The party lives, the class lives, they will triumph! Today, tomorrow . . . ! They will triumph! And you are living, will live, will prevail, will be there![40]

"Solidaritätslied" by Bertolt Brecht and Hans Eisler, composed at the end of the Weimar Republic, gave fervent expression to the concept of solidarity. Brecht's lyrics give musical voice to the famous lines of the Communist Manifesto, "workers of the world, unite!" As performed by Ernst Busch, a leading communist and Brecht interpreter, the song is fast-clipped with obvious martial tones.

> [refrain:]
> Forward, without forgetting
> Where our strength can be seen now to be!
> When starving or when eating
> Forward, not forgetting
> Our solidarity!
> . . . .
>
> Black or white or brown or yellow
> Leave your old disputes behind.
> Once start talking with your fellow

[38] Ludwig Turek, "Ein Prolet erzählt," in Emmerich, *Proletarische Lebensläufe*, 205.
[39] Ibid.
[40] Otto Gotsche, "Märzstürme," in Emmerich, *Proletarische Lebensläufe*, 207.

Men, you'll soon be of one mind.
. . . .

Workers of the world, uniting
That's the way to lose your chains.
Mighty regiments now are fighting
That no tyranny remains!

Forward, without forgetting
Till the concrete question is hurled
When starving or when eating:
Whose tomorrow is tomorrow?
And whose world is the world?[41]

As "Solidaritätslied" indicates, internationalism constituted an essential element of solidarity. Party members believed that theirs was an international struggle that required solidarity among communists and workers across national boundaries. "Freedom for Sacco and Vanzetti!" "Support for the struggling Indian masses!" "Exercise solidarity with the English miners!" the party press bellowed. When chemical workers went on strike in 1922, *Rote Fahne* and local communist papers published countless articles describing the aid sent from near and far—Leipzig construction workers, a Bulgarian consumer cooperative, the Russian chemical association, the French Red Unions.[42] When British miners went on strike in 1926, the KPD tried to mobilize a great campaign of support.[43] The party called on Ruhr workers to refuse overtime, establish control committees in the workplace, and demand of their union the unilateral abrogation of the contract. The party moved into high gear, flooding the Ruhr with leaflets and special issues of *Rote Fahne* and the *Ruhr Echo*. Party members in the factories and mines called meetings of union locals, works councils, party cells, and committees of the unemployed. Resolutions of support for the English strikers were passed, and collections were taken up—in the workplace, by the unions, out in the neighborhoods by Red Aid and the International Workers Aid. The KPD also tried to interfere directly with the mining and shipments of Ruhr coal by calling on miners to limit production, and on dockworkers and seamen to refuse to load or transport coal.

The campaign itself failed. Indeed, as with many other KPD efforts, the unemployed proved the most active, and served as a substitute of sorts for miners,

[41] "Solidaritätslied," lyrics by Bertolt Brecht, music by Hans Eisler, first written 1930 for the film "Kuhle Wampe," revised 1948. The German can be heard on "Eisler: Lieder mit Ernst Busch," Nova recording 8 85 004. This English translation is from *Bertolt Brecht: Poems, 1913–1956*, ed. John Willett and Ralph Manheim with the cooperation of Erich Fried (London: Methuen, 1976), 185–86, by permission.

[42] The headlines are collected in *Zur Geschichte der Kommunistischen Partei Deutschlands*, 111.

[43] For the following see the reports of the BLR Pol-Leitung to the ZK: "Bericht aus der Arbeit des Bezirks Ruhrgebiet im Monat Mai 1926," 1 June 1926; "Bericht der Arbeit im Bezirk Ruhrgebiet in Bezug des englischen Bergarbeiterstreik," 14 June 1926; and "Bericht der Bezirksleitung Ruhrgebiet," 9 December 1926 (which repeats the material in the preceding document), SAPMO-BA, ZPA I/3/18–19/11/154–78, 182–86.

stevedores, and seamen. The unemployed, however, had little power to interrupt coal production and transport. Yet what is significant here is the determined effort to link workers' struggles in Germany with those in other countries. While the party might not have been able to mobilize the mass of workers to risk their livelihoods for English miners, it proved able to raise strike support in working-class neighborhoods and in the mines and factories. In this way, the party promoted a consciousness of internationalism that had very little in common with the strident nationalism that prevailed in German political life and stood in the most direct contradiction to National Socialism. The ideology and practice of international workers' solidarity, one of the most forceful expressions of communist humanism, posed the possibility of a different kind of domestic and international order.

Commitment

Ludwig Turek, a member of the KPD since its founding, mentioned at the end of his autobiography, published in 1929, the organizations of which he and his wife were members in addition to the party: Red Aid, the Union of Popular Health, the Nudist League, the Union of German Book Printers, the Union of Graphical Workers, a consumer cooperative, and the Workers Gymnastic and Sports Association.[44] In June 1924, the Essen KPD organization provided its functionaries with a schedule of party activities. For an activist, almost every weekday evening involved a meeting of one sort or another.[45] And in the winter of 1927/28, the Halle-Merseburg KPD counted for the Central Committee 640 events between 1 November 1927 and 31 January 1928 at which members of the district leadership gave talks, from women's rallies to discussions about Soviet Russia to meetings about local politics.[46]

As these examples demonstrate, to be a communist meant, above all else, a life of commitment to the party and its associated organizations, a life of countless meetings, demonstrations, leaflet distributions, and speeches. Not a few individuals were driven away by the sometimes mind-numbing routine and the unceasing demands on the time and energy of members.[47] But for others, the continual activism of the party gave direction and meaning to their lives, and they threw themselves into party work with astounding dedication.

At a Mansfeld mine, for example, the KPD cell reported in mid-1925 that the ten active members (out of sixty) had read and discussed *Lenin und der*

[44] Ludwig Turek, "Ein Prolet erzählt," in Emmerich, *Proletarische Lebensläufe*, 264–65.

[45] Abschrift, UBL Essen to all Blocks- und Arbeitsgebiete and Ortsgruppen, 14 June 1924, HStAD 16934/41.

[46] "Politischer Bericht des Bezirks Halle-Merseburg für die Monate November und Dezember 1927 und Januar 1928," SAPMO-BA, ZPA I/3/11/16/125.

[47] Party reports are replete with complaints about poor organizational work, the short supply of competent cadres, and the resistance of members to ever-increasing demands from the leadership. State officials who monitored the KPD also noted these problems. See, for example, Lagebericht, RKÜöO, 11 October 1924, BAP RAM 2823/3.

Leninsmus.[48] They had had to share copies, and would next tackle *Was ist Bolschewismus?* They also discussed their working conditions and the improvements that they would like to achieve. They had tried to give every member a specific task for the Reich presidential election, but only a few had actually carried out their work, and they were ready to expel the recalcitrant comrades, many of whom did not even show up for meetings. However, their reading of *Lenin und der Leninismus* had taught them that they should try to "develop each comrade into a professional revolutionary," so they had not proceeded with the expulsions. Despite many obstacles, the cell seemed to manage to distribute a great deal of literature that had stimulated political discussions among their fellow miners. It had "armed" comrades with chalk, and in one day they covered the entire workplace with the slogan, "Elect the worker Thälmann."

The report from the Mansfeld cell, unsigned except for "with communist greetings, Zelle Paulsschact [of the Mansfeld company]," is earnest in the extreme. It evinces the tone of an autodidact striving mightily to improve his own political education and to influence his co-workers against overwhelming odds. It is one small example of the dedication displayed by the communist rank and file and their commitment to self-improvement to serve better the party and the proletarian cause. For such workers, the party provided an outlet for their talents and interests and a means of broadening their experiences and knowledge.

While the Paulsschact communists seem to have undertaken their reading on their own, organized lectures, readings, and courses were a constituent part of party life in the 1920s and early 1930s. For the party leadership, the educational programs served as the means for developing capable and experienced functionaries, always in short supply, and for asserting greater ideological uniformity within the party. For the rank and file, the educational programs provided an opportunity for self-improvement, identity formation as communists, and enhanced possibilities of rising through the party ranks.

The Halle-Merseburg district ran a one-month course in 1929.[49] The leadership selected twenty-six students, only two of whom were women, out of fifty-three who had applied. The applicants were carefully chosen. First they had to take written exams which were graded. A commission established by the district leadership made recommendations for acceptance based on the grades, previous political and party-educational experience, and age between twenty and thirty years (though this seems to have been revised to forty). The final decision lay in the hands of the district leadership. Overwhelmingly, those chosen were workers, and were required to give up employment for four weeks, an astonishing sacrifice. Only four of the participants were already unemployed, and only half were given family subsidies. Two were able to collect unemployment insurance, but most had their claims denied. They were experienced in the labor movement and in the KPD

48 "Bericht der Betriebszelle Paulsschacht, Mansfeld A.G.," 29 May 1925, SAPMO-BA, ZPA I/3/11/21/41–42.

49 For the following, see "Bericht von der 2. Bezirks-Parteischule des Bezirks Halle-Merseburg im Jahre 1929," 3 April 1929, SAPMO-BA, ZPA I/3/11/50/7–16.

in particular, but most were still workers rather than paid functionaries. The two women were housewives.

The course was held in a publicly owned youth retreat outside of Halle, where the participants were housed and fed for a month in quite acceptable conditions, according to the party report. They shared dormitory rooms and partook of solid and plentiful (though simple) fare. Days were spent in seminars, lectures, and study, along with walks and party celebrations. The participants observed the LLL commemoration, for example, while attending the course. They had to write papers on various topics, which were graded by the instructors, most of whom had been sent out from Berlin by the Central Committee and were well received by the participants.

The major topics of study involved Marxian theory, the history of the labor movement, and party work in the trade unions, municipalities, and rural areas. In their evaluations, the students claimed to have found especially worthwhile the deeper understanding they attained of Marx's economic teachings, the theory of imperialism, and the history of the workers' movement, and said that the theory of historical materialism required greater attention than was received in the monthlong course. Most instructors used a seminar approach, which the students appreciated. The students themselves desired further instruction, and proposed an array of programs—from lecture series to additional courses to correspondence courses—to improve their knowledge and abilities, and to extend the advantages of such programs to other party comrades. The instructors expressed satisfaction with the course content and the abilities of the participants.

KPD efforts to develop the talents and skills of enterprising workers were also evident in the Workers Correspondence Movement, which was designed to encourage individual workers to write about the conditions of labor for the party press.[50] By 1926, the Ruhr district reported, the press had developed a "firm and permanent staff of colleagues from the most varied categories of labor."[51] The *Ruhr-Echo*, the leading KPD paper in the district, had a regular column, "From Mine and Mill," later "The Worker" and "Voices of Workers," in which these reports were published. Refined to some extent by the editors, the reports still retained much of the immediacy of the language of workers with minimal formal education. The editorial staff carefully cultivated its relations with the worker correspondents by holding regular meetings and consultations. In the Ruhr, the party had about 110 workers who functioned as permanent correspondents and many others who submitted occasional reports. The Ruhr district leaders wrote, "The best way to develop a permanent corps of [worker correspondents] consists, in our experience, of never throwing a report into the garbage can, but to work over each and every report, even the worst, so long as it contains something positive."[52] Interestingly, most of the correspondents in the Ruhr were miners,

[50] For a general discussion, see W. L. Guttsmann, *Workers' Culture in Weimar Germany: Between Tradition and Commitment* (New York: Berg, 1990), 79–82.

[51] BLR, "Bericht der Bezirksleitung," 9 June 1926, SAPMO-BA, ZPA I/3/18–19/11/216.

[52] Ibid., 217.

which perhaps indicates a line of continuity with miners' long tradition of submitting petitions of grievances to the authorities.[53]

The Workers Correspondence Movement was only one of the innumerable organizations that were either directly under party direction or were one of the broad workers' associations in which the party tried to exercise preponderant influence.[54] As Turek's brief comment implies, these organizations claimed the time and energies of workers. To the chagrin of party leaders, communist workers all too often relished singing in workers' choirs, engaging in chess tournaments in the workers' chess association, and going on trips with the workers' bicycle league at the expense of "party work" in these associations. In Hamm, the Ruhr KPD in 1926 reported to the Central Committee, the comrades in the sports associations were too concerned about sports and not enough about politics. In Dortmund, a strong KPD group existed among the swimmers, while bicyclists in general were reformists. The Gelsenkirchen workers' sports federation had a strong KPD fraction, while in Essen a "hard struggle" had routed the reformists. The Friends of Nature, meanwhile, were too involved with rocks: "The Friends of Nature are a very special class of people who exist in a world of their own. Instead of carrying out party work in their organization they look for rocks and worry about other things."[55]

In time, continued the report, it should be possible to convince even the Friends of Nature that they had to work in line with the direction of the party. Two working-class choir associations existed in the district, which caused the KPD no end of trouble, but the atheists set a record: their Free-Thinker Movement (Freidenkerbewegung) had five different federations in the Ruhr, and communists were represented in all of them.[56] As ever, the leadership complained that comrades had failed to recognize the necessity of carrying party work into the associations and of the need to create a unified free-thinker organization.

The insufficiencies of party work and the radical turn of the third period led the KPD leadership to foment splits in virtually all of the broad-based working-class cultural associations.[57] Communists were now expected to enter separate communist-led sports, chess, free-thinker, and choir associations and federations. In this realm also the KPD narrowed the scope of party work to a small, select group of party members. These developments complemented the KPD's growing isolation as a party of the unemployed, a party of a particular segment of the working class rather than of a broad-based popular movement.

The Reichstag election campaign of 1928 provides one example of the way the

[53] See *Bis vor die Stufen des Throns: Bittschriften und Beschwerden von Bergarbeitern*, ed. Klaus Tenfelde and Helmuth Trischler (Munich: Beck, 1986).

[54] In general on labor movement cultural organizations in the Weimar Republic, see Guttsmann, *Workers' Culture*, and Hartmann Wunderer, *Arbeitervereine und Arbeiterparteien: Kultur- und Massenorganisationen in der Arbeiterbewegung (1890–1933)* (Frankfurt am Main: Campus, 1980).

[55] BLR, "Bericht der Bezirksleitung," 9 December 1926, SAPMO-BA, ZPA I/3/18–19/11/200–202, quote on 202.

[56] Ibid., 202–3.

[57] See Guttsmann, *Workers' Culture*, 97–106, and Wunderer, *Arbeitervereine und Arbeiterparteien*.

party sought to mobilize all the resources available, all the various associations and organizations related to the party, in support of the KPD's cause, and the kinds of involvements expected of the rank and file.[58] An active communist might encounter the party's message in his workplace, neighborhood, the Workers Sports Association, the Free-Thinker Movement, and the RFB. Moreover, he would be expected to propagandize in all of these settings, and in his trade union local and in the works council if he were a member.

For the 1928 election the KPD pulled out all the stops. Naturally, the workplace figured prominently in party calculations. Party groups were to call mass rallies in the factories and mines and to open up their cell meetings to sympathizers. The district leadership provided much of the campaign literature and the speakers. The number of workplace newspapers increased dramatically. In what should have come as no surprise to the leadership, many cells were found not to exist at all or to be almost incapable of effective work. In other cases, the works councils successfully blocked the campaigns of the party cells. Typically, the energies of effective members in the workplace were often taken up by other party responsibilities and by the competing demands of street cells and the citywide organization.

In some union meetings and locals, the KPD did get support. At a DMV meeting in Hamborn and in some mining and construction worker locals, delegates passed resolutions calling on all union members to vote for the KPD. Still, the Ruhr leadership estimated that only 50 percent of the party's union positions were actually used in the electoral campaign. The members still feared firings and exclusions if they sought to turn union meetings into KPD campaign rallies. As a result, the major burden of the electoral campaign fell on the neighborhood organizations.

Communist efforts in the various workers' cultural associations proved more effective than in the workplace. Bicyclists and the sportsmen's music corps were used in demonstrations and rallies, adding a sense of discipline and excitement to the electoral campaign. The Red Women and Girls League and the Communist Youth Organization were set to work, though with indifferent successess. In the Dortmund local of the Union for Atheism and Cremation, the party succeeded in getting a resolution passed that called on the members to vote only for those candidates who had left the church. The resolution was then taken up by other locals and by the Rhineland-Westphalia district leadership. The KPD responded to the resolution positively, the SPD "declined in a fresh and insolent manner."[59] The KPD then subsidized the wider distribution of the free-thinker newspaper that contained articles and documents on the issue. Among the other, rival freethinker associations in the Ruhr, however, the party had no successes.

Unsurprisingly, the KPD's paramilitary organization, the RFB, played the most important role in the campaign, surpassing even the regular party organiza-

[58] For the following, see [BLR], "Bericht über den Wahlkampf im Bezirk Ruhrgebiet," [1928], SAPMO-BA, ZPA I/3/18–19/13/115–36.

[59] Ibid., 118.

tion. Typically, the RFB had become virtually the substitute for mass mobilizations. In the process, the militaristic ethos of the RFB infused the broader culture of German communism. As a party report on the election in the Ruhr indicated, "The RFB has thrown all its energies into the electoral work, and in a model fashion for the entire party. It followed all the requests and directives of the party."[60] The RFB carried out many of the mundane but necessary tasks of electoral campaigns: propaganda marches, public gatherings, agitation in the countryside, poster and leaflet distribution, as depicted in plate 7.7. It helped circulate the *Rote Peitsche (Red Whip)*—a telling name—the electoral supplement to the *Ruhr-Echo.*

Significantly, the unemployed movement, which provided "brilliant support" for the party, seemed to rank only second to the RFB in its electoral activism.[61] The entire apparatus of the movement—in communist hands anyway—was placed in service of the KPD's electoral effort. The unemployed held rallies and demonstrations at which KPD candidates spoke. Their newspaper, *Der Arbeitslose* (The Unemployed), expanded its press run from around nine to thirteen thousand, no doubt with the financial support of the KPD.

The RFB and the unemployed perfected techniques of mass mobilization in the 1928 campaign. Both engaged in semispontaneous street theater, often in the evening to attract the attention of passersby.[62] They adopted the very successful tactic of "flying demonstrations" in which activists would gather at intersections or squares with loudspeakers and the RFB band. They would give a quick street theater performance, complete with music, hold a campaign rally, and then quickly move by auto to another place. The communist youth group's Agitprop Troop performed a "red press review" and a satirical "republican ape theater" to great popular acclaim in the streets. All these efforts were aided by the deployment of a fleet of vehicles, including two RFB "armed propaganda trucks"; autos outfitted with loudspeakers, posters, and banners; two trucks dressed up as prisons; and one truck outfitted as a "colorful model of a worker children's home in the Soviet Union."[63]

The appearance of party leader Ernst Thälmann in Dortmund on 9 April 1928 provided an occasion for mobilizing all the party's resources and supporters. For weeks preceding the rally, the KPD blanketed the city with leaflets, posters, banners, and wreaths. Comrades from throughout the Ruhr and even beyond were sent into the city to bolster the local organization. The party tied the effort into a petition campaign aimed at preventing the banning of the RFB, which the Dortmund police president had threatened. The KPD claimed—correctly—that a local ban would serve as a trial run for a national ban of the RFB.

The 1928 election was a watershed for the KPD. The Ruhr leadership judged it the first time the party had mounted a "grand electoral campaign suitable to the

[60] Ibid., 117.

[61] Ibid., 123.

[62] On this topic generally, see Richard Bodek, "'We are the Red Megaphone': Political Music, Agitprop Theater, Everyday Life and Communist Politics in Berlin during the Weimar Republic" (Ph.D. diss., University of Michigan, 1990).

[63] [BLR], "Bericht über den Wahlkampf im Bezirk Ruhrgebiet," [1928], SAPMO-BA, ZPA I/3/18–19/13/120.

times." Like the NSDAP, the KPD pitched its campaign to ever more defined segments of the electorate, including specific working-class trades as well as different classes, a great advance in the party's own judgment. At the same time, the district leadership argued that at least some propaganda should have been directed at the entire population. Reflecting an attentiveness to modern communications techniques, it advised:

> The large colored posters were too complicated, too involved. In the future it is recommended . . . to put out *one* especially effective *poster* in various sizes and to hammer the masses in the skull. Bourgeois advertisements of each brand of cigarettes demonstrate the theoretical principle: one catch phrase as brief as possible, one clear illustration or dramatic, pictorially pointed scene. Then we will more sharply distinguish ourselves from the hodgepodge and confusion of the other parties.[64]

Also important were the use of camouflaged autos, records, and, "above all else, electoral films, which had a stellar [impact] and were a great help in the electoral struggle."[65] Clearly, the KPD had learned to use the techniques of modern propaganda and advertisement. Along with the mass mobilization of the party rank and file, the intermittent articulation of the new woman and an emancipated sexuality, and the general evocation of a bright socialist future, they demonstrated the modernity of the KPD, one of the reasons for the party's attractiveness.

Enemies

The list of enemies was long, and they were always on the march. Indeed, the concept of struggle would have been meaningless without enemies. They appear in almost any party manifesto and graphically in the pages of the *AIZ*, especially in John Heartfield's many photomontages and in the caricatures used in thousands of party leaflets (plate 7.8). They cascade quickly one into another—capitalists, state officials, social democrats, Junkers, monarchists, priests and pastors, the Entente powers. By the time of the Depression, the cascade had turned into a singular flow when the party dubbed as fascist the Brüning, Papen, and Schleicher governments, as well as social democracy.[66]

"Monarchist reaction," "bourgeois reaction," "the fresh and brutal employers," "the aniline kings"—these are just some of the more moderate terms used to describe the enemies of the early 1920s, who engaged in an "employer offensive," "a monarchistic counterrevolutionary deployment," a "provocative engagement," "a bloody grab at power."[67] The enemies were the traitors of the

[64] Ibid., 124–25.

[65] Ibid., 125.

[66] See the statements collected by Weber, *Deutscher Kommunismus*, 158–59, 182–86.

[67] Terms taken almost at random from the Executive's manifestos, "Gegen Militarismus und Nationalismus! An das deutsche Proletariat! An die sozialistischen Parteien und an den ADGB!" 16 June 1922, and "Solidarität mit den streikenden Anilinarbeitern!" 2 December 1922, in *Zur Geschichte der Kommunistischen Partei Deutschlands*, 105–7, 109–10.

Die Sturm

„Ich gelobe: Stets und immer für die Sowjetunion

Plate 7.7 The varied activities of the RFB, the "storm troops of the proletariat." *Source: AIZ*, 19 June 1927.

The arms of capital.

The three crosses for the workers.

The gallows for the revolutionary proletariat.

Hitler and Severing are the reliable crutches of capital!

Plate 7.8 Social democrats join with the enemies of the working class. *Source:* "Illustrations-Vorlagen für Betriebs- und Häuserblock-Zeitungen," vols. 10 and 11, ed. ZK der KPD, Agitprop (Frankfurt am Main: Rhein-Main-Druck, [early 1930s]). BAK R45/IV/39.

nation or of the class. The rhetoric was so sharp—echoing Luxemburg—that no compromise was conceivable, certainly not with the "stock market hyenas," "those who invent new weapons . . . prepare gas warfare,"[68] or the League of

[68] "An die arbeitenden Klassen Deutschlands!" 11 August 1923; "Solidarität mit den streikenden Anilinarbeitern!" 2 December 1922, "Gegen das Gutachten der amerikanischen Bankiers—das Ar-

Nations, which is the "new Holy Alliance against the proletarian revolution. It is the most dogged and vulgarly dangerous conspiracy of the greedy capitalist robbers against the liberation struggle of the working masses. Its agent in the ranks of the working class is the Second International, the International of MacDonald, the bloody executioner of the Chinese and Indian working masses."[69] Workers endure "rape by the capitalist state power" helped along by "the cowardice of the trade union officials."[70] The KPD's language was designed to make pariahs out of the enemy, to exclude every possibility of mediation and compromise, and to convince workers that the KPD was the "mortal enemy of the bourgeoisie," as Ernst Thälmann put it at the KPD's Eleventh Congress.[71]

The vitriolic rhetoric against the enemy had a basis in the language and ideology of nineteenth-century socialism, and especially in the intransigence and fervency expressed by Luxemburg and Lenin. But the deep-seated rhetorical and ideological hostility toward the enemy also resonated with workers' experiences. In working-class autobiographies and memoirs, enemies are exploitative bosses, feared policemen, and faceless bureaucrats. The bosses move the assembly line at an ever faster pace, resulting in missing limbs, nervous exhaustion, and death. The policemen take pleasure in kicking imprisoned radical workers in the face, breaking their noses, or smashing their faces against steel posts. The bureaucrats laugh in the face of a skilled man who comes looking for work in the midst of the Depression. He leaves, humiliated and infuriated, and as he walks step by step from the office, the reader can imagine the proletarian pounding a hammer or the march of thousands protesting their conditions under the banner of the red flag.[72]

While the right-wing and upper-class enemies had served as leitmotifs of socialist thought and propaganda since the early nineteenth century, the deep hostility toward social democracy was new to the twentieth. Social democrats were the "most unscrupulous traitors to the working class . . . the agents of the class enemy . . . who need to be unmasked and hunted."[73] The responsibility of the SPD for the assassinations of Luxemburg and Liebknecht served as a constant reminder of the calumny of social democracy, which the party press played up especially in the yearly LLL commemorations. No act of treachery was too low for social democrats, who "serve as gendarmes of finance capital to club down every act of proletarian resistance against the slave dictates from London and

beitergutachten!" 4 September 1924, in *Zur Geschichte der Kommunistischen Partei Deutschlands*, 109, 135, 162.

[69] "Manifest der Internationalen Konferenz," 9 October 1924, in *Zur Geschichte der Kommunistischen Partei Deutschlands*, 169.

[70] "Solidarität mit den streikenden Hafenarbeitern!" *RF*, 3 Oktober 1926.

[71] "Manifest des XI. Parteitages der Kommunistischen Partei Deutschlands," 7 March 1927, in *Zur Geschichte der Kommunistischen Partei Deutschlands*, 224.

[72] These examples are from Otto Gotsche, "Aus Märzstürme"; Georg Glaser, "Schluckebier"; Eduard Claudius, "Salz der Erde," all in Emmerich, *Proletarische Lebensläufe*, 206–8, 244–48, 257–59.

[73] "Manifest des XI. Parteitages der Kommunistischen Partei Deutschlands," 7 March 1927, in *Zur Geschichte der Kommunistischen Partei Deutschlands*, 227.

Plate 7.9 The SPD celebrates May Day like a group of the petit bourgeoisie on a beer outing, while . . .

New York."[74] And while communists engaged the struggle, social democrats held pleasurable petit bourgeois parties (plates 7.9 and 7.10).

The level of hostility against the SPD was most pronounced—and most senseless—during the last years of the Weimar Republic, but, as argued through-

[74] "Manifest der Internationalen Konferenz," 9 October 1924, in *Zur Geschichte der Kommunistischen Partei Deutschlands*, 169.

out this book, this sentiment and strategy ran through communist politics from Rosa Luxemburg and the Spartacists to Ernst Thälmann and the KPD of the Weimar Republic and onward to the SED.[75] Indeed, the social fascist line of the

[75] On the KPD in the last years of the Republic and the "social fascist" line, see Hermann Weber, ed., *Die Generallinie: Rundschreiben des Zentralkomitees der KPD an die Bezirke 1929–1933* (Düs-

end phase of Weimar marked no substantive departure, but a logical conclusion, to the KPD's long-standing hostility toward the SPD. The infamous phrase "Hauptstoß gegen die Sozialdemokratie!" (Main blow against social democracy!), echoed Luxemburg's own call for the most resolute struggles against "those hacks of the bourgeoisie, Scheidemann-Ebert."[76]

As with the hostility to bosses and bureaucrats, the KPD's vitriolic opposition to social democracy was not simply an ideological construction imposed on the party from outside. Radical workers had endured scores of bloody encounters with SPD-led security forces, as we saw in earlier chapters. Many communists had lost their jobs through the collusion of social democratic trade unionists. The faceless and hostile bureaucrats they met at the unemployment office were the representatives of a welfare state identified most closely with the SPD. To be sure, there were countercurrents. Some rank-and-file communists deployed the language of solidarity against the intransigence of the third period and sought out contacts and alliances with social democrats.[77] But probably more typical were the experiences in the Halle-Merseburg region, where the hostility between the SPD and KPD was so pronounced in Zeitz and at Leuna that communist and socialist workers in the same enterprises used different train cars in their commute, ate in different sections of the company cafeteria, and changed their clothes in different dressing rooms.[78] The social democratic enemy, like his bourgeois and aristocratic counterpart, took on grisly tones in party propaganda, but it was a portrayal that accorded with the lived experience of many communists.

Factionalism

Little has been said in this book so far about factions within the party, and deliberately so. Certainly, the individual factions—left, right, and center, and various permutations thereof—articulated differing political tendencies. But the historical preoccupation with factional conflict has obscured the very substantial areas of agreement among them.[79] It has been my contention throughout this book that a political culture of communism emerged in the 1920s, and it encompassed all

seldorf: Droste, 1981), and Siegfried Bahne, *Die KPD und das Ende von Weimar: Das Scheitern einer Politik 1932–1935* (Frankfurt am Main: Campus, 1976). For an argument that places the "third period" in the longer context of Comintern history and sees its origins in Nikolai Bukharin's, not Stalin's, politics, see Nicholas N. Kozlov and Eric D. Weitz, "Reflections on the Origins of the 'Third Period': Bukharin, the Comintern, and the Political Economy of Weimar Germany," *JCH* 24:3 (1989): 387–410.

[76] Luxemburg, "Was will der Spartakusbund?" *GW*:4, 448.

[77] See Donna Harsch, *German Social Democracy and the Rise of Nazism* (Chapel Hill: University of North Carolina Press, 1993), 196–200, for examples.

[78] "Politischer Bericht des Bezirks Halle-Merseburg für die Monate September und Oktober," 12 November 1926, SAPMO-BA, ZPA I/3/11/16/43–44.

[79] Weber's *Wandlung* is the standard work on the KPD, but he sees only the conflicts among the factions. Heinrich August Winkler's discussion of the KPD in *Der Schein der Normalität: Arbeiter und Arbeiterbewegung in der Weimarer Republik 1924 bis 1930* (Berlin: J. H. W. Dietz Nachf., 1988), 202–10, 417–65, 661–98, generally follows Weber on this and other points.

the factions. In fact, the significance of factionalism is to be found more in its very existence, in the creation of a communist culture marked very deeply by vituperative internal conflict, less in the tactical, ideological, and personnel differences among the various factions. If communist solidarity invoked some of the finest, most humanistic elements of the socialist tradition, communist factionalism drew on the worst aspects to create an authoritarian and intolerant political practice. There was, indeed, no party life without factional conflict—an essential element of the communist experience that prepared party members to accept the more serious and drastic purges and executions of the 1930s and 1950s.

All of the various groups within the KPD were committed to revolution as the means of social transformation. None of the factions ever posited daily improvements and reforms as goals in and of themselves; nor did any argue, as did social democrats, and also communist parties in the popular front period, that an accumulation of substantive reforms could lead to the supersession of capitalism. Even in the KPD's moderate periods (January 1921, 1922 through the beginning of 1923, 1926–27) no party leadership ventured to deny the essential revolutionary character of the post–World War I epoch. The "right" and "center" tendencies in the KPD argued that the path to revolution lay through active involvement in the daily struggles of the working class, which would result in the creation of a mass party poised to seize power.[80] The "leftist" tendency disparaged practical work in the unions and in the representative institutions of the Weimar Republic. It had a more messianic belief in the innate radicalism of the working class, and argued that the KPD would win support only by demonstrating its revolutionary credentials. But all groups rejected a passive acceptance of existing conditions and the deterministic understanding of social transformation articulated by the SPD. The actualization of revolution depended not merely on the unfolding of events, but on the actions of the party and its supporters which would, in a sense, "force" events.

As Ossip K. Flechtheim noted long ago, it is nearly impossible to draw definitive, causative connections between distinctive social and economic conditions and particular party tendencies.[81] Nonetheless, the regional social and political histories of labor helped enable certain factions to predominate in particular areas. Two party districts will be used here to explore the meaning of factionalism—the Ruhr in the mid-1920s and Halle-Merseburg in the late 1920s and early 1930s. The Ruhr had a reputation as a left-wing district; in Halle-Merseburg the center and right long prevailed. Neither district was uniform, however, and opposing tendencies garnered substantial support. Moreover, members in both districts and of all tendencies were quick to adopt the manipulative and vituperative practices intrinsic to factional conflicts.

[80] See, for example, Jakob Walcher to Nikolai Bukharin, 26 May 1927, SAPMO-BA, ZPA I/6/3/161/5–11. Walcher was a prominent "conciliator" and Bukharin at the time was head of the Comintern.

[81] Though one should note that for the prewar SPD, Adelheid von Saldern has clearly demonstrated for at least one area the small-town origins of reformism. See Adelheid von Saldern, *Auf dem Wege zum Arbeiter-Reformismus: Parteialltag in sozialdemokratischer Provinz Göttingen (1870–1920)* (Frankfurt am Main: Materialis, 1984).

Halle-Merseburg, a diverse industrial area of mostly medium-sized firms—with some significant exceptions like the Leuna works—had constituted the Independent Social Democratic Party's most solid base in the initial postwar years. The SPD had gone over en masse to the new party in 1917 and brought with it a long-standing radical tradition in which the party and the unions were well integrated and the party occupied a solid position in the workplace.[82] The KPD inherited much of this same tradition from the USPD, which in 1920 reprised the earlier party split and went over nearly en masse to the KPD. The firm anchoring in the workplace, which the KPD maintained in Halle-Merseburg until the 1930s, goes far toward explaining the center-right's domination of the district. Few were the communist trade unionists or works councillors who were prepared to throw all their political efforts into demonstrations in the streets. Many were reluctant to abandon completely contacts with social democrats. The orientation toward "practical work," typical of many party trade unionists, aroused the intense ire of the left, but it was held in check until the onset of the "third period." In addition, the quality of the leadership in Halle-Merseburg was quite high and, from 1925 to about 1930, fairly stable. Many leading KPD functionaries, such as Wilhelm and Bernard Koenen and Alfred Oelßner, had been active in the prewar SPD and went on to long and honored careers in the DDR.

The Ruhr was of course Germany's industrial heartland. There has long been a tendency among historians to attribute the radicalism of workers here, including the left-wing tendencies within the KPD, to the immense geographic and social mobility of the war years, which supposedly created a caste of new workers unfamiliar with industrial work and with the traditions of the German labor movement. But the remaking of the working class during the war has often been exaggerated and in any case was very much a temporary phenomenon.[83] More significantly, the entwining of miners and metalworkers, each with their own distinctive traditions of political engagement, made for a particularly volatile mix in the extraordinary circumstances of war and revolution. As a result, the Ruhr became the setting for the most intense conflicts of the early postwar years—the socialization strikes of 1919, the Red Army revolt following the Kapp Putsch, and the civil disturbances during the French occupation. The intermittent but fervent activism of Ruhr workers seemed to lend credence to a political strategy—

[82] See the histories produced in the DDR: Roswitha Mende and Karl-Heinz Leidigkeit, *Von der Jahrhundertwende bis zum Roten Oktober: Geschichte der sozialdemokratischen Bezirksorganisation Halle-Merseburg 1900 bis 1917*, ed. Bezirksleitung Halle der SED (Halle: Druckhaus Freiheit, 1987); Roswitha Mende, "Geschichte der Sozialdemokratie im Regierungsbezirk Merseburg von der Jahrhundertwende bis 1917" (Ph.D. diss., Philisophischen Fakultät des Wissenschaftlichen Rates der Martin-Luther-Universität Halle-Wittenberg, 1985); and Karl-Heinz Leidigkeit and Jürgen Hermann, *Auf leninistischem Kurs: Geschichte der KPD- Bezirksorganisation Halle-Merseburg bis 1933*, ed. Bezirksleitung Halle der SED (Halle: Druckhaus Freiheit, 1979).

[83] See Ute Daniel, *Arbeiterfrauen in der Kriegsgesellschaft: Beruf, Familie und Politik im Ersten Weltkrieg* (Göttingen: Vandenhoeck und Ruprecht, 1989); Eric D. Weitz, "Social Continuity and Political Radicalization: Essen in the World War I Era," *SSH* 9:1 (1985): 49–69; and Merith Niehuss, *Arbeiterschaft in Krieg und Inflation: Soziale Schichtung und Lage der Arbeiter in Augsburg und Linz 1910 bis 1925* (Berlin: Walter de Gruyter, 1985).

continually promoted by the KPD left—based on the expectation of an imminent conflagration. The severity of the repressions that followed each of these events only heightened the intensity of politics, and aroused immense bitterness against the Republic identified with social democrats. Moreover, in Protestant Halle-Merseburg, the KPD, with some exceptions like Magdeburg, exercised an almost uncontested hegemony over labor politics. In the Ruhr the KPD competed for workers' loyalties not only with the SPD, but also with the Center Party. The local and regional leaders of both parties were well connected to their counterparts in Prussia and the Reich—all of which made for even greater communist hostility, which supported the radicalism of the left.

As at the national level, the leftist faction came to dominate the Ruhr in early 1924 in the wake of the disaster of the October Uprising and the governmental ban on the party's activities. Its accession occurred only after conflicts that were fought out with extraordinary bitterness.[84] When the Ruhr KPD held its conference in Essen on 9 March 1924, the police reported that the mood was almost totally in opposition to the old party leadership under Heinrich Brandler, which was held responsible for the failure of the party's 1923 revolt.[85]

Nonetheless, the left leadership soon ran into enormous difficulties with the party's own functionaries and rank and file. Many resisted its directives, and members of all the factions engaged in the poisonous verbal and organizational warfare typical of internal conflicts. During the 1924 miners strike, party members who were miners also struck against their own leaders and refused to call meetings where they worked when communists were scheduled to be the principal speakers or to bring the unemployed into meetings of the workforce.[86] Continual exhortations to the party rank and file to maintain the struggles, work harder, and follow discipline better indicate all too clearly the absence of mass activity and resistance to the left leadership.[87] Realizing that workers were weary of the party's unceasing efforts to organize demonstrations and other activities, many members demanded a return to "practical work." In Essen, the police reported a great sense of demoralization in the party's ranks and a membership and subscription decline of one-third from the previous year.[88] Demoralization turned to bitterness against the party Executive for its heavy-handed tactics in purging local party workers.[89]

After the party's electoral defeat in December 1924, the Essen functionaries erupted in fury at some of their leaders. When the hapless subdistrict secretary

[84] RPD to OBE et al., with accompanying report, 26 March 1924, StAE 102/I/1077. The Ruhr district leadership reported that practically all functionary meetings in the district had come out in favor of the left and demanded the building of a left-wing Executive. "Politischer Bericht Bezirk Ruhrgebiet vom 4. März," [no additional date], SAPMO-BA, ZPA I/3/18–19/11/34.

[85] RPD to OBE et al., with accompanying report, 26 March 1924, StAE 102/I/1077.

[86] For these examples, see RPD to MdI et al., with copies of Rundschreiben, UB Essen KPD, 4 June 1924, HStAD 16961.

[87] RPD to OBE with report on meeting of functionaries of Essen KPD, 24 June 1924, HStAD 16934/78–79.

[88] "Lagebericht (KPD)," 20 October 1924, HStAD 16765.

[89] Ibid.; RPD to MdI, 16 August 1924; "Abschrift (KPD): Lagebericht," 3 November 1924, HStAD 16934; OP Westfalen to RPD, 30 December 1924, HStAD 16923; *AZ*, 17 October 1924.

could not explain the absence of the two district secretaries (Schwan and Kollwitz), who had replaced a well-respected activist purged by the Executive, cries of "cowards, profiteers, fops, whores, swindlers" swirled around the meeting, indicating that the left had no monopoly on harsh rhetoric. Some of the participants were delegated to go find the secretaries, but to no avail.[90] The leadership's efforts to draw optimistic points from the election only further infuriated some of the functionaries, and the meeting passed a resolution demanding a change in party policy. This was a striking, but not untypical, reversal for a local party group that had at the outset of 1924 supported the left—and an indication of how all party groups deployed the vituperative language of factional conflict.

The left viewed itself in a warlike situation with its party opponents. The district leadership complained in a letter to party leader Ruth Fischer that in the Ruhr "a disciplined right-wing fraction has emerged . . . [and] intends . . . to go on the attack." The author of the letter indicated that the Reich leader of the fraction was in the district, as if he had gone undercover, and warned that if the Executive did not fully replace right-wing cadres, the "absolute worst" was to be expected: "the very destiny of the Ruhr district" depended on resolute purges.[91]

Meanwhile, Central Committee instructors described a situation that "is catastrophic. The party Executive must intervene immediately in order to save what there is to save."[92] By this point, the factional conflict had come to dominate completely communist politics and all larger campaigns waned in significance. The situation had not improved upon the instructor's second return in May 1924, nor in the autumn when another instructor visited.[93]

Here, in the left-wing Ruhr district, an intense level of mistrust reigned against the leftist leadership in Berlin. The vituperative language had become a common feature of party life. The moderates and rightists in the party attacked virtually anyone sent out from Berlin. "You're just a criminal like the others!" or charges that Central Committee representatives were police spies were among the favored greetings.[94] The instructor, Wienand Kaasch, seemed especially incensed that these charges were leveled even in public and in the presence of nonmembers.

The left leadership of the Ruhr could not survive the party changes instituted from Moscow in the autumn of 1925, but it managed to hold on to power for quite a while. District secretary Theodor Neubauer charged that a good part of the rightist elements in the party "are social democrats and never will be anything else."[95] Using the pejorative language typical of factional conflicts, Neubauer argued that the "dumb, false, social democratic holdovers of party democracy and criticism"

[90] OP Westfalen to RPD, 30 December 1924, HStAD 16923.

[91] Letter to Ruth Fischer [sender unclear, probably Neubauer], 12 December 1924, SAPMO-BA, ZPA I/3/18–19/11/72.

[92] "Bericht aus dem Ruhrgebiet," 12 May 1924, SAPMO-BA, ZPA I/3/18–19/20/22.

[93] "Bericht über meine zweite Reise nach dem Ruhrgebiet," 22 May 1924, SAPMO-BA, ZPA I/3/18–19/20/24–29, and "Bericht vom Bezirk Ruhrgebiet," 4 October 1924, SAPMO-BA, ZPA I/3/18–19/20/43.

[94] "Bericht vom Bezirk Ruhrgebiet," 4 October 1924, SAPMO-BA, ZPA I/3/18–19/20/43.

[95] BLR to Zentrale, 4 April 1925, SAPMO-BA, ZPA I/3/18–19/11/106.

must be put aside. "Every push in the direction of social democratic 'party democracy' and 'freedom of criticism' must be sharply fought against."[96] Neubauer charged that the ECCI's "Open Letter" of September 1925, which had attacked the left-wing leadership, caused "great confusion" among the members and had allowed all sorts of shadowy elements to emerge.[97]

The Central Committee imposed a new leadership on the Ruhr in the person of Wilhelm Florin, who had a difficult task bringing the party in line.[98] Despite all the hostility toward the left, the commitment to an overtly revolutionary politics extended far deeper than the ideologues of leftism in the Executive and the Reichstag fraction. At one meeting in Buer, for example, at least one worker complained that the Comintern had renounced the slogan "dictatorship of the proletariat" and the idea of councils. Expressing the revolutionary optimism so characteristic of the left, the speaker claimed that the present situation (1926) was, if not comparable to 1919, at least as revolutionary as 1923, yet the Comintern talked about the "relative stabilization of capitalism." "If the present policy is Bolshevik, then we are proud to be anti-Bolsheviks."[99] The speaker went on to levy the usual attacks of the left against the Soviet New Economic Policy and the equivocating tactics of the KPD. The discussion, often punctuated by catcalls and other interruptions, went on all day.[100]

Florin continually made the rounds of the subdistricts, and in mid-1926 found the left still strong in Dortmund, Buer, and other towns. He wrote to the Executive, "the opposition is composed of absolutely solid revolutionary workers" who did not understand why "the fragility of the relative stabilization" was being downplayed.[101] As ever, the left was quick to see signs of an impending revolution.[102] Sentiments against the unions remained high, and members voiced numerous complaints along the lines that "the *Bonzen* [party or union bosses] are traitors!"[103]

Florin thought that many of these comrades could still be kept in the party so long as they saw the party playing an activist role. In an effort to appease the left, he authorized the party press to publish some articles against the "disgusting behavior" of the party's right-wing faction. At the same time he demanded an end to all the "machinations against the party." He warned that those who continued to

[96] Ibid.

[97] "Politischer Bericht des Bezirks Ruhrgebiet für August/September 1925," SAPMO-BA, ZPA I/3/18–19/11/112. See also "Bericht über den Bezirk Ruhrgebiet," [undated, presumably end of 1925 or early 1926], SAPMO-BA, ZPA I/3/18–19/12/83. The Comintern's "Open Letter" was published in *RF*, 1 September 1925. The text is also available in Weber, *Deutscher Kommunismus*, 218–42.

[98] "Bericht über die Bezirksleitungssitzung des Bezirks Ruhrgebiet am 30. December 1925," 20 January 1926, SAPMO-BA, ZPA I/3/18–19/12/118. See also the biographical sketches in Weber, *Wandlung* 2:121–22 (Florin), 231–32 (Neubauer), 298–99 (Schwan).

[99] [Untitled, n.d., presumably August 1926], SAPMO-BA, ZPA I/3/18–19/20/68.

[100] Ibid., 68–77.

[101] "Situationsbericht aus dem Ruhrgebiet," 31 May 1926, SAPMO-BA, ZPA I/3/18–19/11/151.

[102] Ibid.

[103] "Bericht über die Reise nach dem Ruhrgebiet am 17. März 1926," SAPMO-BA, ZPA I/3/18–19/13/1.

engage in such actions would be expelled.[104] Central Committee instructors, meanwhile, continued to express deep-seated misgivings about the operation of the party in the Ruhr. Time after time, the instructors (often Arthur Vogt) complained about the relative quiescence of workers, the passivity of party members and leaders, the failure to follow instructions from the Central Committee, poor communications, and phantom cells.[105] At a time of high unemployment and enhanced employer power, the KPD could do little to stimulate mass uprisings. Instead, factionalism came to dominate party life.

While the leftist Ruhr had to be brought in line behind the Thälmann Central Committee, the opposite problem existed in Halle-Merseburg. With the Comintern's proclamation of the "third period" in 1928, the KPD leadership itself moved to the left. Halle-Merseburg, one of the party's most solid districts, proved of major concern because of its domination by the right and center (the latter often dubbed the "conciliators"). As a result, the Central Committee conducted the Comintern-inspired campaign with reckless enthusiasm in Halle-Merseburg. The invective intrinsic to factional conflicts became even more pronounced and came to dominate almost completely internal party life. Meetings were held all over the region and went on for hours and hours in the effort to rally support for the Thälmann group and, from a distance, the Stalin leadership in the campaign against the right and center.[106]

Even in the factories, where elsewhere the party had such a difficult time establishing itself organizationally, the struggle against the right and center won pride of place. As communists in the Wasag and I. G. Farben chemical plants in Bitterfeld expressed it, they had little occasion to engage in positive work because they "had to concentrate on the struggle against the right-wing comrades."[107] At one meeting in Falkenberg, the two leading speakers addressed the crowd for, respectively, two and one-quarter and one and three-quarter hours, followed by nine comrades who had unlimited speaking time. At a hotly contested meeting in Wittenberg/Piesteritz, Heinrich Brandler, rallying support for the KPD-Opposition, the organization formed by purged rightists and conciliators, spoke for about two hours and the second speaker for one hour.[108]

[104] See BLR, "Bericht der Bezirksleitung Ruhrgebiet," 9 December 1926, SAPMO-BA, ZPA I/3/18–19/11/192.

[105] These impressions are drawn from the collections of instructor reports, SAPMO-BA, ZPA I/3/18–19/12, I/3/18–19/13, and I/3/18–19/14.

[106] The tenor of the campaign against the center and right at the local level can be discerned from the documents in SAPMO-BA, ZPA I/3/11/19, which contains reports of meetings of the subdistricts. For some examples, see the reports about the subdistricts Merseburg, Torgau-Liebenwerda, Sangerhausen-Nordhausen, Wittenberg-Bitterfeld, and Zeitz-Naumburg-Weissenfels, as well as a meeting of the "Brandlerianer" in Wittenberg/Piesteritz, 112–16, 119–23, 150–53.

[107] "Bericht über den Stand der Arbeit der Zelle in den Chemiebetrieben des Bezirks Halle-Merseburg (17. und 18.1.1929)," SAPMO-BA, ZPA I/3/11/19/144.

[108] "Bericht über die Unterbezirkskonferenz Torgau-Liebenwerda in Falkenberg am 2.12.1928," and "Bericht von der öffentlichen Versammlung der Brandlerianer am 26.3.29 in Wittenberg/Piesteritz," SAPMO-BA, ZPA I/3/11/19/115–16, 150–52.

It was not a simple matter to bring the district in line. The subdistrict Sangerhausen-Nordhausen, for example, passed a resolution supporting the decisions of the Sixth Comintern Congress, but at the same time criticized the Politburo for the methods it had adopted in internal party disputes and supported the Halle-Merseburg district leadership.[109] Widely recognized leaders in the district, like Bernard Koenen, angrily countered the Central Committee attacks on the Halle-Merseburg leadership.[110] In at least one meeting, which lasted an entire day, only one lone voice aside from the representative sent from Berlin spoke up for the Central Committee.[111] At Wittenberg/Piesteritz, another meeting of the "Brandlerianer" at which Brandler himself spoke drew four to five hundred mostly supportive individuals.[112] The Central Committee delegate called the situation in the district "catastrophic," but blamed it on unclarity rather than a firm conviction for the center position.[113]

When the Central Committee initiated a control of the Halle-Merseburg district toward the end of 1929, the ensuing report criticized virtually every aspect of party work and party life in the area, including poorly run campaigns against the Young Plan, underestimation of the SPD, insufficient work among women and youth, and the absence of coordination among different party units. While many of the criticisms were no doubt on target, their sweeping character made them weapons in the struggle against the right and center. As the report stated, "the major dangers in the entire district are the extremely strong opportunistic deviations, especially in the functionary corps of the unions and cooperatives."[114] The problem had to be resolved through improvements in the internal political education of the membership and through the strongest organizational measures—that is, purges—against around two hundred functionaries.

In the end, the center and right could do little against a Central Committee acting with the support of the Comintern. "Organizational measures" were carried out, and they brought the district in line behind the party leadership, but at great cost. As we saw in chapter 4, the purges further weakened the communist presence in the workplace and made functionaries and rank-and-file members captive to an intolerant party practice marked by denunciations, invective, and exclusions.

Whatever their differences, the various tendencies in the KPD all contributed to

[109] "Bericht von der Unterbezirkskonferenz Sangerhausen-Nordhausen Bezirk Halle-Merseburg, am 2.12.28," SAPMO-BA, ZPA I/3/11/19/119–20.

[110] "Bericht über die Unterbezirkskonferenz Wittenberg-Bitterfeld am 2.XII.1928," SAPMO-BA, ZPA I/3/11/19/121–23. Koenen then capitulated to the majority, and had a long career in the party and in the DDR, including surviving severe mistreatment at the hands of the Soviet secret police in the 1930s. See Weber, *Wandlung* 2:186–87.

[111] "Bericht über die Unterbezirkskonferenz Wittenberg-Bitterfeld am 2.XII.1928," SAPMO-BA, ZPA I/3/11/19/121.

[112] "Bericht von der öffentlichen Versammlung der Brandlerianer am 26.3.29 in Wittenberg/Piesteritz," SAPMO-BA, ZPA I/3/11/19/150–52.

[113] "Bericht über die Unterbezirkskonferenz Wittenberg-Bitterfeld am 2.XII.1928," SAPMO-BA, ZPA I/3/11/19/122.

[114] "Bericht über die Kontrolle im Bezirk Halle-Merseburg am 21./22.11.29," SAPMO-BA, ZPA I/3/11/19/148.

the creation of a common communist political culture in which factionalism itself played a major role. Many individuals, purged by the party or generally disgusted with the level of internal conflict, retreated altogether from political activity or spent years searching for a new political home. Others, fearing isolation from their comrades and the abandonment of political engagement and their political ideals, became inured to factionalism. Still others relished factional conflict, believing it to be the essence of politics. And those who were good at it were the ones who ultimately triumphed in the party.

Conclusion

For many workers, women and men, support for the KPD meant a journey of sacrifice. In the Weimar Republic they experienced unceasing demands on their time and talents, premature unemployment, prison, beatings, and street fights. But a life in the party meant also a life of meaning, of commitment to the proletarian cause and the socialist future. The party offered people a place to forge identities, to have an impact on their world, to improve themselves. They engaged in an activism designed to surmount truly exploitative conditions at work and the discriminations in the public realm of a class-riven society. Their emancipatory convictions connected them to the long trajectory of German humanism that stretched back to the eighteenth century. In this sense, the KPD, like its socialist forebears, embodied many of the best characteristics of the labor movement.

KPD supporters encountered the language and ideology of communism in the political spaces in which the party entered and in its varied, associated organizations. They learned class, struggle, and solidarity as the guiding principles to a life of incessant conflict with the forces of authority. They also learned factionalism as a necessary element of party life. All these categories gave to communism its dynamic and forceful, and also its militaristic and intolerant, tenor. These latter characteristics gained added sustenance as the Soviet Union won increasing domination over the KPD and contributed its particular intolerant and authoritarian traits to those forged indigenously in the hard-fought social and political conflicts of the Weimar Republic. The Soviet connection made it nearly impossible for the KPD ever to move beyond the circumscribed, though substantial, support that it won in the Weimar Republic. Nonetheless, the Soviet model proved inspirational to many workers and they gave their loyalty willingly.

Fault lines often ran between the demands of the leadership and the activities of the rank and file. Party leaders complained incessantly about the lack of initiative among members, poor attendance at meetings, and failure to carry out directives. The membership, in turn, seems to have resisted efforts to politicize in a party direction every single aspect of working-class associational life. Many apparently enjoyed their bicycle rides, radio clubs, and chess tournaments and were reluctant to break completely with social democratic colleagues. At the same time, many also evinced an arrogance and intolerance that contributed to the

KPD's isolation and drove party leaders to despair. As the Halle-Merseburg KPD wrote:

> [The rank and file and functionaries] adopt a sense of grandeur and superiority in relation to the indifferent and oscillating masses. They persist in a seclusion that sometimes rises to the level of direct aversion toward newcomers or prospective new members, who are just about viewed with pity as immature elements. Those who hesitate and oscillate are in many instances treated with contempt [when they should be] encouraged and strengthened. This is expressed also in the tendency to view the party as way out in front of the masses, or even to place the party in opposition to the decisive strata of the proletariat—which was the case for quite a while with the unorganized, and shows up continually in the crassest manner in relation to SPD workers.[115]

The party culture of the KPD, emancipatory and authoritarian, open and intolerant, developed out of the social historical realities of the Weimar Republic, the ideological and linguistic orientation of German and international communism, and the ever growing predominance of the Soviet Union. The landscape of industrial Germany in the 1920s and early 1930s was its proving ground, and the culture that emerged from it would survive nearly intact despite the political and personal disasters that awaited communists in the 1930s and 1940s.

115 "Ursachen der ungenügenden Entwicklung des Mitgliederstandes und der starken Fluktuation im Bezirk Halle-Merseburg," May 1930, SAPMO-BA, ZPA I/3/11/16/157.

CHAPTER 8

The *Anni terribili*: Communists under Two Dictatorships

Nie wieder Weimarer Demokratie.

—*KPD resister Anton Saefkow*[1]

THE ESTABLISHMENT of the Nazi regime at the end of January 1933 resulted in the immediate and massive repression of German communism. Within weeks the terror exercised by the SA, SS, and regular police rendered any kind of aboveground politics impossible. Individual communists suffered appallingly from the Nazis' systematic application of political violence. By the end of 1933, somewhere between sixty and one hundred thousand communists had been interned by the regime. By 1945, fully half of the three hundred thousand party members in 1932 had endured Nazi jails and concentration camps. About twenty thousand communists were killed by the Nazis, some under the most brutal circumstances.[2]

Many German communists fled to the Soviet Union, and their individual fates were no better. About 60 percent of the exiles were killed in the Stalin terror. More members of the KPD Politburo died at the hands of the Soviet than the Nazi dictatorships. Hundreds, perhaps a few thousand, German citizens wanted by the Nazis were handed over to the Gestapo by the Soviet authorities. Most, but not all, were German communists who had fled the political repression of the Third Reich or had gone to the Soviet Union even earlier to aid in the "construction of socialism."[3]

All told, of the functionary corps in 1932, almost 40 percent were dead by 1945, the vast majority victims of the Nazi or the Soviet dictatorships.[4] Only

[1] "Never again Weimar democracy." Anton Saefkow, member of the KPD's "operative leadership" and leader of the Saefkow-Jacob-Bästlein resistance group, in his political testament written shortly before his execution by the Nazis in 1944. Quoted in Siegfried Suckut, *Die Betriebsrätebewegung in der Sowjetisch Besetzten Zone Deutschlands (1945–1948)* (Frankfurt am Main: Haag + Herchen, 1982), 172.

I have borrowed the title of this chapter from Paolo Spriano, who uses it for his chapter on the Italian communists under the repression of the fascist regime. See *Storia del Partito comunista italiano*, vol. 2: *Gli anni della clandestinità* (Turin: Einaudi, 1969).

[2] Horst Duhnke, *Die KPD von 1933 bis 1945* (Cologne: Kiepenheuer und Witsch, 1972), 104, 525.

[3] Hermann Weber, "Aufstieg und Niedergang des deutschen Kommunismus," *APZ* B40/91 (27 September 1991): 29, and Duhnke, *KPD*, 348, n. 175.

[4] Hermann Weber, "Die deutschen Kommunisten 1945 in der SBZ," *APZ* B31 (5 August 1978): 30.

those who had managed to reach the most far-flung points of exile—Shanghai, Mexico City, Los Angeles—or the safety of Great Britain could be certain of outlasting the Third Reich.

While communists endured imprisonment, beatings, executions, and exile, the Nazi regime in the course of the 1930s managed to win the loyalty of a substantial portion of the working class. The Nazis never completely realized their ideal of a *Volksgemeinschaft*, a racially pure, harmonious "people's community." But the elimination of open political opposition, along with economic growth, social welfare, foreign expansion, and the ideology and practice of racism, reverberated deeply in the populace. The Nazis went a long way toward destroying the solidarities built on the experiences of class—so fundamental to the development of both the socialist and communist movements—and replacing them with the bonds of nation and race.

The Third Reich thereby cast the KPD adrift, tore German communism from its moorings in working-class communities and the organized labor movement. While most communist parties experienced an immense surge of popular support and underwent a dramatic process of political development in the 1930s and 1940s, the KPD became reduced, literally and figuratively, to a party of exiles. German communism won virtually no new members during the twelve years of the Third Reich and found its spaces of activism drastically curtailed. In Weimar, the KPD had been driven from the battlefield and the workplace; under the Nazis, it lost access to the streets, its last domain. Hunted and isolated, the KPD became ever more dependent upon the Soviet Union despite the tragic fate of communists in Soviet exile.

The KPD was not, though, reduced to total silence. From within Germany and abroad thousands of communists kept up a heroic resistance against the Third Reich. Many began to rethink their political conceptions, a process spurred along both by the Comintern's switch to the popular front strategy in 1935 and by the authoritarian practices of Stalin's Soviet Union. Nonetheless, through all the immense transformations experienced by German communists in the twelve years of the Third Reich, the communist political culture forged in the Weimar Republic retained profound resonance, as this chapter will show.

Workers and National Socialism

Catholics and workers proved relatively resistant to the appeal of National Socialism. Nonetheless, the NSDAP won substantial numbers of workers to its side during the last years of the Weimar Republic. Amid the chaos of Germany's political system, the NSDAP become the only group that could claim to be a "*Volkspartei*," a national party with support all across the social spectrum.[5]

Once in power, the stream of support the Nazis had won among workers turned

[5] See Jürgen Falter, *Hitlers Wähler* (Munich: Beck, 1991), and Thomas Childers, *The Nazi Voter: The Social Foundations of Fascism in Germany, 1919–1933* (Chapel Hill: University of North Carolina Press, 1983). The literature is immense on this and every other aspect of National Socialism discussed below. I have kept the notes to a bare minimum.

into a torrent. To be sure, the Nazis' support was never complete. Their claim to represent a unified people rested in the first place on the deliberate, brutal, and ultimately genocidal exclusion of "outsiders," including Jews, the Roma and Sinti ("gypsies"), homosexuals, the mentally and physically handicapped, and the often arbitrarily defined "asocials."[6] Among those allowed into the charmed circle of "das Volk," discontent ran deep, especially on the eve of the war and then, of course, when the war had turned against Germany. But there can be no doubt that the Nazis were enormously successful in building a mass following that extended far beyond the ranks of the party membership.[7]

Hitler himself was an immensely popular figure, among workers as well as the proverbial lower-middle-class supporters of the Nazi movement.[8] Discontent with the policies of the regime was often deflected onto the "little Hitlers," the lower-level Nazi functionaries with whom the population came into daily contact, leaving Hitler's godlike aura untarnished. Even among many who had earlier been ardent anti-Nazis, Hitler's seemingly invincible string of foreign policy successes—until 1942/43—appeared to confirm his political genius and stature as the unquestioned leader of Germany. Workers too reveled in the glory of national aggrandizement and joined in the heady prosperity achieved by pillaging the rest of Europe. Foreign conquest and Hitler's aura were quintessential parts of a fascist aesthetic that glorified—and sexualized—the race, violence, and the leader. Each of these elements had a deep-seated psychological appeal against which socialists and communists had little to offer, try as they might.

The programs targeted specifically at workers also had a great impact.[9] Hitler was only too aware that the success of his regime depended on ending the Depression and eliminating the scourge of unemployment. The revival was slow in coming, and wages rose barely at all through most of the 1930s. But the armaments drive did ultimately put an end to unemployment. And if higher living standards depended on an intensification of the workplace regime—overtime, speedup, piecework—and the entrance of more family members into the paid labor force, nonetheless family incomes did rise, and the popular perception was clearly one of material improvement. Younger workers especially, blocked by Nazi repression from the organizational and cultural experiences of the labor movement, gravitated toward the Third Reich. The vast array of social programs, many of them run through the German Labor Front (Deutsche Arbeitsfront, or DAF), provided

[6] Most recently and thoroughly, Michael Burleigh and Wolfgang Wippermann, *The Racial State: Germany, 1933–1945* (Cambridge: Cambridge University Press, 1991).

[7] For the complex attitudes toward the Third Reich from the vantage point of oral history, see Lutz Niethammer and Alexander Plato, eds. *Lebensgeschichte und Sozialkultur im Ruhrgebiet 1930 bis 1960*, 3 vols. (Berlin: J. H. W. Dietz Nachf., 1983–85).

[8] See especially Ian Kershaw, *The Hitler Myth: Image and Reality in the Third Reich* (Oxford: Oxford University Press, 1987).

[9] Each of the issues that follows remains the subject of much debate. For a fine analysis of the discussion, Ulrich Herbert, "Arbeiterschaft im 'Dritten Reich': Zwischenbilanz und offene Fragen," *GG* 15:3 (1989): 320–60. For a very important contribution, see Carola Sachse et al., *Angst, Belohnung, Zucht und Ordnung: Herrschaftsmechanismen im Nationalsozialismus* (Opladen: Westdeutscher, 1982).

workers with vacations; a form, though sharply delimited, of interest representation; and improved workplace environments.[10] The "honor of labor," a central element of Nazis ideology, found widespread support among those who worked with their hands.[11] It endowed them with social status, even when their material situation changed barely at all, just as the regime's maternalist programs—marriage loans, improved neonatal care, medals and allowances that increased with the number of children—bestowed a new-found sense of honor upon women as mothers.[12]

All of these policies gave people a sense of belonging, of improvement, of hope in the future. And they were all embedded in the racist ideology and practice that constituted the core of National Socialism. Only racially "acceptable" Germans could partake of new jobs, marriage loans, or vacation cruises down the Rhine organized by the DAF. The majority of Germans, workers included, came to accept or at least tolerate the policies that culminated in genocide.[13] While anti-Semitism played a subordinate role in winning the Nazis' popular support in Weimar, racism in the Third Reich provided the ideological cement that bound the people's community together. Racism gave the population clearly defined enemies and a common, collective purpose—to elevate the select group and to subordinate and then murder the others.

The establishment of the dictatorship was also bound up with National Socialist racism. Political opposition challenged the cherished myth of a unified racial community. Moreover, in Nazi eyes, communism and Judaism were identical, placing communist opponents even further beyond the pale. Hence, the regime moved quickly to establish its monopoly of power and destroy the ability of the opposition, primarily communists and socialists, to engage in political organizing. Arbitrary arrests, torture, internment in concentration camps, and murder were all elements of a program of systematic terror designed to contain or eliminate physically the regime's opponents and to spread a climate of insecurity and fear.

[10] Here the classic work is by Timothy Mason, which has finally appeared in an English version: *Social Policy in the Third Reich: The Working Class and the National Community* (Providence: Berg, 1993). Partly critical of his interpretation is Gunter Mai, "'Warum steht der deutsche Arbeiter zu Hitler?' Zur Rolle der Deutschen Arbeitsfront im Herrschaftssystem des Dritten Reiches," *GG* 12:2 (1986): 212–34.

[11] Alf Lüdtke, "'Ehre der Arbeit': Industriearbeiter und Macht der Symbole. Zur Reichweite symbolischer Orientierungen im Nationalsozialismus," in *Arbeiter im 20. Jahrhundert*, ed. Klaus Tenfelde (Stuttgart: Klett-Cotta, 1991), 343–92.

[12] See Claudia Koonz, *Mothers in the Fatherland: Women, the Family, and Nazi Politics* (New York: St. Martin's Press, 1987), and for a review of the controversy surrounding issues of women and gender in the Third Reich, Adelheid von Saldern, "Victims or Perpetrators? Controversies about the Role of Women in the Nazi State," in *Nazism and German Society, 1933–1945*, ed. David F. Crew (London: Routledge, 1994), 141–65.

[13] Alf Lüdtke, "The Appeal of Exterminating 'Others': German Workers and the Limits of Resistance," in *Resistance against the Third Reich, 1933–1990*, ed. Michael Geyer and John W. Boyer (Chicago: University of Chicago Press, 1994), 53–74, and Ulrich Herbert, "Arbeit und Vernichtung: Ökonomisches Interesse und Primat der 'Weltanschauung' im Nationalsozialismus," in *Ist der Nationalsozialismus Geschichte? Zu Historisierung und Historikerstreit*, ed. Dan Diner (Frankfurt am Main: Fischer, 1987), 198–236.

None of this means that the Nazis had created a completely passive and contented population or had successfully eliminated social classes and class conflict. Gestapo, SPD, and KPD reports from the 1930s all indicate widespread discontent with poor wages and insufficient supplies and continual, small-scale conflicts in the workplace and community.[14] When a high DAF official made the rounds of the Ruhr in 1935, for example, he found himself berated by workers who showed him meager lunch pails and complained bitterly about their wages. Even Hitler was not spared protests. When he visited the Krupp factory, many workers hid so they would not have to give the Nazi salute or simply went about their business and ignored the Führer.[15]

Toward the end of the decade the armaments drive strained resources to the breaking point, giving workers renewed bargaining power that led to still more serious conflicts in the workplace and community. Brief strikes and slowdowns, time-honored methods of working-class resistance, emerged more frequently.[16] Already in late 1935 butter, fat, meat, and other essential items were in short supply. Popular unrest intensified, and KPD instructors reported numerous actions in the Ruhr that, on a much smaller scale, recalled those of 1923. Women crowded into stores and demanded that the owners distribute food stocks or harangued SA men who seemed to have privileged access to meat, butter, and coal. On the long lines in front of food stores women complained bitterly about the supposed "*Volksgemeinschaft*" and compared the dire food situation to that of World War I.[17] Within the Nazi hierarchy a major dispute broke out over whether the regime should slow down the pace of armaments production and meet the inchoate but very real popular demands for improved provisions and higher wages. Hitler opted for arms.

However serious, discontent never moved beyond the individual workplace or market, never gelled into more open, popular political challenges to the regime. The fear and insecurity created by repression; the benefits bestowed by economic revival and social welfare; and the ideological and psychological appeal of racism, the "Führer Myth," and national aggrandizement bound workers, as other social groups, ever more tightly to the Nazi state. To a great extent the Nazis undermined the values and social solidarities that had underpinned the socialist and communist

[14] The SPD reports tend to be more sober, less politically colored, than KPD ones. See *Deutschland-Berichte der Sozialdemokratischen Partei Deutschlands (Sopade) 1934–1940*, ed. Klaus Behnken (Frankfurt am Main: P. Nettelbeck, 1980), and for their very effective use, Detlev Peukert, *Inside Nazi Germany: Conformity, Opposition, and Racism in Everyday Life* (New Haven: Yale University Press, 1987). For examples of popular resistance from KPD reports, see [Report], "Ruhrgebiet," [1934]; "Weitere Ergebnisse der Vertrauensrätewahlen," 5 July 1934; "Bericht 9u III," [summer 1934]; "Die Wahl des Vertrauensrates in einem Grossbetrieb im Ruhrgebiet," 6 July 1935, SAPMO, ZPA I/3/18–19/68/20–22, 62, 64, 101–2; "Bericht über die Bezirke Mitte geg. am 19. Mai 1934;" "Bericht über Bezirk Halle-Merseburg," 21 November 1934, SAPMO-BA, ZPA I/3/11/58/34, 97–105.

[15] "Bericht W. Revier," 21 July 1935, SAPMO-BA, ZPA I/3/18–19/68/103.

[16] Mason, *Social Policy*, and the collection of his articles, *Nazism, Fascism and the Working Class: Essays by Tim Mason*, ed. Jane Caplan (Cambridge: Cambridge University Press, 1995).

[17] For examples, see "Schriftlicher Bericht von Leo, November 1935"; "Bericht von Leo. 29.11.1935"; "Bericht Rolf am 29.XI.1935," SAPMO-BA, ZPA I/3/18–19/68/132, 136–38, 144.

movements since the nineteenth century. In place of the bonds of class, the Nazis instituted those of nation and race. In place of workers' partly autonomous, collective organizations in the workplace and community—consumer cooperatives, bicycle clubs, trade unions, political parties—the Nazis provided a top-down, centrally administered welfare state with a clientele restricted to the racially correct. In place of an ideology of egalitarianism, the Nazis promoted a hierarchy of race and individual and collective productivity. Expressions of peace and internationalism were replaced by the warrior ideology and practice of National Socialism. The combination of repression and integration, two sides of the same coin, just about broke the KPD's links to the working class and made the task of organizing a popular, communist-led resistance nearly impossible.

The Problem of the Popular Front

The Nazi seizure of power had, initially, no impact whatsoever on the KPD's political conceptions. To communists, the Nazi regime was just one other form of capitalist rule, every German government from 1929 onward "fascist" of one sort or another. Hence, the KPD was utterly incapable of grasping the enormous and deadly political transformation heralded by Hitler's assumption of the Reich chancellorship on 30 January 1933. The party predicted a brief spell at the helm of the state for Hitler, whose rule would only intensify class conflict and hasten the proletarian revolution. Soviet Russia would soon be freed from its isolation by a Soviet Germany.[18]

Social democrats, not Nazis, remained the major enemy for the KPD. For nearly two years after the Nazi seizure of power, the KPD maintained the strategy of directing the "major blows against the SPD," the "twin brother" of the NSDAP and the "major prop" of capitalism. The language of class—pronouncements in favor of general strikes, proletarian revolution, the "fighting united front," the "determined resistance of the working class"—percolated through underground leaflets and official statements and could hardly be expected to attract non-proletarian antifascists.[19] In May 1933, when thousands of communists were already interned in concentration camps, the Central Committee declared that it had pursued an "absolutely correct political line . . . before and during Hitler's coup," while the "brutal . . . social fascists . . . have openly gone over to the

[18] On the KPD in this period, see Duhnke, *KPD*, 63–100; Hermann Weber, "Die Ambivalenz der kommunistischen Widerstandsstrategie bis zur 'Brüsseler' Parteikonferenz," in *Der Widerstand gegen den Nationalsozialismus: Die deutsche Gesellschaft und der Widerstand gegen Hitler*, ed. Jürgen Schmädeke und Peter Steinbach (Munich: Piper, 1985), 73–85; and Siegfried Bahne, *Die KPD und das Ende von Weimar: Das Scheitern einer Politik 1932–1935* (Frankfurt am Main: Campus, 1976). For the SPD in the last phase of the Republic, see Donna Harsch, *German Social Democracy and the Rise of Nazism* (Chapel Hill: University of North Carolina Press, 1993), and Heinrich August Winkler, *Der Weg in die Katastrophe: Arbeiter und Arbeiterbewegung in der Weimarer Republik 1930 bis 1933* (Berlin: J. H. W. Dietz Nachf., 1990).

[19] See, for example, the very interesting collection of facsimile documents in Margot Pikarski and Günter Uebel, eds., *Der antifaschistische Widerstandskampf der KPD im Spiegel des Flugblattes 1933–1945*, ed. Institut für Marxismus-Leninismus beim ZK der SED (Berlin: Dietz, 1978).

fascists' auxiliary service, where they promote cooperation with the fascist bourgeoisie and applaud the fascist state's control of workers' organizations."[20] In the summer of 1933, seven months into the dictatorship, a leading member of the party wrote to the Comintern that the KPD had succeeded "not only in beating back all the voices of panic, but has also put an end to the retreat. The party has been able to strengthen the cadres and rally the masses for the counterattack. . . . In the last weeks it has become clear that the entire party is on the march and that our authority in the working class is on the rise."[21] Dissonant voices, like that of Politburo member Hermann Remmele, who claimed that the Nazi assumption of power signified a "change of systems" and that the working class had suffered a major defeat, were quickly silenced.

In the Ruhr the KPD fairly brimmed with optimism through the first two years of the Third Reich. In report after report, instructors and local leaders identified growing antifascist sentiment among workers and increasing sympathy for the KPD.[22] The only problem was the party's insufficient organizational strength. Implicitly, better party organization would lead almost automatically to a mass uprising against the Nazis. "We are most definitely the victors of the future!" the Ruhr KPD proclaimed at the end of 1933, and went on to list a catalog of demands centered on proletarian democracy and soviets.[23] It would be a long road to the popular front.

Resistance

Within Germany communists numbering in the tens of thousands pursued active resistance in the 1930s despite the continual rounds of arrests by the Gestapo.[24] Virtually all the activists had been party members before 1933.[25] Their personal profiles conformed to that of the Weimar KPD—male workers, many of whom were skilled or semiskilled, but who had experienced long periods of unemployment. Most were in the prime working ages of the late twenties to early forties. They comprised the Weimar, even more than the World War I, generation.[26]

[20] Central Committee resolution of May 1933, "Zur Lage und den nächsten Aufgaben," in Hermann Weber, ed., *Der deutsche Kommunismus: Dokumente* (Cologne: Kiepenheuer und Witsch, 1963), 343, 345.

[21] "Für unsere Freunde zu Hause," 18 August 1933, SAPMO-BA, ZPA I/6/3/96/22, presumably a clandestine communiqué from an unidentified Politburo member. It was not received in Moscow until December 1933. For similar examples, see "Bericht von Halle," 14 July 1933, SAPMO-BA, ZPA I/3/11/58/12, and Detlev J. K. Peukert, *Die KPD im Widerstand: Verfolgung und Untergrundarbeit an Rhein und Ruhr, 1933 bis 1945* (Wuppertal: Peter Hammer, 1980), 113–14.

[22] See various reports in SAPMO-BA, ZPA I/3/18–19/68. For one example, see "Ruhrgebiet," [early 1934], SAPMO-BA, ZPA I/3/18–19/68/21, 25.

[23] "Arbeitsplan für Januar und Februar," [December 1933], SAPMO-BA, ZPA I/3/18–19/68/9–15.

[24] The figure is from Duhnke, *KPD*, 224. Peukert, *KPD im Widerstand*, 166, estimates some ten to twenty thousand participants in the communist resistance in the Rhein-Ruhr region in the early 1930s.

[25] "All the [functionaries in the Ruhr district] are older comrades," wrote one instructor. "Bericht von Kurt (mündlich) am 30.11.1935," SAPMO-BA, ZPA I/3/18–19/68/126.

[26] See Peukert's analysis based on the records of arrested communist resisters: *KPD im Widerstand*, 171–75.

What did communist resisters do?[27] First and foremost, they sought to maintain the party organization and distribute anti-Nazi literature—*Rote Fahne*, local and regional newspapers, brochures, and leaflets.[28] Communists inside Germany "hungered" for written materials, as one instructor put it.[29] Until 1935, most of the literature was printed in Germany, and resisters spent thousands of hours procuring the basic supplies of ink, paper, and printing machinery. Increasingly, though, party members had to rely on materials printed over the border and smuggled into Germany by couriers—a procedure more efficient and a bit safer, but one which also broke the close ties that had existed between communities and regional and local papers. German communists were aided by Belgian and Dutch stevedores, who smuggled literature along the North Sea and Rhine shipping routes, and by railroad employees who performed similar tasks along their lines.[30]

Amid the severe repression exercised by the Nazis and the communists' own lack of preparation for underground work, it is almost astounding how much literature communists were able to print and distribute. Virtually every local organization managed in the early years of the regime to put out some sort of semiregular newspaper or brochure. In mid-1934, communists in Weissenfels printed and distributed one thousand copies of their own newspaper.[31] In the Halle-Merseburg district, the leadership put out a clandestine edition of the district newspaper, *Klassenkampf*, and over twenty thousand copies of various leaflets in the summer of 1934.[32] The *Westdeutsche Kampfblätter* lasted into the late 1930s and provided its readers with news of illicit anti-Nazi activities. Thousands of leaflets were printed on the reverse side of copied advertisements for Leitz cameras or cigarette brands.[33]

Communists also held secret demonstrations on May Day and painted anti-Nazi slogans on railroad stations and billboards. In Eilenburg red flags with the hammer and sickle were placed on the two highest buildings for May Day.[34] In Essen communists painted on the train station, "May 1 lives! RED FRONT!" A few enterprising souls ran up Soviet flags on the smokestacks of factories and mines.[35] Communists in the workplace helped foster short, wildcat strikes,

[27] In general, see Duhnke, *KPD*; Peukert, *KPD im Widerstand*; Beatrix Herlemann, *Die Emigration als Kampfposten: Die Anleitung des kommunistischen Widerstandes in Deutschland aus Frankreich, Belgien und den Niederlanden* (Königstein im Taunus: Anton Hain, 1982); Klaus Mammach, *Widerstand 1933–1939: Geschichte des deutschen antifaschistischen Widerstandsbewegung im Inland und in der Emigration* (Berlin: Akademie, 1984); and Allan Merson, *Communist Resistance in Nazi Germany* (London: Lawrence and Wishart, 1985).

[28] Peukert, *KPD im Widerstand*, 175–90.

[29] "Bericht von Kurt (mündlich) am 30.11.1935," SAPMO-BA, ZPA I/3/18–19/68/126.

[30] Peukert, *KPD im Widerstand*, 260.

[31] "Bericht der BL Halle-Merseburg," 16 July 1934, SAPMO-BA, ZPA I/3/11/58/60.

[32] "Bericht von der BL-Halle, gegeben Anfang August 1934," SAPMO-BA, ZPA I/3/11/58/65; [untitled report], Bezirk 11, 28 August 1934, SAPMO-BA, ZPA I/3/11/58/80.

[33] Examples in Pikarski and Uebel, *Antifaschistischer Widerstandskampf*.

[34] "Bericht über die Bezirke Mitte geg. am 19. Mai 1934," SAPMO-BA, ZPA I/3/11/58/34.

[35] [Report], 31 May 1934, SAPMO-BA, ZPA I/3/18–19/68/58. On Essen, see also Hans-Joseph Steinberg, *Widerstand und Verfolgung in Essen 1933–1945* (Hannover: Verlag für Literatur und Zeitgeschehen, 1969).

which, as mentioned, became more prevalent in the late 1930s. A few engaged in sabotage, and others channeled vital military information to the Soviet Union. Usually under watch by the Gestapo, they had to act with extreme care. Many kept up loose circles of associations in which they discussed politics and shared news reports listened to clandestinely on the radio. They fell back on the remnants of the working-class and party culture that could exist in the corners of bars and living rooms, but without any wider entrance into the public sphere.

For most communists who remained at large in Germany, these conversations among small circles of friends became the prevailing form of activity.[36] Through these endeavors communists sought to maintain an alternative political culture that could resurface with the defeat of the Third Reich, but only with difficulty can such actions be labeled resistance. Other communists did try to maintain their local party organizations in the face of the greatest adversity, conscious that they were preserving a long tradition of working-class autonomy and self-organization. One instructor report from Halle commented on a sixty-four-year-old financial secretary, who with "proletarian pride" carefully and clandestinely maintained the accounts of the local organization. He was overjoyed that the Central Committee demonstrated interest in his activities however minimal the amount of money he collected.[37] He was one of some 767 members that the Halle-Merseburg district could still count in the summer of 1934 despite repeated arrests, murders, and tortures—three hundred of them in Zeitz alone, a smaller industrial town in the district with a long history of labor organization.[38]

Thousands of communists went into exile, in the 1930s primarily to France, Czechoslovakia, Holland, and Belgium, along with the Soviet Union. With the exception of those in the Soviet Union, most lived illegally and were supported, though meagerly, by the KPD, fellow communist parties, and the Comintern front organization, International Workers Aid. They served as couriers, smuggling people and information in and out of Germany, and engaged in anti-Nazi demonstrations abroad. They wrote and distributed literature. But the hardships and isolation of exile preyed upon them. The outbreak of the Spanish Civil War gave them the opportunity to struggle more actively against the Nazi regime and international fascism. Around three thousand Germans joined the International Brigades, one-sixth of all foreign combatants on the Republican side.[39] About half of the Germans died in Spain; many who survived were interned in southern France, where the Gestapo found them in 1940 and shipped them to concentration camps in Germany. Many of the Comintern operatives sent to Spain were also KPD members, including, notably, Politburo member Franz Dahlem, the

[36] Peukert, *KPD im Widerstand*, 267–68.

[37] [Fragment of a report, 1934], SAPMO-BA, ZPA I/3/11/58/75.

[38] [Untitled report], Bezirk 11, 28 August 1934, SAPMO-BA, ZPA I/3/11/58/79.

[39] Figures in Duhnke, *KPD*, 267. See especially Patrik von zur Mühlen, *Spanien war ihre Hoffnung: Die deutsche Linke im spanischen Bürgerkrieg* (Berlin: J. H. W. Dietz Nachf., 1985), and from the heroic perspective, but with many interesting documents and personal testimonies, Willi Bredel, *Spanienkrieg*, 2 vols. (Berlin: Aufbau-Verlag, 1977).

chief political commissar of the International Brigades, and Erich Mielke, later the long-term Minister for State Security in the DDR.[40]

Repression

The KPD managed to keep intact through the first two years of the Third Reich. But internal party reports, despite a tenor of optimism, indicate just how fragile the organization had become as a result of unending series of arrests and tortures and the widespread use of informants.[41] One illness or one arrest and the contacts between the exiled leadership and local groups were gone. A typical report from Halle-Merseburg in the summer of 1934 began:

> DEAR FRIENDS!
>
> You will already have been informed by the chief advisor that in Halle the Gestapo once again found its way to the party functionary corps. As a result, the previous leading man, friend H., was murdered by the fascist executioners. According to reliable reports, with him 150 to 180 friends of our organization have been arrested.[42]

His murder disrupted everything—contacts to other party members, access to printing machinery and safe houses, the entire leadership of the district.

The repression also rendered extremely fragile the finances of district organizations and the flow of information. Halle-Merseburg, one of the KPD's most important districts, could only support two functionaries for the entire region, while instructors reported in the spring of 1934 that cadres had hardly any knowledge of the recent Central Committee resolutions.[43] Almost all the party's ancillary cultural and social organizations—always crucial elements of the labor movement—had been obliterated. One party instructor grasped hopefully at the reestablishment of contacts in the Leuna works, "where everything had been destroyed," but this amounted to all of two individuals in a workforce of about fifteen thousand.[44]

The Halle-Merseburg KPD nonetheless managed to rebuild its organization.[45] Over the course of a few months in mid-1934, it still proved able to distribute thousands of leaflets, three issues of *Rote Fahne* with one thousand copies each, two thousand copies of *Inprekorr*, and forty of *Die Internationale*. But in the autumn of 1934 the Gestapo again carried out arrests and executions of leading

[40] Other later DDR notables who were in Spain included Hermann Matern, Heinrich Rau, Wilhelm Zaisser, and Willi Bredel.

[41] See the documents in SAPMO-BA, ZPA I/3/11/18–19/68 and I/3/11/58.

[42] "Bericht der BL Halle-Merseburg," 16 July 1934, SAPMO-BA, ZPA I/3/11/58/59.

[43] "Bericht von 11/13," [March and April 1934], SAPMO-BA, ZPA I/3/11/58/67, 68.

[44] "Aus der Aussprache mit dem Berater von 8. bis 13. amd 18.8.33," 19 August 1933, SAPMO-BA, ZPA I/3/11/58/13–14.

[45] The following is based on [Report, October or November 1934]; "Bericht über Bezirk Halle-Merseburg," 21 November 1934; "Bericht über die Vorgänge seit dem 26.1.35 in J. 9," [n.d.]; "Bericht über die Lage im Bezirk Halle-Merseburg Ende Januar 1935," [n.d.]; "Betr. Lage in Halle-Merseburg in der Zeit vom 1.1.–10.4.1935," 20 April 1935; "Bericht über die Lage im Bezirk Halle Merseburg," [n.d.], SAPMO-BA, ZPA I/3/11/58/96–105, 109–16.

communists in Halle and the surrounding region, weakening the organization so painstakingly revived.

In early 1935 the final blow struck the Halle-Merseburg KPD. At the end of January the district leadership gathered for a meeting. The Gestapo, informed beforehand by a well-placed spy, a chief courier by the name of Luise Schröder, raided the meeting and arrested three key individuals—the district political and organizational secretaries and the regional secretary for all of central Germany—along with three others and a bystander who commented too loudly, "The pigs should finally leave the proletariat in peace." Under torture, the communist leaders revealed the names of other resisters. The party's entire technical apparatus in Halle-Merseburg—both personnel and hardware, including typewriters, duplicating machines, and bicycles—was destroyed. The Nazis arrested couriers, contact persons with other party organizations, and the financial secretary, along with other functionaries. The number arrested in Halle climbed to one hundred and fifty. Through Schröder's intimate knowledge of the party organization and the extraction of additional information by torture, the arrests cascaded through the region. About two hundred people were arrested in the Weissenfels district, two hundred and thirty in Wittenberg-Piesteritz, and eighty in Zeitz. One comrade managed to escape the Gestapo net only by staying on the run. He requested higher party officials to send him to the Soviet Union.

By the time an instructor was able to return to the Halle-Merseburg region in the summer of 1935, he found the entire organization destroyed. The few contacts he was able to meet were distrustful and most unwilling to engage in any kind of activism—despite widespread popular unrest. "The mood of those who remained [that is, were not arrested] or have been released is most depressed in relation to the question of reviving [party] work," he wrote.[46]

Matters were no better in the Ruhr and other areas of western Germany.[47] The party lost thousands of cadres to Nazi prisons and concentration camps, where many were severely beaten and systematically tortured. The arrests disrupted contacts, worsened the already strapped financial situation of district organizations, and intensified the wariness and suspicion of the remaining cadres. One report at the end of May 1934 began, "The situation is . . . very bad, everyone has been arrested." No money was available to support functionaries or instructors sent in from abroad because the Nazis had destroyed the district's literature committee, which had earned money for the organization from the clandestine sale of newspapers and brochures. At Krupp, with a workforce about twice the size of Leuna's, ten "firm contacts" were touted as a major achievement. By the end of 1935, however, even those contacts were gone.

By mid-1935 most reports described party members as depressed and demoralized by the waves of arrests. The knowledge that many arrests were the work

[46] "Bericht Mitteldeutschland," 2 September 1935, SAPMO-BA, ZPA I/3/11/58/122.

[47] The following is based on [Report], "Ruhrgebiet," [spring 1934]; [Report], 31 May 1934; [Report, spring 1935]; "Betr. der Lage der Bezirke Ruhr und Mittelrhein," 4 September 1935; "Bericht von Kurt (mündlich) am 30. 11. 1935;" "Betr.: Ruhrgebiet," 26 November 1935; "Bericht von Kurt/mündlich/am 30.11.1935," SAPMO-BA, ZPA I/3/18–19/68/22, 56, 90, 106, 128, 130, 150.

of spies within their own ranks or of information provided by comrades under torture only heightened the sense of fear and insecurity. Those who had been released after brief prison terms had been let out first with efforts to get them to act as spies, then with stern warnings that with the slightest sign of activity for the KPD they would be arrested again. They were extremely hesitant to make contacts with instructors sent into Germany by the border secretaries. Even when an individual agreed to establish contact, he often refused—despite entreaties—to connect the instructor with anyone else. "They don't trust the [KPD's] agents from abroad," the instructor wrote, "and prefer to work with people from their own ranks." Essen he described as "surrounded by a Chinese Wall," because comrades were loathe to talk to him.[48]

Clearly, Gestapo repression not only decimated the KPD organization, but also turned what remained of the party in on itself. The Third Reich accelerated, made still more drastic, the trend already evident in the Weimar Republic, whereby the ties between mass and party activism had become more tenuous. In Weimar, communist activism became more party-specific and had largely failed to serve as the vanguard of a broad-scale public movement. By the mid-1930s the space of activism had been narrowed so drastically that it had become a comrade's kitchen or a small corner of a bar where a few communists would gather and talk. To the eternal lament of the exiled leadership and the instructors sent in by them, party activism had been reduced to talks among like-minded comrades. There were no new recruits, little effort to engage with social democratic or Christian workers. Communists, wrote one instructor, were proud of their party affiliation and their antifascist stand, but did nothing about it. "The greatest error, " he wrote, "is still that instead of attempting to establish a substantial mass base, [party members] continually seek out old former comrades." Duisburg still had a large group of communists, but "in fact they do nothing more than collect membership fees. They are proud of their identification with the party . . . but they don't engage in the essential tasks. The organization itself is the essential goal. . . . They are nothing more than a cashiers' club."[49]

The climate of fear and distrust extended toward social democrats, and only worsened the already slim possibilities for political collaboration. Many communists refused to engage in actions with social democrats because, as one instructor related, they had no assurances that the SPD people would not be Gestapo spies. "Who knows whether the rascals [*Kerle*] are genuine?" he reported one party leader asking.[50] For their part, Gestapo agents, writing in 1937, asserted triumphantly about the KPD, "one can no longer speak at all of an organization in its old form."[51] The vicious repression exercised by the Third Reich had taken its toll.

48 "Bericht von Kurt (mündlich) am 30. 11. 1935," SAPMO-BA, ZPA I/3/18–19/68/126–27. See also "Bericht Rolf am 29.XI.1935," SAPMO-BA, ZPA I/3/18–19/68/145.

49 "Bericht von Leo. 29.1.1935," SAPMO-BA, ZPA I/3/18–19/68/141–42. See also "Bericht Rolf am 29.XI.1935," SAPMO-BA, ZPA I/3/18–19/68/144–45.

50 "Bericht von Leo. 29.11.1935," SAPMO-BA, ZPA I/3/18–19/68/139.

51 "Lagebericht der Gestapo," 1937, in Weber, *Deutscher Kommunismus*, 408.

Strategy

Around mid-1934, some communists began to realize that the party's strategy had failed. Hitler's purge of the SA at the end of June 1934 demonstrated a masterful consolidation of power. The Saarland elections in January 1935, in which 90.8 percent of the population voted for unification with Germany despite an immense propaganda effort by the KPD, provided further evidence of the popularity of the NSDAP and the isolation of the KPD.[52] Some functionaries, swayed by their revolutionary imaginations, could still write that the KPD "has underestimated the [political] maturity of the workers" and was more restrained in exercising its influence than warranted.[53] But more typical was the increasingly sober tone sounded in most internal KPD reports on both the popular mood and the situation of the party. Slowly, inconsistently, inchoately, the longing for a new strategy emerged, a sentiment spurred along by developments within the Comintern hierarchy and the French Communist Party.[54]

The united and popular fronts constituted the crux of the new strategy. "United fronts" meant agreements and coalitions with social democrats, trade unionists, and other working-class representatives. They were intended to promote the immediate "class" interests of the proletariat, hence revolved around demands for higher wages, price controls on essential goods, and labor representation in the councils of government.

United fronts had a lineage that stretched back to 1921; popular fronts constituted the real innovation of the 1930s.[55] They signified an extension of labor movement alliances to the "bourgeoisie"—liberals, social reformers, artists and writers, and religious groups. Popular front programs revolved around demands for social reform, peace, and democratic politics—hardly the stuff of communist revolution. Antifascism served as the glue that made imaginable alliances among these very disparate groups.

On the international level, the popular front originated in the belated recognition that the KPD had suffered an immense defeat, resulting in the greatly enhanced danger of German aggression against the Soviet Union. A number of Comintern strategists, including Dimitri Manuilsky, Palmiro Togliatti, and Georgi Dimitrov, spearheaded the reconsideration of communist tactics, which paralleled Soviet efforts to reach collective security agreements with the western powers. At a roughly comparable moment, the French Communist Party,

[52] See the account in Herlemann, *Emigration als Kampfposten*, 52–65.

[53] "Auszüge aus Politischen Bericht von Westen für die Zeit von Sept. bis Nov. 1934," [late 1934], SAPMO-BA, ZPA I/3/18–19/68/83.

[54] This is one of the major arguments of Peukert, *KPD im Widerstand*, namely, that the transition to a new strategy in 1935 was not only dictated by the Comintern. Herlemann, in contrast, argues that none of the leading figures moved out of their own initiative to the new policy, and that all of them continued to express at least in part the prevailing ultraleftist positions. Herlemann, *Emigration als Kampfposten*, 50–51.

[55] Amid a very substantial literature on the popular fronts, see especially E. H. Carr, *Twilight of the Comintern, 1930–1935* (New York: Pantheon, 1982), and Paolo Spriano, *Storia del Partito comunista italiano*, vol. 3: *I fronti popolari, Stalin, la guerra* (Turin: Einaudi, 1970).

prompted by popular demands for working-class unity against a perceived internal fascist threat, began its own moves toward a broad antifascist alliance.

The KPD was slow to follow. Some communists and social democrats at the local level engaged in joint appeals against the Nazis, acted in defense of the trade unions, and sought to form common means of protection against Nazi repression. At the top level, open political conflict erupted. Ernst Thälmann had been arrested in March 1933, so he was largely out of the picture. (He would languish in prisons and concentration camps until the Nazis executed him in 1944.) By the end of 1933, most of the other leaders had gone permanently into exile and shuttled between Paris, Prague, and Moscow. The Politburo majority held to the intransigent politics of the "third period" and the belief that the Third Reich would soon be consumed by a communist-led revolution. As late as mid-1934, this "left majority"—Hermann Schubert, Fritz Schulte, Franz Dahlem, and Wilhelm Florin—demanded that the KPD in Hesse-Frankfurt break off a united front agreement with the SPD.[56] In opposition, Wilhelm Pieck and Walter Ulbricht, the latter especially attentive to shifts in Comintern attitudes, began to edge away from the complete denunciation of social democracy, and they were soon joined by Dahlem and Paul Merker. Under their influence, the KPD in the second half of 1934 issued some statements replete with contradictions, but notable for at last identifying National Socialism and not the SPD as the major enemy and for raising the possibility of a united front. KPD representatives began to meet with social democrats, though still not with the exiled SPD Executive (Sozialdemokratische Partei Deutschlands/Exilvorstand, or Sopade) in Prague. Left-wing social democratic groups and KPD split-offs—both among the most active in the underground in Germany—complicated the discussions immensely, but the root problem remained the mutual enmity of the KPD and SPD.

Ultimately, only massive pressure from the Comintern in late 1934 and early 1935 enabled the Pieck-Ulbricht group to take over the leadership of the party.[57] Both were communists of long standing.[58] Pieck had been closely associated with Luxemburg and the Spartacus League and had participated in the founding congress of the KPD. Ulbricht, like Pieck active in the pre–World War I SPD, quickly joined the KPD. Both made their careers on their organizational abilities, and they served the KPD and the Comintern in numerous capacities throughout the 1920s and early 1930s. They were, in short, typical functionaries and well suited to a party increasingly under Soviet domination. The ECCI confirmed their position at a high-level meeting in January 1935 that also condemned the previous KPD line as "sectarian" and called for the establishment of a united front with all social democratic groups, including Sopade, and a broad antifascist pop-

[56] Dietrich Staritz, *Sozialismus in einem halben Lande: Zur Programmatik und Politik der KPD/SED in der Phase der antifaschistisch-demokratischen Umwälzung in der DDR* (Berlin: Klaus Wagenbach, 1976), 43.

[57] See Duhnke, *KPD*, 137–50.

[58] See the biographical sketches in Hermann Weber, *Die Wandlung des deutschen Kommunismus: Die Stalinisierung der KPD* (Frankfurt am Main: Europäische Verlagsanstalt, 1969), 2:245–47, 326–27.

ular front. The ECCI also called for the reestablishment in Germany of free trade unions, a notable departure from the long-standing KPD condemnation of the "reformist" unions.

A flurry of activity ensued. The KPD sent letters to Sopade and other groups requesting common action against the Nazi regime. Most importantly, the Comintern convened its long-delayed Seventh Congress in the summer of 1935. With great fanfare, the popular front became the official strategy of international communism, enabling most European communist parties to ride a wave of popular antifascist sentiment. A few weeks later the KPD leadership convened outside of Moscow for a conference. Called publicly the "Brussels" conference in order to disguise the whereabouts of KPD officials, the meeting affirmed the strategy of the popular front and the Pieck-Ulbricht leadership. The KPD abandoned much of the intransigent language of Weimar communism. There was little talk of a "Soviet Germany" or the dictatorship of the proletariat. The final resolution called for a struggle for "all democratic rights and freedoms" and peace and for the revival of the spirit of 1848—not 1917.[59]

The conference also called for far-reaching organizational changes. Belatedly and under strong pressure from functionaries active in the underground, the leadership recognized that efforts to maintain a centralized party organization had only facilitated the Gestapo's penetration of the party.[60] In sharp contrast to all its previous efforts, the KPD adopted a decentralized structure in which border secretaries (the *Abschnittsleitungen*) in Prague, Brussels, Amsterdam, Copenhagen, Zurich, and Forbach (Saar) would maintain contact with small groups of activists in Germany.[61] Following the positions of the Seventh Congress, the KPD also adopted the tactic of the "Trojan horse": communists should work within Nazi organizations to recruit support and undermine the regime. The German Labor Front was the main target of this tactic, but party leaders imagined surreptitious communists active even in the SA and SS.

At long last, and far behind the French, Italian, and Spanish parties, the KPD had joined the most important strategic innovation of the international communist movement. Yet the KPD's implementation of popular front politics can only be described as half-hearted and contradictory.[62] To be sure, many German

59 "Der neue Weg zum gemeinsamen Kampf aller Werktätigen für den Sturz der Hitlerdiktatur: Resolution der 'Brüsseler' Parteikonferenz der KPD (Oktober 1935)," in Weber, *Deutscher Kommunismus*, 328–29. See also the texts in Klaus Mammach, ed., *Die Brüsseler Konferenz der KPD (3.–15. Oktober 1935)* (Berlin: Dietz, 1975), and the secondary account in Arnold Sywottek, *Deutsche Volksdemokratie: Studien zur politischen Konzeption der KPD 1935–1946* (Düsseldorf: Bertelsmann Universitätsverlag, 1971), 55–61.

60 See Beatrix Herlemann, "Communist Resistance between Comintern Direction and Nazi Terror," in *Between Reform and Revolution: Studies in German Socialism and Communism from 1840 to 1990*, ed. David E. Barclay and Eric D. Weitz (Providence: Berghahn, forthcoming), who states that the protocol published by Mammach in the DDR, *Brüsselere Konferenz*, was heavily edited and failed to reveal the depth of rank-and-file anger at the leadership.

61 See especially Herlemann, *Emigration als Kampfposten*.

62 Peukert, *KPD im Widerstand*, 288–95 and passim, wavers a great deal in his assessment of the KPD's trajectory in the 1930s. In a number of places he argues that the party underwent a genuine

communists grasped hopefully at the political potential offered by a broad anti-Nazi alliance. In an important 1936 article, Pieck abandoned talk of a dictatorship of the proletariat and Soviet power as immediate goals of the KPD. For the immediate future, he pledged the KPD's support for the establishment of a democratic republic.[63] Anton Ackermann, newly elevated to the party leadership in the mid-1930s and later to play a leading role promoting the moderate position, leveled in 1937 a sharp critique against the policies of the pre-1933 KPD and introduced into the German party the critical, innovative term, "democracy of a new type."[64] Leaflets distributed within Germany no longer expressed the exclusive language of class, but called for antifascist unity, freedom of conscience, and a democratic Germany, and for opposition to the "insanity of the sterilization, castration, and race laws."[65] Germans, according to one leaflet mailed from England, had only one enemy, Hitler. It made no difference if one were a worker, salesman, or public employee, a social democrat, member of the Confessional Church, communist, or Catholic—all could come together in defense of peace and against the Nazis. The popular front, the leaflet continued, wants simply to govern for, not against, the people in a democratic state marked by freely elected representatives and individual rights.[66]

Other evidence, however, indicates that the KPD approached the popular front with a great deal of hesitation and, in some instances, sought actively to undermine it. Even the resolutions of the Brussels conference continued to malign the "reactionary" segment of the SPD, although the KPD now generously consigned this group to a small minority of social democracy.[67] Raising the possibility of a unified labor party, the KPD attached conditions reminiscent of its intransigent Weimar politics. Such a party could be formed only if its partisans recognized the "necessity of the revolutionary overthrow of the bourgeoisie and the creation of a dictatorship of the proletariat in the form of soviets."[68] Not long after the Brussels conference, Politburo member Wilhelm Florin claimed that the SPD "bore the historic guilt for the victory of fascism."[69] Such statements were not likely to raise confidence among social democrats and others that the KPD had truly committed itself to the popular front movement.

In fact, the KPD never did forge a united or a popular front, unlike virtually

---

transformation in favor of the popular front, but elsewhere he emphasizes the hesitancies and inconsistencies in the KPD's politics. I incline more toward the latter view. See also Sywottek, *Deutsche Volksdemokratie*.

[63] Duhnke, *KPD*, 239–41, and Sywottek, *Deutsche Volksdemokratie*, 71–84.

[64] Anton Ackermann, "Die Volksfront und die demokratische Volksrepublik," *Die Internationale* 3/4 (1937): 36–45.

[65] KPD Gebietsleitung Westen, "Kampfmai 1936," April 1936, in Pikarski and Uebel, *Antifaschistischer Widerstandskampf*, doc. 65.

[66] "An alle deutschen Freunde!" early 1939, in Pikarski and Uebel, *Antifaschistischer Widerstandskampf*, doc. 122. The leaflet was mailed from England to names arbitrarily taken out of phone books.

[67] "Der neue Weg zum gemeinsamen Kampf," in Weber, *Deutscher Kommunismus*, 325.

[68] Quoted in Günter Benser, *Die KPD im Jahre der Befreiung* (Berlin: Dietz, 1985), 12–13.

[69] Quoted in Duhnke, *KPD*, 168.

every other European communist party.[70] In November 1935 Ulbricht and Dahlem finally met with Sopade representatives Friedrich Stampfer and Hans Vogel at the SPD's exile headquarters in Prague. The negotiations led only to a few common anti-Nazi proclamations, but no working agreement. And this was, in fact, the one and only formal meeting between top SPD and KPD representatives in the 1930s.[71] Efforts in Paris to forge a popular front committee never got beyond the issuance of a few proclamations and appeals and endless, wearying negotiations.[72] The same was true of the other exile centers in Holland and Belgium. Willi Münzenberg, the KPD's propaganda genius, won the support of intellectuals and artists for all sorts of antifascist pronouncements and meetings, but he operated under Comintern rather than KPD auspices.[73] For its part, the exiled SPD leadership evinced no interest whatsoever in collaboration with the KPD.[74] On the communist side, Walter Ulbricht, the KPD point man in Paris, acted in kind and played the key role in scuttling efforts at political collaboration. Ulbricht managed to antagonize virtually every noncommunist he encountered. Heinrich Mann, the renowned author and a key figure in all the popular front efforts, felt compelled to write Pieck with a series of complaints about Ulbricht. Pieck's belated reply was opaque.

The situation within Germany was similarly ambiguous.[75] KPD reports from Halle-Merseburg and the Ruhr depicted good contacts with social democrats and even some recruitment from the SPD ranks. But KPD instructors also reported continually that members were hostile to the very idea of collaboration with social democrats.[76] In mid-1934, some six to seven thousand people in Essen marched to the gravesite of a communist who had died in Nazi prison. An SPD man asked a communist work colleague why he had not informed him of the funeral, since he would have gone "to pay his last respects to the antifascist fighter who had died in detention." The communist, a leading functionary in Essen, replied "such people

[70] In general on the KPD and the popular front, see Duhnke, *KPD*, 231–97; Sywottek, *Deutsche Volksdemokratie*; Ursula Langkau-Alex, *Volksfront für Deutschland?* vol. 1 (Frankfurt am Main: Syndikat, 1977); and Herlemann, *Emigration als Kampfposten*, 124–29.

[71] Duhnke, *KPD*, 175.

[72] Even Politburo member Franz Dahlem professed dismay at the lack of progress toward a popular front when he arrived in Paris from Spain. See idem, *Am Vorabend des Zweiten Weltkrieges, 1938 bis August 1939: Erinnerungen*, vol. 1 (Berlin: Dietz, 1977), 68.

[73] Duhnke, *KPD*, 256–60. Helmut Gruber, "Willi Münzenberg's German Communist Propaganda Empire 1921–1933," *JMH* 38:3 (1966): 278–97, covers the earlier part of Münzenberg's career.

[74] For a very insightful analysis of social democratic politics that sees Sopade as quite isolated and at odds with rank-and-file sentiment, see Gerd-Rainer Horn, "The Reorientation of the European Left, 1933–1936" (Ph.D. diss., University of Michigan, 1992), and "Pro-Unity Sentiments in Underground Social Democracy, 1933–1936," in *Between Reform and Revolution*, ed. Barclay and Weitz.

[75] Peukert's conclusion as well in *KPD im Widerstand*, 244, though in other places he tends to give a more positive reading. Herlemann, *Emigration als Kampfposten*, 121–23, argues that social democrats at the base level were no more ready than the Sopade to engage in common actions with the KPD. But compare Horn, "Reorientation."

[76] For example, "Bericht 9u III," [summer 1934]; "Auszüge aus Politischen Bericht von Westen für die Zeit von Sept. bis Nov. 1934," [late 1934]; [Report, spring 1935]; SAPMO-BA, ZPA I/3/18–19/68/64–65, 85, 90.

as [the social democrat], against whom the deceased had always fought, he had simply not invited, because Herbert [the deceased] would most definitely not have wanted to see them at his grave." The communist, in relating the incident, expressed his joy at the "flabbergasted expression of the SPD man."[77]

The official proclamation of the popular front did little to change such attitudes. Collaboration between the two parties remained sporadic and particularly susceptible to discovery and repression by the Gestapo. Only occasionally did cooperation gel into something substantial, such as the organization of a miners union committee among exiled communists and social democrats in France, Belgium, and Holland, which had fairly extensive contacts in the Rhein-Ruhr region.[78] But no other serious efforts at united or popular fronts developed in Rheinland and Westphalia after 1936.[79] In Zeitz in the Halle-Merseburg region, where scores of SPD people went over to the KPD, members saw no reason to agitate among the remaining social democrats. Party instructors lamented that they acted as if the SPD no longer existed in the area, a complaint also aired by instructors in the Ruhr.[80] Even when communists engaged in discussions with social democrats, they talked endlessly and did nothing, according to the complaints of one party functionary in the Ruhr.[81] And the tactic of the "Trojan horse" inspired only confusion and dismay, and absolute hostility from social democrats. For many communists in Germany, contacts with comrades, even in the small circles to which they had been reduced, were vital for their moral and material survival. Identification as a National Socialist was anathema, a violation of everything for which they had suffered so severely.[82] In any case, many argued that no one would believe them if they joined Nazi organizations because their communist pasts were widely known.[83]

Half a year after the Seventh Congress, an instructor noted that the comrades were extremely cautious in their approach to the popular front decisions, expressing views like "We'll have to see whether they can be carried out," or "At the moment we're not so far along the way."[84] Many communists in Germany knew little of the political developments on the outside, or were confused by the new strategy.[85] As late as 1939, one party instructor, operating out of Amsterdam, wrote of a functionary of the Rhein-Ruhr region, "He knows absolutely nothing about the politics that we are pursuing today. He still lives in 1933."[86]

Clearly, the weight of the Weimar past hung heavily on both communists and

[77] "Bericht 9u III," [summer 1934], SAPMO-BA, ZPA I/3/18–19/68/65.

[78] Detlev J. K. Peukert and Frank Bajohr, *Spuren des Widerstands: Die Bergarbeiterbewegung im Dritten Reich und im Exil* (Munich: Beck, 1987).

[79] Peukert, *KPD im Widerstand*, 306.

[80] "Bericht über Bezirk Halle-Merseburg," 21 November 1934, SAPMO-BA, ZPA I/3/11/58/100–101; [Report], 8 June 1934, SAPMO-BA, ZPA I/3/18–19/68/50–52.

[81] [Report, early 1935?], SAPMO-BA, ZPA I/3/18–19/68/89.

[82] Peukert, *KPD im Widerstand*, 321–22; Herlemann, "Communist Resistance."

[83] "Bericht von Leo. 29.11.1935," SAPMO-BA, ZPA I/3/18–19/68/136.

[84] Ibid., 140.

[85] Ibid., 142.

[86] Quoted in Peukert, *KPD im Widerstand*, 251.

social democrats. The KPD's popular front efforts met a stone wall of silence from Sopade, ever distrustful of its communist rivals. The tactic of the "Trojan horse" ran into unrelenting opposition from the SPD, both within and outside Germany. For its part the KPD, at both the leadership and base levels, proved largely unable to surmount the hostility toward the SPD that had been learned at the ideological knees of Luxemburg and Lenin and in active struggle against the SPD-led police forces and trade unions of the Weimar Republic. Moreover, the continued persecution and isolation endured by communists, the bitter experiences of repression and exile, fostered not flexibility, but a desperate desire to hold on to one of the few certainties that remained—communist politics as learned in Weimar. As Detlev Peukert rightly argues, many communists active in the resistance displayed a kind of "conservative-sectarian mistrust" toward the political maneuverings of their own leadership.[87] It was a psychology hardly conducive to the innovation of the popular front.

Moreover, as Peukert also argues, the severities of Nazi repression meant that neither the communist nor the social democratic leadership had to face a popular movement in favor of unity. And German communists lacked the practical experience with coalitions that might have created more fertile soil for the popular front. As much as communist parties were subject to direction from Moscow, in some fashion they also responded to popular sentiment at the base—a fate from which Ulbricht and Pieck, as well as Sopade, were spared by National Socialism.

In the Soviet Whirlwind

Communist efforts at creating popular fronts faced another major obstacle—the onset of the Soviet terror in 1936. The full, social dimension of the terror was not yet known, but the show trials and the executions of leading Bolsheviks gave many social democrats and liberals great pause. Unsurprisingly, the KPD, by now dependent upon the Soviet Union for its very survival, announced its full support for the executions of the "bandits, agents, and provocateurs" and its profound respect for the "genial and beloved leader of the Soviet people and the working people of all countries, comrade Stalin."[88]

The terror did not only affect Soviet citizens and members of the Communist Party of the Soviet Union (CPSU). Its net stretched to include thousands of foreigners, mostly communists, who had found refuge in the Soviet Union and extended abroad to Spain, France, and Mexico. German residents of the Soviet Union, who numbered in the thousands, were among the primary foreign victims and the vast majority were KPD members. The exact number of those caught "in

[87] Ibid., 256–57.

[88] "Resolution des ZK der KPD zu den Konterrevolutionären trotzkistisch-sinowjewistischen Verbrechen gegen die Arbeiterklasse," in Hermann Weber, *"Weiße Flecken" in der Geschichte: Die KPD-Opfer der Stalinschen Säuberungen und ihre Rehabilitierung*, 2d ed. (Frankfurt am Main: isp, 1990), 110–11.

the whirlwind" remains unknown.[89] The most recent, and certainly incomplete, account provides information on over 1,100 Germans who were condemned by the Soviet authorities.[90] Many were executed, including the Politburo members Leo Flieg, Hermann Remmele, Heinz Neumann, Hugo Eberlein, and four others. All had spent years in the communist movement; Eberlein had been one of Rosa Luxemburg's circle and a founding member of the KPD. Other German victims died in the Soviet Gulag or managed to survive its extreme conditions or internal exile to return to the DDR in the 1950s, quite a number only at the end of the decade.[91] As was the case with Soviet citizens, thousands of family members of the convicted, including children, were themselves forced into internal exile or labor camps. Some KPD members survived torture at the hands of agents of the People's Commissariat of Internal Affairs (NKVD), like Bernard Koenen, a leader in the 1920s at Leuna and in the Halle-Merseburg KPD and later a high official in the DDR. Still others, like Margarete Buber-Neumann, endured NKVD prisons to be turned over to the Gestapo in 1940 and then to experience the brutalities of Nazi concentration camps.[92] Hundreds and maybe thousands—the exact figure again is unknown—shared her tragic destiny, many even before the period of the Hitler-Stalin Pact.[93]

Communists within Germany, often unaware even of the popular front decisions, had little information about the terror and certainly no knowledge of its extent. Many, though, already inclined to follow Soviet dictates, were prepared to accept the reports of traitors at hand against whom the most extraordinary measures were required. KPD leaders in Moscow were of course aware of the arrests of their erstwhile comrades. Pieck made some efforts to gain the release of a number of them, as evidence from recently opened archives has demonstrated.[94] There is no documentary record of Ulbricht acting in a similar fashion, and even Pieck's interventions were inconsistent at best. While he defended some German communists, Pieck, Ulbricht, and the rest of the leadership collaborated in the

[89] The term comes from Evgeniia Ginzburg, *Journey into the Whirlwind* (New York: Harcourt, Brace and World, 1967).

[90] *In den Fängen des NKWD: Deutsche Opfer des stalinistischen Terrors in der UdSSR*, ed. Institut für Geschichte der Arbeiterbewegung (Berlin: Dietz, 1991), which uses previously closed KPD archival sources. But the really heroic effort to account for German victims and to expose the SED's long cover-up of the story has been carried out by Hermann Weber. See his *"Weiße Flecken"*. Also informative is David Pike, *German Writers in Soviet Exile, 1933–1945* (Chapel Hill: University of North Carolina Press, 1982).

[91] Susanne Leonhard's memoir, *Gestohlenes Leben: Schicksal einer politischen Emigrantin in der Sowjetunion*, 5th ed. (Herford: Nicolaische Verlagsbuchhandlung, 1968), depicts well the harrowing experience of the Soviet Gulag. She was "fortunate" to be able to return to Berlin in 1948.

[92] Margarete Buber-Neumann, *Als Gefangene bei Stalin und Hitler* (Zurich: Europa, 1949).

[93] Around four thousand Germans were turned over by the Soviets to the German authorities after the Hitler-Stalin Pact, but not all of these were "wanted" by the Gestapo. Weber, *"Weiße Flecken"*, 31, 64, 151, gives a figure of around one thousand in the latter category, Duhnke, *KPD*, five hundred. The most recent account, *In den Fängen des NKWD*, 371, estimates the number as more than 1,200.

[94] A number of Pieck's letters to Comintern officials are published in *ND*, 12 January 1989; *BzG* 31:4 (1989): 488 ff.; and *In den Fängen des NKWD*, 333–43. See also Weber's comments in *"Weiße Flecken"*, 136–38.

persecution of others. At the very least they confirmed the exclusion from the party of hundreds of members, which for those in the Soviet Union amounted to death sentences or long years of internment.[95] Pieck had been in Moscow for too long to venture any kind of bold and probably suicidal action on behalf of all those pursued by the NKVD.

Pieck and Ulbricht's acceptance of the worst excesses of Stalinism indicates the extent to which the German party had become a dependency of the CPSU and its isolation from a social and political base at home. For years factional conflicts had accentuated the authoritarian tendencies in the party. In Soviet exile these conflicts took on a murderous character. Too many of those who survived in leadership positions of the KPD had become accustomed to the notion that political opponents could be dealt with by arbitrary arrest, physical intimidation, and execution. Party members learned to move cautiously and fearfully, ever watchful of shifts in the prevailing political line. The psychology of terror had worked its way into the KPD.

Meanwhile, the KPD's insufficient application of the popular front strategy made it the subject of constant criticism from the Soviet and Comintern leadership, a harbinger of later conflicts between the DDR and the Soviet Union. Once the darling of the Comintern, the KPD had become its bête noire. Year in and year out, the ECCI sharply condemned the "sectarianism" of the KPD and its unwillingness to engage in popular front politics. In the course of the 1930s, as the fears of German aggression against the Soviet Union intensified and the German population appeared mired in passivity, the Comintern criticisms of the KPD became infused with a tone of exasperation and frustration.[96]

The deliberations that began in March 1938, following Franz Dahlem's arrival from Spain via Paris, were typical.[97] They extended over a few months, giving leading members of the ECCI ample opportunity to express their vociferous criticisms of the KPD. The Comintern, fearful of the approaching war, desperately wanted the KPD to raise the level of resistance in Germany and was convinced that party leaders had failed to pursue the popular front vigorously. They demanded greater flexibility from the KPD and a willingness to compromise with political

[95] See the facsimiles of KPD documents in *In den Fängen des NKWD*, 373–78.

[96] This conclusion is drawn from a number of Comintern documents, including an undated and untitled transcription of a meeting of the ECCI with the Politburo of the KPD, SAPMO-BA, ZPA I/6/3/109/3–24; "Resolution über die sektiererischen Fehler der KPD," adopted by Political Secretariat and confirmed by Präsidium [of ECCI] SAPMO-BA, ZPA I/3/110/12–16; and EKKI (Sekretariat Ercoli), "Resolution zu den nächsten Aufgaben der KPD," 17 March 1937, SAPMO-BA, ZPA I/6/3/84/85–95. The attacks on the KPD were often spearheaded by Togliatti, who must have felt sweet revenge for the savaging of his own party and leadership at the hands of German communists, Ulbricht prominent among them, in 1929 at the ECCI's Tenth Plenum.

[97] The following is based on Hermann Wichers, "Zur Anleitung des Widerstands der KPD: Ein Rundschreiben des ZK-Sekretariats an die Abschnittsleitungen vom 29. Juli 1938," *IWK* 26:4 (1990): 526–39, who bases his report on "Chronologische Übersicht über die Behandlung der deutschen Fragen von Februar bis Mai 1938," SAPMO-BA, ZPA I/2/3/20. Wicher states that the documentary evidence largely confirms Dahlem's account in *Am Vorabend*.

allies. Some of the results of the deliberations appeared publicly in a KPD Central Committee resolution of 14 May 1938, which reiterated many of the typical popular front demands, including the establishment of a "democratic republic."

The resolution did not, however, capture the depth and spirit of the Comintern's critique of the German party. An internal communiqué circulated to the border secretaries did, but with an interesting twist. The KPD leadership turned around and laid the blame for "insufficient" work on the lower-level leaders and the cadres. Moreover, the exiled leadership and the ECCI still failed to understand how deeply Nazi ideology had penetrated the working class and the efficiency of the NSDAP's repressive apparatus. The ECCI had called for the transference of the party leadership to Germany, a drastic underestimation of the difficulties involved in maintaining any kind of underground work, let alone party direction, within the Third Reich. So removed was the Central Committee from the situation in Germany that it actually advised the border secretaries to emphasize the Soviet Union and Stalin in their propaganda: "a greater popularization of the Soviet Union and the genial leader of the world proletariat, comrade Stalin, will help show the masses the direct line from our popular front struggle to ever higher forms of democracy and convince them that this is the correct way to reach the socialist goal."[98]

On the Eve of War

The ECCI's critique had little impact. In any case, in the course of 1938 the popular front lost its gleam. The French and Spanish popular fronts deteriorated under the impact of political divisions, the Soviet terror escalated, and the Munich Agreement sounded the death knell for any collective security pact between the Soviet Union and the western democracies. German efforts at creating a popular front in exile had failed, and recriminations flew fast and furiously. In May 1938 the KPD Central Committee, reviving its late Weimar rhetoric, charged that the SPD constituted the main stumbling block to the establishment of a united front. Dahlem claimed that the anti-Soviet pronouncements of some social democratic leaders placed them in the same choir as the fascists.[99] The KPD's intransigent tones were increasingly echoed in Moscow and by other communist parties.

By the time twenty-two KPD leaders gathered outside Paris at the end of January 1939 for the so-called Bern conference, the popular front was all but dead and the KPD a shell of its former existence.[100] Only two delegates at the conference were in direct contact with communists in Germany—as opposed to the 1935 Brussels conference, when two-thirds of the representatives had imme-

[98] Quoted in Wichers, "Zur Anleitung," 536.

[99] Duhnke, *KPD*, 274–75.

[100] See ibid., 313–18, and Klaus Mammach, ed., *Die Berner Konferenz der KPD (30. Januar–1. Februar 1939)* (Berlin: Dietz, 1974).

diate connections with underground work in Germany.[101] The conference reiterated the party's commitment to the popular front, and asserted that it would not make the slightest concession to the regime's "contemptible persecution of Jews. . . . The struggle against anti-Semitism is inseparably united with the struggle against the war and the liberation of the entire people from the yoke of the Hitler dictatorship."[102]

But in many other ways the conference retreated from even the half-hearted innovations that the KPD had adopted in the mid-1930s. Instead of the decentralized structure adopted at Brussels, the KPD called again for a tight organization with a hierarchical leadership. The old barrage of attacks on social democracy reemerged; support for the Soviet Union was made the measure of antifascist commitment. France and Britain were attacked as imperialist powers whose reactionary capitalists sought "to use Hitler as gendarme and the German people as cannon fodder against the Soviet Union" with the goal of weakening both Germany and the Soviet Union. It was "the holy responsibility of communists and socialists" to disseminate the truth about the great socialist power and to obliterate the "campaign of lies of the fascists, their Trotskyist agents, and all their friends."[103]

Clearly, the KPD had reached a dead end. Inside Germany party cells had been decimated by Nazi repression. The mass of workers tolerated the Third Reich, and many actively supported it. Thousands of dedicated communists had perished at the hands of both the Soviets and the Nazis or suffered through the rigors of concentration camps. The Bern conference resolutions were models of confusion. From one of the mass parties of the Weimar Republic, the KPD had been reduced to an isolated grouping able to survive only through the beneficence of the Soviet Union—and that came, like all beneficences, at a price.

The KPD in World War II

The Nazi-Soviet Non-Aggression Pact, signed on 23 August 1939, was greeted with shock and disbelief in many political quarters. For communists the confusion and disorientation ran even deeper.[104] The only consistently antifascist nation had now reached an agreement with the archenemy, fascist Germany. The Nazis had been given a free hand to launch a war of expansion while thousands of German antifascists languished in concentration camps.

The KPD leadership, however, seemed to have little trouble adapting to the changed circumstances. By 1939, Ulbricht, Pieck, and company had witnessed countless changes in official Comintern strategy. They had managed to survive the Stalin terror unscathed. And they were personally dependent on the safe haven offered by the Soviet Union. They had long learned that their chances for

[101] Herlemann, *Emigration als Kampfposten*, 164.

[102] "Resolution der 'Berner' Konferenz der KPD (1939)," in Weber, *Deutscher Kommunismus*, 334.

[103] Ibid., 333, and Herlemann, *Emigration als Kampfposten*, 164–71.

[104] See Peukert, *KPD im Widerstand*, 326–33.

reaching the harbor were much greater if they navigated with the prevailing winds.

Rapidly, the KPD's rhetoric shifted. No longer was antifascist unity against an aggressive Germany the central rallying cry. Instead, the party claimed that the war begun on 1 September 1939 was nothing more than rivalry among imperialist nations. Other countries should simply avoid involvement in the conflict. The Nazi-Soviet Pact, the KPD claimed, lay in the interests of the German people, while foreign powers, notably the British and French, desired a war that would destroy Germany. Ulbricht, in an article that caused great controversy among German exiles and foreign socialists, claimed that Britain was "the most reactionary power in the world" and sought to make Germany a "vassal of English imperialism." German communists, he wrote, think it a crime to want to alter the regime in Germany through a "reactionary war" that will lead to the annihilation of millions of German working people.[105] The SPD's public hostility to the Nazi-Soviet Non-Aggression Pact inspired Florin to claim that the SPD leaders had "sunk deeper than in 1914" and operated as "agents in the pay of English and French imperialism."[106]

With these kinds of statements the KPD came dangerously close to a national-Bolshevik position that implied the possibility of a fundamental modus vivendi with the NSDAP. Ulbricht, a number of Comintern officials, and any number of communists inside Germany believed that as a result of the Non-Aggression Pact, the KPD would be allowed greater room for maneuver and might even be legalized by the Nazi state.[107] Once again the KPD failed to grasp the central dynamic of the regime—the drive to create a racial utopia, which necessitated aggressive expansion and a panoply of murderous policies. Since in Nazi ideology communism blended inextricably with Judaism, there could never be an easing of the repression against the KPD or a long-term peace with the Soviet Union.

In the spring of 1940, Germany escalated the war by invading the Low Countries, Denmark, Norway, and France. The KPD's main western exile points now came under Nazi control, breaking the last links between the border secretaries and the underground. Hundreds and perhaps thousands of German communists (and other antifascists) were captured and sent off to concentration camps. Only a few, like Paul Merker, managed to escape the net to find safe haven across the Atlantic. The gravity of party direction shifted ever more toward Moscow and to the duumvirate of Pieck and Ulbricht, isolated from Germany and from the remnants of the party membership who languished in the underground, concentration camps, or the far-flung points of exile.

The German invasion of the Soviet Union in June 1941 enabled communist parties around the world to return to a clear antifascist position. Distraught at the

[105] Walter Ulbricht, "Hilferding über den 'Sinn des Krieges,'" 9 February 1940, in Weber, *Deutscher Kommunismus*, 364–67. Pieck made very similar points in, "Um was geht es in diesem Krieg?" December 1939, in ibid., 356–57.

[106] Quoted in Staritz, *Sozialismus in einem halben Lande*, 52.

[107] Peukert, *KPD im Widerstand*, 330–31.

dangers posed to the "socialist fatherland," communists were also greatly relieved to leave behind the confused—indeed shameful—period of the Non-Aggression Pact when they had had to mute their hostility toward fascism. Once again, Nazi Germany was the archenemy. Communists in German-occupied Europe launched resistance efforts, which turned into mass movements once the tides of war began to shift in favor of the Allied Coalition. The élan of the popular front years returned, and thousands of new members poured into the French, Italian, Greek, and Yugoslav communist parties. The determined, heroic struggle of communists placed their parties at the center of national coalitions and legitimized their claim to participate in the shaping of the postwar political order.

The KPD, in sharp contrast, remained isolated. From Moscow the party leadership sought to direct communist resistance in Germany, an impossible task given the break in communications that had already occurred. Those few who remained active in Germany struggled bravely, but with virtually no immediate impact. In concentration camps communists could only strive to maintain party discipline and engage in political education.[108] In exile in Buenos Aires, Mexico City, Shanghai, Los Angeles, and elsewhere, communists could do little more than support the Allied effort through pronouncements and newspaper publications, while a very few managed to enlist in the United States or British armed forces.

Within Germany, the wartime communist resistance groups, as in the 1930s, printed and distributed anti-Nazi literature. Some engaged in sabotage, and a few, like the famed Red Orchestra, conducted espionage for the Soviet Union. Most sought to establish cells in the workplace, which, they hoped, would serve as the nuclei for a mass uprising against the Nazi regime. Almost all the activists were communists of long standing, and most, with the notable exception of the Red Orchestra members, came from working-class backgrounds.[109]

The largest communist resistance group, the "Robert Uhrig Group" in Berlin, had about two hundred members and contacts in Bavaria and the Tyrol. Somewhere between one-quarter and one-half of the group were executed by the Gestapo.[110] In late 1942 other Berlin communists formed the Saefkow-Jacob-Bästlein Group, which had cells in thirty Berlin factories. It counted hundreds of members, including about eighty in one Berlin factory alone.[111] Communists also established resistance groups in most of the industrial areas of Halle-Merseburg, including one in the Mansfeld region that escaped the Gestapo's net.[112] In one bread factory in Halle, the resistance cell counted eighteen out of one hundred and twenty workers and had contacts with prisoners of war and forced laborers in the area. They managed to procure twenty rifles, distribute hundreds of copies of illicit materials, and provide support for Italian forced laborers who had gone on strike.

[108] Buber-Neumann, *Als Gefangene*, has scathing words for the exercise of party discipline in the camps.

[109] See Duhnke, *KPD*, 456–529, for a good overview.

[110] Ibid., 460–61.

[111] Ibid., 485–88.

[112] Otto Gotsche, "Unser gemeinsamer Kampf in der Antifaschistischen Arbeitergruppe Mitteldeutschlands," in *Vereint sind wir alles: Erinnerungen an die Gründung der SED* (Berlin: Dietz, 1966), 394–414.

Beginning in late 1942, both the party leadership in Moscow and resisters in Germany sought, once again, to establish a more solid party organization. The Soviets dropped by parachute German communist exiles from the Soviet Union, a number of whom were personally related to leading figures in the party.[113] Virtually all of them were caught and executed. Wilhelm Knöchel, who had directed resistance activities from Amsterdam and elsewhere, managed to reach Berlin in 1942, where he established far-reaching contacts, including intermittent connections to the Central Committee in Moscow. Knöchel had had long years of experience working with the underground and sought to shift the gravity of leadership toward those in Germany. He lent a pronounced national coloration to resistance efforts, claiming that only an internal uprising could save Germany from partition and disaster. He too was eventually caught and executed after being "turned" by the Gestapo into a double agent.[114]

In 1943, the Saefkow-Jacob-Bästlein Group established contacts with resistance groups in Thuringia and Saxony-Anhalt (the former Prussian Saxony with some additional territory), and the three created an internal leadership for the party in Germany, the so-called Operative Leadership composed of Saefkow (Berlin), Theodor Neubauer (Thuringia), and Georg Schumann (Leipzig). They established intermittent contact with the Central Committee in Moscow, but were uncovered by the Gestapo in 1944. The three leaders, along with many others, were executed in 1944.

Most of the members of these groups had spent a good part of the 1930s in Nazi prisons and concentration camps. They had been isolated from the popular front developments of the 1930s; they knew even less about the national front line emanating from Moscow after 1941 or, if they were still alive, the Allied decisions at Yalta that envisaged complete Allied control and partition of Germany.[115] The national front strategy mandated alliances even broader than the popular front and defined the war as a struggle not for socialism, but for democracy, the end of fascism, and the liberation of Soviet territory from German troops. For German communists, who defined the Third Reich as an intrinsically capitalist system, who maintained that Germany's upper classes had installed Hitler in power, who had suffered so greatly at the hands of the regime—for them, cooperation was virtually unimaginable with, say, the officers and aristocrats of the anti-Nazi Kreisau Circle or with businessmen who had suddenly discovered their democratic credentials.

Instead, most resistance groups inside Germany advocated a political line reminiscent of the Weimar KPD.[116] The platform adopted by Neubauer's group in Thuringia, for example, called for a revolution to topple capitalism and the estab-

[113] Duhnke, *KPD*, 367, n. 5.

[114] Knöchel's fate has remained quite controversial. In the DDR he was regarded as a traitor, though Peukert defended his actions in *KPD im Widerstand*, 342–61, 376–81.

[115] DDR historians claimed that the resistance groups in Germany were well informed and acted under the direction of the Central Committee in Moscow, though this was certainly not the case.

[116] See Duhnke's discussion in *KPD*, 502–4, and the documents in Pikarski and Uebel, *Antifaschistischer Widerstandskampf*, and "Am Beginn der letzten Phase des Krieges: Ein neues bedeutsames Dokument aus dem illegalen Kampf der KPD in Deutschland 1944," *BzG* 21:3 (1979): 402–25.

lishment of the KPD as the vanguard of the working class. Neubauer warned party cadres against the efforts of the German bourgeoisie to ally with English and American imperialism. This would result in a peace ten times worse than Versailles, the double enslavement of the German people under foreign and German capitalists. Only one road was open—a national uprising of working people against Hitler and finance capital and alliance with Soviet Russia and the liberated peoples of Europe in a union of socialist republics. "[T]he destruction of German capitalism will begin with the overthrow of Hitler," Neubauer's group claimed, not exactly the U.S. and British, or even the Soviet, understanding of the war.[117]

In an almost astounding lack of political judgement, given all that had transpired since the Nazi seizure of power in 1933, the Leipzig resistance group, echoing the KPD of the late Weimar period, argued that nothing essential divided bourgeois democratic from fascist-authoritarian states.[118] Convinced to the end that the Nazis had failed to penetrate the core of the working class, communist resisters retained the belief that the proletariat would, at long last, rise up against the Nazi dictatorship and fulfill its historical mission.[119] "*Not only Germany, but all of Europe stands on the eve of a powerful revolution.*" Workers throughout the continent would follow the path blazed by the Soviet Union, "*the construction of the power of the working class, of the dictatorship of the proletariat.*"[120]

German refugees outside of the Soviet Union were at least spared the worst excesses of the Stalin and Nazi terror, but exile was always a most difficult situation.[121] With the exception of a handful of luminaries, those who had to flee Nazi Germany faced interminable visa problems and severe material constraints, which only made more arduous the process of psychological adjustment to foreign lands. Few exiles chose their ultimate country of destination; chance, circumstance, and passport bureaucrats determined the direction of their journeys.

In the Soviet Union communists comprised the vast majority of the German exile community. Elsewhere, they constituted a minority among a diverse group with large numbers of liberal and social democratic (and often Jewish) intellectuals and other members of the middle class. The greater the distance from Germany, the more bourgeois and noncommunist the exile communities became. KPD veterans had to learn to work with the diverse range of émigrés and in the most varied political and social settings. Those in exile in the United States, Latin America, Great Britain, Shanghai, and elsewhere accumulated more substantive experience

[117] Leaflet of Neubauer-Poser group, "Hitlers Krieg ist Verloren! Nur Kindsköpfe träumen noch vom Sieg!" September 1943, in Weber, *Deutscher Kommunismus*, 412–13.

[118] Schumann-Engert-Kresse-Gruppe, "Leitsätze über die Liquidierung des imperialistischen Krieges und der Naziherrschaft," February 1944, in Weber, *Deutscher Kommunismus*, 418–21.

[119] "Am Beginn der letzten Phase des Krieges," 409, 411–12.

[120] Ibid., 413, 415, 416–17. See also one of the last statments of the Operative Leadership, Zentralkomittee der Kommunistischen Partei Deutschlands, "An alle Hamburger Kommunisten und revolutionären Arbeiter!" July 1944, in Pikarski and Uebel, *Antifaschistischer Widerstandskampf*, doc. 210.

[121] See Benser, *KPD im Jahre der Befreiung*, 34–59, and the multivolume DDR series, *Kunst und Literatur im antifaschistischen Exil 1933–1945* (Leipzig: Reclam, 1978–83), which is highly informative on the daily lives and politics of the German exile communities.

with the popular and national fronts than their comrades in Germany and the Soviet Union and moved further from the intransigent politics of the Weimar KPD. In countless proclamations and appeals they called for the complete defeat of the Third Reich, the purging of fascists from all posts of influence, nationalization of key industries, and democratization.

All the exiles suffered from insufficient knowledge of conditions in Germany and the Soviet Union. Many retained a faith in the political capacities of the German working class that exceeded all realistic bounds. From the distant shores of Mexico, Paul Merker argued that the working class had remained essentially uncorrupted by the Nazi regime and stood ready to launch active resistance. He anticipated a postwar order defined by a democratic-antifascist-antiimperialist regime that, in an almost natural process, would rapidly transmutate into a socialist society.[122] Wilhelm Koenen, the leading figure among German communist exiles in Britain, responded to Merker with a more moderate, realistic approach. Especially after the Yalta meeting, Koenen—and many others—recognized the fact that the Allied powers would constitute the overwhelming political force in postwar Germany and that socialism was not on the immediate agenda.

As Günter Benser remarks, the dispute between Merker and Koenen demonstrated mainly the tragedy of exile, an experience of isolation, of day-to-day difficulties obtaining residency permits and work, of the reduction of political activism into often sterile arguments. German communist exiles had great hopes for the future; most would find themselves pushed to the margins in the Soviet Occupation Zone and DDR, tainted by their long years of residency in the west.[123]

Communists in the Soviet Union, needless to say, hewed most closely to the Comintern and Soviet line. Many were evacuated from Moscow in the wake of the German invasion. From various points they launched propaganda barrages against the German forces and the population at home. They wrote leaflets that were airdropped over troops, delivered radio reports, and propagandized among German prisoners of war—all to little effect.[124] From mid-1943, the focal point of activity was the "National Committee for a Free Germany" (Nationalkomitee "Freies Deutschland," or NKFD), the first popular front–type organization established successfully by the KPD.[125] The NKFD was composed of German prisoners of war, including officers and regular conscripts, but attracted virtually none of the highest-ranking officers captured at the battle of Stalingrad. The NKFD's initial manifesto reverberated with national-patriotic rhetoric and called on the German population to liberate itself from Nazi tyranny in order to prevent the destruction

[122] As he wrote to Heinrich Mann. See Benser, *KPD im Jahre der Befreiung*, 55–56. On Merker, see Jeffrey Herf, "East German Communists and the Jewish Question: The Case of Paul Merker," *JCH* 29:4 (1994): 627–62.

[123] Benser, *KPD im Jahre der Befreiung*, 56–57; Duhnke, *KPD*, 446–49.

[124] See Pike, *German Writers*, 358–414, who draws effectively on the depictions by Willi Bredel and others of their efforts among German soldiers.

[125] Bodo Scheurig, *Freies Deutschland* (Munich: Nymphenburger Verlagshandlung, 1960), and Sywottek, *Deutsche Volksdemokratie*, 124–47.

and fragmentation of the nation. The issue, the NKFD trumpeted, is the "existence or destruction [*Sein oder Nichtsein*] of our fatherland." The manifesto called for a strong democratic state, which, however, would bear no relation to the tainted Weimar regime.[126]

As the Red Army pushed back the Wehrmacht and the Allies formalized plans to partition Germany, the Soviets had less and less interest in fomenting resistance among German officers. The KPD and the Soviets continued to produce a great deal of propaganda about the NKFD, but its significance waned. Concurrent with the NKFD's founding, the KPD had also established a Working Commission, which increasingly took on the task of planning the party's return to German and, in particular, its participation in the Soviet occupation.[127] Under its auspices Wilhelm Pieck initiated in December 1944 a series of courses for party cadres in the Soviet Union.[128] The KPD's leaders had, at long last, just about given up hope that a national uprising would overthrow Hitler. In lectures presented by Pieck and other leading communists, KPD members heard the charge that the German people—not just German capitalists—bore coresponsibility for the crimes of the Third Reich. The destruction of National Socialism required more than its military defeat. Its roots had to be eliminated as well, which necessitated reeducation of the population, land reforms to eliminate the Junkers, and the establishment of democratic institutions. To fulfill these tasks, a long occupation was to be expected. Hence, communists and other antifascists had to work within the local administration in collaboration with the Soviet authorities. The task was not to accomplish socialism, but to fulfill the bourgeois-democratic program of 1848. This would be the goal of the national front-type coalition, the "bloc of a fighting democracy" (Block der kämpferischen Demokratie) that the KPD intended to establish in the Soviet Occupation Zone.[129]

The democratic goals and coalition government outlined by the KPD's Working Commission in the winter of 1944/45 by no means entailed a rejection of the primary role of the party organization. Clearly, the KPD would play the leading role behind the Soviet authorities in the administration of the planned Soviet Occupation Zone, and KPD leaders expected the party also to play a major role in the western zones. The KPD had to become a mass party again, and party organizations had to be established throughout the institutions of society. But the membership ranks were to be closely guarded. In sharp contrast to the Italian Communist Party, which threw open its membership gates and abandoned the practice of scrutinizing applicants, the KPD called for the exacting examination of prospective members. Ulbricht, true to form, issued directives that social democrats and

[126] "Manifest des Nationalkomitees Freies Deutschland," 15 August 1943, in Weber, *Deutscher Kommunismus*, 388–91.

[127] See the account of Wolfgang Leonhard, "Die 'Gruppe Ulbricht': Erste Schritte zur Macht 1945/46," in idem, *Das kurze Leben der DDR: Berichte und Kommentare aus vier Jahrzehnten* (Stuttgart: Deutsche Verlags-Anstalt, 1990), 13–44.

[128] Ibid., 16–18, and Elly Winter, "An der Seite Wilhelm Piecks in den ersten Monaten des Neubeginns," in *Vereint sind wir alles*, 116. Winter was Pieck's daughter and secretary.

[129] Benser, *KPD im Jahre der Befreiung*, 30–31 and passim.

trade unionists be allowed into the party only if they "have broken with social democracy and have proven themselves in antifascist work." Members of other groups "hostile" to the party—split-offs like the Communist Party-Opposition (Kommunistische Partei-Opposition, or KPO), followers of the former Politburo member (and Soviet purge victim) Heinz Neumann, Trotskyists—were not to be readmitted to the KPD at all.[130] Clearly, exile in the Soviet Union had not served to foster an open and democratic spirit in the KPD.

Conclusion

In the twelve years of the Third Reich the KPD had been battered and buffeted at the hands of two dictatorships. The "party of youth" of the Weimar Republic had become middle-aged and had failed to attract any new members. Thousands of committed communists had been killed in the Soviet and Nazi terrors. Survivors were scattered all over the globe, many embittered by the very immediate, physical experiences of imprisonment, beatings, and exile. Some had fought bravely against fascism in the underground in Germany or on the varied battlefields of Europe; all were dismayed and shaken by the failure of the German population, even at the bitter end, to rise up against the Nazi regime. Not untypical was the fate of a communist activist, who, forced into exile in Belgium and Holland in 1933, smuggled communist literature into and endangered comrades out of Germany, fought in Spain in the International Brigades, served time as a prisoner of Franco's forces, and then, turned over by the Spanish to the Gestapo in 1940, endured five years at Dachau.[131] Not untypical also was the fate of Susanne Leonhard, who had joined the Spartacus Group in 1916 and the KPD at its founding in 1919. After the Nazi takeover she worked for the party underground in Berlin and then emigrated to the Soviet Union in 1935. Caught in the whirlwind of the Soviet terror, she was separated from her young son and condemned to Soviet prisons and labor camps as a "Trotskyist agent." She survived, forever embittered at the Soviet corruption of the ideas of her youth.[132]

As individuals, communists had been cast to fearsome winds; as a party and movement, German communism had been isolated and marginalized, deprived of contact with a mass movement that had given the Weimar KPD its dynamic character. Other communist parties entered the postwar period robust, confident, full of prowess. They had had the experience of leading mass resistance movements and working on a daily basis with socialists, liberals, and conservatives, along with thousands of new, inexperienced recruits to communism. The KPD had had no such opportunities and, as a result, it remained largely mired in the patterns and perspectives developed in its period of popular expansion, the Weimar Republic. Moreover, for German communists the experience of fascism was of the homegrown variant, not of a foreign power that had conquered terri-

[130] Ibid., 14–15, 21–22, 29, and Leonhard, "Die 'Gruppe Ulbricht,'" 15

[131] Interview with Robert Weinand, Essen, 11 June 1980.

[132] Leonhard, *Gestohlenes Leben*.

tory. In the communist understanding fascism always lay rooted in bourgeois society; in the specifically German version, in the bourgeois democracy of Weimar, whose participants were held responsible for the Nazi dictatorship. Hence, the experience of repression under the Third Reich only intensified the hostility toward every manifestation of bourgeois politics and society, a sentiment already inscribed in the party's founding ideology and further developed in the continual and sullen social conflicts the KPD had fostered in the Weimar Republic. The chasm between communism and other forces in German society deepened in the period of the Third Reich, while most other European communist parties had used the opportunities of the popular and national fronts to become truly national movements.

The experience of exile in the Soviet Union further widened the chasm between German communists—at least those who survived—and other elements of German society. The stark, Manichean division of the world typical of communist politics took on absurd and deadly dimensions in the 1930s. Obedience and loyalty, already learned in Weimar, became the absolutely necessary, though by no means sufficient, conditions for bare survival. Such traits, hardly conducive to a democratic political culture, were accentuated by the profound sense of guilt felt by many German communists given the KPD's inability to ignite a popular uprising against the Nazis. Only a rite of national purification, the establishment of a "fighting democracy" in alliance with the Soviet Union, could relieve the burden of guilt shared by all Germans. Unable to locate an anchor of identity in a national resistance movement, the psychological and political dependence on the Soviet Union deepened.

Still, from Shanghai and Mexico City to the Ruhr, Halle-Merseburg, and Moscow, the KPD survivors could justifiably claim a nearly unbroken antifascist stance. In the most adverse circumstances imaginable, many had done what they could to promote the struggle against National Socialism. On 8 May 1945 they looked back with bitterness, but to the future with great hope.

CHAPTER 9

The Weimar Legacy and the Road to the DDR 1945–49

wir einen besonderen deutschen Weg zum Sozialismus unbedingt bejahen.

—*Anton Ackermann*[1]

Die Genossen waren der Meinung, daß wir einen ganz besonderen Weg, ohne Verschärfung des Klassenkampfes gehen. . . . [Jetzt] sind [sie] . . . ein wenig erschrocken.

—*Walter Ulbricht*[2]

IN THE VERY LAST DAYS of the Third Reich, German communists began to stream back to Germany and into the daylight of open political activism. They emerged from exile in the Soviet Union, the underground, concentration camps, and, to a lesser extent initially, exile in the west. Despite all the news accounts, the émigrés were shocked at the desolation they found in Germany.[3] The task of reconstruction and political development, never viewed lightly, now seemed even more formidable.

But what kind of reconstruction? For many German communists, as we have seen, the twelve years of the Third Reich proved less a moment of political reconceptualization than a time to maintain ideological conformity against their most dangerous enemy. The Soviet purges served as a wellspring of much bitterness, but not necessarily of commitment to democracy. For most German communists, the cherished historical reference remained the KPD's emergence as a mass party in the Weimar Republic upon a political strategy of loyalty to the Soviet Union and hard, confrontationist, male proletarian politics fought out in the streets of Berlin, Halle, Essen, and other industrial centers. Communists car-

[1] "*[W]e unconditionally affirm a special German road to socialism.*" Anton Ackermann, "Gibt es einen besonderen deutschen Weg zum Sozialismus?" *Einheit* 1 (February 1946): 31.

[2] "The comrades were of the opinion that we [would] proceed down an entirely unique road, without the intensification of the class struggle. . . . [Now they] are . . . a little shocked." Walter Ulbricht in October 1948, quoted in Dietrich Staritz, "Die SED, Stalin und der 'Aufbau des Sozialismus' in der DDR: Aus den Akten des Zentralen Parteiarchiv," *DA* 24:7 (1991): 691.

[3] Memoirs are quite revealing on this count. See, for example, Wolfgang Leonhard, *Die Revolution entläßt ihre Kinder* (Cologne: Kiepenheuer und Witsch, 1955), and Elly Winter, "An der Seite Wilhelm Piecks in den ersten Monaten des Neubeginns," in *Vereint sind wir alles: Erinnerungen an die Gründung der SED* (Berlin: Dietz, 1966), 115–31.

ried this political culture with them into the years of the underground, exile, and imprisonment under the Nazis and onward to the construction of state socialism in the German Democratic Republic.

Yet a great deal had changed since 1933. The KPD had suffered a profound defeat. The party membership had been decimated by Nazi and Soviet terror and had aged. Nazi dictatorship and total war had drastically transformed political and social conditions. The Comintern had altered its strategy in the 1930s, and the Soviet Union emerged in the 1940s as a world power. All of these developments forced at least some communists to reconsider the political positions held so fervently in, say, 1928 or 1932. Perhaps more importantly, German communists, like the Allied powers, entered in 1944 and 1945 an uncharted and unprecedented situation. The tasks ahead were immense, the prospects of placing their own stamp upon the future invigorating.

Briefly stated, until the autumn of 1948, when the Socialist Unity Party (Sozialistische Einheitspartei Deutschlands, or SED), the KPD's successor, abandoned the attempt to forge a distinctive "German road to socialism" and fell completely in line behind the Soviet model, two political orientations coexisted in uneasy tension within the KPD and SED. The first, which I will call the politics of intransigence, drew on the party's experience in the Weimar Republic, on the Luxemburgist-Leninist ideological heritage, and on the Comintern strategy of the "third period."[4] It was directed at the full assumption of power by the party in the immediate future, its seizure of the state apparatus as the means of engaging the construction of a state socialist system on the Soviet model. The second, which I will call the politics of gradualism, drew on the experiences of working collaboration with socialists and liberals that some communists had gained in the Resistance and exile; on the popular front strategy; and on the wartime coalition of the Allied powers. It envisaged socialism as a relatively distant goal that would be reached through a transitional phase of collaboration with noncommunist groups.

Significantly, these divergent streams were not completely identified with particular individuals or party factions. Most often, the contending positions were embodied in one and the same individuals, and whether one strategy or the other came to the fore depended on the reading, by Germans and by their Soviet sponsors, of the larger political context. This ambiguity contributed greatly to the party's rapid growth in the postwar period, because it permitted tactical flexibility and enabled the leadership to address both old party militants and social groups generally hostile to communism.

The mix of new departures and old conceptions that characterized German communism from 1943 to 1948 also sustained political potentials that extended far beyond the intentions of the major actors. Within the languages and the places of communist politics lay embedded political logics. The rhetoric of democracy and of a "German road to socialism" and the development of multifarious linkages

[4] Note the comments of Christoph Kleßmann, *Die doppelte Staatsgründung: Deutsche Geschichte 1945–1955* (Göttingen: Vandenhoeck und Ruprecht, 1982), that when "the Cold War became the defining element of domestic developments [the SPD and KPD in 1947/48 pursued] . . . in essence their traditions of the Weimar period." (142)

between the party and the population carried the potential of moderating the political stance of the KPD/SED. The moderating logic bore, in turn, the potential for the establishment of a "third way" system in the SBZ/DDR in which the KPD/SED would have functioned as a militant defender of working-class interests, a party rhetorically radical, practically militant, and functionally—for the system overall—supportive. In this setting, German communism would have lent a more egalitarian cast to a social or liberal democratic formation, actions that would have served, ultimately, to help stabilize the system.

In the end, of course, the politics of intransigence prevailed. The pathways leading toward alternate political formations were closed off by the entrenchment of the Cold War, the Soviet decision to construct its own bloc, and, not least, the actions of the KPD/SED leaders, who quickly—far more quickly than their Soviet mentors—sought to force-pace the development of their own state socialist system. And here another logic came into play, the logic of history as a constructed past. For German communists, the politics of intransigence marked also a reversion to the ideological traditions and social historical formation of the party in the Weimar Republic, and for that reason proved so deep-seated, so enduring, so solid. But in the process of re-creating the Weimar traditions of German communism, the party reshaped intransigence from its disruptive and revolutionary meanings in the 1920s and 1930s to a strategy of order and discipline designed to lend legitimacy to a state socialist regime.

The Languages of Communist Politics

One month after the German surrender, one day after the Soviets permitted the establishment of political parties in their zone of occupation, the KPD issued the most remarkable document in its history, the Central Committee's Manifesto of 11 June 1945. Drawn up at the direction of the Soviets, the manifesto laid out a course that diverged sharply from the Luxemburgist-Leninist-Stalinist heritage of the KPD and surprised even leading members of the party. Not one word of socialism graced the document. Instead, the Central Committee called for the establishment of an "antifascist democratic regime, a parliamentary democratic republic with all rights and freedoms for the people," and even declared its commitment to private property rights. Most significantly, the Central Committee specifically rejected the Soviet model as "inappropriate for Germany's stage of development." It called for a completely new departure, "an entirely new way must be blazed!"[5]

Strikingly, the historical reference point was not the Bolshevik and German Revolutions of the World War I era, but the liberal democratic Revolution of 1848, whose legacy could now be brought to fulfillment. When it came to specifics, the Central Committee provided a catalog of the anti-Nazi and democratic

[5] "Aufruf der Kommunistischen Partei Deutschlands," 11 June 1945, in Hermann Weber, ed., *Der deutsche Kommunismus: Dokumente* (Cologne: Kiepenheuer und Witsch, 1963), 431–38, quotes on 434, 435.

demands that had been a fixture of communist appeals since the popular front period and that were fully consonant with the functioning of a bourgeois democratic system. To implement the program, the KPD called for the creation of a bloc of antifascist democratic parties.

For the KPD in particular, the articulation of a moderate-sounding program, the absence of any word about socialism, the rejection of the Soviet path of development, the recognition of private property—all that represented a departure even more dramatic than the Brussels Conference of 1935 or the establishment of the National Committee for a Free Germany in 1943.[6] Over the next two years, the KPD/SED elaborated the political position defined in the Manifesto, especially through the adoption of a new political language, one that departed significantly from the confrontationist language of the Luxemburgist-Leninist tradition. The key, inextricably entwined phrases—the "German road to socialism," "democracy of a new type," "people's democracy"—delineated the possibilities for a "third way" between Soviet-style socialism and western liberal capitalism.

KPD and SED leaders Anton Ackermann and Rudolf Appelt undertook the most sustained efforts to define the new terminology. Ackermann coined the term "the German road to socialism" in a number of speeches in the winter of 1945/46 and then in an article published in the first issue of *Einheit*, the KPD's newly founded theoretical journal.[7] Ackermann framed the argument around the discussions then underway for the unification of the KPD and SPD and expended the greatest amount of ink marshaling quotes from Marx, Engels, and Lenin to demonstrate that the peaceful evolution from capitalism to socialism was only a pipedream and that the proletariat could only seize power through revolution. But then Ackermann issued a notable qualification: if a bourgeois-democratic system has dispensed with the "power apparatus" of militarism and the state bureaucracy, then it could evolve toward socialism.[8] Ackermann argued that the military defeat of Nazi Germany had accomplished just that—the destruction of the reactionary state apparatus. Whether Germany would indeed be able to evolve peaceably toward socialism depended on whether the new German state would be a state of all working people under the leadership of the proletariat. Following a suitable quote

[6] In contrast, DDR accounts presented the picture of a seamless evolution in party policy. See, for example, Günter Benser, *Die KPD im Jahre der Befreiung* (Berlin: Dietz, 1985), 12–13; Horst Laschitza, *Kämpferische Demokratie gegen Faschismus: Die programmatische Vorbereitung auf die antifaschistisch-demokratische Umwälzung in Deutschland durch die Parteiführung der KPD* (Berlin: Deutscher Militärverlag, 1969), who stops short of the Manifesto but whose entire history leads up to it; and the collection of memoirs, *Vereint sind wir alles*.

[7] Ackermann, "Gibt es," and "Fragen und Antworten," 31 pp. brochure (Berlin: Neuer Weg, 1946). Dietrich Staritz, "Ein 'besonderer deutscher Weg' zum Sozialismus?" *APZ* B50–51 (1982): 19–31, provides an account. Glimmers of the "national roads" strategy can be identified in the 1920s during Nikolai Bukharin's tenure as head of the Comintern and the initially hesitant but parallel efforts by Antonio Gramsci and Palmiro Togliatti to work out an appropriate strategy for Italian communism. See my essay "Bukharin and 'Bukharinism' in the Comintern," in *Nikolai Ivanovich Bukharin: A Centenary Appraisal*, ed. Nicholas N. Kozlov and Eric D. Weitz (New York: Praeger, 1989), 59–91.

[8] Ackermann, "Gibt es," 29.

from Lenin, Ackermann concluded, "*we unconditionally affirm a special German road to socialism.*"[9]

Appelt made in 1946 and 1947 one of the most serious efforts to define the term "people's democracy," which in its initial formulation had a much different meaning than that accorded the Soviet-style systems of eastern Europe after 1948.[10] Initially, "people's democracy" was used almost interchangeably with "democracy of a new type," a term with a lineage that reached back to the 1930s. Appelt began an article in *Einheit* with the most remarkable point: people's democracy *(Volksdemokratie)* was sui generis, a "democracy of a new type," distinguishable from both bourgeois *(bürgerliche-kapitalistische)* and the "Soviet-socialist form" of democracy.[11] It arose out of the particular conditions of the imperialist-fascist war, which both exposed and discredited the practices of the old ruling classes and inspired a broad, popular alliance against fascism and for democracy. Its distinguishing characteristic is, first and foremost, that working people (*das arbeitende Volk*) exercise "real influence" on the state. The implementation of laws and decrees is run not through a bureaucracy, but through organs defined by or elected by the people themselves, that is, elected representative bodies or people's committees, which are themselves subject to popular control. Indeed, the people's democracies mobilize the population for participation—in politics, economics, society—on a scale far surpassing that of bourgeois democracies, which are dependent on repressing the interests of the working population.

Moreover, people's democracies undertake major economic reforms, namely land reform and the nationalization (*Verstaatlichung*) of key industries, as well as steps toward economic planning. This does not mean complete socialization: private property and private initiative are protected, but with the proviso that "no one had the right to use private property to the harm of the democratic state. Private property and the public interest must sound in harmony. With large capital that is obviously not the case."[12] Ultimately, Appelt defined people's democracy as a "development that moves in the direction of socialism," a point he developed by quoting and paraphrasing Klement Gottwald, whose brief for a

[9] Ibid., 31.

[10] See Rudolf Appelt, "Ein neuer Typus der Demokratie: Die Volksdemokratien Ost- und Südosteuropas," *Einheit* 1:6 (1946): 339–52, and "Volksdemokratie—ein Weg zum Sozialismus," *Einheit* 2:3 (1947): 304–6. For a thorough discussion, Christoph Kleßmann, "Die deutsche Volksdemokratie: Geschichte, Theorie und Rezeption des Begriffs in der SBZ/DDR," *DA* 8:4 (1975): 375–89. For DDR interpretations of "people's democracy" as part of the seamless process of political development from the "antifascist-democratic revolution," see Ernstgert Kalbe, "Die volksdemokratische Revolution in Europa—eine neue Form des Übergangs zum Sozialismus," *ZfG* 30:10/11 (1982): 899–908, and Günter Benser, "SED und sozialistische Staatsmacht: Ihre Rolle und ihre Wechselwirkung bei der Errichtung der Grundlagen des Sozialismus in der DDR," *ZfG* 30:10/11 (1982): 869–83.

The SBZ and the DDR were never called a "people's democracy" despite the desires of the SED leaders. Nonetheless, the discussion about the term ranged widely in the press and had significant implications for the political character of the SBZ/DDR.

[11] Appelt, "Neuer Typus," 339, 341.

[12] Ibid., 346.

Czech road to socialism carried a subtle critique of the Soviet model of state direction.[13]

Whatever the limits of Appelt's and Ackermann's views—especially the easy identification of popular activism with "the people" in an almost mystical sense and the failure (unlike Gottwald) to distinguish between popular and state control—most striking are the new departures, and in particular the articulation, however restrained the tones, of a gradualist transition to socialism. "People's democracy" and "the German road" signified that socialism could be achieved without the military confrontation of the October Revolution and the subsequent civil war and without the complete state direction of the Stalinist system—the two most important elements of the Soviet experience. Germany could "grow into" socialism, as the Bolshevik leader Nikolai Bukharin explained the social process in a different context. In fact, the people's democracies looked a lot more like the Soviet New Economic Policy of the 1920s that Bukharin defended than the Stalinist model of the 1930s.

The gradualist orientation in the German party emerged as one example of a more general process of political development among the communist parties in the World War II era. Only a few individuals, the Italian communist leader Palmiro Togliatti notable among them, had begun in the 1930s to theorize the popular front as a transitional stage. By the mid-1940s, this had become virtually the standard stuff of communist thinking, and Germans gave it their own tone.[14] Unquestionably, their position was initiated and supported by the Soviets, who sought to maintain the World War II alliance and its domestic corollary, the national front. But the gradualist language also opened up the space for further political development that the Soviets and the German party leadership could control only with difficulty. The gradualist orientation necessarily implied political competition in a multiparty system and political coalitions and cross-class alliances—the very antithesis of the KPD's strategy in the Weimar Republic. Alliances and coalitions implied, in turn, a relatively long-term process of political and social development, a future whose detail could not be foreordained except in the negative—it would *not* be like the Soviet Union. The outcome could have been far more diverse political formations than came to exist in the Soviet bloc and a different kind of international order than that engraved in the Cold War.[15]

[13] Ibid., 352, and "Volksdemokratie." Appelt kept a prudent silence as to how the people's democracies differed from soviet democracy, and gave barely a mention of socialism. He also invoked the Italian experience as a model—one of the few times German communists ever spoke admiringly of the PCI.

[14] See Kleßmann, "Deutsche Volksdemokratie," for many similar formulations from a variety of communist parties and spokespersons. Togliatti had coined the term "democracy of a new type" in relation to the Spanish Republic, and it was used in the 1930s also by Anton Ackermann. Ackermann's talk of a "German road to socialism" predated Togliatti's similar coinage after 1956, while "Volksdemokratie" bore clear similarities to another term, *democrazia progressiva*, that Togliatti coined to describe the transitional regimes of the postfascist period. See Togliatti, *Opere*, vol. 4, pt. 1, ed. Franco Andreucci and Paolo Spriano (Rome: Riunti, 1979), 139–54, and Anton Ackermann, "Die Volksfront und die demokratische Volksrepublik," in *Die Internationale* 3/4 (1937): 36–45.

[15] Staritz, in "Ein 'besonderer deutscher Weg' zum Sozialismus?" reduces the discussion of the

But the language of gradualism was never the only communist political rhetoric, even if it dominated the party press and party gatherings between 1945 and 1947. Other voices were raised within the ranks of the German party and the Soviet Military Administration in Germany (Sowjetische Militäradministration, or SMAD), and they demonstrated the persistence of the politics of intransigence. Among some voices, the language of intransigence echoed the left radicalism of the post–World War I years by invoking the workers and soldiers councils as the key institutions of proletarian power; other voices resonated more clearly with Leninism by emphasizing the party as the source of political truth and the vehicle of political progress. Still others invoked a more Stalinist-inclined vision of communism as a system of authority, of party control and power that German society in particular required because of the corrupting impact of National Socialism. Whatever the shadings in tone, those who rejected the gradualist orientation were united in their revival of the language of class conflict and its international corollary, the anti-imperialist struggle. In contrast to the moderate-sounding appeals for coalitions and alliances, the language of intransigence identified the proletariat as the near-exclusive agent of progress and politics as a combative enterprise.

Memoirs of KPD/SED leaders and studies first by DDR historians indicate that time and again the gradualist orientation had to be fought for in party gatherings.[16] Especially local communists who emerged from the underground or concentration camps and were veterans of the Weimar KPD articulated a kind of left radicalism coupled with commitment to party domination of the political sphere, as we saw in the preceding chapter. As soon as the Nazis were defeated, communists in many localities resurrected the militant language and practices of the Revolution of 1918–20 and the Weimar Republic. In Berlin-Wittenau, they formed a Workers and Soldiers Council. In Meißen, they formed a Council of People's Commissars; in Pirna, the population was advised to greet the new administration with the call "Red Front!" (from the Red Front Fighters League of the Weimar Republic) and to use "comrade" and the "du" form; in Radeburg and Schellerhau communists called for the immediate establishment of the dictatorship of the proletariat.[17] Even

---

German road to the mandates of Soviet interests and the political calculations of KPD leaders striving to accomplish fusion with the SPD. These factors were always present, but Staritz has no sense for the wider resonance of the language, for the process of political development that many parties, including the KPD, had undergone, and for the longer historical lineage of the national roads strategy.

[16] See Wolfgang Leonhard, 'Die 'Gruppe Ulbricht': Erste Schritte zur Macht 1945/46," in idem, *Das kurze Leben der DDR: Berichte und Kommentare aus vier Jahrzehnten* (Stuttgart: Deutsche Verlags-Anstalt, 1990), 13–44; Benser, *KPD im Jahre der Befreiung*; Anton Ackermann, "Der neue Weg zur Einheit," and Fred Oelßner, "Die Anfänge unserer Parteischulung," in *Vereint sind wir alles*, 79–80, 159; Gerhard Mannschatz and Josef Seider, *Zum Kampf der KPD im Ruhrgebiet für die Einigung der Arbeiterklasse und die Entmachtung der Monopolherren 1945–1947* (Berlin: Dietz, 1962), 46; and Ackermann, "Fragen und Antworten," 8–9.

[17] Benser, *KPD im Jahre der Befreiung*, 96, 100. For many more examples, see Norman M. Naimark, *The Russians in Germany: The History of the Soviet Zone of Occupation* (Cambridge, Mass.: Harvard University Press, 1995), 251–75. I am grateful to Prof. Naimark for allowing me to read the manuscript copy of his book.

Walter Ulbricht, writing to Wilhelm Pieck just days after his return to Germany, claimed that the majority of the party comrades were sectarian-minded.[18] In the Ruhr the opposition to the positions delineated in the June Manifesto was so pronounced that the district leadership had to initiate an intensive round of instruction.[19] Party members reacted especially against the Central Committee's attribution of collective guilt to the German people and its support of private entrepreneurship, which struck at the heart of virtually everything the KPD had long supported.

Walter Ulbricht lent a very particular tone to the politics of intransigence, a tone of order, discipline, and power. Even in his most democratic-sounding speeches and writings, he could barely avoid lapsing into the rhetoric of order. In the early months, Ulbricht often used the language of "*Selbstverwaltung*" (self-administration or self-government), a term that had far greater potency than the more hackneyed "democracy" or "democratic."[20] *Selbstverwaltung* resonated both with the long-standing liberal commitment to local self-government and with the more radical working-class conception of workers and soldiers councils in the economy and polity. Yet the frequency with which Ulbricht used *Selbstverwaltung* quickly declined in favor of the far more elusive and infinitely malleable terms of a "democratic order" or an "antifascist-democratic order."[21]

In Ulbricht's hands, this language was often entwined with "*Sauberkeit*," also a malleable term that literally means cleanliness but more often was used to denote moral virtue, purity of purpose, the removal of Nazis from positions of influence, the purge of the party, and, most generally, a kind of conventional petit bourgeois morality.[22] In a speech to Berlin KPD functionaries in October 1945, Ulbricht also distinguished between "honorable" and "apparent" labor: "There are many people in Berlin who only engage in apparent work, who sign up for any kind of pseudo-undertaking in order to avoid honorable labor. One must create order and thereby insure that all those who don't engage in useful work will be put to work where it is necessary in the interests of construction."[23] With these kinds of statements, Ulbricht appropriated and turned around the Nazi and more generally German discourse of "honorable labor," which implied order, diligence, and progress and,

[18] Walter Ulbricht, *Zur Geschichte der deutschen Arbeiterbewegung*, vol. 2, Zusatzband (Berlin: Dietz, 1966), 205.

[19] Mannschatz and Seider, *Zum Kampf der KPD*, 47.

[20] See, for example, "Einigung aller antifaschistisch-demokratischen Kräfte!" 12 June 1945, and "Neue Aufgaben der freien Gewerkschaften," 29 August 1945, both in Walter Ulbricht, *Zur Geschichte der deutschen Arbeiterbewegung: Reden und Aufsätzen*, vol. 2: *1933–1946* (Berlin: Dietz, 1953), 420–24, 454–81. See also Naimark's treatment of Ulbricht and the policies of order in *Russians in Germany*.

[21] See, for example, "Das Programm der antifaschistisch-demokratischen Ordnung," 23 June 1945, and "Das Aktionsprogramm der KPD in Durchführung," 12 October 1945, in Ulbricht, *Reden und Aufsätzen* 2:425–48, 493–94.

[22] For example, "Das Programm der antifaschistisch-demokratischen Ordnung," 23 June 1945, in Ulbricht, *Reden und Aufsätzen* 2:447.

[23] "Das Aktionsprogramm der KPD in Durchführung," 12 October 1945, in Ulbricht, *Reden und Aufsätzen* 2:489.

now, the specifically communist version of the new society. In Ulbricht's hands, the binary opposite—"apparent" labor—is redolent with the misdeeds and immorality of National Socialism and capitalism in general. The KPD, the party promoting "honorable" labor, is also the party of the "active struggle for democracy . . . for the construction of a democratic self-administration of order and moral rectitude. . . . [which] suits the true national interests of the German people."[24] To close comrades he could be even more direct about the need for order, which necessarily meant party control: "Things must look democratic, but we must have everything in our hands," he said in the first days of the reconstruction.[25]

Ulbricht's obsession with order went too far even for many of his Soviet mentors, who complained that he was excessively rigid and needlessly alienated all kinds of potential political allies.[26] His policies, though, reflected not just his Stalinist inclinations, but also a deep-seated distrust of the German population because of its failure to resist the Nazis—a distrust that cut through political divisions among communists, but found special resonance among those who articulated the politics of intransigence. In various forms, the party attributed collective guilt to the German people. Even in the Manifesto of 11 June 1945, the KPD—after twelve years of repression and exile and the loss of thousands of cadres—could hardly resist assuming an air of superiority and attacking the German people at large:

> Not only Hitler is guilty of the crimes that have befallen humanity! Ten million Germans also bear part of the guilt, those who in 1932 in free elections voted for Hitler although we communists warned: "Whoever votes for Hitler votes for war!"
>
> Part of the guilt is also borne by those German men and women who, spineless and without resistance, watched Hitler grab power, watched how he destroyed all democratic organizations, especially those of the labor movement, and locked up, tortured, and murdered the best Germans.
>
> Guilty are all those Germans who saw in the armaments build up a "Greater Germany" and perceived in bestial militarism, in marches and exercises, the sole sanctifying redemption of the nation.[27]

Local communists went still further. In Zeitz in the last days of the war, communists distributed a leaflet that began with a list of rhetorical questions laden with the attribution of guilt:

> Do you know what it means, to lose a war that we, with a criminal lack of responsibility, set off ourselves? . . .

[24] Ibid., 506–7. On the Third Reich's effective use of the concept of honorable labor, see Alf Lüdtke, "'Ehre der Arbeit': Industriearbeiter und Macht der Symbole. Zur Reichweite symbolischer Orientierungen im Nationalsozialismus," in *Arbeiter im 20. Jahrhundert*, ed. Klaus Tenfelde (Stuttgart: Klett-Cotta, 1991), 343–92.

[25] Quoted in Leonhard, "'Gruppe Ulbricht,'" 24.

[26] There are numerous examples of Soviet complaints in Naimark, *Russians in Germany*.

[27] "Aufruf der Kommunistischen Partei Deutschlands," 11 June 1945, in Weber, *Deutscher Kommunismus*, 432–33.

> Do you know what it means, to be hated by the entire world, only because Hitler threatened the entire world?
>
> Do you know what it means, that Hitler and fascism were defeated and overthrown *not by the German people, but by the military* power of the united nations?
>
> You should be clear when you complain about your misery. *The proportion of our people's contribution to the emergence of peace defines the proportion of its participation in the peace.*
>
> Think about it!
>
> And one more thing, when you complain: *We antifascists* were the ones who until the Reichstag fire time and again *warned*:
>
> *Hitler means war!*
> *Hitler means terror!*
> *Hitler means barbarism and suffering!*
>
> You did not listen to us then.[28]

It is difficult to imagine the population of Zeitz responding positively to the litany of charges. But such attitudes constituted one other justification for establishing the tutelary role of the party. If, as Ulbricht charged, the "poison of the gangster ideology [of National Socialism] and militaristic obedience-to-the-death lay deep in the people," then the population certainly needed the leading role of the party.[29] Moreover, the attribution of guilt provided the basis upon which the party could demand work, loyalty, and discipline as a form of redemption from a population that had failed to heed communism and had allowed itself to fall into the grasps of National Socialism. As the KPD of Saxony Province put it quite plainly, through labor came redemption:

> by honorable and dedicated cooperation for the fulfillment of the economic plans for 1946 . . . the *supporters of the Hitler Party* . . . [can] find a way out of the misdirected road they traveled by their own responsibility and shortsightedness. . . . Through conscientious and dedicated fulfillment of the production tasks before them . . . yes, *through enthusiastic participation in the construction* of a new Germany, lies the *road to the community of antifascist-democratic Germany*.[30]

The uneasy coexistence of two political languages—of gradualism and intransigence—is one sign of the relative openness of the postwar political era. Rather than a fixed, immutable language, communist political rhetoric was notably unstable, sometimes within the same speech or article. The same slogans might be deployed with very different intentions and contents. "No Repetition of the Mistakes of 1918!" might mean socialist and communist unity and the neces-

28 Leaflet "Antifaschisten, Bürger!" [n.d.], distributed illegally by "Zeitz friends," LPAH I/2/3/2/4.

29 "Das Programm der antifaschistisch-demokratischen Ordnung," 23 June 1945, in Ulbricht, *Reden und Aufsätzen* 2:426, also 428–31.

30 "Wir meistern den Aufbau! Das Sofortprogramm der KPD für die Wirtschaft der Provinz Sachsen" (13 pp. brochure, 1945), LPAH I/2/3/2/4.

sity for a popular front-type government—a "fighting democracy" in the KPD's language—or party rule and the dictatorship of the proletariat.[31]

But between 1945 and 1948 the gradualist language dominated. The party trumpeted its rhetorical elements—the German road, democracy of a new type, people's democracy—in party gatherings, in the press, on the shop floor, and in local political structures. The terms constituted the linguistic tools through which the party deepened and broadened its social base (as we will see shortly). The political language of class warfare had little appeal and precious little to offer the middle class, the agrarian population, women in general. With that rhetoric, the KPD of the Weimar Republic had become a mass party with a social base largely restricted to the working class, indeed, to the unemployed working class. In contrast, the rhetoric of peaceful development, of cross-class collaboration, of the nation, of an economy marked by mixed private and public ownership—all that resonated deeply with long-standing political traditions in Germany.

At the same time, the ambiguities of communist language constituted one of the major reasons for the early successes the party experienced. If the rhetoric of democracy and national independence found broad resonance in the population, so did the language of order and discipline and the appeal to hard labor as the path out of the national crisis. When Ulbricht spoke of a "democratic order," the emphasis for both speaker and audience may well have been on "order." And when he sought to rally the party and the population with appeals to "exacting labor" as the means of national revival following the "catastrophe of the Hitler war,"[32] his language invoked both the religious and the socialist valoration of labor as the means of creation and redemption. In a situation of immense immiseration and social chaos, the language of *Ordnung und Sauberkeit* had widespread appeal.

The Places of Communist Politics

If the language of communist politics reflected the coexistence of two differing orientations, the politics of intransigence and the politics of gradualism, so did communist activities "on the ground." Determined to surmount its defeated and marginal status, the KPD, with the active support of the SMAD, moved quickly to capture essential positions of administrative power. At the same time, communist politics revolved quite centrally around popular mobilizations, and these the party could never easily channel and contain. Party activism intersected with and supported the upsurge of popular activism engendered, as in 1918/19, by the

[31] For a moderate-sounding application of the slogan, see Wilhelm Pieck in *Deutsche Volkszeitung*, 10 November 1945, and for increasingly intransigent tones, see idem, "Zwei Revolutionen—zwei Ergebnisse," *Einheit* 1:6 (1946): 321–28, and idem, "Zwei Revolutionen—zwei Wege," *Einheit* 2:11 (1947): 993–1004. See also Günter Benser, "'Keine Wiederholung der Fehler von 1918!': Wie KPD und SED im Kampf um die Errichtung der Arbeiter-und-Bauern-Macht die Lehren der Novemberrevolution nutzten," *BzG* 6 (1978): 835–43.

[32] Ulbricht, "Das Programm der antifaschistisch-demokratischen Ordnung," 13 June 1945, in *Reden und Aufsätzen* 2:438.

collapse of the state system. The KPD/SED achieved far wider entrée into the institutional spaces of power and the daily lives of the population than it had ever achieved in the Weimar period. This process was inherently ambivalent. It extended the reach of the party's bureaucratic administration, but also opened up avenues of popular influence in the workplace and the local polity.

Soviet power displayed a similar ambivalence. Ultimately, of course, the Soviets imposed their own system and drastically limited the range of popular and party activism. But the SMAD also helped to create, at least initially, the conditions for wide-ranging popular activism and, consequently, the potential for a different political logic.

In February 1945, Wilhelm Pieck, after consultations with Georgi Dimitrov, issued directives for party work in areas occupied by the Soviet armies. Significantly, these called upon party cadres not to concentrate on the reconstruction of the party organization, but to establish provisional local administrations and to engage in antifascist educational work among the population, both in collaboration with the Red Army.[33] Three so-called Initiative Groups, constituted in Soviet exile, were designated as the major instruments of this policy.[34] Led by Gustav Sobottka, Anton Ackermann, and Walter Ulbricht and directed to Mecklenburg-Pommerania, Saxony, and Berlin, the Initiative Groups moved quickly to reestablish administrative structures in the SBZ. With the significant exception of personnel and security departments, noncommunists were generally placed in leading offices, while communists staffed the secondary positions. By the midsummer of 1945, communists were well established in administrative posts at the local, regional, and provincial level and exercised power over land reform, schools, and purges of ex-Nazis.[35] Some communists complained that party work was being slighted because of all the efforts devoted to administration, but that did not stop the KPD leadership or the Soviets.[36] Before the Postdam Conference, the Soviet authorities established state (*Land*) administrations for Mecklenburg, Saxony, and Thuringia, and provincial administrations for Brandenburg and Saxony-Anhalt. During the Potsdam Conference the SMAD also created eleven (fifteen in 1947) German central administrations, which would later serve as the bases for the ministries of a central government.[37]

[33] See Laschitza, *Kämpferische Demokratie*, and Benser, *KPD im Jahre der Befreiung*, 61–65.

[34] The standard source has been the very interesting eyewitness account of Leonhard, *Revolution*, which has now been supplemented by archival-based studies, notably that of Benser, *KPD im Jahre der Befreiung*. In opposition to directives in Moscow, Communists inside Germany sought first the reorganization of the party or at least the coterminous development of the party and party penetration of administrative structures. See, for example, from Halle, "Organisierung der Partei nach den Kampftagen!" 26 April 1945, LPAH I/2/3/2/1–2, and "Bericht von der Bezirksleitung Sitzung am 29.4.45," 30 April 1945, LPAH I/2/3/2/3 [mislabeled 2].

[35] Benser, *KPD im Jahre der Befreiung*, 264–74.

[36] BLPS, "Bericht über die Entwicklung der Organisation der Kommunistischen Partei im Bezirk Halle," 13 September 1945, LPAH I/2/5/4/5.

[37] Kleßmann, *Doppelte Staatsgründung*, 73. For a thorough study of one of these, the Deutsche Verwaltung für Volksbildung, see David Pike, *The Politics of Culture in Soviet-Occupied Germany*,

Soviet policy, in short, amounted to reliance on the traditional state administrative structure, marking strong lines of continuity with the German past even when quite different individuals occupied the offices.[38] But KPD guidelines and Soviet actions could not in and of themselves determine the nature of party and popular activities in the chaos, confusion, and fluidity of the waning days of the war and the reconstruction. In communities and workplaces throughout Germany "activists of the first hour" emerged, and their engagement blurred the traditional distinctions between work and community. On their own initiative these activists set about preventing the Nazis from blowing up bridges, factories, and mines; clearing rubble; reorganizing production; and ensuring the continued flow of water, gas, and electricity.[39] In a very few areas, such as the Berlin docks and the Mansfeld region, communists at last launched armed actions against the Nazis.[40]

The activists of the first hour were predominantly working class in background, and many—though by no means all—were communists who had emerged from the underground, exile, or concentration camps. They often formed Antifascist Committees (Antifas) and works councils with social democrats, Catholic trade unionists, and others. These committees sprang up all over Germany, especially in the traditional centers of the labor movement, and were in some ways reminiscent of the workers councils of 1918/19.[41] As with the councils, immense variations existed in the composition and activities of the Antifas, and the highpoint of their

---

1945–1949 (Stanford: Stanford University Press, 1992), and for the general developments, the highly informative sections on central administration in the *SBZ-Handbuch: Staatliche Verwaltungen, Parteien, gesellschaftliche Organisationen und ihre Führungskräfte in der Sowjetischen Besatzungszone Deutschlands 1945–1949*, ed. Martin Broszat and Hermann Weber (Munich: Oldenbourg, 1990), 201–96. In contrast to the local administrations, communists had far stronger representation in the leading positions of the central administrative organs.

[38] As Kleßmann points out in *Doppelte Staatsgründung*, 72–73. But for a detailed examination of Soviet administration that emphasizes the confusions and even chaos, especially in the early months, see Naimark, *Russians in Germany*, 9–68.

[39] Examples from "Organisierung der Partei nach den Kampftagen," 26 April 1945, LPAH I/2/3/2/1–2, and Benser, *KPD im Jahre der Befreiung*, 71–73, 77–85. For the Ruhr, Mannschatz and Seider, *Zum Kampf der KPD*, 26–27. For other examples see Lutz Niethammer et al., *Arbeiterinitiative 1945* (Wuppertal: Peter Hammer, 1976); James A. Diskant, "Scarcity, Survival and Local Activism: Miners and Steelworkers, Dortmund 1945–8," *JCH* 24:4 (1989): 547–74; Dietrich Staritz, *Sozialismus in einem halben Lande: Zur Programmatik und Politik der KPD/SED in der Phase der antifaschistisch-demokratischen Umwälzung in der DDR* (Berlin: Klaus Wagenbach, 1976), 92–99; and Siegfried Suckut, *Die Betriebsrätebewegung in der Sowjetisch Besetzten Zone Deutschlands (1945–1948)* (Frankfurt am Main: Haag + Herchen, 1982), 192–214.

[40] Manfred Wille, "Das Ringen der Arbeiterklasse und der anderen Antifaschisten um die Einleitung des Demorkatisierungsprozesses in der Provinz Sachsen (April-August 1945)," *BzG* 22:3 (1980): 431–41; Otto Gotsche, "Unser gemeinsamer Kampf in der Antifaschistischen Arbeitergruppe Mitteldeutschlands," in *Vereint sind wir alles*, 394–414; and Benser, *KPD im Jahre der Befreiung*, 71–73, 77–85.

[41] The major work on the Antifas remains Niethammer et al., *Arbeiterinitiative 1945*. See also Benser, *KPD im Jahre der Befreiung*, and "Antifa-Ausschüsse—Staatsorgane—Parteiorganisation: Überlegungen zu Ausmaß, Rolle und Grenzen der antifaschistischen Bewegung am Ende des zweiten Weltkrieges," *ZfG* 26:9 (1978): 785–802. Benser has counted 500 Antifas (787), but considers the number much too low. See also Staritz, *Sozialismus in einem halben Lande*, 86–99.

activity was already over by midsummer 1945. Both the western Allies and the Soviets were determined to reconstruct and extend regular administrative structures, and the Antifas were too quirky, too unpredictable, too rooted in popular institutions and cultures to be of much use to the authorities, east or west. Never one to mince words, Franz Dahlem put the matter starkly at the beginning of 1946: "The antifascist committees had their rationale so long as no parties existed. The moment that the parties were reestablished, one had to find the means to lead the movement through the common resolve of the antifascist parties."[42]

However, the end of the Antifas as vital institutions did not mean the end of popular mobilizations, nor the closure of political possibilities—the lament of West German studies of the Antifas. Throughout 1945, 1946, and 1947 communists were engaged in all sorts of activities at the local, regional, and zonal level aimed at elevating popular activism and, at the same time, extending party influence through an array of institutions. In the winter of 1945/46 in Saxony Province, for example, life for party members entailed an unending round of both mobilizational activities and bureaucratic work. Party activists directed land reform, making of the event a popular festive occasion complete with music, parades, and speeches. They established rural cooperatives and sent out from the cities labor brigades to help in the sowing and harvesting. In Zeitz and a number of other towns, communist-dominated works councils supervised the city administration, a syndicalist-type activity that dramatically extended the reach of working-class power. In Zeitz and the Mansfeld Seekreis, the mayors delivered public reports to the population at mass rallies, part of the effort to develop democratic practices and to secure the trust of the population for the party, and also a far cry from the bureaucratic tendencies of even socialist municipalities in the Weimar Republic. In workplaces throughout the region, communist-dominated works councils both promoted production and involved workers in negotiations with factory owners and with the Soviet authorities.[43]

Party activists also purged state offices of Nazis and their collaborators and launched campaigns to train rapidly new school teachers—a particularly dire need given the highly successful Nazi penetration of the teaching corps in Germany. After a slow start, communist women organized women's associations that conducted educational and social campaigns, and often won semiofficial status as consultative bodies on city councils.[44] Rallies provided a major focal point of popular mobilization, and internal party reports indicate high attendance at festivities and memorials held on the anniversaries of Engels's birthday, the November

[42] Quoted in Benser, *KPD im Jahre der Befreiung*, 115.

[43] For these examples, see LRLK Merseburg, "Niederschrift über die am 6. Oktober 1945, 15:00 Uhr stattgefunden Enteignung der Güter," 7 October 1945, LPAH IV/414/3/7; [BLPS, Report, December 1945], LPAH I/2/5/4/24, 25; BLPS, "Zum Organisationsbericht für Januar 1946," 7 February 1946, LPAH I/2/5/4/46–50; BLPS, "Zum Organisationsbericht für Februar 1946," 6 March 1946, LPAH I/2/5/4/83–84; "Tätigkeitsbericht der Kommunistischen Partei, Kreisleitung Zeitz, für den Monat Februar 1946," LPAH I/2/3/3a/178; and BLPS, "Stand der Organisation beim Jahreswechsel 1945/46," 7 January 1946, LPAH I/2/5/4/33.

[44] Käthe Kern, "Die Frauen standen mit in vorderster Reihe," in *Vereint sind wir alles*, 87–100.

Revolution, the murder of Luxemburg and Liebknecht, and Wilhelm Pieck's birthday. Local organizations staged highly successful Christmas parties as part of the campaign "Save the Children" and "Help the Children," complete with presents for all who attended. In addition, the KPD and then the SED sought to control price-gouging, ran education programs for members, helped reopen local theaters and concert halls, organized cooperatives, and engaged the very basic work of administration in the communes, counties, and provinces.[45] At the same time, the party engaged in countless negotiations with the SPD over unification and mobilized support in the workplace for union elections.

Of course, all was not sweetness and light. As the leading party in the SBZ, and the one with the greatest access to the SMAD, the KPD/SED had now to take responsibility, in conjunction with the Soviets, for disciplining the population, and labor in particular.[46] In factories and mines throughout the SBZ the KPD/SED exhorted workers to raise production. In conjunction with the SMAD it increased the workday and froze wages.[47] In some instances, party activists went so far as to reinstitute some of the most hated measures of the Weimar factory regime, including body searches at the factory gates and sharp disparities in the pay of men and women.[48] The vast population movements of the immediate postwar period meant that newcomers to a region or a town often formed the core of the party, as in many of the Magdeburg district party groups. Especially in the countryside the local residents viewed the newcomers with mistrust, making party work that much more difficult.[49]

The identification with Soviet power created unending difficulties for German communists. The huge incidence of rape, which continued well past the initial conquest of Germany, was the most horrific aspect of Soviet power and probably the single greatest obstacle to the expansion of communist influence.[50] When Soviet soldiers got into a brawl at a local bar and unloaded their revolvers or

[45] For these examples, see KLM to BLH, 19 January 1946; KLS, "Monatsbericht Dezember," 2 January 1945; KLS, "Monatsbericht Januar," 2 February 1946; "Bericht über die Partei in der Kreisfreien Stadt Magdeburg," 20 December 1945; "Bericht über die Arbeit der Kommunistischen Partei, Ortsgruppe Weissenfels für Monat September 1945;" and "Tätigkeitsbericht für den Monat September 1945 des Zeitzer Unterbezirks der KPD," LPAH I 2/3/3a/7–8, 21–24, 25–27, 75–79, 105–8, 151–56; BLPS, "Stand der Organisation der Kommunistischen Partei in der Provinz Sachsen Anfang November," 28 November 1945, LPAH I/2/5/4/20.

[46] Critical on the SMAD are Naimark, *Russians in Germany*, and Jan Foitzik, "Sowjetische Militäradministration in Deutschland (SMAD)," in *SBZ-Handbuch*, 7–69.

[47] For one example of a local party organization that seems to have fully alienated the workers, see BLPS, "Zum Organisationsbericht für Januar 1946," 7 February 1946, LPAH I/2/5/4/47.

[48] KPD HM, "Diskussion auf der erweiterten BL-Sitzung am 14.2.1946," 18 February 1946, LPAH I/2/3/2/34–37.

[49] BLPS, "Stand der Organisation beim Jahreswechsel 1945/46," 7 January 1946, LPAH I/2/5/4/35–36. In the area of Prussian Saxony, 16.7 percent of the population in December 1945, 24.8 percent in March 1949, were refugees or expelees from the east. See Dieter Marc Schneider, "Zentralverwaltung für deutsche Umsiedler," in *SBZ-Handbuch*, 240.

[50] See Naimark, *Russians in Germany*, 69–140, and Atina Grossmann, "Pronatalism, Nation-Building, and Socialism: Population Policy in the SBZ/DDR, 1945–1960," in *Between Reform and Revolution: Studies in German Socialism and Communism from 1840 to 1990*, ed. David E. Barclay and Eric D. Weitz (Providence: Berghahn, forthcoming).

seized apartments for the billeting of troops, the mood of the population soured even further.[51] The seizure and dismantling of factories for shipment to the east caused still greater bitterness, particularly in light of the employment problem.[52] The KPD in Weissenfels complained that many factories slated for removal to the Soviet Union had had well-functioning party cells, whose impact had now become "illusory."[53] The provincial party leadership in Saxony put the matter succinctly: "The conquest of many areas by Red Army soldiers, the dismantling of factories, the often very disagreeable behavior of those responsible for the dismantling . . . contributed not insignificantly to a hostile attitude toward the Red Army and as a result also toward the Communist Party."[54]

Despite these difficulties and others—including a drastic shortage of experienced functionaries[55]—communists, as the agents of social welfare, economic reconstruction, and, not least, political involvement, won increasing resonance among the population. In the first year or so following the defeat of National Socialism, leading communists displayed a quiet confidence, a sense that party and society were moving forward together. Internal local and regional party reports exude this spirit, a far cry from the litany of complaints expressed in comparable reports of the Weimar period.[56]

Moreover, Antifas, workplace representation in factory management, workers' supervision of local political bodies, mass rallies aimed at vetting the activities of local political authorities—all constituted the terrain of popular political involvement and the institutional and social spaces where party and population met. Through their actions workers, with communist support, laid claim to a decisive voice in the functioning of the factories and mines and local polities. Rarely articulated in a clear programmatic or theoretical manner, these actions nonetheless constituted popular democratic challenges to the distanced, bureaucratic models of representation that prevailed in the Weimar Republic and would come to prevail in both the DDR and the BRD. To the extent that communists were involved in these activities, they promoted democracy at the same time that they sought to capture the bureaucratic levers of power. Communists navigated with difficulty the often unclear, chaotic world of popular involvement and their own tendencies toward bureaucratic administration. But like the gradualist language,

[51] [KLM] to BLH, 4 January 1946 [incorrectly labeled 1945], LPAH I/2/3/3a/8; KLW, "Bericht für den Monat März," 29 March 1946, LPAH I/2/3/3a/121; BLPS, "Zum Organisationsbericht," 7 January 1946, LPAH I/2/5/4/30.

[52] For examples of party complaints about the Soviets, see BLPS, "Zum Organisationsbericht für Januar 1946," 7 February 1946, LPAH I/2/5/4/48, and KLW, "Bericht für den Monat März," 29 March 1946, LPAH I/2/3/3a/121–22. For a thorough examination, Naimark, *Russians in Germany*, 141–204.

[53] KLW, "Bericht für den Monat März," 29 March 1946, LPAH I/2/3/3a/121–22.

[54] BLPS, "Zum Organisationsbericht für Januar 1946," 7 February 1946, LPAH I/2/5/4/48.

[55] See, for example, "Tätigkeitsbericht der Kommunistischen Partei, Kreisleitung Zeitz, für den Monat Februar 1946," LPAH I/2/3/3a/177.

[56] I base this conclusion on the reports of the KPD's Bezirksleitungen, Unterbezirksleitungen, and Kreisleitungen in Saxony Province for 1945 and 1946 in LPAH I/2/3/2, I/2/3/3, I/2/3/3a, I/2/3/4, and I/2/3/4a. The mood of optimism seems to have transcended political differences within the KPD/SED.

the diverse places of communist politics opened the possibilities for a multitude of political formations.

Party Membership and Popular Support

The tension between popular democracy and authoritarian direction is evident also in the character of the KPD/SED's membership and electoral support, both of which rose rapidly and substantially in the SBZ, more slowly but no less significantly in the western occupation zones. No doubt some individuals in the SBZ in particular played the odds and joined the party in an effort to position themselves effectively in the new order or simply to obtain jobs, housing, and other immediate benefits.[57] But in the critical early months of the postwar period, few people could have been certain that communism would come to be the exclusive political force in the SBZ/DDR. The growing support won by the KPD and SED demonstrates that in a mere sixteen months following the defeat of the Third Reich, communists succeeded in re-creating a mass-based movement in Germany, one whose support ran broader and deeper than the old KPD of the Weimar Republic. But as its support grew, opposition also became more pronounced. When the KPD and SED reached their limits of popular support, party leaders and the Soviets grew wary of exposing communism to the vagaries of popular opinion and moved quickly to accentuate the authoritarian tendencies that, initially, had been held in partial abeyance.

Rather quickly, then, the KPD in the SBZ began to draw in new members and support, as internal reports indicate.[58] In the area of the SBZ the KPD already in July 1945 had reached its prewar membership level of one hundred thousand, and by November the figure had almost tripled. Not untypical was the local KPD organization in Zeitz, which reported in September 1945 that only 18 percent of the members had earlier been organized into the KPD.[59] Figure 9.1 shows the trends for Saxony Province, which are exemplary for the SBZ overall.

[57] Party membership certainly enhanced one's access to scarce resources. At the major Brabag works in Zeitz, for example, the predominantly communist authorities purged 450 former Nazis out of a workforce of 4,100, who were replaced with communists or communist sympathizers. As the local organization reported, "New employees were hired essentially according to the criterion of strengthening our party sector in the workplace. . . . As of today, two hundred comrades are employed in the plant." See "Tätigkeitsbericht für den Monat September 1945 des Zeitzer Unterbezirks der KPD," LPAH I/2/3/3a/154. For those party members who remembered the purges of communists from the workplace in the 1920s, such actions in 1945/46 must have constituted sweet revenge.

[58] For a general analysis see Benser, *KPD im Jahre der Befreiung*, 274–86. For some particular examples, see KLS "Monatsbericht Dezember," 2 January 1945; KLS, "Monatsbericht Januar," 2 February 1946; KLW, "Bericht für den Monat März," 29 March 1946; "Tätigkeitsbericht des U.B. Zeitz," [late summer or early autumn 1945], LPAH I/2/3/3a/21, 25, 133, 159; "Monatsbericht der Unterbezirksleitung der KPD Halle-Merseburg," [January 1946]; "Monatsbericht für Januar der Unterbezirksleitung der KPD Halle-Merseburg," LPAH I/2/3/3/33–34, 35, 40.

[59] UBL Zeitz, "Tätigkeitsbericht für den Monat September 1945 des Zeitzer Unterbezirks der KPD," LPAH I 2/3/3a/151–52. Included among the 591 members who had earlier been party members were 220 persons who had suffered under the Nazis 325 years of internment, 260 years of concentration camps, and 95 years of prison.

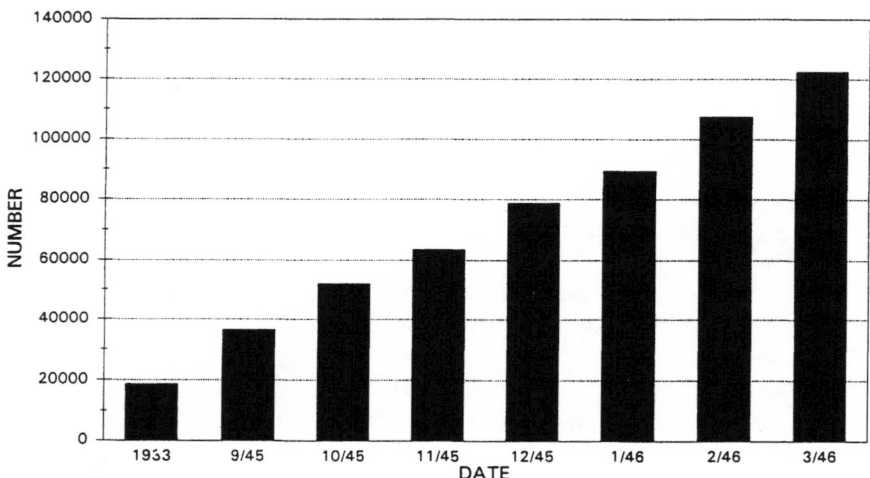

Figure 9.1 KPD Membership Saxony Province, 1933, 1945–46. *Source:* LPAH I/2/5/4/8–14, 20–27, 32–36, 40–45, 64, 85–92, 163; LPAH I/2/5/4a/161–66.

The nature of the KPD's support broadened considerably. According to party statistics, on 31 January 1946, 56.8 percent of the membership in the SBZ were workers (excluding white-collar and agrarian workers), a significantly lower proportion than in the Weimar period. Furthermore, the KPD had acquired far greater support in the agrarian regions than it ever had had in the past. In Brandenburg Province and in Mecklenburg-Vorpommern, the KPD registered, respectively, 113.2 percent and 143.4 percent increases in membership over the Weimar period. As the DDR's leading historian of this period, Günter Benser, argued, the KPD won new members without losing its old cadres.[60] In Weissenfels in the autumn of 1945, the membership was "composed overwhelmingly of workers" and few peasants or women had joined.[61] Yet in March 1946 close to 20 percent of the new members were agricultural workers and peasants, and another 20 percent were invalids or those without a trade.[62] Figures 9.2 and 9.3, which detail the social composition of the KPD membership for two of the party subdistricts in Saxony Province, illustrate the broadened social composition that the KPD achieved.

Among two groups with whom the KPD initially had grave difficulties, women and youth, the party soon made improvements. In the Weimar period, the KPD, like the NSDAP, had an age profile substantially younger than that of the other parties. But by 1945 the party had virtually no members under thirty years of age,

[60] Benser, *KPD im Jahre der Befreiung*, 276–79, 281–82. Despite the strong increase in membership in agrarian regions, Benser argues that the social profile of the party had not essentially changed, which seems incorrect to me.

[61] KLW, "Bericht," 5 October 1945, LPAH I/2/3/3a/80.

[62] KLW, "Bericht für den Monat März," 29 March 1946, LPAH I/2/3/3a/121.

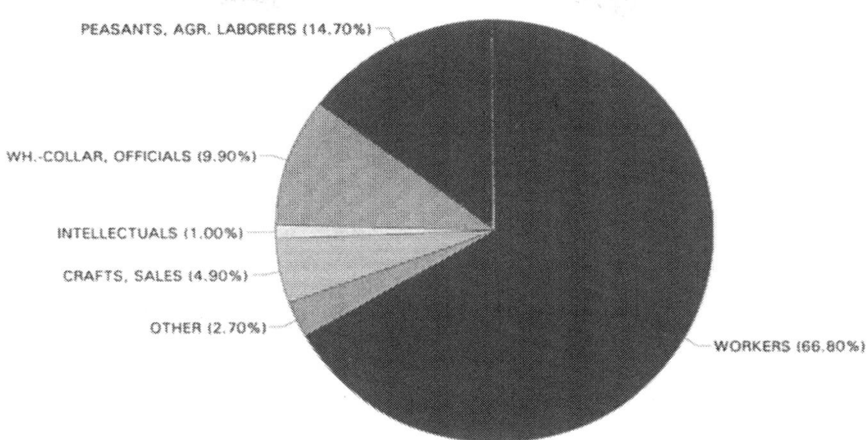

Figure 9.2 Social Composition of KPD Membership Halle-Merseburg Subdistrict, March 1946. *Source:* LPAH I/2/5/4/85–92.

and local party groups commented incessantly on the difficulties of gaining younger members and the general resistance to any kind of political organization after the experience of the Hitler Youth.[63] But as tables 9.1 and 9.2 show, the age structure in at least some subdistricts became less imbalanced in the course of 1945/46.

Among women the party at first did not make much progress at all, despite the dramatic proliferation of women's social roles in the postwar reconstruction and the intense politicization that some women experienced. Most party locals complained in 1945/46 of general weaknesses in the party's work among women.[64] The KPD's rhetorical stress on women's equality still appeared unsettingly radical, especially in the wake of twelve years of Nazi maternalist propaganda and policies. And the party itself sometimes implemented its program with less than stellar consistency. At the important Eisen- und Hüttenwerk Thale, where communists completely dominated the works council and participated in the direction of the firm, leading party members in conjunction with the firm direction opposed granting women employees equal pay for equal work and thereby sacrificed female support.[65] In general, the immense and time-consuming task of searching for the basic necessities of life and maintaining the family left little time and energy for political activism. Most importantly, the devastating experience of rape at the hands of Red Army soldiers resulted in a visceral reaction against

[63] KPDHM, "Protokoll über die Sekretariatssitzung am 14.1.1946;" KPDHM, "Diskussion auf der erweiterten BL-Sitzung am 14.2.1946," 18 February 1946, LPAH I/2/3/2/25, 34; KL Eisleben und Mansfelder Seekreis, "Ergänzung des Tätigkeitsberichtes für den Monat März," 29 March 1946, LPAH I/2/3/3/218; and Benser, *KPD im Jahre der Befreiung*, 306–7.

[64] For just a few examples, see KLW, "Bericht für den Monat März," 29 March 1946, LPAH I/2/3/3a/123, and Benser, *KPD im Jahre der Befreiung*, 311–15.

[65] BLPS, "Zum Organisationsbericht für Januar 1946," 7 February 1946, LPAH I/2/5/4/47.

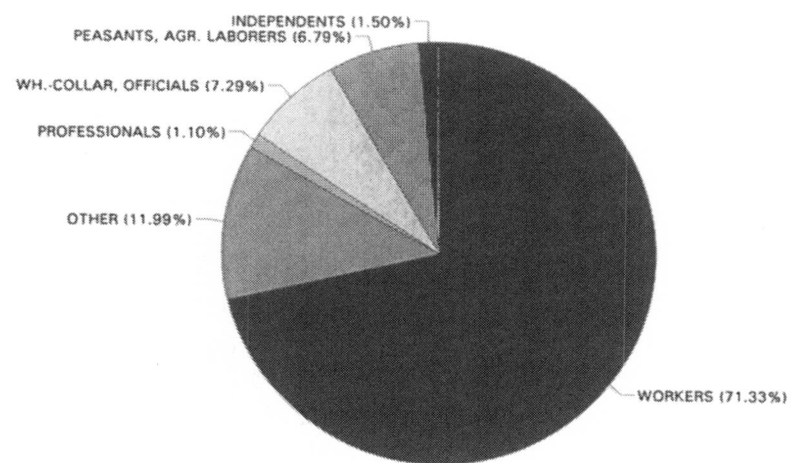

Figure 9.3 Social Composition of KPD Membership Magdeburg Subdistrict, March 1946.
Source: LPAH I/2/5/4/85–92.

TABLE 9.1
Social Composition of KPD Membership Halle-Merseburg Subdistrict, April 1946

Locality	*No.*	*No. Female*	*Pct. Female*	*No. <21 yrs*	*Pct. <21 yrs*	*No. 21–35 yrs*	*Pct. 21–35 yrs*
Torgau	3,227	644	19.96	206	6.38	848	26.28
Eisleben	4,579	887	19.37	451	9.85	1,159	25.31
Weissenfels	4,307	750	17.41	506	11.75	921	21.38
Hettstedt	1,860	372	20.00	130	6.99	600	32.26
Bitterfeld	6,437	1,027	15.95	255	3.96	899	13.97
Herzberg	1,090	338	31.01	53	4.86	105	9.63
Wittenberg	2,414	272	11.27	96	3.98	1,987	82.31
Zeitz	8,437	1,994	23.63	340	4.03	1,341	15.89
Saalkreis	3,574	452	12.65	314	8.79	525	14.69
Querfurt	2,540	428	16.85	135	5.31	338	13.31
Merseburg	6,354	953	15.00	475	7.48	1,014	15.96
Koelleda	1,909	415	21.74	121	6.34	383	20.06
Sangerhausen	2,500	427	17.08	216	8.64	492	19.68
Halle-Stadt	7,649	1,766	23.09	499	6.52	1,166	15.24
Delitzsch	3,517	456	12.97	189	5.37	890	25.31
Liebenwerda	2,140	380	17.76	61	2.85	209	9.77
Total	62,534	11,561	18.49	4,047	6.47	12,877	20.59

Source: LPAH 1/2/3/3/52.

TABLE 9.2

Age Composition of KPD Membership, Halle-Merseburg Subdistrict, 1946

	Halle-Stadt		*Saalkreis*		*Zeitz*		*Weissenfels*	
	Pct. *<21 yrs*	*Pct.* *21–35 yrs*	*Pct.* *<21 yrs*	*Pct.* *21–35 yrs*	*Pct.* *<21 yrs*	*Pct.* *21–35 yrs*	*Pct.* *<21 yrs*	*Pct.* *21–35 yrs*
January	4.14	11.55	11.64	20.95	6.38	21.77	6.82	15.91
March	6.91	20.43	8.53	15.96	4.43	17.76	12.36	21.98
	Merseburg		*Bitterfeld*		*Torgau*		*Schweinitz*	
	Pct. *<21 yrs*	*Pct.* *21–35 yrs*	*Pct.* *<21 yrs*	*Pct.* *21–35 yrs*	*Pct.* *<21 yrs*	*Pct.* *21–35 yrs*	*Pct.* *<21 yrs*	*Pct.* *21–35 yrs*
January	8.42	21.20	6.33	14.22	8.24	10.85	5.76	21.58
March	9.47	20.22	3.23	11.63	6.84	20.96	8.31	20.11
	Wittenberg		*Delitzsch*		*Liebenwerda*		*Mansfeld Seekreis*	
	Pct. *<21 yrs*	*Pct.* *21–35 yrs*	*Pct.* *<21 yrs*	*Pct.* *21–35 yrs*	*Pct.* *<21 yrs*	*Pct.* *21–35 yrs*	*Pct.* *<21 yrs*	*Pct.* *21–35 yrs*
January	3.94	29.59	4.04	27.94	4.31	9.70	6.38	22.32
March	3.91	27.62	6.89	29.81	3.17	8.74	7.41	21.67
	Mansfeld Gebirgekreis		*Sangerhausen*		*Eckartsberga*		*Querfurt*	
	Pct. *<21 yrs*	*Pct.* *21–35 yrs*	*Pct.* *<21 yrs*	*Pct.* *21–35 yrs*	*Pct.* *<21 yrs*	*Pct.* *21–35 yrs*	*Pct.* *<21 yrs*	*Pct.* *21–35 yrs*
January	4.08	22.67	3.69	17.24	8.20	25.16	5.78	29.65
March	3.87	22.61	2.91	13.64	7.02	21.25	8.15	27.78

Source: LPAH I/2/3/4/42, 89.

TABLE 9.3
Proportion of Female Membership, KPD Subdistricts Saxony Province, 1945–46

	Halle-Merseburg			*Magdeburg*			*Dessau*		
Date	*No.*	*No. Female*	*Pct. Female*	*No.*	*No. Female*	*Pct. Female*	*No.*	*No. Female*	*Pct. Female*
11/45	32,741						9,700	1,276	13.15
12/45	37,884	5,576	14.72				10,600	1,800	16.98
1/46	43,579	6,718	15.42	33,267	5,936	17.84	12,700	2,600	20.47
2/46	49,370			41,550			16,636		
3/46	56,811	10,338	18.20	39,085	8,074	20.66			

Source: LPAH I/2/5/4/8-14, 20–27, 32–36, 40–45, 85–92.

communism. Instead, the emergence of a "female discourse" about household, family, and politics constituted a distinctive terrain of women's activism and self-articulation, which could not be easily assimilated, if at all, into the KPD's political conceptions.[66] As a result, the KPD's Halle-Merseburg organization, for example, only counted 18.49 percent female members in early 1946, not much different from the Weimar period.[67]

Nevertheless, table 9.3 indicates that also among women local party organizations could point to improvements in the course of 1945/46 that drove female participation rates above those of the Weimar period. Other party documents also indicate increasing successes among women.[68] Reports from Weissenfels in September 1945, for example, mention a women's meeting with over six hundred in attendance, a very positive send-off, according to the official, for the party's organizational work among women.[69] Some months later, the local again reported well-attended women's rallies and women's active participation in party cells.[70]

On the verge of unity with the SPD in April 1946, the KPD had over six

[66] On the issue of women's discourse and the distinctive terrain of women's activism, Annete Kuhn, "Der Refamilisierungsdiskurs nach '45," *BzG* 33:5 (1991): 593–606, provides a good review of the historiographical debates and some insightful quotes from women in the first postwar period.

[67] "Monatsbericht für Monat März 1946 der U.B.L. der KPD Halle-Merseburg," LPAH I/2/3/3/52. Some individual cities and towns did much better, however, including Halle with somewhat over 23 percent female members and one town, Herzberg, whose membership was almost one-third female.

[68] Compare Naimark, *Russians in Germany*, 129–32, who emphasizes the continued hostility of women to communism and the KPD/SED's inept and insufficient organizational efforts. Even Soviet authorities berated their German comrades for lack of attention to women's issues.

[69] "Bericht über die Arbeit der Kommunistischen Partei, Ortsgruppe Weißenfels für Monat September 1945," LPAH I/2/3/3a/75.

[70] KLW, "Bericht für den Monat März," 29 March 1946, LPAH I/2/3/3a/131–32. For a somewhat similar report, see "Tätigkeitsbericht des U.B. Zeitz," [late summer or early autumn 1945], LPAH I/2/3/3a/164.

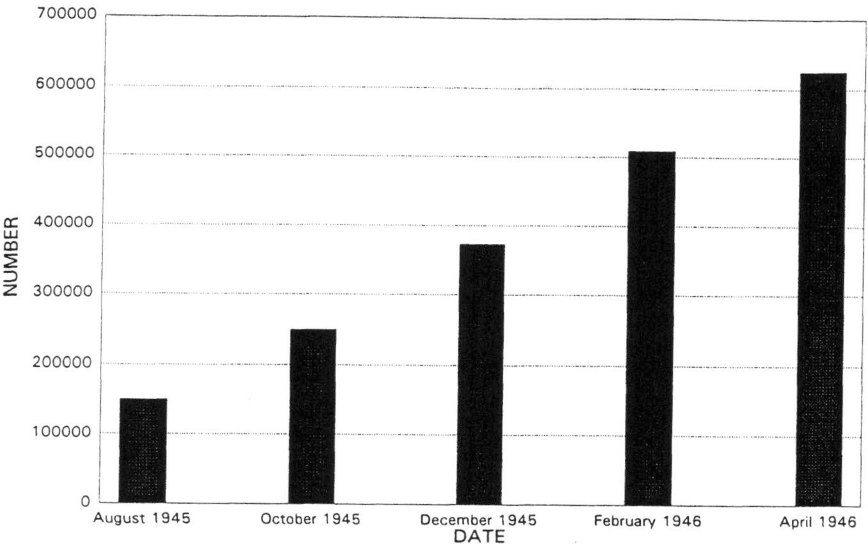

Figure 9.4 KPD Membership SBZ, 1945–46. *Source: SBZ Handbuch*, 458–59.

hundred thousand members (figure 9.4), virtually double the KPD's membership in all of Weimar Germany. For each pre-1933 member, the KPD had five new ones.[71] The KPD had made enormous strides toward becoming a mass-based party, one with far broader and deeper support than communism had achieved in the Weimar Republic. Less than one year after the defeat of the Third Reich, party leaders in Saxony Province reported with a sense of pride and accomplishment that "[t]he continually rising influence of the Communist Party among all circles of the population is shown in the constant upward movement of the membership figures. . . . In the ranks of the party are found mainly workers, but we have also been able to gather in other groups."[72]

The forced march toward unity of the KPD and SPD in the winter of 1945/46 seems only to have aided the popular appeal of the KPD—despite widespread interpretations to the contrary. In the factories and mines especially fusion had an almost elemental and emotional appeal.[73] Internal party reports indicate gener-

[71] Hermann Weber, "Die deutschen Kommunisten 1945 in der SBZ," *APZ* B31 (5 August 1978): 28. The SPD, in contrast, essentially reconstituted its old membership, as Weber points out (30).

[72] BLPS, "Die organisatorische Entwicklung der Kommunistischen Partei in der Provinz Sachsen," 1 February 1946, LPAH I/2/5/4/40.

[73] See the standard account in Dietrich Staritz, *Die Gründung der DDR: Von der sowjetschen Besatzungsherrschaft zum sozialistischen Staat* (Munich: DTV, 1984). For a latter-day, post-DDR effort that largely reiterates the East German view with only a few modifications, Hans-Joachim Krusch and Andreas Malycha, eds., *Einheitsdrang oder Zwangsvereinigung? Die Sechziger-Konferenzen von KPD und SPD 1945 und 1946* (Berlin: Dietz Verlag, 1990). Kleßmann, *Doppelte Staatsgründung*, 139, provides a more nuanced argument, and I largely follow his approach here.

ally strong sentiments, especially in the workplace, for cooperation and unity.[74] Indeed, in Zeitz and Halle SPD members had initially gone over to the KPD en masse and only formed their own organization on command of the Soviet authorities.[75] By March 1946, on the verge of formal unity, the KPD leadership in Saxony Province struck a melodic note by claiming that KPD-SPD unity committees "were sprouting like mushrooms" all over the province and that "unanimous elation" prevailed among the workers about the prospects for a united party.[76] The only gauge of the degree of popular sentiment for unification, the West Berlin referendum of SPD members at the end of March, demonstrated strong hostility to the character of unification—82 percent voted against it—but also powerful sentiments for some kind of coalition or future unification ("*Bündnis*" and "*gemeinsame Arbeit*" were the terms used) with the KPD, for which 62 percent voted in the affirmative.[77]

Whatever the reservations, by 1948, the SED had about two million members, some 16 percent of the adult population of the SBZ.[78] The diversity of the membership accelerated as well (table 9.4) as the SED drew in increasing numbers of white-collar workers, including professionals.[79] Indeed, Walter Ulbricht complained in 1948 about the declining percentage of workers in the SED, leading to a renewed emphasis on party recruitment drives in the workplace and the ideological reassertion of the proletarian character of the SED.[80] The proportion of women in the party increased to 24 percent in 1948,[81] higher than the other German political parties and comparable to the successes of the French and Italian communist parties in the post–World War II period.

In the autumn of 1946 the Soviets permitted a series of elections for representatives at the local, county (*Kreis*), and state (*Land*) level.[82] As in the Berlin referendum on the SPD/KPD merger, the SMAD deployed its powers in support of German

[74] Almost all of the reports from the district and subdistrict leaderships of the KPD in Saxony Province during the winter of 1945/46 support this point. For a few examples, see "Monatsbericht für Monat März 1946 der U.B.L. der KPD Halle-Merseburg," LPAH I/2/3/3/49–52; KLW, "Bericht für den Monat März," 29 March 1946; KL Wernigerode to BLH, 7 February 1946; "Tätigkeitsbericht der Kommunistischen Partei, Kreisleitung Zeitz, für den Monat Februar 1946," LPAH I/2/3/3a/124, 126–28, 149–50, 176; BLPS, "Zum Organisationsbericht," 7 January 1946, LPAH I/2/5/4/29–30.

[75] BLPS, "Bericht über die Entwicklung der Organisation der Kommunistischen Partei im Bezirk Halle," 13 September 1945, LPAH I/2/5/4/6.

[76] BLPS, "Zum Organisationsbericht für Februar 1946," 6 March 1946, LPAH I/2/5/4/82, 83. While the district leadership might have been overstating the case, its reports often carried critical comments about the state of party work, so I am inclined to trust the general appraisal of the situtation.

[77] This is Kleßmann's argument, who observes that the second question on the ballot concerning collaboration has often been ignored. See *Doppelte Staatsgründung*, 141, and Staritz, *Sozialismus in einem halben Lande*, 80–81, who takes a similar position.

[78] Hermann Weber, "Aufstieg und Niedergang des deutschen Kommunismus," *APZ* B40/91 (27 September 1991): 30.

[79] Werner Müller, "Sozialistische Einheitspartei Deutschlands (SED)," in *SBZ-Handbuch*, 489.

[80] Ibid., 450.

[81] Ibid., 489.

[82] On the elections held in the SBZ and early DDR, see Günter Braun, "Wahlen und Abstimmungen," in *SBZ-Handbuch*, 381–431.

Table 9.4
Social Structure of SED Membership, 1947

	No.	*Pct.*
Industrial workers	855,451	47.9
Agricultural workers	64,276	3.6
Peasants	103,457	5.8
Housewives and others	247,195	13.8
Craftsmen and tradesmen	115,749	6.5
Engineers and technicians	17,398	1.0
Teachers	29,416	1.6
Doctors, lawyers, artists	32,083	1.8
Employees	321,113	18.0

Source: SBZ Handbuch, 510.

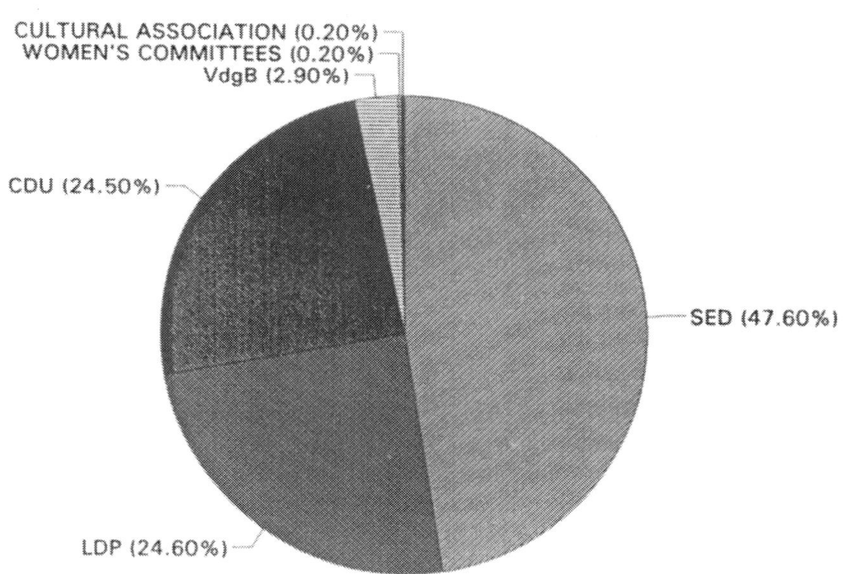

Figure 9.5 Local Elections SBZ, September 1946. *Source: SBZ Handbuch*, 396.
VdgB = Vereinigung der gegenseitigen Bauernhilfe, the SED-dominated peasants' cooperative organization
CDU = Christian Democratic Union
LDP = Liberal Democratic Party

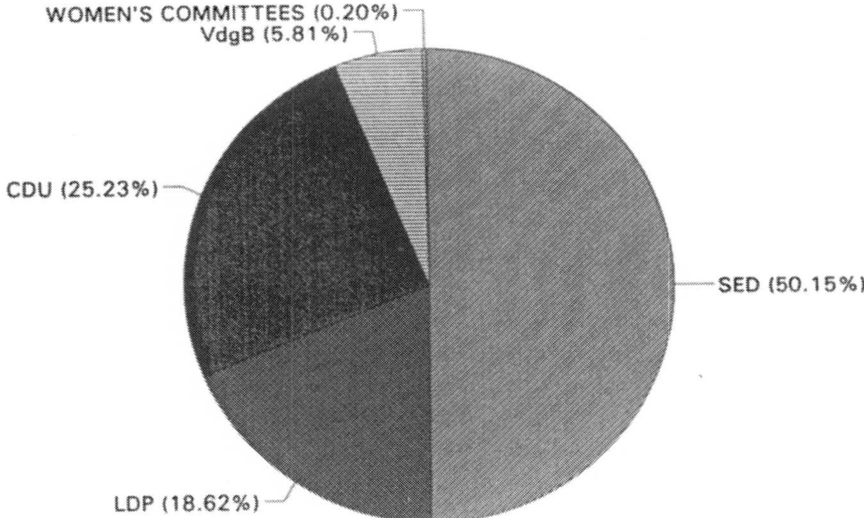

Figure 9.6 County Elections SBZ, October 1946. *Source: SBZ Handbuch*, 396.
VdgB = Vereinigung der gegenseitigen Bauernhilfe, the SED-dominated peasants' cooperative organization
CDU = Christian Democratic Union
LDP = Liberal Democratic Party

communism. The SED received extensive support, the other parties found themselves harassed. They had difficulty obtaining paper and access to the airwaves and holding rallies and demonstrations. Especially in local contests the Christian Democratic Union and the Liberal Democratic Party came under intense pressure and in quite a number of instances were unable to field candidates.

Whatever the limitations, the elections in the autumn of 1946 were reasonably fair and provide one of the few gauges of popular opinion in the SBZ. Figures 9.5 to 9.7 summarize the results. In the local and county elections, the SED won the majority (57.1 percent and 50.3 percent, respectively).[83] At the *Land* level, where the CDU and LDP were better positioned, the SED won a plurality with 47.6 percent of the vote. In the largely agrarian Mecklenburg the SED achieved its greatest success, no doubt as beneficiary of the land reform program. The SED did relatively poorly among women (in contrast to its relatively high female membership), the CDU the best.[84] In areas where substantial SPD opposition to the SPD/KPD merger existed, the SED fared poorly, as in Eisleben, where a strong and intransigent communist group alienated former social democrats. In other traditionally strong KPD regions, like the Mansfelder Seekreis and the

[83] Ibid., 386.

[84] Ibid., 387. In private, SED and Soviet leaders attributed the poor showing among women to the huge incidence of rape committed by Red Army soldiers. See Naimark, *Russians in Germany*, 120–21.

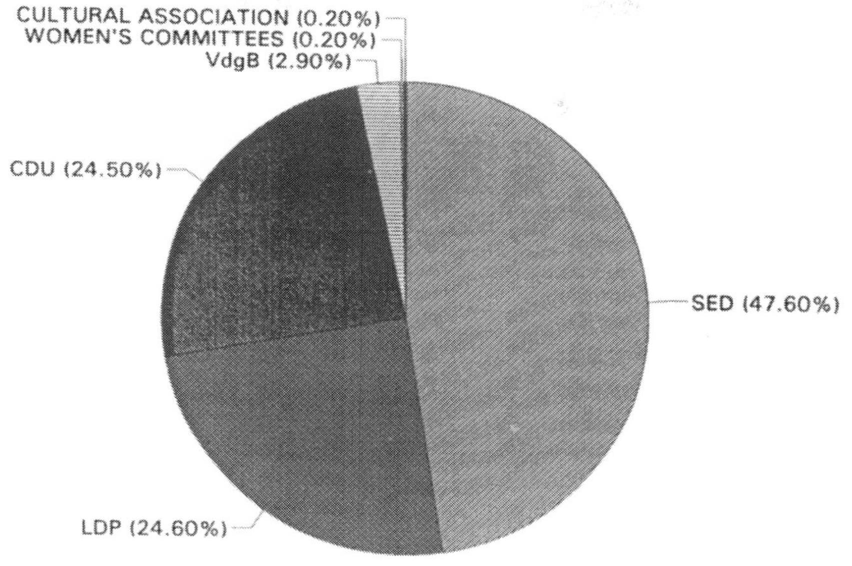

Figure 9.7 Landtag Elections SBZ, October 1946. *Source: SBZ Handbuch*, 397.
VdgB = Vereinigung der gegenseitigen Bauernhilfe, the SED-dominated peasants' cooperative organization
CDU = Christian Democratic Union
LDP = Liberal Democratic Party

Saalkreis, the areas, respectively, around Eisleben and Halle, the SED performed better, obtaining 71.0 percent and 65.6 percent of the vote in the local elections.[85]

Despite the SED's electoral victories, the Soviets and the SED leadership were greatly disappointed. They expected the SED to make a clean sweep and to achieve majority support in nearly all districts of the Zone. In numerous towns and cities the party found itself with only a plurality, and sometimes not even that. The results in Berlin proved especially shocking. Unlike in the SBZ, in Berlin the SPD was able to participate in the election and came out the clear victor. In contrast to the SPD's 48.7 percent of the vote, the SED won only 19.8 percent of the electorate, the fourth position. In the Soviet sector the SED won only 29.9 percent of the vote, the second position. Even in districts that had been solid KPD areas in the Weimar Republic the SED trailed behind the SPD. Only in the Soviet sector was the SED tally comparable to the KPD results in the local election of 1929.[86]

The disappointing results strengthened the hands of those party figures always quick to revert to administrative direction and loathe to expose the party to popular opinion. In fact the elections of 1946 were the last openly contested ones in

[85] Braun, "Wahlen und Abstimmungen," 410–11.
[86] Ibid., 389.

the SBZ aside from a few exceptional local races and two plebescite-like campaigns in support of national unity. Certainly, the electoral results demonstrate a very substantial reservoir of opposition to the SED and its Soviet sponsor—hardly surprising given the magnitude of Germany's defeat in the war, the actions of Red Army soldiers in Germany, and a generalized anticommunism only heightened by twelve years of Nazi propaganda. By the autumn of 1946, the SED and SMAD also had to shoulder the burden of responsibility for the economic insufficiencies and social dislocations in the SBZ. The Berlin election especially demonstrated a wave of opposition to the SED that was bound up with residual hostility to the forced merger of the SPD and KPD.

But the meaning of the elections in the autumn of 1946 is not fully captured by the politics of the moment. From a longer historical vantage point, the electoral results demonstrate that the KPD/SED had become a mass party with a broad base of support. Its overall backing was far higher than the KPD had achieved in the Weimar years, and higher than virtually any other European communist party that contested free elections. While devastating to the party leadership and to the Soviets, the electoral results demonstrate the KPD/SED's successes, not only its failures, in the one and one-half years following the defeat of Nazi Germany. With a new political language and a new strategy, the addition of social democrats to the ranks, and a powerful sponsor, the KPD/SED had begun to move out of the cul-de-sac it had itself helped to create in the Weimar period. The deep disappointment with the results derived from the delusion that a European communist party could ever come to power on the basis of the popular will.

In the western zones the KPD also experienced a surge of support, though with different rhythms and contours. As in central and eastern Germany, communists drew support from popular activism designed to secure infrastructures from the last-minute rampages of the Nazis, locate food supplies, reinstitute production, purge Nazis from positions of responsibility, and establish Antifas.[87] Workers and communists understood many of these initial actions as socialization measures or as the initial steps in the revolutionary transformation of Germany, conceptions that went far beyond the scope of party strategies, let alone the intentions of the occupation authorities. These initiatives blurred the distinctions between community and workplace activism: works councillors got involved in procuring food for their workforces while the Antifas aided in the reconstruction of the workplace, and communists were able to recruit support in both arenas. As one Ruhr miner remembered it, "The communists started first. I went to a big meeting and had a wonderful experience. I heard something I hadn't heard before. . . . The question was one of power, who had it? The communists were highly intelligent and well prepared. They took over everything

[87] For examples see Niethammer et al., *Arbeiterinitiative*; Mannschatz and Seider, *Zum Kampf der KPD*, 26–27; Diskant, "Scarcity, Survival and Local Activism"; and Suckut, *Betriebsrätebewegung*, 120–42. For a more restrained view, see Diethelm Prowe, "Socialism as Crisis Response: Socialization and the Escape from Poverty and Power in Post–World War II Germany," *GSR* 15:1 (1992): 65–85.

and enabled Westhausen to mine coal again. They got together, and simply said: 'We elect . . . the leadership.' "[88]

As a result of these kinds of activities, the KPD's support began to grow. In works council elections in the Ruhr in the autumn of 1945, communists won 666 out of 1716 seats in the mining industry, somewhat over 38 percent, and scored similar victories in 1946.[89] At Victoria Mathias, an Essen mine with a long radical tradition, the KPD won 63.5 percent of the votes for the works councils in October 1945.[90] In the miners union, communists occupied many leading positions, and in the metals industry, communists won 242 works council seats out of 864 in the most important metalworking plants.[91]

Party membership in the Ruhr rose from 24,371 in March 1946 to 50,596 in December 1946, and by January 1947 had reached the membership level of 1932.[92] In all of the western zones, the KPD had one hundred sixty thousand members in February 1946, and around three hundred thousand in 1949.[93] This constituted quite an achievement given the fact that conditions for communist work in the western zones were hardly auspicious. The western allies were notably hostile to communism and popular democratic efforts at the grassroots, and they maintained the ban on political parties until the autumn of 1945 or early 1946, and in some areas even longer. Electorally the KPD also demonstrated greater attractiveness. In a number of states it won more than 10 percent of the vote in Landtag elections. In North Rhine–Westphalia, for example, the KPD garnered 14.0 percent, in Berlin 13.7 percent.

Still desperate living conditions, including serious food and fuel shortages, coupled with the reemergence of managerial authority, often in the person of ex-Nazis, triggered in 1947 the greatest mass protest movement of the postwar years. The KPD again found itself with fruitful arenas of activity that enabled the party to position itself within the traditional domains of labor activism and to assert its claim to be the true defender of working-class interests. Especially in the Ruhr, Hamburg, Bremen, and other traditional centers of the radical labor movement, the KPD drew upon popular activism and deepened its membership base.[94]

[88] Quoted in Diskant, "Scarcity, Survival and Local Activism," 559.

[89] Mannschatz and Seider, *Zum Kampf der KPD*, 52–53, 208, and Christoph Kleßmann and Peter Friedemann, *Streiks und Hungermärsche im Ruhrgebiet 1946–1948* (Frankfurt am Main: Campus, 1977), 69–70 for more statistics.

[90] Kleßmann and Friedemann, *Streiks und Hungermärsche*, 69.

[91] Mannschatz and Seider, *Zum Kampf der KPD*, 208–9.

[92] Ibid., 96, 209.

[93] Weber, "Deutschen Kommunisten 1945," 27.

[94] See Mannschatz and Seider, *Zum Kampf der KPD*, 210–36, and Kleßmann and Friedemann, *Streiks und Hungermärsche*. For important statements on the mix of labor movement traditions and new departures in the western zones after 1945, see Diethelm Prowe, "*Ordnungsmacht* und *Mitbestimmung*: The Postwar Labor Unions and the Politics of Reconstruction," in *Between Reform and Revolution*, ed. Barclay and Weitz; Christoph Kleßmann, "Elemente der ideologischen und sozialpolitischen Integration der westdeutschen Arbeiterbewegung," in *Westdeutschland 1945–1955: Unterwerfung, Kontrolle, Integration*, ed. Ludolf Herbst (Munich: Oldenbourg, 1986), 108–16; and Lutz Niethammer, "Rekonstruktion und Desintegration: Zum Verständnis der deutschen Arbeiterbewegung zwischen Krieg und Kaltem Krieg," in *Politische Weichenstellungen im Nachkriegs-*

In the Ruhr, the actions began in Düsseldorf firms in January 1947 and then took on still greater force in Essen at the beginning of February.[95] On 3 February the workforces of numerous factories and mines left the workplace and marched to the city center. Krupp workers laid down their tools that afternoon, and seventeen thousand marched into the city to join other workers. The next day protests spread to other Ruhr cities and workplaces. Women were very active in these movements, as at a number of mines where they blocked the entrances until miners' demands were accepted. KPD members played leading roles in many of these actions, and the party's program and rhetoric figured largely in the popular demands, including calls for a referendum on the expropriation of the mines and socialization, a thorough purge of Nazis from leading positions in the economy and administration, popular control committees to supervise prices, and the establishment of a central administration for all Germany. In referenda at a number of mines and factories, the workers voted overwhelmingly for expropriation. At the high point of the action, some 334,000 miners struck, despite the opposition of the SPD and other parties. Workers could count significant victories at a number of factories and mines, where works councils and unions achieved, for a brief period, enhanced powers. They also forced the administration of North Rhine–Westphalia to issue a decree confirming the rights of the works councils to control and countersign monthly production records and recognizing control committees.

Yet these victories would prove short-lived. If in the SBZ the SED's claims to political domination aroused increasing opposition, in the western zones the gains won by the KPD became sacrificed to the Cold War. Increasingly, communist support of working-class activism made strikes and demonstrations subject to the charge of treason, which also led to increasingly bitter conflicts in the workplace in the western zones between communists and social democrats.[96] The hard-fought support the party had earned quickly evaporated. The KPD's increasing isolation pushed it into a kind of emotive radicalism reminiscent of the KPD of the Weimar Republic. While the party reached its highest level in 1949 with about three hundred thousand members, thereafter the membership declined precipitously. Similarly, in Landtag elections in 1949 the party's number of seats declined to twenty-nine in five states. It received 5.7 percent of the vote and fifteen mandates in the first Bundestag election on 14 August 1949, and then rapidly declined into near insignificance.[97] The intransigent radicalism of Weimar had little place amid Cold War politics and burgeoning economic prosperity.

---

deutschland 1945–1953, ed. Heinrich August Winkler (Göttingen: Vandenhoeck und Ruprecht, 1979), 26–43.

[95] For the following, see Mannschatz and Seider, *Zum Kampf der KPD*, 214–18 and 223–27, and Kleßmann and Freidemann, *Streiks und Hungermärsche*, 33–49.

[96] Kleßmann and Friedemann, *Streiks und Hungermärsche*, 65–73.

[97] Figures from Hans Kluth, *Die KPD in der Bundesrepublik: Ihre politische Tätigkeit und Organisation 1945–1956* (Cologne: Westdeutscher, 1959), 35–37.

Toward the German Democratic Republic

In the course of the period of reconstruction, the KPD/SED and the Soviet Union abandoned the gradualist orientation for the politics of intransigence and the incorporation of the Soviet Occupation Zone into the emergent Soviet bloc. The steps along the road are clear enough, but the documentary evidence available only since the collapse of the DDR in 1989/90 has more fully demonstrated what scholars have long surmised: the KPD/SED leaders sought the establishment of a separate socialist state in Germany far earlier, far more completely, than their Soviet mentors.[98] German communists tried to force the pace of development in the SBZ, only to be continually restrained by the Soviets. Only when the Soviets abandoned the chimera of a unified, neutralist Germany did the overarching goals of Soviet and German communists converge, a development that culminated in the establishment of the German Democratic Republic on 7 October 1949. Significantly, this process was not linear in nature and not predetermined. At least until the autumn of 1948 the politics of intransigence and of gradualism coexisted.

In the autumn of 1945, the Soviets and the KPD leadership rather suddenly, and in opposition to their earlier position, launched the effort to unify the SPD and KPD.[99] This move marked the first major break with the strategy outlined in the appeal of 11 June 1945, and the reasons for the reversal seem clear. Leading members of the SPD began to express severe reservations about unity or even collaboration with the KPD, rejecting even proposals for joint celebrations (as on the anniversary of the 1918 Revolution). Communist fears of an autonomous, independent, and popular SPD rose, especially in light of the major electoral defeats suffered by the Austrian and Hungarian communist parties in November 1945.

The first preliminary meetings between the SPD and KPD on the subject of unity began in the early winter of 1945. The Soviet authorities exerted strong

[98] The following discussion is based on the critical edition of Wilhelm Pieck's notes of the meetings between KPD/SED leaders and Soviet authorities, *Wilhelm Pieck—Aufzeichnungen zur Deutschlandspolitik 1945–1952*, ed. Rolf Badstübner and Wilfried Loth (Berlin: Akademie, 1993); Rolf Badstübner's preliminary commentary based on Pieck's notes, "Zum Problem der historischen Alternativen im ersten Nachkriegsjahrzehnt: Neue Quellen zur Deutschlandspolitik von KPdSU und SED," *BzG* 33:5 (1991): 579–92, and "'Beratungen' bei J. W. Stalin," *Utopia kreativ* 7 (1991): 99–112; the text "Antworten der SED-Führung auf Fragen Stalins 1948" and Thomas Friedrich's comments, both in *BzG* 33:3 (1991): 364–73; idem, "Das Kominform und die SED," *BzG* 33:3 (1991): 322–35; and the commentary and documents provided by Dietrich Staritz in "Die SED, Stalin und die Gründung der DDR," *APZ* B5/91 (25 January 1991): 3–16, and in "SED, Stalin und der 'Aufbau des Sozialismus.'" For a pre-1989 argument along these same lines, see Dietrich Staritz, "Zwischen Ostintegration und nationaler Verpflichtung: Zur Ost- und Deutschlandspolitik der SED, 1948 bis 1952," in Herbst, *Westdeutschland*, 279–89.

[99] The following account is drawn from Naimark, *Russians in Germany*, 275–84; Leonhard, "'Gruppe Ulbricht'"; Kleßmann, *Doppelte Staatsgründung*, 137–39; and Staritz, *Sozialismus in einem halben Lande*, 62–81. For an earlier study, see Henry Krisch, *German Politics under Soviet Occupation* (New York: Columbia University Press, 1974).

pressure. The SMAD ensured that the KPD had far greater access to scarce printing materials, to the airwaves, to public spaces for demonstrations and meetings. Social democratic proponents of unity received massive support, while those opposed were called before Soviet officers and sometimes detained and arrested. Opposition meetings were banned.

At the same time, the KPD presented a conciliatory face. Old SPD slogans and writings appeared. Ackermann penned his brief for a "German road to socialism" in this period and then contributed a longer pamphlet designed to reassure social democrats that the KPD was sincere in its desire to unify on the basis of equality with the SPD. He warned of the dangers of renewed reaction, and claimed that the KPD now rejected the sectarianism and childish radicalism of Weimar communism. "The KPD of today is no longer the party of 1920 or 1932," he claimed, and it recognized the "national particularities of Germany and of the German labor movement." In more ominous tones, he warned of the revival of reaction and the repetition of the "mistakes of 1918," which led directly to the Nazi victory in 1933, should unification not take place.[100]

In negotiations with the SPD, the KPD agreed to renounce the principle of democratic centralism for the "democratic rights of decision [*Bestimmungsrechts*] of the members" and agreed to parity representation in the leading organs of the new party.[101] Most remarkably, KPD leaders characterized the unified party as something sui generis, a new party that would be neither the KPD nor the SPD of old. At the last KPD congress Ackermann defined the SED as an independent party "because it will be completely free to make its own decisions. It will adapt the basic teachings of Marxism to specific German relations and to the specific German path of development."[102] Echoing Ackermann's earlier comments, Pieck declared "We communists have often applied the experiences of the October Revolution to Germany in a schematic manner. In this way we ignored to a significant extent the national particularities of Germany and of the German labor movement."[103]

The founding congress of the SED convened in April 1946 and passed a program that committed the party to a unified Germany as "an antifascist, parliamentary democratic republic" with a commitment to "economic democracy" through the equal collaboration of the trade unions in the chambers of commerce. It also called for the abolition of capitalist monopolies. Only as a distant goal did the new party envision the transformation of capitalist property into "social property" and the general transition from capitalist to socialist production. The party trumpeted its commitment to a democratic transition to socialism: only if capitalism left the road of democracy would the SED take up the means of revolution.[104] Organizationally, the new party foreswore many of the long-standing

[100] Ackermann, "Fragen und Antworten," 11–15, 27–29, quotes on 28.

[101] I draw on the accounts in Krusch and Malycha, eds., *Einheitsdrang oder Zwangsvereinigung?*; Staritz, *Gründung der DDR*, 112–23; and Kleßmann, *Doppelte Staatsgründung*, 138–42.

[102] Quoted in Leonhard, "'Gruppe Ulbricht,'" 41.

[103] Quoted in ibid.

[104] Staritz, *Sozialismus in einem halben Lande*, 78–79.

characteristics of Marxist-Leninist parties. As agreed upon in the negotiations between the two parties, the statutes established parity representation between the SPD and KPD in the leading organs and a party executive rather than a central committee and politburo, and made no mention at all of democratic centralism.

To many labor movement activists and supporters, the unity of the two parties signified that labor had at last overcome its wrenching division, which, in their eyes, had been the fatal error that had permitted the Nazis to seize power. In the workplace especially powerful sentiments for fusion had developed in the months leading up to the congress. Christoph Kleßmann argues that among social democrats, the emotional pull in favor of unity was so strong that it "threatened ultimately to undermine the authority of the Central Committee [of the SPD] and send it into isolation."[105] On the KPD side, internal reports indicated comparably strong sentiments in favor of cooperation and unity.[106] Many Social Democrats were again reassured when SPD leader Otto Grotewohl declared at the founding congress that "the unfettering of the human personality"[107] was among the major goals of the new society the SED would lead—a formulation that linked the party to the nineteenth-century humanist roots of the socialist movement, rather than to the Leninism of the twentieth century. Grotewohl also declared that with the formation of the SED, there was no longer any need for Russian bayonets, a line greeted with stormy applause at the founding congress.

Ultimately, however, the character of unification undermined the prospects for democracy in the SBZ and marked a major step along the road to the formation of two German states. The forced nature of unification, and the resistance to it on the part of many social democrats, weakened lingering sentiments for labor unity in the west and strengthened the strongly anticommunist hand of the western SPD leader, Kurt Schumacher. Moreover, it led to an alteration in British policy, because the British now viewed communist activity in their zone as a threat and, consequently, drew closer to the United States. Great difficulties arose for rank-and-file communists as social democrats and Christians in the west intensified their efforts to curb communist influence in the works councils and the unions.[108]

In the months following unification, the SED maintained the rhetoric of democracy, national unity, and the German road. At the same time, the SED under communist domination began narrowing the field of democratic practices. The party exerted increasing pressure on political and cultural figures, and the language of order and discipline—coupled with attacks on western "monopolists" and "imperialists" and the "Quisling Dr. Schumacher"—became ever more frequent.[109] As early as the autumn of 1946 the leadership of the SED began floating the idea of a separate socialist state in Germany.[110] In contrast, the Soviets,

[105] Kleßmann, *Doppelte Staatsgründung*, 139.

[106] See n. 74 above.

[107] Quoted in Leonhard, "'Gruppe Ulbricht,'" 41–42.

[108] Kleßmann, *Doppelte Staatsgründung*, 141–42.

[109] Quoted in Pike, *Politics of Culture*, 264–65.

[110] Staritz, "SED, Stalin und die Gründung der DDR," 7.

with larger strategic and international interests, sought to maintain a certain openness in relation to the German question in the hopes of establishing a unified, neutralist nation.

The acceleration of the Cold War, however, pushed the Soviets closer to the claims of German communists for their own state, even in a truncated territory. The critical western moves toward the Cold War—the Marshall Plan; the Truman Doctrine; the removal of communists from the governments of France, Italy, Belgium, Denmark, Luxemburg, Norway, and Iceland; the failure of the London foreign ministers' conference in December 1947—encouraged the Soviet side to tighten its hold on central and eastern Europe, including its occupation zone in Germany. Within the SBZ, the SED faced increasing difficulties and outright public hostility over severely constricted living conditions, continued Soviet dismantling of factories, and the Soviets' refusal to release, or even provide information about, prisoners of war. The SED's obvious dependence on the Soviets, who decided issues great and minor in the Zone, cost the party much of the broad support it had won in 1945/46—despite its ever increasing membership rolls.[111] For the SED leaders, a separate state seemed the only way to secure their powers and free themselves from excessive Soviet interference.

The foundation of the Communist Information Bureau (Cominform) in September 1947 as a successor to the Comintern—which had been abolished at Stalin's behest in 1943—marked the final breach in the allied coalition and a crucial transit station on the way to the establishment of the DDR. At the founding meeting in Sklarska Poremba (Poland) Andrei Zhdanov issued his famed remarks about "two camps." The language was not new, but its reappearance as a general feature of communist political terminology marked a reversion to pre–popular front politics, and especially to the Comintern's "third period" and the language of "social fascism."[112] The official documents from the founding congress of the Cominform stated that the imperialist camp rested on the "political treason of the right-wing social democrats," the "helper's helpers of imperialism" who poison the consciousness of the working class.[113] The SPD specifically charged the Cominform with reviving the communist language of the pre-1933 period, when the KPD and Comintern made social democracy, rather than National Socialism, the main enemy. The SED, in a significant retreat from the gradualist position, replied that it had no intention of renouncing its positions of the late Weimar years.[114]

The SED had not been informed beforehand about the founding of the Cominform in September 1947 and had not been party to the deliberations. It seems that Pieck, Ulbricht, and others were taken aback by the news and sought admission to the international body, but without success. Stalin still wanted to keep his options

[111] For details on the deep level of Soviet involvement in even mundane matters in the Zone, see Naimark, *Russians in Germany*.

[112] The language of two camps had been a fixture of communist doctrine since the October Revolution. Stalin had used the term as early as December 1925 at the Fourteenth Congress of the Bolshevik Party, and in February 1946. See Friedrich, "Kominform und die SED," 323.

[113] Ibid., 324.

[114] Ibid., 326–27, 331.

open in relation to Germany and prevented—for a time—the full incorporation of the SBZ into the emerging Soviet bloc.

Despite their exclusion, the SED leaders could only have reacted with joy. The founding of the Cominform illuminated the green light enabling them to speed along developments in the SBZ. Like the Comintern's proclamation of the "third period" in 1928 and 1929, the founding of the Cominform seemed to confirm the most deeply held convictions of German communists. Both events moved international communist politics into alignment with the intransigent inclinations of the KPD and SED and permitted the party leadership to purge or otherwise render silent the advocates of transitional programs, political alliances, and a German road to socialism. Indeed, the very next month, in October 1947, Ulbricht argued that the time had come to "realize Marxism." The SED had now "to learn" from the Soviet Union and the CPSU and to purge its ranks, and the administrative apparatus, of "opposing" elements, who now acquired the infamous Stalinist appellations of "saboteurs," "agents," "vermin," and "racketeers."[115] The implications were clear—this could only be done by a Leninist "party of a new type" in full possession of political power: in all of Germany if possible, in a truncated state if necessary.

From the foundation of the Cominform and Zhdanov's "two camps" speech, domestic and international events accelerated rapidly, providing ever increasing support for the intransigent line. The Czech coup came in February 1948. The Allied Control Council collapsed the next month. The Soviets granted the German Economic Commission in the SBZ greater powers, and the United States instituted currency reform in the western zones. In April 1948 the Soviets blocked access to Berlin, and in June the American airlift began. Within Germany, the failure of the People's Congress movement, through which the SED sought to rally popular support for a unified Germany, seemed only to confirm the party leadership's position in favor of a separate socialist state.[116]

As a result, over the next year and a half, the SED continually appealed to the Soviets for permission to build a central state apparatus with claims to govern the entire country, but in reality limited to the SBZ.[117] Stalin continually demurred, but the Germans found support among a number of key Soviet officers in Germany, notably Major General Sergei Tulpanov, the chief of the Information Service of the SMAD and a persistent champion of the intransigent position. In May 1948, Tulpanov argued that, in fact, two Germanys now existed, and the SED had to move developments in the direction of a "people's democracy"[118]—a term that by this point had lost the more open and democratic connotations of 1945/46.

[115] Ibid., 330, and Pike, *Politics of Culture*, 267–75, quote on 270.

[116] Dietrich Staritz, *Geschichte der DDR 1949–1985* (Frankfurt am Main: Suhrkamp, 1985), 14–15.

[117] See Loth's introduction and the accompanying documents in *Wilhelm Pieck—Aufzeichnungen*, 32–33 and esp. doc. 60 and 69; Staritz, "SED, Stalin und die Gründung der DDR," 4; and Badstübner, "Zum Problem der historischen Alternativen," 584–85.

[118] Staritz, "SED, Stalin und die Gründung der DDR," 5. See also Badstübner, "Zum Problem der historischen Alternativen," 588–90, and Pike, *Politics of Culture*, 401–9. Pike provides a very revealing discussion of Tulpanov's views based, especially, on notes taken by Anton Ackermann during

Tulpanov's comments must have warmed the hearts of Ulbricht and Pieck, since they went on the rhetorical and ideological offensive at about the same time. Indeed, on 12 May 1948, Pieck, speaking to the SED Executive, called for a "strategic alteration of our struggle." Since the west has separated off, the eastern zone shall "develop as an independent state formation according to socialist principles." In a very significant rhetorical shift, he called the SED a "party of a new type"—the classic Leninist formulation for communist parties—that had to take the leadership of the nation in hand.[119] Pieck's characterization was confirmed by the SED Executive in June 1948, which also announced a two-year economic plan to begin in 1949. Party co-chairman Otto Grotewohl confirmed the new direction: the economic plan means that "[we] *clearly and without any reservation have oriented ourselves to the east!*" though he also professed continued support for the unity of Germany.[120] Ever quick out of the gates, Walter Ulbricht some months later already envisioned the forced construction of socialism: "Our task is . . . to cross the road to the complete elimination and liquidation of capitalist elements in the countryside as well as in the cities. This task is, to put it bluntly, that of socialist construction."[121] This meant, necessarily, the intensification of the class struggle, and Ulbricht, invoking all the manifestations of the Stalinist imagination, warned of opposition and sabotage.

In August 1948 the SED condemned the slogan of a "German road to socialism" as false and as hostile to the party, a sure sign of the triumph of the politics of intransigence. Ackermann had to do penance and was demoted, never again to reach the heights of power.[122] In the autumn and early winter of 1948 and then a number of times through the first months of 1949, SED leaders (Pieck, Ulbricht, and Grotewohl) again met with officials of the SMAD and then were called to Moscow (along with Fred Oelßner as translator) for a meeting with Stalin. In these deliberations, the SED sought support for completing the restructuring of the SED into a "party of a new type" and the SBZ into a "people's democracy." Soviet military commanders in Germany seem to have had no objections to the SED's plans, but Stalin still exercised caution. He counseled that the KPD leaders in the west should not act in too open a manner and that their public ties to the SED should be loosened. The SED itself should pursue a "zigzag" course toward socialism and not use the term "people's democracy." He called on the SED

Tulpanov's conversations (or monologues) with SED leaders. But Pike persistently attributes Tulpanov's views, for which there is ample documentary records in the SED party archive, to Stalin, and assumes, wrongly, a clear, consistent, and uniform position among Soviet policymakers. For far more nuanced interpretations that recognize the limits of Stalin's powers without in anyway calling into question the reality of the dictatorship, see Naimark, *Russians in Germany*, esp. 318–52, and Loth's introduction to *Wilhelm Pieck—Aufzeichnungen*.

[119] Quoted in Staritz, "SED, Stalin und der 'Aufbau des Sozialismus,'" 690.

[120] Quoted in Staritz, *Geschichte der DDR*, 20–21.

[121] Quoted in Staritz, "SED, Stalin und die Gründung der DDR," 6.

[122] See especially the description of the meeting of the SED Executive in September 1948, based on the stenographic record, in Pike, *Politics of Culture*, 414–19.

leaders still to work for the establishment of a provisional all-German government.[123]

Stalin also rejected the SED's appeal for membership in the Cominform and its efforts to intensify dramatically the political situation in the SBZ. At a meeting with Stalin in December 1948, the SED leadership sought permission to characterize the present system as a "higher democratic order," to consider more strongly the "questions of the transition to socialism," and to begin to surmount the constraints on the transition to a people's democracy—all of which went too far for Stalin.[124] Pieck must have taken up his pen with some disappointment when he wrote in his notes on this meeting, "still no unified state, stand not [on the verge of] power."[125]

Stalin, it seems, pushed actively for the transition of the SED into a Soviet-style party, but not for the transformation of Germany into a Soviet-style society—a critical difference completely overlooked by Thomas Friedrich and, partly, by Dietrich Staritz in their recent analyses of these developments. As Staritz writes, "the Stalinist Soviet Union wanted formally to keep open the German question for as long as possible: to underscore its interests in Germany (such as reparations and security) and . . . to be able to use the German question as a means of pressure in the Cold War."[126] This required a loyal party within Germany, but not necessarily a Soviet-style social transformation, which, as Stalin must have understood, would certainly have closed off any options other than the dual state solution.

But the SED made no such distinctions. In contrast to Stalin's cautiousness, the SED understood the movement toward the "party of a new type" as identical with the movement to the "society of a new type," that is, a Soviet-style system in a truncated Germany. (No one talked any longer of a "democracy of a new type," the term associated with the popular front and the gradualist position.) In preparation for their meeting with Soviet leaders, the SED leaders, at Stalin's behest, drew up in late 1948 a series of responses to questions that Stalin had posed—a document quite revealing about the intentions of the party.[127] The SED leaders viewed the division of Germany now as a sign of the intensification of the class struggle and of the attack of capitalist forces against working people. The imperialist forces were

[123] See the quotes provided by Staritz, "SED, Stalin und der 'Aufbau des Sozialismus,'" 692, and "SED, Stalin und die Gründung der DDR," 7.

[124] Staritz, "SED, Stalin und der 'Aufbau des Sozialismus,'" 692. See also Badstübner, "'Beratungen.'"

[125] Quoted in Staritz, "SED, Stalin und der 'Aufbau des Sozialismus,'" 692.

[126] Ibid., 688.

[127] See "Brief der SED-Führung an J. W. Stalin," and "Die sowjetische Antwort," in Staritz, "SED, Stalin und die Gründung der DDR," 11–12, 15–16, and the text and commentary published by Friedrich, "Antworten der SED-Führung." Interestingly, the SED leaders were not shy about requesting various forms of economic and political support from the Soviets. They asked for increased shipments of raw materials and finished products, financial support for the KPD in the west, the release of German prisoners of war in the Soviet Union, and the disbandment of Soviet internment camps in the SBZ, with the release of the inmates to the German authorities or, for those condemned by Soviet organs, their transport to the Soviet Union.

promoting a neofascist revival. In response, the SED had to strengthen the struggle for the unity of Germany (here no mention of a separate socialist state) against the "colonization" of West Germany and struggle against the "factory bosses, the Junkers, and the reactionary bureaucracy as the main force behind the division [of Germany]"[128] Reverting to the language of the Weimar KPD and of Stalinism, the SED leadership claimed that "class enemies" still occupied strong positions in the state, economy, and administration, and have moved to "open sabotage of the democratic economic measures."[129] Therefore—and in contrast to Stalin's call for a campaign for a national government—the SED leaders argued that in the event of the formation of a western German government, the existing administrative apparatus in the SBZ should be consolidated into a "German government for the Soviet Occupation Zone," far closer to a formal state structure than Stalin yet envisioned. In the economic sphere, the SED leaders envisioned bringing large firms under the rubric of state planning, even if they retained the formal status of private ownership.[130] In agriculture, the state units had to be made "model farms" and the peasant cooperatives had to be strengthened. Echoing Stalin's war against the kulaks twenty years earlier, the SED leaders argued that the dominant positions of large peasants in the cooperatives had to be reversed. Similarly, private wholesale trade had to be "systematically restricted . . . so that by the end of 1949 all of wholesale trade would by exercised by state trading organizations and consumer cooperatives."[131] Ideological work in the party had to be strengthened, especially in relation to the role of the CPSU and the Soviet Union and the application of Marxism-Leninism to Germany. Finally, the internal security forces had to be strengthened, especially to protect against sabotage in the workplace, and the party itself "purged."

Clearly, in private deliberations SED leaders expressed their intentions to carry out a Soviet-style transformation in the SBZ.[132] Obviously, actions of such far-ranging import could only be undertaken with Soviet approval. At the same time, they wanted to take over the administration of the zone from the Soviets, at least in part an effort to free themselves from the public hostility that inevitably accompanied their dependence on the Soviet Union.[133] When exactly Stalin gave his endorsement for the establishment of the German Democratic Republic must remain conjecture, but probably not until very late in the game—the summer of 1949—did he finally accede to the wishes of the SED.[134] By that point, of course, the Cold War was well underway, and the prospect of a unified, neutralist Germany

[128] "Antworten der SED-Führung," 367.

[129] Ibid., 368–69.

[130] Ibid., 369.

[131] Ibid., 370.

[132] Though as late as March 1949, Grotewohl argued in an unpublished speech that a separate east German state would be economically unviable and would constitute a drain on the Soviet Union and the socialist bloc. See Badstübner, "Zum Problem der historischen Alternativen," 590.

[133] See Naimark, *Russians in Germany*, 9–68.

[134] Loth, introduction to *Wilhelm Pieck—Aufzeichnungen*, 35, argues that the decision to found the DDR was not made until the end of September 1949, i.e., after the establishment of the government of the Federal Republic.

had proven illusory. Yet Stalin's basically opportunistic approach to the "German question" meant also that a decision made in one context could later be undone. The SED leaders realized this and continually feared that their existence would be sacrificed for the Soviet Union's larger international interests. The dynamic of an intransigent, even provocative, SED seeking to force the hand of a relatively cautious Soviet Union would become a fixed element of postwar international relations.

As the SED moved toward the establishment of the German Democratic Republic, the space for democratic practices narrowed drastically—within the SBZ generally as well as within the party. Intrinsic to the intensification of bureaucratic direction in the SBZ was the adoption of one language—the language of intransigence—and the significant narrowing of the spaces of popular activism and their replacement, in the Soviet Occupation Zone, by specifically party activity and, in the western zones, by the decline of communism into near insignificance. As mentioned, the SED in August 1948 condemned the slogan of a "German road to socialism" as false and as hostile to the party, a sure sign of the triumph of the politics of intransigence. Ackermann published an article in *Neues Deutschland*, "Concerning the single possible road to socialism," which labeled the theory of the German road false and dangerous. In contrast, he now elevated the CPSU to the model for all Marxist-Leninist parties, a position reiterated in all sorts of KPD (of the western zones) and SED documents around this time. Firmly rejecting the Bukharinist position of "growing into socialism," the SED Executive revived, instead, the old KPD and Bolshevik language of revolution as the single path of political progress:

> The path [we have defined] is no special German path toward socialism, which could make possible a peaceful growing into socialism. The attempt to travel a special German road to socialism would mean disregarding the great historical example of the Soviet Union. . . . Our road to socialism is a revolutionary road, which opens up the possibility of proceeding from the fulfillment of the democratic renewal to erecting the political rule of the working class as the precondition for socialism.[135]

In place of the German road, the SED adopted the slogan, "To learn from the Soviet Union means to learn victory!" Concurrently, the SED instituted standard communist organizational practices, including democratic centralism and a politburo and restricted secretariat as the leading organs. And to seal one phase of postwar history and initiate the new, the SED, as mentioned, abandoned discussion of the "democracy of a new type" and substituted the phrase, "party of a new type," a reversion to "pure" Leninist terminology, at its First Conference in January 1949.

Already well established in administrative structures throughout the SBZ, developments in 1947 and 1948 deepened the level of party control and the role of

[135] Quoted in Günter Benser, "'Keine Wiederholung der Fehler von 1918!'" *BzG* 20:6 (1978): 841.

these structures, turning them into unilinear agencies of direction.[136] Henceforth, popular mobilizations would only be permitted in tightly controlled channels. Increasingly the party exercised control over cultural production through a maze of organizations.[137] SMAD Order 32, issued in February 1948, recast the German Economic Commission (Deutsche Wirtschaftskommission, or DWK), founded in 1947, as, for all intents and purposes, a nascent state structure with competence ranging far beyond the economy proper.[138] The DWK was granted power to coordinate the activities of the central administrations—already more heavily staffed with communists than the local and regional bodies—and to issue orders and directives to all German organs within the SBZ. Local organs were increasingly subject to direction from above and deprived of the more interactive relations with the population that had prevailed in 1945/46.

In the economic sphere the party leadership implemented the Soviet model of top-down administration and central planning in place of the more democratic and chaotic models of workers' control or codetermination.[139] A rather drawn-out struggle took place in the SBZ against the works councils, one that paralleled developments in the west but that had deeper irony, perhaps, in the east.[140] The struggle culminated with SMAD Order Number 234 issued in October 1947, which drastically curtailed the scope of the works councils.[141] At the same time, more stringent factory codes and new wage incentive schemes were introduced, which dramatically increased the pressure on workers. The new measures included the extensive application of piecework systems of pay, sharp wage differentials and particular advantages for people in technical and intellectual occupations, and various prizes and awards for highly productive workers, including allotments of shoes, clothing, and other goods. Recalcitrant workers could suffer loss of vacation days. The authorities did not even shy away from using food as a weapon in increasing productivity and labor discipline. According to the SMAD order, firms that did not manage to improve their production were to be deprived of the food supplies needed to provide their workers with a hot midday meal, and recalcitrant workers at any factory might be deprived of admittance to the canteen.[142]

The most grotesque aspect of the new labor regime involved the so-called Activist Campaign, based on the Soviet Stakhanovite program. Its model hero was a Saxon miner named Adolf Hennecke, who supposedly exceeded his plan output by 387 percent. Slogans honoring his achievement blanketed the SBZ, but even

[136] See Naimark, *Russians in Germany*, and the contributions in *SBZ-Handbuch*, 71–348, which detail the process of intensifying central direction.

[137] See Pike, *Politics of Culture*, for a thorough discussion.

[138] Highly informative on the DWK is Wolfgang Zank, "Wirtschaftiche Zentralverwaltung und Deutsche Wirtschaftskommission (DWK)," in *SBZ-Handbuch*, 253–90.

[139] See especially Suckut, *Betriebsrätebewegung*. Kleßmann provides, as usual, a good summary in *Doppelte Staatsgründung*, 272–73, as does Staritz, *Sozialismus in einem halben Lande*, 102–20.

[140] For rather similar moves to curtail the influence of the works councils in the west, see Kleßmann, *Doppelte Staatsgründung*, 126–35.

[141] See especially Suckut, *Betriebsrätebewegung*, 493–526.

[142] Staritz, *Sozialismus in einem halben Lande*, 109–10.

Hennecke was soon surpassed by workers who claimed to have outdone their norms by 1025 percent![143]

The more restrictive and repressive labor regime was not easily imposed. The campaigns created grave difficulties for rank-and-file communists in the factories and mines, who found themselves forced to defend the suppression of working-class power by a self-proclaimed workers' party. For activists with long memories, the productivist program of the nascent East German regime resembled nothing so much as the stabilization measures introduced in Weimar in 1923/24. Like the construction of a central administrative apparatus, the program of labor discipline and labor productivity instituted by the communist authorities demonstrated strong lines of continuity with the German past. Workers, including many communists, sought to undermine the new system through informal slowdowns and other forms of job shirking[144]—practices that echoed popular forms of resistance as far back as the imperial period. Model workers like Hennecke were shunned by their colleagues, as Hennecke himself reported.[145] The works councils, more closely tied to the rank and file, engaged in direct conflict with the trade unions for authority in the workplace. But ultimately, party power triumphed. With the support of the Soviets, the SED redoubled its efforts in the workplace and made the unions, already largely subservient to the party, into the model "transmission belts" of the party, the task Lenin had defined for unions in socialist societies.

Order 234 also extended special privileges that were already being given to intellectuals, such as extra food rations and higher pay, though always contingent on support for the regime. Such measures caused great resentment among the party rank and file and the population at large. Intellectuals were also called upon to develop cultural programs for workers that would make work more pleasant and thereby lead to increased productivity[146]—a rather chilling reminder of the Nazi German Labor Front. Ulbricht, speaking to SED artists and writers, chided them for writing novels about the emigration and concentration camps and painting pictures of "crippled women," instead of a "genuine, realist art that speaks to the people," that depicted land reform and the rebuilding of factories.[147] These were but interim steps toward the total coordination—hence, instrumentalization—of culture that came to fruition with a DWK order on 31 March 1949.[148]

In conjunction with these developments, all the worst characteristics of Stalinism came to the fore in the SBZ and elsewhere in central and eastern Europe—the suppression of other political groups, party purges, establishment of planned economies, declarations of military support for the Soviet Union, enhanced powers of Soviet advisors. The internal security forces, established almost imme-

[143] Suckut, *Betreibsrätebewegung*, 507–9.

[144] Ibid., 502–12.

[145] Staritz, *Sozialismus in einem halben Lande*, 114. For more details, including death threats against Hennecke, see Naimark, *Russians in Germany*, 198–204.

[146] See Pike, *Politics of Culture*, 428–34, 586–612. The privileges were further extended in 1949.

[147] Quoted in ibid., 523–24.

[148] Ibid., 484–536.

diately upon the end of the war, underwent significant expansion.[149] First an agency designed to ferret out Nazis, the police soon began the practices of internal espionage and denunciation of party members and the public at large. The SBZ police forces and the Soviets imprisoned tens of thousands in concentration camps where many died of neglect and disease. An unknown number were deported to the Soviet Union.[150] Some prisoners were Nazis arrested in the immediate weeks following the defeat of the Third Reich, but many others were individuals caught up in the terror-like practices of the security forces. Already in 1947/48 social democrats, nonconformist communists, and others were being arrested in Saxony-Anhalt and elsewhere in the SBZ, including many who had managed to survive the concentration camps of the Third Reich.[151] From the late 1940s to the early 1950s, twenty thousand social democrats lost their jobs, one hundred thousand had to flee to the west, and about five thousand were imprisoned by the East German or Soviet officials, of whom four hundred died in prison.[152] In the cultural sphere, charges of "formalism" and "cosmopolitanism," always linked to "fascism" yet also replete with not very subtle shades of anti-Semitism, flew fast and thick from 1949 into the early 1950s.[153] The obvious parallels between talk of "homeless cosmopolitanism," or the attacks on individuals like the composer Paul Hindemith for being insufficiently German, and the Nazis' own language seems to have escaped most SED and SMAD officials, while the language of "disguised agents" was, as David Pike says, "quintessentially Stalinist."[154]

Whatever lingering reservations Stalin might have had about the establishment of a separate socialist state in Germany were probably erased by elections to the western German Bundestag on 8 August 1949.[155] The elections confirmed beyond a shadow of a doubt the intention of the United States and its allies to support a west German state. Moreover, the western KPD secured only 5.7 percent of the vote, a precipitous decline from its earlier tallies and a way station on the road to the ultimate political irrelevance of the KPD in the Federal Republic.

From the elections to the Bundestag and the formal establishment of the Federal Republic in the summer of 1949 lay only a short path to the foundation of the German Democratic Republic. SED leaders traveled again to Moscow in September 1949 and came prepared—with proposals for establishing the state, with a rough timetable, and even with a list of proposed ministers.[156] They also had a

149 See Naimark, *Russians in Germany*, 353–97.

150 See ibid., 376–78, 385–86.

151 On the repression in Saxony-Anhalt, see Dieter Marc Schneider, "Sachsen-Anhalt," in *SBZ-Handbuch*, 157–58.

152 Hermann Weber, "'Weiße Flecken' in der DDR-Geschichtsschreibung," *APZ* B11/90 (9 March 1990): 8, citing figures collected by the Kurt-Schumacher-Kreis and published in *Vorwärts*, 18 March 1989.

153 See Pike, *Politics of Culture*, 613–56.

154 Ibid., 629–30.

155 Staritz, "SED, Stalin und die Gründung der DDR," 8–9.

156 Wilhelm Pieck, "Zur Einleitung der Besprechung [with the CPSU leaders]," and "Die sowjetische Antwort," in Staritz, "SED, Stalin und die Gründung der DDR," 12–16.

clear idea of the difficulties of their positions given the power and appeal of the west, the evident weakness of the western KPD, the inability to mobilize popular support against western integration of the Federal Republic, and the opposition of the so-called bloc parties in the SBZ.[157] To its leaders, the very survival of the SED now required the establishment of a separate socialist state, and by this point, the Soviets were prepared to agree. With little apparent difficulty, the SED and CPSU agreed on the mechanisms for establishing the state, including the list of ministers in the first government.[158] The Party Executive then, on 4 October 1949, approved the documents and personnel discussed in Moscow, and on 7 October 1949 the founding of the DDR was formally proclaimed. A few days later the legislature elected Pieck president and Grotewohl prime minister. Real power would lie increasingly with Walter Ulbricht as party chairman.

Günter Benser, the leading DDR historian of the initial postwar period, noted with satisfaction in 1978 that from the dual experiences of the successful Bolshevik Revolution and the failed German Revolution of 1918/19, the SED had learned to place in the forefront the issues of state power and party direction.[159] Indeed it had, but the foundation of the DDR signified less the strength of communism, more its weakness and isolation and the party's fear of abandonment by the Soviets.

Conclusion: The German Road and Prospects for a Third Way

The formation of the German Democratic Republic marked the culmination of a drawn-out process of political definition. It was not inscribed in Soviet policy from the outset, though it existed as an available option. Without revisiting the substantial and still controversial debate on the origins of the Cold War, suffice it to say that the Soviet Union would have preferred a unified, neutralist Germany. In the course of 1949, the Soviets themselves became resigned to the inevitable, forced by the familiar markers of the Cold War to recognize the position long advocated by Ulbricht, Pieck, and other SED leaders, who since late 1946 had been promoting the establishment of a state socialist system in a truncated territory. They had been restrained by the Soviet Union's larger strategic interests, which, if need be, would have been purchased at the expense of Ulbricht and company. By some accounts, it was not until 1955 and the failure of yet another Soviet diplomatic effort to prevent West Germany's incorporation into the western bloc that the Soviets finally accepted the existence of the DDR.[160]

The Soviet decision to accept the establishment of the German Democratic Republic ended the prospects for a "third way," a social and political formation

157 The SED's sense of its precarious situation comes across quite clearly in Pieck's notes on the conversations with Soviet leaders. See *Wilhelm Pieck—Aufzeichnungen*.

158 Staritz, "SED, Stalin und die Gründung der DDR," 8–11, 14–16

159 Benser, "'Keine Wiederholung der Fehler von 1918!'" 842–43.

160 Staritz, *Geschichte der DDR*, 91, and Badstübner, "Zum Problem der historischen Alternativen," 591, who takes 1952 and the failure of the Stalin Note as the terminus.

somewhere between western-style liberal capitalism and Soviet-style state socialism. But failure does not mean that the third way was never a possibility.[161] The third way solution lay embedded in the language of a German road, democracy of a new type, and, in its initial formulation, people's democracy, and in the KPD/SED's rapid and relatively successful diffusion into the spaces of social and political life. The many-webbed connections to society in general and workers in particular—in the workplace, the local polity, the sphere of consumption, as well as larger administrative structures—might have served to entrench the gradualist orientation, might have made communist bureaucrats subject in part to the moderating influence of popular interests and popular demands, as happened, for example, to the French and Italian communist parties after World War II, whatever their revolutionary rhetoric. Just as the politics of the streets in the Weimar Republic had its own logic, which accentuated masculinized, confrontationist politics, so the logic of implantation in the multiple spaces of political and social life after World War II might have accentuated the gradualist orientation. It is possible to envision a KPD/SED acting as a militant defender of working-class and more generally popular interests within the confines of a democratic-capitalist system, as a "tributary party" that through its ability to mobilize support in strikes, demonstrations, and elections extracts concessions from economic and political elites.[162] In this fashion, the party could have bestowed a deeper "social content" and greater egalitarianism upon a liberal or social democratic system, and in so doing would have provided workers and other segments of the lower classes with avenues of representation. Indeed, the more Stalinist-minded leaders of the KPD/SED were well aware of this possibility. They were saved from its dangers by the intervention of a different logic, that of the Cold War, which enabled them to recast political space so that the party's wide diffusion into working-class and popular life became the mechanism for unilinear administrative direction of the economy, polity, and social life in general, rather than an interactive stream in which direction was tempered by receptiveness to popular influences.

Clearly, a "third way" solution and the consequent evolution of the KPD/SED itself could only have been realized in a multiparty system, which itself was predicated on the formation of a neutralist, unified Germany. Hence, the prospects for a "third way" were undermined as much by the dynamics of international politics, and in particular the determination of the United States to construct its own bloc, as by the intentions of Walter Ulbricht and company.

Moreover, third way politics depended on continued popular mobilizations,

[161] See Christoph Kleßmann, "Opposition und Dissidenz in der Geschichte der DDR," *APZ* B5 (25 January 1991): 54, who makes a similar argument. For a particularly one-sided, linear view of developments in the SBZ, which sees the KPD/SED clearly and systematically moving toward complete power with the backing of the SMAD, see Werner Müller, "Ein 'besonderer deutscher Weg' zur Volksdemokratie? Determinanten und Besonderheiten kommunistischer Machterringung in der SBZ/DDR 1945 bis 1950," *Politische Vierteljahresschrift* 23:3 (1982): 278–303.

[162] I am following here Georges Lavau's characterization of the role of the French Communist Party in the Fifth Republic in "Le Parti communiste dans le système français," in *Le Communisme en France*, Cahiers de la Fondation Nationale des Sciences Politiques no. 175 (Paris: Armand Colin, 1969), 7–65.

which would have been difficult to sustain even without the party-directed impulses of the KPD/SED. The Antifas and works councils were very much local phenomena, but the devolution of power to the local level was a result of the extraordinary circumstances at the war's end, namely the near-total collapse of administrative structures, economic chaos, and foreign occupation. All the foreign powers and the reconstituted German parties quickly began to rebuild a more traditional bureaucracy in the economy and polity. In a sense, politics became "renationalized." The German population itself longed for a respite from the upheavals and uncertainties that had increasingly enveloped the nation since Stalingrad. In that sense, a popular basis existed for Ulbricht's language of order, one that increasingly supplanted the popular democratic initiatives of 1945/46.

Furthermore, the popular-based left hegemony that existed in Saxony Province, the Ruhr, and elsewhere in 1945–47 was broad but not deep. As shown most clearly by the historians connected with the oral history project on the Ruhr, the twelve-year caesura of National Socialism had had an immense impact on working-class culture.[163] Young people grew up without experience in the organizations and traditions of the labor movement. They returned to Germany from the front or from POW camps feeling deceived, and, at least initially, adverse to politics of all kinds. Older workers, still loyal to labor movement traditions, whether social democratic or communist, had developed individualized strategies for surviving the rigors of National Socialism. They looked to individual forms of satisfaction—doing a good job, the family—rather than to the collective. They viewed younger workers, and many of their former comrades who had quickly defected to the Nazis, with deep distrust. They performed heroic activities in the immediate postwar period, but when conditions began to change, their commitment to the collective waned as well.

To the extent that the KPD/SED's politics opened up possibilities of a third way, its activities were part and parcel of more general trends in communist politics in the 1930s and 1940s. The Soviet and international communist estimations of the political situation at the end of World War II differed dramatically from the evaluation of the situation at the end of World War I. Amid the post–World War I revolutionary wave, communist parties sought the forcible overthrow of the existing regimes and the construction of alternate sources of power—primarily the party and the workers and soldiers councils. The post–World War II situation, in contrast, was seen as the setting for the establishment of democratic-antifascist regimes and the maintenance of the cross-class and cross-political alliances of the Resistance, which would establish the preconditions for the later transition to socialism. This meant, then, not the establishment of institutions of dual power, but of ensconcement within the existing or reconstructed institutions of the state complemented by popular committees of various sorts. Not the party, but the

[163] See especially Lutz Niethammer, ed., *"Hinterher merkt man, daß es richtig war, daß es schiefgegangen ist": Nachkriegserfahrungen im Ruhrgebiet* (Berlin: J. H. W. Dietz Nachf., 1983), and Lutz Niethammer and Alexander von Plato, eds., *"Wir kriegen jetzt andere Zeiten": Auf der Suche nach der Erfahrungen des Volkes in Nachfaschistischen Ländern* (Berlin: J. H. W. Dietz Nachf., 1985), vols. 2 and 3 of *Lebensgeschichte und Sozialkultur im Ruhrgebiet 1930 bis 1960.*

bureaucratic levers of power were most important in this situation. In the west, of course, communists could then be removed from these positions. In central and eastern Europe, this strategy provided communists with influential positions that served as the nuclei of the full assumption of power once Soviet calculations had changed. Ironically, then, it was the very estimation of the postwar situation as nonrevolutionary that provided communists in the SBZ and elsewhere with the institutional sources of power from which they would then carry out the full seizure of power in 1948 and 1949.

For the KPD/SED especially, the move to the politics of intransigence signified not just the absorption of the language of "high Stalinism," but a reversion to the language and culture of communist politics in the Weimar era. Absolutely essential to the SED's politics after 1947 was the clear and conscious reassertion of the legacy of the KPD. This was, to be sure, a carefully constructed reassertion—the "invention of tradition." Luxemburg's democratic tendencies were ignored. Dissident communists were erased from memory. Their living embodiments were purged from leading positions, Anton Ackermann chief among them. But the revival of the confrontationist, class-conflict strategy had such support precisely because it resonated with the lived experience of many German communists, precisely because it was not invented out of whole cloth and was not merely imposed by the Soviet Union. Instead, it drew upon the history of the KPD as a mass party in the Weimar Republic and as a victim of terror in the Third Reich. Their own experiences put many of the leading communists in the camp of those who sought the quick and party-exclusive implementation of a Soviet Germany. They had the lesson of 1918/19 behind them—that is, the failure to implement a thorough social revolution, which allowed then the reassertion of the conservative forces and the triumph of National Socialism. They had faced in Weimar a state system associated with the SPD and in the Third Reich a violent dictatorship rooted in capitalism. The legacy of bitter conflict made it easy for many communists to switch to the intransigent position once Soviet calculations had changed. The revival of the SPD under the strongly anticommunist Kurt Schumacher only facilitated the KPD's own reassertion of its past.

Finally, the essential party leadership consisted of those who had survived the purges of the 1930s in the Soviet Union, not exactly a training ground for democratic practices. Instead, they returned to Germany having absorbed even more deeply the mentality of Stalinism.[164] With some notable exceptions, those communists who had spent the exile years in the west, and even many who had survived the Nazi years in Germany, were rather quickly marginalized from leading positions.

Perched at the summit of power, the statist elements of the KPD/SED became still more pronounced. The disruptive tactics of the Weimar period had to be laid to rest. Discipline, order, and moral rectitude became the guiding principles. The intransigence of the KPD remained, but it was being reshaped from a party strategy of revolution and social disorder to a state strategy of discipline and authority.

[164] See Naimark, *Russians in Germany*, 292–94, for an interesting discussion about the many Russianized Germans who played leading roles in the SBZ and DDR.

CHAPTER 10

The Primacy of Politics: State and Society in the DDR

Das Hauptinstrument bei der Schaffung der Grundlagen des Sozialismus ist die Staatsmacht.

—*Resolution of SED's Second Party Conference*[1]

THE STATE FOUNDED in October 1949 in the Soviet Occupation Zone lasted only a few months beyond its fortieth anniversary, not very long in comparison with many countries. But the DDR existed for almost as many years as Imperial Germany and quite a bit longer than the Weimar Republic and the Third Reich—long enough to have a major impact on the political, social, and cultural patterns in both Germanys.

Its forty years, though, were never completely secure. About 2.7 million citizens fled to the west in the decade before the construction of the Berlin Wall in 1961, while a sullen apathy characterized the attitude of many who remained. The Federal Republic provided a constant allure to the population, and with its refusal to recognize DDR citizenship, a challenge to the very notion of a communist state on German territory. Moreover, the DDR's existence depended ultimately on the protection of its Soviet sponsor, and the party-state had always to fear that it might be sacrificed to the Soviet Union's larger strategic interests.

Hence, throughout the DDR's forty-year history, the leadership of the SED waged an unceasing campaign to secure the existence and legitimacy of its state. As an integral member of the Soviet bloc, the SED deployed all the measures typical of Soviet-style systems. The SED-state patrolled the public sphere, directed the economy, and elevated ideological hostility to bourgeois democracy and liberal capitalism into fixed features of the regime, policies designed to institute ideological and cultural conformity and to "construct socialism" on the Soviet model and in "the colors of the DDR," as the slogan of the 1980s put it.

But in the effort to win the legitimacy it craved, the SED state not only used the standard features of communist systems. It also deployed rhetorics and practices that drew on the specific historical legacy of German communism and on long-standing features of German society in general. Moreover, the SED, like its KPD forebear, operated in a social and political environment that deeply shaped its political culture but over which it had little control. The notable features of the

[1] "The major instrument in the creation of the foundations of socialism is state power." "Beschluß der Zweiten Parteikonferenz der SED," quoted in Christoph Kleßmann, *Die doppelte Staatsgründung: Deutsche Geschichte 1945–1955* (Göttingen: Vandenhoeck und Ruprecht, 1982), 502.

larger environment included the DDR's particular status on the front line of the Cold War in constant, bitter competition with the Federal Republic, and the unanticipated emergence of an increasingly complex, differentiated, and prosperous (at least by Soviet bloc standards) society from the late 1960s onward.

This chapter, then, is designed to explore the SED's ongoing campaign to gain legitimacy for the party and the party-state while it "built socialism." Central to the discussion is an examination of the way the party used and reshaped the legacy of the KPD. The chapter does not provide a comprehensive history of the DDR, nor do I argue that the weight of history provided the exclusive force in the fashioning of the socialist state and society, as the comments above should make clear. But history is inescapable, and nowhere more so than in Germany. The post-1949 reactions even to autonomous, external factors—the oil price rise, say, or changes in Soviet or American policies—were mediated through the experiences and the language of German and international communism from 1914 to 1945. The traditions of the KPD resulted in a set of dispositions that re-created in the altered circumstances of the postwar world many of the intransigent characteristics of German communism of the Weimar Republic and the Third Reich and made the SED and the SED-state particularly impervious to reforms. The traditions were, to be sure, "invented," but not out of blue sky. They were based in the personal experiences and understandings of the SED leadership, the most intact and long-lasting in all the Soviet bloc, and middle-level cadres, some of whose own involvement with communism stretched back to the KPD of the Weimar Republic. Through educational curricula, cultural events, propaganda, and policies, these "traditions" were transmitted to the party cadres and the citizenry of the DDR.[2]

At the same time, the transition from party-movement to party-state impelled the SED to unload a number of the time-honored practices of German communism. A political strategy that promoted civil disorder had no place in the socialist society. The idealization of the rough-hewn male proletarian had to be complemented by images that might appeal to the diverse social classes of a modern and complex society. With responsibilities of governance and a commitment to economic development, the SED promoted stability, and it drew upon and developed the discourses and practices of order and discipline that German regimes since the nineteenth century had promoted. Ironically, the party that had been shaped so decisively by popular protests now sought to control and demobilize the population.

[2] In the most recent studies on the DDR and the programmatic efforts to define its "place" in German history, almost nothing is said about the KPD traditions. I find this a glaring omission. As examples see Jürgen Kocka, ed., *Historische DDR-Forschung: Aufsätze und Studien* (Berlin: Akademie, 1993); idem and Martin Sabrow, eds., *Die DDR als Geschichte: Fragen—Hypothesen—Perspektiven* (Berlin: Akademie, 1994); and Hartmut Kaelble, Jürgen Kocka, and Hartmut Zwahr, eds., *Sozialgeschichte der DDR* (Stuttgart: Klett Cotta, 1994). Notable exceptions are Wolfgang Mommsen's considered essay, "Die Ort der DDR in der deutschen Geschichte," in Kocka, *DDR als Geschichte*, 26–39, and Lutz Niethammer, "Erfahrungen und Strukturen: Prolegomena zu einer Geschichte der Gesellschaft der DDR," in Kaelble, Kocka, and Zwahr, *Sozialgeschichte der DDR*, 95–115.

Building the Party-State: Centralization and Demobilization

Central direction of the economy and polity constituted the essence of the Soviet model. For the SED leaders, schooled in the Marxist-Leninist emphasis on party and state and long subject to the preponderant influence of the Soviet Union, socialism could only be built through central direction. But the Soviets did not simply impose policies on the DDR through German agents. As in so many other realms of the German-Soviet relationship, centralization in the DDR brought to extreme levels tendencies present in the German labor movement since the 1860s and in German society since the eighteenth century, namely, the widely held notion that the state had a major role to play in the construction of society and that solutions to economic and social problems came via the state. Centralization provided the SED with the tools of both repression and beneficence, the twin arms of a strategy of discipline and order designed to demobilize the population from autonomous forms of activism. In the unceasing drive to "construct socialism," popular mobilizations could take place only in carefully delineated channels and in support of goals defined at the center.

As previously discussed, the establishment of central control of the economy, polity, and society was well underway in the last two years of the Soviet Occupation Zone. Its pace only accelerated in the early years of the DDR. In the cultural sphere, the Ministry for Popular Education (from 1954 the Ministry of Culture) took over the censorship powers of the SMAD.[3] In the economic sector, the wide-ranging powers exercised by the DWK were accentuated with the establishment of the Ministry of Planning (from 1950, the State Planning Commission), the founding of industrial ministries, and the institution of the first five-year plan (1951–55), all of which directly mimicked the Soviet model of development. Already by 1950, 76 percent of industrial production occurred within nationalized or Soviet-run firms.[4] Insurance and banking were nationalized, and the relatively small proportion of private producers and merchants suffered under severe state regulations. In agriculture, however, the SED moved cautiously.[5]

But in 1960, the SED went on the full offensive against the still vital private agricultural sector, such that it soon became a relic of a past way of life, and accelerated the pressure on the ever shrinking remains of private trade and industry. Few policies so underscored the rigidity of the SED as the collectivization of agriculture in the DDR at a time when its inefficiencies elsewhere were quite obvious, leading a number of Soviet-bloc countries to abandon the notion entirely and the Soviets themselves to experiment with incentives and private holdings. In perhaps the ultimate folly, under Erich Honecker the DDR in 1972 socialized virtually all that remained of the private sector, which by this time was as distant from the "commanding heights" of the economy as a bathtub sailboat is from a destroyer.

[3] See David Pike, *The Politics of Culture in Soviet-Occupied Germany, 1945–1949* (Stanford: Stanford University Press, 1992), 643–56.

[4] Dietrich Staritz, *Geschichte der DDR 1949–1985* (Frankfurt am Main: Suhrkamp, 1985), 40.

[5] Ibid., 41.

Intrinsic to central control of the economy was a labor regime marked by the elimination of independent forms of representation, intensified exploitation through piecework and other premium wage systems, and, especially in the early 1950s, the deliberate depression of wage levels to fund the expansion of the economy. As discussed in the previous chapter, repressive labor measures had already been introduced on a widespread scale in 1948 with the "activist campaign," the curbing and elimination of the works councils, and the institution of piecework. In the DDR, the complete integration of state and entrepreneurial power made the level of control over workers even more comprehensive. In March 1950, the regime ordered all factories to draw up plans that mandated wage and benefit reductions if the production goals were not met. These plans also codified premium wage systems, so that the proportion of pieceworkers in relation to all industrial workers rose from 40 percent in 1949 to 65 percent at the end of 1951.[6] Shortly thereafter, the regime revised upward production norms, sparking the one great labor protest in the history of the DDR, the 1953 Uprising. The SED was forced to abandon its effort at still greater exploitation of labor. But following the construction of the Berlin Wall in 1961, when the SED no longer feared a reenactment of 1953, it again raised production norms and reinstituted an activist-type drive, reminiscent of the Hennecke campaign of the late 1940s, that encouraged workers to overfulfill their quotas.[7] And while living standards began to rise, never did the party allow independent representation in the workplace. The trade unions served as the "transmission belts" of party control in the offices, mines, and factories of the socialist state, not agencies that articulated workers' grievances and desires.

Beginning in 1948, the party also underwent a series of significant structural changes, the results of which lodged power in an ever smaller group at the center. The establishment of a politburo, secretariat, and central committee, along with the official enshrinement of democratic centralism in the statutes, eliminated any fiction that the SED would constitute some kind of social democratic–communist hybrid.[8] Also in 1948 the leadership initiated the first in a series of purges, which, in the early years, disproportionately affected one-time social democrats. The purge of 1950/51 led to the exclusion of over one hundred and fifty thousand members. The procedure quickly extended to leading members of the party, who, in conjunction with the eastern European show trials of the early 1950s, were removed from leading positions and, in a few cases, lost their lives in mysterious circumstances in prison.[9] In 1951 the SED counted 1.2 million members as op-

[6] Kleßmann, *Doppelte Staatsgründung*, 273; Staritz, *Geschichte der DDR*, 49–50. Conflict at the plant level seems to have been quite pronounced. At Leuna, the workforce three times rejected the contract, but lost its battle nonetheless to secure a 15 percent nighttime differential.

[7] Staritz, *Geschichte der DDR*, 142.

[8] Ibid., 50–54.

[9] Dietrich Staritz, *Sozialismus in einem halben Lande* (Berlin: Klaus Wagenbach, 1976), 62–63, 166–67. Hermann Weber has long argued that only Stalin's death forestalled a show trial in the DDR comparable to the Slansky trial in Czechoslovakia.

posed to two million in 1948, with a higher proportion of functionaries than previously.[10]

These tight measures of control over the party continued until the very end of the regime. While purges became less frequent and extensive, certainly advancement within the party ranks and access to a wide range of material and social privileges depended utterly on conformity to the dictates from above. The goal even in purges was less the removal of questionable cadres than the desire to control the remaining members, to create a party far more disciplined and intimidated, far more willing to accept the dictates of the leadership.[11] In a sense, the SED leadership quite successfully demobilized the party, making it incapable of autonomous expressions and depriving it of the somewhat raucous and ill-disciplined character the KPD/SED had even in the 1940s.

Absolutely essential to the extension of central state power was, of course, the founding of the Ministry for State Security (Ministerium für Staatssicherheit, MfS or Stasi) in February 1950, which developed further the police institutions established right after the war. Widely feared and disliked throughout its history, the full reach of its powers only became clear after the collapse of the DDR. Recent investigations into the files of the MfS have demonstrated its immense powers, including the use of arbitrary imprisonment and torture to intimidate opponents real and imagined. The corruption of everyday life it induced through the widespread use of informants led to countless individual tragedies.[12] These observations exercised over the population were worthy of the grimmest passages in George Orwell's *1984*, but with absurd as well as effective results. In 1956, to use just one example, the DDR regime feared the reverberations from Nikita Khrushchev's secret speech, which exposed the crimes of the Stalin regime. As part of the general ferment in the communist world that ensued, Polish workers in Poznan engaged in strikes, demonstrations, and riots, and an armed uprising broke out in Hungary against the communist party and Soviet control. Just three years after its own experience with a popular revolt, the SED feared the unrest would spread to the DDR. MfS informants kept up a steady stream of information back to Berlin. The reports carry the same tenor as those of Imperial German officialdom, the Reich and Prussian State Commissar for the Supervision of Public Order in the Weimar Republic, and the Third Reich's Gestapo. Every protest, every expression of discontent was worthy of investigation, and like its forebears, the MfS demanded rapid and comprehensive flows of information from the lower levels to the center. When these were not forthcoming, or when the Ministry heard of unrest five weeks after the event, lower-level officials found themselves berated in tones worthy of the most imperious official of the imperial and Weimar bureaucracy.[13]

[10] Staritz, *Geschichte der DDR*, 62, 63.

[11] Staritz, *Sozialismus in einem halben Lande*, 164–65, and *Geschichte der DDR*, 62–63.

[12] See the collection on the MfS edited by Armin Mitter and Stefan Wolle, *"Ich liebe Euch doch alle!" : Befehle und Lageberichte des MfS* (Berlin: Basis, 1990).

[13] See Erich Mielke quoted in Stefan Wolle, "Das MfS und die Arbeiterproteste im Herbst 1956 in der DDR," *APZ* B5/91 (25 January 1991): 44.

Like its predecessors, the MfS fearfully monitored the food situation, ever worried that shortages would set off political protests, and reported sightings of "agents" everywhere. And just as Weimar officialdom continually invoked the specter of 1919 and 1923, the nightmare of the 1953 Uprising haunted the MfS. In the wake of the Poznan events, MfS collaborators reported that some DDR citizens drew the parallel with 17 June 1953 and had even spoken of the need for another uprising in order to gain concessions from the regime. As a result, the MfS assigned agents to watch Sunday cruise outings, because on one of these the supposed plans for the 1953 uprising had been discussed. As Stefan Wolle writes, "One can imagine how on every Sunday the staff of the State Security Service swarmed out to 'operatively secure' the excursion points of the Berlin region."[14]

A severe labor regime, tight control over the party, and repression by the MfS constituted the critical elements of the state's ever more drastic intervention in daily life. But the state also guaranteed the provisioning of the population and made possible substantial social mobility. Through repression and beneficence, the SED state sought to create a passive citizenry *and* fulfill something of its claim to be a "workers' and peasants' state." Its practices, while far more comprehensive and severe than Weimar or Imperial Germany (though certainly not the Third Reich), place it in the long line of continuity of modern German history.

The 1953 Uprising, repressed with the aid of Soviet tanks, established certain limits upon the SED-state. From that point onward, the state ensured that at least basic necessities were available to the population at reasonable prices. Food, housing, and utilities remained heavily subsidized and inexpensive until the very end of the regime. These were touted as among the achievements of socialism, along with extensive social security measures that expanded especially in the 1970s under Erich Honecker's "unity of economic and social policies." Universal health coverage, wide-ranging maternity benefits, and lifetime job security helped establish a stable and relatively comfortable, if hardly prosperous, existence for most of the citizens of the DDR, and served to bind a substantial segment of the population to the regime.[15]

Moreover, many people experienced substantial social mobility. "*Wir haben uns qualifiziert*"—meaning that they had undergone education and training for advancement, often while working—was a phrase that any visitor might hear not long into a conversation with DDR citizens. The members of the "*Aufbaugeneration*" (the post–World War II "construction generation") also maintained a certain pride in their hard-won efforts at reconstruction and development. They were only too aware that they had had no Marshall Plan to help them, but endured the

[14] Ibid., 46–47.

[15] For details on the improvements in material standards, including social welfare, see Staritz, *Geschichte der DDR*, 203–5, 221–22. For a good discussion of the intertwining of economics and politics and the Honecker regime's implicit recognition of the need to improve living standards, see A. James McAdams, *East Germany and Detente: Building Authority after the Wall* (Cambridge: Cambridge University Press, 1985).

precise opposite, Soviet dismantling of factories and infrastructures. That sense of accomplishment also came across in innumerable conversations, and was experienced in the life-course of individuals by their rise to more responsible positions in the workplace and bureaucracy and the improvement in their material well-being. "*Es ging aufwärts*" (things got better), as one of Lutz Niethammer's interviewees said repeatedly in 1987 with evident pride, a sentiment that helped create a certain identity with the DDR.[16]

Material benefits and social mobility alone, however, can be a notably fragile foundation for legitimacy, one that would make toleration and loyalty prone to any interruption in economic advance. Hence, the regime also propagated an ideology of productivism that placed it in line with Germany's entire course of development in the modern era. From the mid–nineteenth century through the Third Reich managers and the state extolled the wonders of German craftsmanship and technology and the benefits that accrued to all through diligence, skill, and hard work. The practice and ideology of "German quality labor" played a major role in the incorporation of workers into prevailing norms from Imperial Germany to both postwar states, as Alf Lüdtke cogently argues.[17] As we have seen in earlier chapters, this discourse was deeply embedded in a hierarchical and repressive understanding of the social order in which those with skill and knowledge and, not least, capital, would be allowed free rein to order the workplace. Likewise, the party-state sought to create a diligent labor force and a disciplined workplace and society through its claim to embody economic progress. More and more, the identity of the DDR was defined in terms of "*hohe Leistung*," of high productivity and material advance.[18] The achievement of technical knowledge became a national campaign in the 1970s. The nightly newscasts were awash with reports of this or that factory surpassing its quota, and even popular magazines depicted men and women most often at work, far less frequently in leisure pursuits or with the family.[19] Even Rosa Luxemburg and Karl Liebknecht were drawn in as exponents of socialist prosperity: shock brigades in different factories took the names of Liebknecht or Luxemburg, and invariably overfilled their

[16] Lutz Niethammer, "Annäherung an den Wandel: Auf der Suche nach der volkseigenen Erfahrung in der Industrieprovinz der DDR," in *Alltagsgeschichte: Zur Rekonstruktion historischer Erfahrungen und Lebensweisen*, ed. Alf Lüdtke (Frankfurt am Main: Campus, 1989), 303–10, and idem, "Das Volk der DDR und die Revolution: Versuch einer historischen Wahrnehmung der laufenden Ereignisse," in *"Wir sind das Volk!" Flugschriften, Aufrufe und Texte einer deutschen Revolution*, ed. Charles Schüddekopf (Reinbek bei Hamburg: Rowhohlt, 1990), 251–79.

[17] See Alf Lüdtke, "'Deutsche Qualitätsarbeit,' 'Spielereien' am Arbeitsplatz und 'Fliehen' aus der Fabrik: Industrielle Arbeitsprozesse und Arbeiterverhalten in den 1920er Jahren—Aspekte eines offenen Forschungsfeldes," in *Arbeiterkulturen zwischen Alltag und Politik: Beiträge zum europäischen Vergleich in der Zwischenkriegszeit*, ed. Friedhelm Boll (Vienna: Europa, 1986), 155–98, and idem, "'Helden der Arbeit'—Mühen beim Arbeiten: Zur mißmutigen Loyalität von Industriearbeitern in der DDR," in Kaelble, Kocka, and Zwahr, *Sozialgeschichte der DDR*, 188–213.

[18] See Sigrid Meuschel, *Legitimation und Parteiherrschaft in der DDR: Zur Paradox von Stabilität und Revolution in der DDR 1945–1989* (Frankfurt am Main: Suhrkamp, 1992), esp. 307.

[19] Irene Dölling, "Continuity and Change in the Media Image of Women: A Look at Illustrations in GDR Periodicals," *Studies in GDR Culture and Society* 9 (Lanham, Md.: University Press of America, 1989), 141.

plan quotas. To a visitor it was strange indeed to see the DDR's production of computer chips touted as the fulfillment of the revolutionary legacy of Luxemburg and Liebknecht.[20]

The discourse and ideology of productivism was never merely a "bourgeois" category that the SED appropriated, as some commentators have argued. The valoration of labor long preceded capitalism, and Marxism itself inspired visions of a technological utopia. The German labor movement glorified productive labor and argued continually that the fetters of capitalism prevented its rational application. The KPD, as we have seen, idealized heroic, male productive labor. The commitment to productivity, technology, and skill resulted not only from "embourgeoisification" of the German labor movement and the DDR, but emerged also out of the life-world of the proletariat, out of a world in which labor occupied so great a part of one's time that its validation bestowed meaning on life and identity on existence.[21]

By marshaling the language and ideology of productivism, the DDR drew on both the general features of German society in the modern era and the specific traditions of the German labor movement including the KPD. In that way, the SED tried to address both its basic constituency in the working class and the broader social strata of an increasingly complex society. To the extent that people derived their identity with the DDR from material progress, social mobility, and technological advance, the regime had succeeded in demobilizing the population from autonomous forms of expression. The concentration on economistic criteria contributed mightily to the reproduction in the DDR of the "unpolitical German," individuals concerned with material progress and devoted to technology, and deprived of and unconcerned with democratic participation.[22] But the hard-won struggle to improve living standards also provided people with creative outlets for their talents and energies. They were active citizens engaged in the project of development—hence their personal identities constructed through labor and their identity with the socialist state—not passive observers of an automatic social process.

There may be little that is specifically socialist about mobility and material progress, but they provided the bases upon which the regime, for a time, won the toleration, if not outright loyalty, of a substantial segment of its citizenry. Many also recognized the differences between their own and West German society.

[20] For just two examples, see "Das Vermächtnis von Karl Liebknecht und Rosa Luxemburg ist in der DDR erfüllt: Wir wissen uns in einer großen Kampftradition," *ND*, 12/13 January 1980, 9, and "Im Geist von Karl und Rosa entschlossen für die Stärkung des Friedens und des Sozialismus," *ND*, 14 January 1980.

[21] Niethammer is too quick, in my view, to condemn economistic measures as simply "bourgeois." See "Annäherung an den Wandel."

[22] From very different vantage points, both Lutz Niethammer and Sigrid Meuschel arrive at the conclusion that DDR citizens were deprived of politics and apolitical, and enmeshed in economistic and technological standards. But the connection between production and technology, on the one hand, and an apolitical stance, on the other, is not automatic, as Meuschel and Niethammer imply. Niethammer's own informants provide a good corrective. See Niethammer, "Annäherung an den Wandel" and "Volk der DDR," and Meuschel, *Legitimation und Parteiherrschaft*, 15–22, 307, and passim.

They respected the social supports provided by the regime and espoused a solidaristic ethos—"no one goes hungry here" was virtually a popular mantra among DDR citizens.[23] At least in this realm, the ethos of solidarity and collective identity, the DDR embodied something of the best traditions of the German labor movement—even within the harsh, centralized structures created by the regime.

In building the socialist state and society, the SED had always to struggle to win the support of the population. It also continually worried about the stability of the Soviet Union's commitment to the DDR. As a result it engaged a strategy, the state socialist "*Flucht nach vorne*" (colloquially, preemptive strike), that bears noteworthy comparisons with that of the KPD in the Weimar Republic and the Third Reich. The KPD presumed that *Kampf*—decisive, active struggle for socialism—would win the party ever greater backing. Similarly, the SED leaders believed that the state-directed leap toward socialism would actually secure the state through enhanced popular support. Moreover, by being more Leninist than their Leninist mentors in Moscow, the SED sought to create conditions that would guarantee continued Soviet support for the DDR.

We have seen this process at work once before, in the late 1940s when the SED pushed for the creation of a separate socialist state in Germany far earlier and far more forcefully than the Soviets were willing to countenance. At least in two other moments, a similar dynamic unfolded: the SED's plans to "construct socialism," announced in 1952, and the building of the Berlin Wall in 1961.

In July 1952, the SED's Second Conference approved a resolution proposed by the Central Committee calling for the planned construction of socialism in the DDR. The Soviet Union, apparently, was not pleased. With the so-called Stalin Note, it had just sought to win western approval for a demilitarized, neutralist Germany. The Korean War was underway. In this setting, the SED's actions seemed deliberately provocative, since there was no conceivable way the west would permit unification with a state in the process of "building socialism." Once again, the SED, pursuing its own interests, went further than the Soviets had planned.[24] The SED leaders might even have felt some sweet revenge in their

[23] And duly related by Niethammer's informants: Niethammer, "Annäherung an den Wandel," 326.

[24] Staritz, *Geschichte der DDR*, 73–78, and new evidence for the conflict between the SED and the CPSU in Wilfriede Otto, "Sowjetische Deutschlandnote 1952: Stalin und die DDR. Bisher unveröffentlichte handschriftliche Notizen Wilhelm Piecks," *BzG* 33:3 (1991): 374–89. But for a challenge to Otto's interpretation, see Ernst Wurl, "Entscheidung 'gegen das Konzept Stalins'? Zu Wilfriede Ottos Dokumentation von Notizen W. Piecks, *BzG*, 3/1991," *BzG* 33:6 (1991): 767–70. Staritz, "Die SED, Stalin und der 'Aufbau des Sozialismus' in der DDR: Aus den Akten des Zentralen Parteiarchiv," *DA* 24:7 (1991): 686–700, is particularly critical of Otto's view that the SED acted on its own.

For the argument that the Soviet Union stood behind the forced pace development in the DDR, see Gerhard Wettig, "Zum Stand der Forschung über Berijas Deutschland-Politik im Frühjahr 1953," *DA* 26:6 (1993): 674–82, and idem, "Die Deutschland-Note vom 10. März 1952 auf der Basis diplomatischer Akten des russischen Außenministeriums: Die Hypothese des Wiedervereinigungsangebots," *DA* 26:7 (1993): 786–805, and numerous responses in following issues. For a far more nu-

actions: the Soviets had informed them in detail of the Stalin Note only one day before the public announcement.[25] At the beginning of April, they had journeyed to Moscow for deliberations with Stalin and other Soviet leaders. Pieck's notes indicate the SED leadership's desire to intensify policies—arm the police, create a People's Army, end the "pacifist period," and extend military training. But Stalin, as he had through the spring of 1949, held on to hopes for an agreement with the west and counseled the SED only to intensify agitation for national unity. According to Dietrich Staritz,

> although Stalin did not brake the further reconstruction of DDR society, [he] wanted to hold on to the "zigzag" policy. The conversation was certainly not satisfying in terms of the domestic situation of East Germany. The Soviet leader referred to the old concepts and, according to Pieck's catchwords, said: "Unity, peace treaty—further agitate." In its entirety the balance of the conversation was not brilliant for the SED.[26]

In the next weeks the SED followed the Soviets' directives. But then, in an abrupt change of course, the party, in a letter to Stalin, declared that the unity of the working class and peasantry had been secured; the tasks of the bourgeois-democratic revolution had been fulfilled; and the socialist planned economy had taken hold—all just three years after the foundation of the state. Hence, "the decisive preconditions have been created for the turn to the construction of socialism and the establishment of the bases of socialism in the agrarian economy."[27] A few days later, on 8 July 1952, the CPSU Politburo responded and granted approval of the drive to implement socialism, which opened the way for the SED Party Conference's confirmation of the policy. The reasons for the Soviet reversal are not totally clear, but Staritz surmises the driving force was the fact that, by this point, the Stalin Note had obviously failed. Once again the west had rejected Soviet overtures. In 1949, this resulted in the Soviet acquiescence to the foundation of the state. In 1952, it led to the Soviet acceptance of the "construction of socialism."[28] The ultimate outcomes might not have differed, but in both instances the SED acted as the Leninist rabbit, the pacesetter of the race that the Soviet Union brought to successful conclusion.

The "construction of socialism" was not the last race that the SED initiated. After Khrushchev's 1956 speech, the SED tried to limit the impact of de-

---

anced interpretation, see Elke Scherstjanoi, "Die DDR im Frühjahr 1952: Sozialismuslosung und Kolletivierungsbeschluß in sowjetischer Perspektive," *DA* 27:4: (1994) 354–63, who sees the Soviets as more cautious than the SED. But her claim that the Second Conference marked no new departures is misplaced.

[25] Staritz, "SED, Stalin und der 'Aufbau des Sozialismus,'" 694.

[26] Ibid., 697.

[27] Ibid., 698–99.

[28] Ibid., 698, 700. However, the Soviets soon reversed course and were harshly critical of SED policies both immediately before and after the June 1953 Uprising. See the CPSU Politburo resolution, "Über die Maßnahmen zur Gesundung der politischen Lage in der Deutschen Demokratischen Republik," recently published by Rolf Stöckigt in "Ein Dokument von großer historischer Bedeutung vom Mai 1953," *BzG* 32:5 (1990): 648–54, and Monika Kaiser's contribution to the discussion on the 1953 Uprising, "Der 17. Juni-vierzig Jahre danach," in Kocka, *DDR als Geschichte*, 50–52.

Stalinization. It also sought constant reassurances from the Soviet Union and the socialist bloc states that the DDR would not be sacrificed to the general interests of European disarmament and Soviet strategic concerns. The Soviets, no fools when it came to evaluating the relative importance of the Germanys, tried, instead, to lure Bonn from the western camp with the siren song of national unification. As a result, it had to contain its communist German ally, always ready to raise the stakes, as when the SED tried to win Soviet approval for the complete incorporation of Berlin into the DDR.

But the DDR had other cards to play. Sixty percent of agriculture was still in private hands in 1959. In a new round of the battle "to build socialism," virtually all of agriculture was collectivized within three months in 1960.[29] This was soon followed by the socialization of large segments of private business and trade, as mentioned previously. The actions of the party-state only intensified the stream of refugees who fled to the west, heightening the acute domestic and international crisis that the SED faced.[30] But the crisis enabled the SED to assert that population loss threatened the entire Soviet bloc. At around the same time, Soviet diplomatic initiatives to the west on the Berlin and German issues again ran aground. The DDR was able to argue convincingly that the building of a protective wall in Berlin would aid the development of the entire socialist bloc.[31] The SED heightened domestic tensions as the international situation worsened, narrowing the options for the Soviets and leading them to acquiesce to the construction of the Berlin Wall.

The state socialist "Flucht nach vorne" was, then, an integral part of the political strategy that entwined central direction with voluntarism, the notion that decisive action by an enlightened vanguard would rally the population behind the cause and cow the opposition. This kind of thinking sailed over objective limitations to politics, whether of material resources or popular attitudes. In pursuing this strategy, the German communists never merely followed Soviet orders; the dynamic between the two parties displayed in the post–World War II period reached back to the mid-1920s.[32] At that time, the Soviets initiated the removal of Ruth Fischer and a more realistic strategy for the KPD. In the 1930s, they ruthlessly criticized the KPD's resistance to the popular front. In the late 1940s they tried to brake the SED's headlong rush to the establishment of the socialist state, in 1952, the SED's forced-pace construction of socialism. In 1960/61 the

[29] Figures in McAdams, *East Germany and Detente*, 23.

[30] On the dire situation of the DDR in the early 1960s, see Michael Lemke, "Kampagnen gegen Bonn: Die Systemkrise der DDR und die West-Propaganda der SED 1960–1963," *VfZ* 41:2 (1993): 153–74.

[31] See Staritz's discussion in *Geschichte der DDR*, 131–38. See also Hope M. Harrison, "Ulbricht and the Concrete 'Rose': New Archival Evidence on the Dynamics of Soviet–East German Relations and the Berlin Crisis, 1958–1961," Cold War International History Project, Woodrow Wilson International Center for Scholars, Working Paper no. 5 (1993).

[32] In contrast to the position I am arguing here, some ex-DDR historians, in the first flush of the collapse of the state, suddenly discovered that the Soviet Union dictated everything that happened in the DDR. For just one example, with very interesting documentation nonetheless, see Stöckigt, "Ein Dokument von großer historischer Bedeutung."

Soviets tried to put off for as long as possible such drastic measures as the building of the Berlin Wall. In 1970/71, they helped depose Ulbricht, whose New Economc System had degenerated into a voluntaristic leap into the future that ignored the objective limitations of the existing economy.[33] More radical—and with much less to lose—than their Soviet mentors, the KPD and SED pursued their own strategic conceptions as far as possible. German communists, at critical junctures, established a menu of options that limited Soviet choices. While the Soviets sought an all-German solution to the "German question," when threatened, they threw their weight behind their ally. The intransigence and determination displayed by German communists were only partly learned at the feet of the Soviet mentors; they were also developed out of their own experiences in the social and political conflicts of modern German society.[34]

Class, Nation, and Gender: Formulas of Legitimacy

Centralization, material progress, and the preemptive strike were all part of a strategy designed to secure the socialist state. The SED also marshaled an array of ideological and rhetorical formulas and programs designed to give meaning to the socialist state and the enterprise of constructing socialism. The SED trumpeted the DDR as the political embodiment of the proletariat and as the expression of the grand national characteristics of the German people. Moreover, the socialist state, it asserted, had established the equality of women and men and had freed women to combine both paid employment and motherhood in a creative and fulfilling manner.

Fault lines ran between and within the SED's languages and policies on class, nation, and gender. But these categories enabled the SED leaders to invoke both the German and the specifically KPD past and proved at least partly successful in giving the DDR a degree of stability and legitimacy, at least until the latter half of the 1980s. By invoking especially the communist past, the SED leaders drew upon their own experiences as party veterans; they also drastically limited the "political imaginary," keeping it encased in the era of coal and steel, armed revolution, and hard-fought street battles.

First and foremost, the SED, like its KPD forebear, always defined itself, and its state, in class terms. However much all sorts of ancillary formulations varied over its forty-year history, the DDR was always the state of "workers and peasants." As the party expressed it in 1961: "This state [the DDR] is the work of the working class led by the revolutionary Marxist-Leninist party, which exercises

[33] See Gerhard Naumann and Eckhard Trümpler, *Von Ulbricht zu Honecker: 1970—ein Krisenjahr der DDR* (Berlin: Dietz, 1990), especially the analysis of Günter Mittag's pronouncements, 26–27.

[34] Michael Lemke, "Die Deutschlandspolitik der DDR zwischen Moskauer Oktroi und Bonner Sogwirkung," and Ludolf Herbst, "Abhängigkeit oder Interdependenz," in Kocka, *DDR als Geschichte*, 181–90, both recognize a degree of tension in the relations between the DDR and the Soviet Union. But their analyses, in my view, are a bit too cautious.

power in alliance with the peasantry of the cooperatives and the working strata."[35] Nearly every other aspect of the identity of the socialist state derived from its class character. Class meant that the SED and its members were engaged in continuous struggle to build socialism and international peace. The proletariat was the agent of historical progress, the party served the proletarian cause, and the party-state served as the main instrument in the struggle.

Class even underpinned the antifascism that was so fundamental to the identity of the DDR.[36] Since in the SED understanding, National Socialism was inextricably rooted in capitalist society, the heroic resistance waged by the KPD was also an act of resistance against capitalism. The DDR's very existence maintained the struggle against resurgent fascism in West Germany and ensured that at least from its part of Germany, no war of conquest would emerge. Antifascism, in daily life found in street names, wall plaques, national celebrations, and school curricula, demarcated the DDR from the BRD and served as a critical element of legitimation.

Class also meant, of course, loyalty to the Soviet Union, the great protector, the "socialist brother," the inspiration and the source of "help" in the construction of socialism. As late as 1988, the relationship to the Soviet Union and the CPSU remained the "touchstone for revolutionary thought and action," and the SED expressed its "brotherly friendship" and "indestructible fighting alliance with the party and country of Lenin."[37]

Class and struggle entailed reviving the deep commitments of the party's founders, even if in symbolic form. In the annual march to the gravesite to commemorate the assassinations of Luxemburg and Liebknecht and the death of Lenin—the "LLL" commemorations—*Neues Deutschland*, the SED's major newspaper, depicted crowds dressed for the winter and marching under a sea of umbrellas. They carried giant posters of Liebknecht and Luxemburg and fought the elements to honor the revolutionary martyrs.[38] The famous line from Luxemburg's last article, "Ich war—ich bin—ich werde sein" (I was—I am—I shall be), displayed on banners carried by demonstrators and at the monument to socialist militants at Friedrichsfelde, linked Luxemburg's unwavering commitment

[35] "Aus dem 'Gesetzbuch der Arbeit,'" 12 April 1961, in Hermann Weber, ed., *DDR: Dokumente zur Geschichte der Deutschen Demokratischen Republik 1945–1985* (Munich: DTV, 1986), 249.

[36] See Konrad H. Jarausch, "The Failure of East German Antifascism: Some Ironies of History as Politics," *GSR* 14:1 (1991): 85–102, and Eve Rosenhaft, "The Uses of Remembrance: The Legacy of the Communist Resistance in the German Democratic Republic," in *Germans against Nazism: Nonconformity, Opposition and Resistance in the Third Reich. Essays in Honour of Peter Hoffmann*, ed. Francis R. Nicosia and Lawrence D. Stokes (New York: Berg, 1990), 369–88.

[37] "70 Jahre Kampf für Sozialismus und Frieden, für das Wohl des Volkes: Thesen des Zentralkomitees der SED zum 70. Jahrestag der Gründung der Kommunistischen Partei Deutschlands," *ND*, 14 June 1988, 3–8, quote on 7. See also Hermann Weber's comments on the double-edged character of these pledges of loyalty in the context of the Gorbachev reforms: "Geschichte als Instrument der Politik: Zu den Thesen des ZK der SED 'Zum 70. Jahrestag der Gründung der KPD,'" *DA* 21:8 (1988): 863–72.

[38] "Mit der Stärkung unserer Republik erfüllen wir ihr revolutionäres Vermächtnis: Rede von Egon Krenz in der Gedenkstätte der Sozialisten," *ND*, 18 January 1988, 3, and "Aufmarsch von über 200 000 Berlinern an den Gräbern von Karl und Rosa," *ND*, 18 January 1988, 1, 3.

to the socialist cause with the current generation of party members working to develop still further the socialist state.[39]

Commitment also meant reviving the cult of militarism that the KPD had propagated in the Weimar Republic. In the "LLL" demonstrations, the workplace-based, paramilitary "Kampfgruppen" of the DDR marched in the lead and gave visual representation to the militancy of the socialist struggle. Disseminated through the party press and television news, these visual representations of idealized revolutionaries as physically powerful men marching in disciplined formation reprised the role of the Red Front Fighters League of the 1920s.[40] The glorification of the National People's Army, which reached new heights under Honecker, performed a similar role.

The militaristic style of the KPD also found echoes in the uniforms and activities of the Free German Youth, in school curricula, and in political language with its evocations of the battlefield and the military dimension of the class struggle. "Storm the Fortress of Science" proclaimed the Free German Youth (Freie Deutsche Jugend, or FDJ) at its 1950 conference, signaling changes in higher education policies.[41] "For us art and literature are weapons for socialism," trumpeted Kurt Hager, Secretary for Science, Institutions of Higher Education, and Popular Education in 1957.[42] Margot Honecker, the Minister of Culture, conveyed the essence of struggle:

> Under the changed conditions of the class struggle in the present, the direct confrontation of both opposed systems and the increasing ideological diversions of our opponents take on greater and greater meaning. We have to convey to [our youth] the knowledge that what we have today has been won over from the imperialists in a hard class struggle, that it is now being defended against them, and that it must be further developed.[43]

Especially following the abandonment of reform efforts, those of 1956–58, the late 1960s, and the mid-1970s (to be discussed below), the party reasserted the centrality of class by extolling proletarian militancy and proletarian culture. Resurrecting the KPD's proletarian correspondent campaign of the 1920s, the SED in 1958 called on workers to write to help supersede the division of art and life. "Pick up the pen, miner: The socialist national culture needs you!" ran the slogan.[44] As in 1948, the SED promoted a new "activist campaign" in the workplace, which both idealized labor and pressured workers to overfulfill their production quotas.[45] Intellectuals were called upon to practice socialist realism and depict proletarian life in their artistry. Just two years after Khrushchev's secret

[39] For example, "Ich war—ich bin—ich werde sein," *ND*, 18 January 1949, 1–2.

[40] As late as the 1980s, *Neues Deutschland*'s report on the demonstration accorded prominent place to the parade of the *Kampfgruppen*. See *ND*, 14 January 1980, and the photos of the all male *Kampfgruppen* accompanying the reports in *ND*, 18 January 1988, 3 and 16 January 1989, 3.

[41] Kleßmann, *Doppelte Staatsgründung*, 286.

[42] Ibid., 288.

[43] Quoted in McAdams, *East Germany and Detente*, 132.

[44] Staritz, *Geschichte der DDR*, 126.

[45] Ibid., 126–27.

speech, all of this marked a reversion not only to the Stalinist style, but also to the proletarian militancy of the KPD. The sharpening of internal measures of control following the construction of the Wall only intensified the picture of Stalinism redux, and with a language that recalled the KPD of the 1920s and 1930s as well as the Soviet Union—attacks on traitors and enemies who deserved to be "pounded on the nose"; on the imperialist United States and its Bonn lackeys; on the social democratic leaders Kurt Schumacher and Erich Ollenhauer who reprised the assassination of Luxemburg and Liebknecht with their attacks on the DDR.[46]

But the class identity of the socialist state, associated with proletarian masculinity, class warfare, and militarism, did not suffice for a nation whose very existence was always subject to doubt and whose own multiclass society became increasingly diverse and complex. The SED also laid claim to German national identity, a claim staked and defended with particular fervency because of the competition with the BRD. The identification of the party and the party-state as the embodiment of "all that was progressive" in the history of the German people dates from the very founding of the DDR, not only from the 1970s and 1980s, as is often presumed.[47]

In broad terms, two strands of nationalist claims coexisted in uneasy fashion. The first simply absorbed nation into class in a kind of national-Bolshevik formulation, one that bore distinct echoes of Karl Radek's "Schlageter speech" of 1923 and the KPD's 1931 "Program for the National and Social Liberation of the German People." In this perspective, the proletariat represented the "true" interests of the German nation and was the single and final heir to a long history of heroic struggle. Promoting the proletarian cause promoted, at one and the same time, the national cause. However problematic, this formulation was articulated down to the very end of the DDR. In the worst periods of Stalinism, it achieved some notably absurd versions, such as the contention that Beethoven could only be truly appreciated under socialism, or that the destruction of German fascism by the Red Army opened the way for a "true, objective evaluation and appreciation of Bach."[48] More typical were Wilhelm Pieck's claim that Liebknecht and Luxemburg were the "true defenders of the national interests of the German people,"[49] and Walter Ulbricht's call for the study of history as of critical significance for the "struggle for the national unity of Germany and for the fostering of all the great traditions of the German people."[50]

[46] Examples are from Staritz, *Geschichte der DDR*, 141–42; "Den Toten die Ehre—uns die Pflicht," *ND*, 16 January 1949, 3; and Wilhelm Pieck, "Wir erfüllen das Vermächtnis unserer Toten," *ND*, 15 January 1950, 3.

[47] See especially Meuschel, *Legitimation und Parteiherrschaft*, for a profound discussion of the intertwining of class and nation over the long course of the DDR's history.

[48] SED Executive, cited in Staritz, *Geschichte der DDR*, 58.

[49] Wilhelm Pieck, "Wir erfüllen das Vermächtnis unserer Toten," *ND*, 15 January 1950, 3.

[50] For a good overview see Georgi Verbeeck, "Kontinuität und Wandel im DDR-Geschichtsbild," *APZ* B11/90 (9 March 1990): 30–42, quote on 31–32.

The second strand sought to connect the identity of the DDR not specifically to the heroic progressive tradition, but to certain values and ideas long condemned in party circles as representative of "bourgeois" culture. The SED propagated in particular a social conservatism defined by such key terms as "*Sauberkeit*" (cleanliness, moral virtue), "*Anständlichkeit*" (propriety, moral rectitude), and that holy trinity, "*Ordnung, Fleiß und Sparsamkeit*" (order, diligence, and thrift). These terms stood in marked contrast to the disruptive elements of proletarian militancy that had characterized the KPD of the Weimar Republic. Indeed, their active propagation by the party required a continual and unresolved struggle against "*Proletkult*," the elevation of rough proletarian militancy into the hallmark of revolutionary commitment. Amid the revolutionary claims of the SED, the effort to appropriate "*Bürgerlichkeit*" lent a profoundly conservative and traditional tone to DDR society, one that, especially in the 1950s, bore remarkable parallels to the tenor of West German society.

Walter Ulbricht, for example, never abandoned his obsession with order already evident upon his return to Germany in 1945. In the 1950s, he offered the catechism-like "Ten Commandments of Socialist Morality," which called on the populace to "love . . . the Fatherland," "exercise . . . good deeds for socialism," "strive to improve your productivity, be thrifty, and maintain socialist labor discipline," and live "in a moral and upright manner" (*sauber und anständing*).[51] Erich Honecker, leading the campaign against writers and artists in the mid-1960s, claimed that "the DDR is a virtuous (*sauber*) state" in which reigns an unshakable level "of ethics and morals, of rectitude and propriety."[52] Americans, in sharp contrast, were "culture barbarians," a position that reprised long-standing attitudes on both the right and the left in Germany and was eerily redolent of National Socialist propaganda: "The American culture barbarians and their lackey desecrate the memory of Beethoven by misusing Bonn, his birthplace, for the most pernicious national dishonor. From Bonn is undertaken the cosmopolitan attempts to undermine the great German cultural values in order to destroy the national consciousness of the German people."[53]

In the 1950s, jazz, abstract art, blue jeans, and other artifacts of the burgeoning mass consumption culture of the West were all said to represent western degeneracy in contrast to DDR-*Anständlichkeit*. The charge that West Germany and its "agents" in the DDR, including such old communists as Paul Merker and Franz Dahlem, stood for "cosmopolitanism," "formalism," and "finance capital"—all charges that had pronounced anti-Semitic connotations—connected the DDR not only to the worst excesses of Stalinism, but also to the German conservative-national and fascist discourses about the nation.[54]

[51] Walter Ulbricht, "10 Gebote der sozialistischen Moral," 10 July 1958, in Weber, *DDR: Dokumente*, 237.

[52] Quoted in Kleßmann, "Opposition und Dissidenz in der Geschichte der DDR," *APZ* B5/91 (25 January 1991): 59.

[53] Central Committee of the SED, quoted in Staritz, *Geschichte der DDR*, 58–59.

[54] Meuschel, *Legitimation und Parteiherrschaft*, 112–16, and Jeffrey Herf, "East German Communists and the Jewish Question: The Case of Paul Merker," *JCH* 29:4 (1994): 627–62.

The propagation of profoundly conservative cultural norms as a means of linking the DDR to the national past is also evident in the broad popularity of etiquette books in the 1950s and early 1960s, such as Karl Smolkas's *Gutes Benehmen von A-Z*, which went through three printings and 235,000 copies between 1957 and 1961, and Walter Schweickert and Gert Hold's *Guten Tag, Herr von Knigge*, which went through fourteen editions between 1957 and 1963.[55] Anna-Sabine Ernst argues that these books differed hardly at all from their West German counterparts. DDR citizens were advised that clothing should be "appropriate," "unobtrusive," and "solid." The most important and worthy guests were to be seated on the left of the hostess. "Elegance is always simple," ran one maxim.[56] All of this was entwined with the effort to set a "good tone" for the new society, to elevate human relations to a "defined civilized level."[57] In so doing, the SED sought to win over the middle class to the new socialist state and to "elevate" workers and peasants. Workers would become worthy of their leading role in the state, and the DDR, by laying claim to the "civilized" nature of German culture and society, would become a model for other countries: "Since the majority of Central Europeans behave this way, we should do the same. If people have cut potatoes with the edge of their forks for the past 200 years, why should we suddenly decide to use knives?"[58]

The etiquette book authors had to do sharp battle with the received understanding of "Proletkult," which often signified the deliberate challenge to bourgeois conventions. In the socialist state, they argued, such behavior was no longer necessary. Wild disruptions and loud laughter at the table, indiscipline and slothful behavior, deliberate nonrecognition of rules—all this now had to be replaced by "good tone" and appropriate behavior.[59] What may have been appropriate for the Weimar Republic or Imperial Germany should no longer set the standards for the developing socialist society of the DDR. "'Proletkult' quickly becomes as sterile as earlier bourgeois [demeanor]," claimed one etiquette book author, and "boorish behavior is not proletarian deportment."[60]

Much like the argument that Beethoven and Bach could only be properly heard under socialism, the SED argued that truly appropriate behavior had degenerated into mere formality under capitalism, but that under socialism form and content would be integrated. As Schweikert and Hold stated in their etiquette book: "The

[55] I draw here on Anna-Sabine Ernst, "Vom 'Du' zum 'Sie': Die Rezeption der bürgerlichen Anstandsregeln in der DDR der 50er Jahre" (ms., 1992), paper delivered at the 1992 Annual Meeting of the German Studies Association, and idem, "The Politics of Culture and the Culture of Daily Life in the DDR in the 1950s," in *Between Reform and Revolution: Studies in German Socialism and Communism from 1840 to 1990*, ed. David E. Barclay and Eric D. Weitz (Providence: Berghahn, forthcoming).

[56] These examples are from Ernst, "Vom 'Du' zum 'Sie,'" 2.

[57] Ibid., 6.

[58] Smolka, quoted in Anna-Sabine Ernst, "Middle Class Values and the Socialist Concept of Mass Culture: Etiquette Books in the GDR in the 1950s" (ms., 1992: English translation and compression of the above cited essay), 3.

[59] Ernst, "Vom 'Du' zum 'Sie,'" 7–8.

[60] Karl Kleinschmidt quoted in ibid., 13.

human being of the socialist society, when it has fully flowered, will have no possibility, no occasion, and no desire any longer to behave badly. He will not dissemble, cringe, or swindle. In the same manner that he will no longer steal, no longer rob, no longer exploit, he will not eat fish with a knife or drink champagne out of a red wine glass."[61] The proletariat had also to learn proper attire; work-clothes should no longer be trend-setting for committed socialists as they had been in the Weimar Republic: "A suit for festive occasions is simply part of culture, particularly socialist culture. . . . After ten years of the DDR, is it really necessary to go to the theater in a plaid jacket?"[62]

Recommendations for upstanding, cultured behavior involved more than the ethereal claims to the German bourgeois past. They had also a direct, functional purpose: to enhance social discipline and, of course, productivity, the bête noire of the DDR's existence, and to ameliorate (at least) the opposition to the administrative direction of state and society. Ulbricht himself argued, in effect, that politeness and appropriate behavior on the part of party functionaries would go a long way toward easing the opposition to party rule, and the etiquette books and articles followed suit.[63] In particular, the conflicts between the intelligentsia and party and state functionaries drawn substantially from the working class would be eased through appropriate behavior, it was hoped. Hence the recommendation to use the formal "Sie" instead of "du," accompanied by open admission of the hierarchical nature of the workplace.[64]

A virtual straight line of continuity connects the calls for upstanding and "correct" behavior in the 1950s and early 1960s with the somewhat more sophisticated discussion conducted by historians and other academics in the late 1970s and 1980s about "*Erbe*" (inheritance) and "*Tradition*." The latter term was reserved for the specific, formative elements of the past that helped shape the DDR, like the KPD legacy. "*Erbe*" is a more general term that enabled the SED to appropriate, at times critically, the totality of the German past.[65] Through both terms the SED sought, once again, to weld class and nation together.

Practically, this resulted in renewed interest in local and regional history and the distant past, and the resurrection and incorporation into the "Erbe" of the DDR of such minor figures as Luther, Frederick the Great, and Bismarck. Like the recommendations for *Sauberkeit* and *Anständlichkeit*, the discussion about these figures—and, importantly, about Prussia itself—enabled the SED to incorporate profoundly conservative aspects of the German past into the "inheritance" of the

[61] Ibid., 11.

[62] "Festkleidung hebt die Stimmung," in *ND*, 31 October 1959, quoted in ibid., 13.

[63] See the quote from his speech to the Volkskammer on 4 October 1960 in ibid., 14.

[64] Ibid., 15–17.

[65] See the discussion in Irma Hanke, "Sozialistischer Neohistorismus? Aspekte der Identitätsdebatte in der DDR," and Sigrid Meuschel, "Auf der Suche nach Madame L'Identité? Zur Konzeption der Nation und Nationalgeschichte," in *Die DDR in der Ära Honecker: Politik—Kutlur—Gesellschaft*, ed. Gert-Joachim Glaeßner (Opladen: Westdeutscher, 1988), 56–76, 77–93, both of which have full references to the East German literature. See also the collection of essays from the debate, *Erbe und Tradition in der DDR: Die Diskussion der Historiker*, ed. Helmut Meier and Walter Schmidt (Berlin: Akademie, 1988), and Konrad H. Jarausch, ed., *Zwischen Parteilichkeit und Professionalität: Bilanz der Geschichtswissenschaft der DDR* (Berlin: Akademie, 1991).

DDR. Helmut Hanke, one of the major academic partisans of the effort, even found some value in Prussian militarism, which alongside mindless drill, obedience, and pettiness conveyed to the nation "also cultivation and a specific sense of honor."[66] In Irma Hanke's exposition of the "*Erbe und Tradition*" discussion, the conservative inheritance bestowed "the particular sense of work among the Germans and their special sense of family, the strict separation of the public and private realms. [Helmut Hanke] claimed these virtues for socialism: The general tendency for a life in social security and private safety could also be seen as evidence of the stabilization and solidification of the socialist way of life."[67]

Even the "*Kleinstaaterei*" of the Holy Roman Empire, scorned by every German progressive worthy of his or her name since the War of Liberation in 1809, found its advocates in the DDR of the 1980s. In the realm of architecture and city planning, academicians and officials, acting as if they had just read Jane Jacobs, rediscovered the virtues of urban neighborhoods with their population mix and small shops, as opposed to the massive Stalinist-type architecture that had dominated the DDR for most of its history.[68] Practically, this at least led to some substantial efforts in the late 1970s and 1980s to rehabilitate older housing stock in the central cities of the DDR.

The renewed interest in the nation signified an effort to imbue national sentiments with a socialist content and socialist sentiments with a national content. In Honecker's words, as quoted and paraphrased by Sigrid Meuschel, the citizens of the DDR are able " 'because of its socialist formation, to bind closer together their own locality [*Heimat*] with the socialist fatherland' and to call in mind local and regional traditions that belong 'to our national identity, to the progressive and humanistic history of our people.' "[69] And as Walter Schmidt and Alfred Kosing, two of the most active proponents of the new DDR nationalism, put it in a striking reworking of classic Marxian categories: "Through the 'evolution of a new socialist defined national self-understanding and national consciousness' the nation will [develop] from 'a nation in itself to a nation for itself. It will consciously [make] its national identity and thereby [become] an historical subject to the fullest extent.' "[70]

All of these efforts were designed to elevate the emotional commitment of the population to the DDR, to enhance its identity, and thereby to serve an integrative, system legitimizing function. As Hermann Weber writes, the assertion of national-conservative values was designed to make the DDR attractive to the diverse strata of the population and assert its place in the lineage of German history.[71]

But the new nationalism never replaced the specific party and class traditions that the regime also consciously propagated and venerated. Indeed, in the late 1970s and 1980s the SED invoked with new vigor the glorious *Kampftraditionen* of the KPD and the language of proletarian militancy. As an institution the SED

66 Quoted in Hanke, "Sozialistischer Neohistorismus?" 69–70.

67 Ibid., 69.

68 Ibid., 65–68.

69 Meuschel, "Auf der Suche nach Madame L'Identité?" 86.

70 Quoted in ibid.

71 Weber, "Wandlungen im Selbstverständnis der SED unter Honecker," 295.

was "celebrated as never before" in the Honecker years, according to one observer.[72] The party placed renewed emphasis on the proletariat as the centerpiece of its social conception and reasserted its militant proletarian legacy—even though these conceptions bore little semblance of reality with the DDR's own increasingly modern and complex social order.[73]

Moreover, the conservative social norms propagated by the SED were never exclusively the province of the German bourgeoisie. Discipline and order also constituted part of the tradition of the German labor movement. In the KPD, they found expression in the continual calls for proletarian and party discipline, and, in extreme version, in Stalinist *Kadavergehorsamkeit* (obedience to the very end). Indeed, so-called bourgeois values provided a powerful legitimizing function for the regime precisely because they allowed the SED-state to lay claim to both the bourgeois, national liberal heritage of the late eighteenth and nineteenth centuries and the culture of the labor movement from the Lassalleans of the 1860s to the SPD of Imperial Germany and, of course, to the KPD of the Weimar Republic. Clearly, contradictions and fault lines existed in this kind of cultural appropriation; it was well-nigh impossible to reconcile the proletarian *Kampftraditionen* of the KPD, with its disruptive, street-fighting connotations, and bourgeois *Anständlichkeit*. But seamless integration may not be the most effective form of constructing legitimacy. By laying claim to multiple traditions that could be variously deployed, the SED may well have gone a long way toward establishing successfully the socialist nation—at least until the end of the 1980s.[74]

Similarly, in its commitment to gender equality, the SED drew on both the specifically socialist support for women's emancipation and the more standard emphasis on the family and women's maternal roles that cut through all sorts of political divisions. The first constitution of 1949 established the legal equality of men and women and equal pay for equal work. The revised family code, which entered into force on 1 April 1966, reaffirmed legal equality and the mutual responsibility of men and women in the family. They were implored to order their relationships such that women could combine motherhood with "professional and social activity."[75] About 80 percent of women worked in the paid labor force; 90 percent of women in the relevant age groups either worked or studied. Half of the labor force was composed of women.[76]

With one of the highest female labor participation rates in the developed world, DDR women by the 1980s were also the beneficiaries of one of the world's most egalitarian educational programs and most extensive maternalist social welfare programs. From the 1960s onward educational opportunities were equivalent for boys and girls. Proportionately many more women were trained for advanced

[72] McAdams, *East Germany and Detente*, 130.

[73] Meuschel, *Legitimation und Parteiherrschaft*, 232–42, and Staritz, *Geschichte der DDR*, 171–75.

[74] Niethammer makes a related point in "Annäherung an den Wandel," 326.

[75] See the discussion in Gisela Helwig, "Staat und Familie in der DDR," in Glaeßner, *DDR in der Ära Honecker*, 468–69.

[76] Hildegard Maria Nickel, "Frauen in der DDR," *APZ* B16–17/90 (13 April 1990): 39–45.

positions than in the Federal Republic. By the 1980s, "variations in the level of formal professional qualifications for men and women . . . [had] essentially ceased to exist for those under forty years old."[77] The "unity of economic and social policy" in the 1970s and 1980s provided DDR women with year-long paid leaves from work following the birth of a child, family allowances, a forty-hour work-week for mothers with at least two children, an extensive system of child-care centers, and additional days for vacation and for the care of sick children.[78] These measures seem to have turned around the birthrate decline, which in 1980 again reached the 1968 level.[79] The regime continually touted the welfare programs as one of the great accomplishments of "real existing socialism" and evidence of the establishment of equality between men and women in the DDR.

The SED, reviving the KPD's perspective, always articulated the establishment of gender equality within the formal language and standards of Marxism-Leninism and denied the category of gender any independent analytical or political significance. To quote Inge Lange, the longtime head of the Central Committee's Women's Department: "[T]he women's question is not a question between the sexes, but is a class question."[80] The party argued that the path of emancipation lay through the coupling of communist party power with the participation of women in the productive sphere.[81] Typically, party advocates resorted to the socialist classics, especially Engels's *Origins of the Family, Private Property, and the State* and its materialist perspective, to explain the subordination of women under capitalism and the tasks ahead for the development of socialist society.[82] Any evaluation of the status of women in the DDR invariably began with a compilation of statistics on women's involvement in the paid labor force. As Lange put it, "the inclusion of women in social production is the most important and most fundamental step [in their emancipation]."[83] Lange even argued for policies that would deprive women of the choice of part-time work, since that would slow their emancipation—and weaken the regime's productivist drive.[84]

Especially in the 1950s and 1960s, the SED reprised the KPD's hostility to the

[77] Hildegard Maria Nickel, "Geschlechtertrennung durch Arbeitsteilung," *Feministische Studien* 8 (1990): 10.

[78] Helwig, "Staat und Familie," provides a good summary of the programs, which were improved and made more generous through the last two decades of the DDR.

[79] By DDR evaluations, the social policy measures relating to time off had more impact on reversing the natality decline than financial incentives. See Ulrike Enders, "Kinder, Küche, Kombinat—Frauen in der DDR," *APZ* B6–7 (1986): 32, who cites the relevant DDR literature.

[80] Inge Lange, "Die Frau im gesellschaftlichen Leben der DDR," *Einheit* 30:9 (1975): 2.

[81] For some examples, see Lange, "Frau im gesellschaftlichen Leben," and Eva Schmidt-Kolmer and Heinz H. Schmidt, "Über Frauenarbeit und Familie," *Einheit* 17:12 (1962): 89–99.

[82] See Inge Lange, *Die Frauen—aktive Mitgestalterinnen des Sozialismus: Ausgewählte Reden und Aufsätze*, ed. Institut für Marxismus-Leninismus beim ZK der SED (Berlin: Dietz, 1987), for many typical statements.

[83] Inge Lange, "Im Geiste Lenins die Gleichberechtigung der Frauen im Leben verwirklichen" (1970), in Lange, *Frauen*, 30. Or see the title of one of Lange's many articles and speeches, "Die Rolle der Frau im Produktionsprozeß bestimmt ihre Stellung in der sozialistischen Gesellschaft," *Einheit* 24 (1969): 329–47.

[84] "Aktuelle Probleme der Arbeit mit den Frauen bei der weiteren Verwirklichung der Beschlüsse des VIII. Parteitages der SED" (1974), in Lange, *Frauen*, 81–82.

individual household, which was viewed as a relic of presocialist society. The tenor of many commentaries denigrated women who might have desired to stay at home with their children and certainly slighted the social role of motherhood in favor of large-scale social institutions.[85] Just as individual production had been superseded by social production under capitalism, so educative and social functions formerly conducted within individualized families would now be superseded by the far superior forms of socialized education and housework.[86] Lange, after delineating the participation of women in the workforce, invariably presented statistics on the proportion of household wash carried out in industrial enterprises and on the percentage of the population that had a warm meal from the company or school canteen.[87] All of this also placed the DDR firmly within one long-standing German tradition—the recourse to the state and to technology as the near-automatic solution to social problems.

The denigration of the individual household went so far that the affective aspects of motherhood—the "mystifying mother-child relationship" charted by psychoanalysis, "overly ardent love ['*Affenliebe*'] and . . . excessively strong concentration on the interests of [a mother's] own children"—were often condemned.[88] Yet at the same time, the SED promoted very traditional family patterns—again reprising the KPD, whose contradictory mix of imagery in relation to women we have already seen, as well as long-standing bourgeois patterns. According to the etiquette books of the 1950s and 1960s, women belonged in the workplace, but they should conduct themselves in a feminine manner, avoiding coarse jokes and improper behavior.[89] Men should remember that their wives and daughters might be the recipients of rude behavior. At dances women should never approach men, but should wait to be asked to dance. Nor should they initiate conversation; that too remained the prerogative of men. The passive role was considered part of the "natural" character of the female sex. Women's nature allows them to elevate family life, to "define the tone that reigns in the family." They do the same in the firm, whose internal life they elevate by their politeness and upstanding behavior. Should women appear out of the kitchen in an apron, then family life is threatened. No one is happy to be with a mother who allows her outer appearance to wane, and then, step by step, "the feelings of love and affection become dulled and the inner cohesion of the family wanes."[90]

These "traditional values" gained a new lease on life in the 1970s and 1980s in the context of the regime's expansion of social welfare measures.[91] The "unity of

[85] See, for example, Schmidt-Kolmer and Schmidt, "Über Frauenarbeit und Familie."

[86] Ibid., 92.

[87] See, for example, Lange, "Im Geiste Lenins die Gleichberechtigung der Frauen im Leben verwirklichen" (1970); "Die Erfahrungen der DDR im Kampf um die Befreiung der Frau—Teil des allgemeinen Kampfes um Demokratie und Sozialismus" (1970); and "Aktuelle Probleme der Arbeit mit den Frauen bei der weiteren Verwirklichung der Beschlüsse des VIII. Parteitages der SED" (1974), all in Lange, *Frauen*, 34, 51, 77–79. See also Schmidt-Kolmer and Schmidt, "Über Frauenarbeit und Familie," 98.

[88] For example, Schmidt-Kolmer and Schmidt, "Über Frauenarbeit und Familie," 97, 99.

[89] Ernst, "Vom 'Du' zum 'Sie,'" 17–21.

[90] Karl-Heinz Tomaschewsky, quoted in ibid., 21.

[91] Nickel, "Geschlechtertrennung," 11, and Elke Mocker, Beate Rüther, and Birgit Sauer,

employment and motherhood," another oft-cited slogan of the Honecker era, captured the SED's version of the model socialist woman. The regime tended now to invoke the glories of motherhood both for the socialist woman and as a social function of the highest order. But in Hildegard Nickel's pithy phrase, the DDR accomplished "patriarchal equality of rights instead of social equality."[92] Labor force segmentation along gender lines remained quite high and women were concentrated in lower-paying sectors.[93] Social welfare policies, highly progressive in many respects, clearly invested women with the primary responsibilities in the family and sought ways of making paid labor and motherhood (not gender-neutral parenting) more efficient. The law providing leave days for the care of sick children, for example, specifically stated that fathers could be granted such leave only in exceptional circumstances, and required an affidavit from a doctor that their wives were too ill to fulfill their child-care responsibilities.[94] The larger cultural world of the DDR also reproduced "traditional" gender patterns. In the proletarian novels touted by the regime, for example, males almost always represented heroic revolutionary fighters. Uncommitted men, in contrast, are depicted as weak and submissive—"feminine" characteristics—while women, when they are depicted at all, are divided, in very traditional fashion, into "good" or "fallen" women.[95]

Both the achievements and the limitations of the DDR's policies were rooted in perspectives on gender articulated by the German labor movement and the KPD in particular and in long-standing conceptions of separate spheres that stretched back to the late eighteenth century.[96] The heroic male fighter, that essential element of party culture forged in the Weimar Republic, was reproduced in all sorts of ways in the DDR—in the continual invocation of the glorious traditions of the party; in the composition of the nearly all male party and state leadership; in the use of the masculinized language of *Kampf* to describe everything from efforts to raise production to the campaign for nuclear disarmament; in social and cultural policies that defined the household as primarily a woman's sphere. The fixation on class, struggle, and production had its corollary in the refusal to admit any independent significance to gender. The oppression of women under capitalism and their emancipation under socialism were mere epi-

---

"Frauen- und Familienpolitik: Wie frauenfreundlich war die DDR?" *DA* 22:11 (November 1990): 1700–1705.

[92] Nickel, "Frauen in der DDR," quote on 39. The discussion below follows ibid. as well as idem, "Geschlechtertrennung," and Rainer Geißler, "Soziale Ungleichheit zwischen Frauen und Männern im geteilten und im vereinten Deutschland," *APZ* B14–15/91 (29 March 1991): 13–24.

[93] See Mocker, Rüther, and Sauer, "Frauen- und Familienpolitik," 1702; Christiane Lemke, "Frauen, Technik und Fortschritt: Zur Bedeutung neuer Technologien für die Berufssituation von Frauen in der DDR," in Glaeßner, *DDR in der Ära Honecker*, 481–98; and Nickel, "Geschlechtertrennung."

[94] Helwig, "Staat und Familie," 473–74.

[95] See the very interesting analysis of Julia Hell, "At the Center an Absence: Foundationalist Narratives of the GDR and the Legitimatory Discourse of Antifascism," *Monatshefte* 84:1 (1992): 23–45. For a different kind of example, see Dölling, "Continuity and Change."

[96] See Karin Hausen, "Family and Role-Division: The Polarisation of Sexual Stereotypes in the Nineteenth Century—An Aspect of the Dissociation of Work and Family," in *The German Family*, ed. Richard J. Evans and W. R. Lee (London: Croom Helm, 1981), 51–83.

phenomena of the respective social systems, each defined essentially by the nature of property relations.

But the SED also asserted "traditional," conservative values. Social welfare programs reinscribed the family and household as primarily women's domains. The advocacy of a patriarchal family structure—even if often contradicted by the more emancipatory claims of the regime—was designed to create order and stability and to win the loyalty of social groups identified by the party as conservative and traditional. The strength of these efforts rested on the fact that the SED mobilized the traditions of both proletarian and middle-class Germany.

The assertion of traditional values had a functional purpose as well, especially in the 1950s and 1960s when social supports were at a minimum. Many women cared for multigenerational households and labored in the workplace. They carried the burdens in the household of insufficient state supports and they were drawn into production in ever increasing numbers since female labor was absolutely critical to economic development and to the support of families. The reprivatization of the household and social reproduction went hand in hand with the enormously high labor participation rates of women.[97]

The centrality of women to the regime's goals of order, discipline, and socialist development meant that issues relating to women became party-political concerns when they threatened the productivist goals of the regime, as when increasing numbers of women took to part-time work and when the birthrate dropped precipitously.[98] Precisely at these moments the state intensified its exhortations to women and expanded its social welfare programs. Even the widely touted system of state-run day-care centers had its origins in the drive to increase the efficiency of the labor force, to enable women to manage more effectively household and paid labor. A pluralist conception of freeing women for more individual pursuits hardly lay at the heart of the DDR's social welfare policies, which were reduced to functionality for the system.[99]

Ultimately, gendered politics under state socialism were highly instrumental in nature, subservient to the primary task of increasing production and protecting the stability of the "workers' and peasants' state." The regime touted the achievements of gender equality as a means to accomplish legitimacy, and it partially succeeded. Its policies were in many ways greatly beneficial for women. But by the 1980s, "real existing socialism" had produced all the emancipation of which it was capable.

The Problem of Reform

Through social welfare policies, economic development, and, not least, blatant repression, the SED state successfully demobilized the population. The intense, open forms of political and social conflict that had characterized working-class life in the Weimar Republic especially, but also in Imperial Germany and the

[97] Niethammer, "Volk der DDR," 256–57.

[98] Helwig, "Staat und Familie," 467.

[99] Nickel, "Frauen in der DDR," esp. 44.

immediate post–World War II years—conflicts that had markedly shaped the character of German communism—had been laid to rest. The party leadership operated in a political field defined by Soviet power, the Cold War, and its own ideological proclivities, but not by popular influence exercised through collective action. The SED established the primacy of its politics over society.[100]

Not even the SED, however, could completely stamp out challenges to its reign. On 17 June 1953, workers rose up in strikes and demonstrations in protest against excessive production norms and low wages.[101] Quickly, demands escalated into calls for free elections and the removal of the government. In its prairie fire–like spread to many of the traditional centers of the labor movement, the 1953 movement bore distinct similarities to other waves of working-class protest in Germany in previous decades.[102] Sporadic strikes broke out again in 1956, the year of great ferment throughout the communist world that began with Khrushchev's secret speech to the Twentieth Congress of the CPSU denouncing the crimes of Stalin. On the job, workers in the DDR engaged in the array of informal protests perfected already in Imperial Germany, which were designed to carve out some measure of autonomy in the factory and mine.[103] And all the regime's vaunted efforts to establish its uncontested authority and inculcate its values ran into sullen, societal opposition.[104]

Within the party reform efforts emerged in the wake of the 1953 Uprising and especially in the years 1956–58.[105] In the latter period, discussions quickly spilled over to society at large. In the universities, academies, and artistic associations of the DDR, intellectuals demanded an easing of state censorship and a general reduction in party claims to direct all aspects of life. Party reformers sought an end to "one-person rule" and, in some cases, an end to the SED's monopoly of power.[106] Ironically, Ulbricht himself inspired a new round of re-

[100] Or as Jürgen Kocka puts it, "the political basis of social processes" rather than "the social basis of political processes." See "Eine durchherrschte Gesellschaft," in Kaelble, Kocka, and Zwahr, *Sozialgeschichte der DDR*, 547.

[101] Recent work on the Uprising based on newly available archival materials include Detlef Hansel et al., eds., *Der 17. Juni 1953—Die SED-Führung zwischen Ohnmacht und Macht: Originaldokumente des Politbüros und des Zentralkomitees der SED vom Juni bis Juli 1953* (Berlin: Akademie, 1993); Armin Mitter and Stefan Wolle, *Untergang auf Raten: Unbekannte Kapitel der DDR-Geschichte* (Munich: Bertelsmann, 1993); and "Der 17. Juni—vierzig Jahre danach: Podiumdiskussion," in Kocka, *DDR als Geschichte*, 40–66.

[102] See Kleßmann, "Opposition und Dissidenz," 55.

[103] Lüdtke, "'Helden der Arbeit.'"

[104] See ibid. and Christiane Lemke's important study, *Die Ursachen des Umbruchs: Politische Sozialisation in der ehemaligen DDR* (Opladen: Westdeutscher, 1991).

[105] See especially Meuschel, *Legitimation und Parteiherrschaft*, 152–68, and Staritz, *Geschichte der DDR*, 109–18. Generally, see Karl Wilhelm Fricke, *Opposition und Widerstand in der DDR* (Cologne: Wissenschaft und Politik, 1984).

[106] For the most wide-ranging effort from within the party, see "Aus der politischen Plattform Wolfgang Harichs und seiner Freunde," November 1956, in Weber, *DDR: Dokumente*, 227–29. The Central Committee's response to Khrushchev's secret speech was so composed and contradictory that a reader would hardly know that the CPSU's Twentieth Congress constituted one of the major political events of the twentieth century. The text was published in *ND*, 8 July 1956.

form efforts in the 1960s. Through his New Economic System, the SED tried to invigorate the economy by giving wider scope to individual initiative and by emphasizing self-sustaining technological development.[107] Inevitably, the discussion moved beyond the confines of the economy into issues of party control over other aspects of society.[108]

Since the collapse of the DDR in 1989/90, archival evidence, especially from the MfS files, has indicated that these reform efforts and overt challenges to SED rule were more wide-ranging than most observers had imagined.[109] Nonetheless, until the autumn of 1989, the overall picture remained one of extremely limited efforts at change from within, with the one exception of the June 1953 Uprising. If anything characterizes the DDR, it is the roads not taken, the reforms widely touted and quickly abandoned.[110] Notable are not the ruptures and new departures, but the maintenance of the basic structures and ideological orientations over the forty-year history of the state.[111] The DDR had no Prague Spring, no Solidarity, no *samizdat* movement among intellectuals. The impact of 1956 was probably more limited in the DDR than anywhere else in the communist world. Serious reforms of the economic sector under Ulbricht in the 1960s and Honecker in the 1970s were abandoned for the SED's almost instinctual response, recentralization.[112] Communist party leaderships fell all over Europe in the wake of 1956 and in some cases following 1968 (the Prague Spring) and 1981 (the Polish Solidarity movement) as well. The SED leadership, however, remained in place, the most long-lasting and intact in the communist world. In short, the SED's claim to embody democracy and socialist development went largely uncontested in the public political realm.

Why was reform so limited in the DDR? As ever, the competition with the Federal Republic strongly influenced the contours of the socialist state. With West Germany just over the border, DDR reformers could hardly raise the cry of national independence, as could Poles, Czechs, and Hungarians. Any serious reform effort

[107] For a concise and effective summary on economic reform efforts, see Doris Cornelsen, "Die Wirtschaft der DDR in der Honecker-Ära," in Glaeßner, *DDR in der Ära Honecker*, 357–70. On the emergence of the technical intelligentsia, the classic studies are Peter Christian Ludz, *Parteielite im Wandel: Funktionsaufbau, Sozialstruktur und Ideologie der SED-Führung. Eine empirisch-systematische Untersuchung* (Cologne: Westdeutscher, 1968), and Thomas A. Baylis, *The Technical Intelligentsia and the East German Elite: Legitimacy and Social Change in Mature Communism* (Berkeley and Los Angeles: University of California Press, 1974).

[108] For a very similar trajectory of reform discussions in the Soviet Union, see Moshe Lewin, *Political Undercurrents in Soviet Economic Debates: From Bukharin to the Modern Reformers* (Princeton: Princeton University Press, 1974).

[109] For 1956, see Wolle, "MfS und die Arbeiterproteste," who corrects the earlier, widely propagated view that workers had not been involved at all in the ferment of that year.

[110] Kleßmann, "Opposition und Dissidenz," in my view, goes too far in asserting continuity in dissident expressions in the DDR, while Meuschel, *Legitimation und Parteiherrschaft*, is perhaps too astringent in her denial of any kind of opposition in the DDR.

[111] Gert-Joachim Glaeßner, "Vom 'realen Sozialismus' zur Selbstbestimmung: Ursachen und Konsequenzen der Systemkrise in der DDR," *APZ* B1-2/90 (5 January 1990): 4.

[112] See Staritz, *Geschichte der DDR*, 192–209, 221–26; the cogent summary by Doris Cornelsen in "DDR-Wirtschaft: Ende oder Wende?" *APZ* B1–2/90 (5 January 1990): 33–38; and Naumann and Trümpler, *Von Ulbricht zu Honecker*.

would almost inevitably reopen the "German question," which for the DDR had to place in question its very existence. On the front lines of the Cold War, the SED had always to look over its shoulders and worry that Bonn would use any opening to destabilize the DDR. The flood of refugees to the west throughout the 1950s only intensified the nervousness of the SED leadership. Moreover, many reformers left the DDR for West Germany in the 1950s or were forcibly expelled there in the 1970s and 1980s.[113]

Furthermore, the sheer repressive powers of the state can never be underestimated in explaining the limited scope of reform. While there existed clear limits to the abuses practiced by the regime—nothing of the mass murder and terror exercised by many other twentieth-century dictatorships—innumerable personal tragedies traverse the history of the DDR. If outright execution rarely took place, the threats were ever present to livelihood and to the small realms of independence that people were able to carve out for themselves. The regime never gave up its claim to monopolize the economy, the polity, and truth itself. While the DDR's own development created a substantial stratum of the scientific and technical elite, the regime continually deprived this and every other group of the autonomy needed to forge a truly modern, differentiated society.[114] The space of political articulation remained limited in the extreme.

In addition, the divide between workers and intellectuals was quite pronounced in the DDR and was expressively conveyed by reports of the factory-based *Kampfgruppen* descending on student gatherings in 1956 to prevent their escalation into demonstrations.[115] In Poland, Hungary, and Czechoslovakia, the two realms were far more permeable than in the DDR. The repression of 1953 induced greater caution among workers, while at the same time the regime granted them concessions and material conditions improved. Worker demands after 1953, in turn, remained limited to material concerns. Intellectuals, materially quite privileged in the DDR, had almost nothing to say about, gave virtually no support to, workers' economic demands.

Perhaps even more significantly, the experience of fascism had made intellectuals extremely chary of popular activism. They had enormous, if latent, fears that mass participation would signify a reemergence of fascist sentiments.[116] They considered state-sanctioned and enforced antifascism sacrosanct, which made it nearly impossible to challenge the essence of state power. Furthermore, DDR intellectuals, whatever the rhetoric of solidarity, had also imbibed that very traditionally German overrespect for the educated, which made them loathe to engage in common cause with an undisciplined, rank-and-file, workers' movement.

Moreover, the younger DDR generation of the 1950s had had little in the way of independent political experience. Even the "activists of the first hour" in 1945/46

[113] Kleßmann, "Opposition und Dissidenz," 53.

[114] See Meuschel, *Legitimation und Parteiherrschaft.*

[115] Wolle, "MfS und die Arbeiterproteste," 45.

[116] A major point of Meuschel's very important work, *Legitimation und Parteiherrschaft.* See also Mommsen, "Ort der DDR."

had been drawn from the pool of Weimar veterans who had grown up in the independent organizations of the labor movement. The first DDR generation, in contrast, had been socialized in the Third Reich and was accustomed to political passivity within highly structured mass organizations. As Lutz Niethammer cogently argues, a certain symbiosis emerged between the older, Stalinist-schooled SED leadership and the new cadre generation, both committed to order, discipline, and individual and collective economic advance. It was not a fertile social base for dissent and reform.[117]

Typically, the party reform discussions, however democratically inspired, however much an advance over the SED's complete reliance on the powers of the state, did not entail any notion of grassroots democracy. Even such models as workers and soldiers councils, easily legitimated through reference to the KPD's past, barely surfaced. Reform programs involved, at best, a loosening of étatisme. Reformers wanted the party to be more attentive to society, less fixated on the primacy of politics practiced by the SED under Ulbricht. But they never questioned the bases or goals of party power. Even Robert Havemann, later to become the leading dissident of the DDR, made his first oppositional statements fully within the framework established by Khrushchev's secret speech. And intellectuals never reached beyond their own circles and never challenged the bases of party power, only its corruption under Ulbricht.

Yet no state lives by repression alone. As discussed above, the SED did succeed in winning legitimacy for the socialist state, especially in the 1970s and early 1980s when Honecker's program, "the unification of economic and social policy," proved initially successful in raising living standards. Moreover, many took seriously the antifascist identification of the DDR, personified in a party and state leader who had spent the greatest part of the Nazi years in prison. Others were able to retreat into their own "niches," the small circles of friends and relations in which people pursued their private interests and pleasures.[118] These niches functioned socially as the postmodern equivalent of workers moving from mine to mine in search of better conditions—individualized forms of self-expression that, while sustaining of personal identities, also helped reproduce the existing structures.

The retreat to the niche was coupled with an expectation that the state would provide social security and social services. The long-standing German tendency to look to the state for social solutions—in this case, the state as the agency of social provisioning—reached new heights in the DDR as the regime itself made this practice a source of legitimacy. Its corollary was, however, a certain depoliticization, an expectation that the state would provide and that the social services bureaucracy, by its very nature, needed no popular input. Herein lies at least part of the explanation for the rapid transformation in loyalties in the winter of 1989/90.[119] With the DDR on the verge of collapse, loyalties shifted to the Federal

[117] Niethammer, "Erfahrungen und Strukturen," and also Lüdtke, "'Helden der Arbeit.'"

[118] The term "Nischengesellschaft" was coined by Günter Gaus in *Wo Deutschland liegt: Eine Ortbestimmung* (Hamburg: Hoffmann und Campe, 1983) and has become a standard feature of analyses of DDR society.

[119] Jan Wielgohs and Marianne Schulz, "Reformbewegung und Volksbewegung: Politische und soziale Aspekte im Umbruch der DDR-Gesellschaft," *APZ* B16-17/90 (13 April 1990): 23–24.

Republic as the new source of social provisioning, a shift drastically accelerated by Helmut Kohl's promises of prosperity around the corner.

Conclusion

On the eve of its collapse, the DDR was widely touted as a stable, relatively successful social system.[120] Virtually no one foresaw the transformation that came with unprecedented rapidity. The structures so painstakingly created over forty years quickly fell victim to the winds of change emanating from the Soviet Union and racing through the entire Soviet bloc.

Yet the DDR had achieved a measure of stability and legitimacy until the mid-1980s. The populace benefited from improved living standards and a tightly webbed safety net of social welfare programs. However unstable some of the joints, the welding of nation and class proved partly successful in giving the regime—and its citizens—an identity rooted in the specific traditions of the German labor movement and broader, cross-class characteristics of German society since the eighteenth century. Similarly, the regime could assert that its policies improved the status of women while protecting motherhood and the family. Even the claim to represent order and discipline had a measure of popular appeal. While the SED state mobilized tools of repression specific to Soviet-type societies, it also drew on the discourses and practices common to German regimes in the modern era.

But in the 1980s the economy faltered and prospects for further improvements in living standards appeared increasingly dim. The regime, with its unending faith in central direction, proved unable to respond to a more complex economic world. Material insufficiencies and long-standing frustration with the SED's authoritarian practices created stockpiles' worth of discontent that made the public highly receptive to Mikhail Gorbachev's reform course.

Ultimately, a party and state whose claims to legitimacy rested, to a substantial degree, on the history of communism in Germany could never be secure because that history was itself so contested. While the KPD had become a mass party in the Weimar Republic, it was never a majority party, not even among workers. Moreover, the KPD's culture of struggle lay increasingly distant from the realities of the modern and complex society that the DDR had become. Yet the history of the KPD constituted the reservoir of language and experience that governed the practices of the SED leadership, the most intact among the Soviet bloc states in Europe. The formative experiences had been the party of the Weimar Republic and then the harsh experiences of internment and underground struggle in the Third Reich and exile in the Soviet Union. Whatever reforms or changes the leadership instituted came "not through breaks with existing policies, but through conservative renewal."[121] The continual recourse to central state

[120] See, for example, the important collection edited by Glaeßner, *DDR in der Ära Honecker*, including his introduction, which asserts the enhanced stability that the DDR had achieved under Honecker.

[121] Hanke, "Sozialistischer Neohistorismus?" 73.

power as the agent of socialist development; the sharp demarcation drawn between state socialism and liberal capitalism; the language of unceasing struggle and popular mobilization; the near-obsessive emphasis on the productive sphere as the wellsprings of progress and emancipation—all of that refracted the strategy and culture of German communism of the Weimar Republic. By the end of the 1980s, the DDR population had grown intensely weary with a political language and political policies rooted in the 1920s and increasingly removed from the concerns and realities and desires of everyday existence.

CONCLUSION

The End of a Tradition

Ohne uns läuft nichts mehr.

—*DDR demonstrators*[1]

TO THE BITTER END, the SED adhered tightly to the mechanisms of central direction constructed from the late 1940s onward. Yet by virtue of the system's own development, DDR society had become increasingly complex and differentiated.[2] Segments of society developed their own normative values and communicative forms, but their abilities to articulate their interests and goals in a more public and effective manner remained closed off by the rigid authoritarianism of the regime. The chasm between society and the party-state reached monumental proportions. Increasingly, the regime became ensconced in a fabled world of make-believe, cut off from the ferment underway in society and capable only of recourse to the rhetoric of communism of the 1920s and 1930s and the tools of repression developed over the forty years of the DDR. Lacking the possibility of public articulation, DDR society became, in the effective and renowned phrase of Günter Gaus, the Federal Republic's first representative in the DDR, a "Nischengesellschaft," a society of niches into which small circles of people retreated and sought their own individualized or small-group forms of satisfaction in hopeful isolation from the larger currents in the political system. That even the "niches" had been deeply penetrated by the state through the MfS's extensive network of informants only became clear after the collapse of the system.

Yet from these niches emerged, slowly and hesitantly, a civil society that posed the first serious challenge to the party-state since 1953 and that departed dramatically from the languages and forms of protest developed since the nineteenth century. A citizens', not a workers', movement emerged in the DDR, and its institutional expression was found in the proliferation of groups comparable to the new social movements that have preoccupied western sociologists and political scientists for the last twenty years or so.[3] From Neues Forum (New Forum) to

[1] "Without us nothing runs any longer." Marlies Menge, *"Ohne uns läuft nichts mehr": Die Revolution in der DDR* (Stuttgart: Deutsche Verlags-Anstalt, 1990), quoting demonstrators in the DDR.

[2] See Sigrid Meuschel, *Legitimation und Parteiherrschaft in der DDR: Zur Paradox von Stabilität und Revolution in der DDR 1945–1989* (Frankfurt am Main: Suhrkamp, 1992), and for a very good overview, Gert-Joachim Glaeßner, "Vom 'realen Sozialismus' zur Selbstbestimmung: Ursachen und Konsequenzen der Systemkrise in der DDR," *APZ* B1–2/90 (5 January 1990): 3–20.

[3] For a good summary of the difference between the citizens groups and traditional political

Demokratisches Aufbruch (Democratic Awakening), these organizations were composed disproportionately of the educated, including many academics and intellectuals. Their demands were focused on political liberties, on the creation of democratic institutions throughout society, on the establishment of humane standards of human interaction, on environmentalism.[4]

Even the Marxian categories that the opposition by and large retained—a point of much subsequent criticism—were invested with the language of new social movements. Its Marxism lay in a commitment to socialism as a general goal and form of organization, socialism in the sense of a solidaristic society. The opposition groups posited anything but a "scientific" Marxism, none of the proletarian element that formed the core of the organized socialist and communist movements and ideologies in the era of high modernity, and certainly little of the Marxian commitment to totality. In short, they posited a Marxian humanism notable more for its elusiveness than its scientific rationalism. Moreover, they welded this Marxism to the liberal notion of a constitutional state and the particularist commitments typical of the new social movements. They promoted the goals of pacifism, environmentalism, women's emancipation, and social (rather than state) control. All of this lay embedded in an overarching framework that sought the reconstitution of civil society—better put, of civil societies. In place of the all-encompassing claims of the party-state, on the one hand, and the multitudinous, depoliticized "niche society" on the other, the opposition movements articulated a vision of a polity infused by multiple discourses emerging out of multiple civil societies in which citizens, not workers or peasants, exercised influence within the institutions that encompassed their lives. Their political concept entailed a hazily defined, but no less real, vision of a "third way" between the bureaucratized, liberal capitalist order of the BRD and the state socialism of the DDR.

The overt political activism of the opposition groups converged with the completely unexpected, semichaotic surge of people into foreign embassies and the streets of the DDR to create the extraordinary mass movement of 1989/90. But amid the vibrant protests, the glaring silence was that of the workplace. Workers were among those who crammed into the Federal Republic's mission in East Berlin and its embassies in Prague and Budapest. Workers took to the streets with others in Leipzig, Halle, and elsewhere. But nowhere was the workplace a central focus of popular protest, at no time did demands specifically related to the workplace figure centrally in the popular movement. Far from conceiving of it as the focal point of a

parties, see Hubertus Knabe, "Politische Opposition in der DDR: Ursprünge, Programmatik, Perspektiven," *APZ* B1–2/90 (5 January 1990): 23.

[4] See the documentary collections: *"Wir sind das Volk!" Flugschriften, Aufrufe und Texte einer deutschen Revolution*, ed. Charles Schüddekopf (Reinbek bei Hamburg: Rowohlt, 1990); *Die deutsche Vereinigung: Dokumente zu Bürgerbewegung, Annäherung und Beitritt*, ed. Volker Gransow and Konrad H. Jarausch (Cologne: Wissenschaft und Politik, 1991); *DDR Journal: Zur Novemberrevolution August bis Dezember 1989*, 2d ed. (Berlin: taz, 1990); and *DDR Journal Nr. 2: Die Wende in der Wende Januar bis März 1990* (Berlin: taz, 1990). See also the very interesting set of interviews conducted by Dirk Philipsen in *We Were the People: Voices from East Germany's Revolutionary Autumn of 1989* (Chapel Hill: Duke University Press, 1992), and Konrad H. Jarausch's account in *The Rush to German Unity* (New York: Oxford University Press, 1993).

new political order, the activists of 1989/90 viewed the workplace as but one of a nexus of spheres through which democratic and humanitarian standards had to percolate.

Clearly, the DDR's self-designation as a "workers' and peasants' state" retained some resonance, limiting the extent of the popular movement. As discussed in the previous chapter, workers were relatively well provisioned and opportunities existed for social advancement. While many DDR citizens complained about the inefficiencies of their labor, many were also quite aware that westerners worked far harder and in far more competitive circumstances. The workplace was by no means democratically structured in the DDR, but it was less regimented, and there were perhaps greater avenues for individualized forms of nonacquiescence (not protest) than in the west. Moreover, the DDR had become a highly modern society, with a well-educated labor force and a developed (if backward by western standards) tertiary sector.

Hence, the glaring discontents experienced by the population were not so much in the productive sphere as in the spheres of social reproduction, of politics and consumption. It is fitting, therefore, that the spaces of political contestation were not the factories and mines, but city plazas, streets, and churches, all of them spatially linked to one another, which enabled mass meetings to unfold easily into deliberative and peaceful demonstrations. It is also fitting that women played critical roles in a number of the citizens' opposition groups, and that an autonomous feminist movement emerged in the course of the civic revolution of 1989/90.[5]

DDR citizens did not, then, merely reprise western political forms. They became the standard bearers of postmodern politics by welding together conceptions of a constitutional state that guarantees natural rights with the particularist and anti-centralist concerns of the new social movements. They were doing much, much more than the "catch-up revolution" described so condescendingly and flippantly by Jürgen Habermas.[6] In strange company, Habermas found himself in agreement with Joachim Fest, the conservative editor of the *Frankfurter Allgemeine Zeitung*, who characterized the events as "a revolution that, for the first time, had no preeminent thinkers, generally had no intellectual participation." For Fest, this point only sharpened the distinction between the DDR and other state socialist systems, in which a vibrant intellectual opposition had developed.[7]

Habermas, Fest, and many others blithely overlooked the chief characteristic of the dissident groups of the 1980s and the Revolution of 1989/90, namely, their

[5] See the *taz* reports, "Aufbruch der Frauen gegen die 'mittlemäßigen Männer,'" and "Gleichstellungsgesetz," 3 December 1989 and 5 December 1989, reprinted in *DDR Journal*, 165, and "DDR-Opposition: Null Bock auf Emanzen," 17 January 1990, reprinted in *DDR Journal 2*, 57–58.

[6] Jürgen Habermas, "Nachholende Revolution und linker Revisionsbedarf: Was heißt Sozialismus heute?" in idem, *Die nachholende Revolution: Kleine Politische Schriften VII* (Frankfurt am Main: Suhrkamp, 1990), 179–204.

[7] Joachim Fest, "Schweigende Wortführer, Überlegungen zu einer Revolution ohne Vorbild," *Frankfurter Allgemeine Zeitung*, 30 December 1989, quoted in Christoph Kleßmann, "Opposition und Dissidenz in der Geschichte der DDR," *APZ* B5/91 (25 January 1991): 52–62.

"newness." The political conceptions and forms of organization marked, for a brief time, a new synthesis, one rooted in the social achievements of the DDR, the liberalism of the west, and the postmodern particularist concerns of new social movements. If anything, the DDR's civic revolution resembled more post-1968, leftist politics in the west than any of the internal party oppositions of the SED or the dominant West German political parties. The dissident movements that developed in the course of the last decade of the DDR were themselves the outcome of the construction of a modern, highly differentiated society, while the KPD and the SED were rooted in the "classic" era of labor representation. While the dissidents had ties to earlier oppositionists, notably Robert Havemann, and invoked communist heroes of the past like Rosa Luxemburg, they really stood on the edge of transition to a new historical era. In that sense, also, their actions were deeply revolutionary.

In the course of the 1980s, in association with the ever increasing signs of crises and the reformist course of the Gorbachev regime, growing discontent and protest became evident also in the ranks of the SED.[8] The regime's efforts to protect its citizenry from the dangerous influences now emanating from the east and the west seemed to many the height of hypocrisy. The ultimate act, the seizure of the Soviet German-language journal *Sputnik*, set off thousands of protests within the party. Yet even these protests remained atomized, and the public realm remained closed to an open discussion. Ultimately, the reform forces in the SED were unable to establish a coherent, effective opposition.

And in contrast with other Soviet bloc nations, the East German opposition remained until the 1980s within the ranks of the party. Only the convergence of intensified political repression, the grand hopes inspired by Gorbachev's reforms, and the political rigidity of the SED led the internal opposition to initiate some contacts with the dissident movements. Typically, provocations by the regime inspired the intensification of opposition. In November 1987, the police searched the East Berlin Environmental Library, a focal point of some elements of dissident activity. In January 1988 it carried out widespread arrests in the wake of a counter-demonstration at a Liebknecht-Luxemburg commemoration in which demonstrators had unfurled a banner with Luxemburg's famous line "*Freiheit ist immer Freiheit der Andersdenkenden*" (Freedom is always the freedom of those who think differently).

The regime's repressive actions resulted in a "forced politicization" of the opposition,[9] which received further sustenance from additional outrages, most clearly the obvious fraud in conjunction with the communal elections of May 1989. Egon Krenz, chairman of the electoral commission, reported a 98.5 percent vote in support of the SED-dominated "National Front" list. Local activists in some areas estimated that 20 percent of the voters returned ballots marked with

[8] See the discussion in Jan Wielgohs and Marianne Schulz, "Reformbewegung und Volksbewegung: Politische und soziale Aspekte im Umbruch der DDR-Gesellschaft," *APZ* B16–17/90 (13 April 1990): 15–24.

[9] Ibid.

"no" or with nothing at all.[10] Granting the Karl Marx Order to Nicolai Ceausescu in November 1988 and the demonstrative expression of solidarity with the Chinese Communist Party in the wake of Tiannamen Square only added elements of the grotesque to the SED's increasing isolation from the population.

The citizens who fled the DDR or took to the streets in October and November 1989 demonstrated the still-vital power of mass movements in the twentieth century. They toppled the longest-lasting leadership in the Soviet bloc and, for a brief period, articulated a vision of a new kind of politics in central Europe. They also closed an epoch that stretched back to the formation of the organized labor movement in the late nineteenth century and lasted as long as a self-described workers' party, the Socialist Unity Party, retained power.

While the citizens' movement destroyed an existing regime and put the seals on an historical era, it failed to establish a new kind of politics. The denouement is now known.[11] In the elections of March 1990, the DDR citizenry voted decisively for Helmut Kohl's Christian Democratic Union and for unification. "Experiments" suddenly seemed dangerous, and the citizenry longed for "normalcy" and material security, both of which Kohl promised in abundance. Little could withstand the power, not just of the Bundesbank and its D-Mark, but also of the West German political parties determined to bring enlightenment to the east. Ex-DDR citizens soon discovered that all was not sweetness and light, and a reservoir of bitterness remains. Its full political impact has yet to be determined.

In the "coming to terms" with the DDR past that has gripped both the ex–West Germany and the ex–East Germany since 1989, the favored term of explanation has been "Stalinism" and, subsequently, "totalitarianism." The original sin of the system, in virtually all accounts, was Stalinism; the eternal sin, in virtually all accounts, the maintenance of Stalinism longer even than in the Soviet Union itself, let alone the neighboring socialist states of Poland, Czechoslovakia, and Hungary.[12]

As a shorthand explanation for the mechanisms of rule in the party-state, "Stalinism" is an effective rhetorical tool. As an historical explanation, the term is gravely deficient. It projects a power of explanation that overrides a great deal of historical nuance and that overlooks the complexity of the historical sources that shaped the development of the German Democratic Republic. "Stalinism" directs the analytical gaze exclusively eastward and derives from Russian and Soviet history the patterns of development in Soviet-occupied Germany.

The purpose of this book, however, has been to show that "Stalinism" was never merely a Soviet strain forcibly planted in German soil after 1945. As I have tried to show, German communism was shaped also by social, ideological, and political

[10] These incidents are recounted by Knabe, "Politische Opposition," 24–25.

[11] See especially Jarausch's account, *Rush to Unity*. On the importance of the flight from the DDR for the subsequent collapse of the regime, see Norman M. Naimark, "'Ich will hier raus': Emigration and the Collapse of the German Democratic Republic," in *Eastern Europe in Revolution*, ed. Ivo Banac (Ithaca: Cornell University Press, 1992), 72–95.

[12] See, for example, Glaeßner, "Vom 'realen Sozialismus,'" and Hermann Weber, "Aufstieg und Niedergang des deutschen Kommunismus," *APZ* B40/91 (27 September 1991): 25–39.

factors indigenous to Germany, or, alternately posed, by aspects of transnational developments indigenous to Europe in the era of high modernity, which received a particular coloration—as they did in each nation-state—in Germany. These factors helped forge a political culture of German communism that retained potency—even when consciously manipulated and constructed—down to the very end of the DDR in 1989/90. "Stalinism" in no way captures the complexity of this historical process; "Stalinism" reduces history to a Russian/Soviet characteristic transported through Europe by the Red Army. But the critical issues, for Germany as for other countries, involve the complex ways in which Soviet power intermingled with party and national contexts.

As an analytical device, "Stalinism" also truncates chronologically the important history: it reduces the causative factors of DDR history to the post-1945 period. Obviously, the immensity of Soviet power in the SBZ/DDR cannot be seriously challenged, but, as this book has also tried to suggest, the critical historical factors that shaped the KPD and, subsequently, the SED stretch back decisively to the Weimar period and, even further, to the period of high industrialization that began around 1890—to the strategies adopted by elites for establishing order in German society, and the political challenges to these efforts posed by labor. None of this is captured by the term Stalinism.

Moreover, it remains debatable, at the very least, whether the entire history of the DDR can really be characterized as "Stalinist," yet this has been a virtually unquestioned presumption in recent debates. However ugly the various aspects of the German party-state, they bear little comparison to the drastic practices of the Stalin "revolution from above." While "Stalinist purges" may have characterized the 1950s in the DDR, the extent, the arbitrary character, and the brutality—certainly repressive and inhumane—nonetheless pale in comparison with the Soviet 1930s. And as a system, "Stalinism" implies more than arbitrary rule, the exercise of terror, and the monopoly of power by the party. The term also encompasses the immense, state-directed social transformations of forced collectivization and rapid industrialization, the creation in the 1930s of a staggeringly mobile, unsettled "quicksand society."[13] Stalinism, in other words, should not be understood as a descriptive concept of political rulership separated from the social history of the Soviet Union.

"Totalitarianism" is no less problematic as a descriptive term for the DDR. Clearly, the party-state exercised immense powers, and no realm of life remained immune from its reach—a *durchherrschte* society, in the effective term of Alf Lüdtke and Jürgen Kocka.[14] But totalitarianism neglects drastically the societal realm and presumes that the regime could exercise its will irrespective of social

[13] The term is Moshe Lewin's in *The Making of the Soviet System: Essays in the Social Histoy of Interwar Russia* (New York: Pantheon, 1985).

[14] Alf Lüdtke, "'Helden der Arbeit'—Mühen beim Arbeiten: Zur mißmutigen Loyalität von Industriearbeitern in der DDR," and Jürgen Kocka, "Eine durchherrschte Gesellschaft," in *Sozialgeschichte der DDR*, ed. Hartmut Kaelble, Jürgen Kocka, and Hartmut Zwahr (Stuttgart: Klett Cotta, 1994), 188–213, quote on 188, and 547–53.

and historical constraints.[15] Yet as I have tried to show in this study, the weight of both the KPD and the more generally German past bore heavily on the SED, providing it with a set of dispositions that both enabled and drastically limited its range of policies. Moreover, the regime had to respond to all sorts of societal and political factors, many of them completely unanticipated. And if the SED-state for many years successfully quashed open opposition, it had always to deal with the only weapon left to the populace, sullen non-compliance.[16]

Even less justified, in my view, are the continual comparisons and identities drawn since 1989 between the DDR and the Third Reich. Such efforts are comforting to those who wish to condemn every aspect of the DDR and German communism, to make of the DDR a pariah, and, at the same time, to elevate West German politics and society to saintly status. However repressive the practices of the SED-state, however many personal tragedies traverse its history, the DDR remained linked ideologically to the Enlightenment humanism of Marxism. It never practiced genocide, never made race and nation—the battle cries of the two world wars begun in Germany—the essence of its politics. The effort to identify the DDR and the Third Reich serves political purposes; it offers little analytical insight into the history of German communism or the workings of the party-state.

Amid the rapid developments of the autumn of 1989, the SED finally, belatedly, underwent the most far-reaching changes in its history. On 17 October 1989 Honecker was deposed in a palace coup led by his protégé, Egon Krenz. Then on 3 November 1989, one day before the great East Berlin demonstration, the Politburo met and deposed five leading members. Krenz promised significant reforms and a dialogue with the nation. The ferment within the party had become almost unstoppable. On 3 December, Krenz had to step down, and a new working committee, composed of leading party reformers, was established as an interim group. It called for a new, "modern socialist party," and a radical break with the "Stalinist-imprinted basic structures" and for a "free, just, and solidaristic society."[17] On 8 and 9 December and then again on 15 and 16 December 1989 the party met in an

[15] Meuschel's *Legitimation und Parteiherrschaft* is a learned and profound study of the DDR, and she is not inattentive to society. But the ultimate impact of her analysis is to demonstrate the success of, not the societal constraints on, the party-state, bringing it in line with the totalitarian model. See also idem, "Überlegungen zu einer Herrschafts- und Gesellschaftsgeschichte der DDR," *GG* 19:1 (1993): 5–14, and M. Rainer Lepsius, "Die Institutionenordnung als Rahmenbedingung der Sozialgeschichte der DDR," in Kaelble, Kocka, and Zwahr, *Sozialgeschichte der DDR*, 17–30. Less effective uses of the totalitarian model can be found in "Totalitäre Herrschaft—totalitäres Erbe," ed. Wolfgang-Uwe Friedrich, *GSR* special issue (1994).

[16] Important correctives to the totalitarian model include Christiane Lemke, *Die Ursachen des Umbruchs: Politische Sozialisation in der ehemaligen DDR* (Opladen: Westdeutscher, 1991); Lutz Niethammer, "Erfahrungen und Strukturen: Prolegomena zu einer Geschichte der Gesellschaft der DDR," in Kaelble, Kocka, and Zwahr, *Sozialgeschichte der DDR*, 95–115; Lüdtke, "'Helden der Arbeit'"; and Ralph Jessen, "Die Gesellschaft im Staatssozialismus: Probleme einer Sozialgeschichte der DDR," *GG* 21:1 (1995): 96–110.

[17] Quotes and chronology from Glaeßner, "Vom 'realen Sozialismus,'" 11–16.

extraordinary congress. In the meantime, membership had sunk from 2.3 million to 1.8 million.[18] Gregor Gysi, who had emerged as the leader of the reform group, called for a "complete break with . . . Stalinist, that means administrative, centralized, socialism in our country," and for a "third way of a socialist character" defined by "radical democracy and a constitutional state, humanism, social justice, environmental protection, and the. . .true equal status of women." The party should base itself upon "social democratic, socialist, non-Stalinist communist, antifascist, and pacifist traditions."[19] The congress voted to abandon the long-standing structural features of communist parties, the central committee, politburo, and central control commission, for the more neutral-sounding chairmanship, presidium, and party executive. Gysi, with 95.32 percent of the vote, was elected chairman, Hans Modrow, almost unanimously, deputy chairman.[20] In deference to the old guard, the congress did not abandon entirely the tarnished "SED," but gave the party the unwieldy new name of "Socialist Unity Party—Party of Democratic Socialism."

But the epoch of communism is over. The links to the past proved a burden in the new Germany, and the former KPD and SED became simply the PDS, the Partei des Demokratischen Sozialismus (Party of Democratic Socialism). It retains important support especially in the "new federal states," the former DDR, where discontent with the results of unification runs deeply.[21] It remains divided between reform elements who want to broaden and modernize the party's appeal and those still enamored of the SED. To the extent that the PDS remains a viable party, it has increasingly to shed its past and join the ranks of the postmodern opposition groups. The other option, functioning as a "normal" party in the Bonn-Berlin matrix, remains closed to it—despite some contacts with the SPD—so long as the DDR remains in the eyes of the German political elite a regrettable episode outside the pale of German history.

The breaching of the Berlin Wall and the subsequent political developments closed the books on many accounts: the DDR citizenry's claims against the regime under which it lived; some of the territorial divisions that resulted from World War II; the lingering, if only titular, claims of the four powers over German sovereignty. But these events also closed the books on the last, direct political legacy of the Weimar Republic—the formation of a mass-based communist party committed to continual confrontation with the institutions of bourgeois society and to the construction of a central state with massive powers of direction.

[18] Ibid., 13.

[19] Ibid. Gysi, and others, also called for the continued existence of the party despite calls, mostly outside of the ranks of the party, for its dissolution. The historian and party veteran Jürgen Kuczynski, one month earlier in *ND*, had called for a "return to Lenin," probably the least realistic, least meaningful slogan raised in the course of the Revolution of 1989/90. See ibid., 17–18, and *ND*, 8 November 1989, 4.

[20] Glaeßner, "Vom 'realen Sozialismus,'" 14.

[21] See David P. Conradt et al., eds., *Germany's New Politics*, special issue of *GSR* (1995), and especially Gerald R. Kleinfeld, "The Return of the PDS," 193–220.

BIBLIOGRAPHY

Primary Sources

Archives

Betriebsarchiv der Leuna-Werke (BLW)
  Arbeits- und Lohnverhältnisse
  Tätigkeit des Arbeiterausschußes
  Tätigkeit der Betriebsvertretungen
  Entwicklung des Werkes
Bundesarchiv Koblenz (BAK)
  Reichskanzlei—Kommunistische Parteien und Bestrebungen R43 I
  Reichskanzlei—KPD R45 IV
  Clara Zetkin, letters to Maria Reese Kl. Erw. 379-1
Bundesarchiv Potsdam (BAP)
  Reichsministerium des Innern (RMdI)
  Reichsarbeitsministerium (RAM)
  Reichs- und Staatskommissar für gewerbliche Fragen in Westfalen
  Reichskommissar für die Überwachung der öffentlichen Ordnung (RKÜöO)
Geheimes Staatsarchiv preußischer Kulturbesitz Merseburg (GStAKM)
  Ministerium des Innern Rep. 77
  Ministerium für Handel und Gewerbe Rep. 120
  Preußische Abgeordnetenhaus bzw. Landtag Rep. 169
Hauptstaatsarchiv Düsseldorf (HStAD)
  Rheinisches Behördenarchiv Abt. 2
    Regierung Düsseldorf—Politische Akten
    Regierung Düsseldorf—Polzei
    Essen Landratsamt
Historisches Archiv der Fried. Krupp GmbH (HA Krupp)
  Werksarchiv (WA)
  Familienarchiv Hügel (FAH)
Hoover Institution Archives (HIA)
  NSDAP Hauptarchiv
Landeshauptarchiv Sachsen-Anhalt Magdeburg (LHSAM)
  Oberpräsidium Magdeburg C20 Ib
  Regierung Merseburg C40 Ie
Landesverband Sachsen-Anhalt der Partei des Demokratischen Sozialismus,
  Landesparteiarchiv-Halle (LPAH)
  KPD I 2/3
  KPD I 2/5
  KPD IV 474
Stadtarchiv Essen (StAE)
  Hauptamt Rep. 102 Abt. I
  Handel und Gewerbe Rep. 102 Abt. XVI
  Stoppenberg Rep. 124
Stadtarchiv Halle (StAH)
  Centralbüro

Stiftung Archiv der Parteien und Massenorganisationen der DDR im Bundesarchiv, Zentrales Parteiarchiv (SAPMO-BA, ZPA)
Bezirk Halle-Merseburg I 3/11
Bezirk Ruhrgebiet I 3/18–19
Kommunistische Internationale, Deutsche Vertretung I 6/3
Rosa Luxemburg Nachlaß
Roter Frauen-und Mädchenbund I 4/3
Victoria Mathias Verwaltungsgesellschaft m.b.H.
Geschäftsberichte
Employment records

Periodicals

Arbeiter-Illustrierte-Zeitung (Berlin)
Arbeiter-Zeitung (Essen)
Inprekorr (Berlin, Moscow)
Klassenkampf (Halle)
Kommunistische Internationale (Berlin, Moscow)
Neues Deutschland (Berlin)
Rote Fahne (Berlin)
Ruhr-Echo (Essen)

Other Primary Sources

Ackermann, Anton. "Fragen und Antworten," 31 pp. brochure. Berlin: Neuer Weg, 1946.
———. "Gibt es einen besonderen deutschen Weg zum Sozialismus?" *Einheit* 1:1 (1946): 22–32.
———. "Die Volksfront und die demokratische Volksrepublik." *Die Internationale* 3/4 (1937): 36–45.
"Am Beginn der letzten Phase des Krieges: Ein neues bedeutsames Dokument aus dem illegalen Kampf der KPD in Deutschland 1944." *Beiträge zur Geschichte der Arbeiterbewegung* 21:3 (1979): 402–25.
Andert, Reinhold, and Wolfgang Herzberg. *Der Sturz: Erich Honecker im Kreuzverhör.* Berlin: Aufbau, 1990.
Appelt, Rudolf. "Ein neuer Typus der Demokratie: Die Volksdemokratien Ost- und Südosteuropas." *Einheit* 1:6 (1946): 339–52.
———. "Volksdemokratie—ein Weg zum Sozialismus." *Einheit* 2:3 (1947): 304–6.
"Die Arbeiterschaft der Kruppschen Gußstahlfabrik: Zur Denkschrift 'Die Firma Krupp im Weltkriege.'" Ms., n.d. Historisches Archiv der Fried. Krupp GmbH, Werksarchiv f1105/Kd 75.
A. Riebeck'sche Montanwerke: Die Geschichte einer mitteldeutschen Bergwerksgesellschaft. Zum 25 Jahre Carl Adolph Riebeck und 50 Jahre A. Riebeck'sche Montanwerke AG, 1858–1933. Munich: F. Bruckmann, 1933.
Baade, Fritz. "Die November-Revolution von 1918." *Die Heimatstadt Essen* 12 (1960/61): 49–60.
Badstübner, Rolf. "'Beratungen' bei J. W. Stalin." *Utopia kreativ* 7 (1991): 99–102.
Badstübner, Rolf, and Wilfried Loth, eds. *Wilhelm Pieck—Aufzeichnungen zur Deutschlandspolitik 1945–1952.* Berlin: Akademie, 1993.
Behnken, Klaus, ed. *Deutschland-Berichte der Sozialdemokratischen Partei Deutschlands (Sopade) 1934–1940.* Frankfurt am Main: P. Nettelbeck, 1980.

Brecht, Bertold. *Poems, 1913–1956*. Ed. John Willett and Ralph Manheim with the cooperation of Erich Fried. London: Methuen, 1976.

Brecht, Bertolt, and Hans Eisler. "Solidaritätslied," lyrics by Bertolt Brecht, music by Hans Eisler, first written 1930 for the film "Kuhle Wampe," revised 1948. "Eisler: Lieder mit Ernst Busch," Nova recording 8 85 004.

Buber-Neumann, Margarete. *Als Gefangene bei Stalin und Hitler*. Zurich: Europa, 1949.

"Chronik der Stadt Essen," 1910–25. Typescript, Stadtarchiv Essen.

Dahlem, Franz. *Am Vorabend des Zweiten Weltkrieges, 1938 bis August 1939: Erinnerungen*, vol. 1. Berlin: Dietz, 1977.

———. "Keine Wiederholung der Fehler von 1918." *Deutsche Volkszeitung*, 9 November 1945.

———. "Nachgelassenes, Ausgelassenes: Über einen Prozeß und die Schwierigkeiten seiner richtigen Beurteilung." *Beiträge zur Geschichte der Arbeiterbewegung* 32:1 (1990): 17–25.

DDR Journal: Zur Novemberrevolution, August bis Dezember 1989. Vom Ausreisen bis zum Einreißen der Mauer. Berlin: taz, 1990.

DDR Journal 2: Die Wende in der Wende, Januar bis März 1990. Berlin: taz, 1990.

Dokumente und Materialien zur Geschichte der KPD-Bezirksorganisation Halle-Merseburg bis 1933. Ed. Bezirksleitung Halle der SED, Kommission zur Erforschung der Geschichte der örtlichen Arbeiterbewegung. Halle: n.p., 1982.

Durch Kampf zum Sieg! Jubiläumsschrift der Sozialdemokratischen Partei im Halle und dem Saalkreis. Halle: Hallesche Genossenschafts-Buchdruckerei, 1914.

Emmerich, Wolfgang, ed. *Proletarische Lebensläufe: Autobiographische Dokumente zur Entstehung der Zweiten Kultur in Deutschland*, 2 vols. Hamburg: Rowohlt, 1974–75.

Friedrich, Thomas. "Antworten der SED-Führung auf Fragen Stalins 1948." *Beiträge zur Geschichte der Arbeiterbewegung* 33:3 (1991): 364–73.

Führer durch die Essener Wohnsiedlungen der Firma Krupp. Essen: Graphische Anstalt der Fried. Krupp AG, 1920.

50 Jahre Mitteldeutscher Braunkohlen Bergbau: Festschrift zum 50jährigen Bestehen des Deutschen-Braunkohlen-Industrie-Vereins E.V. Halle (Salle) 1885–1935. Halle: Wilhelm Knapp, n.d.

Ginzburg, Evgeniia. *Journey into the Whirlwind*. New York: Harcourt, Brace and World, 1967.

Gotsche, Otto. "Unser gemeinsamer Kampf in der Antifaschistischen Arbeitergruppe Mitteldeutschlands." In *Vereint sind wir alles: Erinnerungen an die Gründung der SED*, 394–414. Berlin: Dietz, 1966.

Grandke, Anita. "Festigung der Gleichberechtigung und Förderung bewußter Elternschaft." *Neue Justiz* 26:11 (1972): 313–19.

Gransow, Volker, and Konrad H. Jarausch, eds. *Die deutsche Vereinigung: Dokumente zu Bürgerbewegung, Annäherung und Beitritt*. Cologne: Wissenschaft und Politik, 1991.

Hansel, Detlef, et al., eds. *Der 17. Juni 1953—Die SED-Führung zwischen Ohnmacht und Macht: Originaldokumente des Politbüros und des Zentralkomitees der SED vom Juni bis Juli 1953*. Berlin: Akademie, 1993.

Honecker, Erich. "Erich Honecker vor Gericht." *Deutschland Archiv* 26:1 (1993): 97–105.

Humbert-Droz, Jules. *De Lénine à Staline: Dix Ans au Service de l'Internationale communiste 1921–1931. Memoires de Jules Humbert-Droz*, vol. 2. Neuchâtel: Editions de la Baconnière, 1971.

Kaasch, Wienand. "Die soziale Struktur der KPD." *Die Kommunistische Internationale* 9:19 (1928).

Karski [Julian Marchlewski]. *Die Sozialisierung des Bergbaues*, Vortrag gehalten auf der Konferenz der Bergarbeiter-Delegierten des rheinisch-westfälischen Industrie-Gebietes am 5. März 1919 in Essen. Essen: Bezirksleitung der "Kommunistischen Partei" für Rheinland-Westfalen, 1919.

Kelly, Alfred, ed. and trans. *The German Worker: Working-Class Autobiographies from the Age of Industrialization*. Berkeley and Los Angeles: University of California Press, 1987.

Kern, Käthe. "Die Frauen standen mit in vorderster Reihe." In *Vereint sind wir alles: Erinnerungen an die Gründung der SED*, 87–100. Berlin: Dietz, 1966.

Koenen, Emmy. "Exil in England." *Beiträge zur Geschichte der Arbeiterbewegung* 22:4 (1980): 540–63.

Könnemann, Erwin, ed. *Arbeiterklasse siegt über Kapp und Luttwitz*, 2 vols. Glashütten/Taunus: Auvermann, 1971.

Krupp: A Century's History of the Krupp Works, 1812–1912. N.p., n.d.

Krusch, Hans-Joachim, and Andreas Malycha, eds. *Einheitsdrang oder Zwangsvereinigung? Die Sechziger-Konferenzen von KPD und SPD 1945 und 1946*. Berlin: Dietz, 1990.

Lange, Inge. "Die Frau im gesellschaftlichen Leben der DDR." *Einheit* 30:9 (1975): 954–61.

———. "Die Frauen—aktive Mitgestalter der sozialistischen Demokratie." *Einheit* 41:4/5 (1986): 329–33.

———. *Die Frauen—aktive Mitgestalterinnen des Sozialismus: Ausgewählte Reden*. Berlin: Dietz, 1987.

———. "Die Rolle der Frau im Produktionsprozeß bestimmt ihre Stellung in der sozialistischen Gesellschaft." *Einheit* 24 (1969): 329–47.

Laschitza, Annelies, ed. *Rosa Luxemburg und die Freiheit der Andersdenkenden: Extraausgabe des unvollendeten Manuskripts "Zur russischen Revolution" und anderer Quellen zur Polemik mit Lenin*. Berlin: Dietz, 1990.

Leonhard, Susanne. *Gestohlenes Leben: Schicksal einer politischen Emigrantin in der Sowjetunion*, 5th ed. Herford: Nicolaische Verlagsbuchhandlung, 1968.

Lüdtke, Alf, ed. *Mein Arbeitstag—mein Wochenende: Arbeiterinnen berichten von ihrem Alltag 1928*. Hamburg: Ergebnisse, 1991.

Luther, Hans. "Zusammenbruch und Jahre nach dem ersten Krieg: Erinnerungen des Oberbürgermeisters der Stadt Essen." *Beiträge zur Geschichte der Stadt und Stift Essen* 73 (1958).

Luxemburg, Rosa. *Gesammelte Briefe*, 5 vols. Ed. Institut für Marxismus-Leninismus beim ZK der SED. Berlin: Dietz, 1982–84.

———. *Gesammelte Werke*, 5 vols. Ed. Institut für Marxismus-Leninismus beim ZK der SED. Berlin: Dietz, 1970–75.

Mammach, Klaus, ed. *Die Berner Konferenz der KPD (30. Januar–1. Februar 1939)*. Berlin: Dietz, 1974.

———. *Die Brüsseler Konferenz der KPD (3.–15. Oktober 1935)*. Berlin: Dietz, 1975.

Meyer-Leviné, Rosa. *Inside German Communism: Memoirs of Party Life in the Weimar Republic*. London: Pluto, 1977.

Mitter, Armin, and Stefan Wolle. *"Ich liebe Euch doch alle!" : Befehle und Lageberichte des MfS*. Berlin: Basis, 1990.

Neuner Kommission. "Die Sozialisierung des Bergbaues und der Generalstreik im rheinischen-westfälischen Industriegebiet." Brochure, 1919.

Noakes, Jeremy, and Geoffrey Pridham, eds. *Nazism 1919–1945*, vol. 1: *The Rise to Power, 1919–1934*. Exeter: Exeter University Publications, 1983.

Orlopp, Josef. "Die Munitionsarbeiterstreik 1917 in Essen." In *Die Novemberrevolution und die deutschen Gewerkschaften*, 2. Halbband: *Erinnerungen aus Veteranen der deutschen Gewerkschaftsbewegung an die Novemberrevolution (1914–1920)*. Berlin: Tribüne, 1958.

Otto, Wilfriede. "Sowjetische Deutschlandnote 1952: Stalin und die DDR. Bisher unveröffentlichte Notizen Wilhelm Piecks." *Beiträge zur Geschichte der Arbeiterbewegung* 33:3 (1991): 374–89.

Petzina, Dietmar, Werner Abelshauser, and Anselm Faust. *Sozialgeschichtliches Arbeitsbuch*, vol. 3: *Materialien zur Statistik des Deutschen Reiches 1914–1945*. Munich: Beck, 1978.

Philipsen, Dirk, ed. *We Were the People: Voices from East Germany's Revolutionary Autumn of 1989*. Chapel Hill: Duke University Press, 1992.

Pieck, Wilhelm. "Zwei Revolutionen—zwei Ergebnisse." *Einheit* 1:6 (1946): 321–28.

———. "Zwei Revolutionen—zwei Wege." *Einheit* 2:11 (1947): 993–1004.

Pikarski, Margot, and Günter Uebel, eds. *Der antifaschistische Widerstandskampf der KPD im Spiegel des Flugblattes 1933–1945*. Institut für Marxismus-Leninismus beim ZK der SED. Berlin: Dietz, 1978.

Prussia, Ministerium für Handel und Gewerbe. *Jahresbericht der Preussischen Regierungs- und Gewerberäte und Bergbehörden*, 1900–1928.

Rabbich, Heinrich. "Protokoll: Gespräch mit Heinrich Rabbich 27.7.77: Novemberrevolution 1918 in Essen." Interview conducted by Ernst Schmidt, Archivsammlung Ernst Schmidt 1918–7 (Essen).

———. "60 Jahre Essener 'Freie-Arbeiter-Jugend.'" Ms., 1965, Archivsammlung Ernst Schmidt (Essen).

Rive, Richard Robert. *Lebenserinnerungen eines deutschen Oberbürgermeisters*. Ed. Schriftenreihe des Vereins zur Pflege Kommunalwissenschaftlicher Aufgaben e.v. Berlin, vol. 5. Stuttgart: W. Kohlhammer, 1960.

Schabowski, Günter. *Der Absturz*. Berlin: Rowohlt, 1991.

———. *Das Politbüro: Ende eines Mythos. Eine Befragung*, ed. Frank Sieren und Ludwig Koehne. Reinbek bei Hamburg: Rowohlt, 1991.

Schmidt-Kolmer, Eva, and Heinz H. Schmidt. "Über Frauenarbeit und Familie." *Einheit* 17:12 (1962): 89–99.

Schüddekopf, Charles, ed. *"Wir sind das Volk!" Flugschriften, Aufrufe und Texte einer deutschen Revolution*. Reinbek bei Hamburg: Rowohlt, 1990.

Spartakusbriefe. Ed. Institut für Marxismus-Leninismus beim ZK der SED. Berlin: Dietz, 1958.

Staritz, Dietrich. "Die SED, Stalin und der 'Aufbau des Sozialismus' in der DDR: Aus den Akten des Zentralen Parteiarchiv." *Deutschland Archiv* 24:7 (1991): 686–700.

———. "Die SED, Stalin und die Gründung der DDR." *Aus Politik und Zeitgeschichte* B5/91 (25 January 1991): 3–16.

Stöckigt, Rolf. "Ein Dokument von großer historischer Bedeutung vom Mai 1953." *Beiträge zur Geschichte der Arbeiterbewegung* 32:5 (1990): 648–54.

Tenfelde, Klaus, and Helmuth Trischler, eds. *Bis vor die Stufen des Throns: Bittschriften und Beschwerden von Bergarbeitern*. Munich: Beck, 1986.

Thälmann, Ernst. "Einige Fehler in unserer theoretischen und praktischen Arbeit und der Weg zu ihrer Überwindung." *Die Internationale* 14:11–12 (1931): 481–509.

Togliatti, Palmiro. *Opere*, vol. 4, pt. 1. Ed. Franco Andreucci and Paolo Spriano. Rome: Riuniti, 1979.

Ulbricht, Walter. *Zur Geschichte der deutschen Arbeiterbewegung*, vol. 2, Zusatzband. Berlin: Dietz, 1966.

———. *Zur Geschichte der deutschen Arbeiterbewegung: Aus Reden und Aufsätzen*, vol. 2: *1933–1945*. Berlin: Dietz, 1953.

Vereint sind wir alles: Erinnerungen an die Gründung der SED. Berlin: Dietz, 1966.

Weber, Hermann, ed. *DDR: Dokumente zur Geschichte der Deutschen Demokratischen Republik 1945–1985*. Munich: DTV, 1986.

———. *Der deutsche Kommunismus: Dokumente*. Cologne: Kiepenheuer und Witsch, 1963.

———. *Die Generallinie: Rundschreiben des Zentralkomitees der KPD an die Bezirke 1929–1933*. Quellen zur Geschichte des Parlamentarismus und der politischen Parteien, 3d series, vol. 6. Düsseldorf: Droste, 1981.

———. *Der Gründungsparteitag der KPD: Protokoll und Materialien*. Frankfurt am Main: Europäische Verlagsanstalt, 1969.

———. *Unabhängige Kommunisten: Der Briefwechsel zwischen Heinrich Brandler und Isaac Deutscher 1949 bis 1967*. Berlin: Colloquium, 1981.

Weinert, Erich. *Gesammelte Gedichte*, vol. 3. Berlin: Aufbau-Verlag, 1971.

Weinert, Erich, and Hans Eisler. "Der heimliche Aufmarsch," lyrics by Erich Weinert, music by Hans Eisler, composed 1929. "Eisler: Lieder mit Ernst Busch," Nova recording 8 85 004.

Wichers, Hermann. "Zur Anleitung des Widerstands der KPD: Ein Rundschreiben des ZK-Sekretariats an die Abschnittsleitungen vom 29. Juli 1938." *Internationale wissenschaftliche Korrespondenz zur Geschichte der deutschen Arbeiterbewegung* 26:4 (1990): 526–39.

Winter, Elly. "An der Seite Wilhelm Piecks in den ersten Monaten des Neubeginns." In *Vereint sind wir alles: Erinnerungen an die Gründung der SED*, 115–31. Berlin: Dietz, 1966.

Wollenberg, Erich. Memoirs. Typescript, n.d., Hoover Institution Archives.

Zetkin, Clara. "Richtlinien für die Kommunistische Frauenbewegung." *Die Kommunistische Internationale* 3:15 (1921): 530–55.

Zur Geschichte der Kommunistischen Partei Deutschlands: Eine Auswahl von Materialien und Dokumenten aus den Jahren 1914–1946, ed. Marx-Engels-Lenin-Stalin-Institut beim Zentralkomitee der SED, 2d ed. (Berlin: Dietz, 1955).

Secondary Sources

Abrams, Lynn. *Workers' Culture in Imperial Germany: Leisure and Recreation in Rhineland and Westphalia*. London: Routledge, 1992.

Agnew, John A. *Place and Politics: The Geographical Mediation of State and Society*. Boston: Allen and Unwin, 1987.

Anderson, Perry. "Communist Party History." In *People's History and Socialist Theory*, ed. Raphael Samuel, 145–56. London: Routledge and Kegan Paul, 1981.

Angress, Werner. *Stillborn Revolution: The Communist Bid for Power in Germany, 1921–1923*. Princeton: Princeton University Press, 1963.

Arendt, Hans-Jürgen. "Eine demokratische Massenbewegung unter Führung der KPD im Frühjahr 1931: Die Volksaktion gegen den Paragraphen 218 und gegen die päpstliche

Enzyklika 'Casti connubii.'" *Zeitschrift für Geschichtswissenschaft* 19:2 (1971): 212–23.

———. "Der erste Reichskongreß werktätiger Frauen Deutschlands 1929." *Beiträge zur Geschichte der Arbeiterbewegung* 20 (1972): 467–79.

———. "Der Kampf der Kommunistischen Partei Deutschlands um Einbeziehung der werktätigen Frauen in die revolutionäre deutsche Arbeiterbewegung in der Periode der Weltwirtschaftskrise (1929–1932)." Ph.D. diss., Karl-Marx-Universität Leipzig, 1970.

———. "Zur Rolle der Frauen in der Kontrollausschußbewegung 1922/23." *Wissenschaftliche Studien der Pädagogischen Institute Leipzig* 1 (1971): 22–27.

———. "Das Schutzprogramm der KPD für die arbeitende Frau vom 15. Oktober 1931." *Beiträge zur Geschichte der Arbeiterbewegung* 11 (1969): 291–311.

———. "Weibliche Mitglieder der KPD in der Weimarer Republik—Zahlenmäßige Stärke und soziale Stellung." *Beiträge zur Geschichte der Arbeiterbewegung* 19 (1977): 652–60.

Arendt, Hans-Jürgen, and Werner Freigang. "Der Rote Frauen- und Mädchenbund—die revolutionäre deutsche Frauenorganisation in der Weimarer Republik." *Beiträge zur Geschichte der Arbeiterbewegung* 21 (1979): 249–58.

———. "Zur proletarischen Frauenbewegung unter Führung der KPD." *Geschichte und Staatsbürgerkunde* 11 (1968): 1019–32.

Bade, Klaus J. "Arbeitsmarkt, Bevölkerung und Wanderung in der Weimarer Republik." In *Weimarer Republik: Belagerte Civitas*, ed. Michael Stürmer, 160–87. Königstein/Ts.: Anton Hain, 1980.

Badstübner, Rolf. "Die Geschichtsschreibung über die DDR zwischen Krise und Erneuerung." *Beiträge zur Geschichte der Arbeiterbewegung* 32:4 (1990): 481–91.

———. "Zum Problem der historischen Alternativen im ersten Nachkriegsjahrzehnt: Neue Quellen zur Deutschlandspolitik von KPdSU und SED." *Beiträge zur Geschichte der Arbeiterbewegung* 33:5 (1991): 579–92.

Badstübner, Rolf, et al. *Deutsche Geschichte*, vol. 9: *Die antifaschistisch-demokratische Umwälzung, der Kampf gegen die Spaltung Deutschlands und die Entstehung der DDR von 1945 bis 1949*. Berlin: Deutscher Verlag der Wissenschaften, 1989.

Bahne, Siegfried. "Die Erwerbslosenpolitik der KPD in der Weimarer Republik." In *Vom Elend der Handarbeit: Probleme historischer Unterschichtenforschung*, ed. Hans Mommsen and Wilfried Schulze, 477–96. Stuttgart: Klett-Cotta, 1981.

———. *Die KPD und das Ende von Weimar: Das Scheitern einer Politik 1932–1935*. Frankfurt am Main: Campus, 1976.

———. "'Sozialfaschismus' in Deutschland: Zur Geschichte eines politischen Begriffes." *International Review of Social History* 10:2 (1965): 211–45.

Bähr, Johannes. *Staatliche Schlichtung in der Weimarer Republik: Tarifpolitik, Korporatismus und industrieller Konflikt zwischen Inflation und Deflation 1919–1932*. Berlin: Colloquium, 1989.

Barclay, David E. *Rudolf Wissell als Sozialpolitiker 1890–1933*. Berlin: Colloquium, 1984.

Bartel, Horst. "Erbe und Tradition in Geschichtsbild und Geschichtsforschung der DDR." *Zeitschrift für Geschichtswissenschaft* 29:5 (1981): 387–94.

Bauer, Karin. *Clara Zetkin und die proletarische Frauenbewegung*. Berlin: Oberbaum, 1978.

Baylis, Thomas A. *The Technical Intelligentsia and the East German Elite: Legitimacy and Social Change in Mature Communism*. Berkeley and Los Angeles: University of California Press, 1974.

Benenson, Harold. "The 'Family Wage' and Working Women's Consciousness in Britain, 1880–1914." *Politics and Society* 19:1 (1991): 71–108.

———. "Victorian Sexual Ideology and Marx's Theory of the Working Class." *International Labor and Working Class History* 25 (1984): 1–23.

Benser, Günter. "Antifa-Ausschüsse—Staatsorgane—Parteiorganisation: Überlegungen zu Ausmaß, Rolle und Grenzen der antifaschistischen Bewegung am Ende des zweiten Weltkrieges." *Zeitschrift für Geschichtswissenschaft* 26:9 (1978): 785–802.

———. "Das Jahr 1945 und das Heute: Brüche—Rückgriffe—Übergänge." *Beiträge zur Geschichte der Arbeiterbewegung* 32:4 (1990): 472–80.

———. "'Keine Wiederholung der Fehler von 1918!' Wie KPD und SPD im Kampf um die Errichtung der Arbeiter-und-Bauern-Macht die Lehren der Novemberrevolution nutzten." *Beiträge zur Geschichte der Arbeiterbewegung* 20:6 (1978): 835–43.

———. *Die KPD im Jahre der Befreiung*. Berlin: Dietz, 1985.

———. "SED und sozialistische Staatsmacht: Ihre Rolle und ihre Wechselwirkung bei der Errichtung der Grundlagen des Sozialismus in der DDR." *Zeitschrift für Geschichtswissenschaft* 30:10/11 (1982): 869–83.

Beradt, Charlotte. *Paul Levi: Ein demokratischer Sozialist in der Weimarer Republik*. Frankfurt am Main: Europäische Verlagsanstalt, 1969.

Berlanstein, Lenard, ed. *Rethinking Labor History: Essays on Discourse and Class Analysis*. Urbana: University of Illinois Press, 1993.

Bessel, Richard. "'Eine nicht allzu große Beunruhigung des Arbeitsmarktes': Frauenarbeit und Demobilmachung in Deutschland nach dem Ersten Weltkrieg." *Geschichte und Gesellschaft* 9:2 (1983): 211–29.

———. *Germany after the First World War*. Oxford: Clarendon, 1993.

———. "Militarisierung und Modernisierung: Polizeiliches Handeln in der Weimarer Republik." In *"Sicherheit" und "Wohlfahrt": Polizei, Gesellschaft und Herrschaft im 19. und 20. Jahrhundert*, ed. Alf Lüdtke, 323–43. Frankfurt am Main: Suhrkamp, 1992.

———. "Unemployment and Demobilisation in Germany after the First World War." In *The German Unemployed: Experiences and Consequences of Mass Unemployment from the Weimar Republic to the Third Reich*, ed. Richard J. Evans and Dick Geary, 23–43. New York: St. Martin's Press, 1987.

Blackbourn, David, and Geoff Eley. *The Peculiarities of German History: Bourgeois Society and Politics in Nineteenth-Century Germany*. New York: Oxford University Press, 1984.

Bock, Hans Manfred. *Syndikalismus und Linkskommunismus von 1918-1923*. Meisenheim am Glan: Anton Hain, 1969.

Bodek, Richard. "Communist Music in the Streets: Politics and Perceptions in Berlin at the End of the Weimar Republic." In *Elections, Mass Politics, and Social Change in Modern Germany: New Perspectives*, ed. Larry Eugene Jones and James Retallack, 267–86. Cambridge: Cambridge University Press, 1992.

———. "'We are the Red Megaphone': Political Music, Agitprop Theater, Everyday Life and Communist Politics in Berlin during the Weimar Republic." Ph.D. diss., University of Michigan, 1990.

Borchardt, Knut. "Wirtschaftliches Wachstum und Wechsellagen 1800–1914." In *Handbuch der deutschen Wirtschafts- und Sozialgeschichte*, vol. 2, ed. Hermann Aubin and Wolfgang Zorn, 198–275. Stuttgart: Ernst Klett, 1976.

Borkenau, Franz. *World Communism: A History of the Communist International*. New York: Norton, 1939.

Brady, Robert A. *The Rationalization Movement in German Industry: A Case Study in the Evolution of Economic Planning*. Berkeley and Los Angeles: University of California Press, 1933.

Brandt, Willy. *Ernst Reuter: Ein Leben für die Freiheit*. Munich: Kindler, 1957.

Braunthal, Julius. *History of the International*, vol. 2: *1914–1943*. New York: Praeger, 1967.

Bremme, Gabriele. *Die politische Rolle der Frau in Deutschland: Eine Untersuchung über den Einfluß der Frauen bei Wahlen und ihre Teilnahme in Partei und Parlament*. Göttingen: Vandenhoeck und Ruprecht, 1956.

Bridenthal, Renate, and Claudia Koonz. "Beyond *Kinder, Küche, Kirche*: Weimar Women in Politics and Work." In *When Biology Became Destiny: Women in Weimar and Nazi Germany*, ed. Renate Bridenthal, Atina Grossmann, and Marion Kaplan, 33–65. New York: Monthly Review Press, 1984.

Broszat, Martin, et al., eds. *Von Stalingrad zur Währungsreform: Zur Sozialgeschichte des Umbruchs in Deutschland*. Munich: Oldenbourg, 1988.

Brüggemeier, Franz-Josef. *Leben vor Ort: Ruhrbergleute und Ruhrbergbau 1889–1919*. Munich: Beck, 1983.

Brüggemeier, Franz-Josef, and Lutz Niethammer. "Schlafgänger, Schnapskasinos und schwerindustrielle Kolonie: Aspekte der Arbeiterwohnungsfrage im Ruhrgebiet vor dem Ersten Weltrkieg." In *Fabrik, Familie, Feierabend: Beiträge zur Sozialgeschichte des Alltags im Industriezeitalter*, ed. Jürgen Reulecke and Wolfhard Weber, 133–75. Wuppertal: Peter Hammer, 1978.

Burawoy, Michael. *The Politics of Production: Factory Regimes under Capitalism and Socialism*. London: Verso, 1985.

Burleigh, Michael, and Wolfgang Wippermann. *The Racial State: Germany, 1933–1945*. Cambridge: Cambridge University Press, 1991.

Busch, Otto, and Gerald D. Feldman, eds. *Historische Prozesse der deutschen Inflation 1914 bis 1924: Ein Tagungsbericht*. Berlin: Colloquium, 1978.

Campbell, Joan. *Joy in Work, German Work: The National Debate, 1800–1945*. Princeton: Princeton University Press, 1989.

Camparini, Aurelia. *Questione femminile e Terza Internazionale*. Bari: De Donato, 1978.

Canning, Kathleen. "Class, Gender, and Working-Class Politics: The Case of the German Textile Industry, 1890–1933." Ph.D. diss., Johns Hopkins University, 1988.

———. "Feminist History after the Linguistic Turn: Historicizing Discourse and Experience." *Signs* 19:2 (1994): 368–404.

———. "Gender and the Culture of Work: Ideology and Identity in the World Beyond the Mill Gate, 1890–1914." In *Elections, Mass Politics, and Social Change in Modern Germany: New Perspectives*, ed. Larry Eugene Jones and James Retallack, 175–99. Cambridge: Cambridge University Press, 1992.

———. "Gender and the Politics of Class Formation: Rethinking German Labor History." *American Historical Review* 97:3 (1992): 736–68.

Caplan, Jane. *Government without Administration: State and Civil Service in Weimar and Nazi Germany*. Oxford: Clarendon, 1988.

———. "Postmodernism, Poststructuralism, and Deconstruction: Notes for Historians." *Central European History* 22:3/4 (1989): 260–78.

Carr, E. H. *Twilight of the Comintern, 1930–1935*. New York: Pantheon, 1982.

Childers, Thomas. *The Nazi Voter: The Social Foundations of Fascism in Germany, 1919–1933*. Chapel Hill: University of North Carolina Press, 1983.

———. "The Social Language of Politics in Germany: The Sociology of Political Discourse in the Weimar Republic." *American Historical Review* 95:2 (1990): 331–58.

Claudin, Fernando. *The Communist Movement: From Comintern to Cominform*. New York: Monthly Review Press, 1975.

Conradt, David P., et al., eds. *Germany's New Politics*. *German Studies Review* special issue (1995).

Cornelsen, Doris. "DDR Wirtschaft: Ende oder Wende?" *Aus Politik und Zeitgeschichte* B1–2/90 (5 January 1990): 33–38.

———. "Die Wirtschaft der DDR in der Honecker-Ära." In *Die DDR in der Ära Honecker: Politik—Kultur—Gesellschaft*, ed. Gert-Joachim Glaeßner, 357–70. Opladen: Westdeutscher, 1988.

Crew, David F. "*Alltagsgeschichte*: A New Social History from Below?" *Central European History* 22:3/4 (1989): 394–407.

———. "Bedürfnisse und Bedürftigkeit: Wohlfahrtsbürokratie und Wohlfahrtsempfänger in der Weimarer Republik, 1919–1933." *Sozialwissenschaftliche Information* 18:1 (1989): 12–19.

———. "'Eine Elternschaft zu Dritt'—staatliche Eltern? Jugendwohlfahrt und Kontrolle der Familie in der Weimarer Republik 1919–1933." In *"Sicherheit" und "Wohlfahrt": Polizei, Gesellschaft und Herrschaft im 19. und 20. Jahrhundert*, ed. Alf Lüdtke, 267–94. Frankfurt: Suhrkamp, 1992.

———. "German Socialism, the State and Family Policy, 1918–33." *Continuity and Change* 1:2 (1986): 235–63.

———. "Gewalt 'auf dem Amt': Beispiele aus der Wohlfahrtsverwaltung der Weimarer Republik." *WerkstattGeschichte* 4 (1993): 33–42.

———. "A Social Republic? Social Democrats, Communists, and the Weimar Welfare State, 1919–1933." In *Between Reform and Revolution: Studies in German Socialism and Communism from 1840 to 1990*, ed. David E. Barclay and Eric D. Weitz. Providence: Berghahn, forthcoming.

———. "'Wohlfahrtsbrot ist bitteres Brot': The Elderly, the Disabled and the Local Welfare Authorities in the Weimar Republic 1924–1933." *Archiv für Sozialgeschichte* 30 (1990): 217–45.

Cronin, James E. "Labor Insurgency and Class Formation: Comparative Perspectives on the Crisis of 1917–1920 in Europe." In *Work, Community, and Power: The Experience of Labor in Europe and America, 1900–1925*, ed. idem and Carmen Sirianni, 20–48. Philadelphia: Temple University Press, 1983.

Dalchow, Irmtraud. "Die Hallesche Maschinenfabrik und Eisengiesserei AG von ihrer Gründung bis zum Jahre 1918." *Aus der Geschichte der halleschen Arbeiterbewegung*, vol. 7, ed. Stadtleitung Halle der SED. Halle: Druckhaus Freiheit, n.d.

Daniel, Ute. *Arbeiterfrauen in der Kriegsgesellschaft: Beruf, Familie und Politik im Ersten Weltkrieg*. Göttingen: Vandenhoeck und Ruprecht, 1989.

Davis, Belinda. "Reconsidering Habermas, Gender, and the Public Sphere: The Case of Wilhelmine Germany." In *Society, Culture, and the State in Germany, 1870–1930*, ed. Geoff Eley. Ann Arbor: University of Michigan Press, forthcoming.

Deppe, Rainer, Helmut Dubiel, and Ulrich Rödel, eds. *Demokratischer Umbruch in Osteuropa*. Frankfurt am Main: Suhrkamp, 1990.

Diehl, James M. *Paramilitary Politics in Weimar Germany*. Bloomington: Indiana University Press, 1977.

Diskant, James. "Scarcity, Survival and Local Activism: Miners and Steelworkers, Dortmund 1945–8." *Journal of Contemporary History* 24:4 (1989): 547–74.

Döblin, Alfred. *A People Betrayed.* New York: Fromm, 1983.

Dölling, Irene. "Continuity and Change in the Media Image of Women: A Look at Illustrations in GDR Periodicals." In *Studies in GDR Culture and Society* 9, 131–43. Lanham, Md.: University Press of America, 1989.

Domansky, Elisabeth. "Militarization and Reproduction in World War I Germany." In *Society, Culture, and the State in Germany, 1870–1930*, ed. Geoff Eley. Ann Arbor: University of Michigan Press, forthcoming.

———. "Der 'Zukunftsstaat am Besenbinderhof.'" In *Arbeiter in Hamburg: Unterschichten, Arbeiter und Arbeiterbewegung seit dem ausgehenden 18. Jahrhundert*, ed. Arno Herzig, Dieter Langewiesche, and Arnold Sywottek, 373–85. Hamburg: Erziehung und Wissenschaft, 1983.

Domansky-Davidsohn, Elisabeth. "Der Großbetrieb als Organisationsproblem des Deutschen Metallarbeiter-Verbandes vor dem Ersten Weltkrieg." In *Arbeiterbewegung und industrieller Wandel: Studien zu gewerkschaftlichen Organisationsproblemen im Reich und an der Ruhr*, ed. Hans Mommsen, 95–116. Wuppertal: Peter Hammer, 1980.

Dorpalen, Andreas. "SPD und KPD in der Endphase der Weimarer Republik." *Vierteljahrshefte für Zeitgeschichte* 31:1 (1983): 77–107.

Drachkovitch, Milorad M., and Branko Lazitch, eds. *The Comintern: Historical Highlights.* New York: Praeger, 1966.

Duhnke, Horst. *Die KPD von 1933 bis 1945*. Cologne: Kiepenheuer und Witsch, 1972.

Eley, Geoff. "Class, Culture, and Politics in the Kaiserreich." *Central European History* 27:3 (1994): 355–75.

———. "Is All the World a Text? From Social History to the History of Society Two Decades Later." In *The Historical Turn in the Human Sciences*, ed. Terrence McDonald. Ann Arbor: University of Michigan Press, forthcoming.

———. "Labor History, Social History, *Alltagsgeschichte*: Experience, Culture, and the Politics of the Everyday—A New Direction for German Social History?" *Journal of Modern History* 61:2 (1989): 297–343.

———. "Reviewing the Socialist Tradition." In *The Crisis of Socialism in Europe*, ed. Christiane Lemke and Gary Marks, 21–60. Durham: Duke University Press, 1992.

———. "Wie denken wir über die Politik? Alltagsgeschichte und die Kategorie des Politischen." In *Alltagskultur, Subjektivität und Geschichte: Zur Theorie und Praxis von Alltagsgeschichte*, ed. Berliner Geschichtswerkstatt, 17–36. Münster: Westfälisches Dampfboot, 1994.

Eley, Geoff, and Keith Nield. "Why Does Social History Ignore Politics?" *Social History* 5:2 (1980): 249–71.

Eliasberg, Georg. *Der Ruhrkrieg von 1920*. Bonn-Bad Godesberg: Neue Gesellschaft, 1974.

Enders, Ulrike. "Kinder, Küche, Kombinat: Frauen in der DDR." *Aus Politik und Zeitgeschichte* B/6–7 (1986): 26–37.

Erger, Johannes. *Der Kapp-Lüttwitz Putsch: Ein Beitrag zur deutschen Innenpolitik 1919/20*. Düsseldorf: Droste, 1967.

Ernst, Anna-Sabine. "Middle Class Values and the Socialist Concept of Mass Culture: Etiquette Books in the GDR in the 1950s." Ms., German Studies Association annual meeting, 1992.

———. "The Politics of Culture and the Culture of Daily Life in the DDR in the 1950s." In *Between Reform and Revolution: Studies in German Socialism and Communism from 1840 to 1990*, ed. David E. Barclay and Eric D. Weitz. Providence: Berghahn, forthcoming.

———. "Vom 'Du' zum 'Sie'": Die Rezeption der bürgerlichen Anstandsregeln in der DDR der 50er Jahre." Ms., 1992.

Evans, Richard J. "Introduction: William II's Germany and the Historians." In *Society and Politics in Wilhelmine Germany*, ed. idem, 11–39. London: Croom Helm, 1978.

———. "Politics and the Family: Social Democracy and the Working-Class Family in Theory and Practice before 1914." In *The German Family: Essays on the Social History of the Family in Nineteenth- and Twentieth-Century Germany*, ed. Richard J. Evans and W. R. Lee, 256–88. London: Croom Helm, 1981.

———. *Proletarians and Politics: Socialism, Protest, and the Working Class in Germany before the First World War*. New York: Berg, 1991.

Evans, Richard J., and Dick Geary, eds. *The German Unemployed: Experiences and Consequences of Mass Unemployment from the Weimar Republic to the Third Reich*. New York: St. Martin's Press, 1987.

Falter, Jürgen W. *Hitlers Wähler*. Munich: Beck, 1991.

———. "Warum die deutschen Arbeiter während des 'Dritten Reiches' zu Hitler standen: Einige Anmerkungen zu Gunther Mais Beitrag über die Unterstützung des nationalsozialistischen Herrschaftssystems durch Arbeiter." *Geschichte und Gesellschaft* 13:2 (1987): 217–31.

Falter, Jürgen W., and Dirk Hänisch. "Die Anfälligkeit von Arbeitern gegenüber der NSDAP bei den Reichstagswahlen 1928–1933." *Archiv für Sozialgeschichte* 26 (1986): 179–216.

Feldman, Gerald D. *Army, Industry, and Labor in Germany, 1914–1918*. Princeton: Princeton University Press, 1966.

———. "Economic and Social Problems of the German Demobilization, 1918–1919." *Journal of Modern History* 47:1 (1975): 1–23

———. "German Business between War and Revolution: On the Origins of the Stinnes-Legien Agreement." In *Entstehung und Wandel der modernen Gesellschaft: Festschrift für Hans Rosenberg zum 65. Geburtstag*, ed. Gerhard A. Ritter, 312–41. Berlin: Walter de Gruyter, 1970.

———. *The Great Disorder: Politics, Economics, and Society in the German Inflation, 1914–1924*. New York: Oxford University Press, 1993.

———. *Iron and Steel in the German Inflation, 1916–1923*. Princeton: Princeton University Press, 1977.

———. "The Origins of the Stinnes-Legien Agreement: A Documentation." *Internationale wissenschaftliche Korrespondenz zur Geschichte der deutschen Arbeiterbewegung* 19/20 (1973): 45–103.

———. "Saxony, the Reich, and the Problem of Unemployment in the German Inflation." *Archiv für Sozialgeschichte* 27 (1987): 103–44.

Feldman, Gerald D., Eberhard Kolb, and Reinhard Rürup. "Die Massenbewegung der Arbeiterschaft in Deutschland nach dem Ersten Weltkrieg." *Politische Vierteljahresschrift* 13:3 (1972): 84–105.

Feldman, Gerald D., and Irmgard Steinisch. "Die Weimarer Republik zwischen Sozial- und Wirtschaftsstaat: Die Entscheidung gegen den Achtstundentag." *Archiv für Sozialgeschichte* 18 (1978): 353–439.

Feldman, Gerald D., et al., eds. *Die deutsche Inflation: Eine Zwischenbilanz*. Berlin: Walter de Gruyter, 1982.

Fischer, Alexander. "Die Bewegung 'Freies Deutschland' in der Sowjetunion: Widerstand hinter Stacheldraht?" In *Der Widerstand gegen den Nationalsozialismus: Die deutsche

Gesellschaft und der Widerstand gegen Hitler, ed. Jürgen Schmädeke and Peter Steinbach, 954–73. Munich: Piper, 1985.

Fischer, Conan J. "Class Enemies or Class Brothers? Communist-Nazi Relations in Germany, 1929–1933." *European History Quarterly* 15:3 (1985): 259–79.

———. *The German Communists and the Rise of Nazism*. New York: St. Martin's Press, 1991.

———. "The KPD and Nazism: A Reply to Dick Geary." *European History Quarterly* 15:4 (1985): 465–71.

Fischer, Ruth. *Stalin and German Communism*. New Brunswick: Transaction Books, 1982, first published 1948.

Fischer, Wolfram. "Bergbau, Industrie und Handwerk 1914–1970." In *Handbuch der deutschen Wirtschafts- und Sozialgeschichte*, vol. 2, ed. Hermann Aubin and Wolfgang Zorn, 198–275. Stuttgart: Ernst Klett, 1976.

Flechtheim, Ossip K. *Die KPD in der Weimarer Republik*. Hamburg: Junius, 1986, first published 1948.

Fowkes, Ben. *Communism in Germany under the Weimar Republic*. New York: St. Martin's Press, 1984.

Frevert, Ute. *Women in German History: From Bourgeois Emancipation to Sexual Liberation*. New York: Berg, 1989.

Fricke, Karl Wilhelm. *Opposition und Widerstand in der DDR*. Cologne: Wissenschaft und Politik, 1984.

Friedländer, Saul, ed. *Probing the Limits of Representation: Nazism and the "Final Solution"*. Cambridge, Mass.: Harvard University Press, 1992.

Friedrich, Thomas. "Das Kominform und die SED." *Beiträge zur Geschichte der Arbeiterbewegung* 33:3 (1991): 322–35.

Friedrich, Wolfgang-Uwe, ed. "Totalitäre Herrschaft—totalitäres Erbe." *German Studies Review* special issue (1994).

Fülberth, Georg. *Die Beziehungen zwischen SPD und KPD in der Kommunalpolitik der Weimarer Periode 1918/19 bis 1933*. Cologne: Pahl-Rugenstein, 1985.

———. *KPD und DKP 1945–1990: Zwei kommunistische Parteien in der vierten Periode kapitalistischer Entwicklung*. Heilbronn: Diestel, 1990.

Funk, Nanette, and Magda Mueller, eds. *Gender Politics and Post-Communism: Reflections from Eastern Europe and the Former Soviet Union*. New York: Routledge, 1993.

Gaus, Günter. *Wo Deutschland liegt: Eine Ortbestimmung*. Hamburg: Hoffmann und Campe, 1983.

Geary, Dick. "Identifying Militancy: The Assessment of Working-Class Attitudes towards State and Society." In *The German Working Class 1888–1933: The Politics of Everyday Life*, ed. Richard J. Evans, 220–46. London: Croom Helm, 1982.

———. "Nazis and Workers: A Reply to Conan Fischer's 'Class Enemies or Class Brothers?'" *European History Quarterly* 15:4 (1985): 453–64.

Geißler, Rainer. "Soziale Ungleichheit zwischen Frauen und Männern im geteilten und im vereinten Deutschland." *Aus Politik und Zeitgeschichte* B14–15/91 (29 March 1991): 13–24.

Geschichte der Sozialistischen Einheitspartei Deutschlands, vol. 1: *Von den Anfängen bis 1917*, ed. Institut für Marxismus-Leninismus beim ZK der SED. Berlin: Dietz, 1989.

Geschichte der VEB Leuna-Werke "Walter Ulbricht" 1916 bis 1945, ed. Kreisleitung der SED des VEB Leuna-Werke "Walter Ulbricht." Leipzig: Deutscher Verlag für Grundstoffindustrie, 1989.

Geschichte der VEB Leuna-Werke "Walter Ulbricht" 1945 bis 1981, ed. Kreisleitung der SED des VEB Leuna-Werke "Walter Ulbricht." Leipzig: Deutscher Verlag für Grundstoffindustrie, 1989.

Geyer, Michael. "Nation, Klasse und Macht: Zur Organisierung von Herrschaft in der Weimarer Republic." *Archiv für Sozialgeschichte* 26 (1986): 27–48.

Gladin, Albin. "Die Streiks der Bergarbeiter im Ruhrgebiet in den Jahren 1889, 1905 und 1912." In *Arbeiterbewegung am Rhein und Ruhr: Beiträge zur Geschichte der Arbeiterbewegung in Rheinland-Westfalen*, ed. Jürgen Reulecke, 111–48. Wuppertal: Peter Hammer, 1974.

Glaeßner, Gert-Joachim. "Vom 'realen Sozialismus' zur Selbstbestimmung: Ursachen und Konsequenzen der Systemkrise in der DDR." *Aus Politik und Zeitgeschichte* B1-2/90 (5 January 1990): 3–20.

Glaeßner, Gert-Joachim, ed. *Die DDR in der Ära Honecker: Politik—Kultur—Gesellschaft*. Opladen: Westdeutscher, 1988.

Glaeßner, Gert-Joachim, and Fred Klinger. "The Three Cultures: Social Forces and Socialist Modernization in the GDR." In *Studies in GDR Culture and Society* 9: 1–20. Lanham, Md.: University Press of America, 1989.

Goldman, Wendy Z. *Women, the State, and Revolution: Soviet Family Policy and Social Life, 1917–1936*. Cambridge: Cambridge University Press, 1993.

Grossmann, Atina. "Abortion and Economic Crisis: The 1931 Campaign against Paragraph 218." In *When Biology Became Destiny: Women in Weimar and Nazi Germany*, ed. Renate Bridenthal, Atina Grossmann, and Marion Kaplan, 66–86. New York: Monthly Review Press, 1984.

———. "'Girlkultur' or Thoroughly Rationalized Female: A New Woman in Weimar Germany." In *Women in Culture and Politics*, ed. Judith Friedlander, 62–80. Bloomington: Indiana University Press, 1986.

———. "The New Woman and the Rationalization of Sexuality in Weimar Germany." In *Powers of Desire: The Politics of Sexuality*, ed. Ann Snitow, Christine Stansell, and Sharon Thompson, 153–71. New York: Monthly Review Press, 1983.

———. "Pronatalism, Nation-Building, and Socialism: Population Policy in the SBZ/DDR, 1945–1960." In *Between Reform and Revolution: Studies in German Socialism and Communism from 1840 to 1990*, ed. David E. Barclay and Eric D. Weitz. Providence: Berghahn, forthcoming.

———. *Reforming Sex: The German Movement for Birth Control and Abortion Reform, 1920–1950*. New York: Oxford University Press, 1995.

———. "'Satisfaction Is Domestic Happiness': Mass Working Class Sex Reform Organizations in the Weimar Republic." In *Toward the Holocaust: The Social and Economic Collapse of the Weimar Republic*, ed. Michael N. Dobkowski and Isidor Wallimann, 265–93. Westport, Conn.: Greenwood, 1983.

Gruber, Helmut. *Red Vienna: Experiment in Working-Class Culture, 1919–1934*. New York: Oxford University Press, 1991.

———. *Soviet Russia Masters the Comintern: International Communism in the Era of Stalin's Ascendancy*. New York: Anchor Books, 1974.

———. "Willi Münzenberg's German Communist Propaganda Empire 1921–1933." *Journal of Modern History* 38:3 (1966): 278–97.

Guttsmann, W. L. *Workers' Culture in Weimar Germany: Between Tradition and Commitment*. New York: Berg, 1990.

Habermas, Jürgen. *Die nachholende Revolution*. Frankfurt am Main: Suhrkamp, 1990.

Hagemann, Karen. *Frauenalltag und Männerpolitik: Alltagsleben und gesellschaftliches Handeln von Arbeiterfrauen in der Weimarer Republik.* Bonn: J. H. W. Dietz Nachf., 1990.

Haimson, Leopold H., and Charles Tilly, eds. *Strikes, Wars, and Revolutions in International Perspective: Strike Waves in the Late Nineteenth and Early Twentieth Centuries.* Cambridge: Cambridge University Press, 1989.

Hanke, Irma. *Alltag und Politik: Zur politischen Kultur einer unpolitischen Gesellschaft.* Opladen: Westdeutscher, 1987.

———. "Sozialistischer Neohistorismus? Aspekte der Identitätsdebatte in der DDR." In *Die DDR in der Ära Honecker: Politik—Kultur—Gesellschaft,* ed. Gert-Joachim Glaeßner, 56–76. Opladen: Westdeutscher, 1988.

Harrison, Hope M. "Ulbricht and the Concrete 'Rose': New Archival Evidence on the Dynamics of Soviet–East German Relations and the Berlin Crisis, 1958–1961." Cold War International History Project, Woodrow Wilson International Center for Scholars, Working Paper no. 5 (1993).

Harsch, Donna. *German Social Democracy and the Rise of Nazism.* Chapel Hill: University of North Carolina Press, 1993.

Hartewig, Karin. *Das unberechenbare Jahrzehnt: Bergarbeiter und ihre Familien im Ruhrgebiet.* Munich: Beck, 1993.

Harvey, David. *The Condition of Postmodernity: An Enquiry into the Origins of Cultural Change.* Oxford: Basil Blackwell, 1989.

———.*Consciousness and the Urban Experience: Studies in the History and Theory of Capitalist Urbanization.* Baltimore: Johns Hopkins University Press, 1985.

Harvey, Elizabeth. "Serving the Volk, Saving the Nation: Women in the Youth Movement and the Public Sphere in Weimar Germany." In *Elections, Mass Politics, and Social Change in Modern Germany: New Perspectives,* ed. Larry Eugene Jones and James Retallack, 201–21. Cambridge: Cambridge University Press, 1992.

———. *Youth and the Welfare State in Weimar Germany.* Oxford: Clarendon, 1993.

Hausen, Karin. "Family and Role-Division: The Polarisation of Sexual Stereotypes in the Nineteenth Century—An Aspect of the Dissociation of Work and Family." In *The German Family,* ed. Richard J. Evans and W. R. Lee, 51–83. London: Croom Helm, 1981.

Hayes, Peter. *Industry and Ideology: IG Farben in the Nazi Era.* Cambridge: Cambridge University Press, 1987.

Heer-Kleinert, Lore. *Die Gewerkschaftspolitik der KPD in der Weimarer Republik.* Frankfurt am Main: Campus, 1983.

Hell, Julia. "At the Center an Absence: Foundationalist Narratives of the GDR and the Legitimatory Discourse of Antifascism." *Monatshefte* 84:1 (1992): 23–45.

Helwig, Gisela. "Staat und Familie in der DDR." In *Die DDR in der Ära Honecker: Politik—Kultur—Gesellschaft,* ed. Gert-Joachim Glaeßner, 466–80. Opladen: Westdeutscher, 1988.

Helwig, Gisela, and Hildegard Maria Nickel, eds. *Frauen in Deutschland 1945–1992.* Berlin: Akademie, 1993.

Hentschel, Volker. "Das System der sozialen Sicherung in historischer Sicht, 1880 bis 1975." *Archiv für Sozialgeschichte* 18 (1978): 307–52.

Henze, Jochen. *Sechsstundenschicht im Ruhrbergbau 1918–1920: Ursachen und Verlauf eines Arbeitszeitkonflikts.* Freiburg: Burg, 1988.

Herbert, Ulrich. "Arbeit und Vernichtung: Ökonomisches Interesse und Primat der 'Weltanschauung' im Nationalsozialismus." In *Ist der Nationalsozialismus Geschichte?*

Zu Historisierung und Historikerstreit, ed. Dan Diner, 198–236. Frankfurt am Main: Fischer, 1987.

———. "Arbeiterschaft im 'Dritten Reich': Zwischenbilanz und offene Fragen." *Geschichte und Gesellschaft* 15:3 (1989): 320–60.

———. *A History of Foreign Labor in Germany, 1880–1980: Seasonal Workers/Forced Laborers/Guest Workers*. Ann Arbor: University of Michigan Press, 1990.

Herbst, Ludolf. "Abhängigkeit oder Interdependenz." In *Die DDR als Geschichte: Fragen—Hypothesen—Perspektiven*, ed. Jürgen Kocka and Martin Sabrow, 181–90. Berlin: Akademie, 1994.

Herbst, Ludolf, ed. *Westdeutschland 1945–1955: Unterwerfung, Kontrolle, Integration*. Munich: Oldenbourg, 1986.

Herf, Jeffrey. "East German Communists and the Jewish Question: The Case of Paul Merker." *Journal of Contemporary History* 29:4 (1994): 627–62.

———. "Multiple Restorations: German Political Traditions and the Interpretation of Nazism, 1945–1946." *Central European History* 26:1 (1993): 21–55.

Herlemann, Beatrix. "Communist Resistance between Comintern Direction and Nazi Terror." In *Between Reform and Revolution: Studies in German Socialism and Communism from 1840 to 1990*, ed. David E. Barclay and Eric D. Weitz. Providence: Berghahn, forthcoming.

———. "Der deutschsprachige Bereich an den Kaderschulen der Kommunistischen Internationale." *Internationale wissenschaftliche Korrespondenz zur Geschichte der deutschen Arbeiterbewegung* 18:2 (1982): 205–29.

———. *Die Emigration als Kampfposten: Die Anleitung des kommunistischen Widerstandes in Deutschland aus Frankreich, Belgien und den Niederlanden*. Königstein im Taunus: Anton Hain, 1982.

———. *Kommunalpolitik der KPD im Ruhrgebiet 1924–1933*. Wuppertal: Peter Hammer, 1977.

Hickey, Stephen H. F. *Workers in Imperial Germany: The Miners of the Ruhr*. Oxford: Clarendon, 1985.

Hinrichs, Peter, and Peter Lothar. *Industrieller Friede? Arbeitswissenschaft, Rationalisierung und Arbeiterbewegung in der Weimarer Republik*. Cologne: Pahl-Rugenstein, 1976.

Hobsbawm, Eric. "Man and Woman: Images on the Left." In idem, *Workers: Worlds of Labor*, 83–102. New York: Pantheon, 1984.

Hobsbawm, Eric, and Terence Ranger, eds. *The Invention of Tradition*. Cambridge: Cambridge University Press, 1983.

Hoffmann, Walter. *Der Mansfelder Kupferschieferbergbau: Ein Beitrag zur mitteldeutschen Wirtschaftsgeschichte*. Ed. Mitteldeutschen Kulturrat e.v. Bonn. Meisenheim am Glan: Anton Hain, 1957.

Hoffmann, Walther G. *Das Wachstum der deutschen Wirtschaft seit der Mitte des 19. Jahrhunderts*. Berlin: Springer, 1965.

Homburg, Heidrun. "Anfänge des Taylorsystems in Deutschland vor dem Ersten Weltkrieg." *Geschichte und Gesellschaft* 4:2 (1978): 170–94.

———. *Rationalisierung und Industriearbeit: Arbeitsmarkt- Management-Arbeiterschaft im Siemens-Konzern Berlin 1900–1939*. Berlin: Haude und Spener, 1991.

———. "Vom Arbeitslosen zum Zwangsarbeiter: Arbeitslosenpolitik und Fraktionierung der Arbeiterschaft in Deutschland am Beispiel der Wohlfahrtserwerbslosen und der kommunalen Wohlfahrtshilfe." *Archiv für Sozialgeschichte* 25 (1985): 251–98.

Hong, Young-Sun. "The Contradictions of Modernization in the German Welfare State: Gender and the Politics of Welfare Reform in First World War Germany." *Social History* 17:2 (1992): 251–70.

Horn, Gerd-Rainer. "Pro-Unity Sentiments in Underground Social Democracy, 1933–1936." In *Between Reform and Revolution: Studies in German Socialism and Communism from 1840 to 1990*, ed. David E. Barclay and Eric D. Weitz. Providence: Berghahn, forthcoming.

———. "The Reorientation of the European Left, 1933–1936." Ph.D. diss., University of Michigan, 1992.

Hull, Isabel V. "Feminist and Gender History through the Literary Looking Glass: German Historiography in Postmodern Times." *Central European History* 22:3/4 (1989): 279–300.

In den Fängen des NKWD: Deutsche Opfer des stalinistischen Terrors in der UdSSR. Ed. Institut für Geschichte der Arbeiterbewegung. Berlin: Dietz, 1991.

James, Harold. *The German Slump: Politics and Economics, 1924–1936*. Oxford: Clarendon, 1986.

Jarausch, Konrad. "Divided by Words: Constructing German Unification as History." Ms., 1992.

———. "The Failure of East German Antifascism: Some Ironies of History as Politics." *German Studies Review* 14:1 (1991): 85–102.

———. *The Rush to German Unity*. New York: Oxford University Press, 1993.

Jarausch, Konrad, ed. *Zwischen Parteilichkeit und Professionalität: Bilanz der Geschichtswissenschaft der DDR*. Berlin: Akademie, 1991.

Jarausch, Konrad, and Larry Eugene Jones. "German Liberalism Reconsidered: Inevitable Decline, Bourgeois Hegemony, or Partial Achievement?" In *In Search of a Liberal Germany: Studies in the History of German Liberalism from 1789 to the Present*, ed. idem, 1–23. Providence: Berg, 1990.

Jessen, Ralph. "Die Gesellschaft im Staatssozialismus: Probleme einer Sozialgeschichte der DDR." *Geschichte und Gesellschaft* 21:1 (1995): 96–110.

———. "Unternehmerherrschaft und staatliches Gewaltmonopol: Hüttenpolizisten und Zechenwehren im Ruhrgebiet (1870–1914)." In *"Sicherheit" und "Wohlfahrt": Polizei, Gesellschaft und Herrschaft im 19. und 20. Jahrhundert*, ed. Alf Lüdtke, 161–86. Frankfurt am Main: Suhrkamp, 1992.

Jones, Larry Eugene, and James Retallack, eds. *Elections, Mass Politics, and Social Change in Modern Germany: New Perspectives*. Cambridge: Cambridge University Press, 1992.

———. "German Conservatism Reconsidered: Old Problems and New Directions." In *Reform, Reaction, and Resistance: Studies in the History of German Conservatism from 1789 to 1945*, ed. idem, 1–30. Providence: Berg, 1993.

Juin, Hubert. *Victor Hugo*, vol. 3: *1870–1885*. Paris: Flammarion, 1986.

Kaelble, Harmut, Jürgen Kocka, and Hartmut Zwahr, eds. *Sozialgeschichte der DDR*. Stuttgart: Klett Cotta, 1994.

Kalbe, Ernstgert. "Die volksdemokratische Revolution in Europa—eine neue Form des Übergangs zum Sozialismus." *Zeitschrift für Geschichtswissenschaft* 30: 10/11 (1982): 899–908.

Kämpfendes Leuna (1916–1945): Die Geschichte des Kampfes der Leuna-Arbeiter, Teil 1: 1. Halbband. Ed. Kreisleitung der SED VEB Leuna-Werke "Walter Ulbricht." Berlin: Tribüne, 1961.

Kaplan, Temma. *Red City, Blue Period: Social Movements in Picasso's Barcelona*. Berkeley and Los Angeles: University of California Press, 1992.

Katznelson, Ira, and Aristide R. Zolberg, eds. *Working-Class Formation: Nineteenth-Century Patterns in Western Europe and the United States*. Princeton: Princeton University Press, 1986.

Kent, Susan Kingsley. *Making Peace: The Reconstruction of Gender in Interwar Britain*. Princeton: Princeton University Press, 1993.

Kershaw, Ian. *The Hitler Myth: Image and Reality in the Third Reich*. Oxford: Oxford University Press, 1987.

Kertzer, David I. *Ritual, Politics, and Power*. New Haven: Yale University Press, 1988.

Kleinfeld, Gerald R. "The Return of the PDS." In *Germany's New Politics*, ed. David P. Conradt et al., 193–220. *German Studies Review* special issue (1995).

Kleßmann, Christoph. "Betriebsparteigruppen und Einheitsgewerkschaft: Zur betrieblichen Arbeit der politischen Parteien in der Frühphase der westdeutschen Arbeiterbewegung 1948–1952." *Vierteljahrshefte für Zeitgeschichte* 31:2 (1983): 272–307.

———. "Betriebsräte und Gewerkschaften in Deutschland 1945–1952." In *Politische Weichenstellungen im Nachkriegsdeutschland 1945–1953*, ed. Heinrich August Winkler, 44–73. Göttingen: Vandenhoeck und Ruprecht, 1979.

———. "Die deutsche Volksdemokratie: Geschichte, Theorie und Rezeption des Begriffs in der SBZ/DDR." *Deutschland Archiv* 8:4 (1975): 375–89.

———. *Die doppelte Staatsgründung: Deutsche Geschichte 1945–1955*. Göttingen: Vandenhoeck und Ruprecht, 1982.

———. "Elemente der ideologischen und sozialpolitischen Integration der westdeutschen Arbeiterbewegung." In *Westdeutschland 1945–1955: Unterwerfung, Kontrolle, Integration*, ed. Ludolf Herbst, 108–16. Munich: Oldenbourg, 1986.

———. "Opposition und Dissidenz in der Geschichte der DDR." *Aus Politik und Zeitgeschichte* B5/91 (25 January 1991): 52–62.

———. *Zwei Staaten, eine Nation: Deutsche Geschichte 1955–1970*. Göttingen: Vandenhoeck und Ruprecht, 1988.

Kleßmann, Christoph, and Peter Friedemann. *Streiks und Hungermärsche im Ruhrgebiet 1946–1948*. Frankfurt am Main: Campus, 1977.

Kluge, Alexander, and Oskar Negt. *Öffentlichkeit und Erfahrung: Zur Organisationsanalyse von bürgerlicher und proletarischer Öffentlichkeit*. Frankfurt am Main: Suhrkamp, 1972.

Kluge, Ulrich. *Die deutsche Revolution 1918/1919: Staat, Politik und Gesellschaft zwischen Weltkrieg und Kapp-Putsch*. Frankfurt am Main: Suhrkamp, 1985.

———. "Essener Sozialisierungsbewegung und Volksbewegung im rheinisch-westfälischen Industriegebiet 1918/19." *Internationale wissenschaftliche Korrespondenz zur Geschichte der deutschen Arbeiterbewegung* 16 (1972): 56–65.

Kluth, Hans. *Die KPD in der Bundesrepublik: Ihre politische Tätigkeit und Organisation 1945–1956*. Cologne: Westdeutscher, 1959.

Knabe, Hubertus. "Politische Opposition in der DDR: Ursprünge, Programmatik, Perspektiven." *Aus Politik und Zeitgeschichte* B1–2/90 (5 January 1990): 21–32.

Koch, Max Jürgen. *Die Bergarbeiterbewegung im Ruhrgebiet zur Zeit Wilhelms II*. Düsseldorf: Droste, 1954.

Koch-Baumgarten, Sigrid. *Die Märzaktion der KPD 1921*. Cologne: Bund, 1987.

Kocka, Jürgen. "Eine durchherrschte Gesellschaft." In *Sozialgeschichte der DDR*, ed. Hartmut Kaelble, Jürgen Kocka, and Hartmut Zwahr, 547–53. Stuttgart: Klett Cotta, 1994.

———. *Klassengesellschaft im Krieg: Deutsche Sozialgeschichte 1914–1918*. Göttingen: Vandenhoeck und Ruprecht, 1973.

———. *Vereinigungskrise: Zur Geschichte der Gegenwart*. Göttingen: Vandenhoeck und Ruprecht, 1995.

Kocka, Jürgen, ed. *Historische DDR-Forschung: Aufsätze und Studien*. Berlin: Akademie, 1993.

Kocka, Jürgen, with Ute Frevert, eds. *Bürgertum im 19. Jahrhundert: Deutschland im europäischen Vergleich*, 3 vols. Munich: DTV, 1988.

Kocka, Jürgen, and Martin Sabrow, eds. *Die DDR als Geschichte: Fragen—Hypothesen—Perspektiven*. Berlin: Akademie, 1994.

Koenker, Diane P., William G. Rosenberg, and Ronald Grigor Suny, eds. *Party, State, and Society in the Russian Civil War: Explorations in Social History*. Bloomington: Indiana University Press, 1989.

Kolb, Eberhard. *Die Arbeiterräte in der deutschen Innenpolitik*. Düsseldorf: Droste, 1962.

Kolb, Eberhard, ed. *Vom Kaiserreich zur Weimarer Republik*. Cologne: Kiepenheuer und Witsch, 1972.

Könnemann, Erwin. *Einwohnerwehren und Zeitfreiwilligenverbände: Ihre Funktion beim Aufbau eines neuen imperialistischen Militärsystems (November 1918 bis 1920)*. Berlin: Deutscher Militärverlag, 1971.

Könnemann, Erwin, and Hans-Joachim Krusch. *Aktionseinheit contra Kapp-Putsch*. Berlin: Dietz, 1972.

Könnemann, Erwin, et al. *Halle: Geschichte der Stadt in Wort und Bild*. Berlin: Deutscher Verlag der Wissenschaften, 1983.

———. *Vereint auf dem Weg zum Sozialismus: Geschichte der Landesparteiorganisation Sachsen-Anhalt der SED 1945 bis 1952*. Ed. Bezirksleitungen Halle und Magdeburg der SED, Kommissionen zur Erforschung der Geschichte der örtlichen Arbeiterbewegung. Halle and Magdeburg: Druckhaus Freiheit, 1986.

Kontos, Silvia. *"Die Partei kämpft wie ein Mann!" : Frauenpolitik der KPD in der Weimarer Republik*. Frankfurt am Main: Roter Stern, 1979.

Koonz, Claudia. *Mothers in the Fatherland: Women, the Family, and Nazi Politics*. New York: St. Martin's Press, 1987.

Korff, Gottfried. "From Brotherly Handshake to Militant Clenched Fist: On Political Metaphors for the Worker's Hand." *International Labor and Working Class History* 42 (1992): 70–81.

———. "Rote Fahnen und geballte Faust: Zur Symbolik der Arbeiterbewegung in der Weimarer Republik." In *Fahnen, Fäuste, Körper: Symbolik und Kultur der Arbeiterbewegung*, ed. Dietmar Petzina, 27–60. Essen: Klartext, 1986.

———. "Rote Fahnen und Tableaux Vivants: Zum Symbolverständnis der deutschen Arbeiterbewegung im 19. Jahrhundert." In *Studien zur Arbeiterkultur*, ed. Albrecht Lehmann, 103–40. Münster: F. Coppenrath, 1984.

———. "Volkskultur und Arbeiterkultur: Überlegungen am Beispiel der sozialistischen Maifesttradition." *Geschichte und Gesellschaft* 5:1 (1979): 83–102.

Krabbe, Wolfgang R. *Die deutsche Stadt im 19. und 20. Jahrhundert: Eine Einführung*. Göttingen: Vandenhoeck und Ruprecht, 1989.

Krisch, Henry. *German Politics under Soviet Occupation*. New York: Columbia University Press, 1974.

Krusch, Hans-Joachim. "Neuansatz und widersprüchliches Erbe: Zur KPD 1945/1946." *Beiträge zur Geschichte der Arbeiterbewegung* 33:5 (1991): 615–27.

Kruse, Wolfgang. *Krieg und nationale Integration: Eine Neuinterpretation des sozialdemokratischen Burgfriedensschlusses 1914/15*. Essen: Klartext, 1993.

Kuhn, Annette. "Der Refamilialisierungsdiskurs nach '45." *Beiträge zur Geschichte der Arbeiterbewegung* 33:5 (1991): 593–606.

Kunst und Literatur im antifaschistischen Exil 1933–1945. Leipzig: Reclam, 1978–83.

Ladd, Brian. *Urban Planning and Civic Order in Germany, 1860–1914*. Cambridge, Mass.: Harvard University Press, 1990.

Langewiesche, Dieter. "The Impact of the German Labor Movement on Workers' Culture." *Journal of Modern History* 59:3 (1987): 506–23.

———. "Politik—Gesellschaft—Kultur: Zur Problematik von Arbeiterkultur und kulturellen Arbeiterorganisationen in Deutschland nach dem 1. Weltkrieg." *Archiv für Sozialgeschichte* 22 (1982): 359–402

———. "Wanderungsbewegungen in der Hochindustrialiserungsperiode: Regionale, interstädtische und innnerstädische Mobilität in Deutschland 1880–1914." *Vierteljahrschrift für Sozial- und Wirtschaftsgeschichte* 64:1 (1977): 1–40.

Langewiesche, Dieter, and Klaus Schönhoven. "Arbeiterbibliotheken und Arbeiterlektüre in Wilhelminischen Deutschland." *Archiv für Sozialgeschichte* 16 (1976): 134–204.

Langkau-Alex, Ursula. *Volksfront für Deutschland?* vol. 1. Frankfurt: Syndikat, 1977.

Laschitza, Horst. *Kämpferische Demokratie gegen Faschismus: Die programmatische Vorbereitung auf die antifaschistisch-demokratische Umwälzung in Deutschland durch die Parteiführung der KPD*. Berlin: Deutscher Militärverlag, 1969.

Lavau, Georges. "Le Parti communiste dans le système français." In *Le Communisme en France*, Cahiers de la Fondation Nationale des Sciences Politiques no. 175: 7–65. Paris: Armand Colin, 1969.

Lechtape, Heinrich. "Der Einfluß des Weltkrieges auf die Bevölkerung der Stadt Essen (Ruhr)." Ph.D diss., Universität zu Greifswald, 1923.

Leidigkeit, Karl-Heinz, and Jürgen Hermann. *Auf leninistischem Kurs—Geschichte der KPD-Bezirksorganisation Halle-Merseburg bis 1933*. Ed. Bezirksleitung Halle der SED, Kommission zur Erforschung der Geschichte der örtlichen Arbeiterbewegung. Halle: Druckhaus Freiheit, 1979.

Leidigkeit, Karl-Heinz, et al. *Gegen Faschismus und Krieg: Die KPD im Bezirk Halle-Merseburg 1933 bis 1945*. Ed. Bezirksleitung Halle der SED, Kommission zur Erforschung der Geschichte der örtlichen Arbeiterbewegung. Halle: Druckhaus Freiheit, 1983.

Lemke, Christiane. "Beyond the Ideological Stalemate: Women and Politics in the FRG and the GDR in Comparison." *German Studies Review*, DAAD Special Issue (1990): 87–94.

———. "Frauen, Technik und Fortschritt: Zur Bedeutung neuer Technologien für die Berufssituation von Frauen in der DDR." In *Die DDR in der Ära Honecker: Politik—Kultur—Gesellschaft*, ed. Gert-Joachim Glaeßner, 481–98. Opladen: Westdeutscher, 1988.

———. "Political Socialization and the 'Micromilieu': Toward a Political Sociology of GDR Society." In *The Quality of Life in the German Democratic Republic: Changes and Developments in a State Socialist Society*, ed. Marilyn Rueschemeyer and Christiane Lemke, 59–73. Armonk, N.Y.: M. E. Sharpe, 1989.

———. *Die Ursachen des Umbruchs: Politische Sozialisation in der ehemaligen DDR*. Opladen: Westdeutscher, 1991.

Lemke, Christiane, and Gary Marks, eds. *The Crisis of Socialism in Europe*. Durham: Duke University Press, 1992.

Lemke, Michael. "Die Deutschlandspolitik der DDR zwischen Moskauer Oktroi und Bonner Sogwirkung." In *Die DDR als Geschichte: Fragen—Hypothesen—Perspektiven*, ed. Jürgen Kocka and Martin Sabrow, 181–85. Berlin: Akademie, 1994.

———. "Kampagnen gegen Bonn: Die Systemkrise der DDR und die West-Propaganda der SED 1960–1963." *Vierteljahrshefte für Zeitgeschichte* 41:2 (1993): 153–74.

Leonhard, Wolfgang. *Das kurze Leben der DDR: Berichte und Kommentare aus vier Jahrzehnten*. Stuttgart: Deutsche Verlags-Anstalt, 1990.

———. *Die Revolution entläßt ihre Kinder*. Cologne: Kiepenheuer und Witsch, 1955.

Lepsius, M. Rainer. "Die Institutionenordnung als Rahmenbedingung der Sozialgeschichte der DDR." In *Sozialgeschichte der DDR*, ed. Hartmut Kaelble, Jürgen Kocka, and Hartmut Zwahr, 17–30. Stuttgart: Klett Cotta, 1994.

Lewin, Erwin. "Einige Aspekte der Wirkung von Stalins Luxemburg-Urteil 1931 in der Komintern." *Beiträge zur Geschichte der Arbeiterbewegung* 33:4 (1991): 483–93.

Lewin, Moshe. *The Making of the Soviet System: Essays in the Social History of Interwar Russia*. New York: Pantheon, 1985.

———. *Political Undercurrents in Soviet Economic Debates: From Bukharin to the Modern Reformers*. Princeton: Princeton University Press, 1974.

Lidtke, Vernon. *The Alternative Culture: Socialist Labor in Imperial Germany*. New York: Oxford University Press, 1985.

Linton, Derek. *Who Has the Youth Has the Future*. Cambridge: Cambridge University Press, 1990.

Lösche, Peter, and Franz Walter. "Auf dem Weg zur Volkspartei? Die Weimarer Sozialdemokratie." *Archiv für Sozialgeschichte* 29 (1989): 75–136.

———. "Zur Organisationskultur der sozialdemokratischen Arbeiterbewegung in der Weimarer Republik: Niedergang der Klassenkultur oder solidargemeinschaftlicher Höhepunkt?" *Geschichte und Gesellschaft* 15:4 (1989): 511–36.

Lucas, Erhard. *Märzrevolution 1920*, 3 vols. Frankfurt am Main: Roter Stern, 1970–78.

———. "Ursachen und Verlauf der Bergarbeiterbewegung in Hamborn und im westlichen Ruhrgebiet 1918/19." *Duisburger Forschungen* 15 (1971): 1–119.

———. *Zwei Formen von Radikalismus in der deutschen Arbeiterbewegung*. Frankfurt am Main: Roter Stern, 1976.

Lüdtke, Alf. "The Appeal of Exterminating 'Others': German Workers and the Limits of Resistance." In *Resistance against the Third Reich, 1933–1990*, ed. Michael Geyer and John W. Boyer, 53–74. Chicago: University of Chicago Press, 1994.

———. "Arbeiterpolitik versus Politik der Arbeiter: Zu Unternehmensstrategien und Arbeiterverhalten in deutschen Großbetrieben zwischen 1890 und 1914/20." In *Arbeiter und Bürger im 19. Jahrhundert: Varianten ihres Verhältnisses im europäischen Vergleich*, ed. Jürgen Kocka, 202–12. Munich: Oldenbourg, 1986.

———. "Cash, Coffee-Breaks, Horseplay: *Eigensinn* and Politics among Factory Workers in Germany circa 1900." In *Confrontation, Class Consciousness and the Labor Process: Studies in Proletarian Class Formation*, ed. Michael Hanagen and Charles Stephenson, 65–95. Westport, Conn.: Greenwood, 1986.

———. "'Deutsche Qualitätsarbeit', 'Spielereien' am Arbeitsplatz und 'Fliehen' aus der Fabrik: Industrielle Arbeitsprozesse und Arbeiterverhalten in den 1920er Jahren—Aspekte eines offenen Forschungsfeldes." In *Arbeiterkulturen zwischen Alltag und Politik: Beiträge zum europäischen Vergleich in der Zwischenkriegszeit*, ed. Friedhelm Boll, 155–98. Vienna: Europa, 1986.

———. "'Ehre der Arbeit': Industriearbeiter und Macht der Symbole. Zur Reichweite symbolischer Orientierungen im Nationalsozialismus." In *Arbeiter im 20. Jahrhundert*, ed. Klaus Tenfelde, 343–92. Stuttgart: Klett Cotta, 1991.

———. *Eigen-Sinn: Fabrikalltag, Arbeitererfahrungen und Politik vom Kaiserreich bis in den Faschismus*. Hamburg: Ergebnisse, 1993.

———. "'Helden der Arbeit'—Mühen beim Arbeiten: Zur mißmutigen Loyalität von Industriearbeitern in der DDR." In *Sozialgeschichte der DDR*, ed. Hartmut Kaelble, Jürgen Kocka, and Hartmut Zwahr, 188–213. Stuttgart: Klett Cotta, 1994.

———. "Organizational Order or *Eigensinn*? Workers' Privacy and Workers' Politics in Imperial Germany." In *Rites of Power: Symbolism, Ritual, and Politics since the Middle Ages*, ed. Sean Wilentz, 303–33. Philadelphia: University of Pennsylvania Press, 1985.

———. "Wo blieb die 'rote Glut'? Arbeitererfahrungen und deutscher Faschismus." In *Alltagsgeschichte: Zur Rekonstruktion historischer Erfahrungen und Lebensweisen*, ed. idem, 224–82. Frankfurt am Main: Campus, 1989.

Lüdtke, Alf, ed. *Alltagsgeschichte: Zur Rekonstruktion historischer Erfahrungen und Lebensweisen*. Frankfurt am Main: Campus, 1989.

———. *Herrschaft als soziale Praxis: Historische und sozialanthropologische Studien*. Göttingen: Vandenhoeck und Ruprecht, 1991.

———. *"Sicherheit" und "Wohlfahrt": Polizei, Gesellschaft und Herrschaft im 19. und 20. Jahrhundert*. Frankfurt am Main: Suhrkamp, 1992.

Ludz, Peter Christian. *Parteielite im Wandel: Funktionsaufbau, Sozialstruktur und Ideologie der SED-Führung. Eine empirisch-systematische Untersuchung*. Cologne: Westdeutscher, 1968.

McAdams, A. James. *East Germany and Detente: Building Authority after the Wall*. Cambridge: Cambridge University Press, 1985.

———. *Germany Divided: From the Wall to Reunification*. Princeton: Princeton University Press, 1992.

McCreary, Eugene C. "Social Welfare and Business: The Krupp Welfare Program, 1860–1914." *Business History Review* 42:1 (1968): 24–49.

McElligott, Anthony. "Mobilising the Unemployed: The KPD and the Unemployed Workers' Movement in Hamburg-Altona during the Weimar Republic." In *The German Unemployed: Experiences and Consequences of Mass Unemployment from the Weimar Republic to the Third Reich*, ed. Richard J. Evans and Dick Geary, 228–60. New York: St. Martin's Press, 1987.

———. "'. . .und so kam es zu einer schweren Schlägerei': Straßenschlachten in Altona und Hamburg am Ende der Weimarer Republik." In *"Hier war doch alles nicht so schlimm": Wie die Nazis in Hamburg den Alltag eroberten*, ed. Maike Bruhns et al., 58–85. Hamburg: VSA, 1984.

———. "Workers' Culture and Workers' Politics on Weimar's New Housing Estates: A Response to Adelheid von Saldern." *Social History* 17:1 (1992): 101–13.

Mai, Gunther. "Die nationalsozialistische Betriebszellen-Organisation: Zum Verhältnis von Arbeiterschaft und Nationalsozialismus." *Vierteljahrshefte für Zeitgeschichte* 31:4 (1983): 573–613.

———. "'Warum steht der deutsche Arbeiter zu Hitler?' Zur Rolle der Deutschen Arbeitsfront im Herrschaftssystem des Dritten Reiches." *Geschichte und Gesellschaft* 12:2 (1986): 212–34.

Mai, Gunther, ed. *Arbeiterschaft in Deutschland 1914–1918: Studien zu Arbeitskampf und Arbeitsmarkt im Ersten Weltkrieg*. Düsseldorf: Droste, 1985.

Maier, Charles S. "Between Taylorism and Technocracy: European Ideologies and the

Vision of Industrial Productivity in the 1920s." *Journal of Contemporary History* 5:2 (1970): 27–61.

———. "The Collapse of Communism: Approaches for a Future History." *History Workshop Journal* 31 (1991): 34–59.

———. *Recasting Bourgeois Europe: Stabilization in France, Germany, and Italy in the Decade after World War I.* Princeton: Princeton University Press, 1975.

Mallmann, Klaus-Michael. "Milieu, Radikalismus und lokale Gesellschft: Zur Sozialgeschichte des Kommunismus in der Weimarer Republik." *Geschichte und Gesellschaft* 21:1 (1995): 5–31.

Mammach, Klaus. *Widerstand 1933–1939: Geschichte des deutschen antifaschistischen Widerstandsbewegung im Inland und in der Emigration.* Berlin: Akademie, 1984.

Mannschatz, Gerhard, and Josef Seider. *Zum Kampf der KPD im Ruhrgebiet für die Einigung der Arbeiterklasse und die Entmachtung der Monopolherren 1945–1947.* Berlin: Dietz, 1962.

Mason, Timothy. "Massenwiderstand ohne Organisation." In *Aufstieg des Nationalsozialismus: Untergang der Republic, Zerschlagung der Gewerkschaften*, ed. Ernst Breit, 197–212. Cologne: Bund, 1984.

———. *Nazism, Fascism and the Working Class: Essays by Tim Mason*, ed. Jane Caplan. Cambridge: Cambridge University Press, 1995.

———. "Gli scioperi di Torino del marzo 1943." In *L'Italia nella seconda guerra mondiale e nella Resistenza*, ed. Ferratini Tosi et al., 399–422. Milan: Franco Angeli Libri, 1988.

———. *Social Policy in the Third Reich: The Working Class and the National Community.* Providence: Berg, 1993.

———. "Women in Germany, 1925–1940: Family, Welfare and Work," 2 parts. *History Workshop Journal* 1 (1978): 74–111 and 2 (1978): 5–32.

Maynes, Mary Jo. "Autobiography and Class Formation in Nineteenth-Century Europe: Methodological Considerations." *Social Science History* 16:3 (1992): 516–37.

———. "*Genossen und Genossinnen*: Gender Identity and Socialist Identity in Imperial Germany." In *Between Reform and Revolution: Studies in German Socialism and Communism between 1840 and 1990*, ed. David E. Barclay and Eric D. Weitz. Providence: Berghahn, forthcoming.

———. *Schooling for the People: Comparative Local Studies of Schooling History in France and Germany, 1750–1850.* New York: Holmes and Meier, 1985.

———. *Taking the Hard Road: Life Course in French and German Workers' Autobiographies in the Era of Industrialization.* Chapel Hill: University of North Carolina Press, 1995.

Meier, Helmut, and Walter Schmidt. *Erbe und Tradition in der DDR: Die Diskussion der Historiker.* Berlin: Akademie, 1988.

Meisel, G. "Der Kampf der Werktätigen des Leunawerkes in den Jahren 1919–1921." Diss., Institut für Gesellschaftswissenschaften beim ZK der SED, 1961.

Mende, Roswitha. "Geschichte der Sozialdemokratie im Regierungsbezirk Merseburg von der Jahrhundertwende bis 1917." Ph.D. diss., Philisophischen Fakultät des Wissenschaftlichen Rates der Martin-Luther-Universität Halle-Wittenberg, 1985.

———. *Karl Liebknecht und Rosa Luxemburg im Bezirk Halle.* Ed. Kommission zur Erforschung der Geschichte der örtlichen Arbeiterbewegung bei der Bezirksleitung Halle der SED. Halle: Druckhaus Freiheit, 1981.

Mende, Roswitha, and Karl-Heinz Leidigkeit. *Von der Jahrhundertwende bis zum Roten Oktober: Geschichte der sozialdemokratischen Bezirksorganisation Halle-Merseburg 1900 bis 1917.* Ed. Bezirksleitung Halle der SED. Halle: Druckhaus Freiheit, 1987.

Menge, Marlies. *"Ohne uns läuft nichts mehr": Die Revolution in der DDR*. Stuttgart: Deutsche Verlags-Anstalt, 1990.

Merson, Allan. *Communist Resistance in Nazi Germany*. London: Lawrence and Wishart, 1985.

Metzmacher, Helmut. "Der Novemberumsturz in der Rheinprovinz." *Annalen des historischen Vereins für den Niederrhein* 168/169 (1967): 135–265.

Meuschel, Sigrid. "Auf der Suche nach Madame L'Identité? Zur Konzeption der Nation und Nationalgeschichte." In *Die DDR in der Ära Honecker: Politik—Kultur—Gesellschaft*, ed. Gert-Joachim Glaeßner, 77–93. Opladen: Westdeutscher, 1988.

———. *Legitimation und Parteiherrschaft in der DDR: Zur Paradox von Stabilität und Revolution in der DDR 1945–1989*. Frankfurt am Main: Suhrkamp, 1992.

———. "Überlegungen zu einer Herrschafts- und Gesellschaftsgeschichte der DDR." *Geschichte und Gesellschaft* 19:1 (1993): 5–14.

———. "Wandel durch Auflehnung: Thesen zum Verfall bürokratischer Herrschaft in der DDR." In *Demokratischer Umbruch in Osteuropa*, ed. Rainer Deppe, Helmut Dubiel, and Ulrich Rödel, 26–47. Frankfurt am Main: Suhrkamp, 1991.

Milatz, Alfred. *Wähler und Wahlen in der Weimarer Republik*. Bonn: Bundeszentrale für politische Bildung, 1965.

Miller, Susanne. *Die Bürde der Macht: Die deutsche Sozialdemokratie 1918–1920*. Düsseldorf: Droste, 1978.

———. *Burgfrieden und Klassenkampf: Die deutsche Sozialdemokratie im Ersten Weltkrieg*. Düsseldorf: Droste, 1974.

Milward, Alan S., and S. B. Saul. *The Development of the Economies of Continental Europe, 1850–1914*. Cambridge, Mass.: Harvard University Press, 1977.

Mitter, Armin, and Stefan Wolle. *Untergang auf Raten: Unbekannte Kapitel der DDR-Geschichte*. Munich: Bertelsmann, 1993.

Mocker, Elke, Beate Rüther, and Birgit Sauer. "Frauen- und Familienpolitik: Wie frauenfreundlich war die DDR?" *Deutschland Archiv* 22:11 (1990): 1700–1705.

Mommsen, Hans. *Arbeiterbewegung und nationale Frage*. Göttingen: Vandenhoeck und Ruprecht, 1979.

———. "Die Bergarbeiterbewegung an der Ruhr 1918–33." In *Arbeiterbewegung am Rhein und Ruhr: Beiträge zur Geschichte der Arbeiterbewegung in Rheinland-Westfalen*, ed. Jürgen Reulecke, 275–314. Wuppertal: Peter Hammer, 1974.

———. *From Weimar to Auschwitz*. Trans. Philip O'Connor. Princeton: Princeton University Press, 1991.

———. *Der Nationalsozialismus und die deutsche Gesellschaft: Ausgewählte Aufsätze*. Ed. Lutz Niethammer and Bernd Weisbrod. Reinbek bei Hamburg: Rowohlt, 1991.

———. "Soziale und politische Konflikte an der Ruhr 1905 bis 1924. In *Arbeiterbewegung und industrieller Wandel: Studien zu gewerkschaftlichen Organisationsproblemen im Reich und an der Ruhr*, ed. idem, 62–86. Wuppertal: Peter Hammer, 1980.

———. *Die verspielte Freiheit: Der Weg der Republik von Weimar in den Untergang 1918 bis 1933*. Frankfurt am Main: Propyläen, 1990.

Mommsen, Hans, ed. *Arbeiterbewegung und industrieller Wandel: Studien zu gewerkschaftlichen Organisationsproblemen im Reich und an der Ruhr*. Wuppertal: Peter Hammer, 1980.

Mommsen, Wolfgang J. "Die Ort der DDR in der deutschen Geschichte." In *Die DDR als Geschichte: Fragen—Hypothesen—Perspektiven*, ed. Jürgen Kocka and Martin Sabrow, 26–39. Berlin: Akademie, 1994.

Mommsen, Wolfgang J., and Hans-Gerhard Husung, eds. *The Development of Trade Unionism in Great Britain and Germany, 1880–1914*. London: George Allen and Unwin, 1985.

Moore, Barrington. *Injustice: The Social Bases of Obedience and Revolt*. White Plains, N.Y.: M. E. Sharpe, 1978.

Moreau, Patrick. "Krisen und Anpassungsstrategien der kommunistischen Strömungen in der Bundesrepublik Deutschland und der ehemaligen DDR." *Aus Politik und Zeitgeschichte* B/46–47/90 (9 November 1990): 38–53.

———. "Die PDS: Eine postkommunistische Partei." *Aus Politik und Zeitgeschichte* B5/92 (4 January 1992): 35–44.

Morgan, David. *The Socialist Left and the German Revolution: A History of the German Independent Social Democratic Party, 1917–1922*. Ithaca: Cornell University Press, 1975.

Mühlen, Patrik von zur. *Spanien war ihre Hoffnung: Die deutsche Linke im spanischen Bürgerkrieg*. Berlin: J. H. W. Dietz Nachf., 1985.

Müller, Dirk H. *Gewerkschaftliche Versammlungsdemokratie und Arbeiterdelegierte vor 1918: Ein Beitrag zur Geschichte des Lokalismus, des Syndikalismus, und der entstehenden Rätebewegung*. Berlin: Colloquium, 1985.

Müller, Werner. "Ein 'besonderer deutscher Weg' zur Volksdemokratie? Determinanten und Besonderheiten kommunistischer Machterringung in der SBZ/DDR 1945 bis 1950." *Politische Vierteljahresschrift* 23:3 (1982): 278–303.

———. *Die KPD und die "Einheit der Arbeiterklasse"*. Frankfurt am Main: Campus, 1979.

———. *Lohnkampf, Massenstreik, Sowjetmacht: Ziele und Grenzen der "Revolutionären Gewerkschafts-Opposition" (RGO) in Deutschland 1928 bis 1933*. Cologne: Bund, 1988.

Naimark, Norman M. "'Ich will hier raus': Emigration and the Collapse of the German Democratic Republic." In *Eastern Europe in Revolution*, ed. Ivo Banac, 72–95. Ithaca: Cornell University Press, 1992.

———. "Revolution and Counterrevolution in Eastern Europe." In *The Crisis of Socialism in Europe*, ed. Christiane Lemke and Gary Marks, 61–83. Durham: Duke University Press, 1992.

———. *The Russians in Germany: A History of the Soviet Zone of Occupation, 1945–1949*. Cambridge, Mass.: Harvard University Press, 1995.

Naumann, Gerhard, and Trümpler, Eckhard. *Von Ulbricht zu Honecker: 1970—ein Krisenjahr der DDR*. Berlin: Dietz, 1990.

Nettl, Peter. *Rosa Luxemburg*, abridged ed. Oxford: Oxford University Press, 1969.

Neumann, Robert Paul. "The Sexual Question and Social Democracy in Imperial Germany." *Journal of Social History* 7:3 (1974): 271–86.

Nickel, Hildegard Maria. "Frauen in der DDR." *Aus Politik und Zeitgeschichte* B16–17/90 (13 April 1990): 39–45.

———. "Geschlechtertrennung durch Arbeitsteilung." *Feministische Studien* 8 (1990): 10–19.

Nicosia, Francis R., and Lawrence D. Stokes, eds. *Germans against Nazism: Noncompliance, Opposition and Resistance in the Third Reich. Essays in Honour of Peter C. Hoffmann*. Leamington Spa: Berg, 1990.

Niehuss, Merith. *Arbeiterschaft in Krieg und Inflation: Soziale Schichtung und Lage der Arbeiter in Augsburg und Linz 1910 bis 1925*. Berlin: Walter de Gruyter, 1985.

Niethammer, Lutz. "Annäherung an den Wandel: Auf der Suche nach der volkseigenen Erfahrung in der Industrieprovinz der DDR." In *Alltagsgeschichte: Zur Rekonstruktion historischer Erfahrungen und Lebensweisen*, ed. Alf Lüdtke, 283–345. Frankfurt am Main: Campus, 1989.

———. "Erfahrungen und Strukturen: Prolegomena zu einer Geschichte der Gesellschaft der DDR." In *Sozialgeschichte der DDR*, ed. Hartmut Kaelble, Jürgen Kocka, and Hartmut Zwahr, 95–115. Stuttgart: Klett Cotta, 1994.

———. "Rekonstruktion und Desintegration: Zum Verständnis der deutschen Arbeiterbewegung zwischen Krieg und Kaltem Krieg." In *Politische Weichenstellungen im Nachkriegsdeutschland 1945–1953*, ed. Heinrich August Winkler, 26–43. Göttingen: Vandenoeck und Ruprecht, 1979.

———. "Das Volk der DDR und die Revolution: Versuch einer historischen Wahrnehmung der laufenden Ereignisse." In *"Wir sind das Volk!" Flugschriften, Aufrufe und Texte einer deutschen Revolution*, ed. Charles Schüddekopf, 251–79. Reinbek bei Hamburg: Rowohlt, 1990.

Niethammer, Lutz, ed. *Wohnen im Wandel: Beiträge zur Geschichte des Alltags in der bürgerlichen Gesellschaft*. Wuppertal: Peter Hammer, 1979.

Niethammer, Lutz, and Alexander von Plato, eds. *Lebensgeschichte und Sozialkultur im Ruhrgebiet 1930 bis 1960*, 3 vols. Berlin: J. H. W. Dietz Nachf., 1983–85.

Niethammer, Lutz, Alexander von Plato, and Dorothee Wierling. *Die Volkseigene Erfahrung: Eine Archäologie des Lebens in der Industrieprovinz der DDR*. Berlin: Rowohlt, 1991.

Niethammer, Lutz, et al. *Arbeiterinitiative 1945: Antifaschistische Ausschüsse und Reorganisation der Arbeiterbewegung in Deutschland*. Wuppertal: Peter Hammer, 1976.

———. *Bürgerliche Gesellschaft in Deutschland: Historische Einblicke, Fragen, Perspektiven*. Frankfurt am Main: Fischer, 1990.

Niggemann, Heinz. *Emanzipation zwischen Sozialismus und Feminismus: Die sozialdemokratische Frauenbewegung im Kaiserreich*. Wuppertal: Peter Hammer, 1981.

Nolan, Mary. "Economic Crisis, State Policy, and Working-Class Formation in Germany, 1870–1900." In *Working-Class Formation: Nineteenth-Century Patterns in Western Europe and the United States*, ed. Ira Katznelson and Aristide R. Zolberg, 352–93. Princeton: Princeton University Press, 1986.

———. "'Housework made Easy': The Taylorized Housewife in Weimar Germany's Rationalized Economy." *Feminist Studies* 16:3 (1990): 549–73.

———. *Social Democracy and Society: Working-Class Radicalism in Düsseldorf, 1890–1920*. Cambridge: Cambridge University Press, 1981.

———. *Visions of Modernity: American Business and the Modernization of Germany*. New York: Oxford University Press, 1994.

Oertzen, Peter von. *Betriebsräte in der Novemberrevolution: Eine politikwissenschaftliche Untersuchung über Ideengehalt und Struktur der betrieblichen und wirtschaftslichen Arbeiterräte in der deutschen Revolution 1918/19*. Düsseldorf: Droste, 1963.

———. "Die Großen Streiks der Ruhrbergarbeiterschaft im Frühjahr 1919." *Vierteljahrshefte für Zeitgeschichte* 6:3 (1958): 231–62.

Die Oktoberrevolution und Deutschland. Ed. Kommission der Historiker der DDR und der UdSSR. Berlin: Akademie, 1958.

Orlow, Dietrich. "Preussen und der Kapp-Putsch." *Vierteljahrshefte für Zeitgeschichte* 26:2 (1978): 191–236.

———. *Weimar Prussia, 1918–1925: The Unlikely Rock of Democracy*. Pittsburgh: University of Pittsburgh Press, 1986.

———. *Weimar Prussia, 1925–1933: The Illusion of Strength*. Pittsburgh: University of Pittsburgh Press, 1991.

Ozouf, Mona. *Festivals and the French Revolution*. Cambridge, Mass.: Harvard University Press, 1988.

Patton, Craig. "Patterns of Protest in the German Inflation: Labor Militance and Political Radicalism in Four Chemical Communities, 1914–1924." Ms., 1993.

Peterson, Brian L. "The Politics of Working-Class Women in the Weimar Republic." *Central European History* 10:2 (1977): 87–111.

———. "The Social Bases of Working-Class Politics in the Weimar Republic: The Reichstag Election of December 1924." Ph.D. diss., University of Wisconsin, Madison, 1976.

Petro, Patrice. *Joyless Streets: Women and Melodramatic Representation in Weimar Germany*. Princeton: Princeton University Press, 1989.

Petzina, Dietmar, ed. *Fahnen, Fäuste, Körper: Symbolik und Kultur der Arbeiterbewegung*. Essen: Klartext, 1986.

Peukert, Detlev J. K. *Grenzen der Sozialdisziplinierung: Aufstieg und Krise der deutschen Jugendfürsorge von 1878 bis 1932*. Cologne: Bund, 1986.

———. *Inside Nazi Germany: Conformity, Opposition, and Racism in Everyday Life*. New Haven: Yale University Press, 1987.

———. *Jugend zwischen Krieg und Krise: Lebenswelt von Arbeiterjungen in der Weimarer Republik*. Cologne: Bund, 1987.

———. *Die KPD im Widerstand: Verfolgung und Untergrundarbeit an Rhein und Ruhr 1933 bis 1945*. Wuppertal: Peter Hammer, 1980.

———. "Volksfront und Volksbewegungskonzept im kommunistischen Widerstand—Thesen." In *Der Widerstand gegen den Nationalsozialismus: Die deutsche Gesellschaft und der Widerstand gegen Hitler*, ed. Jürgen Schmädeke and Peter Steinbach, 875–88. Munich: Piper, 1985.

———. *Die Weimarer Republik: Krisenjahre der Klassischen Moderne*. Frankfurt am Main: Suhrkamp, 1987.

———. "Wohlfarhtsstaat und Lebenswelt." In *Bürgerliche Gesellschaft in Deutschland: Historische Einblicke, Fragen, Perspektiven*, ed. Lutz Niethammer et al., 348–63. Frankfurt am Main: Fischer, 1990.

Peukert, Detlev J. K., and Frank Bajohr. *Spuren des Widerstands: Die Bergarbeiterbewegung im Dritten Reich und im Exil*. Munich: Beck, 1987.

Piechocki, Werner. "Der Volkspark als Kultur- und Bildungsstätte der halleschen Arbeiter (1907–1914)." *Aus der Geschichte der halleschen Arbeiterbewegung* no. 6. Ed. SED Stadtleitung Halle, Bildungsstätte Kommission zur Erforschung der Geschichte der örtlichen Arbeiterbewegung. Köthen: Aufbau-Druckerei, 1968.

Pike, David. *German Writers in Soviet Exile, 1933–1945*. Chapel Hill: University of North Carolina Press, 1982.

———. *The Politics of Culture in Soviet-Occupied Germany, 1945–1949*. Stanford: Stanford University Press, 1992.

Pohl, Karl Heinrich. "Sozialdemokratie und Gewerbeinspektion: Zum Verhältnis von Staat, Arbeiterbewegung und Arbeitgebern zwischen 1890 and 1914." *Vierteljahrschrift für Sozial- und Wirtschaftsgeschichte* 75:4 (1988): 457–82.

Prager, Eugen. *Geschichte der U.S.P.D.: Entstehung und Entwicklung der Unabhängigen Sozialdemokratischen Partei Deutschlands*. Berlin: Verlagsgenossenschaft "Freiheit," 1921.

Preller, Ludwig. *Sozialpolitik in der Weimarer Republik*. Stuttgart: Franz Mittelbach, 1949.

Prowe, Diethelm. "*Ordnungsmacht* und *Mitbestimmung*: The Postwar Labor Unions and the Politics of Reconstruction." In *Between Reform and Revolution: Studies in German*

Socialism and Communism from 1840 to 1990, ed. David E. Barclay and Eric D. Weitz. Providence: Berghahn, forthcoming.

———. "Socialism as Crisis Response: Socialization and the Escape from Poverty and Power in Post–World War II Germany." *German Studies Review* 15:1 (1992): 65–85.

Quataert, Jean H. "Workers' Reactions to Social Insurance: The Case of Homeweavers in the Saxon Oberlausitz in the Late Nineteenth Century." *Internationale wissenschaftliche Korrespondenz zur Geschichte der deutschen Arbeiterbewegung* 20:1 (1984): 17–35.

Reisberg, Arnold. *An den Quellen der Einheitsfrontpolitik: Der Kampf der KPD um die Aktionseinheit in Deutschland 1921–1922*, 2 vols. Berlin: Dietz, 1971.

Reißig, Rolf, and Gert-Joachim Glaeßner, eds. *Das Ende eines Experiments*. Berlin: J. H. W. Dietz Nachf., 1991.

Reulecke, Jürgen. "Bürgerliche Sozialreformer und Arbeiterjugend im Kaiserreich." *Archiv für Sozialgeschichte* 22 (1982): 299–329.

Reulecke, Jürgen, and Wolfhard Weber, eds. *Fabrik, Familie, Feierabend: Beiträge zur Sozialgeschichte des Alltags im Industriezeitalter*. Wuppertal: Peter Hammer, 1978.

Ricke, Gabriele. *Die Arbeiter-Illustrierte-Zeitung: Gegenmodell zur bürgerlichen Illustrierten*. Hannover: Internationalismus, 1974.

Rimlinger, Gaston V. *Welfare Policy and Industrialization in Europe, America, and Russia*. New York: John Wiley and Sons, 1971.

Ringer, Fritz. *Education and Society in Modern Europe*. Bloomington: Indiana University Press, 1979.

———. *Fields of Knowledge: French Academic Culture in Comparative Perspective, 1890–1920*. Cambridge: Cambridge University Press, 1992.

Ringer, Fritz, Detlef K. Müller, and Brian Simon, eds. *The Rise of the Modern Educational System: Structural Change and Social Reproduction, 1870–1920*. Cambridge: Cambridge University Press, 1987.

Ritter, Gerhard A. *Die Arbeiterbewegung im Wilhelminischen Reich: Die Sozialdemokratische Partei und die Freien Gewerkschaften 1890–1900*. Berlin: Colloquium, 1959.

———. "Entstehung und Entwicklung des Sozialstaates in vergleichender Perspektive." *Historische Zeitschrift* 243:1 (1986): 1–90.

———. *Social Welfare in Germany and Britain: Origins and Development*. Leamington Spa: Berg, 1986.

———. "Workers' Culture in Imperial Germany: Problems and Points of Departure for Research." *Journal of Contemporary History* 13:2 (1978): 165–89.

Ritter, Gerhard A., with Elisabeth Müller-Luckner, eds. *Der Aufstieg der deutschen Arbeiterbewegung: Sozialdemokratie und Freie Gewerkschaften im Parteiensystem und Sozialmilieu des Kaiserreichs*. Munich: Oldenbourg, 1990.

Ritter, Gerhard A., and Klaus Tenfelde. *Arbeiter im Deutschen Kaiserreich 1871–1914*. Bonn: J. H. W. Dietz Nachf., 1992.

Roberts, Mary Louise. *Civilization without Sexes: Reconstructing Gender in Postwar France, 1917–1927*. Chicago: University of Chicago Press, 1994.

Rohrwasser, Michael. *Saubere Mädel, starke Genossen: Proletarische Massenliteratur?* Berlin: Roter Stern, 1975.

Rose, Sonya O. *Limited Livelihoods: Gender and Class in Nineteenth-Century England*. Berkeley and Los Angeles: University of California Press, 1991.

Rosenberg, Hans. *Große Depression und Bismarckzeit*. Berlin: Walter de Gruyter, 1967.

Rosenhaft, Eve. *Beating the Fascists? The German Communists and Political Violence, 1929–1933*. Cambridge: Cambridge University Press, 1983.

———. "The Uses of Remembrance: The Legacy of the Communist Resistance in the German Democratic Republic." In *Germans against Nazism: Nonconformity, Opposition and Resistance in the Third Reich. Essays in Honour of Peter Hoffmann*, ed. Francis R. Nicosia and Lawrence D. Stokes, 369–88. New York: Berg, 1990.

———. "Women, Gender, and the Limits of Political History in the Age of 'Mass' Politics." In *Elections, Mass Politics, and Social Change in Modern Germany: New Perspectives*, ed. Larry Eugene Jones and James Retallack, 149–73. Cambridge: Cambridge University Press, 1992.

———. "Working-Class Life and Working-Class Politics: Communists, Nazis and the State in the Battle for the Streets, Berlin 1928–1932." In *Social Change and Political Development in Weimar Germany*, ed. Richard Bessel and E. J. Feuchtwanger, 207–40. London: Croom Helm, 1981.

Roth, Ralf. "'Bürger' and Workers, Liberalism and the Labor Movement, 1848–1914." In *Between Reform and Revolution: Studies in German Socialism and Communism between 1840 and 1990*, ed. David E. Barclay and Eric D. Weitz. Providence: Berghahn, forthcoming.

Rueschemeyer, Marilyn. "East German Women in Transition." Harvard University Minda de Ginzburg Center for European Studies, Program on Central and Eastern Europe Working Paper Series no. 12, 1991.

Rueschemeyer, Marilyn, and Christiane Lemke, eds. *The Quality of Life in the German Democratic Republic: Changes and Developments in a State Socialist Society*. Armonk, N.Y.: M. E. Sharpe, 1989.

Rürup, Reinhard. "Demokratischer Revolution und 'dritter Weg': Die deutsche Revolution von 1918/19 in den neueren wissenschaftlichen Diskussion." *Geschichte und Gesellschaft* 9:2 (1983): 278–301.

———. "Problems of the German Revolution 1918–19." *Journal of Contemporary History* 3:4 (1968): 109–35.

Ryan, Mary. "The American Parade: Representations of the Nineteenth-Century Social Order." In *The New Cultural History*, ed. Lynn Hunt, 131–53. Berkeley and Los Angeles: University of California Press, 1989.

———. "Gender and Public Access: Women's Politics in Nineteenth-Century America." In *Habermas and the Public Sphere*, ed. Craig Calhoun, 259–88. Cambridge, Mass.: MIT Press, 1992.

Sachse, Carola. *Siemens, der Nationalsozialismus und die moderne Familie: Eine Untersuchung zur soziale Rationalisierung in Deutschland im 20. Jahrhundert*. Hamburg: Rasch und Rohring, 1990.

Sachse, Carola, et al. *Angst, Belohnung, Zucht und Ordnung: Herrschaftsmechanismen im Nationalsozialismus*. Opladen: Westdeutscher, 1982.

Sachße, Christoph, and Florian Tennstedt, eds. *Soziale Sicherheit und soziale Disziplinierung: Beiträge zu einer historischen Theorie der Sozialpolitik*. Frankfurt am Main: Suhrkamp, 1986.

Saldern, Adelheid von. *Auf dem Wege zum Arbeiter-Reformismus: Parteialltag in sozialdemokratischer Provinz Göttingen (1870–1920)*. Frankfurt am Main: Materialis, 1984.

———. "Gewerbegerichte im Wilhelminischen Deutschland." In *Wissenschaft, Wirtschaft und Technik: Studien zur Geschichte. Wilhelm Treue zum 60. Geburtstag*, ed. Karl-Heinz Manegold, 190–203. Munich: Bruckmann, 1969.

———. "Neues Wohnen, Wohnverhältnisse und Wohnverhalten in Groß-Wohnanlagen der

1920er Jahre." In *Massenwohnung und Eigenheim: Wohnungsbau und Wohnen in der Großstadt seit dem Ersten Weltkrieg*, ed. Axel Schidt and Arnold Sywottek, 201–21. Frankfurt am Main: Campus, 1988.

———. "Sozialdemokratie und kommunale Wohnungsbaupolitik in den 20er Jahren—am Beispiel von Hamburg und Wien." *Archiv für Sozialgeschichte* 25 (1985): 183–237.

———. "Victims or Perpetrators? Controversies about the Role of Women in the Nazi State." In *Nazism and German Society, 1933–1945*, ed. David F. Crew, 141–65. London: Routledge, 1994.

———. "Wilhelminische Gesellschaft und Arbeiterklasse: Emanzipations- und Integrationsprozesse im kulturellen und sozialen Bereich." *Internationale wissenschaftliche Korrespondenz zur Geschichte der deutschen Arbeiterbewegung* 13:4 (1977): 469–505.

———. "The Workers' Movement and Cultural Patterns on Urban Housing Estates and in Rural Settlements in Germany and Austria during the 1920s." *Social History* 15:3 (1990): 333–54.

Sanford, Gregory W. *From Hitler to Ulbricht: The Communist Reconstruction of East Germany, 1945–46*. Princeton: Princeton University Press, 1983.

Saul, Klaus. "Repression or Integration? The State, Trade Unions and Industrial Disputes in Imperial Germany." In *The Development of Trade Unionism in Great Britain and Germany, 1880–1914*, ed. Wolfgang J. Mommsen and Hans-Gerhard Husung, 338–56. London: George Allen and Unwin, 1985.

———. *Staat, Industrie, Arbeiterbewegung im Kaiserreich: Zur Innen- und Aussenpolitik des Wilhelminischen Deutschland 1903–1914*. Düsseldorf: Bertelsmann Universitätsverlag, 1974.

SBZ-Handbuch: Staatliche Verwaltungen, Parteien, gesellschaftliche Organisationen und ihre Führungskräfte in der Sowjetischen Besatzungszone Deutschlands 1945–1949, ed. Martin Broszat and Hermann Weber. Munich: Oldenbourg, 1990.

Scharrer, Manfred. "Demokratie und Diktatur bei Rosa Luxemburg." *Beiträge zur Geschichte der Arbeiterbewegung* 33:4 (1991): 469–74.

Scherstjanoi, Elke. "Die DDR im Frühjahr 1952: Sozialismuslosung und Kollektivierungsbeschluß in sowjetischer Perspektive." *Deutschland Archiv* 27:4: 354–63.

Scherstjanoi, Elke, ed. *"Provisorium für längstens ein Jahr": Die Gründung der DDR 1949*. Berlin: Akademie, 1993.

Scheurig, Bodo. *Freies Deutschland*. Munich: Nymphenburger Verlagsshandlung, 1960.

Schiffmann, Dieter. *Von der Revolution zum Neunstundentag: Arbeit und Konflikt bei BASF 1918–1924*. Frankfurt am Main: Campus, 1983.

Schmädeke, Jürgen, and Peter Steinbach, eds. *Der Widerstand gegen den Nationalsozialismus: Die deutsche Gesellschaft und der Widerstand gegen Hitler*. Munich: Piper, 1985.

Schmitz, Hubert. "Ausgewählte Kapitel aus der Lebensmittelversorgung der Stadt Essen in der Kriegs- und Nachkreigszeit." *Beiträge zur Geschichte von Stadt und Stift Essen* 58 (1939).

Schöck, Eva Cornelia. *Arbeitslosigkeit und Rationalisierung: Die Lage der Arbeiter und die kommunistische Gewerkschaftspolitik 1920–1928*. Frankfurt am Main: Campus, 1977.

Schoenhals, Kai P. *The Free Germany Movement: A Case of Patriotism or Treason?* Westport, Conn.: Greenwood, 1989.

Schönhoven, Klaus. *Expansion und Konzentration: Studien zur Entwicklung der Freien Gewerkschaften im Wilhelminischen Deutschland 1890 bis 1914* (Stuttgart: Klett-Cotta, 1980).

———. *Reformismus und Radikalismus: Gespaltene Arbeiterbewegung im Weimarer Sozialstaat*. Munich: DTV, 1989.

Schorske, Carl E. *German Social Democracy 1905–1917: The Development of the Great Schism*. Cambridge, Mass.: Harvard University Press, 1955.

Schultz, Eberhard. *Der Kampf um die revolutionäre Massenpartei der Arbeiterklasse in ehemaligen Regierungsbezirk Halle-Merseburg (1917–1920)*. Beiträge zur Geschichte der Arbeiterbewegung im Bezirk Halle. Halle: n.p., 1972.

Schuster, Kurt G. P. *Der Rote Frontkämpferbund 1924–1929: Beiträge zur Geschichte und Organisationsstruktur eines politischen Kampfbundes*. Düsseldorf: Droste, 1975.

Seidl, Helmut. *Streikkämpfe der mittel- und ostdeutschen Braunkohlenbergarbeiter von 1890 bis 1914*. Ed. Rektor der Bergakademie Freiberg, Freiberger Forschungshefte D47. Leipzig: Deutscher Verlag für Grundstoffindustrie, 1964.

Sewell, William H., Jr. "Collective Violence and Collective Loyalties in France: Why the French Revolution Made a Difference." *Politics and Society* 18:4 (1990): 527–52.

———. *A Rhetoric of Bourgeois Revolution: The Abbé Sièyes and "What Is the Third Estate?"* Durham: Duke University Press, 1994.

Sheppard, Eric, and Trevor J. Barnes. *The Capitalist Space Economy: Geographical Analysis after Ricardo, Marx and Sfarra*. London: Unwin Hyman, 1990.

Shorter, Edward, and Charles Tilly. *Strikes in France, 1830–1968*. Cambridge: Cambridge University Press, 1974.

Sodaro, Michael J. *Moscow, Germany, and the West from Khrushchev to Gorbachev*. Ithaca: Cornell University Press, 1990.

Spencer, Elaine Glovka. *Management and Labor in Imperial Germany: Ruhr Industrialists as Employers, 1896–1914*. New Brunswick: Rutgers University Press, 1984.

Spethmann, Hans. *Zwölf Jahre Ruhrbergbau: Aus seiner Geschichte von Kriegsanfang bis zum Franzosenabmarsch 1914–1925*, 5 vols. Berlin: Reimar Hobbing, 1928–31.

Spittmann, Ilse. "Sozialismus in den Farben der DDR." *Deutschland Archiv* 22:3 (1989): 241–44.

Spriano, Paolo. *Storia del Partito comunista italiano*, 5 vols. Turin: Einaudi, 1967–75.

Stachura, Peter. *The Weimar Republic and the Younger Proletariat: An Economic and Social Analysis*. New York: St. Martin's Press, 1989.

Stachura, Peter, ed. *Unemployment and the Great Depression in Weimar Germany*. London: Macmillan, 1986.

Staritz, Dietrich. "Ein 'besonderer deutscher Weg' zum Sozialismus?" *Aus Politik und Zeitgeschichte* B/51-52 (1982): 15–31.

———. *Geschichte der DDR 1949–1985*. Frankfurt am Main: Suhrkamp, 1985.

———. *Die Gründung der DDR*. Munich: Beck, 1987.

———. "Die Kommunistische Partei Deutschlands." In *Parteien-Handbuch: Die Parteien der Bundesrepublik Deutschland 1945–1980*, vol. 32, ed. Richard Stöss, 1663–1809. Opladen: Westdeutscher, 1984.

———. *Sozialismus in einem halben Lande: Zur Programmatik und Politik der KPD/SED in der Phase der antifaschistisch-demokratischen Umwälzung in der DDR*. Berlin: Klaus Wagenbach, 1976.

———. "Zwischen Ostintegration und nationaler Verpflichtung: Zur Ost- und Deutschlandspolitik der SED, 1948 bis 1952." In *Westdeutschland 1945–1955: Unterwerfung, Kontrolle, Integration*, ed. Ludolf Herbst, 279–89. Munich: Oldenbourg, 1986.

Stein, Eberhard. "Die Entstehung der Leuna-Werke und die Anfänge der Arbeiterbewegung in den Leuna-Werken während des Ersten Weltkrieges und der Novemberrevolution." Ph.D. diss., Martin-Luther-Universität Halle-Wittenberg, 1960.

———. "Salpeter für Ludendorff und die IG: Zwei Beiträge zur deutschen Stickstoffchemie im Ersten Weltrieg." Ed. IML an der Technischen Hochschule für Chemie Leuna-Merseburg. N.p., 1963.

Steinberg, Hans-Joseph. *Widerstand und Verfolgung in Essen 1933-1945*. Hannover: Verlag für Literatur und Zeitgeschehen, 1969.

———. "Workers' Libraries in Imperial Germany." *History Workshop Journal* 1 (1976): 166–80.

Steinberg, Heinz Gunther. *Die Entwicklung des Ruhrgebietes: Eine wirtschafts- und sozialgeographische Studie*. Düsseldorf: Landbezirk Nordrhein-Westfalen Deutscher Gewerkschaftsbund, 1967.

Steinisch, Irmgard. *Arbeitszeitverkürzung und sozialer Wandel: Der Kampf um die Achtstundenschicht in der deutschen und amerikanischen Eisen- und Stahlindustrie 1880–1929*. Berlin: Walter de Gruyter, 1986.

Steinmetz, George. "The Local Welfare State: Two Strategies for Social Domination in Urban Imperial Germany." *American Sociological Review* 55:6 (1991): 891–911.

———. *Regulating the Social: The Welfare State and Local Politics in Imperial Germany*. Princeton: Princeton University Press, 1993.

———. "Workers and the Welfare State in Imperial Germany." *International Labor and Working Class History* 40 (1991): 18–46.

Stollberg, Gunnar. *Die Rationalisierungsdebatte 1908–1933: Freie Gewerkschaften zwischen Mitwirkung und Gegenwehr*. Frankfurt am Main: Campus, 1981.

Stolle, Uta. *Arbeiterpolitik im Betrieb: Frauen und Männer, Reformisten und Radikale, Fach- und Massenarbeiter bei Bayer, BASF, Bosch und in Solingen (1900–1933)*. Frankfurt am Main: Campus, 1980.

Stößel, Frank. *Positionen und Strömungen in der KPD/SED 1945–1954*. Cologne: Wissenschaft und Politik, 1985.

Strobel, Georg W. "Die Legende von der Rosa Luxemburg: Eine politsch-historische Betrachtung." *Internationale wissenschaftliche Korrespondenz zur Geschichte der deutschen Arbeiterbewegung* 28:3 (1992): 373–94.

Suckut, Siegfried. *Die Betriebsrätebewegung in der Sowjetisch Besetzten Zone Deutschlands (1945–1948): Zur Entwicklung und Bedeutung von Arbeiterinitiative, betrieblicher Mitbestimmung und Selbstbestimmung bis zur Revision des programmatischen Konzepte der KPD/SED von "besonderen deutschen Weg zum Sozialismus"*. Frankfurt am Main: Haag + Herchen, 1982.

Sywottek, Arnold. *Deutsche Volksdemokratie: Studien zur politischen Konzeption der KPD 1935–1946*. Düsseldorf: Bertelsmann Universitätsverlag, 1971.

———. "Revolutionäre Perspektiven des kommunistischen Widerstands." In *Der Widerstand gegen den Nationalsozialismus: Die deutsche Gesellschaft und der Widerstand gegen Hitler*, ed. Jürgen Schmädeke and Peter Steinbach, 475–96. Munich: Piper, 1985.

Tammen, Helmuth. *Die I. G. Farbenindustrie Aktiengesellschaft (1925–1933): Ein Chemiekonzern in der Weimarer Republik*. Berlin: Helmuth Tammen, 1978.

Tampke, Jürgen. "The Rise and Fall of the Essen Model, January-February 1919." *Internationale wissenschaftliche Korrespondenz zur Geschichte der deutschen Arbeiterbewegung* 13:2 (1977): 160–72.

Tarrow, Sidney. *Power in Movement: Social Movements, Collective Action and Politics*. Cambridge: Cambridge University Press, 1994.

Tenfelde, Klaus. "Linksradikale Strömungen in der Ruhrbergarbeiterschaft 1905 bis 1919." In *Glück auf, Kameraden! Die Bergarbeiter und ihre Organisationen in Deutschland*, ed. Hans Mommsen, 199–224. Cologne: Bund, 1979.

———. "Mining Festivals in the Nineteenth Century." *Journal of Contemporary History* 13:2 (1978): 377–412.

———. "1914 bis 1990—Einheit der Epoche." *Aus Politik und Zeitgeschichte* B40/91 (27 September 1991): 3–11.

———. "Probleme der Organisation von Arbeitern und Unternehmern im Ruhrbergbau 1890–1918." In *Arbeiterbewegung und industrieller Wandel: Studien zu gewerkschaftlichen Organisationsproblemen im Reich und an der Ruhr*, ed. Hans Mommsen, 38–61. Wuppertal: Peter Hammer, 1980.

———. *Proletarische Provinz: Radikalisierung und Widerstand in Penzberg/Oberbayern 1900–1945*. Munich: Oldenbourg, 1982.

———. *Sozialgeschichte der Bergarbeiterschaft an der Ruhr im 19. Jahrhundert*. Bonn-Bad Godesberg: Neue Gesellschaft, 1977.

Tenfelde, Klaus, ed. *Arbeiter im 20. Jahrhundert*. Stuttgart: Klett-Cotta, 1991.

Tenfelde, Klaus, and Heinrich Volkmann, eds. *Streik: Zur Geschichte des Arbeitskampfes in Deutschland während der Industrialiserung*. Munich: Beck, 1981.

Tennstedt, Florian. *Sozialgeschichte der Sozialpolitik in Deutschland*. Göttingen: Vandenhoeck und Ruprecht, 1981.

———. *Vom Proleten zum Industriearbeiter: Arbeiterbewegung und Sozialpolitik in Deutschland 1800 bis 1914*. Cologne: Bund, 1983.

Tilly, Charles. "Contentious Repertoires in Great Britain, 1758-1834." *Social Science History* 17:2 (1993): 253–80.

Treue, Wilhelm. "Die Technik in Wirtschaft und Gesellschaft 1800–1970." In *Handbuch der deutschen Wirtschafts- und Sozialgeschichte*, vol. 2, ed. Hermann Aubin and Wolfgang Zorn, 51–121. Stuttgart: Ernst Klett, 1976.

Trotnow, Helmut. *Karl Liebknecht (1871–1919): A Political Biography*. Hamden, Conn.: Archon Books, 1984.

Tschirbs, Rudolf. *Tarifpolitik im Ruhrbergbau 1918–1933*. Berlin: Walter de Gruyter, 1986.

Ueberhorst, Horst. *Frisch, Frei, Stark und Treu: Die Arbeitersportbewegung in Deutschland 1893–1933*. Düsseldorf: Droste, 1973.

Ullmann, Hans-Peter. "Unternehmerschaft, Arbeitgeberverbände und Streikbewegung 1890–1914." In *Streik: Zur Geschichte des Arbeitskampfes in Deutschland während der Industrialisierung*, ed. Klaus Tenfelde and Heinrich Volkmann, 194–208. Munich: Beck, 1981.

Usborne, Cornelie. *The Politics of the Body in Weimar Germany: Women's Reproductive Rights and Duties*. Ann Arbor: University of Michigan Press, 1992.

———. "Pregnancy Is the Women's Active Service: Pronatalism in Germany during the First World War." In *The Upheaval of War: Family, Work, and Welfare in Europe, 1914–1918*, ed. Richard Wall and Jay Winter, 389–416. Cambridge: Cambridge University Press, 1988.

Verbeeck, Georgi. "Kontinuität und Wandel im DDR-Geschichtsbild." *Aus Politik und Zeitgeschichte* B11/90 (9 March 1990): 30–42.

Voß, Angelika, Ursual Büttner, and Hermann Weber. *Vom Hamburger Aufstand zur politischen Isolierung: Kommunistische Politik 1923–1933 in Hamburg und im Deutschen Reich*. Hamburg: Landeszentrale für politische Bildung, 1983.

Wall, Richard, and Jay Winter, eds. *The Upheaval of War: Family, Work, and Welfare in Europe, 1914–1918*. Cambridge: Cambridge University Press, 1988.

Ward, J. J. "'Smash the Fascists . . .': German Communist Efforts to Counter the Nazis, 1930–31." *Central European History* 14:1 (1981): 30–62.

Watts, Dan. "Electoral Success and Political Failure: The KPD in Mannheim in the Last Years of the Weimar Republic." *European History Quarterly* 18:4 (1988): 439–54.

Weber, Hermann. "Die Ambivalenz der kommunistischen Widerstandsstrategie bis zur 'Brusseler' Parteikonferenz." In *Der Widerstand gegen den Nationalsozialismus: Die deutsche Gesellschaft und der Widerstand gegen Hitler*, ed. Jürgen Schmädeke and Peter Steinbach, 73–85. Munich: Piper, 1985.

———. *Aufbau und Fall einer Diktatur: Kritischen Beiträge zur Geschichte der DDR*. Cologne: Bund, 1991.

———. "Aufstieg und Niedergang des deutschen Kommunismus." *Aus Politik und Zeitgeschichte* B40/91 (27 September 1991): 25–39.

———. "Die deutschen Kommunisten 1945 in der SBZ." *Aus Politik und Zeitgeschichte* B31 (5 August 1978): 24–32.

———. *Die DDR 1945–1986*. Munich: Oldenbourg, 1988.

———. "Geschichte als Instrument der Politik: Zu den Thesen des ZK der SED 'Zum 70. Jahrestag der Gründung der KPD.'" *Deutschland Archiv* 21:8 (1988): 863–72.

———. *Kommunismus in Deutschland 1918–1945*. Darmstadt: Wissenschaftliche Buchgesellschaft, 1983.

———. *Kommunistische Bewegung und realsozialistischer Staat: Beiträge zum deutschen und internationalen Kommunismus. Hermann Weber zum 60. Geburtstag*. Ed. Werner Müller. Cologne: Bund, 1988.

———. "Die KPD in der Illegalität." In *Widerstand und Verweigerung in Deutschland 1933 bis 1945*, ed. Richard Löwenthal and Patrik von zur Mühlen, 83–101. Bonn: J. H. W. Dietz Nachf., 1982.

———. "Die SED und die Geschichte der Komintern: Gegensätzliche Einschätzung durch Historiker der DDR und der Sowjetunion." *Deutschland Archiv* 22:8 (August 1989): 890–903.

———. *Die Wandlung des deutschen Kommunismus: Die Stalinisierung der KPD in der Weimarer Republik*, 2 vols. Frankfurt am Main: Europäische Verlagsanstalt, 1969.

———. "'Weiße Flecken' in der DDR-Geschichtsschreibung." *Aus Politik und Zeitgeschichte* B11/90 (9 March 1990): 3–15.

———. *"Weiße Flecken" in der Geschichte: Die KPD-Opfer der Stalinschen Säuberungen und ihre Rehabilitierung*, 2d ed. Frankfurt am Main: isp, 1990.

Weber, Hermann, ed. *Parteiensystem zwischen Demokratie und Volksdemokratie*. Cologne: Wissenschaft und Politik, 1982.

Weber, Stefan. *Ein kommunistischer Putsch? Märzaktion 1921 in Mitteldeutschland*. Berlin: Dietz, 1991.

Weisbrod, Bernd. *Schwerindustrie in der Weimarer Republik*. Wuppertal: Peter Hammer, 1978.

Weitz, Eric D. "Bukharin and 'Bukharinism' in the Comintern, 1919–29." In *Nikolai Ivanovich Bukharin: A Centenary Appraisal*, ed. Nicholas N. Kozlov and Eric D. Weitz, 59–91. New York: Praeger, 1989.

———. "Conflict in the Ruhr: Workers and Socialist Politics in Essen, 1910–1925." Ph.D. diss., Boston University, 1983.

———. *Popular Communism: Political Strategies and Social Histories in the Formation of the German, French, and Italian Communist Parties, 1919–1948*. Western Societies Program Occasional Paper no. 31. Ithaca: Cornell University Institute for European Studies, 1992.

———. "'Rosa Luxemburg Belongs To Us!': German Communism and the Luxemburg Legacy." *Central European History* 27:1 (1994): 27–64.

———. "Social Continuity and Political Radicalization: Essen in the World War I Era." *Social Science History* 9:1 (1985): 49–69.

———. "State Power, Class Fragmentation, and the Shaping of German Communist Politics, 1890–1933." *Journal of Modern History* 62:2 (1990): 253–97.

Weitz, Eric D., and David E. Barclay, eds. *Between Reform and Revolution: Studies in German Socialism and Communism from 1840 to 1990.* Providence: Berghahn, forthcoming.

Weitz, Eric D., and Geoff Eley. "Romantisierung des Eigen-Sinns? Eine e-mail-Kontroverse aus Übersee." *WerkstattGeschichte* 10 (1995): 57–64.

Weitz, Eric D., and Nicholas N. Kozlov. "Reflections on the Origins of the 'Third Period': Bukharin, the Comintern, and the Political Economy of Weimar Germany." *Journal of Contemporary History* 24:3 (1989): 387–410.

Weitz, Eric D., and Nicholas N. Kozlov, eds. *Nikolai Ivanovich Bukharin: A Centenary Appraisal.* New York: Praeger, 1989.

Wettig, Gerhard. "Die Deutschland-Note vom 10. März 1952 auf der Basis diplomatischer Akten des russischen Außenministeriums: Die Hypothese des Wiedervereinigungsangebots." *Deutschland Archiv* 26:7 (1993): 786–805.

———. "Zum Stand der Forschung über Berijas Deutschland-Politik im Frühjahr 1953." *Deutschland Archiv* 26:6 (1993): 674–82.

Wheeler, Robert F. "German Women and the Communist International: The Case of the Independent Social Democrats." *Central European History* 8:2 (1975): 113–38.

———. "The Independent Social Democratic Party and the Internationals: An Examination of Socialist Internationalism in Germany, 1915–1923." Ph.D. diss., University of Pittsburgh, 1970.

Wickham, James. "Working-Class Movement and Working-Class Life: Frankfurt am Main during the Weimar Republic." *Social History* 8:3 (1983): 315–43.

Wiel, Paul. *Wirtschaftsgeschichte des Ruhrgebietes: Tatsachen und Zahlen.* Essen: Siedlungsverband Ruhrkohlenbezirk, 1970.

Wielgohs, Jan, and Marianne Schulz. "Reformbewegung und Volksbewegung: Politische und soziale Aspekte im Umbruch der DDR-Gesellschaft." *Aus Politik und Zeitgeschichte* B16–17/90 (13 April 1990): 15–24.

Wilke, Manfred, Hans-Peter Müller, and Marion Brabant. *Die Deutsche Kommunistische Partei (DKP): Geschichte, Organisation, Politik.* Cologne: Wissenschaft und Politik, 1990.

Wille, Manfred. "Das Ringen der Arbeiterklasse und der anderen Antifaschisten um die Einleitung des Demokratisierungsprozesses in der Provinz Sachsen (April-August 1945)." *Beiträge zur Geschichte der Arbeiterbewegung* 22:3 (1980): 431–41.

Winkler, Heinrich August. "Klassenbewegung oder Volkspartei? Zur Programmdiskussion in der Weimarer Sozialdemokratie." *Geschichte und Gesellschaft* 8:1 (1982): 9–54.

———. "Nationalismus, Nationalstaat und nationale Frage in Deutschland seit 1945." *Aus Politik und Zeitgeschichte* B40/91 (27 September 1991): 12–24.

———. *Der Schein der Normalität: Arbeiter und Arbeiterbewegung in der Weimarer Republik 1924 bis 1930.* Berlin: J. H. W. Dietz Nachf., 1988.

———. *Von der Revolution zur Stabilisierung: Arbeiter und Arbeiterbewegung in der Weimarer Republik 1918 bis 1924.* Berlin: J. H. W. Dietz Nachf., 1984.

———. *Der Weg in die Katastrophe: Arbeiter und Arbeiterbewegung in der Weimarer Republik 1930 bis 1933.* Berlin: J. H. W. Dietz Nachf., 1990.

Winkler, Heinrich August, ed. *Politische Weichenstellungen im Nachkriegsdeutschland 1945–1953.* Göttingen: Vandenhoeck und Ruprecht, 1979.

Wohlgemuth, Heinz. *Die Entstehung der Kommunistischen Partei Deutschlands 1914 bis 1918.* Berlin: Dietz, 1968.

Wolle, Stefan. "Das MfS und die Arbeiterproteste im Herbst 1956 in der DDR." *Aus Politik und Zeitgeschichte* B5/91 (25 January 1991): 42–51.

Woods, Roger. *Opposition in the GDR under Honecker, 1971–1985*. London: Macmillan, 1986.

Wunderer, Hartmann. *Arbeitervereine und Arbeiterparteien: Kultur- und Massenorganisationen in der Arbeiterbewegung (1890–1933)*. Frankfurt am Main: Campus, 1980.

———. "Materialien zur Soziologie der Mitgliedschaft und Wählerschaft der KPD zur Zeit der Weimarer Republik." *Gesellschaft: Beiträge zur Marxschen Theorie* 5 (1975): 257–77.

Wurl, Ernst. "Entscheidung 'gegen das Konzept Stalins'? Zu Wilfriede Ottos Dokumentation von Notizen W. Piecks." *Beiträge zur Geschichte der Arbeiterbewegung* 33:6 (1991): 767–70.

Zang, Gert. "Die KPD besetzt den 'öffentlichen Raum.'" In *Arbeiterleben in einer Randregion: Die allmähliche Entstehung der Arbeiterbewegung in einer rasch wachsenden Industriestadt, Singen a.H. 1895–1933*, ed. idem, 218–27. Konstanz: Südkurier, 1987.

Zwahr, Hartmut. *Ende einer Selbstzerstörung: Leipzig und die Revolution in der DDR*. Göttingen: Vandenhoeck und Ruprecht, 1993.

———. "Der rote Distelfink unter der Pickelhaube: Namen, Symbole, Identitäten Geächteter im 19. Jahrhundert." Ms., German Studies Association annual meeting, 1990.

INDEX

ABOUT THE AUTHOR

ERIC D. WEITZ is Associate Professor of History at St. Olaf College. Among his books is *Between Reform and Revolution: Studies in German Socialism and Communism from 1840 to 1990*, coedited with David E. Barclay (forthcoming).

Made in the USA
Middletown, DE
08 December 2021

54561244R00276